LARGE PRINT

RANDOM
HOUSE
LARGE
PRINT

I Alone
Can Fix It

Also by Carol Leonnig and Philip Rucker
Available from Random House Large Print

A Very Stable Genius

I Alone
Can Fix It

DONALD J. TRUMP'S
CATASTROPHIC FINAL YEAR

Carol Leonnig and
Philip Rucker

RANDOM HOUSE
LARGE PRINT

The Library of Congress has established a Cataloging-in-Publication record for this title.

ISBN: 978-0-593-50387-4

www.penguinrandomhouse.com/large-print-format-books

FIRST LARGE PRINT EDITION

Printed in the United States of America

10 9 8 7 6 5 4 3 2 1

This Large Print edition published in accord with the standards of the N.A.V.H.

To Naomi, Clara, Karen, and Lee

To John, Molly, and Elise

CONTENTS

Authors' Note

We never anticipated we would write a second book about Donald Trump's time in the White House. Our first, **A Very Stable Genius,** brought readers deep inside his chaotic and impulsive presidency. Our story ended as Trump was about to face impeachment for pressuring a foreign country to investigate his political rival, well into his third year. We expected his presidency would follow its established pattern and rhythms. Then came the year 2020. Trump's final year in office turned out to be by far his most consequential and, for many Americans, the most frightening. We felt compelled to pick up where we left off. Our minds raced with questions anew. We felt a responsibility, for history, to reveal what was happening behind the scenes as Trump stared down his first true crisis, the coronavirus pandemic, and chose to spawn another, the subversion of democracy, an act that led him to be the first U.S. president ever to be twice impeached.

This book is based on hundreds of hours of interviews with more than 140 sources, including the seniormost Trump administration officials, career government officials, friends, and outside advisers to the forty-fifth president, as well as other witnesses to the events described herein. Some of our interviews with key figures extended for more than five hours in a single sitting as the sources recounted their experiences in meticulous detail. Most of the people we interviewed agreed to speak candidly only on the condition of anonymity, to share private accounts of moments that profoundly challenged or shook them, to protect their future careers, or to fend off retaliation from Trump or his allies. Many of them provided their accounts in a background capacity, meaning we were permitted to use the information they shared so long as we protected their identities and did not attribute details to them by name. A few of our sources agreed to speak on the record, including Trump, whom we interviewed for two and a half hours.

We are objective journalists who seek to share the truth with the public. In this book, we aimed to provide the closest version of the truth that we could determine based on rigorous reporting. We carefully reconstructed scenes to present Trump unfiltered, showing him in action rather than telling readers what to think of him. These scenes were reconstructed based on firsthand accounts and, whenever possible, corroborated by multiple sources and buttressed by our review of calendars, diary entries, slideshow decks, internal memos, and other correspondence among principals. Dialogue cannot always be exact but is based here on people's memories of events and, in some cases, contemporaneous notes taken by witnesses. In a few instances, sources disagreed substantively about the facts in an episode, and when necessary, we note that in the pages, recognizing that different narrators sometimes remember events differently.

This book is an outgrowth of our reporting for **The Washington Post.** As such, some of the details in our narrative first appeared in stories we authored for the newspaper, some of them in collaboration with other colleagues. However, the overwhelming majority of the scenes, dialogue, and quotations are original to our book and based on the extensive reporting we conducted exclusively for this project.

To reconstruct episodes that played out in public, we relied upon video of events, such as presidential speeches, many of which are archived on C-SPAN's website. We also relied on contemporaneous news reports in the **Post** as well as in other publications. We have also drawn from the government record, including internal government reports and private email exchanges. In most instances we built upon the published record with our own original reporting. Material gleaned from such accounts is properly attributed, either with a direct reference in the chapter text or in the endnotes.

I Alone
Can Fix It

Prologue

On January 20, 2017, Donald John Trump coronavirus became president, unskilled in the machinery of government and unmoved morally by the calling of the position, but aglow in his unmatched power. The first three years of Trump's term revealed a presidency of one, in which the universal value was loyalty—not to the country, but to the president himself. Scandal, bluster, and uninhibited chaos reigned. Decisions were driven by a reflexive logic of self-preservation and self-aggrandizement. Delusions born of narcissism and insecurity overtook reality.

In those early years, which we chronicled in our book **A Very Stable Genius,** Trump's advisers believed his ego and pride prevented him from making sound, well-informed judgments. His management style resembled a carnival ride, jerking this way and that, forcing senior government officials to thwart his inane and sometimes illegal ideas. Some of them concluded that the president was a long-term and immediate danger to the country that he had sworn an oath to protect, yet they took comfort that he had not had to steer the country through a true crisis.

Trump's actions and words nevertheless had painful consequences. His assault on the rule of law degraded our democratic institutions and left Americans reasonably fearful they could no longer take for granted basic civil rights and untainted justice. His contempt for foreign alliances weakened America's leadership in the world and empowered dictators and despots. His barbarous immigration enforcement ripped migrant children out of the arms of their families. His bigoted rhetoric emboldened white supremacists to step out of the shadows.

But at least Trump had not been tested by a foreign military strike, an economic collapse, or a public health crisis.

At least not until 2020.

This book chronicles Trump's catastrophic fourth and final year as president. The year 2020 will be remembered in the American epoch as one of anguish and abject failure. The coronavirus pandemic killed more than half a million people in the United States and infected tens of millions more, the deadliest health crisis in a century. Though the administration's Operation Warp Speed helped produce vaccines in record time, its overall coronavirus response was mismanaged by the president and marred by ineptitude and backbiting.

The virus was only one of the crises Trump confronted in 2020. The pandemic paralyzed the economy, plunging the nation into a recession during which low-wage workers, many of them minorities, suffered the most.

The May 25 killing of George Floyd, a Black man, under the knee of a white police officer in Minneapolis ignited protests for racial justice and an end to police discrimination and brutality. Yet Trump sought to exploit the simmering divisions for personal political gain, quickly declaring himself "your president of law and order" and relentlessly pressuring Pentagon leaders to deploy active-duty troops against Black Lives Matter protesters.

The worsening climate crisis, meanwhile, was almost entirely ignored by Trump, who earlier in his term had rolled back environmental regulations and withdrawn the United States from the Paris Agreement. The president was instead preoccupied with stoking doubts about the legitimacy of the election. After he lost to Joe Biden, Trump fanned the flames of conspiracies and howled about fraud that did not exist. His false claims of a "rigged election" inspired thousands of people to storm the Capitol in a violent and ultimately failed insurrection on January 6, 2021.

The year 2020 tested the republic. Yet the institutions designed by the Founding Fathers were still standing by the time Trump left office. America's democracy withstood the unrelenting assault of its president. Trump's cries summoned tens of thousands of angry citizens to Washington to overturn the election, but Vice President Mike Pence and scores of lawmakers followed their constitutional duties.

"There is a good news story here," General Mark Milley, chairman of the Joint Chiefs of Staff, told the military brass at the conclusion of Trump's presidency. "It's the strength of the country. There is polarization. But at the end of the day, the country did stand tall. There was a peaceful transfer of power. There weren't tanks in the streets. And the line bent, but it didn't break."

Senator Mitt Romney, who often stood alone among fellow Republicans in his criticisms of Trump, said the president's attacks on democratic institutions amounted to one of the greatest failings of any president.

"I think as we all recognize, democracy is more than taking a vote," Romney said. "We've had a number of countries take votes to quickly fall into disrepair from a democratic standpoint in part because they don't have the institutions that allow democracy to survive. Attacking the institutions here puts democracy itself in jeopardy, whether it's our judicial system, our freedom of the press, our intelligence community, the FBI—these things underpin the strength of our democratic republic. So he attacked those along the way and then, as a final act, attacked election integrity itself. Those things have real consequences."

The characteristics of Trump's leadership, blazingly

evident through the first three years of his presidency, had deadly ramifications in his final year. He displayed his ignorance, his rash temper, his pettiness and pique, his malice and cruelty, his utter absence of empathy, his narcissism, his transgressive personality, his disloyalty, his sense of victimhood, his addiction to television, his suspicion and silencing of experts, and his deception and lies. Each trait thwarted the response of the world's most powerful nation to a lethal threat.

"The last year you see what happens when you actually have erosion in the capacity of government to respond, when you have a president and appointees who don't take governing seriously and honestly don't know how to use it," said Margaret O'Mara, a professor of history at the University of Washington. "That's the great tragedy. It shows how fundamentally oblivious the president was to governing and the immense power for good at his disposal."

Most of Trump's failings can be explained by a simple truth: He cared more about himself than the country. Whether managing the coronavirus or addressing racial unrest or reacting to his election defeat, Trump prioritized what he thought to be his political and personal interests over the common good.

"There come moments where you have to decide, am I going to do something that's purely in my own self-interest if it is contrary to the interests of the people I represent," one of Trump's advisers remarked. "And in those moments, you've always got to pick the people you represent. The fact is that in 2020 Donald Trump put himself ahead of the country. When you do that as a leader, the people notice—and when they notice, they kick your ass out."

Throughout his presidency, Trump cast himself as a long-suffering, tormented victim. He believed himself to be persecuted by what he called the "deep state," a reference to any number of national security, intelligence, and law enforcement officials. Because some of these officials investigated his campaign's contacts with Russian operatives amid Russia's effort to help Trump win in 2016, he saw them as enemies. He branded any investigation pertaining to his conduct—whether it was Robert Mueller's investigation of Russian interference in the 2016 campaign, probes into his finances, or an impeachment inquiry into his pressure on Ukraine to help him smear Biden—a "witch hunt." He also claimed the media were running a sophisticated disinformation operation to puncture his popularity. And he demanded apologies for criticisms and slights.

Trump's incessant complaining ran counter to what had long been a core tenet of the Republican Party: personal responsibility. Yet Trump's strategy of self-victimization yoked him to his supporters, who similarly felt disrespected by elites in Washington and felt wronged by the fast-changing global economy.

Trump's standard tool kit for getting out of trouble—bullying, bluster, and manipulation—was useless in managing the pandemic. He tried to cloak reality with happy talk. He promised cures that would never be realized. He floated dangerous and unproven treatments, such as injecting bleach into patients' bodies. He muzzled experts like Dr. Anthony Fauci who challenged his shaky claims and became more popular than the president. He refused to lead by example and wear a mask. He picked feuds with health officials and state governors scrambling to respond to emergency outbreaks, striking out at those who didn't praise his haphazard response. Not only did he fail to keep Americans safe; he couldn't even keep himself safe. Trump was hospitalized with COVID-19 in October 2020, zapping his false air of invincibility.

The coronavirus changed the world, altering how people worked, how families lived, and what constituted a community. These profound changes were accelerated by the recession and heightened by the tensions in the aftermath of Floyd's killing. Trump, however, principally governed for a minority of the country—his hard-core political supporters—and chose neither to try to unite the nation nor to reimagine a postpandemic America. He egged on the anger and disaffection among many white people who felt economically threatened and culturally marginalized. He pitted groups of Americans against one another. He uttered racist phrases and used his immense social media platforms to spread messages of hate. He stoked fear and egged on violence.

"His view of America is provincial, it's parochial, it's sullied, it's any other adjective that calls up a sense of narrowness and ugliness," said Eddie Glaude Jr., chair of the Department of African American Studies at Princeton University. "In so many ways, Donald Trump represents the death rattle of an old America, and it's loud and it's violent."

A senior government official who worked closely with the president drew a parallel between Trump's handling of the Black Lives Matter protests of 2020 and Adolf Hitler's rise to power in Nazi Germany.

"People either singularly or in crowds are interested in personal survival and stability and safety," this official said. "When you are experiencing confusion and chaos and things you can't quite make sense of, and you see this phenomena around you that's getting scary—the economy and COVID and losing your job and immigrants crossing the border—along comes a guy who takes fuel, throws it on the fire, and makes you scared shitless. 'I will protect you.' That's what Hitler did to consolidate power in 1933."

Nancy Pelosi, the Democratic House Speaker whose opposition to Trump was as resolute as any, twice presided over his impeachment—in 2019 for seeking help from Ukraine in his reelection, and in 2021 for instigating the Capitol insurrection. After he left office, she told us in an interview that she was grateful democracy had prevailed but feared another president might come along and pick up where Trump left off.

"We might get somebody of his ilk who's sane, and that would really be dangerous, because it could be somebody who's smart, who's strategic, and the rest," Pelosi said. "This is a slob. He doesn't believe in science. He doesn't believe in governance. He's a snake-oil salesman. And he's shrewd. Give him credit for his shrewdness."

That shrewdness, coupled with shamelessness and unnatural political stamina, allowed Trump to deliver on many of his campaign promises. He pleased his conservative base by remaking the federal judiciary, including with three nominations to the Supreme Court; cutting taxes on corporations and the wealthy; expanding the military; toughening border enforcement; and weakening the regulatory state. Trump also forged new bilateral trade agreements, negotiated peace accords in the Middle East, and won concessions from European allies he had argued were taking advantage of the United States.

Trump nearly won a second term. More than 74 million people voted to reelect him—the second-highest vote total ever recorded, the highest being Biden's 81 million. Were it not for Biden's victories in a handful of swing states, Trump would have won the electoral college and secured four more years in office. It would be foolhardy then to dismiss his presidency as a failure and to turn the page on this period. Rather, we must try to understand what made him appealing to so many, and what that reveals about the country.

Trump almost certainly would have achieved more had he governed effectively and nurtured a professional and productive work culture. Instead, he allowed his White House to become a nest of vipers, with senior officials often advancing their personal agendas and vendettas instead of a collective mission. "It was by far the most toxic environment I could imagine working in, and I'm not a fragile person," a senior White House official recalled. "People were deeply cruel to each other."

By his fourth year in office, Trump had surrounded himself as much as he could with enablers and loyal flatterers. Power in the West Wing consolidated around Jared Kushner, the president's son-in-law and senior adviser, and Mark Meadows, the White House chief of staff who prioritized campaign politics and believed it was his duty to execute the president's wishes.

"Where are the adults?" one Cabinet secretary lamented. "They are supposed to be in the White House advising the president. That's a big part of the story of this administration. The people he has around him are putting things in his ears, but they aren't giving him careful, thought-through advice. There are no adults."

A few sturdy guardrails remained. Milley, Defense Secretary Mark Esper, and Attorney General Bill Barr were there when the president wanted to deploy the military to American cities. Barr, despite loyally looking out for the president's interests at the Justice Department, also fended off some of his efforts to prosecute and punish his enemies. The leaders of federal health agencies prevented Trump from corrupting the coronavirus vaccine development by rushing approvals before Election Day. And then there was Pence, who certified Biden's electoral college victory, after four years of unflinching fealty to Trump.

"Even though almost everybody who worked with Trump ended up taking a lot of grief and having reputational risk as a result of it, there were a number of good people who tried to prevent the worst at the White House over the years," said a senior Republican lawmaker. "Clowns in one camp and people genuinely trying to prevent the worst in the other camp. There were some heroes there."

"Good people at key moments taught him a lesson that the system is more important than anybody, including the president," this lawmaker added.

These are conclusions drawn from our four years of reporting about Trump's presidency and reflect the experiences and opinions of many of the most senior principals who served in the final year of his administration. They divulged, some for the very first time, what they witnessed firsthand, to tell the truth about this extraordinary year for the benefit of history.

As with **A Very Stable Genius,** the title of this book borrows Trump's own words. On July 21, 2016, when he accepted the Republican presidential nomination in Cleveland, Trump vowed, "I alone can fix it." He offered himself to the forgotten men and women of America as their sole hope for redemption, and as a president, he was powered by solipsism. He governed to protect and promote himself. "I alone can fix it" was the tenet by which he led.

What follows is the story of Trump's final year in office told from the inside. Some events have indelibly marked our nation's collective memory; many behind-the-scenes episodes have never been reported until now. Some moments show perseverance and resilience; others expose cowardice and callousness. It is an attempt to make sense of a year of crisis, at the heart of which was a leadership vacuum. It is the story of how Trump stress-tested the republic, twisting the country's institutions for personal gain and then pushing his followers too far. And it is the story of how voters, both fearful for their own futures and their country, finally discharged him.

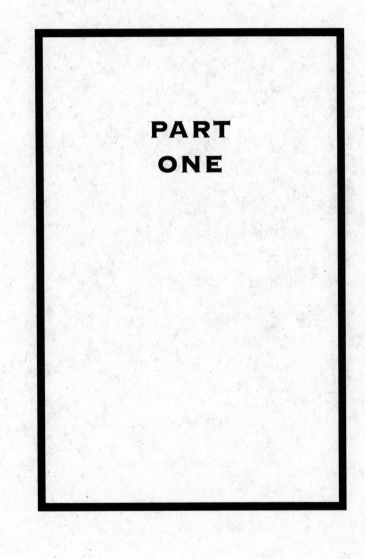

PART ONE

One

Deadly Distractions

President Trump rang in 2020 at Mar-a-Lago, the landmark mansion in Palm Beach built nearly a century ago by Marjorie Merriweather Post, at his members-only social club's annual New Year's Eve gala. Arriving on the red carpet outside the ballroom doors at about 9:30 p.m., as a band could be heard performing Daft Punk's "Get Lucky," the tuxedo-clad president stopped to parry questions from a gaggle of reporters, with the first lady at his side. Militiamen earlier that day had attacked the U.S. embassy in Baghdad, and the United States held Iran responsible. Would Trump retaliate?

"This will not be a Benghazi," he said disdainfully, referring to the attack in 2012 on a U.S. consulate in Libya that had long dogged then secretary of state Hillary Clinton.

Was he prepared for his upcoming Senate impeachment trial?

"It's a big fat hoax," Trump said dismissively.

What about Kim Jong Un, the North Korean dictator with whom Trump had boasted of exchanging love letters, who over the holidays menacingly had warned of a "Christmas present" for the United States?

"I hope his Christmas present is a beautiful vase," Trump quipped, seeming to make light of the possibility of nuclear war, as Melania, silent and statuesque in shimmering gold sequins, broke into a momentary smile.

"We're going to have a great year, I predict," he said. "I think it's going to be a fantastic year." He added, "Our country is really the talk of the world. Everybody's talking about it."

On that same day, December 31, 2019, a curious email landed in the inboxes of top officials at the Centers for Disease Control and Prevention, whose Atlanta headquarters was lightly staffed over the holidays. It was a short alert from a small team of scientists at the CDC's outpost in Beijing about reports of a series of unexplained pneumonia-like cases in the interior Chinese port city of Wuhan. Few Americans had ever heard of Wuhan, though the city of eleven million on the Yangtze River served as a massive manufacturing and transportation hub, as well as the cultural and urban center for central China. Some dubbed it the Chicago of China. The scientists in the CDC's office in Beijing wrote that they were working to learn more about what was going on.

For some CDC leaders, the email didn't set off flashing alarms. Yet Dr. Robert Redfield, the center's director, was concerned. A highly esteemed virologist and infectious disease physician with decades of research under his belt, Redfield was spending the holidays with his wife, their five grown children, and eleven grandchildren at a rented house in Deep Creek Lake in the mountains of western Maryland, near the Pennsylvania and West Virginia borders. He was disturbed by the words "unexplained pneumonia." "This seems significant," Redfield told his chief of staff, Kyle McGowan. "I need to know what they find."

Redfield had worried about the possibility of a mystery virus like this for months. After joining the Trump administration in March 2018, the CDC director had visited Capitol Hill to meet with key lawmakers who authorized the center's budget or conducted oversight of its operations. Chatting with him about his twenty years as an army doctor and his work on HIV and AIDS, a few members of Congress had asked Redfield variations on the same question: What disease or public health threat keeps you up at night? Redfield had told them that he dreaded an infectious respiratory disease for which most humans had no immunity, probably some strain of bird flu that could quickly become a pandemic akin to the 1918 influenza, known as the Spanish flu.

Little more than a year later, Redfield was confronted by that very possibility. From that moment on, Redfield's relaxing family get-together, complete with matching Christmas-plaid pajamas for everyone, was hijacked. The man whose pajama top read "Grandpa" in thick lettering routinely had to leave the living room or the dining table to take work calls. The CDC leader directed his aides to give him and the leadership of the Department of Health and Human Services a "sitrep"—a situation report—the next day. And he asked McGowan to set up a call as soon as possible with his counterpart in China, Dr. George Fu Gao, the director of China's Center for Disease Control and Prevention.

That December 31 email was a critical red flag that the Chinese government was holding its cards close to the vest about a global public health threat. Following the 2003 SARS outbreak, the United States, China, and many other countries had agreed they would all participate in a global software system called ProMED, in which they were obliged to report the appearance of any new or unusual virus and send up a digital flare for all to see. But the CDC was learning of these strange illnesses in Wuhan not because of an official alert, but instead because at midnight on December 30, somewhere in Asia an anonymous doctor had uploaded to the hotline a report about emergency guidance for Wuhan hospitals that had leaked to a news outlet outside of China. The Chinese government had not officially shared the information itself.

On January 1, 2020, the CDC's immunization and respiratory diseases staff and China team produced the sitrep with all the available intel on the Wuhan illness, as Redfield had requested. The next day, Redfield briefed a senior staffer on the National Security Council, who at the same time was managing the risk of Ebola outbreaks in Africa.

On January 3, Redfield finally connected with Gao by phone. The Chinese virologist offered what seemed like calming news. Gao said the virus had originated in a seafood market in Wuhan that sold exotic game; officials believed the virus had jumped from an infected animal to a human. He said that regional health authorities and the Wuhan government appeared to have it contained and that there were a little more than two dozen cases.

"What about human-to-human transmission?" Redfield asked. The issue of transmission was key, because a contagious virus would be much more difficult to control.

"We don't have any evidence of that," Gao said, explaining that the only consistent link among the patients was the market.

Redfield was not entirely convinced about this, because in a few more conversations that day he heard Gao say that at least three of the cases involved patients whose family members were also infected. He found it hard to believe that a man, his wife, and their child had walked through the market and each been independently infected there.

"But, George, you've got three clusters," Redfield said. He told Gao he remained concerned there was human-to-human transmission. Redfield offered to send a team of twenty to thirty infectious disease experts from the CDC to Wuhan to help investigate the virus. Gao agreed that would be helpful and said he would get back to him about this offer.

Redfield hung up, feeling more unsettled. First, he was surprised that Gao seemed to have only recently learned about this virus in Wuhan. He suspected that such a virus would surely have been circulating for some time, so how could the head of the Chinese CDC only know as much as Redfield had learned from reading unofficial media reports? "I think there's something more here we're not seeing," he told an aide.

Redfield wasn't alone in his suspicions. Dr. Anthony Fauci, one of the world's leading immunologists, had tracked viral infections for nearly four decades as director of the National Institute of Allergy and Infectious Diseases. He knew that the first outbreak of SARS had been traced to a fishmonger in China's Guangdong Province, but had soon spread human-to-human. The contagion transferred first to nurses and doctors treating the patient who had contracted it, then one of them traveled to Hong Kong and infected people there. Before long, people in twenty-nine countries were sick.

Fauci was apprehensive about the Chinese explanation of the mysterious new virus transferring from animals to humans at a wet market. He also couldn't believe that everybody who contracted the disease was infected by an animal. A virus is unlikely to jump species so many times at a single wet market. Surely, Fauci thought, there must be human-to-human spread.

Redfield talked to Gao several more times over the next several days, as much as two and three times a day. On one of those calls, Redfield asked Gao to explain the case definition that Wuhan officials were using to analyze the patients with suspicious pneumonia. Gao explained they were focusing on examining people with an unspecified respiratory infection who had contact with the market. Redfield warned Gao that by doing so, they could be missing a much larger problem.

"You're making a mistake there," Redfield said. He urged them to look for pneumonia cases that had no link to the market.

Redfield could tell Gao was getting increasingly uncomfortable with his questions. He sounded torn about sharing information. Gao started speaking in a stilted, formal way. This was not the good old George who had casually bantered a year earlier about their plans for visiting each other's countries. Gao at times now sounded like a prisoner trying secretly to signal in some type of code. Redfield felt sure Chinese "minders" or spies were listening in on their calls, as they typically did, and wondered if that was the cause of Gao's awkwardness.

The conversation became more uncomfortable

when Redfield pressed Gao about his earlier offer to send a CDC team to investigate the virus— a routine move given the expertise of America's scientists. Gao said he couldn't extend the invitation and that Redfield should issue a formal request to the Chinese government.

By the time they spoke again a day or two later, Gao sounded distraught. He reported that health officials had looked beyond the market as Redfield suggested and found many, many more cases of the virus with no link to that area or to purchases there. Hundreds of them. He broke down on the phone.

"We may be too late," Gao said.

On January 6, Redfield wrote a formal request to the Chinese government on U.S. Department of Health and Human Services letterhead, asking for permission to send a CDC team to Wuhan. He never received a reply.

U.S. officials would not fully realize for some time how much Chinese authorities were hiding. A full week before Redfield's January 3 call with Gao, Chinese health authorities already had significant anecdotal evidence of human-to-human transmission. A Wuhan hospital's chief of respiratory diseases had reported to her superiors that she had nearly incontrovertible evidence on December 26. While examining two patients with very similar lung damage on their CT scans, she discovered they were wife and husband. Not long after, their son, who came to their apartment to help them while they were sick, also came down with the same symptoms. This was human-to-human transmission. A novel corona-virus. It was just as Redfield and Fauci had suspected. The nightmare the CDC director had been dreading was here.

Trump, meanwhile, was preoccupied with a threat in the Middle East. In late December 2019, tensions with Iran, which had been simmering since 2018 when the president withdrew the United States from the nuclear agreement that President Barack Obama had previously brokered, had reached a boil. A rocket attack in Iraq by what U.S. authorities identified as an Iranian-backed militia had killed an American contractor. American intelligence agencies had learned that Iran's top security and intelligence commander, Major General Qassim Soleimani, was orchestrating a broad campaign against American embassies, consulates, and personnel in Syria, Iraq, and Lebanon. The intelligence was, in the assessment of General Mark Milley, the chairman of the Joint Chiefs of Staff, "compelling," "imminent," and "very, very clear in scale [and] scope."

On December 29, Milley, Defense Secretary Mark Esper, Secretary of State Mike Pompeo, and National Security Adviser Robert O'Brien converged on Palm Beach to brief Trump on the intelligence and possible retaliatory measures—including killing Soleimani. As they gathered around a long table in a compact, secure room at Mar-a-Lago, Trump said he wanted to strike back somehow against Iran. He firmly believed that weakness would invite aggression. He went around the table asking each man what he counseled. Some warned that attacking Soleimani would be risky because Iran could respond by escalating even further. Trump had long said he wanted to avoid a war with Tehran, especially in 2020, when he stood for reelection. The last to weigh in was the president's top military adviser, Milley, an undaunted, no-bones army four-star, who had seen ample combat after deploying in five U.S. wars and invasions.

"Mr. President, you will be held criminally negligible for the rest of your life if you don't do this," Milley said. "American lives are at stake here. We're going to lose Americans if we don't take action right away."

Acknowledging the risks, Milley told Trump, "They're not going to just take it. They're going to react."

Trump was not one for studying intelligence. He had a low tolerance for briefings of any kind, but he struck his advisers as unusually focused, even clinical, that day as they laid top-secret plans for taking out Soleimani.

On December 31, a mob of Shiite militiamen and other Iranian sympathizers stormed the U.S. embassy in Baghdad. Trump brooded over video footage of smoke billowing from the embassy, with pro-Iranian demonstrators protesting outside. He wrote on Twitter that Iran would "pay a very BIG PRICE! This is not a Warning, it is a Threat."

Trump had discussions over the subsequent days about the forthcoming operation, including receiving intelligence updates tracking Soleimani's whereabouts. In one such conversation, Keith Kellogg, a retired army lieutenant general who was close to the president and served as Vice President Mike Pence's national security adviser, summed up the geostrategic imperative for both Trump and Pence.

"This is the guy that needs killing," Kellogg told them. "He's been fomenting the problems we've had in the Middle East. This guy is the lynchpin."

"He's got American blood on his hands, and the civilized world won't miss him at all," Kellogg added. Speaking directly to Trump, he said, "Look, sir, this is a win-win for you. It's going to make a pretty strong point. They're not going to stop screwing around with us until we do something dramatic."

Some of Trump's advisers believed it would be difficult to kill Soleimani because he would be unlikely to leave Iran, given how tense the situation had become. But Soleimani had a history of traveling freely within the Middle East, and intelligence reports in early January indicated that Soleimani was preparing a trip.

"This arrogance will kill him," Kellogg told Trump and Pence.

"What are you talking about?" Pence said.

"He will travel," Kellogg replied. "Trust me."

When Trump authorized the strike plan, he asked his advisers, "Do you think we can get him?" The president was assured they could. "Okay," he said, "let's do it."

On January 3, Soleimani flew from Damascus to Baghdad, where he was to meet with Iraqi prime minister Adil Abdul-Mahdi. After the Iranian general got into a vehicle to drive away from Baghdad International Airport, a U.S. drone fired several missiles on the motorcade, killing Soleimani and nine others.

Trump would later regale campaign donors at a Mar-a-Lago fundraiser with a play-by-play account of watching the assassination from "cameras that are miles in the sky," according to an audio recording of the January 17 event obtained by CNN's Kevin Liptak.

"Two minutes and eleven seconds to live, sir," Trump recalled military officials telling him as they narrated the silent footage. "They're in the car. They're in the armored vehicle. Sir, they have approximately one minute to live, sir. Thirty seconds. Ten, nine, eight . . . They're gone, sir. Cutting off."

Trump still spoke with awe about this feat more than a year later, when he sat down with us at Mar-a-Lago for an interview for this book. "It was sort of an amazing thing," he said of killing Soleimani. Trump recalled a conversation with Pakistani prime minister Imran Khan. "I was with Khan of Pakistan. A great athlete. Did you know he was the Mickey Mantle of cricket? He was a great athlete, handsome guy, and I met with him and he said to me, 'President, I've been through a lot in my life. I've been a star.' He's a big, big athletic star and very popular in Pakistan. He said, 'When Soleimani was taken out it was the single biggest thing I can ever remember happening in my life.'"

It was typical of Trump to be an overly dramatic and indiscreet braggart. But he had reason to crow. Soleimani was the second successful assassination of a top terrorist target he had ordered in under three months. On October 26, 2019, U.S. forces had killed Islamic State leader Abu Bakr al-Baghdadi.

During the al-Baghdadi raid by Delta Force operators, supported by a heroic dog (a Belgian Malinois named Conan), Milley narrated the black-and-white thermal video feed for the president in the White House Situation Room. Trump sat calmly as the operation unfolded, until he saw the explosions and Milley said, "We got the guy."

In early January, U.S. intelligence agencies began including warnings about the novel coronavirus and updates about the contagion's spread in the President's Daily Brief, a top-secret catalogue of the government's latest information about emerging security threats and conflicts around the globe. Yet Trump ignored the alerts. He rarely read his written PDB, and he would later claim that the coronavirus did not rise to his attention in those early days.

But all around him, Trump's advisers were growing

increasingly alarmed. Matthew Pottinger, the White House's deputy national security adviser, had been monitoring Redfield's reports but felt his first pang of worry shortly after January 10, while traveling for work to India and the United Kingdom. Pottinger had lived through the SARS outbreak, covering it from China as a foreign correspondent for **The Wall Street Journal,** and he feared the Communist government would try to conceal key information about this new pathogen—anything it considered potentially embarrassing to the nation. While on the road, he saw an article quoting a respected Chinese doctor he knew, who registered grave concern about the virus. Pottinger sent his staff an email: "If this doctor is concerned, then I'm concerned." He authorized Anthony Ruggiero, a director for weapons of mass destruction and biodefense, to convene daily NSC meetings to provide the latest on the virus, starting January 14.

At the CDC, meanwhile, officials were growing increasingly alarmed. That same day, on January 10, the Shanghai Public Health Clinical Center, a Chinese lab that had a partnership with a Wuhan hospital, was the first to publish the genome sequence of the virus, using samples from Wuhan patients. The lab's researchers uploaded the information into a publicly available website for medical investigators to share pathogen research and ideas.

The genome data was a huge leap forward for the world health community for two reasons. First, it confirmed the virus was a novel coronavirus, a version of SARS, and very likely derived from bats. Second, it gave labs everywhere critical information they needed to start developing a test to detect the virus. A crucial way to prevent an outbreak was to identify those who had the virus and keep them isolated.

But the release of the genome sequence gave a false impression that the Chinese were willing to share important and helpful information about the virus. In fact, several other labs that had confirmed the genomic sequence were blocked by the Chinese government from publishing information, and one of them was ordered not to discuss the virus with the media. After the Shanghai lab published its information online, government health officials were privately furious and, as punishment, temporarily shuttered the lab. In public, they would later point to the publication as proof of their scientists' talent and dedication to sharing information.

For Fauci, this was déjà vu. He had learned during the SARS outbreak not to trust that the Chinese were necessarily sharing the full story. His red flag went up. "Here we go again," he told associates. "Let's keep an open mind about this." Fauci called the Virus Research Center to tell them to use the Chinese genome sequencing to begin developing a vaccine.

Initially, Fauci and his boss, Dr. Francis Collins, the longtime director of the National Institutes of Health, were concerned this might have been a human-engineered virus that had gotten loose in China, either accidentally or, worse, intentionally. But

after convening several experts on viral genome evo-
lution to study that possibility, it was ruled out. Only
nature could have designed this virus, they concluded.

On January 12, the Chinese government formally
shared the genomic sequence with the World Health
Organization, which provided the optimistic assessment that there was no evidence of widespread transmission and that the outbreak was a small cluster that
Chinese authorities appeared to have under control.

But the very next day, January 13, Thailand reported a patient infected by the novel coronavirus,
a woman from Wuhan but the first known case outside China. Redfield and Fauci both recognized the
significance: The virus was no longer contained to
Wuhan or the surrounding Hubei Province. It was
spreading fast. Redfield got Gao on the phone and
the Chinese CDC director confirmed what Redfield
didn't really want to hear: Wuhan doctors were reporting that the disease appeared to transmit easily,
based on the growing number of patients in the area.

At this moment, America's frontline defense against
the virus known as COVID-19 was being led by
Redfield and Fauci as well as Alex Azar, the secretary
of health and human services. Unbeknownst to this
trio, the first patient with COVID-19 had entered
the United States that very day. A Chicago woman
in her sixties was traveling home from Wuhan after
a trip to take care of her sick father there. She arrived at Chicago's O'Hare International Airport feeling fine, but within a few days would call her doctor

complaining of strained breathing and was admitted to a local hospital. Days after that, her physicians realized she had also infected her husband.

On January 14, China's top health minister privately warned provincial health officials that the virus was likely on its way to becoming a pandemic. In a secret teleconference, the minister urged nationwide screening for the illness and declared the public health peril so grave it required a "Level One" emergency response, the highest in China. The country had embarked on building the first of five new hospitals to handle the flood of cases. Furthermore, since late December Chinese health officials had been urging doctors and nurses to take extreme precautions, such as wearing personal protective equipment when treating patients infected with the virus and creating isolation wards in which to treat them.

Yet, on the eve of announcing a major trade deal with the United States, the Chinese kept these fears and precautions hidden from the general public and even from the WHO. That same day the organization parroted Beijing's insistence that the virus was not spreading from human to human. "Preliminary investigations conducted by the Chinese authorities have found no clear evidence of human-to-human transmission of the novel #coronavirus (2019-nCoV) identified in #Wuhan, #China," the WHO said on its official Twitter account. This was a lie of gross omission. But the timing of the lie was important for a Chinese government obsessed with reputation and public optics. And luckily for them, Trump's political goals played right into their hands.

The next day, January 15, Trump hosted a signing ceremony with Chinese officials to execute the first phase of a trade deal between the two countries. Appearing in the grandeur of the East Room of the White House, adorned with rich gold drapery and three giant crystal chandeliers, Trump crowed about the accord for forty-eight minutes in a rambling monologue. Some attendees, including House Republican leader Kevin McCarthy, had to leave midspeech to get back to the Capitol for votes. Even the high-level Chinese delegation, confident they had outnegotiated the Americans, looked somewhat stiff and pained while waiting for the president to wrap up.

"I want to thank President Xi, who is watching as we speak—and I'll be going over to China in the not-too-distant future to reciprocate. But I want to thank President Xi, a very, very good friend of mine," Trump told his assembled guests.

According to the agreement, China would buy roughly $200 billion in U.S. goods, mostly agricultural, over two years in exchange for U.S. companies expanding access to Chinese markets and adding intellectual property protections. But experts doubted how much the deal benefited the United States, considering Trump had waged a trade war with China that damaged U.S. businesses and drove up the price of Chinese-manufactured appliances and other goods.

Still, Trump had what he wanted: a deal that he could boast was "great for America," signed at the dawn of his reelection year.

About an hour after Trump finished speaking, a thirty-five-year-old man from Washington State arrived at Seattle-Tacoma International Airport on a commercial flight from China, returning home from a business trip to an area just outside Wuhan. He didn't know it at the time, but he was carrying the virus. A few days after getting home, the man would suffer severe flu-like symptoms and be taken to a hospital in Everett, a bedroom community of Seattle.

He would become the second person known to enter the United States with this mystery respiratory disease. But the Trump administration would not learn about the man's case until five days after he had landed at Sea-Tac airport.

On January 16, Trump awoke in an especially foul mood. His impeachment trial was set to formally begin at the Capitol that day. He had been impeached a month earlier by the Democrat-controlled House—only the third president in history to receive that momentous rebuke—for abuse of power and obstruction of Congress in soliciting help for his reelection campaign from the Ukrainian government. Now, he faced trial in the Senate. The upper chamber was controlled by Republicans, who complained the accusations were unfair and the impeachment a

Democratic hit job, so his acquittal seemed a fore-gone conclusion, yet still the trial promised to be excruciating for the president.

Shortly before noon, the seven Democratic House impeachment managers solemnly entered the Senate chamber to deliver their articles of impeachment. One of them, Representative Adam Schiff, the Democratic House Intelligence Committee chairman and a favorite Trump foil, read out the articles in a formal, almost dour manner. Schiff explained that Trump had acted with "corrupt motive" when he pressured the newly elected president of Ukraine to announce an investigation of his leading Democratic challenger, former vice president Joe Biden, and his son Hunter Biden.

Chief Justice John Roberts of the Supreme Court, who had also drawn Trump's wrath over the years, took the rostrum and was sworn in to preside over the trial, and senators took their oath swearing to "do impartial justice" and decide whether the president should be removed from office.

Trump passed word to his aides to tell reporters he wasn't watching the proceedings because he was so busy with work in the Oval Office, yet the president seemed to know exactly what was transpiring in the Senate Chamber. That afternoon at 3:39 he tweeted, "I JUST GOT IMPEACHED FOR MAKING A PERFECT PHONE CALL!"

Later that day, a little after 5:00, Trump met with some of his campaign advisers. At the time, the Trump team thought Senators Bernie Sanders or Elizabeth Warren might be the Democratic nominee, and both were running on expanding health-care access as signature issues. The Trump campaign's data showed that voters trusted Democrats more than Republicans on health care, especially when it came to protecting coverage for those with preexisting conditions, and that the president's plan to repeal the Affordable Care Act was unpopular. Trump also faced a polling deficit on the issue of prescription drug pricing.

Tony Fabrizio, a longtime Republican pollster who worked on Trump's 2016 and 2020 campaigns, argued that health care would be top of mind to voters, especially in Florida and some other battleground states, and that if Trump could sign an executive order or otherwise enact policies protecting those with preexisting conditions he might fare better against the Democrats. Reminded that the White House counsel's office was drafting some such orders, Trump lashed out.

"Yeah, like they work on everything else," Trump said. "They're so fucking slow."

Trump was already smarting that week over a series of ads Michael Bloomberg, the former New York mayor running for the Democratic presidential nomination, was airing, criticizing Trump's failure to produce a health-care plan despite his campaign promise to do so. The polling presentation sent him into a rageful fury.

"This vaping ban shit is hurting me," Trump said,

referring to the administration's push led by Azar to ban flavors in e-cigarettes in the fall of 2019.

Brad Parscale, Trump's campaign manager, spoke up to say he, too, believed the e-cigarette ban was suppressing Trump's support with voters who vape.

"Get me Azar on the phone!" Trump cried out to his assistant.

Once the health secretary was reached on his cell phone, the president tore into him, and put the line on speakerphone to make the campaign advisers listen in.

"I'm losing on drug pricing," Trump told Azar. "I'm getting killed on drug pricing. The polling shows the Democrats are beating me on drug prices. You've got to fix that."

"Mr. President," Azar responded, "you're losing on drug pricing because you've done literally nothing on drug pricing."

"What do you mean?" Trump asked.

"Literally everything I've tried to do on cutting drug costs, you have killed it," Azar replied.

The president then pivoted to e-cigarettes.

"I never should have done this vaping thing," Trump said. "I'm going to get fucked on this."

"You lost me the election, Alex," he continued. "Everywhere I go, every rally I go to, they are holding signs: 'I vape. I vote.' They told me you have hurt me in the polls. We should have left it alone. You should have let me leave it alone. I shouldn't have done any of that."

As Trump bellowed, Azar thought he was living

in a bad movie. Trump had picked this same fight with Azar nearly half a dozen times since rolling out the e-cigarette policy in September 2019. At the time Trump embraced the ban on flavors and told reporters that he and his wife had been antivaping advocates in part because their teenage son had become curious about vaping. The president acknowledged telling Barron, "Don't vape! Don't vape!"

"That's how the first lady got involved," Trump said. "She's got a son . . . a beautiful young man, and she feels very, very strongly."

But Trump's resolve melted away as soon as Parscale had told the president the vaping regulations could backfire with part of his political base. The day after the announcement, Azar was in the Democratic Republic of Congo for a visit related to the deadly Ebola outbreak when his cell phone rang. It was the president, and he was screaming.

"You have lost me the election!" Trump yelled at the secretary. It was all about Azar pushing Trump to ban flavored e-cigarettes. "Brad tells me I'm going to lose the election now because the vapers are my core constituents and they're not going to show up and vote!"

From his hotel room in Kinshasa, Azar tried to calm Trump down and explain that the ban on flavored e-cigarettes had a huge upside with voters, too. "Every suburban mom thanks you—you've taken these horrific products out of the hands of their children," Azar said. "I have won you the election!"

But Trump was not to be reasoned with. "It's your fault if I lose, Alex!" he yelled.

From that moment on, Azar was solidly in the president's doghouse.

The January 16 conversation felt to Azar like a broken record. Azar once again tried to reason with his boss.

"You've gotten praised in every editorial page in the country," he told Trump. "You have parents thanking you for empowering them. You have teachers thanking you. These long-haired hippie vapers, if they voted for you before, aren't going to switch sides now."

Azar dismissed the people holding signs. "These are professional protesters, paid by the vape industry, Mr. President," he said. "I'm sure your polling data will tell you that you are winning on vaping."

Trump had had enough.

"Okay," Trump said. "Goodbye."

The call was over.

Azar's chief of staff, Brian Harrison, had been listening on another line. Once the president hung up and he and Azar were alone on the line, Harrison said, "You really shouldn't speak to the president of the United States like that."

Azar understood his point but disagreed, given the president's modus operandi. Azar had long ago grown accustomed to gut punches from the president and he felt that Trump would respect him more if he punched back. Trump would call Azar unscheduled up to three times a day. Early in the morning or in the middle of the day or late at night, sometimes with a compliment but more often angry about something he saw on a cable news show. He would demand Azar fix it, whatever the problem might be.

That night, Azar had an opportunity to give Trump a freebie on his favorite medium: television. The secretary had a prescheduled interview that would air at 11:00 p.m. on the Fox News Channel with host Shannon Bream. The appearance came on National Religious Freedom Day. Religious freedom was not typically a front-and-center issue for a U.S. health secretary, but it was for many Trump voters, so Azar touted Trump's commitment to protecting the freedom to pray in school.

"We have in President Trump the greatest protector of religious liberty who has ever sat in the Oval Office," Azar told Bream and her Fox viewers.

By mid-January, as the CDC began implementing public health screenings at a handful of major international airports, coronavirus was already silently pouring into the United States, carried by unwitting travelers. It was too late to stop the contagion. On the morning of Saturday, January 18, Azar rose early with a nagging concern. While health agencies and the NSC had been rapidly preparing for a potential pandemic, he hadn't had a deep conversation of any kind with Trump about the virus. He knew Trump was at Mar-a-Lago for the weekend, consumed with

his impeachment trial. He figured it was doubt-
ful the president knew much if anything about the
virus. From his den at home in a Maryland suburb,
Azar reached acting White House chief of staff Mick
Mulvaney, who was golfing at Trump International
Golf Club in West Palm Beach, near Mar-a-Lago.

"Mick, we've got this novel coronavirus," Azar
said. He described how it resembled its predecessors,
SARS and MERS, and how this virus could quickly
turn into a global threat. He explained the airport
screenings and that the Chinese government had
admitted to having forty-five cases, which almost
certainly meant there were a lot more. Plus, there
were reports the virus had already spilled into other
Asian countries.

"I'm very nervous about the president and whether
you guys have educated him about this," Azar said.

Mulvaney said nothing about briefing Trump on
the virus.

"Mick, I've gotta talk to the president," Azar said.
"I've got to fill him in on this if you guys haven't
already."

Several hours passed. At about 6:00 p.m., at
Mulvaney's suggestion, Trump called Azar, who
happened to be back in his den. The president immediately began laying into his health secretary
on vaping.

"You should have left them alone!" Trump said of
the e-cigarette industry.

Azar was burning out on the subject and cursed back.

"I won you the fucking election," he said. "This is gold with suburban women, the people you most need."

Trump didn't engage on that point, and instead issued instructions.

"You need to come up with a plan to quickly get those flavors back on the market," he said.

Azar sighed, thinking how he could move the conversation to the virus, but the president started peppering Azar about something else.

"How's our health-care plan?" Trump said. "Where's the new plan to replace Obamacare? How about our lawsuit? Where the fuck are we, Alex?"

After Azar answered, Trump said he had to get going.

"No, no, Mr. President," Azar said hurriedly. He explained that he wanted to talk about the coronavirus that so far had sickened dozens of people that they knew of in Wuhan, and that the symptoms mimicked a lethal pneumonia and looked a lot like SARS.

"What's a coronavirus?" Trump asked.

"It can be really dangerous," Azar said. "This could kill a lot of people. It's already in China."

Azar gave the president a quick lesson on the SARS outbreak nearly two decades earlier and said this new virus could be just as bad and required vigilance.

"We're working to try to catch cases as people come into the country, but it's a really big deal," Azar said. "It is a potentially very serious health situation."

Trump didn't ask any questions. He sounded peeved, said he needed to get off the phone, and hung up. The president had a party to get to, the Palm Beach Policemen's and Firemen's Ball, hosted at Mar-a-Lago. He put on his tuxedo, shook hands in the ballroom, and gave a special toast.

Two

Totally Under Control

On January 21, 2020, President Trump jetted off to the snow-capped Swiss Alps, where he addressed the World Economic Forum the next day. This was a pilgrimage to the Mecca of moneyed global elites—the kind of people Trump had long resented for looking down on him and not taking him seriously—to rub it in their faces that his "America First" agenda was bearing fruit. The unemployment rate had fallen, the stock markets were up, and Trump had a new trade deal with China to boot.

Never mind that the coronavirus was fast spreading, or that China was still refusing to allow a team of U.S. scientists into Wuhan for an inspection, or that Matt Pottinger and Trump's top doctors feared China once again was trying to cover up an internal problem. Trump wished to project optimism. The last thing he wanted was to alarm Americans, which could depress the economy and sink his reelection chances.

White House aides booked an interview for Trump in Davos with CNBC's Joe Kernen, hoping to give the president a forum to tout the economy. But the **Squawk Box** cohost asked about the virus, which was still only garnering modest mentions in national news. Kernen referenced the Washington State man having recently been declared the first confirmed U.S. case.

"Are there worries about a pandemic at this point?" Kernen asked.

"No, not at all," Trump said. "We have it totally under control. It's one person coming in from China, and we have it under control. It's going to be just fine."

When Kernen asked whether he trusted China was sharing everything the U.S. government needed, Trump said he had no worries there either.

"I do. I do," he said. "I have a great relationship with President Xi. We just signed probably the biggest deal ever made. It certainly has the potential to be the biggest deal ever made. And it was a very interesting period of time, but we got it done, and no, I do. I think the relationship is very, very good."

Public health officials were aghast. The president had said the novel coronavirus was "under control" when they were learning new and worrisome things about it practically by the hour. What's more, the phrase "under control" was a defined, scientific phrase meaning that the number of infections had been steadily reducing, essentially that the threat was petering out. The coronavirus was absolutely, definitively **not** under control.

Francis Collins was also in Davos that day for meetings with other leading global infectious disease experts about the coronavirus. The NIH director represented the U.S. delegation in a meeting with Dr. Tedros Adhanom Ghebreyesus, the director general of the World Health Organization, during which he sought to persuade the global institution to declare an international public health emergency. He was directly undercut by his boss, Trump. For Collins and his colleagues at the NIH, this was the beginning of the dramatic divergence between the scientific consensus and the president's public statements.

Alex Azar was shopping at a music store in Washington's Tenleytown neighborhood when he connected by phone with Robert O'Brien, who was flying back to Washington from Davos. Azar stepped outside into the cold for privacy to share his exasperation with the national security adviser.

"The president was pretty dismissive with me, Robert," Azar said. "I can take that. But it's really important that the president not be dismissive like he was on TV. This is a big deal. This is a really big problem."

Azar had hoped O'Brien would say something like "Yeah, we're on it," or "You're right. I'll tell him." As they spoke, Azar paced back and forth on the sidewalk, holding his phone to his ear with one hand and gesticulating with the other, scowling. Azar wasn't upset with O'Brien but with the situation. He didn't feel the White House leadership was treating this threat seriously.

Trump arrived back in Washington to face turf battles, which were flaring up in the West Wing and among the agencies. Distrust between the president's political appointees and career health officials and other professionals was deepening. This was the consequence of him having spent three years molding the government in his own image. The White House had largely abandoned the pretense of following a methodical policy process to make decisions or crafting long-term strategic plans. The driving imperative for those at the top was to survive the daily news cycle by diagnosing every problem as a public relations crisis. Senior officials were on edge about their employment. This weakened the chain of command and risked paralyzing the administration at the very moment the machinery of government needed to be running at maximum tilt. Mick Mulvaney, who had been acting White House chief of staff for thirteen months, still had not shaken the "acting" from his title, which was interpreted fairly or not as an indicator the president lacked confidence in him.

Azar, having angered Trump over e-cigarettes and delays in health-care reforms Trump had promised on the campaign trail, had alienated a slew of administration colleagues before the coronavirus hit and was seen as vulnerable. A lawyer who had recently run pharmaceutical giant Eli Lilly's U.S. division, he was a longtime Republican with the résumé to match. He'd worked as a law clerk to Justice Antonin Scalia, on the Whitewater investigation embroiling the Clintons, and in the George W. Bush administration as both a deputy and general counsel for the Department of Health and Human Services. As a big pharma executive, he had been a demanding taskmaster and was used to calling the shots. But now in government, his subordinates bristled at times at his C-suite manner. He rubbed the president the wrong way, too, with his detailed, laborious recitations on everything from legal precedent to vaccine clinical trials.

Azar had a long-simmering rivalry with Joe Grogan, director of the White House's Domestic Policy Council, dating from their disagreements over prescription drug pricing and other health-care policies. One of their colleagues described it as "a big dick-swinging contest" between them. Azar also had a feud going with Seema Verma, the Centers for Medicare & Medicaid Services director, who reported to him, that grew so acrimonious and personally nasty that, by the end of 2019, it had required interventions from senior White House aides Kellyanne Conway, Chris Liddell, Mulvaney, and ultimately Trump himself. It was in this poisonous, disloyal atmosphere that the White House tried to mount a coronavirus response.

While Trump and his entourage were in Davos, Grogan became increasingly worried by media reports about the coronavirus, as well as conversations he was having with Scott Gottlieb, a friend who had recently departed as Food and Drug Administration commissioner. The two men spoke early in the morning on January 19 and Gottlieb was stressed about the emerging threat. Until this point, the government response was largely being handled by Azar and the CDC and other agencies that reported to him, with relatively little White House involvement outside of the National Security Council. But after talking to Gottlieb, Grogan thought to himself, **Oh, fuck. I'm going to have to deal with this.**

On Monday, January 20, Grogan came to work and scheduled a series of meetings on the coronavirus to get himself and his team up to speed. The NSC had been having its own coronavirus meetings for at least a week, which meant health agency officials now had to brief dueling groups of White House aides.

During one of Grogan's first coronavirus meetings in the Roosevelt Room, aides discussed the CDC's recent discovery of the thirty-five-year-old man who had traveled home to Washington State from Wuhan, the first known case of the coronavirus in the United States. Hogan Gidley, the principal deputy press secretary, cornered Grogan with an urgent concern.

"This is gonna leak," Gidley said, worried about how news of a U.S. case might impact the president.

Gidley wanted to make sure the White House got in front of the story so people wouldn't panic.

"I don't know what to tell you," Grogan replied. "We've got a goddamn U.S. case. It is going to get out."

The CDC publicly announced the case a day later, on January 21.

Azar was furious that Grogan was convening his own coronavirus meetings. In his January 22 call to O'Brien, he unloaded on what he called the "mayhem" of the government response. He said experts at the CDC and FDA, whose leaders reported to Azar, risked burnout if they had to keep briefing multiple groups of White House officials. O'Brien told Azar that he would task his deputy, Pottinger, to run coronavirus meetings so there would not be repetition, even though Mulvaney had already blessed Grogan's lead role.

On January 23, the day after the return of the Davos delegation, Mulvaney convened a meeting of White House aides in his office to get a handle on the coronavirus. Pottinger and Grogan were there, as well as Conway, legislative affairs director Eric Ueland, press secretary Stephanie Grisham, Gidley, and Keith Kellogg. There was growing apprehension about the political consequences of the virus. Video footage out of China was frightening—trucks rolling through the streets of cities spraying fog, people wearing smocks and other protective gear around their bodies, deaths piling up. Imagine how voters might react if these images played out in America, too?

"This could cost us the election," Grogan said. "Look, guys, one of the criticisms we're getting on the left on Twitter is that we eviscerated the NSC because [former national security adviser John] Bolton shut down the global health security directorate, and that is true."

"Okay, Grogan, what do you want to do?" Mulvaney asked.

"We need to bring a czar in, like Ron Klain was for Ebola," Grogan said, referring to the Obama administration's handling of the Ebola outbreak in 2014 and 2015. "We need somebody who can do media and project, 'We're in charge of it.' It doesn't need to be a doctor. It needs to be somebody who has good communication skills and good political instincts."

The group discussed an array of people who could be the face of the administration's response but found fault with all of them. Some thought Anthony Fauci, though a leading expert on infectious diseases, would look too old on television; Azar sounded too condescending; Robert Redfield came off as too much of a professor and lacked political chops. They considered the merits of luring Gottlieb back into the administration.

But the idea of a coronavirus czar was tabled. And Mulvaney started to chair meetings on the crisis, a feeble attempt to unite the overlapping internal efforts.

On January 24, Azar met with Trump and updated the president on his department's coronavirus work.

"How's China doing?" Trump asked.

"They are being relatively transparent compared to SARS," Azar said. "But it's China, so you never know what you don't know."

Azar continued: "They've got to let the CDC in and they've got to give us samples. Under WHO regulations, they are in violation because they haven't done that."

The president appeared to hear only the first—and most optimistic—thing his health secretary had said.

"You know, I'm going to send out a tweet praising them," Trump said out of nowhere. "Praising China."

Azar was speechless. Trump had been on a pro-China roll for weeks, so excited before and after signing the trade deal on January 15, which he felt was a huge plum for his reelection campaign. He made clear he didn't want to insult Chinese president Xi Jinping.

Trump then yelled out for Dan Scavino, who sat in a small, windowless cubbyhole of an office just outside the Oval Office. Scavino was the director of social media, which meant he was one of the only people with access to Trump's vaunted Twitter account and often pecked out messages the boss dictated.

Azar's shoulders tightened. He knew what Trump

was about to do—dictate a tweet about China to Scavino—and wanted desperately to stop him.

"Mr. President, that is a big give to Xi," Azar said hurriedly. "You should not do that lightly. His response is not going well. You endorsing him will shore up his power structure. This is not something you should do lightly." He stressed that they didn't know whether China was being transparent.

But Trump waved his hand and said he would praise China anyhow. He signaled he was done with Azar's briefing, and kept barking out for Scavino, who soon appeared at the door. Azar couldn't change Trump's mind, not at this pace. So he left the Oval and headed toward O'Brien's corner office. He found the national security adviser inside.

Azar told O'Brien about Trump's tweet plan and then blurted out, "You've got to tell the president he can't praise Xi. I can't get him to stop. He can't send this tweet. I can't convince him. And I can't take the phone out of his hands."

The president's next scheduled meeting was with Mike Pompeo. Azar hoped the two of them could convince Trump. The intervention was not to be, however. Trump tweeted: "China has been working very hard to contain the Coronavirus. The United States greatly appreciates their efforts and transparency. It will all work out well. In particular, on behalf of the American People, I want to thank President Xi!"

———

On January 28, at around 7:30 a.m., Pottinger was driving himself to work at the White House when his cell phone rang with a callback he had been waiting for. On the other line was a doctor in China whom Pottinger knew well. Pottinger had been reaching out with increasing urgency to a list of old sources and friends in Asia from his time there as a journalist. Now he had one of those trusted contacts on the phone. The doctor told Pottinger the virus was spreading rapidly, already far beyond the province of Hubei. There were hundreds of cases traced to community spread. And there was something worse.

"This is wholly unlike SARS in 2003," the doctor said. It was spreading asymptomatically, the doctor noted, estimating that as many as half of China's cases at that point had been spread by people without symptoms.

"This isn't SARS 2003," the doctor said. "This is 1918."

The Spanish flu had infected roughly a third of the world's population over two years and was estimated to have killed at least fifty million people.

Pottinger thought, **Okay, this is scaring the shit out of me.**

He then shared this new information with O'Brien, who suggested Pottinger join him at Trump's regular intelligence briefing later that morning. The two men, CIA briefer Beth Sanner, Mulvaney, and several other senior officials gathered in the Oval sometime around 11:30, with O'Brien and Sanner taking chairs in front of the Resolute Desk and Pottinger sitting on a sofa just behind them.

Sanner began going through a long list of hot topics, then eventually turned to the coronavirus in China. The president interjected.

"What do you think of this thing?" he asked O'Brien.

O'Brien said the NSC saw evidence that the virus was becoming very serious.

"This is going to be the most severe national security threat of your presidency," O'Brien said.

Sanner then recited the available facts, none of them terribly alarming. New stats on the infection spread in China. The status of the Chinese government's travel bans in and out of Wuhan.

"Is this going to be worse than the 2003 outbreak of SARS?" Trump asked.

Sanner said it wasn't clear at this point.

O'Brien suggested Pottinger add a few new things he had learned. The deputy national security adviser, a Marine by training, stood up from his sofa seat.

"Mr. President, I want to convey some things I just learned because I think it's important," Pottinger said. "This thing is spreading asymptomatically. This is going to be more akin to the 1918 flu outbreak."

Noting that he agreed with O'Brien about the seriousness of the threat, Pottinger explained that if people without symptoms were spreading the infection, it would be harder to identify those who were infected. Without symptoms, they wouldn't be able to isolate and control the contagion, as they had done with SARS.

"You can't do temperature checks and expect to find this thing, so it's really going to be much more challenging," Pottinger said.

And he warned the president that the Chinese government was not being transparent about these worrisome facts.

"Do you think I should shut off travel from China?" Trump asked.

This was a topic that O'Brien and Pottinger had been preliminarily discussing following the Wuhan lockdown. Both advisers told the president he should restrict travel from China.

"I think we should, because it's clear to me they are not being forthcoming," Pottinger said, referring to Chinese government officials. "I'm getting much more detailed information from personal phone calls than the entire global health establishment is getting."

Trump did not commit to a decision, and Sanner moved along to the next topic. In a forty-five-minute discussion of a globe full of problems, they devoted roughly ten minutes to talking about the virus. The meeting ended and the president's advisers dispersed.

As they were walking out the door, Mulvaney turned to Pottinger with a stern face. At this point a skeptic of the virus morphing into a domestic crisis, Mulvaney was irate that Pottinger had raised reports from a single contact to effectively scare the president into taking action. "That was totally inappropriate," the acting chief of staff told Pottinger. "You won't come to another one of these."

Downstairs in the Situation Room, Mulvaney gathered some members of the fledgling coronavirus task force. The topic turned to the idea of restricting travel from China into the United States, as a bulwark against the virus spreading in America. This would be a severe course of action. Various advisers highlighted the risks in doing so, including choking off commerce between the world's two largest economies.

Fauci raised other concerns: Historically, travel bans have not worked to contain infectious diseases, and it would not be feasible to restrict travel worldwide.

As Fauci spoke, White House trade adviser Peter Navarro was incredulous. Navarro was a Trump World original, having advised then candidate Trump during the 2016 campaign, and had fashioned himself as the ultimate loyalist, earning a reputation as a sycophant. He was also an ideologue, advocating an isolationist approach to foreign policy and an adversarial posture toward China. Navarro titled his two books on that subject **The Coming China Wars** and **Death by China.**

This was the first time Navarro had met Fauci, who had been widely respected through Democratic and Republican administrations alike. Looking across the table at Fauci, however, Navarro thought to himself, **That's the most arrogant, dumb guy I've ever met—just full of himself, just absolutely full of himself, like his excrement didn't stink and he was**

God. Navarro had found his antagonist—the archrival he would plot to undermine and cut down at every turn. Navarro went home the night of January 28 determined to convince Fauci and other task-force members of the imperative of restricting travel.

Late that night, the first in a series of charter flights to repatriate Americans from China touched down in Anchorage for fuel and an infection check. Its 201 passengers—staffers from the U.S. consulate in Wuhan and other private citizens based there—were among 800 people the State Department was seeking to evacuate as soon as possible. After the passengers were screened twice for possible infection in Alaska, the plane continued to its destination: March Air Reserve Base outside Riverside, California. There, they were supposed to stay in special barracks until health officials could be sure they wouldn't infect the general public.

The next day, January 29, Navarro submitted a memorandum to the NSC and coronavirus task force advocating for "swift containment and mitigation measures" and noting that the most readily available option was to issue a travel ban to and from the source of the outbreak, China. He presented his case using game theory. Navarro calculated that the cost of stopping travel from China to the United States for one month would be approximately $2.9 billion, and if the virus became like a seasonal flu outbreak or was contained, travel would be able to resume after that. But he calculated that the economic costs of a pandemic without any containment measures would be catastrophically higher, $3.8 trillion.

By the time some task-force members read Navarro's memo, however, they had already come around to the presumption that Trump would restrict travel from China, considering both how quickly the virus was spreading there and the extraordinary steps the Chinese government itself was taking to try to contain it and to treat the infected. China was officially reporting some 6,000 cases of the virus and 132 deaths, but U.S. officials reasoned the actual toll was considerably higher.

At sixty-eight, Redfield had toiled for four decades as an army doctor, virologist, and university lab director before taking the CDC job. He figured he should be retired and relaxing with his wife and grandchildren. Yet here he was, in the fourth iteration of his public health career, and a worldwide health catastrophe was occurring on his watch. Since Redfield's first call in early January with George Gao, the disturbing events came at him nonstop. He was terribly sleep-deprived. His wife kept waking up in their Baltimore home to find him at 2:00 and 3:00 a.m. in dark rooms talking on the phone with people in faraway time zones, such as CDC scientists in China, WHO officials in Europe, or public health officials in California or Washington State.

The morning of January 30, Redfield felt like

everything was starting to explode. Illinois officials had contacted the CDC the previous night to report the husband of the Chicago-area woman in her sixties was now also infected. He became the sixth U.S. case. This was irrefutable evidence that the infection spread from human to human. Then Redfield's staff alerted him to a seventh U.S. case. The double whammy solidified Redfield's resolve about something he initially had resisted: restricting travel from China.

Like Navarro, O'Brien and Pottinger had been pushing for the travel ban for several days. They strongly believed that China had been consistently misleading the United States about how badly the virus was spreading, even beyond China's border. Redfield, like Fauci, was not initially in favor of shutting down borders and announcing travel bans, which they believed could cause panic while doing little to stop diseases from spreading. The public health mantra to stop the spread was to identify the infected, trace their contacts, and isolate the exposed.

Now, though, Redfield felt this virus was galloping past them and decided the ban was critical. Fauci concluded the same. They spoke to Azar during a previously scheduled meeting around 11:00 a.m. that day to let him know they had changed their minds. Azar was quickly on board, too. Azar's wife, Jennifer, had been asking him about this issue recently. "This is going on in China," she said. "Why are we letting people come in from China?" Azar thought that was a good question.

Trump had no idea about the anxiety building among his experts. He departed the White House at about 1:15 p.m. to fly west for a pair of campaign rallies later that day in Michigan and Iowa. But his White House operation kept humming along. Mulvaney had a deputies' meeting on coronavirus at 3:00, in the small Situation Room. A possible China travel ban wasn't on the agenda, but given the urgency Azar was getting from Redfield and Fauci, he told Mulvaney they needed to make it the central topic. The group discussed the new cases and the evidence of human-to-human transmission. Then they discussed implementation of the "212(f)"—their shorthand for the proposed travel restriction, referring to the section of the statute spelling out the president's authority to ban entry to the country in times of danger or crisis. They also agreed to endorse the State Department's plan to fly four more evacuation flights of Americans out of Wuhan and surrounding areas. Nearly everyone agreed both the ban and the repatriation flights were no-brainers. Mulvaney told the team they would gather to present the recommendation to the president the next day.

As the meeting wrapped, Mulvaney asked Azar to walk with him to his office upstairs so they could call the president, who was aboard Air Force One, to get his buy-in on evacuating the additional Americans. Mulvaney stood near his standing desk by the fireplace in his office, with Azar hovering, and got Trump on the line. Mulvaney's national security aide, Rob

Blair, and legal adviser, Mike Williams, sat on nearby couches, while Deputy Secretary of State Steve Biegun was connected by the White House operator.

"Mr. President, we've got something that Biegun and Azar need to run by you," Mulvaney said.

Biegun opened with what he and the group thought would be a basic overview of the effort to bring home diplomats and permanent residents, as well as protections to ensure the evacuated Americans didn't spread the virus after returning. The president wanted to know how many people. Biegun estimated it would be several hundred right away, and eventually could be a couple of thousand.

Trump exploded.

"We're not letting them come back," he said. "You risk increasing my numbers. You won't increase my numbers."

Trump didn't want sick Americans landing on U.S. soil, even if they were working for the State Department, or else the government would have to report a rise in infections, and that would make the public—the voters—nervous. The president was always thinking about the political ramifications for himself, even during a crisis.

Biegun and Azar explained the measures under way to screen and isolate the passengers who had already landed in California.

"The first flight was a mistake," Trump said. "Those people shouldn't have been in China in the first place."

Azar and Mulvaney exchanged a look. The president

was talking about Americans who had gone to China to serve the U.S. government as if they had irresponsibly or illegally crossed into a foreign country. Biegun compared their situation in Wuhan to a war zone. United States government employees deserved protection and services that could not reliably be provided to them in a city where the virus had overrun hospital wards and created a true emergency.

"It would be like leaving a man on the field of battle," Biegun added.

Azar urged the president to consider his mantra of placing America—and thus Americans—first.

"This would be contrary to your brand of protecting Americans, Mr. President," he said.

O'Brien walked into Mulvaney's office midconversation. Trump said he thought doing so amounted to a dangerous risk. But Biegun and Azar stuck to their guns. They appealed to Trump's media instincts, telling him it would look horrible not to bring Americans home when there was a relatively safe way to do so. Trump gradually eased back, and by the end of the call he described himself as supporting the flights. The president said there was no other choice. Then he hung up. In the coming weeks, Trump would fully embrace the repatriation of Americans after hearing the first-person accounts of some of the early evacuees.

"All right," Mulvaney said, turning to the group. "The president approved the flights."

Azar warned Mulvaney he wasn't sure the president was entirely on board. After his painful e-cigarette experience with Trump, Azar wondered who the president would blame for this later down the road.

"Mick, the president is not at rest on the issue," he said.

Azar took the opportunity of this smaller meeting with the acting chief of staff to complain, as he regularly had, about a string of damaging leaks about him in media reports, and pointed to Grogan as the culprit.

"This has got to stop," Azar said. "I'm literally here working nonstop with the White House. He's your guy, and he's leaking every day and making crap up."

"You don't know who did it," Mulvaney said. "Everyone leaks here."

He added, "You just have to put up with it."

That same day, the WHO, which had been deferential to China and slow to hit the panic button, finally declared the coronavirus a global health emergency. But at an event that day in Warren, Michigan, Trump told a roaring rally crowd that they had nothing to worry about.

"We think we have it very well under control," he said. "We have very little problem in this country at this moment—five—and those people are all recuperating successfully."

Joining Trump at the rally was the vice president, who had been notably disengaged from the coronavirus response to date. Pence had been represented in task-force meetings by Olivia Troye, a career national security professional who was serving as his homeland security adviser. But Troye sometimes had difficulty getting through to Pence and his chief of staff, Marc Short, with virus updates.

Such was the case the night of January 30. Aware that a presidential decision was imminent about restricting travel from China, Troye called Short several times to try to brief him and the vice president on the matter, but he didn't pick up. He and Pence were preoccupied with the rally and preparing remarks for an anti-human-trafficking event scheduled the next day. Troye sent a memo to Air Force Two outlining the travel decision but received no acknowledgment that Pence or Short had read it.

The next day, January 31, Mulvaney summoned everyone to the Oval Office. The doctors. The economists. The national security chiefs. The vice president. Though Trump was leaning toward it, Mulvaney wanted him to hear from all his advisers before officially deciding about travel from China.

When the Oval session was hastily added to Pence's calendar, Short called Troye and asked her to rush to the vice president's office right away to brief him on this. She was irritated because she had been trying to get their attention the day before, and now suddenly everyone was scrambling. But she was ready. She was given five minutes to lay out the facts for the vice president and Short, as well as Kellogg, who was in the room.

Pence and Short asked her what she expected in the Oval when the travel ban came up.

"I think you should expect to implement this," Troye said.

Short rolled his eyes and scoffed at her. "Can you believe this?" he said, looking at Pence.

"There's no way," Pence said.

As they hurried toward the Oval, Kellogg said to Troye, "You're doing your job, and you're doing it well. You're nailing it, kid."

Once the meeting began, Redfield did a lot of the talking. He told the president that he would be failing in his job as CDC director to protect the American public's health if they didn't block flights coming from China.

"This pathogen is transmissible human-to-human, it's clear it's now starting to leak out of China, and we need to shut down air travel from China," Redfield said. "It's obviously spreading quickly."

Trump had questions. What did they know about the virus so far? How many cases did they trace to China? How quickly was it spreading?

Speaking in neutral scientific terms, Redfield warned that the same ghoulish scenes playing out in China soon could replay in American cities. The NSC had some intelligence that also indicated bodies were literally piling up in hospitals and morgues in Wuhan. Reports flagged that the Chinese government

was in the process of building or repurposing buildings to create five new hospitals. Later intelligence
would confirm reports that state crematoriums in the
region were working round the clock in late January,
at a rate of six times the incineration they had done
before the virus.

"The evidence we have right now is that the virus in
Wuhan is having significant mortality," Redfield told
Trump. At the time, they estimated eight out of every
one hundred people infected in Wuhan would end
up dead in a few weeks. Even those who recovered
needed long stays in the hospital, filling intensive care
wards. "It is totally overwhelming their health system,
bringing their health system to its knees," he said.

O'Brien and Pottinger chimed in that Wuhan had
just effectively quarantined eleven million people,
shutting down travel in and out of the entire Hubei
province surrounding the city. The top national security aides told the president a reaction this substantial reasonably cleared the path for terminating travel
from China.

As many as fourteen thousand people a day were
traveling from China to the United States. "The problem is, Mr. President, they're still flying the planes out
of Wuhan, and we need to shut those planes down,
so they at least don't land in America," Redfield said.

Trump would later say he alone pushed for the
China ban and claimed that in so doing he had protected "millions" of Americans from death. But in
the decision meeting, almost all of the president's

advisers were on board with restricting travel, including Mulvaney.

Tomas Philipson, the chairman of the Council of Economic Advisers, was a rare voice of opposition, warning the ban on travel from a major economic partner would take a huge financial toll and calling it an "overreaction." And Treasury Secretary Steven Mnuchin raised similar concerns, arguing that restricting travel would violate free-market principles.

Conway, a pollster by trade who was a specialist in political messaging and had worked on the administration's response to the opioid epidemic, did not oppose the restrictions but offered a note of caution about how it might reverberate with Trump's core supporters.

"I wanted you to be tougher on China from the get-go," she told the president. "So how are we going to tell moms all over the country that we never stood up to China when they were pouring fentanyl into our communities, our kids' veins, and our coworkers, but we're doing it now?"

The president was listening intently, and in a departure from the norm, sticking to the subject at hand. He made a decision in just twenty minutes. Flights would be suspended from China to the United States. Pence, who was just getting up to speed on the issue, supported Trump's decision.

Yet Trump wasn't excited to announce the order himself. He didn't explain why, but some advisers in the room believed that the president making this statement could make a big splash and he didn't want to spook the stock markets.

"Alex, you go out and you announce it," Trump said to Azar.

As Azar later told aides, he was immediately suspicious. Trump was not normally shy about grabbing a chance at the lectern. He suspected the president wanted to see how this would be received politically and in the markets. "If this doesn't play well," Azar later told an aide, "he will hang me out to dry."

Azar went to the Roosevelt Room to prepare an announcement. His staff hustled to draft his remarks. "Total scramble," one aide recalled. "Par for the course in the Trump administration."

It seemed odd to Azar's team of aides that no one from the White House press shop weighed in on his speech. When Azar signed the formal declaration of a public health emergency before his news conference, his chief of staff, Brian Harrison, took a picture with his personal cell phone.

Azar stepped under the bright lights of the White House press briefing room before a hastily assembled press corps to announce that travel from China would be banned effective 5:00 p.m. on February 2. He said American residents returning from China would have to be screened prior to entry and quarantine in their homes for two weeks after returning. And he declared that the coronavirus constituted a public health emergency in the United States.

Before the markets closed for the day, the Dow

Jones Industrial Average fell a whopping six hundred points, an overall market loss of 2 percent. The markets would bounce up and down over the next few days in reaction to the travel restrictions. This was only a preview of what was still to come.

Redfield and Fauci had been alarmed in recent days about a few reports of asymptomatic transmission in Germany and elsewhere. But because the CDC still hadn't received a virus specimen from the Chinese nor been permitted to send a team there to investigate, they were somewhat in the dark in late January, thinking this virus was similar to SARS, which was—in the main—easy to spot based on obvious symptoms.

Three

Seeking Revenge

The first week of February 2020 was one of triumph for President Trump. On February 2, he boasted in an interview, which aired during the Super Bowl, that the coronavirus was nothing to worry about thanks to his new travel restrictions. "We pretty much shut it down coming in from China." Trump's reelection campaign also spent $10 million to buy sixty seconds' worth of advertising during the 49ers-Chiefs game—a political muscle flex intended to signal the president's financial dominance, but that many veteran operatives considered a colossal waste of money surely designed to satisfy the president's supersized ego rather than win a campaign.

Two days later, Trump strode into the House Chamber to deliver his annual State of the Union address, a speech complete with dramatic reveals and live spectacles befitting a former reality television producer president. He interrupted his address to award the Presidential Medal of Freedom, the nation's highest civilian honor, to an emotional Rush Limbaugh, the controversial and highly partisan conservative radio host.

But the week's exclamation point came the day after, February 5, when the Senate voted not to convict Trump in his impeachment trial. As had been broadly expected, Democrats fell short of the two-thirds majority required to remove Trump from office, as the Republican-controlled chamber voted 52–48 to clear Trump of the abuse-of-power allegation and 53–47 to acquit him of obstructing justice related to his attempts to pressure Ukraine. Senator Mitt Romney of Utah was the lone Republican who voted to convict the president on the first article, but Romney also acquitted him on the second.

Trump celebrated his "VICTORY on the Impeachment Hoax," as he put it on Twitter. The morning after the Senate vote, Trump sat in his private dining room off the Oval Office with copies of that day's **New York Times, Washington Post,** and other newspapers. They all had banner headlines with some variation of "Trump's acquitted." The president was giddy with delight.

"Look at all these headlines," he told aides. "I've never had press coverage like this. This is amazing! I should be impeached more often."

The excitement did not come without a cost. Not only had the three-week impeachment trial

distracted the president and his top aides from focusing on the coronavirus threat, but it also sowed
dissent inside the West Wing. White House counsel
Pat Cipollone and Mick Mulvaney had been waging
war internally and were barely on speaking terms,
owing in part to Cipollone's shock and frustration
at Mulvaney's public admission in October 2019 of
a presidential quid pro quo. The extreme distrust between Trump loyalists and the career professionals
who they derisively referred to as members of the
"deep state"—a group that included Army Lieutenant
Colonel Alexander Vindman and other officials who
had testified about Trump's conduct with Ukraine
in the impeachment inquiry—was also incapacitating
the administration.

Olivia Troye was also considered part of that group
of career officials. She had been a career intelligence
officer at the Department of Homeland Security
when she was asked early in the Trump administration to transfer to the White House and work for Vice
President Pence. When Keith Kellogg interviewed her
for the job, he asked, "Why do you want to work
here?" Troye responded, "Because I want to serve my
country and I want to make a difference."

But in early February, as Troye was logging long
hours trying to stay on top of an emerging public
health calamity, she was being mocked by some colleagues on the vice president's staff as "deep state."
It didn't help that her office was next door to that of
Jennifer Williams, a Pence foreign policy adviser who

had testified before the congressional inquiry and who had a similar public service background.

After his acquittal, Trump began a retribution campaign to root out the so-called deep state foes and punish his perceived enemies within his government, including anyone he believed contributed to his impeachment or had otherwise crossed him in the Ukraine saga. Escaping accountability had emboldened Trump. The president told aides it was really his enemies who were responsible for him having been impeached. Their crimes were that, when subpoenaed to testify before Congress, they told the truth under oath.

Within two days, Trump tapped his first victims. Vindman and his brother, Yevgeny Vindman, were removed from their NSC posts and reassigned to the Defense Department. Hours later, news broke that Gordon Sondland, the U.S. ambassador to the European Union, who also had delivered damning testimony to Congress, would be recalled.

By month's end, Trump would order Joseph Maguire, the acting director of national intelligence, to vacate his office. Maguire's crime? His office had privately briefed a bipartisan group of key members of Congress, as the law required, on intelligence—specifically that Russia was interfering in the 2020 election and had developed a preference for Trump. The president would tell Maguire that he had just handed Democrats great ammunition to use against him in the campaign.

In addition, John Rood, the Defense Department's undersecretary for policy, who had certified that Ukraine could receive U.S. aid at a time when Trump lawyer Rudy Giuliani was trying to block it, would be forced to resign. And by early March, Elaine McCusker, a career public servant who had warned White House officials about the risks of withholding aid from Ukraine, would have her nomination to be Pentagon comptroller withdrawn.

Trump's rash and retaliatory dismissal of Maguire would compel retired Admiral William McRaven, who oversaw the Navy SEALs raid that killed Osama bin Laden, to write: "As Americans, we should be frightened—deeply afraid for the future of the nation. When good men and women can't speak the truth, when facts are inconvenient, when integrity and character no longer matter, when presidential ego and self-preservation are more important than national security—then there is nothing left to stop the triumph of evil."

In early February, around the time of Trump's acquittal, his job approval rating in the Gallup daily tracking average reached 49 percent, its highest measure in his entire presidency. The data collected privately by Trump's campaign pollsters were just as strong.

This marked a significant turnabout. Tony Fabrizio had been deeply concerned about the president's standing when he began work on Trump's reelection in the spring of 2019. Fabrizio conducted a round of polls in seventeen states the campaign identified as battlegrounds, such as Florida, Michigan, and Pennsylvania. The data identified a key vulnerability for Trump: Voters perceived the economy to be healthy, booming even, but did not feel it improving their own lives. Roughly six in ten voters thought the economy was moving in the right direction under Trump, but when asked whether they were better off personally, a majority said they felt no difference in their personal financial situation.

Fabrizio and other Trump advisers believed the president's reelection would hinge on the economy—and to win he had to close the gap with these voters. This was a psychological challenge as much as a financial one. They advised Trump to stop talking about the economy through the prism of Wall Street and whether stocks were up or down, but instead focus on working people, their wages, and the availability of jobs.

In early February 2020, Fabrizio went back into the field in those seventeen battleground states and found Trump's position had completely reversed. Not only were economic perceptions still strong and even a little bit higher than the year prior, but now instead of a majority saying their personal financial situation had not improved, a plurality and in some states a majority said it had. This helped lift Trump's approval rating in those states—so much so that he was leading his Democratic challengers, outside the margin of error, in states whose electoral college votes totaled 278, and he was likely to win in states totaling an additional 40 electoral college votes. If the economy continued to improve, Fabrizio believed, Trump would easily crest 300 electoral college votes in November, clearing the 270 needed to win.

Around this time, Brad Parscale met with the president in the Oval Office and made a bold prediction. "Look, we're going to win on policy," the campaign manager said. "You're going to lose on personality, but the economy you're the winner on, and you're going to win in a landslide."

Trump was beside himself. He had survived impeachment, and now the pros running his campaign were telling him he was headed toward a landslide victory. He got to talking about what he would do in his next four years as president. And Parscale, always striving to score points with the boss, continued to fluff him up.

"Look how much you've gone up," he said. "You're winning New Hampshire. You're winning Nevada. You're almost winning New Mexico. You're close in Minnesota."

"I don't understand," Trump said, confused about how he could be so popular after such an ugly impeachment saga.

"Americans don't like a false prosecution," Parscale told him. Democrats, he argued, "look petty now. And we're in a good place. Just don't make a mistake and you've got this in the bag."

After a month of prodding, the Chinese government still refused to open its doors to a U.S. team of virus investigators. Robert Redfield tried to press for access through his Chinese counterpart, George Gao. Alex Azar tried calling his counterpart, Chinese health minister Ma Xiaowei. Both men struck out, politely rebuffed by the Chinese.

Redfield's and Azar's exasperation was shared by Robert O'Brien and Matt Pottinger at the White House, who by the end of January had concluded the best way to possibly break the logjam would be for Trump to personally appeal to Xi Jinping.

When his advisers first suggested this play at the end of January, Trump was wary. He didn't want to insult the Chinese president, with whom he had bragged of having a great relationship, and he didn't want to antagonize the leader of a nuclear power. But by early February, the president agreed to give it his best shot. "Set it up," Trump told O'Brien and Pottinger.

After a few days of negotiations between Washington and Beijing, a call between the two presidents was scheduled for February 7. Trump gently broached with Xi the idea of having a team of Americans from the CDC visit Wuhan, and he tried to couch it in a way to allow Xi to save face.

"I know you've got this well in hand. You've got

good people," Trump told Xi. "We've also got good people. I think we can be helpful. It would also be useful to us to know more about this."

Xi listened as Trump continued.

"They're ready to go," Trump said. "I've got the team ready to go. All you have to do is issue the visas and they'll be there."

Xi's response was cool.

"We have this in hand," he told Trump. "We're waging a people's war against this virus. It's going to be fully contained in short order."

Then Xi signaled his annoyance with Trump's recent decision to restrict travel from China to the United States.

"We urge the United States not to overreact," Xi said, adding that the coronavirus was "easily defeated" in warmer weather. He even stated an approximate temperature at which the virus started to die off: the high 50s Fahrenheit.

"We're going to be in very good shape," he said.

Xi never directly answered Trump's request to allow a CDC team in Wuhan. So Trump circled back to his original ask.

"We can have people there," he said. "They're ready to go."

Then Xi gave the most direct "no" without actually saying the word "no."

"Well," the Chinese president said, "we're working through the WHO."

O'Brien hoped they could try again and eventually

get Xi's buy-in. They didn't know how firmly set China was on stonewalling the Americans.

The weekend of February 8, state governors converged on Washington for their annual National Governors Association meeting. It was a jam-packed few days of policy discussions and po-litical confabs, fancy dinners and receptions—and, importantly, an all-hands briefing on the coronavirus led by Anthony Fauci, Redfield, and other govern-ment health leaders, who warned that this virus was far more contagious than SARS and would spread in only a matter of time.

The South Korean embassy hosted the governors, with President Moon Jae-in beaming in on a video conference to welcome them—a warm reminder of the close diplomatic and economic ties between South Korea and the United States. Moon offered a special greeting to Maryland governor Larry Hogan, a Republican who chaired the NGA and whose wife, Yumi, was born in South Korea and immigrated to the United States in her twenties. Moon called him "a son-in-law to the Korean people."

The next night, at a private dinner for the Republican Governors Association, Trump gave a rambling address during which he sprayed in-sults far and wide—his remarks so disjointed and long that the catering staff, who were loath to walk around the room while the president was talking, held off delivering entrees to increasingly hungry governors and their spouses. Trump brought up South Korea.

"Why should we even defend them?" Trump asked, referring to the extensive U.S. military presence in the Korean peninsula. "They're not paying us enough."

Trump went on to make fun of Moon, as if they were schoolyard rivals.

Yumi Hogan was nearly in tears and thought about walking out, but she kept her composure and the Hogans stayed.

The next night, February 9, at the Governors Ball, a black-tie affair hosted every year on NGA weekend at the White House, Yumi Hogan still couldn't shake Trump's attacks on her homeland. It turned out the Hogans were seated for dinner at the ball next to Pence and his wife, Karen. The two couples were relatively close, and the Hogans knew that Pence's father was a veteran of the Korean War.

"Your father fought for freedom in South Korea," Yumi Hogan told the vice president. "I wouldn't be here without your dad."

Then Maryland's first lady cut to the chase.

"Mr. Vice President, you have to talk to the president," Yumi Hogan said. "Did you hear what he said about South Korea?"

Pence turned slightly red in the face and shook his head. Ever loyal to Trump, the vice president appeared to be searching for words and quickly changed the subject.

Roger Stone was a lifelong dirty trickster, a political operative with a carnival huckster style and, most important at this juncture in the sixty-seven-year-old's life, a loyal defender of Trump. He had used smears and sleights of hand to help his political clients—including, for many years, Trump—make their opponents look foolish or guilty, stretching all the way back to his work for Richard Nixon at the start of his career.

Stone had been found guilty in November 2019 of obstructing a congressional probe and witness tampering while dodging Special Counsel Robert Mueller's Russia investigation. A jury concluded Stone had lied repeatedly to a congressional committee about his advance knowledge of the Russian hack of emails that could embarrass Hillary Clinton during the 2016 election, and that he later threatened to hurt a person who could expose his lies.

In early February 2020, prosecutors in the U.S. Attorney's Office in Washington faced a judge's deadline to recommend the prison sentence befitting his crimes. It was a hot-button case as well as one that Attorney General Bill Barr would soon take a strong interest in.

Barr had just arranged to change leadership in the U.S. Attorney's Office, pressuring the U.S. Attorney Jessie Liu over the Christmas holidays and through January to give up her job so he could install one of his closer advisers in that role. Liu was awaiting confirmation hearings for the number three job at Treasury, and though nominees usually got to remain in their job until confirmed for the new one, Barr kept pressing her to go. In an awkward January 9 meeting, Liu asked the attorney general why he wanted to rush her out the door. "We don't want the uncertainty," Barr told her. His explanation didn't make sense. He gave her February 1 as a deadline to leave. As that date approached, Barr announced his former counselor Tim Shea would become the new U.S. attorney and start work February 3. This was less than a week before line prosecutors in the office would present a recommendation for Stone's punishment.

On February 5, the four prosecutors in the D.C. office handling the Stone case recommended a prison sentence of seven to nine years. But over the next several days, they received warnings from their supervisors that this proposal wasn't going to fly with their new boss. They said Shea felt pressure to "cut Stone a break" and was "afraid of the president." One of the prosecutors, Aaron Zelinsky, a former Mueller prosecutor who had worked on the Stone team the longest, said he would withdraw from the case rather than sign a politically manipulated recommendation.

On February 10, Shea told Barr the prosecutors in his office were pushing to recommend a seven- to nine-year sentence for Stone. Barr told Shea that was ridiculous. He wanted prosecutors to let the judge decide Stone's punishment without pushing for the tough sentence they were technically entitled to seek. Shea said he thought he had a good compromise on a recommendation that would satisfy both the prosecutors and Barr. Shea promised to take care of it.

That night, the prosecutorial team got word they could file their recommendation of seven to nine years, if they deleted a section describing Stone's threatening behavior. Barr, who didn't closely monitor the news, heard reports of the tough new sentencing recommendation. "What the hell happened?" Barr asked an aide. He couldn't reach Shea. But the attorney general felt the prosecutors were way out of line. White-collar criminals charged with obstructing a criminal probe or lying to federal agents rarely did more than two years in jail. He wasn't wrong about that. On the other hand, Stone's conduct had been unusually egregious. In addition to threatening to kill a witness and ruin his life, he had also released an image of crosshairs over the face of the judge presiding over his trial. Barr debated that night with his chief of staff, Brian Rabbitt, about the holy hell they believed he would spark if he reduced the proposed punishment, but decided lessening Stone's recommended sentence was the right thing. "We're going to have to fix this in the morning," Barr said.

Over at the White House, Trump didn't like what he was seeing on the news either. In a sign of how little he slept when he was worked up, Trump issued a fiery tweet at 2:48 a.m. on February 11. "This is a horrible and very unfair situation," he wrote. "The real crimes were on the other side, as nothing happens to them. Cannot allow this miscarriage of justice!"

Later that morning at the Justice Department, Barr was discussing the new sentencing recommendation with staff when Deputy Attorney General Jeffrey Rosen walked in. It was about 8:30 a.m.

"So, did you see the president's tweet?" Rosen asked. Aides looked at their phones and read it aloud.

"Holy shit," Barr said. "Now what do I do?"

Should he proceed with reducing the recommendation or stand down? Barr decided to go forward. It looked to prosecutors across the country—and many in the general public—like Barr was dutifully obeying Trump's Twitter instructions. Trump and Barr insisted they never spoke about what to do about Stone, but that hardly mattered. Trump's wishes about going easy on Stone were easy for anyone to see. Barr's decision only cemented the view that the attorney general was manhandling the independent Justice Department to do Trump's bidding.

At Barr's instruction, Shea told the court his office wasn't pushing for a specific penalty. It was too much for the four prosecutors on the case—Zelinsky, Jonathan Kravis, Adam Jed, and Michael Marando—who each left the case or resigned from the department altogether. This was a deafening version of what lawyers call "a noisy withdrawal"—a notice that signals to the court that lawyers are disgusted with the client or the handling of the case. In this case, both.

Liu, meanwhile, was preparing for her upcoming

Senate confirmation hearing for the Treasury job, re-lieved she had had no role in the Stone decision, when she got a strange call from Treasury Secretary Steven Mnuchin's office asking her to meet with Mnuchin to discuss "the stuff in the news today."

When they met, an apologetic Mnuchin told Liu that she wouldn't get the job because the White House decided to withdraw her nomination.

"Can you tell me why?" she asked.

"I'm sorry," the secretary said. "I cannot."

Trump had been convinced by conspiracy-minded supporters that Liu was part of the "deep state" and had gone too easy on former acting FBI director Andrew McCabe, a villain in Trump's mind, and gone too hard against Stone. Their list of objections to Liu was longer still, but this was enough. In Trump's view, she was disloyal, and she was out.

Furious that his reputation was taking a beating, Barr knew he could not change the minds of the Stone prosecutors, but he was determined to estab-lish for the record that the president wasn't pulling his strings. He also knew he had to get through to the so-called audience of one, Trump. Barr's staff arranged for him to sit for an interview with Pierre Thomas of ABC News on February 13, explaining the Stone case. They did not give the White House a heads-up; Barr wanted Trump to watch it and understand he meant business.

"I think it's time to stop the tweeting about Department of Justice criminal cases," Barr told

Thomas. "I'm not going to be bullied or influenced by anybody . . . whether it's Congress, a newspaper editorial board, or the president. . . . I cannot do my job here at the department with a constant background commentary that undercuts me."

Not more than two minutes after the interview aired, Barr's cell phone rang. It was the audience of one. Barr's message had been received. Instantly.

"Hey, I thought that was cool," Trump told him. "There's no problem."

"I meant what I said, Mr. President," Barr replied. "You can't be doing that kind of thing."

The president wasn't in the mood to fully comply, however. In a volley that had become familiar, Trump tried to get the last word. Early in the morning of February 14, the president was back on Twitter, quoting the part of Barr's interview where he said the president had never asked him to interfere in the Stone case.

"This doesn't mean that I do not have, as President, the legal right to do so, I do, but I have so far chosen not to!" Trump wrote.

Later that day, however, Trump got a taste of the Justice Department's independence, though the timing was strictly coincidental. The department notified McCabe's lawyers they were dropping their investigation of him and would not charge him for lying about disclosing information to the media. Trump raged about this development to his aides, furious the "deep state" former FBI honcho wasn't going to be roughed up by prosecutors. That afternoon, Trump bellyached to Barr that this wasn't fair. He wanted to know why the government couldn't bring a case against McCabe.

Barr put his foot down. "I'm not talking to you about that," he said.

By mid-February, the coronavirus had killed some two thousand people around the world and sickened seventy-five thousand. The vast majority of cases were in China, but the contagion was spreading quickly, with infections now reported in at least twenty-eight other countries, including the United States. World leaders were on edge, but the kind of global stewardship the United States had often provided at moments of international crisis was nonexistent.

Jeremy Farrar, one of the world's leading infectious disease experts, who was based in London, was so exasperated by the lack of engagement by the White House that he called Tom Bossert, who had served as Trump's homeland security and counterterrorism adviser earlier in the administration. In the mid-2000s, as a staffer on President George W. Bush's National Security Council, Bossert had helped write a pandemic response strategy, and Farrar saw him as an ally in trying to contain the coronavirus.

"There's nobody we can talk to," Farrar told Bossert. "Nobody's answering our calls."

Bossert took Farrar's plea to heart. He put in calls to Trump and Pence, and even tried to track down a private number for Melania Trump, hoping to scare them into action on the virus, but had no luck. He was convinced that Jared Kushner, Trump's son-in-law and senior adviser, who was the most powerful aide in the West Wing, and Marc Short were blocking his calls as an act of retaliation after Bossert had criticized in an ABC News interview Trump's phone call with the Ukrainian president.

When Bossert got through to Trump's assistant, Molly Michael, he told her, "Either Marc Short or Jared are standing in front of your desk. Tell them, 'Fuck you. Mr. Bossert wants to talk to the president.' Put me through to the president and let him decide."

Michael suggested Bossert talk to Pence, but when Bossert was connected to the vice president's office, Short picked up. "Sorry," he said, "the VP isn't interested in talking to you right now. He's busy."

"Come on, Marc, this is serious," Bossert replied, and went into a spiel about just how devastating the infection rate and death toll could soon be.

"We've got plenty of smart people working on this, but none of them have numbers that agree with yours," Short said. "It's not that bad. Thanks for your call. We'll figure it out."

Short told Pence about Bossert's outreach and tried to arrange a follow-up conversation, but it was unclear if the two ever spoke. Bossert, who was warning that the virus would leave ninety-eight million people sick, twelve to fifteen million hospitalized, and five hundred thousand dead, never got to speak with Trump.

Bossert confided his frustrations in Fauci, whom he had known for years.

"Listen," Fauci told him, "I just present the facts. I wish you were still in the White House. I'm not the one that runs the CDC. I'm the infectious disease person that does the research."

Fauci told Bossert that he felt little urgency about the virus from the White House. Trump wasn't attending task-force meetings, for instance, and the federal response efforts were not being properly coordinated. It was a mess.

Trump had long considered the stock markets his political weathervane, so the week of February 24, when markets tanked amid reports the coronavirus was spreading across South Korea and Italy, brought gale-force winds. The president was on a two-day visit to India, where Prime Minister Narendra Modi played to his ego by staging a massive, hundred-thousand-person stadium rally called "Namaste Trump."

Back in the United States, Nancy Messonnier, the head of the CDC's National Center for Immunization and Respiratory Diseases, held her daily media teleconference on February 25 to update the public on the rapidly evolving coronavirus situation. She spoke the truth.

"I understand this whole situation may seem overwhelming and that disruption to everyday life may be severe," Messonnier told reporters. "But these are things that people need to start thinking about now. I had a conversation with my family over breakfast this morning and I told my children that while I didn't think that they were at risk right now, we as a family need to be preparing for significant disruption of our lives. You should ask your children's school about their plans for school dismissals or school closures. Ask if there are plans for teleschool. I contacted my local school superintendent this morning with exactly those questions. You should think about what you would do for childcare if schools or day cares close, if teleworking is an option for you. All of these questions can help you be better prepared for what might happen."

Messonnier's warnings of impending disruptions to everyday life quickly became banner headlines on television news. The markets' reaction was deafening, with the Dow Jones Industrial Average falling another 879 points that afternoon. Aides watching from the West Wing were gobsmacked, and some believed Messonnier had been overly alarmist. "This is ridiculous," Short said, shaking his head.

At about the same time, Trump boarded Air Force One in India for his return to Washington. The president stayed awake for the entire fourteen-hour turbulent flight home, watching market reports and news coverage. He was fuming about Messonnier, becoming obsessed with a CDC scientist he had never met. Trump called Azar from the plane.

"What the hell is this woman doing?" he said. "What are these statements? The market has collapsed."

The president added, "She's scaring people! This is killing me!"

Azar said Messonnier's only failing was getting out in front of the president in explaining it to the public.

"What she said is true and we're actually planning to meet with you at five p.m. the day you get back to go through all of this," Azar said.

"You gotta keep her away from the microphone," Trump ordered. "You gotta get out there and clear this up. Get the market calm again."

Azar tried to sound agreeable and understanding, having learned that when Trump was in a true frenzy, it was better to absorb his rage rather than argue. He said he had a press briefing of his own scheduled within the next hour or so.

"We'll get this clarified," Azar said.

Also on the flight home, Melania Trump tried to talk some sense into her husband. "You have to take this more seriously," the first lady told the president. "This is going to be a big problem and you need to get out in front of it. . . . You can't be telling people it's just going to go away, that you have it handled, because we don't and you need to stop."

Concerned that he might not listen to her, Melania

Trump then enlisted former New Jersey governor Chris Christie, an old friend of the president's, to help reinforce her message with him. When Christie called him, Trump casually dismissed him. "You sound just like Melania," Trump told Christie. "You two worry too much."

The morning of February 26, Trump took to Twitter to accuse the media and Democrats of exaggerating the coronavirus threat, though he misspelled the name of the virus. "Low Ratings Fake News MSDNC (Comcast) & @CNN are doing everything possible to make the Caronavirus look as bad as possible, including panicking markets, if possible. Likewise their incompetent Do Nothing Democrat comrades are all talk, no action. USA in great shape! @CDCgov . . ."

Trump called a coronavirus news conference for 6:00 p.m. Redfield was out of town, so his deputy, Anne Schuchat, was due to sub in for him at the event. It would be her first time meeting the president. Azar called her to warn, "Please make sure he knows you're not Nancy Messonnier or he's going to scream at you!"

When he arrived at the White House, Azar first went to Mulvaney's office. The chief told him Trump was thinking of naming Pence as coronavirus czar. Azar had been chairing the task force and had just told Trump that he wasn't convinced a czar was ideal, so he was a little perplexed. When they joined the president in the Oval, Trump said he was "thinking about" installing the vice president as czar. But within minutes, it was clear this was already cooked and decided. The president announced at the news conference that Pence was taking over the task force. Afterward, Pence asked Azar and other task-force members to follow him.

"Let's huddle in my office, you can brief me on the process," Pence said.

Once inside, Pence turned to Azar. "This is a very serious moment in our nation's history. We should begin with the secretary leading us in prayer," something the evangelical Christian vice president often did when chairing important meetings.

A devout Catholic and member of an Eastern Orthodox church, Azar wasn't used to praying in government offices, but said a prayer at the vice president's urging.

"I think what we have here is a communication discipline issue," Pence said. "My number one issue is getting a handle on communications." He talked about the importance of clear, consistent messaging in any crisis, something he had learned firsthand as governor of Indiana.

In consultation with Mulvaney and others, Trump also had considered former Food and Drug Administration commissioner Scott Gottlieb and Christie to lead the task force but settled on Pence. They worried that if the vice president were in charge, the White House would own any problems, but they also felt the crisis had become bigger than Azar seemed able to handle. Mulvaney in particular wanted the coronavirus response to be brought in-house and controlled by the White House, and he thought Pence was the obvious choice. Already peeved with Azar over e-cigarettes and other issues, Trump told other senior officials that he blamed the health secretary for the floundering virus response and a public relations mess.

Kushner would later explain to Azar that Trump picked Pence because he wanted someone to focus solely on telling people the virus was under control, and because the vice president wasn't particularly busy. Pence had spent much of his time traveling do-mestically, trying to keep the religious faithful and conservative base engaged for the reelection, but that travel was ending because of coronavirus fears.

"He didn't have anything else to do," Kushner told Azar. A senior administration official said Kushner did not recall the conversation.

Pence and his aides moved quickly to take over all communications related to the virus. Mulvaney sent a memo to administration officials instructing that all talking points, press releases, and interview bookings first be approved by Short or Katie Miller, Pence's communications director, fresh off her wed-ding less than two weeks earlier to Stephen Miller, Trump's senior policy adviser and chief speechwriter. Katie Miller and Short wanted every task-force mem-ber delivering the same message, and they wanted to avoid another Messonnier incident.

Azar's press aide Caitlin Oakley called the secretary

late that evening. "All your press bookings are cancelled," she told him.

The health secretary was being put in a closet, effectively demoted and muzzled because a CDC scientist had told the truth.

On February 29, Pence convened the coronavirus task-force meeting to order and turned to the agenda. Just then, Trump walked in, surprising those in attendance—not merely because it was a Saturday and Trump was not known to work on weekends, but also because he had shown so little interest in their work before. Pence, seated at the head of the table, welcomed the president and scooched his chair over to the left to let Trump sit at the head. Azar decided to broach the topic of the virus's spread to all continents. He thought it was past time the World Health Organization declare COVID-19 a pandemic, as it by now had met the criteria for that grim label.

"Mr. President, we need to start calling this a pandemic because it is one," Azar said. "The WHO is not going to say it now, because they don't want to embarrass China. The WHO is going to wait until cases are rising in the U.S. Then, Tedros will have air cover to call it a pandemic to embarrass us. We need to get ahead of it and call it a pandemic now."

Azar was referring to Tedros Adhanom Ghebreyesus, director-general of WHO. While considered the preeminent global health agency, the WHO had also become increasingly sensitive to not alienating the Chinese government, which had dramatically increased its funding of the group in recent years to try to compete with the United States. The WHO had publicly taken China at its word and praised the ruling Communist Party leadership for its work on the virus, even amid growing evidence the Chinese government was concealing information about it.

At hearing Azar's suggestion about using the p-word, though, Trump blew a gasket. The memory of Messonnier and the precipitous market drop still was fresh.

Trump said no way.

"This will cause panic," he bellowed. "We will not call it a pandemic."

Trump had reason to worry. Fabrizio was in Israel around this time advising Prime Minister Benjamin Netanyahu on his election there. Netanyahu was a keen observer of American politics, having spent part of his youth in the Philadelphia area, attended the Massachusetts Institute of Technology, and worked for the Boston Consulting Group. He and Fabrizio got to talking about the Democratic primary campaign, which had been heating up all month.

"Let me tell you something, Tony," Netanyahu told Trump's pollster. "None of these Democrats can beat Donald Trump."

"Really?" Fabrizio said.

"Yeah," Netanyahu replied. "The only thing that can beat President Trump is coronavirus."

"Are you serious, Mr. Prime Minister?" Fabrizio asked.

"Yeah," he said. "If you don't understand what a pandemic is and the mathematics behind how this will spread if we don't contain it, it will collapse economies, and that changes the ball game tremendously."

Four

The P-Word

In February 2020, Dr. Deborah Birx was working in South Africa, meeting with public health experts and other leaders from around the globe to combat the global AIDS epidemic, when she received increasingly worrisome messages from an old contact, Matt Pottinger. At sixty-three, Birx had worked for four decades in immunology, conducting HIV/AIDS vaccine research and developing therapeutics. A physician who began her career in the army, she rose to become an ambassador-at-large and U.S. global AIDS coordinator. She and Pottinger had known each other for years; his wife, Yen, a virologist, once worked in Birx's lab. Pottinger knew Birx could help steer the administration's response to the coronavirus, which was fast becoming a catastrophe. Day after day, he appealed to her to come work in the White House.

Although Birx had been appointed to her

ambassadorship by President Obama in 2014, she prided herself on remaining apolitical as a civil servant. She knew enough about the daily dramas in Trump's Washington to want to stay away. As Birx confided to associates, she would have to be an idiot to sign up to work in the White House. Doing so, she figured, could be terminal to her long public health career. Serving Trump was the last thing she wanted to do.

But Pottinger persisted. Birx was studying the infection curves from Wuhan and Italy and was worried about the administration's approach given this virus had significant asymptomatic spread. She was alarmed by the Trump administration's initial moves, especially its public statements that the virus posed a very low risk to people's livelihoods. She started to think she could help make a difference.

"You can save American lives," Pottinger told her, appealing to her military background and sense of duty.

By month's end, Birx was on board, after Robert O'Brien arranged with Mike Pompeo to move her to the White House. She would become the White House coronavirus response coordinator, reporting to Vice President Pence, who now chaired the task force. On the long flight home from Africa the weekend of February 29, Birx wrote an action plan. She wanted to convene immediately a series of meetings with important outside stakeholders, including private-sector labs who could help ramp up testing capacities and medical correspondents in the media, such as CNN's Sanjay Gupta, to help them communicate the seriousness of the emerging pandemic.

Birx's first day on the job was March 2. On MSNBC that morning, anchor Chris Jansing told viewers, "We've got some breaking news. One of the main people in charge of fighting the deadly coronavirus in the U.S. now says it has indeed reached outbreak proportions and likely pandemic proportions." The network then rolled tape of correspondent Richard Engel interviewing Anthony Fauci.

"What are we dealing with with this coronavirus, COVID-19?" Engel asked.

"We're dealing with clearly an emerging infectious disease that has now reached outbreak proportions and likely pandemic proportions," Fauci said. "If you look at, you know, by multiple definitions of what a pandemic is, the fact is, this is multiple sustained transmissions of a highly infectious agent in multiple regions of the globe."

Jansing returned to the screen to make the significance clear to viewers. "So Dr. Anthony Fauci, who is widely regarded as the number one expert in the country . . . talking for the first time about a pandemic."

Within the hour, Marc Short was on the phone to Brian Harrison. Though Short recognized it was just a matter of time before the coronavirus was declared a pandemic, he nonetheless didn't want Fauci or any other task-force member straying from precoordinated talking points.

"You've got to get Fauci on message," Short told Alex Azar's chief of staff. "He is saying things that are too extreme."

Harrison didn't make any promises, but said he'd relay the message. Short's call came as a shock at HHS headquarters, in part because the White House had never tried to control Fauci's comments or interview appearances on public health. But Pence was now leading the task force, and its focus immediately became more political. Azar huddled with Harrison, deputy chief of staff Judy Stecker, and Caitlin Oakley. Azar told his aides they wouldn't be monkeying with what Fauci had to say because that would only backfire and make them look like tools of the White House.

"We aren't going to harness or silence CDC or NIH on scientific matters," Azar said. "It is just stupid." Some had complained, in fact, that Azar did try to control the scientists' message when he determined it was important to do so, but he resisted Short's instruction.

For thirty-six years in his role, Fauci had had the same philosophy on speaking with presidents, from Ronald Reagan to Donald Trump. Each time he walked into the White House, Fauci told himself that this might be his last time doing that, because he might have to tell the president something he didn't want to hear. Fauci knew that could mean banishment.

On March 2, Trump met with pharmaceutical executives at the White House. With Fauci present, the president predicted a rather optimistic timeline for a coronavirus vaccine.

"So you're talking over the next few months, you think you can have a vaccine?" Trump asked one of the pharmaceutical executives.

"You won't have a vaccine," Fauci interjected. "You'll have a vaccine to go and get tested."

When an executive explained the phases of testing would take many months, Trump asked, "All right, so you're talking within a year?"

"Like I've been telling you, Mr. President, a year to a year and a half," Fauci corrected.

"I like the sound of a couple of months better, let's be honest," Trump said.

It was clear to Fauci and other health professionals in the room that Trump did not understand the steps involved in developing, testing, approving, and ultimately injecting into people's arms a vaccine.

The next day, Trump toured Fauci's lab, the NIH Vaccine Research Center, as part of the White House effort to showcase the president's determination to speed up the creation of a vaccine. Fauci again reminded Trump that getting a vaccine in a year was wildly optimistic. At the end of the tour, Fauci and Azar drove with the president across Wisconsin Avenue from the NIH campus to the helipad at Walter Reed National Military Medical Center, where Marine One awaited to fly Trump back to the White House.

"So how's Francis Collins doing?" the president

asked Azar, referring to the NIH director they had just said goodbye to.

"He's really helped us on the fetal tissue ban," Azar said. He referred to Trump's 2019 decision to dramatically cut government funding at NIH and elsewhere for medical research that relied on tissues of aborted fetuses. This was a move to please anti-abortion conservatives, a key part of the president's political base. Collins didn't agree with the policy, Azar told Trump, but was "being very professional in implementing it."

Azar was surprised when Trump asked, "Is that fetal tissue issue going to slow down the vaccine and therapies?" When he learned the answer was yes, the president said he wanted them to reverse the ban, but that never happened.

With Pence firmly in charge of the task force the first week of March, priorities shifted noticeably to public relations and election-year politics. As the vice president's top aide, Short took on an outsized role, setting the agenda and even seating arrangements for meetings. Short was among the most conservative members of the team and felt there should be limits on the role of the government, even in a public health emergency. He worried about Pence being responsible for the coronavirus response, calculating that any missteps could accrue to the political detriment of his boss, who had his eye on a presidential run of his own in 2024. But Pence's attitude was, okay, this is my job, and I'm going to try to do the best I can.

Short, fifty, formed a power center with Katie Miller, twenty-eight, who was so aggressive in her advocacy for Pence that she would scream at reporters on the phone, sometimes so loudly that other aides had to leave the room because they found her end of the conversations insulting. Short and Miller tightly controlled which task-force members could speak to the media and what they would say, though they did not see their actions as muzzling experts. Their objective was to silence alarmism and to keep Fauci and other health professionals from scaring the public—which in turn could further jolt the already jittery stock markets and weaken the president's political fortunes—even if it meant shading the truth. When the facts seemed too scary to the public, Miller would ask task-force members, "Can we not word it that way?"

At press briefings, which Pence was leading at the time, Short and Miller would decide which doctors stood at his side and where they would be positioned onstage. Olivia Troye sometimes helped speechwriter Brian Bolduc script the opening remarks Pence would deliver, a daily update on infections and other relevant statistics. Troye was adamant they be entirely factual and apolitical. One day in a workspace off the Situation Room, as Troye was drafting Pence's remarks on her computer, Miller kicked Troye out of her chair.

"Olivia, move," Miller said. She had just come down from Pence's office, where the vice president had given her instructions to add some points to his script. "I'm going to type this," Miller told Troye. "You don't know Pence. I know what he wants. He doesn't even know what he wants. But I know what he needs."

Keith Kellogg later counseled Troye, "Don't let her touch the remarks. You should take control of that situation. You know your stuff. [Pence] wants the facts and he trusts you. . . . Don't let her bully you."

Task-force meetings took on a fresh intensity, attracting long-standing members as well as new ones, including Seema Verma. She reported to Azar, her longtime rival, and when he ran the task force he hadn't included her, arguing that the CMS administrator wasn't necessary like experts such as Fauci and Redfield. But Verma had deep ties in the White House. From Indiana, she had served as an outside health-care adviser to Pence's administration when he was governor and advised Trump on his health-care policies during the 2016 campaign. After Pence took over the task force, Verma appealed to Short, explained that her agency regulates nursing homes, where some of the worst outbreaks were occurring, and Pence immediately added her to the task force.

Pence also brought on two other officials who reported to Azar and had been left off the task force when he ran it: Dr. Jerome Adams, the surgeon general, whose job was to serve as a public health spokesperson, who had served as Indiana's state health commissioner in Pence's administration; and Dr. Stephen Hahn, the Food and Drug Administration commissioner, who was a radiation oncologist who had just joined the administration in December 2019 and was new not only to Trump World but to politics altogether. Many mornings, Hahn would have 7:00 or 7:30 calls with Joe Grogan for guidance about navigating task-force personalities and political land mines.

Hahn was wise to worry about interpersonal dynamics. Tensions were high among many task-force members, including between Redfield and Azar. The bad blood between them dated to Redfield's early weeks as CDC director. When he agreed to take the job in March 2018, Redfield gave up a medical professorship that earned him about $700,000 a year. Under a federal salary program called Title 42, which was designed to attract high-earning scientists with unique and critical skills into the government, Redfield was paid $375,000. After news reports later revealed Redfield's salary, emphasizing that he was making nearly double what his predecessor at the CDC had earned, and more than Azar's pay of $199,000, Azar confronted Redfield.

"How did you negotiate a salary like that?" Azar asked.

Redfield, who reported to Azar, said there were a number of fellow "Title 42s" making salaries in the high three hundreds and he assumed Azar had approved it.

"If I had known that you were going to have to be paid this much, I would have probably asked to look for somebody else," Azar snapped, his voice loud and his tone sharp.

"Mr. Secretary, let's just be real clear here," Redfield said. "I came in to do this job for the mission, not the money, so if you feel a need to change my salary, change my salary."

Azar did just that, slashing Redfield's pay to $185,000, comfortably below his own. Later during the coronavirus response, when Azar sought to blame Redfield for delays in fixing a flawed CDC test, the CDC director's mind raced back to the salary fight. "I should have known from the beginning this guy didn't have my back," Redfield told Kyle McGowan, his chief of staff.

Complicating matters internally was the evolving guidance provided by health officials. At first, Fauci and others argued that face coverings were not a necessary precaution, even as mask usage was widespread in Asia.

"Masks I don't believe do very much," Fauci said in an early task-force meeting. "It might make you feel better."

In February and March, Fauci and Adams made similar comments publicly, arguing that masks were only needed for health workers. At the time, although masks were proven to protect against contagions in hospitals and other medical settings, there was not yet strong evidence that masks were effective in other environments. In addition, Fauci and Adams were concerned about a run on masks, which were in low supply, and wanted to preserve them for hospital workers and other first responders. By the end of March, however, once the evidence of asymptomatic spread by airborne transmission became overwhelming and studies showed that face coverings were effective in all settings, Fauci, Adams, and other task-force members would change their tune and advocate widespread mask usage.

Although Trump had previously seemed uninterested in the details of the pandemic, when the virus came to dominate the news cycle in late February and early March, Trump suddenly took a keen interest in the task force and began attending both the public briefings and the closed-door meetings. At one of the latter sessions in the Situation Room, Trump offended some of his aides by interrupting a briefing on the health crisis to identify what he considered a silver lining.

"I don't know, maybe this COVID thing is a good thing because I don't have to shake hands with people," the germaphobe president said, according to Troye. "I was a businessperson in New York and I shook a lot of hands, but when you're a politician, you really have to shake a lot more hands. I have to shake hands with these disgusting people. It's disgusting. And now I don't have to shake their hands. Maybe it's a good thing." Trump said through a spokesman that he always hated shaking people's hands and denied that he said this in relation to COVID.

In the first week of March, the possibility of having to impose further travel restrictions—including on the cruise industry—weighed heavily on task-force members. Cruise ships were turning into floating COVID cities, super-spreaders at sea. The CDC had been struggling for weeks with what to do about the **Diamond Princess,** a cruise ship quarantined off the coast of Japan, on which hundreds of passengers, some of them U.S. citizens, had tested positive for the virus. But in early March, officials were learning of a cluster of COVID cases coming off another cruise ship, the **Grand Princess,** which had returned home to port after embarking on its journey from San Francisco in mid-February with thirty-five hundred passengers. To top it off, an elderly passenger on that voyage had suffered extreme respiratory distress upon disembarking. On March 3, she tested positive for COVID-19 and died on March 4.

Gathered in the Situation Room, several advisers urged Pence to consider a full ban on cruises setting sail on new voyages. Pence, ever mindful of alienating corporate America, said he wasn't ready. On March 5, the pressure to do something about the floating viral vessel ratcheted up. Redfield, who had the authority to order a ban on cruises, was most emphatic, and Azar agreed. They explained that worldwide three hundred thousand Americans had recently been passengers on these ships and many could have become infected.

Ken Cuccinelli, a senior official at the Department of Homeland Security, warned they needed a decision—and soon. He told Pence that an estimated hundred thousand more passengers would set sail in two days, as most cruises departed on Saturdays, and stressed that the Coast Guard would need twenty-four hours' notice to issue a no-sail order.

As the discussion continued, Pence and Short grew concerned that some of the doctors—who in this and other meetings disparaged cruises as "petri dishes" and made comments like, "I don't know why anyone would go on a cruise"—harbored a bias against the industry. They worried about the precedent it could set if the government imposed harsher restrictions on cruise liners than on commercial airlines, for instance. Task-force members saw Short pass Pence a note. Then the vice president said, "I think we need to study that some more. I'm not ready for that."

Pence told the group he planned instead to meet with the cruise ship CEOs that coming Saturday, March 7, in Fort Lauderdale, a primary port of call in South Florida, in order to see what health precautions the industry was taking to control spread aboard their vacations at sea.

Trump also was bound for Florida that weekend, but there were some coronavirus hiccups in his travel plans on Thursday and Friday. Trump was scheduled to fly to CDC headquarters in Atlanta for a press event on March 6 to showcase the hard work going on to increase testing capacity. But the evening of March 5, Azar urged Mick Mulvaney to cancel the event because a CDC staffer on the campus appeared to have tested positive for COVID. The acting White House chief of staff agreed.

The next morning, at a White House event, Trump motioned to Azar.

"Why the fuck did we cancel the trip to the CDC?" the president demanded.

"There's a case we thought was positive," Azar said, though in the intervening hours they would learn it was a false positive.

"Screw that," Trump said. "We're going."

Trump hollered over to an aide: "Make it happen. I'm going."

The Secret Service went into overdrive to replan a canceled trip in less than four hours. Once he got to Atlanta for the CDC tour, Trump didn't mince words in reacting to the troubling news that roughly half of the people tested on the **Grand Princess** ship being held in the waters off San Francisco— twenty-one out of forty-six passengers—had tested positive for COVID. Trump told reporters he didn't think the infected people should disembark, although public health officials said it was an unhealthy place to quarantine and would likely result in increased infections.

"Frankly, if it were up to me, I would be inclined to say leave everybody on the ship for a period of time and you use the ship as your base, but a lot of people would rather do it a different way," Trump said. "They'd rather quarantine people on the land. Now, when they do that, our numbers are going to go up. Our numbers are going to go up."

The answer revealed Trump's consistent focus on political optics, public health be damned. He wanted the cruise business to keep chugging along—and most of all, he wanted to keep from having to count cruise ship infections in "our numbers." Wearing a red cap emblazoned with his reelection campaign slogan, "KEEP AMERICA GREAT," and flanked by Redfield and Azar, Trump claimed to have special scientific expertise.

"I like this stuff," he said. "My uncle is a great person who was at [the Massachusetts Institute of Technology]. He taught at MIT for, I think, a record number of years. He was a great, super genius. Dr. John Trump. I like this stuff. I really get it. People are surprised that I understand it. Every one of these doctors said, 'How do you know so much about this?' Maybe I have a natural ability. Maybe I should have done that instead of running for president."

This natural ability did not prevent the president from ignoring medical advice. At a time when most Americans were avoiding social interactions out of fear of spreading the virus, Trump spent the weekend at Mar-a-Lago, where he had dinner with the Brazilian president and members of his delegation, three of whom tested positive for the virus. He also attended a thousand-person campaign fundraiser and a large birthday bash for Kimberly Guilfoyle, his son Donald Trump Jr.'s girlfriend, who was turning fifty-one.

Absent from the CDC visit was Mulvaney, who typically accompanied the president on his travels. Once Trump got to Mar-a-Lago the evening of March 6, he announced on Twitter that he was appointing a new chief of staff, Mark Meadows, a former Republican congressman from North Carolina and one of Trump's fiercest defenders on Capitol Hill, who had long been a thorn in the side of the party establishment. Aside from being appointed U.S. special envoy to Northern Ireland as a consolation prize, Mulvaney's dumping was unceremonious.

Trump's selection of Meadows surprised no one. After three years of grinding through the guardrails, the president finally had found the ultimate enabler to be his chief of staff. Meadows had proved his loyalty to Trump during the impeachment proceedings, helping lead the president's defense strategy and appearing frequently on the Fox News Channel to attack the investigation. He had cultivated a close relationship with the president, Jared Kushner, and other members of the Trump family. He had recently dined with the president at the steakhouse in the Trump International Hotel in Washington and, unlike Mulvaney, sat with him at the head table at the February 16 wedding of Stephen and Katie Miller. Meadows's transition would be delayed by a couple of weeks because he had been exposed to someone with the coronavirus, so he self-isolated at home before reporting to work at the White House.

The next day, March 7, Pence, accompanied by Redfield, met with the cruise ship executives, just as a new cycle of cruise ships tossed off their lines at the ferry docks and set sail. The CEOs told the vice president they were working on their plan; Pence announced they would be allowed to keep sailing.

When the task force met on March 8, Azar told Pence they needed to take bolder steps.

"We've got to ban cruise ships," Azar said. "We've got to stop travel with Europe and get our travel advisories up."

Pence nodded, listening attentively, and smiled when Azar finished talking.

"Yes, we need to be bold here," Pence said. "But we need to set up a process to think about that."

Public health officials were beside themselves at the inaction since Pence had taken the reins. The vice president's first instincts were to delay decisions. Pottinger commiserated about the paralysis, telling another official, "They can't seem to get to a decision." As an outside adviser to the president explained at the time, "Pence is just drifting around. There's no decision being made at the task-force level. The decisions are all Trump, or they're not getting made."

———

Grogan awoke on March 9, anxious about the hugely consequential workweek ahead of him. He had been emailing with Birx and Redfield over the weekend, and they all agreed that this week would be make or break for the virus. "We can't pussyfoot around," Grogan said. Big decisions would need to be made about travel restrictions and other measures. Early that Monday morning, he reached out to Ivanka Trump and Kushner. "This is going to be a really momentous week," he told the couple. "I may need you guys to say something to the president to get him focused."

Two days later, on March 11, the issue of further restricting travel came to a head. Pence convened a meeting in the Roosevelt Room. Azar, Redfield, Fauci, Birx, Grogan, and Kellogg were there. So were Steven Mnuchin, Mike Pompeo, Robert O'Brien, and Acting Secretary of Homeland Security Chad Wolf. Chris Liddell, a deputy White House chief of staff, asked Kushner to join them, considering the magnitude of the decision facing the president. They also were joined by Hope Hicks, Trump's longtime communications adviser who had left the White House in 2018 but returned in early March 2020 as a counselor to the president.

There was consensus around the table to shut down inbound travel from Europe, although Mnuchin argued against it because such restrictions would constrain the transcontinental flow of goods and people and therefore inhibit commerce. Larry Kudlow, the

National Economic Council director, shared that view and was adamant that cargo flights be permitted to continue unimpeded. Mnuchin and Kudlow both said restricting transcontinental travel would be economically catastrophic.

The group then moved to the Oval Office to present their recommendation to the president. Redfield felt the issue was so urgent that when it came time for him to lay out his recommendation, he stood up, walked toward Trump, and put his hands on the Resolute Desk.

"Mr. President, we need to shut down all air travel to and from Europe," the CDC director said.

"Are you serious?" Trump asked, looking incredulous. He had a lot of questions, but the first was the obvious one. "Why?"

Redfield explained that the pathogen was spreading through the United States very quickly and they desperately needed to slow down the rate of spread by stopping new cases from flying in.

"I wish that we had come to you to suggest that two weeks ago," Redfield said. "Clearly this coronavirus is getting seeded throughout our country from a virus that's gone from China to Europe, Europe to America, and we need to shut down all air travel."

Mnuchin shook his head and firmly objected. Trump asked him some questions. Then he turned to Birx.

"Do you agree with Redfield?" he asked.

She said she did.

"Fauci, do you agree with Redfield?" Trump continued.

"I do, sir," Fauci replied. He chimed in to explain that Italy's numbers of infections—and deaths—were astronomical. Anyone in Italy could travel almost anywhere else in Europe.

Mnuchin continued to make the case that the economy wouldn't recover.

"You can't do that, Mr. President," he said. The Treasury secretary warned of an economic meltdown far grimmer than a recession. "We're not talking about the r-word here. We're talking about the d-word. This will be a depression; you'll never get out of it throughout your presidency."

But the doctors in the room were predicting a grim death toll if they didn't block the pathogen at the border.

"Let me give you the data, Steve," Birx said. "We've got infections right now in thirty-five states. Thirty of those states have infections from European sources. Only five states have infections that originated in China. . . . If we don't do something, we're talking about deaths that could be a massive, massive number."

Mnuchin continued to push back about a market collapse. O'Brien said, "This is something we have to do. We're talking about saving thousands of lives. How do you think the markets are going to react when thousands of people die from this?"

Kushner thought the debate had gotten too

emotional and tried to buy time. "Let's not make [the decision] right now. Let's give the president a couple hours to think about this and let's come back to him with a set of clear options," he said, suggesting they meet among themselves in the meantime and try to dial the temperature down.

The group moved to the Cabinet Room, where although Pence chaired the task force it became awkwardly clear to those in the room that Kushner was really in charge. He led the meeting, questioned Birx on her virus data, and challenged other speakers.

At moments, Pence sounded like a supplicant to the president's son-in-law. "Jared, what do you think?" the vice president asked. "Jared, what would you do?" One attendee said it was "nauseating" to watch Pence defer to Kushner, considering only one of them actually had been elected by the American people.

The advisers then returned to the Oval and recommended to Trump that he shut down travel from Europe. They argued it was the right thing to do medically, and that if the virus threat dissipated, they could always reverse the restrictions at a later point. Trump's mind was made up. He had sided with the doctors.

"We can always rebuild the economy," the president said. "We can't get these lives back. We can make the money back. We've got to shut it down."

Mnuchin came around to supporting Trump's decision, but stressed that the government had to take aggressive steps to protect the economy from the anticipated aftershocks.

Trump was scheduled to meet next with Blackstone Group chairman Stephen Schwarzman and other business leaders.

"I should speak to those guys about it," Trump said, hesitating about his decision.

"Mr. President, if you do that and reverse your decision to shut down travel, just be aware that the story in the press will be that you reversed your decision after talking to a bunch of billionaires," Grogan said.

"I can ask them," Trump said.

As the president's advisers dispersed, O'Brien took a shortcut to his office through the West Wing reception area. There, Fauci stopped him and patted him on the arm. "Bob, thank you," Fauci said. "You saved a lot of lives today."

Trump stuck with the travel restrictions and, at Kushner's recommendation, made plans to deliver a televised address to the nation that evening from the Oval Office at arguably the most sobering moment of his presidency. "You have to show a real commitment to the fact that you are taking this seriously," Kushner told Trump.

The speech was hastily prepared, written quickly by Kushner, Stephen Miller, and staff secretary Derek Lyons, with considerable input from Pence. The script was ready to be spoon-fed to the president via the teleprompter in front of him as he sat behind the Resolute Desk.

Some of Trump's top advisers stood in a semicircle behind the cameras, facing the president. Trump looked up at Azar, the health secretary he barely tolerated, and teased him.

"Do you wanna do this instead of me?" Trump asked, partly joking.

Azar laughed and said: "Nope. All yours."

But just as they were readying to go live, the president looked down and cursed. One of the black-inked Sharpies he liked to use had bled onto his shirt, its cap having wriggled off.

"Oh, fuck," Trump said. "Uh-oh, I got a pen mark. Anybody, anybody have any white stuff?"

The president of the United States had suffered a wardrobe malfunction. Hicks dashed up to his desk and gently tugged at his jacket and tie to make sure it covered the black spot. In a matter of moments, she had fixed the problem.

The president began. The speech was going reasonably well, his aides felt. But then Trump veered off script and mistakenly said the U.S. government was shutting off all transportation from Europe, which left the impression no ships could bring cargo to American ports. In addition, he neglected to specify that U.S. citizens would be exempt and allowed to return home.

Trump's aides, who knew the travel ban did not include cargo restrictions, cringed. **Oh, shit, why didn't he just read the script?** Azar thought.

Still, when Trump finished, the small cluster of

aides around Trump told him a version of the same thing: "Home run, boss."

Trump was beaming, thinking he had sounded decisive and strong. But he acknowledged to aides right away that he had made a mistake in describing the travel ban. Kushner sought to reassure him by saying the White House would correct his misstatement, and Trump sent a cleanup tweet of his own. "The restriction stops people not goods," he wrote.

The ten-minute speech drew sharp criticism—not only because it was riddled with errors, but also because of its nationalist and xenophobic tone and the president's lack of empathy and boasts instead about his own decisions. Trump seemed ill at ease. His delivery was labored and monotone, as he twiddled his thumbs, struggling at times to read the words on the teleprompter. Aides speculated that his heart simply wasn't in it. As one of them recalled, "He didn't say he didn't want to do it, but he wasn't gung-ho about it, and when he's not one hundred percent in it, it's not a good result typically."

The speech was intended to reassure the nation that he had the coronavirus crisis under control. It had the opposite effect, raising more questions than providing answers. Futures for the Dow Jones Industrial Average fell in real time with virtually each word Trump uttered, a preview of the bloodbath in the stock markets to come the next morning. Absorbing the criticism made Trump apoplectic.

The lack of clear instructions in Trump's announcement set off chaos in airports on both sides of the Atlantic. Americans about to leave on flights bound for Europe ditched their plans out of fear they wouldn't be able to get back, while Americans abroad panicked and scrambled to return home.

The administration had done little to actually implement the ban and to make sure it was done safely. Who would enforce the restrictions? Who would decide the method for screening travelers' health? Who would ensure knowledgeable teams were available at airports to receive what would no doubt be thousands of Americans seeking to return home?

At the same time, the ground was shifting in communities across the country, just as Nancy Messonnier had predicted two weeks earlier. All manner of businesses—from law firms and Fortune 500 companies to manufacturing plants and hotels—began telling their nonessential workers to stay home until further notice. State and municipal officials started announcing bans on large gatherings and forcing the closure of schools, restaurants, gyms, and other businesses where people congregate. Doctors complained they could not conduct tests on patients they suspected were infected because of very narrow CDC testing guidelines. Local leaders complained about the terribly small supply of tests, not to mention the long delays to receive results. An enormous coronavirus data-track operation managed by Johns Hopkins University produced daily counts on U.S. testing and new cases of infections, which showed the United States lagging terribly behind other countries.

The virus was spreading silently through communities.

On March 12, Fauci and Redfield testified at a House Oversight Committee hearing about the testing problem that was sparking considerable outrage. They acknowledged that a CDC coronavirus test that was supposed to be a model for public health labs to copy had been delivering inconclusive results—a glitch they were working to fix. But the bigger problem was that the public health system hadn't invested in producing a massive supply of tests for new pathogens at a rapid rate. It relied largely on the private sector, which only rushed to make tests on its own timetable and based on its own bottom line.

So far, Fauci and Redfield told the lawmakers, only about eleven thousand Americans had been tested for coronavirus in the first seven weeks of the outbreak. That was less than the roughly twenty thousand tests South Korea was then conducting daily.

"That is a failing," Fauci said. "Let's admit it."

"Failing" was not a word Trump was going to let stand. The next day, at a White House news conference, the president tried to correct the media's conclusion—based on hard data and bolstered by Fauci's admission—that the U.S testing program was a failure and being rapidly outrun by the virus.

When asked by NBC's Kristen Welker if he took any responsibility for the slow rate of testing, Trump replied, "No, I don't take responsibility at all."

Trump was derided on talk shows and on editorial board pages for his denial of responsibility. It was eating him up. And then over the weekend, scenes of chaos overtook the nation's busiest airports. Terminals were packed with hundreds of anxious international passengers, who were queried as part of "enhanced entry screenings." Delayed and rerouted flights to and from Europe only added to the dysfunction. And there was no coherent messaging from Washington.

Photos of mayhem at Chicago's O'Hare International Airport taken by frustrated travelers went viral on social media. Illinois governor J. B. Pritzker, a Democrat, went ballistic as he saw the images and heard reports from O'Hare. He tried calling the White House but couldn't get through to anyone with answers. Late at night on March 14, he tweeted directly at Trump and Pence: "The crowds & lines O'Hare are unacceptable & need to be addressed immediately. @realDonaldTrump @VP since this is the only communication medium you pay attention to—you need to do something NOW." Pritzker added in a follow-up tweet, "The federal government needs to get its s@#t together. NOW."

Later that evening, Pritzker got an apology from an official at U.S. Customs and Border Protection. And he got a call from a midlevel White House aide, Doug Hoelscher, the director of intergovernmental affairs, who berated the governor. Hoelscher told Pritzker it was "irresponsible and juvenile" to "tweet angry tweets" and to criticize the president.

"Are you kidding me?" the flabbergasted governor said.

Pritzker pointed out to Hoelscher that his boss, Trump, was a proud Twitter harasser.

Pritzker and other governors at the time had been scrambling to get ventilators as well as personal protective equipment and other medical supplies into their states. On a March 16 conference call with the nation's governors, Trump effectively told them they were on their own and not to think of the federal government as stocking clerks.

"Respirators, ventilators, all of the equipment—try getting it yourselves," Trump said. "We will be backing you, but try getting it yourselves. Point of sales, much better, much more direct if you can get it yourself."

Governors listening in were surprised. At a time of national crisis, the commander in chief was abdicating responsibility to the states.

"I just got a pit in my stomach," Rhode Island governor Gina Raimondo, a Democrat, later recalled. "Like, wow, we're really on our own here. We better get to work. There's no one else coming, as they say in the military."

Later in the day on March 16, Trump rolled out detailed public health guidance—under the banner "15 Days to Slow the Spread"—recommending closing schools, restaurants, bars, gyms, and other such venues, and limiting gatherings to no more than ten people. The president's demeanor was notably changed from his previous coronavirus briefings, as when he had promised six days earlier that "it will all go away." This time, Trump was deadly serious. "We have an invisible enemy," the president said, adding, "This is a very bad one."

By the middle of that week, after days of coverage of the airport chaos and of his failure to take responsibility for the testing problems, Trump had had enough. On the morning of March 18, just after 8:30, Azar took a call from the boss unlike any he'd had in his career. As he rode to the White House for another task-force meeting, Azar answered his cell phone and took the equivalent of a sustained lion's roar in the face. The president never even said hello.

"Alex, testing is killing me," Trump bellowed. "It's going to lose me the election! What idiot decided to have the federal government do testing?"

Azar was taken aback, both by the volume of Trump's yelling and the mention of testing. Nearly a week earlier, Kushner had arranged a Rose Garden news conference to roll out a half-baked plan for streamlined drive-through testing sites across the country. Azar thought well of Kushner, but also felt the announcement was largely for the appearance of action without any real action. He assumed the president was referring to that.

"Um, the whole testing idea was Jared's, Mr. President," Azar said.

"Jared didn't fuck this up," Trump retorted. "Who fucked this up? Jared is the one fixing your problem. Why is the CDC doing testing?"

Azar explained that the CDC had a duty to create tests whenever a new pathogen was detected, to help create a model for public health labs and hospitals. And he noted that every major country did the same thing.

"CDC never should have done this. Never!" Trump yelled. He added, "We should have left this to the states and the private sector. We shouldn't have owned this."

With that, Trump's concern was coming into focus.

"Who is responsible for this disaster of testing?" Trump demanded. "Who did the testing?"

"Well, it was the CDC," Azar said, thinking to himself that this fact had been well established in many of Trump's previous briefings.

"So who does CDC report to?" Trump asked.

Was the president playing him, or poking him for sport? The question hung there. Two months into a pandemic, after multiple meetings and briefings, was it possible the president didn't know the chain of command for the critical public health agencies on the front lines?

"It reports to me," Azar finally said.

"Well, then. I have my answer," Trump said with

a harumph. "This was gross incompetence. Just gross incompetence."

The president was furious at the CDC, and his primary reason was not that it created a contaminated and malfunctioning COVID test that took weeks to fix, not that America lacked enough tests that could have traced and controlled the spread. He was angry because the CDC had created a political problem for him by agreeing to create a test for the virus in the first place. Barely missing a beat, the president spun to another topic.

"Larry Ellison called me. He tells me remdesivir works," Trump said. "So get the FDA to approve it today. And Laura says chloroquine works as a cure. So the FDA has to approve it also." He was referring to the Oracle founder and to Laura Ingraham, the Fox News Channel host.

Azar, still a little punch drunk from the testing conversation, explained the FDA didn't do same-day approvals of drugs or therapies and that it would have to conduct studies to make sure the drugs were safe.

"Larry, he's the smartest person I know," Trump said. "He says it's safe. Get it approved."

"Just because Laura Ingraham takes chloroquine when she goes to Africa, just because Larry Ellison is extremely smart, doesn't mean we can approve it," Azar said. "We do what is called clinical trials to study this. We are literally putting it in people's bodies. It has to be safe."

Azar explained that chloroquine treatments,

including hydroxychloroquine, were antimalarial drugs that had shown a risk of serious side effects, including blindness, liver toxicity, and heart issues. Although some doctors were prescribing it, the FDA had not approved hydroxychloroquine for safe treatment for the coronavirus.

"No, these products are safe," Trump said. "Laura says she takes it all the time and nothing happens. Just approve them. I want these approved today."

Azar was an intense, detail-oriented former CEO and lawyer. Though he and the president had often disagreed, Trump's treatment of him had reached a degrading level he had never expected when he joined the Cabinet. Plenty of critics felt Azar was Machiavellian, always looking for credit and dodging blame, and he could be hard with his subordinates, some of whom chafed at his demands and felt undermined by him. But Azar felt he was being wronged, too. He had worked hard for the president, fought to get him to pay attention to the virus when it grew serious, gotten blamed for mistakes he didn't consider his own, and been crucified on Capitol Hill for boneheaded positions the White House forced him to take. Riding to the White House after the president hung up, Azar had never felt more demoralized.

When he walked into the West Wing, Azar paid a visit to Meadows to brief the new chief of staff on his heated conversation with Trump and discuss the very real possibility he might be fired. Meadows listened silently as Azar recounted the president's tirade.

"There are many people in the White House who want you removed, but the president has not brought it up with me," Meadows said.

Azar and Meadows believed they knew who those people were. They thought Grogan and Short, among others, were gunning for him. Azar decided to set some boundaries with Meadows, in case the president decided to follow through on his critics' wishes.

"If he ever tweets against me, I will quit that day. I will never let myself become a Jeff Sessions," Azar said, referring to Trump's first attorney general, whom he had tormented relentlessly for more than a year before firing him in November 2018.

Azar also warned Meadows about the political risk of trying to make him a scapegoat for the administration's coronavirus response. "'The outside world views me as the competent one," Azar said.

Meadows listened, appearing to size up Azar's points. "I got you, buddy," he said.

After a few moments, Meadows said: "We gotta figure out how we work on rehabilitating you over here. Listen, you have to follow the law, but you gotta do something to show the president we're making therapies available. The media is showing all these people being cured from these therapies. Even zinc. We should approve all these products that the media say work."

Trump was increasingly worried about what the pandemic was doing to his political standing and

reached out to an old friend for advice. He called
Chris Christie, who had been one of the first establishment Republicans to endorse his candidacy in
2016 and had stood by him through scandals aplenty,
and asked him to come to the White House. "No
one's better in a crisis than you. I need you down
here," Trump told Christie, who had won bipartisan
plaudits for his aggressive and empathetic leadership
in the aftermath of Hurricane Sandy in 2012.

On March 19, Christie drove himself to
Washington from New Jersey and spent about ninety
minutes with the president in the Oval Office. They
were alone most of the time, other than the roughly
ten minutes when Pence joined them, and brief appearances by Kellyanne Conway and Pat Cipollone.
Christie tried to appeal to Trump to rethink his
approach to the coronavirus.

"There is a way to handle a crisis where you meet
people's expectations regardless of how the crisis
is playing out," Christie said. "The way to do that is
they expect you to be out there. They expect you to
prove to them that you understand why they're afraid
and that no matter how long it takes you're going to
fix the problem.

"But you're not doing that," Christie continued.
"You're telling people that it's going to just go away, it's
going to magically go away. People don't want to hear
that. You tell people that we've got it under control,
but it's clear that we don't, and so I'm very concerned
that what you're doing is you're setting yourself up

for failure and that people will not believe you after a while."

"I'm not going to scare people," Trump said. "It's not my job. My job is to reassure people and not scare them."

"Yeah, but you only reassure them with the truth, not with the stuff that they know from a common-sense perspective can't be true," Christie replied. "No, it's not under control. No, it's not just going to go away magically one day. They know that. That's commonsensical. It's not like medical training. You just know that.

"By the way," Christie added, "if it does, you get all the freaking credit anyway. Who cares? But if you go further out there, extend yourself in terms of your level of concern, your level of preparedness for what the worst-case scenario is, you can always bring it back. If you go short of the mark in the beginning, you can't ever extend it."

Trump told Christie he would rather "tell them it's going to go away. Chris, when the weather gets warm, it's going to go away."

"Mr. President, if that happens, you'll get credit for it," Christie said. "You don't need to keep saying it. Talk about it as if it's serious, and if it gets better, you win anyway. Play worst-case on this."

Christie encouraged Trump to reframe his presidency around the pandemic as a way to inspire all Americans, not just Republicans, to rally behind him.

"Say, 'You know, up until today the position of

president was a job, but now it's a mission, and I'm not going to leave here until the mission is completed,'" Christie said. "That's what I said during Sandy: 'Being governor was a job—a great job, but it was a job. Now it's a mission, and I'm not going to let anybody knock me off of the mission that I have to accomplish for the people of New Jersey, which is to rebuild the state that we love.' Say it over and over and over and over and over again and people believe it because you keep saying it over and over again, because it comes from a place that's seen as genuine."

Trump nodded as he listened, but was noncommittal. It was clear the president didn't buy into Christie's advice.

Like many other big states, Illinois was running low on ventilators, masks, gowns, and other supplies and equipment. Pritzker repeatedly had asked the Trump administration for help but seemed to get nowhere. The governor had reached his last resort and decided to call the president.

Pritzker loathed Trump. Campaigning for governor in 2018, he would assail the president in his stump speeches as "racist," "misogynistic," "homophobic," and "xenophobic." Curiously, though, Trump had a soft spot for Pritzker. He was a multibillionaire, and Trump liked to suck up to the uber-rich. The Pritzker family, one of America's wealthiest, founded and developed the Hyatt hotel chain, and New York's Grand Hyatt was one of Trump's proudest real estate deals.

In December 2018, when Pritzker and other governors-elect first visited the White House following their elections, Trump made a beeline past Florida's Ron DeSantis and other political allies to shake hands with the Democrat from Chicago. "J. B., you come from a great family. A great family," Trump said, patting Pritzker on the shoulder. "Congratulations on your win, and I just want you to know, you come from a great family."

Now at a loss for how to bring supplies into Illinois, Pritzker called Trump on March 23 in an attempt to play to the president's ego. He wrote out a script for himself, knowing he might get angry and wanting to stay calm and collected.

"Like you, Mr. President, I'm a former businessman," Pritzker told Trump. "I normally don't like government interfering with the commercial market. But with regard to ventilators and PPE, if you could invoke the [Defense Production Act], it would stop the price gouging and put some order into the market. As it is, states are competing with each other and against foreign countries, too. You have the power to save lives, to control distribution of these goods, and we need your help."

"What do you need?" Trump asked.

Pritzker ticked through his list, from masks to ventilators to gowns and gloves.

"Let me see what I can do," Trump said, and ended the call.

About half an hour later, Pritzker's phone rang. It was Peter Navarro, Trump's trade adviser, who had taken on a new role coordinating manufacturing and Defense Production Act policies.

"I think I can help you out," Navarro told the governor. "I've got three hundred ventilators in our private stock and I can send those to you. And I've got three hundred thousand N95 masks. I can get those out of our private stock and I can get them to you in Trump time."

"Wow, Trump time?" Pritzker replied. "That sounds pretty fast. When do you think we could see those?"

"I'll get it to you by Sunday," Navarro said, which was six days later. He had one favor to ask of Pritzker, according to people with knowledge of the conversation: "Make sure when you're on TV next you are grateful to the president."

Navarro denied that he asked Pritzker to praise Trump and said he only asked the governor to "tone down his partisan rhetoric."

Nothing arrived on Sunday. When the federal shipment showed up several days late, it contained the three hundred ventilators, but the three hundred thousand masks were of the surgical variety, not nearly as efficacious as N95 masks. Navarro told Pritzker he would investigate what went wrong with the order. A couple of weeks later, Navarro called Pritzker to follow up.

"Listen, I've got six hundred gallons of hand sanitizer," he told the governor. "Do you need hand sanitizer?"

Pritzker needed N95 masks, not hand sanitizer. He accepted the shipment, happy to just get something from Washington. But "Trump time," he concluded, was nothing more than a clever and deceptive sales pitch.

Five

Rebelling Against the Experts

President Trump decided on March 16 to effectively shut down the country for fifteen days. But the doctors on his task force knew they would need more time to control the spread of the coronavirus. They immediately started working to convince Trump to extend the lockdown. Mark Meadows, Steven Mnuchin, Larry Kudlow, and other advisers, who believed the shutdown would mean unnecessarily destroying the economy, opposed them. Trump, who saw the economy as key to his re-election chances, was predisposed to agree. He made that much clear on March 23 when, amid the administration's review of extending shutdown recommendations, he tweeted in all caps, "WE CANNOT LET THE CURE BE WORSE THAN THE PROBLEM ITSELF."

The country at this point was gripped by fear, and the president fixated on being the savior. When NBC's Peter Alexander asked him at the March 20 coronavirus briefing, "What do you say to Americans who are watching you right now who are scared," Trump snapped. "I say that you are a terrible reporter. That's what I say. I think it's a very nasty question. I think it's a very bad signal that you are putting out to the American people. They're looking for answers and they're looking for hope. And you're doing sensationalism."

Trump had never managed to show empathy during his presidency, and even in this crisis, he still did not summon compassion for others.

The president decided he wanted the country to reopen and arbitrarily picked a date of April 12, which happened to be Easter, because he assumed voters would be heartened by images of church pews packed with parishioners on Easter Sunday and families out celebrating over brunch in neighborhood restaurants. Some of his advisers warned him this could be perilous.

"Mr. President, this is a huge mistake," Kellyanne Conway told him. "You don't own the deaths right now, but you'll own all the deaths if you do this."

Easter Sunday, Conway argued, was "too soon. You can't put an artificial date on reopening the economy."

"No, no, no," Trump replied. "We have to open. It's killing people."

"I get it," Conway said. "But we can't even see this

virus. It's transmitted through the air. And if you reopen now, you'll own it."

As a counterweight to the economic and political concerns dominating the thinking inside the White House, Anthony Fauci, Deborah Birx, Robert Redfield, and Stephen Hahn formed an alliance. They began meeting as a "doctors' group" three to four times a week to strategize for when they faced off later against Meadows, Mnuchin, Kudlow, and others at the broader task-force meetings.

Birx and Fauci analyzed publicly available data, including from the CDC, to model dire projections of deaths without continued social distancing and other mitigation efforts. As many as 1.6 million to 2.2 million Americans would die, their analysis showed, whereas by continuing the lockdown the estimated fatality total would be 100,000 to 240,000. They presented the findings to Trump, arguing that keeping restrictions in place would save lives. Birx knew that Trump was moved by anecdotes and personal connections, and at the time, Elmhurst Hospital, a public hospital in Queens near where he grew up, was being overrun with COVID cases. Cable news channels were showing footage from Elmhurst of body bags piling up.

"These hospitals that are serving our most vulnerable Americans are all over the United States," Birx told Trump. "We have six thousand–plus hospitals in the United States. You could, right off the bat, have a thousand Elmhursts."

"Are you sure that this will create more Elmhursts?" Trump asked her, referring to a spike in cases if the economy reopened prematurely.

"Yes, I'm sure," Birx said.

Trump was persuaded. On March 29, the president announced from the Rose Garden that the strict federal guidelines that effectively shut down businesses would be extended for an additional thirty days, through April 30.

"Nothing would be worse than declaring victory before the victory is won," Trump said. "That would be the greatest loss of all."

Trump said the ghastly scenes from Elmhurst helped convince him.

"I've been watching that for the last week on television, body bags all over in hallways," Trump said. "I have been watching them bring in trailer trucks, freezer trucks—they are freezer trucks because they can't handle the bodies, there are so many of them. This is essentially in my community in Queens—Queens, New York. I have seen things I've never seen before. I mean, I've seen them, but I've seen them on television in faraway lands."

The doctors had prevailed, but their win would prove short-lived.

Max Kennedy Jr. was an unlikely candidate to work for the Trump administration's coronavirus response—unlikely both because he was a lifelong Democrat and a grandson of the late Robert F. Kennedy Jr., and because he was twenty-six years old and had neither expertise in public health nor experience in crisis management. But that didn't stop Jared Kushner from bringing Kennedy on board, along with roughly a dozen other twentysomething consultants and private-equity analysts. Kushner figured these financial whiz kids, volunteering directly for him and outside the strictures of government health agencies, could bust through bureaucratic logjams and solve problems like the supply chain for personal protective equipment. If only it had been that easy.

Kennedy said that when he first reported to work on March 22, he stepped into chaos. He was assigned to the "sourcing team," meaning his job would be to source test kits, hand sanitizer, masks, and other equipment from manufacturers overseas. He and the other volunteers cold-called factories in China on their personal cell phones asking if they would sell goods to the U.S. government. He said they conducted business over their Gmail accounts and had to copy someone with a ".gov" email address to confirm they were reaching out on behalf of the government. They weren't dummies; Kennedy had graduated from Harvard and worked as a consultant at McKinsey & Company before joining Insight Partners, a midsized equity firm. But he and the other volunteers were the first to admit they had no idea what they were doing.

The supervisor on this sourcing project, Rachael Baitel, didn't know much more. She was a former executive assistant to Ivanka Trump and Goldman Sachs analyst. No one on the team had existing manufacturing relationships or was versed in FDA regulations or understood federal procurement policies. Kennedy said that another superior in the operation, Michael Duffey, instructed him never to put anything in writing to him—no emails, no text messages. Kennedy thought that was strange, then he Googled Duffey and learned he had been the Office of Management and Budget official who withheld aid to Ukraine, and some of his emails had become evidence in Trump's impeachment investigation.

The volunteers worked out of the Federal Emergency Management Administration's headquarters, where khaki-clad employees nicknamed the newcomers the Slim Suit Crowd for their natty attire. In the West Wing, Kushner's group was mocked more derisively; "that whizbang crew of numb nuts" was how one senior official described it. In their FEMA offices, nobody wore masks or socially distanced. When Vice President Pence visited them, he walked around a small conference room shaking people's hands and patting them on the back, as if the virus somehow couldn't penetrate their bubble.

Kushner was a self-styled fixer, establishing himself as the administration's key conduit for federal agency officials, state governors, and business executives—especially when it came to the PPE supply chain. The thirty-nine-year-old had only ever worked in real estate and had no expertise in international logistics.

He had never marshaled a response to a crisis, much less a pandemic. But because of his exalted status as husband to the president's favorite child, Kushner carried himself with supreme confidence and could spur swift responses from across the administration, where one's power was measured by loyalty and proximity to Trump. He gave his cell-phone number to government procurement officials and instructed them to communicate directly with him to approve international orders. Kushner wanted money to be wired to manufacturers within minutes, not days, lest the United States lose out to another country, and he personally called the chief executive officers of FedEx and UPS to deploy their planes to deliver freight.

Kushner would pay frequent visits to the volunteer team and issue decrees. He had an air of self-importance, as if he alone could bust through barriers. When volunteers flagged problems, Kushner vowed to get them solved right away. Some things got fixed, but chaos endured.

Kushner expected his team to follow up on every lead about sourcing or delivering PPE. Kennedy said the team became easily distracted by incoming ideas or requests from VIPs, which the volunteers had been instructed to prioritize—including an email from Dallas Mavericks owner Mark Cuban; repeated calls and emails from the Fox News Channel host Jeanine Pirro requesting a hundred thousand masks be redirected to a hospital she favored; a lead on PPE procurement from Charlie Kirk, a Trump loyalist who founded Turning Point USA, a network of young conservative activists; and a lead from Tana Goertz, a former contestant on **The Apprentice.**

Brad Smith, the deputy administrator at the Centers for Medicare & Medicaid Services, was a trusted ally of Kushner's and took on a special assignment working with the volunteers. The CDC data modeled by Birx and Fauci suggested a far more catastrophic scenario than Kushner and other political advisers to Trump wanted to believe. Kennedy said Smith asked him and another volunteer to devise a new model.

"I don't know anything about disease modeling," Kennedy told Smith.

"That's okay," Smith said. "Just put a growth rate on it and make sure it ends up at the right numbers. It just needs to be a model that shows a worst case of one hundred thousand people dying and a low case of twenty thousand. Look around. Does it feel like two hundred fifty thousand people are going to die?"

Kennedy recalled, "I was looking around like, I'm in a FEMA building, there's military officers everywhere. To me, this feels pretty serious."

Smith disputed Kennedy's description of their conversation. "The only model I asked the team to build in late March and early April 2020 was a model to project PPE needs through July 2020," Smith said. "To calculate PPE needs, the model used hospitalizations and deaths as inputs. The mean version of the model assumed one hundred sixty-nine thousand deaths by July 2020 and the worst-case version of the model assumed three hundred twelve thousand deaths by July 2020. According to the CDC, there were approximately one hundred sixty thousand deaths as of July 30, so the model's assumptions proved to be very accurate."

Three weeks in, Kennedy resigned, distressed and disgusted by his experience. He filed a whistleblower complaint to the House Oversight Committee, hoping that Congress might investigate what he saw as malfeasance on the part of Trump's political appointees. Kennedy refused to follow through on Smith's order, but political appointees cooked up a fatality model to satisfy Trump's alternate reality. Unbeknownst to Birx at the time, Kevin Hassett, an economist who had served as Trump's chairman of the Council of Economic Advisers until 2019, returned to the White House with a special assignment: to work with a small team and quietly build an econometric model to show far fewer fatalities.

Birx continued to toil in her windowless closet of an office on the ground floor of the West Wing, analyzing CDC data to present to the task force. But shortly after Trump agreed to extend the shutdown guidelines, Birx found her projections of rising numbers of infections and deaths undercut by the rogue Hassett model, which many in the White House interpreted to suggest the death toll would peak by mid-April and then drop off substantially. It was embraced by Kushner and guided the mindset inside the

White House to prioritize the economy over public health. The Hassett model affirmed the skepticism of many of Trump's political advisers of the severity of the virus.

Meadows also routinely challenged Birx's data analysis. "Debbie, I don't know what this data is," he said in a task-force meeting. "It seems specious to me." Channeling Trump's instincts to focus on the economy, the chief of staff argued, "We've got to get moving again. We've got to open things up."

Soon, Birx found her access to Trump cut off. She was no longer invited regularly into the Oval Office and was asked to brief Pence instead. Birx had a relatively productive relationship with Kushner, though in some meetings he aggressively challenged the veracity of her data and questioned her analysis, as if to suggest he knew more about infectious disease and epidemiology than she did. Frustrated by the office politics, Birx asked Grogan, one of the few White House officials she had known before the virus hit, what Kushner was really like.

"Look, Debbie, he's not like anybody you've worked with," Grogan said. "He's not like a four-star general who's going to scream at you and call you 'Sugar Tits' and be a prick. He's not like any asshole who lies and misrepresents data. He is a zero-sum-game motherfucker from New York. And if you can't get your head around that, it is not going to go well for you."

Michael Caputo had gotten used to life in lockdown in East Aurora, a picturesque village outside of Buffalo, New York. He sat at home with his wife and six- and eight-year-old kids watching Governor Andrew Cuomo's daily news conference, then Trump's daily news conference, taking notes when something seemed important. Caputo was especially freaked out about catching COVID-19. He went grocery shopping in a mask and goggles, and when he returned home he stripped down in the mudroom and put his clothes in a plastic bag so he wouldn't risk the contagion spreading among his family. He would tell neighbors, "If you're not wearing a mask, you're part of the problem."

Caputo cut an unusual figure as a public health evangelist. A former conservative radio commentator, he was a longtime fixture in Trump World, having started as Trump's driver and worked on Trump's 2014 bid to buy the Buffalo Bills, before becoming a communications adviser on his 2016 presidential campaign. Caputo, who had personal and business ties in Moscow, had been ensnared as a witness in the Russia investigation.

One day in early April, Caputo was sitting at his kitchen table eating lunch when his phone rang. It was the president.

"I need help," Trump said. "Do you want to join the administration?"

"Well, sure," Caputo replied.

"Johnny's right here," Trump said, referring to

Johnny McEntee, the twenty-nine-year-old director of presidential personnel whom Trump had empowered to root out his perceived enemies from government and to seed the bureaucracy with loyalists. "We want to know if you want to be assistant secretary for public affairs at HHS and help with the communications on COVID. They're all fucked up."

"Sure," Caputo said.

"The sound that you hear is my pen to paper, so pack your bags," Trump said.

McEntee then texted Caputo, "We're counting on you," and a week later Caputo was in the White House being sworn in, with McEntee standing at his side. The location of Caputo's swearing-in symbolized the fact that he was Trump's choice and would have personal access to the president. In fact, Caputo's boss, Azar, had no role in hiring him and was surprised by the appointment.

At the time, Azar was taking incoming arrows from several administration officials, and in particular from Grogan. Azar quickly began to confide in Caputo and seek his help trying to hold on to his job and rehabilitate his image. In huddles with Caputo, Azar would lose his temper about Grogan and complain about negative news stories as "a Grogan trap" or "a Grogan hit piece," convinced that his West Wing rival was leaking damaging information about him to reporters. When he got especially worked up, Azar would talk like a hen, bobbing and pecking his head, his voice growing ever higher and louder.

"Fuck this," Azar would tell Caputo, pacing back and forth in his office. "This is the end. I can't believe this is happening. This is so fucking unfair. Fucking Grogan."

Caputo figured Azar would become the fall guy for the administration's early failure to control the virus. This was reinforced by Trump's comments. The president would call Caputo and ask, "How's Alex doing? What do you think of Alex?" This was a tell tale sign that Trump was losing confidence.

But Caputo tried to stick up for Azar. "He's on board with your program," he told Trump. "He's always going to be throwing punches for you." And Caputo would try to get positive comments about Azar into stories in the five newspapers he knew Trump read in print: **The New York Times, The Washington Post, The Wall Street Journal,** the **New York Post,** and the **New York Daily News.**

Even if it put him at odds with Trump, Caputo believed one of his missions at HHS was to help share public health information, and he thought the best messengers were the doctors—first and foremost, Fauci. So he tried to cultivate a partnership with Fauci, who had him at his home near American University in Northwest Washington for breakfast early in his tenure. It was 6:30 a.m., and Fauci welcomed Caputo to his deck, where they removed their masks, sat overlooking a leafy backyard, and had scrambled eggs, bacon, toast, and coffee.

They got to talking about Trump, and Fauci

surprised Caputo when he said, "I have nothing personal against the president. I certainly don't dislike him; in fact, he has some things about him that are attractive."

"The coronavirus task force is a battle of ideas," Fauci said. "There's a lot of disagreement on the task force and we try to reach consensus by the end of the meetings."

By early April, Joe Biden was the presumptive Democratic presidential nominee and had his sights set squarely on Trump. Out of the makeshift television studio he built in the basement of his home in Wilmington, Delaware, the former vice president assailed Trump's management of the pandemic. Polls showed Trump had lost the small bumps in job approval he saw in February and March following his acquittal in the impeachment trial and the early outbreaks of the virus. Now, Trump trailed Biden, in whom voters had greater confidence to steer the country out of the converging health and economic crises.

Trump's campaign advisers test-drove lines of attack against Biden, which ranged from hinting that at the advanced age of seventy-eight there were signs of senility in Biden's behavior, to suggesting his son Hunter was corrupt, to criticizing his background as a lifelong career politician. None seemed to move the needle much, so long as the president failed to manage the crises of the day. Still, Brad Parscale believed the key to a Trump victory would be a relentlessly negative assault on Biden.

"We've got to make Biden look bad and make the country see him as a good ole Uncle Joe," Parscale advised Trump. "We should make him look like a pedophile, womanizing, senile guy who can't keep his wits together."

Trump thought that line of attack was fruitful. In fact, the president had long ago nicknamed Biden "Sleepy Joe" and routinely cast doubt on his mental acuity. He enjoyed when his campaign used images of Biden that made him look old and ugly. But Trump did not want his campaign spending much money on advertisements about his challenger. He wanted the advertising budget to primarily be spent promoting himself. Trump wanted the election to be a referendum on himself and what a great job he was doing as president. Besides, Trump thought he could count on Bill Barr to fire the magic bullet. For all of 2019, the attorney general had been the president's golden boy. As Dan Scavino once explained to Barr, "In the Cabinet, you're up here and everyone else is down here." Scavino raised an arm above his head before lowering it. Trump liked Barr's smarts, toughness, and willingness to fight on his behalf.

Two moves stood out for Trump: Barr's suggestion to the public that Robert Mueller's Russia investigation had found no evidence of obstruction of justice by the president, when in fact the opposite was true; and his subsequent appointment of prosecutor John Durham to investigate the origins of the FBI's 2016 probe of the Trump campaign. The president thought that the "Crossfire Hurricane" investigation had been launched by a corrupt FBI to frame him. He assumed Durham would produce evidence proving it and perhaps prosecute former FBI director James Comey, former CIA director John Brennan, and other top Obama administration officials. Trump hoped this would give him an edge in his reelection.

On April 8, 2020, Barr made the unusual prediction that Durham's far-from-finished investigation would prove the FBI engaged in gross misconduct and abused their power in their pursuit of Trump. "What happened to him was one of the greatest travesties in American history," Barr told Laura Ingraham in a Fox News interview. "Without any basis, they started this investigation of his campaign, and even more concerning actually is what happened after the campaign—a whole pattern of events while he was president . . . to sabotage the presidency—or at least have the effect of sabotaging the presidency."

Many prosecutors and Justice Department alumni felt their skin crawl. Here he goes again, they said, Barr trying to use the department's powers to give Trump some political ammunition. Normally prosecutors didn't breathe a word about an ongoing investigation. Comey had endured a public tarring from Republicans and Democrats alike for violating that norm as FBI director when in 2016 he had discussed the investigation of Hillary Clinton's use of a private email system for her government work.

Trump had been antsy to see Durham's findings—and by giving him the false hope that it might wrap up soon, Barr had made a tactical error. The attorney general had wanted to put the "pedal to the metal" on this probe, as he told aides, and release findings well before the election. But two things dramatically slowed Durham's progress. The Connecticut prosecutor had to hold off on much of his work while the Justice Department's inspector general finished an overlapping investigation in December 2019. Then came the coronavirus, which made convening grand juries and traveling the world to interrogate witnesses rather difficult.

But Trump didn't let up. He repeatedly pressed Meadows to ask Barr what was going on with the Durham investigation. Though he did not direct Barr to indict anyone specifically, the president frequently brought up the probe during their Oval Office meetings that spring. His questions were frequently some version of, "When do you think something might come out of that?" Barr didn't feel comfortable responding with details and tried to manage the president's expectations. He would provide responses like, "Mr. President, whether or not John Durham indicts somebody is not going to affect this election outcome."

"It makes us look weak," Trump often grumped. Bringing his enemies "to justice," the president argued, showed strength.

B y mid-April, as U.S. deaths from the coronavirus topped thirty thousand, Trump faced a political imperative to find someone to blame. Trump's search for a scapegoat fit a pattern of his presidency. "He's never at fault for anything," explained David Lapan, a former senior official in Trump's Department of Homeland Security. "It's Fauci's fault. It's China's fault. It's Obama's fault. It's always someone else, somewhere else. He doesn't want to hear the bad news. He doesn't take responsibility for the bad news and wants to gloss over it and change the subject."

Trump decided to use his trademark hyperbole to draw a bull's-eye for the American people around the real villains: China and the World Health Organization. On April 14, he formally announced he was suspending U.S. funding to the WHO while his administration conducted a review of the group's "role in severely mismanaging and covering up the spread of coronavirus." He argued that the WHO failed to call out China's lack of transparency about the Wuhan outbreak, although he had repeatedly praised China's handling of the virus in January and February. Trump's blame game was easily chalked up to a preelection push to sidestep his own role in failing to protect Americans. But in several corners of government, many career experts agreed with the facts behind Trump's critique. Officials who vehemently disagreed with each other on other coronavirus decisions were aligned in finding fault in the WHO for parroting China's lies and shielding it from scrutiny.

Mike Pompeo, Robert O'Brien, and Matt Pottinger repeatedly stressed to the president that the WHO had blood on its hands. "I believe the whole world is the collateral damage of the way China handled this episode," Pottinger told colleagues.

Redfield, too, was increasingly convinced Tedros Adhanom Ghebreyesus had stonewalled him in trying to get a CDC team into China early on. He told confidants he had to conclude the WHO had not been an honest broker.

Some administration officials homed in on the Wuhan Institute of Virology, a prestigious Chinese lab recognized for its expertise on bat coronaviruses. Pottinger, Pompeo, and other top national security officials had been urging government investigators and intelligence officials to look more deeply into a theory percolating among Chinese-based scientists and right-wing U.S. media figures that the Wuhan lab had either accidentally or intentionally leaked the novel coronavirus—SARS-CoV-2—into the world. The claim resembled the plot of a sci-fi thriller, but at least one part of it was firmly rooted in real risks at the lab. No serious person believed this was an intentional leak of a manufactured bioweapon by the Chinese, but several national security and intelligence officials believed an accident was possible and even likely.

This was not the first time U.S. officials had concerns about the Wuhan Institute of Virology, which
China had designed as a world-class research facility
to study some of the deadliest pathogens, especially
coronaviruses. In early 2018, after State Department
science diplomats had toured the lab, they warned
U.S. officials that the lab suffered a serious shortage of staff with adequate containment training and
needed help to meet the very high safety standards
for the dangers they were handling. They also warned
that a team led by Dr. Shi Zhengli, the well-known
head of the lab's bat virus research, was working with
SARS-like coronaviruses they found could interact
with human cell receptors and might easily transmit
to people. Known as China's "Bat Woman," Shi had
been studying how coronaviruses could infect humans and manipulating the spike proteins that the
virus used to enter human cells.

After the outbreak in Wuhan, some argued it was
just too much of a coincidence. The epicenter of
the virus was in the same city that boasted one of the
world's largest repositories of coronavirus specimens.
Perhaps the virus accidentally infected lab staff. Shi
has angrily dismissed the idea that her lab had anything to do with the novel virus. But Trump's intelligence officers reported that they had credible
information indicating some Wuhan lab workers had
suffered COVID symptoms in the fall of 2019. If
true, they would have been the earliest known cases of
infection. The intelligence community briefed Trump

in late March that it had revised its classified assessment from early January that "the outbreak probably occurred naturally." Now they were adding the possibility that the new coronavirus emerged "accidentally" due to "unsafe laboratory practices" at either the Wuhan Institute of Virology or its partner lab near the Wuhan market.

Trump found it hard to keep this new intelligence to himself. He brought it up with campaign advisers, domestic policy aides, and health officials.

On April 18, Trump confirmed at a White House coronavirus press briefing that intelligence agencies were digging into evidence that suggested an accident or shoddy conditions at the Wuhan lab were connected to the outbreak. "A lot of people are looking at it," he told reporters. "It seems to make sense." But the assessment was greeted with deep suspicion in the scientific community and in the media. Trump and some of his allies were looking for a scapegoat, and a Chinese lab screw-up provided a convenient one.

Critics of the Wuhan lab theory discounted the warnings from Pottinger, who was well known as a skeptic of nearly everything the Chinese government claimed, as a China-hawk fever dream. But Pottinger knew from past experience not to automatically buy what Beijing was selling. When he was a reporter in Beijing, the Chinese government covered up a 2004 accident at a Beijing lab studying SARS and similar coronaviruses, which led to an outbreak that infected nine people and killed at least one.

To try to suss out the likely sources of the virus, Pottinger consulted with doctors and other experts he had met while covering the 2003 SARS outbreak. Pottinger also got a summary from the NSC's virology expert, Philip Ferro, about how zoonotic diseases typically jumped from animals to humans and spread through a population. Sifting through the information he received from SARS experts, intelligence reports, and Ferro, he was taken aback by three key facts. What Pottinger didn't know at this early stage was that the director of the CDC was zeroing in on those same facts with increasing conviction that a lab leak was the likely source of this unusually lethal and contagious virus.

First, COVID-19 had in a few weeks' time become a zoonotic pathogen that boasted one of the most rapid and efficient transmissions of any virus in modern human history. That was not normal for zoonotic viruses that jumped from animal to human. An animal host of the virus, like a bat, could potentially infect another animal species, which would then infect a human. The virus could make the next animal species very ill and even kill them. But this type of virus that jumped from animal to human had a much harder time replicating—and spreading rapidly.

Second, though the Chinese government claimed the virus emanated from a seafood market in Wuhan that also sold wild and exotic game, a team of scientists in China published research in January noting that a sizable portion of the initial cluster of cases in Wuhan had no known contact with the market. Later research would establish that this quickly embraced and dominant theory about the virus's source—that it started at the wet market—was almost certainly wrong.

Third, the Wuhan lab had a Level Four designation, giving it permission to handle the riskiest biohazards despite the U.S. government's earlier concerns about the lab's safety. Its sister lab, down the street from the market, had a much lower Level Two designation and harvested bat viruses.

Redfield shared Pottinger's concerns—but he was assessing these facts as a seasoned virologist, not as a national security expert suspicious of China. He strongly believed the Wuhan lab was the source, but primarily because he knew from years of lab work that a virus jumping from animal to human had never replicated and spread as easily as COVID-19 had. Over time a chorus of scientists studying the virus would agree that they'd never seen a virus like this one. Interestingly, scientists began to learn something else as they studied the novel coronavirus's spike protein that helped the virus enter a human cell and invade its host: their spikes were amazingly adaptable and the most successful ever seen in their quest to attach to human cells. "Zoonotic diseases that transition for the first time to man, these are not highly infectious to man," Redfield would explain to colleagues. "This virus, in my view, is too infectious to man to assume that last January it jumped from bat to man."

Redfield was clear that he didn't think the virus was released intentionally or deployed as a weapon but was unshakable in this belief that the lab was the coronavirus's epicenter: "It unintentionally escaped, probably by infecting laboratory technicians."

The origin of this potent virus would remain a mystery throughout the year. Many experts dismissed the lab-leak theory as highly unlikely, while a growing number of American and European scientists insisted it had never been properly investigated. Two profound failures prevented the world from knowing the answer about the origin. First, the Chinese government dissembled and tried to keep anyone outside the country from looking closely. Secondly, the Trump administration let China get away with that. This second flaw showcased Trump's consistent focus on optics over facts. His administration primarily deployed the lab theory as a useful anti-China talking point, a convenient boogeyman, rather than a hypothesis that required rigorous stress-testing and unimpeachable data. In the early days of the outbreak when it mattered most, the U.S. president did not demand that a CDC team be allowed into Wuhan to conduct an independent investigation that could have ruled a lab accident in or out. Trump was too busy touting his "great" relationship with President Xi Jinping and their trade deal. Even when Trump was later personally rebuffed in seeking to send in investigators, he still took no action to punish China or hold it to account.

Through late March and early April, the president heard a steady drumbeat of anecdotal testimony that the untested, antimalarial drug hydroxychloroquine could treat COVID-19. The evangelists in his ear ranged from Rudy Giuliani to Ingraham, who, with Meadows's help, arranged to bring doctors who were regular on-air guests on her Fox show to the White House for private meetings with Trump to talk up the drug.

Hydroxychloroquine was still in the testing stages and not yet approved by the FDA as a treatment for COVID-19, although doctors were permitted to prescribe it to hospitalized patients. Medical professionals believed it had dangerous side effects, and Fauci privately pleaded with the president to be more cautious about advocating the drug. But Trump, who famously said he trusted his gut more than anything an expert could counsel him, was so desperate to make the virus disappear that he pitched the drug as "a very special thing."

"What do you have to lose?" the president asked again and again.

Doctors around the country watching the president's reckless promotion were stunned. If he wasn't the president, they noted, he could be prosecuted for off-label promotion of a drug—pushing a medicine for an unauthorized and not fully tested use. In the pursuit of FDA emergency use authorizations for hydroxychloroquine and other therapeutics, Meadows was Trump's enforcer. He regularly browbeat Hahn, demanding to know why data from the clinical trials was not yet available. He wanted results immediately, and applied pressure on the FDA chief to speed up the process.

"We've got to get it done," Meadows would tell Hahn. "You're not working fast enough."

Hahn would explain that it took months to complete clinical trials and get data. What's more, the FDA was concerned that with so many hospitalized COVID patients taking hydroxychloroquine, there was a sudden shortage of the drug for people with lupus, for which hydroxychloroquine was an approved treatment.

Hahn was concerned about how political the hydroxychloroquine debate had become and worried it was a dry run for the pressure he fully expected to receive from Trump and Meadows to speed up FDA approval of vaccines before the election. He and Caputo went on walks along the National Mall to talk through the personalities and politics involved. They both agreed that if the White House tried to manipulate the FDA during the vaccine approval process, government scientists would sooner climb to the roof at the FDA's White Oak offices in suburban Maryland and light themselves on fire than take a political action. As Caputo joked with Hahn, "None of those electric cars in the parking lot at White Oak have Trump bumper stickers."

On April 13, Azar entered Meadows's office for a meeting and found him waving a spiral-bound report and yelling. "If this goes out, the president will fire you," Meadows said.

The report had been prepared by the National Institute for Allergy and Infectious Diseases, which Fauci ran. It urged that there be Phase Three clinical trials of therapies, including hydroxychloroquine, that Trump wanted authorized immediately as miracle cures. Clinical trials would take time—time that Trump considered unnecessary and wasteful. Azar defended the multistage trials, explaining that the government endorsement of such therapies should rightly come only after thorough research on benefits, side effects, and unusual reactions. There was alarm in the scientific community that hydroxychloroquine, when combined with azithromycin, could cause heart arrhythmias.

"The president wants this now, Alex," Meadows said. "It works."

A senior member of the task force observed, "Meadows was so consistently abusive, so dismissive of the medical professionals—repeatedly. They deserved to be challenged and questioned, but kicking the shit out of them for your own amusement and trying to browbeat them was so counterproductive, and it was just an absolute disaster over time."

Providing backup was Peter Navarro, the zealous trade adviser who had concluded that Hahn and the other task-force doctors had "hydroxy hysteria." So he joined a task-force meeting around this time to try to strong-arm a consensus on approving hydroxychloroquine. Navarro arrived in the Situation Room with a stack of papers that he said were nearly two dozen retrospective reviews of hydroxychloroquine as a COVID treatment. Other officials questioned the credibility of the writings and noted that some were from Chinese doctors.

Navarro handed Hahn the papers. "Look, this is not high-level evidence to support what you want to do," Hahn said. "We have to wait for the clinical trials to be done."

"I know the literature," Navarro said. "This is highly supportive."

Fauci jumped into the conversation to back up Hahn and explain that the evidence thus far was inconclusive. At that, Navarro challenged Fauci's medical credentials and argued that he was the only task-force member who had read all of the studies about the drug.

"You have blood on your hands," Navarro told Hahn and Fauci, charging that many more Americans would die if they did not immediately approve hydroxychloroquine.

The argument escalated until Pence put an end to it and the meeting broke up. Hahn's and Fauci's instincts proved right. On April 24, the FDA would caution against using hydroxychloroquine for treatment of COVID-19 because of the risk of "serious heart rhythm problems." And on June 15, the

FDA would revoke its emergency use authorization because it was no longer believed to be effective against COVID-19.

When Birx began work in March, she drew up a list of her top ten scientific questions about the coronavirus that she wanted to be able to answer for the public. One of them was simple: Does the virus still spread on surfaces outdoors? Scientists at the Department of Homeland Security set about trying to find Birx an answer. They tested different disinfectants outdoors, timed sunlight exposures, and tried to see how long the virus would last on an outdoor surface that people touch but that is blocked from sunlight, such as the undersurface of a swing set.

The answer came on April 23, when one of the DHS scientists, William Bryan, came to the White House to brief the task force on their preliminary findings. He said the life span of droplets containing the virus was shorter when exposed to sunlight or heat, such as summer weather, and that it would be more practical for the government to encourage people to be active outdoors, though he cautioned that there was no proof that the virus was less contagious or spread less aggressively in warmer climates.

After the task-force meeting broke up, some advisers went to the Oval Office to meet with Trump before his daily news conference. (Birx, who by then was cut out of most Oval meetings, went to her downstairs office.) They brought Bryan with them, figuring the president would be interested in hearing what he had to say. Indeed, he was—so much so that Trump asked Bryan to join him at the press briefing.

As officials lined up to get ready to walk into the briefing room, Bryan spotted Birx and told her he got to go into the Oval. "It was really exciting," he said. "The president thinks this could be a treatment," meaning sunlight. Trump, Birx, and Bryan stepped into the briefing room, and Bryan presented his findings. Then Trump ruminated aloud about the presentation, as if he were conversing with Bryan, only live on television with millions of Americans watching.

"So, supposing we hit the body with a tremendous, whether it's ultraviolet or just very powerful light, and I think you said that hasn't been checked, but you're going to test it," Trump said. "And then I said, supposing you brought the light inside the body, which you can do, either through the skin or in some other way. And I think you said you're going to test that, too. Sounds interesting, right? And then I see the disinfectant, where it knocks it out in a minute, one minute. And is there a way we can do something like that by injection inside or almost a cleaning, because, you see, it gets in the lungs and it does a tremendous number on the lungs, so it'd be interesting to check that."

Birx, seated alongside the podium, looked uncomfortable and slightly distraught as Trump mused about injecting a household disinfectant such as bleach into the human body. She smirked at first and then stared down, trying to keep a straight face. She later told confidants she felt as if the earth had swallowed her up. **This cannot be happening,** she thought to herself. It was not in Birx's DNA to stand up and yell, "This is not a treatment! Do not inject bleach!" So Birx sat silently, declining to correct the president. She was, after all, an army doctor—a "chain-of-command gal," as she liked to tell people—and Trump was her commander in chief.

After the news conference ended, Birx unloaded on Trump's aides. She was screaming, crazed about how Bryan was even allowed into the Oval in the first place. "Who let [Bryan] see the president?" she asked them. "Who let him in there?"

Olivia Troye couldn't believe the president would suggest on national television during a pandemic that people inject themselves with bleach and it might make them immune from the virus. "I remember walking away from that moment and thinking, Tonight there is going to be some family probably somewhere who's going to [inject bleach] because they believe everything he says," Troye later recalled. "Some of his supporters are loyal, unwavering people. And God, I hope tonight there isn't a family out there somewhere who actually does this."

Another member of the task force recalled thinking, "I don't know what the fuck was going through his head. It was inconceivable that the president believes you can shoot yourself up with disinfectant.

Was he tired? Was he misspeaking? Did he use the wrong word? He said he was being facetious. He told me privately, 'I was being facetious.' I don't believe that's true."

The bleach moment went viral and was held up across the media as an example of Trump's willingness to spread misinformation about the pandemic. The president had a communications crisis. For weeks now, Trump's daily news conference performances had been erratic, combative, grandiose, and, yes, saturated with falsehoods. His political advisers had come to believe that they were hurting him in the polls.

"We're in a global pandemic," Conway told Trump during this time. "People are watching. It's become must-see TV. But not because you're sparring with the press. It's must-see TV because people want information. They have information underload when it comes to the pandemic."

Conway warned Trump his daily performances could swing the election. "We get you two hours a night and we get an hour a week of Joe Biden," she told the president. "That's good for Joe Biden."

A coordinated procession of Trump allies visited with the president around this time to implore him to change his tune or risk losing reelection. Among them was Republican senator Lindsey Graham, arguably Trump's closest friend in the Congress, who himself was facing a tough reelection challenge in South Carolina.

"Mr. President, it's not working," Graham told

Trump, referring to the daily briefings. "You're getting too combative. You're getting in pissing contests with thirty-five-year-old reporters. And that's not helping you. You were very reassuring at first and then you got to be in competition—'We're doing better,' 'Our numbers are better than Europe,' 'I'm doing a great job,' versus, 'The country is suffering.'"

Bleach day was the breaking point. Parscale called Kushner and said, "We're going to lose in a landslide. You've got Doctor Trump up there all day. We're still going down in the polls. We're losing and nothing's changing."

"I know," Kushner replied. "This is horrible."

This turned out to be Trump's final time answering questions at a coronavirus news conference for a while. Starting April 24, when the U.S. death toll reached fifty thousand, Trump attended the news conference and made brief remarks. "Our country is a great place and it's going to be greater than ever before," the president said. Earlier in the day, he signed the Paycheck Protection Program and Health Care Enhancement Act, which provided $320 billion for businesses harmed by the shutdowns to keep employees on payroll. These programs were created as part of the historic $2.2 trillion coronavirus relief package Trump signed in late March. When it came time for reporters to ask questions, however, Trump turned the show over to Pence and Hahn. Finally, he had heeded his advisers' advice to pare back his briefing room performances.

As one of Trump's advisers later explained, "He's a poor communicator to the public. He makes it about him, and it can't be. All he had to do to win the election was if he walked up to a glass wall at a hospital and said, 'I'm America's president. The whole force of the United States government is behind you. I'll do everything I can do to save lives.' A little teary-eyed, and he'd win the election. But he said, 'No, no, this isn't true.' 'There's a miracle drug.' 'We're all going to survive.' 'Let's open the country.'"

"Even if that's right," this adviser continued, "you don't fucking say that."

Six

Refusing to Mask Up

B ill Barr is a political junkie. He studied campaigns and voters' attitudes closely. As spring wore on, he came to believe that President Trump was squandering his hopes for re-election. It felt all too familiar. He had experienced this same premonition of an election slipping away when he had been attorney general in the final year of George H. W. Bush's presidency. Barr had no role in the coronavirus response, but he was fed up watching Trump's undisciplined press briefings and ad hominem attacks, and knew they were damaging his popularity among voters otherwise inclined to support him.

Barr had come out of a comfortable and easy semi-retirement to work for Trump, vowing to give him the solid advice he badly needed and to do his bit to keep the Republican Party in charge of the executive branch. Like many Trump appointees, Barr had taken a personal and professional beating for decisions he made in service to the president. Like a receiver, he didn't mind getting tackled after catching the ball for another first down. But Barr didn't appreciate having taken these hits only to watch Trump fritter away these advantages. As he confided privately to his advisers, Trump seemed programmed for overkill. "He's never had a good hand he didn't overplay," Barr told them.

In April 2020, Barr decided to make the most of his standing as the rare Cabinet member to talk straight to the boss—to tell Trump he was losing, which Lindsey Graham and a few other trusted allies also did that month. Barr scheduled a meeting with Trump in the Oval Office, just the two of them alone. He wanted a truly private conversation.

Barr opened the discussion with a plea for patience, hoping to short-circuit Trump's standard soliloquy at the start of every meeting. "Mr. President, I have something very important I want to talk to you about, and I'm hoping you actually listen to what I have to say," Barr said, according to the account he shared with confidants.

"Okay," Trump said, a bit taken aback.

"I feel you are going to lose the election," Barr said. "I feel you are actually losing touch with your own base."

Barr explained that in his travels around the country, he had talked to a lot of people in law enforcement and other solid Trump supporters who were uncomfortable with the president's focus on skewering his perceived enemies rather than on clear, consistent plans to steer the country safely through the pandemic and shore up the economy.

"I have yet to meet anybody who supports you who hasn't said to me, 'We love the president, but would you please tell him to turn it back a bit?'" Barr said. "You're going to lose because there's going to be enough people who otherwise would vote for you who are just tired of the acrimony, the pettiness, the punching down and picking a fight at every moment, and the apparent chaos, and they're just going to say, 'We're tired of this shit.'"

Barr warned Trump that he risked turning off some of his 2016 backers—enough to lose the election, especially with Joe Biden as the Democratic nominee.

"You're trying to jack up your base, but you can jack up your base without pissing off this important segment," Barr said.

Barr explained that Trump had won the 2016 election narrowly, in large part because he had been scared straight one month before the election by the release of the shocking **Access Hollywood** recording in which he bragged that his celebrity status gave him the power to sexually assault women. Republican officials, including then party chairman Reince Priebus, predicted he would lose badly, and Trump became convinced to stick to a disciplined script crafted by Kellyanne Conway and strategist Steve Bannon, among others.

"The only reason you won last time, Mr. President, is because of the 'grab them by the pussy' comment," Barr said, according to the account he shared with others. "It actually scared you enough to listen to Kellyanne. And for the last several weeks you behaved yourself and you won by a hair. This time it's different. You cannot wait until the end."

Barr saw two reasons that the 2020 campaign was different, but he told Trump only one of them.

"It's different because then people were willing to give you a chance," Barr said. "They sort of wanted a change. You were an outsider who would be an agent of change. Now most people know who you are and you're going to have to start much earlier to smooth over some of the rough edges."

Barr left unsaid the second reason. In 2016, Trump had been a neophyte and knew enough to listen to seasoned advisers like Conway. But now, Trump insisted he was the true political genius—after all, he had defied so many of the pros by winning—and in his hubris, he was disinclined to follow people's advice.

Barr told Trump that he was motivated to talk to him that day because he'd been spurred by an old memory of a similar heart-to-heart. He recounted how in 1992, Barr and Jack Kemp, then the secretary of Housing and Urban Development, went in to see Bush in the Oval.

"Our message to the president was, 'You're going to lose this election,' and unfortunately we turned out to be right," Barr told Trump. "We were right because we felt that he was falling prey to and was not addressing the image of him as someone who was out of touch with what was happening in the country, and that there was a lot that he could do to address that."

"I feel a sense of déjà vu, which is, I think you're going to lose this election," Barr continued. "I think that if you wanted to you could walk into a second term, COVID and all. You could go down in history as an amazing president and it's yours for the taking. But it's about you, and you're turning off enough people to lose this election."

Trump was oddly silent, not interrupting or trying to regain the floor as he usually did. The president had listened without emoting for a long time. He didn't ask any questions. He didn't push back. Now, as Barr's spiel came to an end, Trump nodded, and said he appreciated the advice. Barr left hopeful that the president had really taken his message to heart, but he couldn't be sure.

On the morning of April 25, Alex Azar got a call from two aides reaching out to him together with bad news.

"CNN is about to report that you're being fired," one of them said.

Azar's job had seemingly been on life support all year, yet a news report that his dismissal was imminent was next level. He called Mark Meadows.

"That's not even being discussed," Meadows told Azar.

Azar needed to clear his head, so he took a five-mile walk around his neighborhood and nearby trails. Shortly after the CNN story was published, Azar's phone rang. It was Jared Kushner, who had broken Sabbath on this Saturday to make the call.

"Alex, this story is just false," Kushner said. "Completely false. But this crap with Grogan and Seema. We gotta get this straight."

Kushner was suggesting the CNN story might be the handiwork of Joe Grogan and Seema Verma, two of Azar's fiercest critics in the administration, though he could not prove that either were sources for the report.

As disappointed as he was with Azar's dysfunctional early response to the pandemic, Kushner believed the secretary had begun turning things around. Operations had improved by ramping up the supply of ventilators and masks, and Kushner believed firing Azar would only add unnecessary drama. He suggested Azar join him the next day at the home of Adam Boehler to talk about mobilizing HHS in the right direction. Boehler was Kushner's former Harvard roommate who had gone on to work in private equity investing in health-care technology and services and became part of the so-called Slim Suit Crowd. Kushner had earlier arranged for FEMA to take charge of key aspects of the virus response, but he had since become frustrated by the bureaucracy there—not to mention unflattering leaks to the media about Kushner's work at FEMA—and decided HHS would make a better command center.

The morning of April 26 brought a downpour of rain in Washington. The Sunday talk shows were still abuzz with the news that Azar would be fired. Azar got a call from Meadows before 10:00.

"Alex, the stories are false," the White House chief of staff assured him. "There cannot be sources who are familiar with discussions that haven't occurred. This is all coming from one source, and that will be dealt with."

Meadows didn't say who he meant, but Azar assumed he was referring to Grogan.

That afternoon, Azar met Kushner at Boehler's mansion off Foxhall Road. In a sweet hostess gesture, Boehler's wife used her new air fryer to make Azar, who had celiac disease, a plate of air-fried vegetable crisps. They sketched out plans for how to score some wins for Team Trump by stockpiling protective equipment and helping speed up vaccines.

That afternoon, after Azar got home, Trump called him. The president was mild mannered, something Azar had not experienced in many weeks.

"Listen, I'm not getting rid of you," Trump said. "Why would I get rid of you with six months to go? Even if you were mediocre I wouldn't do that. And you're great, so why would I do that?"

Azar thanked him for the reassurance.

"Who's generating all these stories?" Trump asked. "Where's all this shit coming from?"

Azar had one word: "Grogan!"

"So what should we do?" Trump asked.

"You have to get rid of him," Azar said. "He is a cancer on your presidency."

Grogan was a cancer, to be sure, but far more on Azar's future in the administration than on Trump's presidency. Regardless, Grogan already had decided to leave the administration at the end of May. He had promised his wife he would not stay in the government a day longer than Memorial Day, as they were eager for him to make more money in the private sector and have more time to spend at home.

Azar told the president what Michael Caputo had encouraged him to keep in mind: attacks on Azar were equivalent to attacks on Trump.

"These leaks hurt you, not me," Azar said. "I have not leaked in my life to hurt you. I will defend myself. But I have never leaked to hurt you. We are a team and we are in this together. Together, we have to win in six months."

"Yeah, you're right," Trump said. "We are together. You need me to look good for you to look good."

Then the president gave the instructions that would end their months of friction.

"I'm going to post a tweet disputing this story," Trump said. "You tweet this is 'fake news' and I want you to put out a whole list of all the great things we did together on COVID."

Azar agreed. Trump went first at 5:53 p.m.: "Reports that H.H.S. Secretary @AlexAzar is going

REFUSING TO MASK UP

to be 'fired' by me are Fake News. The Lamestream Media knows this, but they are desperate to create the perception of chaos & havoc in the minds of the public. They never even called to ask. Alex is doing an excellent job!"

About twenty minutes later, Azar tweeted: "Reports of President Trump looking to replace me are #FakeNews. The media continues to smear @POTUS and his Administration's fight against #COVID19 and grossly overlook the historic whole-of-government response that we've been delivering under the President's leadership. While the #FakeNews media and their leaker allies collude to destroy this President, his Administration is following his leadership 24/7 to protect Americans and end a global health crisis."

Several agency chiefs who reported to Azar, including Robert Redfield, Stephen Hahn, and Verma, watched this unfolding Twitter volley with confusion and, frankly, disappointment. They had been hearing for weeks from colleagues in the White House that Azar would soon be canned, and they were rooting for it privately. They considered him the worst boss. Azar and his senior aides seemed entirely focused on him claiming credit for successes and pinning blame on agency chiefs below him whenever something went south. They considered Azar untrustworthy and completely overwhelmed by the pandemic. Vice President Pence recognized these problems, too, but held his tongue and did not intervene. He had recommended

Trump hire Azar as health secretary. Both men knew each other from when Pence was governor and Azar was CEO of Indianapolis-based Eli Lilly. Therefore, Azar's downfall would have reflected poorly on Pence's judgment.

What Azar didn't know was just how close he had come to losing his job. Trump had not been honest with him when he said he thought he was doing "great." The president repeatedly had planted the idea of firing the health secretary, including directly with some of Azar's subordinates. And he went to great lengths to undermine Azar publicly. Trump tightly choreographed the daily coronavirus press briefings in March and April. Sometimes he would make sure all the other administration officials had messages to deliver but left nothing for Azar to say. He also instructed aides to have Azar stand at the edge of the platform, putting him out of camera view. Well aware of Azar's rivalry with Verma, Trump sometimes told her, "Seema, we want you right over my shoulder," as if he were trying to antagonize Azar or to make him paranoid.

Yet in a sign of just how much the president encouraged a **Fight Club** mentality in his administration, Trump separately told Azar to try to tolerate Verma and that he would get rid of her after he won the election.

After saving Azar's job, Trump brought up the topic in a call with Verma.

"Well, Alex is really close to the edge," Trump

told Verma. "I saved him. People think he needs to go."

The president acknowledged Azar's troubles in the job and told Verma that he decided to keep him for a simple political reason: "It's not a good idea to change the secretary before the election," he said.

But as a senior task-force member later explained, keeping Azar may have been a political mistake, as that left nobody to shoulder the blame for the failed coronavirus response. "Had they taken Azar out, they could've said it was all his fault," this official said. "The fall guy became the president and everybody else in the White House."

After the CDC issued guidance on April 13 urging people to wear masks when in public settings where social distancing is difficult, a deep divide emerged at the White House. Redfield and his fellow public health leaders wanted administration officials, who often stood close together at news conferences, to lead by example. Redfield knew masks were a critical defense against the virus, and that Americans would take cues from leaders in Washington. He wanted administration officials to present a united "face"—their noses and mouths covered by blue-and-white medical masks. Redfield's mantra was "Wear a mask. Wear a mask. Everyone wear a mask."

Trump, however, would not wear one, and that meant people who wanted to stay in the president's good graces resisted wearing masks as well, including members of the Secret Service. Task-force members learned from a top Secret Service official that some agents and officers felt masks did not look manly. As the president had put it to reporters on April 3, "Somehow sitting in the Oval Office behind that beautiful Resolute Desk, the great Resolute Desk, I think wearing a face mask as I greet presidents, prime ministers, dictators, kings, queens—I don't know, somehow I don't see it for myself. I just, I just don't."

In the intervening weeks, Redfield took it as a personal mission to convince the president and vice president to wear masks. Redfield prodded them gently at every opportunity—especially Pence, whom he considered a softer target. "It's so important for you to set the example," Redfield told Pence after a task-force meeting. Pence said he was confident he didn't have the virus—he was being tested regularly—so a mask seemed redundant. The truth was he wanted to follow Trump's lead.

On April 28, the White House resistance to masking came to a head when Pence flew to Rochester, Minnesota, to tour the Mayo Clinic. He visited with patients and staff and toured facilities at the renowned medical center that were supporting COVID-19 research, but did not wear a mask, a violation of the Mayo Clinic's policy. Video of Pence's maskless interactions, including greeting a patient in bed, went viral. Here was the chair of the coronavirus task force flouting a hospital's policy, not to mention the CDC's recommendations. Everyone else in the video clips wore masks.

Pence at first defended his decision not to wear a mask, saying he was tested for the virus regularly. "Since I don't have the coronavirus, I thought it'd be a good opportunity for me to be here, to be able to speak to these researchers, these incredible health-care personnel, and look them in the eye and say, 'Thank you,'" Pence said.

Two days later second lady Karen Pence would claim on Fox News that her husband hadn't known about the mask requirement until after the clinic visit. But that wasn't the full truth. Pence's staff did know the policy. The Mayo Clinic tweeted on its official social media account, "Mayo Clinic had informed @VP of the masking policy prior to his arrival today." The tweet was soon deleted, after Marc Short yelled at clinic officials for attempting to embarrass the vice president and for drawing media attention away from the convalescent plasma research Pence had flown to Rochester to promote.

There was yet more evidence of the Pence team's prior knowledge of the masking policy. Before the trip, Pence's office shared guidance with reporters traveling with the vice president about the clinic's mask mandate and explicitly instructed journalists to wear masks on the trip.

Two days after the Mayo visit, Redfield got a happy surprise. Pence finally wore a face mask. In a rare public about-face for the Trump administration, the vice president on April 30 visited a General Motors plant in Indiana that had been converted into a ventilator factory—and was photographed wearing a mask as he toured the facility. He would almost always wear it in close public spaces from then on.

Still, the mask story would continue to dog Pence until May 3, when he acknowledged his lapse in judgment at the Mayo Clinic. "I didn't think it was necessary, but I should have worn a mask at the Mayo Clinic," he said at a Fox News town hall event.

Meanwhile, Redfield's efforts to convince Trump to wear a mask in public were less successful. He leaned on Dr. Sean Conley, the president's physician in the White House Medical Unit, for help.

"Sean, you gotta get the president to wear a mask," Redfield told him one day around this time. "You gotta get him to wear it for his own protection."

Another time, Redfield pressed again, worried about several instances of people in and around the White House testing positive.

"Sean, you gotta get the president to understand he needs to do this," Redfield told Conley. "You gotta tell him. You're his doctor. You gotta tell him."

Conley insisted he was trying and he would keep at it. But he turned the dilemma back on Redfield: Didn't he have patients who didn't take his advice?

On May 1, a new White House press secretary—Trump's fourth in three years—stepped to the lectern in the James S. Brady Press Briefing Room: Kayleigh McEnany.

It had been 417 days since a White House press secretary had held a briefing and much had changed. For starters, the number of journalists allowed to attend had shrunk considerably in observance of social distancing rules. McEnany's predecessor, Stephanie Grisham, never deigned to hold a briefing in her eight months in the job, making her the first White House press secretary in history to abdicate that important responsibility.

McEnany, thirty-two, was a Harvard Law graduate and had earned Trump's approval in her fiery cable television appearances. Recruited by Meadows and Kushner, she was attractive, petite, and blond—just the kind of spokeswoman they knew the casting-director president would want as his on-camera defender in the run-up to the election. In her first briefing, McEnany revealed a special talent for bending the facts to Trump's benefit. Reporters were scarred by three straight years of lies and caustic attacks—from the president, his succession of spokespeople, and countless other administration officials—and wondered whether McEnany would be just the latest in Trump's rotating cast of fabulists and tricksters.

"Will you pledge never to lie to us from that podium?" Associated Press reporter Jill Colvin asked.

"I will never lie to you. You have my word on that," McEnany said, not a frown to be seen.

It was a striking claim, not only because she worked

for Trump, but also because truth had not been a priority for her in the recent past. As a spokesperson for the Trump campaign, McEnany had insisted in late February 2020 that the coronavirus simply wouldn't reach the United States because Trump would keep it at bay.

"He will always protect American citizens," McEnany had told Fox Business Channel host Trish Regan. "We will not see diseases like the coronavirus come here. We will not see terrorism come here. And isn't it refreshing, when contrasting it with the awful presidency of President Obama?"

McEnany made this ridiculous comment even though the White House already had confirmed dozens of U.S. cases.

In the May 1 briefing, despite promising never to lie to reporters, McEnany proceeded to repeatedly stretch the truth. She misrepresented what FBI records showed about agents' strategy before their famous interview with then national security adviser Michael Flynn. She claimed Robert Mueller's Russia investigation cost taxpayers $40 million; it had cost $32 million. She claimed the Mueller probe resulted in "the complete and total exoneration of President Trump"; in fact, the Mueller team concluded there was substantial evidence that the president obstructed a criminal probe and that they could not exonerate him. The actual words of the report's conclusion said: "while this report does not conclude that the president committed a crime, it also does not exonerate him."

McEnany ended the briefing by reminding everyone watching of Trump's top priority: high ratings. "Everyone should watch the Fox News town hall with the president from seven to nine p.m.," she said. "It'll be can't-miss television, much like the highly rated President Trump coronavirus task-force briefings have been."

McEnany's arrival, along with the hiring of Alyssa Farah as communications director, cemented Meadows's control over the administration's coronavirus messaging, which had been the domain of Pence's office. Farah had a long-standing relationship with Meadows from the five years she spent on Capitol Hill, first as Meadows's communications director and later as the spokeswoman for the conservative House Freedom Caucus. She then joined the Trump administration, first as Pence's press secretary and then as Defense Secretary Mark Esper's press secretary.

Meadows tried to exert complete control over all virus communications, including dramatically scaling back the media appearances by Fauci and other health officials, who too often corrected Trump's misinformation about the virus. Meadows directed Farah to block television appearances and other media interview requests for the doctors. Francis Collins, Fauci's boss, repeatedly had to intervene personally with Meadows to get approval for bookings. The doctors were trying to communicate the best health guidance to the public during a pandemic and needed to do as much media as possible.

Meadows sometimes agreed, but only reluctantly, and with conditions.

"You've got to tell Tony to talk about why this is actually going better now," Meadows told Collins on one such occasion. "You've got to talk to Tony: 'Don't be such a fearmonger.'"

In other words, Fauci could go on TV, but only if he did "happy talk."

Collins replied, "I don't think that's what Tony's going to do. I will pass on your message."

Collins and Fauci spoke every evening to compare notes from the day not only about scientific advances, but political struggles, too. With tensions so fraught on the task force, the two longtime colleagues felt it was essential there never be daylight between them. When Collins shared Meadows's request that Fauci put a more positive spin on the trend lines, they both laughed about it. In the interview, Fauci told the truth.

Michael Caputo also tried to intervene to get the White House to approve bookings for Fauci, Redfield, Jerome Adams, and other health officials. He suggested they appear on shows that Farah and her White House colleagues considered too liberal, such as **The Rachel Maddow Show** on MSNBC, or on random podcasts that they thought would be a waste of time. Farah preferred the doctors appear on more apolitical shows with high ratings, such as ABC's **Good Morning America,** where they might be less likely to be asked questions that made the president look bad. Caputo's emails and calls to Farah often got no replies. At one point in the spring, he ran out of patience. He decided to book the doctors on several television shows, with or without Farah's approval.

Caputo wrote an email to Meadows, Farah, and McEnany that said something along the lines of, "Look, I can't get you on the phone. I can't get you to reply. I'd love to have you involved, but if you can't, that's fine. I'm not booking Sunday shows. I'll leave that to you. But I'm booking these six doctors on as many shows as will take them. As long as the interviews don't interfere with their work at the agencies, that's what they're doing. We need more public health information, not less. These are all smart people and they'll make the president look good."

Caputo presented himself in the email as the doctors' champion and an advocate for sharing accurate health information with the public. But subsequent reporting by Dan Diamond, then of **Politico,** would reveal that Caputo had played a key role behind the scenes in trying to manipulate federal data, reports, and guidelines to align with Trump's claims that fears about the virus were overstated. Caputo and other Trump appointees, including Paul Alexander, a health adviser who worked closely with Caputo, demanded to review and seek changes to the CDC's Morbidity and Mortality Weekly Report, a weekly digest authored by career scientists that analyzed for medical professionals and the public how COVID-19 was spreading and which kinds of people were at risk, according to the **Politico** report.

Farah already had doubts about Caputo's competence and suspicions about his intentions, and sometimes had booked Fauci and other doctors without looping him in. She was furious about the email, which she thought Caputo intentionally sent knowing it would become part of the public record and might burnish his image in history books.

Meadows called Caputo. "Come to the office immediately," the chief of staff said. "I'm of the mind to fire you right now."

"Have you passed that by the president?" Caputo asked.

"I can fire anybody I want," Meadows said.

"I believe you can, sir, but I think this is something we should talk to the president about," replied Caputo, who was banking on Trump having his back, considering their long history together.

Before Caputo showed up, Farah had acknowledged to Meadows, "I could be nicer to him. I shouldn't be as harsh. But I'm warning you guys, this guy is a liability." When Caputo arrived in the chief of staff's office, he assumed he was walking into his execution. Meadows, Farah, and McEnany were there. At one point, Azar joined them. Meadows dressed Caputo down about how all media appearances had to be approved by the White House communications office, which Farah ran. He said the doctors were not the right messengers on television and argued that Azar would be a better political spokesperson for the administration's virus response.

Then Meadows turned genteel.

"Let's hit restart on this relationship," he said. "Kayleigh, can we do that?"

"I think we can," McEnany said.

"Alyssa, can we do that?" Meadows asked.

"Sure," Farah responded.

"Michael, can we do that?" Meadows asked.

"Hope dies last," Caputo replied.

Meadows, puzzled, asked, "Michael, what do you mean?"

"I hope so," Caputo said. "Palms up."

On their way out of the meeting, Farah addressed Caputo: "I want to say one thing to you: You wrote that email to leak."

"I don't leak against the president of the United States," Caputo said.

"Yes you did," Farah shot back.

"Alyssa," he said, "I'm not you."

As task-force doctors used whatever means they could to preach to the public to wear masks and avoid large gatherings, their place of work suddenly turned into a coronavirus petri dish. On May 6, a military service member who served as one of Trump's personal White House valets started having symptoms of COVID-19, and the next day tested positive.

For the germaphobe president, who once had infamously admonished Mick Mulvaney for coughing in his presence, the virus's breach not only of the

heavily fortified White House complex, but also of
Trump's personal bubble, was alarming. It should not
have been surprising, however. Other than requiring
regular testing of senior aides and others who came
into proximity with Trump, the White House staff
eschewed its own health recommendations. In fact,
Trump continued to meet in person with groups
of strangers, including a May 8 gathering of World
War II veterans.

Some of Trump's advisers were afraid of catching
the coronavirus at work. Deborah Birx was militant
about wearing a mask in the White House. She remembered how masks had protected her from any
number of diseases when she traveled the world's
hot zones researching respiratory illnesses. She knew
many of the young people on Trump's staff believed
they were invincible and gathered socially after hours.
She also knew Secret Service agents used small com-
munal break rooms on the complex, where the risk
of exposure was high. She was fearful of bringing the
virus home.

Similarly militant about masking was Matt
Pottinger, whom other West Wing aides teased for
covering up part of his face. The deputy national security adviser was so concerned about the likelihood of
the maskless White House becoming an incubator
of infection—and of staff dropping like flies—that in
mid-March he made an urgent outreach to the Taiwan
government. He procured hundreds of thousands
of Taiwanese masks, primarily for U.S. health-care

workers, and thirty-six hundred masks for the use of White House personnel.

Most others had a carefree attitude about masks, however, including Katie Miller, who in her role running Pence's communications was a fixture at task-force meetings and worked closely with its members. Though she had an office in the Eisenhower Executive Office Building, Miller often worked out of Short's cramped cubby-sized office in the West Wing, sitting sometimes on the floor, as did other vice-presidential aides. The two were overheard gossiping about and making fun of task-force doctors.

On May 7, Pence delivered boxes of personal protective equipment from FEMA to a nursing home in Alexandria, Virginia. Miller staffed him for the photo op. As she talked near a gaggle of reporters without wearing a mask, Miller coughed. She had tested negative earlier that day, but when she got tested again on May 8, her results came back positive. She had COVID.

The news of Miller's positive test delayed Pence's departure that morning for Iowa. Air Force Two sat on the tarmac at Joint Base Andrews for nearly an hour as staffers who had been exposed to Miller disembarked. Pence and Short stayed on, despite having been in close proximity to Miller, and they continued on to Des Moines.

Back at the White House, Olivia Troye was distraught. She had been working closely with Short, Miller, and others on the staff. In the privacy of her office, Troye broke down in tears. She was afraid she had COVID and would get her immunocompromised husband sick. She took vitamin C and washed her hands obsessively that day, so much so that they felt raw by the time she got home.

Troye wasn't alone in her fears. Other vice-presidential staffers came into her office, closed the door behind them, and privately asked for advice. They were scared about traveling with Pence in the future. "When you're in these mass gatherings, never take off your mask," Troye told them. "Don't listen to Marc. Wash your hands all the time. Don't shake any hands. Carry sanitizer with you. When you're at rallies, stay behind the stage and in your own pod, where you know the people you're traveling with have been tested. Don't go to the front and take photos or interact with strangers. Protect yourself."

Fear of the virus outbreak permeated the White House staff that weekend. Kevin Hassett gave voice to the concerns on May 10, when he said on CBS's **Face the Nation,** "It is scary to go to work." He added, "I think I'd be a lot safer if I was sitting at home than I would be going to the West Wing."

Even though the virus dominated the administration's focus, Trump continued through the spring with his postimpeachment tour of vengeance. He wanted to sack anyone who did not move loyally in lockstep with him. He had long been eyeing Chris Wray, the FBI director whom Trump had tapped in

2017 after he fired James Comey. Their honeymoon had been short-lived.

Soon after being confirmed as attorney general in early 2019, Barr noticed Trump would hammer away constantly at how much he hated the FBI and wanted to make a change in the leadership there. Trump said he wished Wray would do more to punish the FBI agents who "came after me." Trump also had an allergic reaction to Wray's just-the-facts style and even-handed manner in public interviews. Trump preferred the pugilistic and unapologetic mode Barr displayed.

As Trump said to Barr in one such meeting, "He's just so weak. He contradicts you! You should be mad! When they ask him, do you agree on this, he always weasels out of it. You should be mad!"

Barr explained that the FBI director played a different role than the attorney general, which is a more political position. Though both are nominated by the president, the FBI director typically served a ten-year term and was expected to work with both parties and avoid political sparring. Barr was a big fan of Wray and succeeded in tempering the president's impulse to fire him. Barr had a standard line. "Mr. President, he and I are working well together," Barr would say. "I understand the bureau and the kind of relationship that's important to build, and I think we're doing that with Chris Wray."

With gallows humor, Barr then would joke with aides that he had become the FBI director's "human heat shield."

Trump also wanted to dump the FBI's deputy director, Dave Bowdich, who was the bureau's most senior agent. Trump had called Bowdich "a Comey guy," a deduction he and Meadows made after reviewing Bowdich's past job titles in his twenty-five-year FBI career. For instance, when Comey was FBI director, Bowdich had served as associate director overseeing budget and administration. Trump and Meadows seemed to think, Aha! Barr's eyebrows rose at this Wikipedia method of ferreting out friend or foe. The attorney general told the president that he thought highly of Bowdich and said the fact that he served in a senior career job during Comey's directorship didn't make him a Comey acolyte.

Most alarming to Barr, though, were Trump's suggestions for replacements for Wray and Bowdich. Barr had heard that Trump was considering making Kash Patel deputy director. In Trump's view, Patel was gold, having toiled to discredit the Russia investigation as an aide to Congressman Devin Nunes, the top Republican on the House Intelligence Committee. In 2018, Patel had authored a memo for Nunes that claimed the Obama administration relied on anti-Trump sources to justify surveilling a Trump campaign aide. The memo made some accurate and some false claims while cherry-picking facts, and reached its conclusion based on information secretly provided by the White House. He was an ideological firebrand and highly controversial, even in conservative circles. In private conversations with colleagues,

Barr called Patel a "walking disaster." He thought
Rudy Giuliani and Patel bore a good deal of responsibility for the president's impeachment, as both were
accused of feeding him misinformation alleging base-
lessly that Ukraine had interfered in the 2016 election on behalf of Democrats, and of encouraging him
to strong-arm the country to boost his reelection.

"Mr. President, if you try to make Kash Patel the
deputy director I will resign immediately. No ifs,
ands, or buts," Barr told him the first time Trump
broached the idea. "No fucking way."

Barr said the FBI's rank and file would never accept a nonagent in any senior position other than
the directorship, according to the account Barr
gave confidants.

"Mr. President, the FBI is like the Marine Corps,"
Barr added. "They're all agents, they've all gone
through agent school. You are nobody at the FBI unless you're an agent. The only person who is not an
agent is the director. The deputy director has been
an agent and has always been an agent and always
will be an agent, otherwise you cannot run that place.
And to take a clown like him, who has no background,
and make him deputy is just beyond the pale."

In the first week of May, Trump's interest in terminating Wray moved from festering pique to imminent
action. In court papers filed the previous week, Flynn
argued to the judge presiding over his case that the
FBI had engaged in misconduct by bringing charges
against him. Though he twice had pleaded guilty to

the charges, Flynn and his lawyer, Sidney Powell, said newly unsealed documents showed the FBI had planned to close their investigation of him but kept it open when they learned about his call with a Russian ambassador. It was unclear why it would be misconduct for the FBI to keep a case open upon learning new information. A group of Trump supporters, including attorney Joseph diGenova, conservative commentator Dan Bongino, and former White House official Sebastian Gorka, publicly called for Trump to fire Wray over how the FBI handled its Flynn investigation. "Why does Christopher Wray still have a job?" Bongino said on May 4 on Gorka's radio show. "I asked the president directly about it. . . . I cannot for the life of me understand how the current director of the FBI is still in his position."

On May 7, at Barr's direction, the Justice Department did a 180-degree turn and tossed out the prosecution of Flynn on the recommendation of a special prosecutor Barr had appointed to reinvestigate the case. To the president's delight, Barr concluded that the lies that Flynn told to FBI agents and denials about his conversations with a Russian ambassador were not a crime because there was no official investigation under way at the time. This was another brutal affront to the line prosecutors working the Flynn case, and fresh evidence that Barr intervened to show mercy when the defendants were Trump allies. The day of the new filing, Trump applauded Flynn as "an even greater warrior" and called the senior FBI and Justice Department officials who pursued him "human scum."

That morning, Bill Evanina, a former FBI agent who headed up the National Counterintelligence and Security Center, got an urgent call from an assistant to Robert O'Brien. "Can you get down here as quick as possible?" she asked.

Evanina said he would. He arrived at O'Brien's office to find the national security adviser and Ric Grenell, the acting director of national intelligence, inside. Grenell told Evanina that Wray's firing was imminent and they were looking for possible replacements. They informed him that when Comey was fired, Evanina had been one of the top names recommended to replace Comey as an acting director.

"Would you be interested?" O'Brien asked.

Evanina said it didn't make sense because Wray was doing a great job. O'Brien and Grenell explained that it didn't matter. Wray was on his way out.

"Of course I would take it," Evanina said. "Who wouldn't?"

With that, Evanina was shuttled over to Kushner's office for what ended up being a fairly substantive, albeit brief, fifteen-minute meeting. Grenell had pushed Kushner to meet Evanina, boasting about his law enforcement bona fides, though Kushner was not of the mind to fire Wray. Sitting across from Evanina, Kushner had one last question before they parted: "Who put you in the job you're in now?"

Evanina answered: "President Obama."

Kushner stared at him for a minute. Evanina explained that technically former director of national intelligence James Clapper had hired him, but they worked under Obama. They said their goodbyes.

Evanina then was taken to the Oval to chat with Trump, where the president asked him mostly about his family, their roots in Pennsylvania coal country, and his work as an FBI agent in New Jersey. He asked whether Evanina had ever appeared before his sister, Maryanne Trump Berry, a now-retired federal judge. Then he asked about Evanina's sister, who was an FBI agent. Trump wondered: Did she like Comey? At one point, Evanina mentioned the patron saint of New Jersey, Bruce Springsteen, in passing. Trump was displeased to hear this name. But the two parted genially, with the president telling Evanina: "Keep up the good work! And keep Navarro in line."

Evanina left the White House feeling that this wasn't a normal job interview. He was completely unaware that he'd been paired with Patel as a possible replacement team. But he did discover the president was pretty normal and personable in a one-on-one conversation.

"He's not the guy you see on TV," Evanina later told a confidant. "He's not the guy the IC is all worked up about."

Evanina concluded nothing would ever come of it. He never heard another word about being director.

The same day, Barr went to the White House for what he expected would be a standard meeting with

Meadows. But Trump had been on the warpath against Wray all week. Into this cauldron walked Barr and his chief of staff, Will Levi. An assistant told them their meeting that day would be in the Roosevelt Room. Barr remarked that was strange but waited with Levi in the empty room. Within a few moments, Johnny McEntee strode in with Evanina. Barr got an uncomfortable look on his face and glanced at Levi, then excused himself and walked out of the room. Evanina and Levi continued to make small talk.

There was a reason Barr fled the room. McEntee was Trump's loyalist and enemy hunter, the director of the White House Office of Presidential Personnel with a personal mandate from the president to get rid of the "Never Trumpers" suspected of working at various agencies and to install "more of my guys," as Trump put it. If he was squiring a new person through the White House, it suggested someone else was about to get fired.

McEntee had followed a highly unusual path to becoming a senior White House adviser. A former University of Connecticut quarterback, McEntee was a low-level Fox News employee in 2015 when he had emailed the Trump campaign several times hoping to get a job interview, but got no response. He finally broke through when he suggested that the campaign needed someone to help answer emails. McEntee was hired, and his prep-school-boy good looks and Trump fandom fueled a steady rise, becoming the candidate's personal assistant, known as a "body man." McEntee continued that role in the White House, catering to the president's needs and carrying his overcoat and boxes of papers. He was trusted by Trump and his family, including Kushner and Ivanka Trump, because of his loyalty and discretion.

"Loyalty is everything to the president," a former senior White House official said. "Johnny certainly seemed like a loyal guy. Always there, carrying bags and jackets. I saw a 'yes' man. No original thought."

McEntee lost his job in March 2018. He had been carrying the president's top-secret briefing materials but did not yet have a permanent security clearance. Investigators warned then White House chief of staff John Kelly that McEntee appeared to have won hundreds of thousands of dollars in online gambling over a few years, but they saw no evidence he had reported the winnings on his tax returns. Kelly confronted McEntee and told him he was sorry, but he couldn't stay in the White House. Disappointed, McEntee headed to a job at the Trump campaign, where he waited out Kelly's tenure and eventually got rehired by Trump in February 2020.

After McEntee had greeted Barr and Levi, Barr marched over to Meadows's office and asked what the hell was going on. He asked, was Trump appointing Evanina as FBI director and putting in Patel as deputy director? Meadows looked a little surprised.

Meadows and Barr then walked upstairs to Pat Cipollone's office. Cipollone and Meadows explained that the president had called in O'Brien and Grenell to talk about replacing Wray and his deputy, Bowdich. There had been some "spitballing" with the president about candidates. The president seemed to like the idea of Evanina and Patel.

"Not over my dead body," Barr said, according to the account he gave other senior officials.

The attorney general told Meadows he didn't have anything personally against Evanina, though he very much preferred Wray. He was deeply concerned, however, about Patel. Barr warned that if they removed Wray, they would have to have someone so eminently qualified and with such stature that there could be no credible objection. And they could not install a nonagent as deputy director.

Barr threw himself on top of the grenade, and he won the day. Trump did not remove either Wray or Bowdich as planned.

The next morning, Trump did an hour-long call-in interview on **Fox & Friends.** He praised Barr as "a man of unbelievable credibility and courage" for his handling of the Flynn matter, and said "he's going to go down in the history of our country."

Wray's fate was less clear in Trump's rambling remarks. First, he suggested he wasn't going to fire Wray. "I learned a lot from Richard Nixon," Trump said. "Don't fire people."

Then Trump intimated there were surprise developments on the horizon. He called Wray's performance in reviewing the FBI's work on the Russia investigation "disappointing." He added,

"Let's see what happens with him. Look, the jury's still out."

There was another tension point in Barr's relationship with Trump around this time: the lack of any public sign of progress in John Durham's probe of the origins of the FBI investigation. In May, Trump started making noise again about Durham's work and claimed the prosecutor was likely to indict Obama and Biden. On May 10, which was Mother's Day, Trump showered social media with an extraordinary 126 tweets or retweets—including one labeling these alleged crimes against his presidency "OBAMAGATE."

Barr tried to shut off that talk by telling reporters that neither Obama nor Biden was under investigation. But Trump was peeved at the attorney general for undercutting him and brought it up to Barr sometime later.

"You didn't indict Comey . . . none of these things have panned out," Trump said, raising old grievances about enemies who got away. "And Obama and Biden—you said they weren't being investigated."

"They're not," Barr said. He told Trump that claiming otherwise was counterproductive. "The more you talk about it, the more you're pulling the rug out from under John Durham."

He continued: "This is just going to discredit Durham's work. There's a lot of people working, doing serious work on this stuff and you're just going to [get them] discredited by suggesting that this is going after Obama. We're not going after Obama."

As the weeks went on, Trump would keep pecking curiously, asking Barr about Durham's investigation. The president and his Republican allies in Congress were hoping Durham would publish a bombshell report revealing seamy details of investigative abuses by the Obama administration and the intelligence community—and, if they were lucky, nail a few scalps to the wall.

The president would grow antsy into the summer, usually peppering Meadows with questions, and then Meadows would call Barr for some kind of timeline on new developments. Barr would tell Meadows he was hopeful they would have some news that summer. Privately, the attorney general had reason to believe another government official was going to be prosecuted, but it wasn't one of the big fishes Trump was looking to catch.

Trump had told Barr that not indicting Comey, Clapper, former CIA director John Brennan, and other officials hurt his image. "It makes us look weak," the president would say.

Barr always tried to manage expectations. "Mr. President, whether or not John Durham indicts somebody is not going to affect this election outcome," he had told the president. What would affect the election, Barr told Trump, was the president staying on message and consistently highlighting his accomplishments.

O n May 13, Karl Rove, the former strategist for President George W. Bush's campaigns, visited the White House. A few days earlier, Rove had received two successive calls from Trump advisers sounding him out on the president's latest theory: Biden was such a weak candidate that President Obama and his allies would soon orchestrate a coup, replacing him as the presumptive Democratic presidential nominee with New York governor Andrew Cuomo, who was riding a surge in popularity thanks to his nationally televised coronavirus briefings. That wasn't all. Trump thought former first lady Michelle Obama would join the ticket as Cuomo's vice-presidential running mate. Rove thought to himself, **This is completely insane.** But in Trump's mind, it was plausible if not bound to happen.

Trump asked Rove to fly to Washington to prepare a strategy to run against a possible Cuomo-Obama ticket. When Rove walked into the Oval Office, there were at least a dozen people in the room, including Meadows and Brad Parscale.

"Karl, Karl, thank you for coming," Trump said, welcoming his guest. Turning to his advisers, the president joked, "Karl's been so good to me the last year. Not so much before, but he's been good now."

Trump rolled out his theory. He sized up Cuomo: "He'd be tough. So tough. I'd beat him, but he'd be tough."

Then he took stock of Obama: "You know, Michelle, she could be his running mate. I'd beat them, but that'd be tough."

Rove, trying to be polite, said, "This is not going to happen. This is not real." He added, "Michelle Obama wants nothing to do with politics. She was unhappy with politics, she suffered through politics so her husband could be president, but she is not Hillary Clinton. She does not want to occupy the office. She wants to enjoy the life that she's now having."

Trump then told the group he thought they should hold off on attacking Biden for the time being because he did not want to weaken the presumptive Democratic nominee and give the Obama forces in the party reason to boot him from the ticket.

Rove was gobsmacked by what he was hearing.

"Mr. President, that's wrong," Rove said. "If you began now, today, to say we want to launch a full-throated attack on Biden, it would take you 'til June to get it together. So you start June first. You have five months. You have four months until people [start to] vote. In 2012, Barack Obama gave a speech on April first attacking Mitt Romney by name, depicting him as a heartless plutocrat. That was April. Six weeks ago. We attacked John Kerry in February of 2004. We then had a grand total of eight months and Obama had a grand total of seven months—and you'd have only five months to make the case.

"You're running out of time," Rove added. "You've

chewed up a lot of the clock that other [incumbents] have used to their advantage."

The meeting lasted about two hours. By the end, Trump was persuaded that a Cuomo-Obama ticket was probably not going to materialize.

May 15 was a perfect Washington spring day: 84 degrees, relatively low humidity, a slight breeze, and only passing clouds. The ideal setting for a major announcement in the Rose Garden: Operation Warp Speed.

Operation Warp Speed was the Trump administration's version of the Manhattan Project, the U.S. government–led effort to develop an atomic bomb during World War II. The public-private partnership was designed to help seed, fund, and fuel the rapid development of vaccines, as well as therapeutic treatments and other diagnostic tools, and then distribute them quickly to the public. The priority was creating a vaccine by the end of the year—an exceptionally ambitious deadline that the president hounded his advisers to strive to keep. Of course, Trump wanted to beat that deadline and announce a vaccine—a "cure," as he put it—before voters went to the polls in November.

The Warp Speed name was derived from **Star Trek**'s imaginary USS **Enterprise**'s ability to travel at a speed faster than light. The Trump administration needed an emergency response, and though the government did not make vaccines, they could speed up the approval for such drugs. Most importantly, the government could provide the pharmaceutical industry a multibillion-dollar carrot, promising to buy tens of millions of doses of the future vaccines, which encouraged companies to ramp up work by guaranteeing future sales. The government also could use the Defense Production Act to get companies to produce critical ingredients and transform their manufacturing facilities to help ramp up vaccine production.

To Redfield, Operation Warp Speed had a great chance of success because it had three critical features of the Manhattan Project. First, the president set a clear goal of developing a vaccine by the end of the year and never let up. Second, there were powerful players in critical roles. The Oppenheimer, a scientist beyond compare, was Moncef Slaoui, a researcher who had developed five vaccines as chairman of research and development at GlaxoSmithKline. And the General Groves, a logistics commander who could push manufacturing capability, was General Gustave Perna, a four-star who led the army's Materiel Command. Finally, the operation could not rely on one promising vaccine, but had to invest in multiple vaccine candidates, which would increase the chances for success.

It took some convincing from a number of advisers for Trump to agree to make massive early investments in developing vaccines. There was no guarantee of success. Kushner told him, "Look, I really believe this is smart. I know there's a chance we'll lose twelve billion dollars, but if it hits, this will be the best investment you'll make. . . . And if it doesn't work, I think we'll be glad we tried."

"Let's do it," Trump said. "Give it a shot."

Trump rolled out the new program with great fanfare. He had task-force members Pence, Slaoui, and Perna join him at the announcement event. As the principals gathered in the Oval Office before heading out to the Rose Garden, they all were wearing masks, other than Trump.

"We're not going to go out there and have our masks on," Trump told them. "I don't think the masks are a good look."

Fauci chimed in. "With all due respect, Mr. President, I am not going out there without a mask. I've been telling people to wear masks, and when I go out there, I'm going to keep my mask on."

"Okay," Trump said. Then he turned to the handful of military officers in uniform and said, "You guys keep your masks off. I don't think it's going to be good for us being out there with masks on."

The officers followed their commander in chief's orders. Fauci, Birx, and Collins were among the only officials wearing masks.

As Operation Warp Speed got under way, an unlikely hero emerged. Several of the doctors advising the president believed Kushner was a force for good when it came to vaccines and tried to steer the president in a helpful direction. When he entered a meeting, Kushner listened for a while as the group debated why something wouldn't work, and then asked the critical question: What do we need to make it work?

"I just found him as a problem solver," an Operation Warp Speed adviser recalled. "When Jared Kushner was involved, he would grab hold of the discussion in a decisive way, so we started to more systematically get the plan of action to solve the problem."

Five days after the rollout, Azar thought he had succeeded in delivering a golden egg to his impatient king. After reading a late February report that found a new experimental Oxford-AstraZeneca vaccine was highly effective in blocking transmission of the virus, Azar and his department began reaching out to the British company's leadership. On May 20, the U.S. government brokered a $1.2 billion deal to purchase three hundred million of the first one billion doses the company planned to produce.

From his kitchen at home, Azar called Kushner. "Jared, we got it," he said. "We got AstraZeneca! Three hundred million doses!"

Kushner said that sounded great, but asked Azar to hold on. He was at the White House late that night with the president. Kushner put Trump on the phone.

"Mr. President, we just got the first deal with

AstraZeneca," Azar said. "It's the first one ever. It's incredible."

Azar explained how sensitive it was.

"It's going to be announced at four o'clock tomorrow," he said. "You can't talk about it. It will be released when the British stock market opens."

"What?" Trump asked. "It's a British company?"

"They are the first one with a vaccine, Mr. President," Azar said.

Trump sounded deflated. "I'm going to get killed," he said. "Oh, this is terrible news. Boris Johnson is going to have a field day with this."

Azar wasn't sure what to say about the British prime minister.

"Why aren't we doing this with an American company?" Trump asked.

"This is the first one that is available," Azar explained.

"I don't want any press on this," Trump said. "Don't do any press on this. Let's wait."

Azar was stunned. He'd been angry and frustrated before in this job, many times. But in this moment, he was flat-out depressed. He had imagined the president would thank him. Instead, Trump had acted as if Azar had failed him.

Kushner, Hope Hicks, and Dan Scavino were in the room and heard Trump's end of the conversation. They were surprised.

"Secretary Azar has just delivered you a vaccine and you just yelled at him," Hicks told Trump. "Why did you do that?"

"This is great news," Scavino added. "We should be promoting this."

Kushner, too, tried to correct the president.

"This is a really big advance," he told his father-in-law. "That was not helpful."

PART
TWO

PART
TWO

Seven

Bunkers, Blasts, and Bibles

A h! They'll kill me. They'll kill me. I can't breathe. I can't breathe."

Shortly after 8:00 p.m. on May 25, George Floyd, a forty-six-year-old Black man, was hand-cuffed and pinned against the pavement outside a south Minneapolis convenience store. He pleaded for his life. He cried out for his children and for his mother. He said, "I can't breathe," more than twenty times. A white officer, Derek Chauvin, knelt on Floyd's neck for nine minutes. Floyd gasped, "They'll kill me. They'll kill me." His pleas grew faint and then silent. His body went limp. Paramedics could not re-suscitate him. Floyd, having struggled with addiction and unemployment, having contracted COVID-19 and survived, died under the knee of a police officer.

That night the police had received a radio call about

a man trying to pass a counterfeit $20 bill to buy cigarettes. Responding to the scene, a pair of officers noticed Floyd nearby with a friend inside his car, and suspected they were doing drugs. They handcuffed Floyd, who complained about being placed in a squad car, and two additional officers arrived. His arrest rapidly turned into a savage show of force and brutality, as Chauvin knelt on Floyd's neck and Floyd cried out again and again, "I can't breathe." Horrified bystanders gathered, some recording video on their phones.

The next morning, May 26, videos circulated widely online. People reacted with overwhelming revulsion. By that afternoon, the Minneapolis Police Department had fired all four officers involved. The city's mayor, Jacob Frey, appeared near tears in a news conference. "It was malicious and it was unacceptable," he said of Floyd's death. "There is no gray there."

Video of Floyd's final breaths played on a loop in the media, becoming indelible in the nation's conscience. Another Black American who posed no threat had died at the hands of the police. Eric Garner. Tamir Rice. Walter Scott. Philando Castile. Alton Sterling. Stephon Clark. Breonna Taylor. And now, George Floyd.

For many Americans, this unending cycle of police brutality was too much to bear.

Breaking the normally inviolable solidarity of police, law enforcement leaders around the country condemned Chauvin's knee hold on Floyd. "There is no need to put a knee on someone's neck for

NINE minutes. There IS a need to DO something," Chattanooga police chief David Roddy tweeted. "If you wear a badge and you don't have an issue with this . . . turn it in."

On May 26, President Trump had a relatively light schedule. In the Oval Office just after noon, he swore in his new director of national intelligence, Congressman John Ratcliffe, who was being rewarded with a plum administration post for having energetically and unconditionally defended Trump in the impeachment hearings. Trump had a meeting that afternoon with Mike Pompeo and made remarks in the Rose Garden about protecting seniors from diabetes.

After Trump first saw the video of Floyd's dying moments, he reacted with what aides described as rare, visceral emotion. The president had on occasion registered disgust and disapproval for what he considered police overreaction that led to a person's death, whether the victim was Black or white. He reacted more strongly than his advisers might have expected given his embrace of the "Thin Blue Line" flag and frequent calls for "law and order," including when in 2017 he suggested police rough up suspects when putting them in a "paddy wagon."

That evening, angry protesters took to the streets in Minneapolis to demand action for what they rightly called a police murder. Protests would erupt the next day in cities across the country, from Los Angeles to Chicago to Memphis. Before long, demonstrations were taking place practically everywhere.

On May 27, Trump met with Bill Barr to review what had happened in Minneapolis. Barr told Trump the Justice Department was launching a civil rights investigation, following the local authorities' own investigation, and went over the key questions the legal team would seek to answer in deciding whether to charge the officers. Trump was visibly disturbed by Floyd's death. He exhibited more genuine empathy than his advisers had ever seen in him. The president was agitated about what he believed to be obvious abuse.

"What the fuck? What happened here?" Trump asked.

This was not a first for Trump. In July 2019, when Barr had decided that the Justice Department would not charge police in the killing by choke hold of Garner in Staten Island, New York, Trump had had a similar reaction. He had wanted to know why Barr wasn't going after bad cops.

"That was bad. That was really bad—that cop, you know," Trump said at the time. "I grew up with guys like that in Queens."

Barr explained the officer's actions looked bad but did not cause Garner's death.

"Mr. President, they were sent there to arrest the guy, and the guy was doing that," Barr said. "But the bottom line is, he started off in an authorized hold, the guy was bucking around and his arm slipped into a position, but it was for seven seconds and it did not cause his death."

But Trump's preeminent concern was typical:
how to play Floyd's death for the cameras. Kayleigh
McEnany also joined the meeting to discuss what
Trump would say publicly. Trump debated how much
of his personal outrage to make public.

"What should I say about this?" Trump asked
his attorney general and press secretary. Some of his
other advisers proposed a toned-down version of
his disgust. That was fine with the president. He
wasn't pushing to make a big statement right away,
and later that day Trump tweeted that Floyd's death
was "very sad and tragic." He also proposed that the
FBI and Justice Department investigate the police for
a possible civil rights violation.

On May 28, the third straight day of protests in
Minneapolis, some of them violent, Minnesota governor Tim Walz activated the National Guard to
restore peace to the Twin Cities. But protests continued. A large group of demonstrators surrounded the
3rd Precinct police station, forcing police to abandon
the building, which was soon set ablaze by protesters.
Crowds spilled into neighboring St. Paul, burning
and vandalizing more storefronts and buildings in
a commercial district. Not even the announcement
that Chauvin had been arrested and charged with
second- and third-degree murder could calm the unrest in the streets.

At about 1:00 a.m. on May 29, after watching
television footage of the precinct station fire, Trump
tweeted that the Minneapolis mayor was "very

weak" and that the protesters were "thugs who are dishonoring the memory of George Floyd." Trump then tweeted, "when the looting starts, the shooting starts," a phrase that echoed the brutal crackdown on civil rights protests in Black neighborhoods in Miami in the 1960s.

Later that day, Trump spoke by phone with Floyd's family. "I just expressed my sorrow," Trump said of the call, adding that what happened in Minneapolis "should never happen" and that "the family of George is entitled to justice." Aides later described the president as "gracious" and "sympathetic" in his conversation with Floyd's brother Philonise Floyd and said he had invited the family to visit the White House. But Philonise Floyd offered a different interpretation. "It was so fast. He didn't give me an opportunity to even speak," Philonise Floyd said in an interview with civil rights leader Al Sharpton on MSNBC. "It was hard. I was trying to talk to him, but he just kept, like, pushing me off, like, 'I don't want to hear what you're talking about.'" The brother added, "I just told him, 'I want justice.' I said, 'I can't believe that they committed a modern-day lynching in broad daylight. I can't stand for that.'"

On May 28, as the Black Lives Matter movement was erupting, the nation reached a tragic milestone: one hundred thousand coronavirus deaths. Trump had claimed the death toll would never rise this high. On February 26, he had famously said that the number of coronavirus cases "within a couple of days is going to be down to zero," and the next day had declared, "It's going to disappear. One day—it's like a miracle—it will disappear."

The president chose not to honor the occasion. There was no moment of silence or somber commemoration. There was no opportunity for Americans, frightened by the relentless power of the "invisible enemy," as Trump had termed it, to grieve collectively.

Instead Trump focused on other matters. In the days leading up to the milestone, he played golf at his private club in Virginia, at the entrance to which his motorcade zipped past a small group of protesters holding up a sign that read: "I care do U? 100,000 dead." And he was especially active on social media, tweeting or retweeting messages mocking the weight of Georgia Democratic leader Stacey Abrams, calling Hillary Clinton a "skank," and promoting a baseless conspiracy theory that former congressman and MSNBC host Joe Scarborough may have had an affair with and killed a former staffer.

Then, finally, Trump directly addressed the death toll, refusing to take responsibility. He tweeted on May 26: "For all of the political hacks out there, if I hadn't done my job well, & early, we would have lost 1 1/2 to 2 Million People, as opposed to the 100,000 plus that looks like will be the number. That's 15 to 20 times more than we will lose."

Michael Gerson, President George W. Bush's chief

speechwriter on September 11, 2001, and during the crisis that followed, highlighted Trump's lack of public statement. "There's maybe a fundamental problem here in the ability to feel and express empathy, and that's a serious problem in the aftermath of loss of life and a kind of crisis that involves the loss of American lives," he said in an interview with **The Washington Post**'s Ashley Parker.

Most of the protests of Floyd's death and displays of solidarity with the Black Lives Matter movement across the country were peaceful, but in some places there was unrest, violence, and looting. Between May 27 and May 29, police in forty-eight U.S. cities arrested more than fourteen thousand people during protest-related activities. During that time, Trump and his advisers warily monitored the situation and conferred with governors, mayors, and law enforcement leaders about how to quell the unrest. But on the evening of Friday, May 29, the demonstrations literally came to the president's front yard.

In anticipation of civil unrest in the nation's capital, officials in Washington had taken some modest security precautions. The Justice Department brought in a few dozen U.S. marshals and Bureau of Prisons officers who had been trained in prison riots to protect the department's Pennsylvania Avenue headquarters over the coming weekend. The U.S. Park Police, which has jurisdiction over the National

Mall, monuments, and other federal lands in the city, and the Secret Service set up a temporary perimeter of waist-high sections of metal fencing, resembling bike racks, a few yards out from the White House's northern fence line. This essentially created a buffer on Pennsylvania Avenue, the most exposed side of the eighteen-acre complex. Other than that, however, there was no planning for or expectation of the protests that would come that evening.

The first crowds began gathering in small clusters throughout the city that Friday evening at about 5:00. At Fourteenth and U Streets NW, the epicenter of Black culture in Washington, which was scarred by the 1968 riots but had been reborn in the twenty-first century as a diverse, vibrant, gentrified neighborhood, roughly two hundred people assembled peacefully but noisily. Some in the group chanted "I can't breathe," and a speaker led the crowd in reciting a list of names of unarmed Black men and women killed by police. Then the crowd marched south on Fourteenth Street, toward the White House. As people flowed into Lafayette Square in front of the White House, a small skirmish ensued between protesters—many of them young people chanting "Black Lives Matter!"— and the Park Police and Secret Service officers. Some protesters tossed plastic bottles at the officers' heads. Police surrounded one man.

Shortly after 7:00 p.m., the crowd swelled considerably. To the surprise of officers, there were now as many as five hundred people. The protesters were no longer standing back and chanting, a routine the officers knew well from hundreds of protests outside the White House over the years. Now members of the crowd rushed to the perimeter of temporary fencing. Many tugged at the metal racks, hopped over them where they could, and in some spots, pushed them over entirely.

Secret Service officers radioed an alert. A young man with dark hair and a yellow shirt had hopped over the fencing around the Treasury Building, adjoining the White House complex and officially part of its grounds. Though it was 350 yards from the East Wing of the White House, the Treasury fencing was a known weak spot that "jumpers" had used twice before to reach the White House grounds and approach the mansion. The suspected jumper was taken into custody by officers, and three more protesters believed to have jumped over police barricades were also arrested and charged with unlawful entry at 1600 Pennsylvania Avenue. Additional demonstrators had scaled iron bars near the Treasury and scrawled "Fuck Trump" in large letters on the window behind the bars.

The threats sent up a flare in the Secret Service's Joint Operations Center. Protesters were overwhelming officers to the point that officers feared the arrival of more. The threat level at the White House was elevated from "Condition Yellow" to "Condition Red," indicating a breach that put the president in potential danger. Members of the president's security detail rushed up a flight of stairs to his private quarters and quickly guided Trump, along with Melania and Barron, down a narrow tunnel to the emergency shelter under the East Wing. The Secret Service decision reflected the real danger the Trumps faced.

Secret Service officers would later remark that the forcefulness of the demonstrators that night was like nothing they had experienced before, calling to mind clashes between police and Vietnam War protesters in the 1960s. The night was so harrowing that Keith Kellogg later brought Georgetown Cupcakes from the specialty cupcake shop to the office to hand out to agents as a token of appreciation. When he commended a young female agent for her bravery and asked her what it was like that night, she told him, "We were standing there and people were spitting on us and telling us all kinds of names. All I'm trying to do is do my job and protect the White House."

The next morning, May 30, Trump also commended the Secret Service in a series of messages on Twitter. "I was inside, watched every move, and couldn't have felt more safe," he wrote. The president added, "Big crowd, professionally organized, but nobody came close to breaching the fence. If they had they would have been greeted with the most vicious dogs, and most ominous weapons, I have ever seen. That's when people would have been really badly hurt, at least." Trump also claimed that Secret Service agents wanted to engage the protesters. He wrote that he had been told, "We put the young ones on the front line, sir, they love it, and good practice."

Trump's suggestion of siccing "vicious dogs" on Black Lives Matter protesters evoked ugly memories of police brutality and racism. This language, coupled with a later tweet blaming D.C. mayor Muriel Bowser for the unrest, prompted a scornful rebuttal from the Black Democrat. "There are no vicious dogs & ominous weapons," Bowser wrote on Twitter. "There is just a scared man. Afraid/alone."

The protests continued in Washington all weekend, including in front of the White House, and though they were peaceful during the day, at night violence increased. Several dozen law enforcement officers were treated for injuries. Downtown stores and office buildings were vandalized, as was the Hay-Adams hotel on Lafayette Square. On Sunday night, protesters set fire to the basement of St. John's Episcopal Church, an historic place of worship on Lafayette Square attended at least once by every president since James Madison in the early 1800s.

The nation was reeling from an unprecedented confluence of health, economic, and social crises and crying out for leadership. Pictures of shattered glass, charred vehicles, bruised bodies, and graffiti-tagged buildings told the story of America from coast to coast. Yet Trump seemed unwilling or unable to unite Americans. His political strategy was to pit groups of people against one another. Indeed some in the public arena suggested the president should simply stay in the background.

"He should just stop talking," Atlanta mayor Keisha

Lance Bottoms, a Black Democrat, said on May 31 on CNN. Invoking Trump's equivocal response to the deadly 2017 white supremacist rally, she continued, "This is like Charlottesville all over again. He speaks, and he makes it worse. There are times when you should just be quiet. And I wish that he would just be quiet."

That weekend, Tom Rath, a longtime Republican official in New Hampshire, also lamented Trump's tendency toward conflict: "On his automatic transmission, there is one speed. It is not conciliate. It is not comfort. It is not forge consensus. It is attack. And the frustration right now is that nobody is in charge. Anarchy rules."

On May 31, as protesters took to the streets in Washington for the third day straight, **The New York Times** reported that Trump had been taken to the bunker two nights earlier. The report, which was confirmed by other outlets and replayed heavily on cable news, infuriated the president because he thought it made him appear scared and weak. Trump demanded to know who had leaked this news to Maggie Haberman and Peter Baker of the **Times.** He told Mark Meadows, "Mark, you have to catch whoever leaked that. They should be in prison. They should be tried for treason. This is treasonous!"

"I'm on it," Meadows said. "I'm on it."

The bunker story would become an obsession of the new chief of staff's—and he would spend hours pursuing possible leads on the identity of the leaker, though the release of this White House gossip didn't constitute a crime and Meadows's fixation got in the way of his job managing the entire executive branch. Meadows would tell other aides that he suspected the leak originated from the first lady's office, but he would never uncover solid enough evidence to make a convincing case.

A few days later, Trump would deny what had happened. "It was a false report," Trump said in a call-in interview with Fox News Radio's Brian Kilmeade. "I went down during the day, and I was there for a tiny, little, short period of time, and it was much more for an inspection."

Trump's risible explanation was a lie. His aides knew it. His Secret Service agents knew it.

Going into that weekend, Trump gathered Meadows, Defense Secretary Mark Esper, Joint Chiefs of Staff Chairman Mark Milley, and other top advisers in the Oval Office to plan an end to the protests. The president wanted to deploy the military, both in Washington and elsewhere in the country. Sitting in front of the Resolute Desk, facing the president, Esper and Milley warned Trump that deploying active-duty troops on American streets was almost never a good idea, and especially not to handle civil unrest. Milley's opposition to the use of military force domestically was well known throughout the Pentagon.

From the back of the room, Stephen Miller piped up. Though Miller had previously only worked as a congressional staffer and had zero military experience, he was highly regarded by the president for his hard-edged nationalism and innate understanding of how to cater to Trump's political base. He egged on Trump to use armed troops.

"Mr. President, you have to show strength," Miller said. "They're burning the country down."

Milley, nothing if not blunt with his counsel, whipped his head around and locked eyes with Miller. The general didn't like much of anything that Miller had to say about dealing with protests. He had told aides he considered him a Rasputin character, always whispering devilish ideas in the king's ear. Milley raised his arm to point a finger in Miller's direction, staring at him as he did so.

"Stephen, shut the fuck up," Milley snapped. "They're not burning the fucking country down."

Then he turned back to Trump. The president's obsession with tapping the military's might led the Pentagon to keep at the ready data it had never needed before, so Milley could fight fire with facts. The chairman's office got updated counts of the total number of law enforcement officers and National Guard available in every major city in the United States.

"Mr. President," Milley said, "there are two hundred seventy-six cities in America with over one hundred thousand people in them. We track this all the time." In the last twenty-four hours, Milley said, there were only two cities with violent protests so large that local authorities might have needed reinforcements. Otherwise, he said, "there was some vandalism and some rioting, but they were handled by local police."

Then he turned back to Miller.

"Stephen, that's not burning the country down," he said.

Miller pushed back. "Let me get this straight," he said. "We're supposed to say, Sorry, your city's being burned down. Too bad your mayor doesn't want to do anything about it. That's our argument? We can't possibly take the position that the people are free to riot for as long as they want to in this country. This is a completely untenable position."

Still, Milley's firmness made an impression on Trump, who watched silently and eagerly, as if the argument between his advisers were a pay-per-view fight on HBO. Miller was pressed on the ropes in the first round. Milley was setting a boundary with a president who saw none, something he would have to do far more often in the coming months. Yes, some protests were violent, but they were not enveloping entire cities, and it was the Pentagon's assessment that law enforcement authorities could control the situations.

This same weekend, Esper called Larry Hogan with a special request. He asked—pleaded, really—for the Maryland governor to deploy National Guard soldiers to Washington. Hogan's gut reaction was no. He

BUNKERS, BLASTS, AND BIBLES

needed them on standby at home in case protests in Baltimore or elsewhere in Maryland got intense. More important, though, Hogan had mixed feelings about deploying his National Guard for the Trump administration. In 2015, he had called up the National Guard to assist law enforcement officers in keeping protests peaceful in Baltimore following the killing of Freddie Gray. Hogan was proud of the state's response then and deeply uncomfortable with an additional military response to civil unrest, believing demonstrators need space to express their frustrations.

"Look," Hogan told Esper, "we're always willing to help our next-door neighbor, but what are they going to be used for? We have nine hundred guys in Baltimore outside the city waiting if they're needed and we don't have a defined mission. What is it that you want to use them for?"

"Here's the situation," Esper said. "The president wants me to use active-duty military troops and that's the last thing I want to do. The citizen-soldiers in the National Guard, that's what they're for, but D.C. doesn't have enough."

"No, we don't want to do that," Hogan said.

The governor consulted with the guard's adjutant general, who explained he didn't have enough troops and did not want to send them on some undefined mission. Hogan called back Esper to negotiate. Esper urged Hogan to change his mind, noting that he was also asking a handful of neighboring states, including New York, New Jersey, and Pennsylvania to send National Guard soldiers. Hogan agreed to send one hundred National Guard members, and Esper was pleased, although the governor insisted upon a defined mission.

"We're not doing anything on protesters," Hogan said. "We'll go protect the monuments."

So Maryland's soldiers stood guard around the Lincoln Memorial, far from the violence in front of the White House.

Meanwhile, despite Milley whacking Miller's argument, the issue of deploying troops came up in a subsequent White House meeting. Trump asked why it couldn't be done. Protesters were looting stores and vandalizing buildings. The president reasoned that they had to be stopped just like when troops were used in the 1960s to bring order to the streets.

"Mr. President, it doesn't compare anywhere to the summer of sixty-eight," Milley said. "It's not even close."

Miller piped up again. "It's an insurrection!" he said.

This time, the general didn't bother turning toward the young aide. Though Milley had been sharp with Miller before, he tried to stay calm with the president now. Milley pointed at the painting of President Lincoln that hung on the wall to the right of the Resolute Desk.

"Mr. President, that guy had an insurrection," Milley said. "You don't have an insurrection. When guys show up in gray and start bombing Fort Sumter, you'll have an insurrection. I'll let you know about it. You don't have an insurrection right now."

The Insurrection Act, enacted in 1807, had last been used in 1992 during the riots in Los Angeles after officers were found not guilty of beating Black motorist Rodney King. Invoking it was considered the very last resort—a nuclear option. And Milley was not about to let it happen on his watch. Some other key voices in Trump's ear backed up Milley, including Kellogg, who told Trump, "Leave it alone. Let the governors worry about this with the National Guard." Kellogg said invoking the Insurrection Act was "always something to keep in your back pocket, but don't do it."

"The problem is, with all these riots going on, it'd have to be a massive group. You can't just send troops to one location," Kellogg told Trump. "And what you don't want to do is seem like you're doing martial law, putting federal troops into a bunch of states. What I would do is reserve them, but don't bring federal troops into cities until we find out something has become uncontrollable."

Trump believed troops in battle dress were the only way to show he meant business, to be the "law and order" president he styled himself as. Again and again, he would argue that cities were falling prey to violent extremists and he was needed to stop the chaos and prevent destruction. Each time, Milley could counter with the number of officers already on the ground prepared to enforce the peace.

Milley hoped to calm Trump down: "Mr. President, that's not what's happening. Some protests are getting violent, but the cops got it. Law enforcement has got it. There's no insurrection. There's no need for troops."

The morning of Monday, June 1, Trump awoke early and lost his temper at the news coverage of the White House protests and his trip to the bunker. His advisers were on edge. Trump had been mulling a plan to personally dominate the situation: He would personally walk into Lafayette Square and, in the words of a military commander, retake that hill.

Trump summoned Esper, Milley, Meadows, Barr, and deputy White House chief of staff Tony Ornato, his former Secret Service detail leader who oversaw operations and security, to the Oval Office. He wanted to get the mess on his front lawn straightened out. Trump complained about how weak he must look to other foreign leaders with fires burning in plain view of the White House.

"How do you think this looks to hostile countries?" Trump asked. "They see we can't even control our own capital city and the space around the White House!

"I had to be fucking taken down," Trump said of the trip to the bunker that he had earlier denied took place. "This is crazy."

Trump again proposed bringing in military troops. Speaking in a herky-jerky style, effectively brainstorming aloud, he threw out random numbers—ten thousand! five thousand!—of troops he could order to Washington. He asked about calling in the 82nd Airborne. He wanted reinforcements lining the White House perimeter. He suggested they invoke the Insurrection Act immediately. Neither Trump's attorney general nor his Pentagon leaders liked the idea of active-duty soldiers patrolling city streets. Milley explained to the president that the 82nd Airborne would take a long time to mobilize and transport to Washington: troops could not just hop on a cargo plane and fly in immediately. Esper explained why the Insurrection Act was a dramatic move for civilian protests when there were so few dangerous lawbreakers.

"Mr. President, the National Guard is best suited to do this," Esper said. "This is a job for law enforcement. Law enforcement has the lead. The military should be in the back of the line and the active duty should be dead last."

Trump slammed on the Resolute Desk and yelled that Esper wasn't helping him fix the problem. Everyone in the room went quiet for a bit. Trump then suggested Milley, whose tough bravado the president admired, could be the commander of an operation to restore order in the city. The chairman of the Joint Chiefs of Staff poured cold water on that idea, realizing the president didn't understand he didn't command troops.

"No, no, Mr. President," Milley said. "There's

a civilian leadership. I'm not in an operational role here."

Milley tried to explain that Americans had a constitutional right to protest and the military should not be used to stop them.

"You can't say that!" Trump interjected.

"Well, I just did," Milley said. "I'm your military adviser. I have to tell you that."

Now red in the face, Trump demanded that somebody give him a solution because this chaos in the streets required an immediate and deafening response. Milley held his tongue, figuring there was no winning this argument. Others stayed silent, too, and the president grew more frustrated.

"You're all fucked up," Trump thundered. "Every one of you is fucked up."

Then he turned to look at Vice President Pence, who had been silent the entire time, and exclaimed: "Including you!"

Barr, fortunate to not also be on the receiving end of this tirade, was listening. He had enjoyed an unusually good relationship with Trump compared to other Cabinet members and had aligned with Milley and Esper at times to help persuade the president. At this tense juncture, Barr sided with the Pentagon duo and urged Trump not to use active-duty troops. But despite Esper, Milley, and Barr all singing from the same hymn sheet, Esper sensed the president was on the verge of giving them a direct order to activate soldiers. Since Trump had suggested ten thousand troops, Esper proposed one tolerable way to get to the president's number.

"Mr. President, why don't we do this?" Esper said. "Let me go back to the Pentagon, I will get the guard moving." He said he thought he could get governors from neighboring states to loan five thousand National Guard members to team up with the five thousand members of law enforcement agencies under the Justice Department provided by Barr. Barr reconfirmed that he could do that. The truth was the Justice Department had very few officers who could provide this kind of help, and even fewer with the proper training. Bureau of Prisons officers were ideal for controlling riots in prisons. U.S. marshals were trained to track down fugitives. Neither force had much experience with the nuanced work of corralling civilian protesters exercising their right to free speech.

There was a long pregnant pause. Trump was hardly overjoyed. But Esper's proposal was good enough for now. Trump seized on this "plus-up" plan and turned to Barr: "You're going to run this thing."

The attorney general had no control over, or even practical communication with, most of the agencies involved in the law enforcement response. He had no chain of command to the Park Police, the Secret Service, or the National Guard. But Trump's goal was simple, and so were his solutions. He wanted to show he was dominating the streets of Washington, and he needed a commander.

The attorney general shrugged and accepted his assignment: "Yes, Mr. President."

Barr relished his role as the go-to guy for the president, but also for Milley and Esper, who counted on him to talk sense into Trump. He didn't really like to say no or give the impression he couldn't handle something. But that Monday, Barr didn't stop to point out to the president—or perhaps, even, to seriously consider for himself—all the minefields that stood in his way. This was a strategy that some senior advisers and Cabinet members had developed after months of working for Trump: get him to a palatable decision during a meeting—and then move to end the meeting and leave as soon as possible. "Get up and get out," as one former Cabinet member said. It was risky to continue the discussion with Trump because a new and far worse plan could be proposed at any moment.

Immediately after their tense meeting in the Oval, Trump and the others moved to the Situation Room for a conference call with the nation's governors. It was contentious right off the bat, with the heated conversation in the Oval essentially overflowing into the next meeting.

In his opening remarks, Trump said, "General Milley is here, who's head of [the] Joint Chiefs of Staff, a fighter, a war hero, a lot of victories and no losses, and he hates to see the way it's being handled in the various states. And I just put him in charge." Having just explained why this was not possible, Milley could be seen blanching at the suggestion.

Trump then said of his attorney general, "We will activate Bill Barr and activate him very strongly. . . . We're strongly looking for arrests."

Then the president berated the governors. "You have to get much tougher," he said, adding, "You have to dominate. If you don't dominate, you're wasting your time. They're going to run all over you, you'll look like a bunch of jerks. You have to dominate, and you have to arrest people, and you have to try people and they have to go to jail for long periods of time."

Barr then came on the line and backed up the president. "Law enforcement response is not gonna work unless we dominate the streets, as the president said," Barr told the governors. "We have to control the streets. If we treat these as demonstrations, the police are pinned back, guarding places, and don't have the dynamic ability to go out and arrest the troublemakers."

Esper, who was on the clock to get governors to activate National Guard units to arrive by nightfall, hoped to encourage this step on the call. He praised Walz's deployment of the National Guard in Minneapolis to reduce tensions and to deter further trouble there. Esper and Milley both chimed in about the need to "dominate the battle space," a fairly mundane military phrase, but which sounded jarring to some of the governors' ears. Several governors chimed in with overnight updates on the protests in their states. And then, when J. B. Pritzker was called to speak, the Illinois governor confronted Trump.

"I wanted to take this moment . . . to say that I'm extraordinarily concerned with the rhetoric that's been used by you," Pritzker said. "It's been inflammatory and not okay. . . . And I need to say that we are feeling real pain out here and that we've got to have national leadership on this that is calling for calm and for making sure that [people can have] legitimate peaceful protests. That will help us bring order."

"Well, thank you very much, Jay," Trump responded. "I don't like your rhetoric, either."

After the call wrapped up, Pritzker and his aides suspected Trump was on the verge of a serious escalation. The governor's chief of staff, Anne Caprara, called his chief of strategy, Emily Bittner, to say, "You've got to watch the news. Donald Trump is going to do something crazy."

One part of the plan that emerged from the White House meeting, and which Barr agreed with, was to expand the northern security perimeter around the White House, both to protect the complex and St. John's, where protesters had previously set fire to the basement. Park Police, aided by the Secret Service, would bring in reinforcements from D.C. police; the Justice Department's units; law enforcement in neighboring Arlington, Virginia; and National Guard members. Once new fencing material arrived and enough forces were on location, they would move the protest barricade one block north, from H Street to I Street. But beyond that, there was not much of a plan. After their meetings at the White House, Meadows, Esper, Barr, and Milley met privately—without the president—to discuss how this was all going to work. Milley kept shaking his head.

"What the fuck?" Milley asked the group.

It was crystal clear Trump had no understanding of how the various departments of his administration worked, or of how civilian and military roles diverged at the Pentagon, or even of the sacred importance of the First Amendment. A president could not merely do away with it to impress some foreign leaders. But Barr, wanting to find a way to be helpful, had just said yes to overseeing something vague and ominous.

About 2:00 that afternoon, Barr headed to the Strategic Information and Operations Center, the FBI's global command center, known as SIOC, to check on the status of protests in Washington and around the country. Pointing at a map on an electronic board, Barr explained how he expected the northern White House perimeter would be moved by one block.

At roughly the same time, Ivanka Trump was cooking up a plan for her father to make a dramatic show of strength that evening. The president would deliver an address from the Rose Garden extolling the importance of "law and order," and then exit the White House, walk across Lafayette Square, and pay

a visit to St. John's. Ivanka's conceit was for Trump
to show the country that violent protests weren't
the answer.

"You're not hunkered down. You're not hiding," she
told her father. "Why don't you walk to the church,
go inside, say a prayer, and show people they should
not be afraid. We can't tear our country apart and
burn it to the ground."

Hope Hicks also suggested the president do something once he got to St. John's, such as read Scripture
or visit with faith leaders, to make the event more
meaningful. She worried that the image of him
merely standing in front of the church would come
across as awkward. But Trump nixed that idea. He
decided he would simply carry a Bible symbolically
and hold it aloft.

Sometime close to 4:00 p.m., Barr had moved to
the FBI's Washington Field Office—where representatives of many of the various law enforcement agencies in Lafayette Square were stationed—to coordinate
security around the city and White House. Watching
the live video feeds of the square, Barr noticed the
perimeter hadn't been moved yet. Someone told
him the crowd in the square was very small, maybe
150 people, so it seemed to him it would be a good
time to push out the perimeter. But some of the fencing reinforcements had not yet been delivered to the
scene. The perimeter extension would have to wait.

At about 5:00, Esper called Milley, who by now
had joined Barr at the WFO, to talk over rules of

engagement, the plan for the night, and their coordination with local law enforcement. Milley told Esper he was going to change out of his stiff dress uniform, with its chest full of medals, into his more comfortable camouflage battle fatigues because he would be out on the streets with National Guard units late into the night. Milley and Barr got bored in the command center and decided to venture out to Lafayette Square to check on the scene themselves. A few minutes after 6:00, Milley and Barr walked into the square from behind the security perimeter. They saw the crowd by now was substantially larger than 150 people, many of them holding up their arms and chanting "Hands up! Don't shoot!" Some of the protesters recognized the attorney general and yelled at him. Barr spoke with a Park Police commander in charge of the scene. Ornato, who coordinated presidential movements but was not in charge of perimeter security, came out to join them.

"Why haven't you moved the perimeter yet?" Barr asked the Park Police commander.

The commander said they had been waiting on more backup forces, including some National Guard units that were just arriving, but they planned to make the move soon.

"When is the president coming out?" Barr then asked.

Barr had been told earlier in the day the president was coming out to the square, and he presumed it was to survey the scene.

Ornato pulled Barr aside and, with an indoor voice,

said: "He's coming out, but we're not telling anyone about that."

Milley was a few steps away. His cell phone rang, and he stepped away to answer it. It was his wife, Hollyanne.

"I'm seeing you on TV," she said. "Are you okay?"

"Everything's fine," Milley assured her.

Milley then talked to some of the National Guard members, including Major Adam DeMarco. Milley sensed a tension in the air and sought to defuse it. "We defend the Constitution, and the First Amendment gives you the right to protest and freedom of speech," Milley told the guard members on one corner of the park. "Keep your cool. No matter what happens here, stay cool."

With Barr and Milley still conferring on the square and surveying the police lineup at the perimeter, D.C. police commanders got a radio alert that the president would soon be making an unscheduled movement in the area. Minutes later, the D.C. police were warned on the same system that Park Police would soon begin using munitions to move the protesters and for officers to take cover. The police hadn't seen the crowd engage in any specific violence that day. So far the worst thing that had happened was that a few protesters had thrown their water bottles over the perimeter fencing.

About twenty clergy members from around the city had spent the day on the patio of St. John's, handing out granola bars and bottles of water to protesters to keep them cool in the heat and humidity. As the Reverend Gini Gerbasi remembered, it had been a day of inspiration and hope that perhaps the country might someday overcome the racism that infected it.

At this moment, Barr told Milley he had just learned the president wanted them at the White House for an update. Esper, then being driven downtown to survey the troops, got the same message and headed to the White House. At about 6:25, Barr and Milley left the park area and headed toward the Northwest Gate. As they walked away, Barr heard a warning to disperse over a loudspeaker. Arriving in the West Wing, they found an unusual flurry of activity and many people scurrying about. They learned the president was about to speak in the Rose Garden. Behind them, however, something far more dramatic and shocking was unfolding.

At about 6:30, a half hour before the city's 7:00 p.m. curfew, federal police in riot gear fired gas canisters, flash-bang shells, and exploding munitions that released rubber pellets to force largely peaceful demonstrators out of the area. They struck protesters with batons and slammed into them with their shields. They sought to rush them by riding at them on horseback.

"The air was just crackling with something as the police were piling up," Gerbasi recalled. "And suddenly, there were screams and explosions. . . . I looked up and saw a smoky trail coming from the park out to the street, and then just billowing smoke from that. We're seeing people starting to run toward us, and running toward us with their faces just red and their eyes burning. . . . The police on horseback, they're driving people down. Tear gas. It's like a war scene."

While peaceful protesters were being charged, shot at with rubber pellets, and routed out by flash grenades, Trump strode into the Rose Garden to declare before cameras, "I am your president of law and order and an ally of all peaceful protesters."

Esper arrived as instructed at the White House and found nearly twenty people milling around in the anteroom just outside the Oval. He turned to an assistant.

"I'm here for the meeting, where's the meeting?" Esper said.

"There is no meeting," the aide said. "The president is out talking to the press. He's giving remarks."

Esper said he needed to go and check out the security situation, then.

"No, no," the aide said. "Just hang tight. He may want to go to the church afterward."

Esper figured he'd at least get some work done while he waited, so he went to find Robert O'Brien.

Milley, who arrived a little later than Esper, also did not attend the speech.

"Do you know what's going on?" Esper asked him.

"No, I really don't know," Milley replied.

A little later an aide explained to Esper that the president wanted to head over to the church because he wanted to see the damage from the previous night. Milley was sitting in the Cabinet Room and heard applause, indicating the president had finished speaking in the Rose Garden. Esper called out to him. It was time to walk with the president.

Then Trump came by.

"Okay, you guys ready to go?" he asked. "I'm going to go walk to the church."

Dozens of aides quickly gathered to accompany Trump for his grand surprise exit from the White House. Conspicuously absent was Pence—in part because Marc Short had sensed the church photo op could backfire politically and decided to keep the vice president away from the scene. Trump saw that Ivanka had brought her purse and asked her to carry in her bag the Bible he intended to use as a prop. Milley, Esper, and Barr were in the first row directly behind Trump as he stepped out of the West Wing. All of them felt their spidey sense go off as soon as the walk began.

As if staging a Hollywood production, some White House aides told Barr, Esper, and Milley to trail several paces behind Trump, allowing him to lead the entourage alone. Within a few steps, the group could smell pepper spray. Esper's face—usually expressive and easy to read—had a look of, **Whoa. This is weird.** Milley, still in his battle camouflage, got almost all the way to the church. He was a few yards away when he saw Trump stop in front of the entrance. An aide guided the president on where he should stand, and his daughter handed him the Bible she had been carrying in her $1,540 MaxMara purse. **This is fucked up,** Milley thought. Concerned about the appearance of a uniformed military leader joining in a political photo op, Milley looked at his aide and said, "Let's get out of here." Like a running back on a football field, he looked for an opening and took it. He headed off to the right, saw some cops at an intersection, and struck up a conversation with them. Then he took a circuitous route back to the White House.

As a civilian political appointee, Esper had less to worry about in participating, but he likewise stayed at a distance from the church, trying to avoid any chance of being pulled into the photo.

Barr accompanied Trump all the way to the church door but tried to stand offstage left so he wouldn't be in the picture. Trump insisted and summoned Barr to stand by his side. Trump held the Bible aloft, but did not read from it or deliver a prayer as Hicks had proposed, and said only a few words. When a reporter asked whether it was a family Bible, Trump responded only that it was "a Bible." He did not go inside the church to inspect the fire damage.

It was impossible for Trump or any of his deputies to argue the clearing they executed at Lafayette Square was for a security purpose. This was purely a political show.

Trump campaign aides almost immediately circulated the resulting propaganda-style photographs online. The clergy members were disgusted and distraught. A seminarian, Julia Domenick, sent Gerbasi a text message that read: "Did we just get fucking tear gas for a fucking photo op?"

Gerbasi burst into tears. "It answered all the questions," she later explained. "The apocalypse. People tend to think it means the end of the world or the zombies are coming. But the word 'apocalypse' means an unveiling, a revealing. . . . And that is what happened there. People of faith everywhere were able to see."

When the president and his entourage returned to the White House, the entryway was lined with two rows of Secret Service officers holding their shields in front of them, standing at attention like the president's own Praetorian Guard.

Among the participants, bitter disagreements remain about what actually happened that day at Lafayette Square and why. Barr later told aides he thought there was consensus to move the perimeter back as soon as possible that morning, had embraced that decision, and pushed to make it happen. He claimed to them that he heard Trump was going to come out to inspect the square but did not know he had planned to walk across it to take a picture at the church. He also told aides that he didn't actually give the tactical order to clear the park, but that after White House officials identified him as the person who gave the order, he chose to take the heat and responsibility rather than correct the record.

D.C. Metropolitan Police Chief Peter Newsham said the timing of the urgent push to remove protesters was directly connected to the president's walk across the park a half hour later. DeMarco also disputed Barr's claim that there was an agreed-upon plan to move the perimeter. Both Newsham and DeMarco said the fencing materials needed to create the expanded perimeter did not arrive until 9:00 p.m.— hours after Barr asked the Park Police why they hadn't yet pushed it out.

Acting Park Police Chief Greg Monahan said his team moved to clear the square because protesters had grown increasingly violent. He said a decision had been made late in the day to create an expanded perimeter on the White House's north side but declined to say by whom. But the part of his account alleging violence has been roundly rejected.

Ornato has not answered questions about how the planning of Trump's walk across the park shaped the frightening charge on the protesters. He and the Secret Service had a responsibility to clear the park of any risk before the president crossed it.

For the trio walking with Trump that evening, Lafayette Square was a wake-up call. Barr realized Trump couldn't help but spike the football and look smaller for it. Esper recognized that Trump was willing to trample the spirit of public service that had been instilled in him since his earliest days at West

Point. "We were played," he would tell confidants late that night. And Milley decided he wasn't going to get caught in Trump's web like that again. He was going to have to draw very bright boundaries with this president.

"He burned me," Milley told aides. "Fuck these guys. I'm not playing political games."

Eight

Staring Down
the Dragon

After accompanying President Trump on his triumphant walk across Lafayette Square on June 1, Mark Esper and Mark Milley surveyed the streets of Washington late into the night, talking with National Guard soldiers, learning where they were from and what they had seen. When they returned to the FBI's Washington Field Office after 10:00, they finally put together all the pieces of what had happened. Despite their best efforts, Esper and Milley had dragged the U.S. military into an ugly scene and there would be a fierce backlash. They realized they had to explain themselves to the public, even if doing so would rupture their relationships with the president. They had to make clear they did not condone the use of force against people exercising their constitutional right to protest. That night, Esper instructed his spokesperson to ready a statement he wanted to send out to thank the entire force, stressing their important role defending those rights and staying above politics.

On June 2, NBC News and other media reported that Esper thought he was walking with Trump to visit a vandalized bathroom in Lafayette Square, but not whether Esper knew that the walk was a staged photo opportunity or whether law enforcement had been ordered to clear the park. Regardless, Esper's bathroom explanation became a punch line of sorts on cable news, with some analysts poking fun at the idea of the defense secretary inspecting toilets. Meanwhile, the president had only amped up his rhetoric about bringing in the military to put down the "thugs."

The night of June 2, Esper decided he had to correct the record in his own words. He told confidants that he was motivated by a sense the country was out of control like a runaway car, and somebody needed to grab the wheel. Trump had inflamed the Floyd protesters, and set the country on edge with the events of June 1. Esper feared what fresh violence might be set off in this volatile moment and would later tell associates he felt he needed to "break the fever." He stayed up until 2:00 a.m. trying to strike the right notes. The morning of June 3, he gathered Milley; General John Hyten, the vice chairman of the Joint Chiefs of Staff; Deputy Defense Secretary David Norquist; and a few other trusted advisers around a table, with some joining by phone, to help him get his message just right.

Esper knew Trump would not like what he had to say. Milley said, "This is the right thing to do and you're going to hit it out of the park."

Later that morning, Esper stood before reporters in the Pentagon's press briefing room and began to speak. He first offered his condolences to George Floyd's friends and family and said the police officers on the scene "should be held accountable for his murder." Then Esper stressed that the military values diversity and that the right of people to protest systemic racism is part of the Constitution that "every member of this department has sworn an oath to uphold and defend."

Esper had not shared his remarks with White House officials ahead of time, but Trump was watching the defense secretary's statement on television with rapt attention. The next few sentences would set him off. Esper said he had always felt the National Guard, of which he had been a member, was better suited to supporting police in times of civil unrest—and, importantly, that he did not support invoking the Insurrection Act.

"The option to use active-duty forces in a law enforcement role should only be used as a matter of last resort, and only in the most urgent and dire of situations," Esper said. "We are not in one of those situations now."

Esper also touched on what happened at Lafayette Square and said some of the reporting on his role had been flawed. "I did know that following the president's remarks on Monday evening that many of us were going to join President Trump and review the damage in Lafayette Park and at St. John's Episcopal Church," Esper told the reporters. "What I was not aware of was exactly where we were going when I arrived at the church and what the plans were once we got there."

In other words, Esper didn't know the walk was staged as a presidential photo op and didn't know officers had used force to clear the protesters. "Look, I do everything I can to try to stay apolitical and try and stay out of situations that may appear political," Esper said. "And sometimes I'm successful at doing that, and sometimes I'm not as successful, but my aim is to keep the department out of politics, to stay apolitical."

Esper also did Milley a favor, seeking to dispel the notion that the chairman of the Joint Chiefs of Staff had donned his camouflage uniform to look tough for Trump. Esper noted that it was standard protocol for military leaders to wear their field uniforms when meeting with troops on location, as Milley had done when he visited National Guard members.

Milley joined Esper as he walked back to his office and told the secretary he thought the speech was great. He had stepped up to the plate and offered his views plainly. Milley didn't say so, but he also knew Esper's remarks would land like a turd in the White House. Within fifteen minutes, Mark Meadows called Esper, who put the White House chief of staff on speakerphone. Esper's office filled with the sound of Meadows yelling.

"What the fuck?" Meadows said. "The president is apoplectic! He's really pissed. He's going to rip your face off."

As luck would have it, Esper and Milley were both due at the White House shortly for an 11:30 a.m. briefing on Afghanistan with Trump. They were to be joined by Kenneth McKenzie, a Marine Corps general who headed up U.S. Central Command. Esper ended the call with Meadows without resolution. Esper was not looking forward to the meeting.

"I'm just going to get my face ripped off," Esper said.

"Yeah, it's true, you are," Milley said, then tried to joke a little. "But you need to stare the dragon down. You need to just do it. Mr. Secretary, just pretend you're back at West Point on the Plain and you just brace like a cadet."

Esper paced in his office, thinking. He knew it would be better to let the president cool down, but that was no longer an option.

"Let's go get this over with," Esper told Milley. "If there's going to be a showdown, let's get it over with."

Esper grabbed his suit jacket and they went out to the secretary's waiting vehicle and rode across the Potomac River to the White House.

Esper and Milley headed into the Situation Room, where they planned to brief the president at 11:30 a.m. But an aide said, "The president wants to see you immediately." So they went upstairs to the

Oval Office. Chairs were arranged in a half-moon around the Resolute Desk, with Vice President Pence, Bill Barr, Robert O'Brien, Meadows, and a few others gathered around. Two chairs sat empty in front of the desk.

When Esper and Milley entered the room, the others facing the president put their heads down, as if praying in church. Milley told aides he thought to himself, **Oh, boy, this is going to be classic.** Esper took his seat, and as Milley put his hands on the back of his chair to begin to sit down, the nuclear bomb exploded.

"You betrayed me!" Trump screamed at Esper. "You're fucking weak! What is this shit? **I** make the decisions on the Insurrection Act. **I'm** the president, not you. You're taking options away from the president. This is about presidential authority. This is about presidential prerogative. And you're not the fucking president!"

Trump continued his open-mouthed roar. "You took away my authority!" he said.

Esper, looking straight at the president, chose a calm, even tone.

"Mr. President, I didn't take away your authority," he said.

"That is not your position to do that," Trump said.

"Mr. President, I didn't say it was my position. I said it was my recommendation," Esper said.

Several in the room were blown away by how viciously Trump tore into his defense secretary, but they had to give Esper credit. He sat there, leaning forward in his chair, and took it. The scene resembled a grunt in basic training getting laced by a drill sergeant. Esper didn't flinch. He still held the dark-blue folder containing the Afghanistan briefing materials that he planned to present.

Once Trump's tongue-lashing had slowed, Esper tried to push back with a few facts about the law.

"Mr. President, the Insurrection Act is . . ." Esper began.

But he didn't get far. Trump went off again, this time at an even higher decibel.

Trump accused Esper of insubordination as well as several other apostasies, but the president was talking so fast it was hard to make out what they all were. He accused Esper of saying several things Esper remembered were not in the speech he himself had written.

"Mr. President, I did not say that. Here's what I said," Esper told him. He then began to repeat the correct phrases.

Trump interrupted: "No, you said it!"

Esper had brought a copy of the transcript of his remarks that morning and had highlighted key sentences. When the president again insisted, Esper pulled the transcript out of his jacket, reached over to the Resolute Desk, and slid the paper directly under his nose.

"Mr. President, here's what I said," Esper said.

Arms folded, Trump looked down at the paper. He

didn't appear to read it. But he fell silent for a moment. Then another complaint came to him.

"You did it during the hearing!" Trump said.

Esper looked confused. **What hearing?** He would later learn the president was talking about a Senate Judiciary Committee hearing that Chairman Lindsey Graham had held that morning to highlight the FBI's alleged abuse of power for investigating Trump and his campaign in 2016. The president thought Esper had coordinated his news conference to distract from press coverage of the hearing, which Trump was counting on for good talking points for his reelection campaign.

Everyone in the room was silent. Once Trump's latest explosion subsided, they went to the Situation Room for the Afghanistan briefing. As they left the White House that afternoon, Esper told Milley it was all over.

"I'm going to get fired," Esper said. Then, a few moments later, he said, "I'm going to resign."

"Hang in there," Milley replied. "You did good. Hold your head high."

It was easy for Milley to say; his face hadn't been ripped off. Many in the Oval that day suspected that despite his anger, Trump would not actually fire Esper—not with his election only five months away, not when he needed to counter the narrative of his presidency as chaotic and dysfunctional in the midst of several crises. David Urban, an outside political adviser to Trump who was close to top Pentagon officials, and whom Trump had appointed to West Point's board of visitors, called Milley that afternoon.

"Esper really fucked up today. He was trying to fix the situation and he made it far worse," Urban said, noting that the defense secretary had angered Trump with his attempt to explain his Insurrection Act comments. But, Urban added, "Look, the president clearly can't fire him right now because the world's a tinderbox. Everything's too volatile."

Ever since Trump's campaign ground to a halt in March because of the pandemic, the president had been itching to return to the trail. He missed his Make America Great Again rallies, which were re-branded "Keep America Great" for his reelection. He missed having the big stage all to himself, the bright lights on him, the sea of red-capped fans hanging on to his every word. MAGA rallies fed his soul.

Watching the coverage of thousands of people marching in cities across America, Trump thought this could be the green light to restart his rallies, ir-respective of his own government's recommendations against mass gatherings. So he called Brad Parscale.

"I see all these people out there," Trump told his campaign manager. "Why can't we do rallies if they do these protests?"

"We can get away with it if we do it outside," Parscale said. "Let's call them protests."

Staging a political rally during the pandemic carried

significant risks. It would be fresh evidence that the president was not taking the virus seriously. Then there was the actual risk that he or his supporters might get infected. What if his rallies became super-spreader events? But the president wanted to hold a rally, and Parscale knew he wouldn't be able to stop him, so he got to work planning one. He thought first of Florida, a critical battleground state, where the Republican governor, Ron DeSantis, had some of the nation's most lax coronavirus policies.

Parscale suggested an outdoor rally at the Florida State Fairgrounds in Tampa where some small measure of social distancing would be possible. "If you really want people, let's do a tailgate in Tampa," he told Trump. "Let's do a giant tailgate with people having parties in the back of their cars, twelve feet apart."

"No, I don't want to do that," Trump said. He wanted the image of a packed crowd, not people spread far apart.

Then Parscale proposed an outdoor rally in Pensacola, where the ocean breeze might help cut into Florida's oppressive heat and humidity this time of year. He got an initial sign-off from DeSantis, but then the governor appealed directly to the president. DeSantis talked Trump out of holding his first rally during the pandemic in Pensacola by arguing that doing so would kill his chances of winning Florida. The governor suggested Trump and his team find another state to host them.

Parscale later ran into Pence in the hallway outside

the Oval Office. Who better to advise on which state to hold a rally than the head of the coronavirus task force?

"Sir, what's the most open state to have an indoor rally?" Parscale asked.

Pence's answer was easy: "Oklahoma."

Parscale called Governor Kevin Stitt, a Republican, who gave his blessing. "Yeah, come on," Stitt said.

Parscale presented the plan to Trump in the Map Room of the White House. Pence was there, as were Meadows, Jared Kushner, and a handful of other advisers. Most of them pushed Trump to do the Oklahoma rally outdoors, where the virus spread much less easily. But the president was adamant about doing it indoors. He wanted to convince the country that the threat of the virus was gone, that it finally was safe to fully reopen, congregate en masse, and return to normal.

"This is a bad idea," Parscale told Trump. "Sir, you don't know if people will show up. I was in the airport this morning at DCA and was the only person there."

He pulled out his cell phone to show Trump a photo he had taken of the nearly empty terminal at Washington's Reagan National Airport. The president snapped.

"You don't know that people won't show up," he said.

"I don't know," Parscale replied. "That's the point."

"They'll show up for me," Trump insisted. "They're not going to believe this virus stuff."

Nearly three months into the pandemic, Trump

still did not appreciate the seriousness and endurance of the threat, nor the time it would take for life to return to normal. When campaign aides presented him polling data that showed his approval rating taking a hit because of his mismanagement of the pandemic, Trump would say, "Fucking virus!" He had become conspiratorial in his mindset about COVID-19, telling Parscale that the continuation of public health restrictions into the summer was in part an elaborate plot to keep him from holding rallies and therefore deny him a second term.

"People will show up," Trump told Parscale.

"Okay, I'll do it," the campaign manager said. "I'll have to go all-out."

There was a curious presence in the Map Room that day. Mike Lindell, the founder and chief executive of MyPillow, was visiting from his home in Minnesota. MyPillow was one of the biggest advertisers on Fox News, and Lindell was the product's on-camera pitchman. The jingle went, **For the best night's sleep in the whole wide world, visit MyPillow dot com.** Over the years, Lindell had garnered a lot of facetime with Trump via the television screen. It didn't hurt that he was an outspoken Trump booster and a minor celebrity at MAGA rallies.

Trump had come to believe that Parscale's television advertising strategy was flawed. He didn't think the campaign was placing ads smartly, and he thought MyPillow had great rates from Fox. In the Map Room meeting, Trump suggested that Lindell might do a superior job and asked him to take over the Trump campaign's TV ads. Unwilling to cede control over the campaign's ads, with millions of dollars at stake for himself and other consultants, Parscale said, "Let's compete."

Turning to Kushner, who controlled all major decisions on the campaign, Parscale said, "Jared, give us a hundred thousand dollars—fifty thousand dollars to my company and fifty thousand dollars to MyPillow's company—and have the ads on Fox say, 'If you're going to support Donald Trump, grab your phone now and dial 88022 now.' Prospecting commercials. See which one gets more sign-ups for less cost."

Off they went. After the ads ran, it turned out Parscale's ad generated more responses, by a large margin, and Kushner convinced the president to drop the idea of outsourcing ads to Lindell.

One of the president's advisers remarked later, "Trump is so bad at marketing, you don't understand. He's great at marketing ideas, great at branding— unbelievable brander. Obviously great at messaging because he's the best gaslighter in history. But horrible at how marketing works—how to buy TV ads, how digital works. He doesn't understand."

On June 8, Francis Collins was working at the NIH when he got a strange message from the White House summoning him to meet with Trump later that day. There was no agenda, and as Collins made his way downtown from his Bethesda offices, he could only wonder, **What is this all about?**

The subject on Trump's mind was hydroxy-chloroquine, which had become a personal obsession and was then under review by the FDA. The antimalarial drug was untested as a treatment for COVID-19, the FDA had warned against its use outside of hospitals, and a study in **The Journal of American Medical Association** had shown it was ineffective against the virus and associated with cardiac problems. Still, Trump believed it to be a "game changer," as he put it back in March—so much so that in mid-May, after the corona-virus outbreak at the White House, the president had announced he was taking hydroxychloroquine for two weeks as a prophylactic.

When Collins arrived in the Oval Office on June 8, Trump immediately set out to compel the NIH di-rector to see hydroxychloroquine as he did: a magical cure-all. The president offered up firsthand evidence.

"Let me just get Jack Nicklaus on the phone," Trump said. "He'll tell you what happened."

Nicklaus, eighty, a champion golfer nicknamed "The Golden Bear" who spent a lot of time in the Palm Beach area, was an old friend of Trump's. Trump asked his assistant to get Nicklaus on the phone, and for half an hour or so the golfer talked on speakerphone to Trump and Collins about how he and his wife, Barbara, had had COVID-19 in March. He said the president had urged him to take hydroxychloroquine, which they did, and they had recovered. The conversation was surreal.

After the call with Nicklaus ended, Collins told Trump, "Anecdotes where people draw a cause-and-effect conclusion are dangerous. They have led us down the wrong path for medical issues for centuries. We don't want to make that mistake here. I'm glad Jack Nicklaus got better. I'm glad his wife got better. I'm glad you think that this has been helpful. But Mr. President, the data, when you look at it in a rigorous way, does not support this."

Trump was unpersuaded. He wasn't completely sold on the scientific process already underway to assess the drug—not when his friend Jack had a story to tell.

A week later, on June 15, the FDA revoked its emergency use authorization of the drug. The FDA announced that, based on emerging scientific data, chloroquine and hydroxychloroquine were unlikely to be effective in treating COVID-19 and that there were potentially serious side effects, including adverse cardiac events, associated with the drug.

As it did in many institutions, George Floyd's killing forced an uncomfortable racial reckoning in the military. In early June, Pentagon leaders decided to do something about the use of Confederate symbols, which were seen as perpetuating racism. The Marine Corps became the first service to prohibit the Confederate battle flag from being hung, while the army considered renaming ten bases honoring Confederate generals. That list included three of the five most populous bases: Fort Bragg in North Carolina, Fort Hood in Texas, and Fort Benning in Georgia.

As momentum grew among advocacy groups to change the names of the bases, Trump called Milley at home one night. It was late, about 10:00, and Milley was in bed at the chairman's official residence, high on a hilltop at Fort Myer in Arlington, Virginia, overlooking Washington's monuments to democracy and valiant soldiers.

"General, what do you think about renaming these Confederate bases?" Trump asked.

"Mr. President, I think it's absolutely the right thing to do," Milley said, according to an account of the conversation he shared with aides.

"But my base, my base . . ." Trump said, referring to his political base and his assumption that his supporters would oppose the renaming.

"Mr. President, I don't know anything about your base," Milley replied. "But we should rename these bases."

A few days later, in the Oval Office, Milley had an unrelated meeting with the president and a group of other advisers, including Pence, Esper, Meadows, O'Brien, Keith Kellogg, Pat Cipollone, and Stephen Miller. Trump shifted the topic to the debate, now raging in public. He put Milley on the spot.

"General, what do you think about the Confederate bases?" Trump asked, knowing his answer already but seeming to hope the chairman might have had a change of position since their last conversation.

"Mr. President, are you sure that you want me to answer that?" Milley said. "Do you want to hear it again?"

Trump said he did.

"Okay, I think you should change the names of all the Confederate bases," Milley said. "I don't think Confederate flags and statues should be in the public space. These guys were traitors. Thirty-eight of them were indicted for treason. And more importantly, Mr. President, they lost the war. They're losers, Mr. President. They betrayed the country. We absolutely should change the names of those bases."

Trump fell silent.

"I know that opinion is different from many people in this room," Milley said. "Mr. Meadows over here is from North Carolina. He firmly believes the opposite. But I wear Union blue. We won the war. It's over."

Trump went around the room asking others for their advice.

"Sir, I think it's a mistake," Kellogg said. "I'm a Fort Bragg, North Carolina, guy. Ninety-nine percent of the soldiers at Fort Bragg couldn't tell you who Fort Bragg was named after. They don't know who the hell Braxton Bragg is. It's a power-projection platform of the army, and when people say they're from Bragg, it means a lot."

Kellogg continued. "This 'cancel culture' is a mistake," he said. "I don't know where it ends. This reminds me of what the Taliban did when they blew up statues. You start destroying your culture. Learn from your history. Nobody says American history is perfect, but learn from it."

At one point in the discussion, Milley said, "Robert E. Lee was a traitor." That set Kellogg off.

"Wait a second, Mark," Kellogg said. He pointed to the White House residence out the window of the Oval Office. "That discussion was held over one hundred and fifty years ago. Andrew Johnson wanted to court-martial Robert E. Lee for being a traitor and U. S. Grant told him, 'You do that, you find a new general. Let him go home.' Mark, you better learn your history, because that decision was made a long time ago."

Kellogg added, "Mark, what happens when they want to take away one of the largest monuments in Arlington National Cemetery, the [Confederate] Memorial? What about disinterring the Confederates? Where does this all end?"

Milley responded by drawing Trump into the conversation.

"Mr. President, as you well know, all the graves in Arlington are in rows, except those Confederates, and they're in a circle with their names facing inward," he said. "And the symbolism of that, Mr. President, is they turned their back on the union and the Constitution. They turned their back at the

272 I ALONE CAN FIX IT

time, they turned their back in death, and they will be traitors for eternity."

Trump looked at Milley with an expression of canine curiosity. He merely said, "Okay."

Trump's advisers concluded that the president didn't really care about whether military bases were named after Confederate generals. He had no ideology, much less a nuanced understanding of history and the nation's sordid legacy on race. All he cared about was making sure the people who voted for him in 2016 would vote for him again in November. He was a transactional president. After all, renaming military bases would go against his well-established assault on political correctness.

On June 10, Trump announced a decision on Twitter: "These Monumental and very Powerful Bases have become part of a Great American Heritage, and a history of Winning, Victory, and Freedom. The United States of America trained and deployed our HEROES on these Hallowed Grounds, and won two World Wars. Therefore, my Administration will not even consider the renaming of these Magnificent and Fabled Military Installations. . . . Our history as the Greatest Nation in the World will not be tampered with. Respect our Military!"

The Lafayette Square incident on June 1 reverberated deeply in the military community. In the days afterward, retired generals and admirals spoke out against Trump's efforts to politicize the armed forces. No one felt the heat more acutely than Milley, who, unlike Esper, had not yet publicly explained his actions and values.

One of Milley's predecessors as chairman, retired Navy Admiral Mike Mullen, wrote on June 2 that he felt compelled to finally break his silence about Trump's leadership. "Whatever Trump's goal in conducting his visit, he laid bare his disdain for the rights of peaceful protest in this country, gave succor to the leaders of other countries who take comfort in our domestic strife, and risked further politicizing the men and women of our armed forces," Mullen wrote in **The Atlantic.**

A bigger shoe dropped the next day, June 3, when Trump's first defense secretary, retired Marine Corps General Jim Mattis, finally went public with his disdain for the president. Mattis had long insisted it would be improper for him to criticize a sitting president, but after seeing military personnel on the scene as officers forcibly cleared peaceful protesters at Lafayette Square, he decided he had a duty to speak out.

"Donald Trump is the first president in my lifetime who does not try to unite the American people—does not even pretend to try. Instead, he tries to divide us," Mattis wrote, also in **The Atlantic.** "We are witnessing the consequences of three years of this deliberate effort. We are witnessing the consequences of three years without mature leadership."

Mattis also criticized Milley for having jeopardized the military's independence when he walked, in battle fatigues, with the president. The nonpartisan military that Mattis had served for nearly five decades was being used as decoration for a political photo op, and the president was using the leaders who replaced him at the Defense Department to further divide the nation, Mattis fumed to friends.

"When I joined the military, some 50 years ago, I swore an oath to support and defend the Constitution," Mattis wrote. "Never did I dream that troops taking that same oath would be ordered under any circumstance to violate the Constitutional rights of their fellow citizens—much less to provide a bizarre photo op for the elected commander-in-chief, with military leadership standing alongside."

Mattis nursed a grudge against Milley. He believed Milley had flattered and humored the president to get his job. Mattis had wanted Trump to nominate his ally, General David Goldfein, then the Air Force chief of staff, as chairman when the position opened in 2018 with the retirement of General Joseph Dunford. But when Trump interviewed Milley, they hit it off and the president offered him the job on the spot. Milley believed Mattis held it against him; several times since then, Mattis had given him the cold shoulder, literally greeting others in a line but bypassing Milley.

It irked Milley, as well as Esper, that Mattis had not called them first to share his concerns before writing a public condemnation. Like Esper, Milley also knew that he was going to have to say something to correct the horrible impression that walk had left. Milley was a devout Catholic and was raised to believe that the only way to recover from a mistake was to confess.

Milley had often remarked to others that the United States had the only military in the world whose members do not take an oath to a monarch, leader, tribe, religion, or country. They take an oath to the Constitution—a living, dynamic document—and to the idea that American citizens are born free and equal and can rise to the level of their merit, skills, and hard work.

He was scheduled to speak to the graduating class of the National Defense University on June 10 and thought that would be the perfect venue to confess his mistake. He had a commencement address ready to go, but starting the night of June 1, he began re-writing most of it. He sat with a legal pad in the living room of his Fort Myer home and scribbled out an apology. Milley wanted to speak in a way that didn't appear political, and to address racism head-on. He asked a Black executive officer to help him with the speech.

Milley did not give Trump, Meadows, or even Esper any advance warning. After all, this speech wasn't going to be about them. It was going to be about the military's values, systemic racism, and the Constitution. **If they want to fire me,** he thought, **I don't care. Screw it.**

Addressing the graduates, Milley said the protests reflected not just one man's death but "centuries of injustice toward African Americans."

"What we are seeing is the long shadow of our original sin in Jamestown four hundred and one years ago, liberated by the Civil War, but not equal in the eyes of the law until one hundred years later in 1965," Milley said. "We are still struggling with racism, and we have much work to do. Racism and discrimination, structural preferences, patterns of mistreatment, unspoken and unconscious bias have no place in America, and they have no place in our Armed Forces."

Milley then addressed June 1.

"As many of you saw, the results of the photograph of me in Lafayette Square last week, that sparked a national debate about the role of the military in civil society," Milley told the graduates. "I should not have been there. My presence in that moment, and in that environment, created the perception of the military involved in domestic politics."

After Milley finished speaking, Meadows called.

"You should've cleared that," he said.

"Well, Chief, I don't think so," Milley said. "It wasn't about the White House. Listen to the whole speech. It's a good speech."

"It looks like you're opposing the president," Meadows said.

"I'm not opposing the president at all," Milley said. "This was about me going to confession, Chief. This is about no politicization of the military. Chief, we should not politicize the military."

Kellogg had seen the apology speech as well and called Milley up to offer an apology of his own.

"I feel so bad," Kellogg said. "I knew what was going to happen. I knew that was a political event. I knew what they were orchestrating.

"Shit," Kellogg added. "Mark, you shouldn't have been there. And it's my fault. . . . I'm kicking myself because I knew better. I should've not let you do it. I should've said, 'Mark, you're the only one in uniform. Go get lost.'"

Milley shook his head.

"I appreciate that, but what's done is done," he said. "At the end of the day, I own it."

A couple of days later, Milley met with Trump in the Oval. He could tell the president was furious. There were other people in the room, but Trump focused on Milley.

"Why did you apologize?" he asked. "Apologies are a sign of weakness."

"Mr. President, not where I come from they're not," Milley replied. "The way I was brought up is, when you make a mistake you apologize, and you get it over with."

"What's wrong with walking with your president?" Trump asked.

"Mr. President, this has nothing to do with you," Milley said. "This had to do with me and the uniform and not politicizing the uniform. I'm not apologizing for you. I was apologizing for me."

Trump gave Milley a quizzical look.

"Mr. President, I don't expect you to get that," Milley said. "But I'm a soldier, and I can never allow the politicization of this uniform. I can't do it. It's wrong. And that's why I apologized."

After the meeting wrapped, Milley and Meadows went to the chief of staff's office for a heart-to-heart.

"Chief, never again—never," Milley said. "We're not politicizing this uniform. We're not politicizing this military. It's wrong. It's way fucking wrong. It's had a dramatic effect on the military. And it will have a dramatic effect on you guys."

Meadows shook his head and said using the military wasn't political—and indeed was appropriate in some situations.

"I'm a professional. I owe you professional and candid feedback," Milley said. "You're chief of staff of the White House. And I'm giving it to you right now.

"You don't want the military in politics," Milley said. "It's fundamental to the survival of the republic."

Something else changed for Milley after June 1. That summer, he kept hearing Trump warn that he might not trust the November election results, that if he did not win by a landslide, the vote was rigged. Milley told aides that he had reached out to a trusted confidant soon after Lafayette Square. He had a plan, and he needed someone to hold him accountable to it.

"I have four tasks from now until the twentieth of January, and I'm going to accomplish my mission," Milley told this confidant, referring to the Inauguration in 2021. "Mission One is to get us from now until the election without U.S. troops on the streets of America killing Americans. Mission Two is no overseas war with Iran. Mission Three is maintaining the integrity of the U.S. military. Mission Four is maintaining my own personal integrity.

"That's my mission and I commit to you that mission," he continued. "And our mission is to ensure the United States of America has a free and fair election with no U.S. military involvement whatsoever."

Nine

A Sea of Empty Seats

E ver since the release of the Mueller report in 2019, which he had overseen a few months after becoming attorney general, Bill Barr had been labeled as a puppet of Trump. Barr bristled at the notion that he let the president call any prosecutorial decisions at the Justice Department. In reality, however, Trump didn't need to exercise control over the department by fiat or suggestion. Barr was a political operator and a lifelong conservative, dedicated to empowering Trump and advancing the Republican cause as long as it was reasonable, lawful, and part of his job. Barr didn't need instructions from Trump because he was already unapologetic in his belief that every Cabinet member should be trying to help re-elect the president.

In 2020, Barr was on a glide path to exerting more control over major U.S. Attorney's Offices around the country, those that his top aides called "offices of consequence." The two most important were in New York and Washington, in that order. These offices also happened to have most of the cases that mattered personally to the president. Barr had pushed out Jessie Liu as the U.S. attorney in Washington in January and replaced her with a loyalist. By mid-June, Barr decided it was time to pull the trigger in the Southern District of New York, too. The office had been investigating Trump's 2016 campaign, his businesses, and his longtime ally and personal lawyer, Rudy Giuliani. Anything could happen in any of these cases at any time to wreak havoc on the president's reelection campaign—as Trump was all too aware.

"That office has a bunch of [partisan prosecutors] who are after me," Trump once told Barr.

Since becoming attorney general, Barr had clashed several times with the U.S. attorney for the Southern District, Geoffrey Berman. Barr didn't like Berman's proclivity for pushback against directives from "Main Justice," as the Washington headquarters was known. And Berman didn't like how Barr second-guessed his office's handling of criminal investigations connected to the president. Barr wanted to be personally briefed on investigations that held some importance—or liability—for Trump. Berman concluded that the attorney general was playing the role of fixer for the president.

Their most heated dispute had come in June 2019, when Barr had urged Berman to drop the prosecutions of two Turkish defendants accused of using Halkbank, a Turkish bank, in a scheme to bypass U.S. sanctions against Iran. Turkish president Recep Erdogan had repeatedly pressed Trump to drop the case, and Trump had been eager to acquiesce, even though doing so would undermine U.S. national security interests in the Middle East. Trump had significant business interests in Turkey—his company made roughly $2.6 million a year from properties there—but he also felt a brotherly bond with Erdogan, telling aides he liked his authoritarian strength and Darth Vader–like baritone voice. Berman told Barr he wouldn't drop the charges midinvestigation without asking those charged to cooperate in the probe. "This is not how we do things in the Southern District," Berman said.

In June 2020, Berman again defied Main Justice. Barr's deputies were asking Berman to sign a letter criticizing New York mayor Bill de Blasio for his enforcement of social distancing rules to curb the spread of COVID-19. They wanted Berman to join the head of the department's civil rights division, Eric Dreiband, in objecting to the mayor endorsing large George Floyd protests while curtailing or banning religious gatherings—an effort seemingly designed to curry favor with Christian conservatives. On June 18, as Barr's office prepared to release the letter, Berman said it was a political "stunt" that would unnecessarily provoke city leaders, and he refused to sign.

Barr was scheduled to fly to New York on June 19 to tape a sit-down interview with Fox Business anchor

Maria Bartiromo. He decided to fix his problem in the Southern District while he was in town. On June 18, Barr's scheduler emailed Berman to say the boss wanted to meet him for lunch the next day at the Pierre hotel. The email didn't say what Barr wanted to discuss, and Berman didn't ask. But he was pretty sure the conversation, like most of his with Barr recently, would be unpleasant.

Berman had a few friends at Main Justice who had warned him that Barr was a bully who rammed his decisions down the throats of department chiefs, many of whom didn't dare to speak up for fear of hurting their careers. Berman knew Liu had felt browbeaten and mistreated by Barr; she called Berman to seek his advice when Barr and his then chief of staff, Brian Rabbitt, were pressuring her to step down.

"Tell Brian to go fuck himself," Berman counseled Liu. "Then go on vacation."

They had both chuckled grimly. But Liu relented, surrendering her post within a few weeks. Now, as he awaited their lunch date at the Pierre, Berman wondered: **What did Barr want?** Barr wanted precisely what he had done with Liu: to make sure the U.S. attorney was someone more firmly in his—and consequently the president's—court. Barr saw an opportunity to "upgrade" in the Southern District, as he put it to others, and to let Trump scratch an itch. Barr hoped by getting rid of the Southern District's chief, he might hold the president off from terminating other officials, such as Chris Wray at the FBI.

Barr had learned that Jay Clayton, the chairman of the Securities and Exchange Commission and a golfing buddy of Trump's, wanted to transfer to New York so he could get back to his family there. Barr's attitude was that he had better seize opportunities when they came along. Clayton was available. It seemed like ideal timing to make a switch. Barr didn't know of any imminent actions in Southern District cases that critics could argue he was trying to steer or squelch. This could work out elegantly, he thought. He'd offer Berman a job as head of the civil division or as assistant attorney general, and Barr would get in Clayton a prosecutor he could rely on in an important spot. Barr wasn't bothered a bit by Clayton's lack of prosecutorial experience; Barr had none himself when he became attorney general the first time.

On Friday, June 19, when Berman arrived at Barr's suite at the Pierre, he walked into a small living area just off the bedroom, with two chairs facing each other. There were sandwiches set out on a table. Barr was in a calm, almost placid mood. His voice was monotone. They were in a confined indoor space, but Barr did not wear a mask. Berman removed his own mask, feeling he didn't have a choice.

Barr got straight to the point.

"We want you to take another job," he said. Barr told Berman he could head the civil rights division.

As he later confided in others and described to the House Judiciary Committee, Berman was shocked, and immediately thought of how disgracefully Liu had been shoved out the door. He thought to himself: **This is not going to happen to the Southern District.** He made a point of not raising his voice; he didn't want to appear rattled. But in a burst, he told Barr he would not resign. Barr warned Berman he would be fired if he didn't leave on his own accord, and that would look bad on his résumé. He urged Berman to think about it and asked for his cell phone number.

"I'm going to call you later tonight," Barr said.

"I'm always open to a phone call," Berman said. "But I want your expectations to be realistic. I'm not going to resign."

After forty-five minutes, Berman said he had to go, though neither man had touched the sandwiches. Immediately afterward, Berman called his private attorneys and told them what Barr had demanded. Berman explained his legal theory that Barr couldn't remove him because he had been appointed by a panel of federal judges, after the Trump administration did not put a confirmed nominee in the job. Legally, Berman argued, only the court could remove him, or the president. He hadn't told Barr this, but he believed it was his protection.

"I may very well be fired in the next twenty-four hours and I want paper put together to oppose it," Berman told the lawyers, who got to work on an emergency motion they could file in court if necessary.

At about 7:20 p.m., Berman realized someone with a 202 area code had called his phone much earlier, and dialed the number. It was Barr. He offered the U.S. attorney what seemed like a shiny bauble.

"How would you like to be chairman of the SEC?" Barr asked.

Berman thought, **Wow. He really wants me to resign.**

"My position hasn't changed," Berman told Barr. "I want to talk to my staff about all this."

"Why do you have to talk to them?" Barr asked. "This is about you."

"This is about the office," Berman said.

"The change is going to be made, Geoff," Barr said.

"I need to think about it until Monday," Berman said. "Give me until Monday."

Barr said he'd call Berman on Sunday. But when he hung up, he sensed Berman was secretly playing him—or "grin-fucking" him, as Barr would later describe it to others. Instinctively, Barr began plotting how to beat Berman to the punch.

Just after 9:00 that night, Berman and his wife, Joanne Schwartz, were about to pull into their driveway in New Jersey, returning home from their day in the city. Berman was driving and Schwartz noticed her phone was beeping and glowing with text messages and emails from friends. "Oh, I'm so sorry," and "What happened?," they said. What in the world were they talking about? She googled and found Barr had issued a news release announcing that Berman was stepping down from his post as U.S. attorney. The statement also said that Trump planned to nominate

Clayton to replace him, and that Craig Carpenito, the U.S. attorney in New Jersey, would immediately step into the job until the Senate confirmed Clayton.

It had all come to a boil much faster than Berman had expected. And it all confirmed his worst suspicions, the U.S. attorney would tell his deputies that night: Barr wanted someone he could control in the run-up to the election.

After conferring with his aides, Berman decided to publicly punch back at Barr. He used the precise language of the obstruction of justice statute, to emphasize that Barr's efforts to remove him should not impede or interfere with ongoing criminal investigations. Sharing drafts back and forth with his staff for the next hour, he released a statement after 11:00 that night.

"I learned in a press release from the Attorney General tonight that I was 'stepping down' as United States Attorney," Berman said. "I have not resigned, and have no intention of resigning, my position, to which I was appointed by the Judges of the United States District Court for the Southern District of New York. I will step down when a presidentially appointed nominee is confirmed by the Senate. Until then, our investigations will move forward without delay or interruption. I cherish every day that I work with the men and women of this Office to pursue justice without fear or favor—and intend to ensure that this Office's important cases continue unimpeded."

Berman knew he would lose his job: you couldn't

call the attorney general a liar and expect to show up for work the next day like everything was normal. But he was going to at least try to stop this hostile take-over of the Southern District. If anyone monkeyed around with the Southern District's ongoing cases, Berman figured, it would come back to haunt both Barr and Trump.

The next day, June 20, Barr called Trump and gave him the rundown of what had happened in New York. He told Trump he wanted to remove Berman, but he would now need the president's authorization.

"Once I've told [Berman] I'm going to do this, I have to carry it out," Barr told Trump. "I have to follow through."

Trump didn't want his firing of Berman to create a bigger news story, but he understood Barr's position and agreed. In a stinging letter he publicly released after 3:00 that afternoon, Barr notified Berman and the world that Trump had removed him from his post. Barr also scoffed at the implication that his personnel move threatened the progress of important cases.

"Your statement also wrongly implies that your continued tenure in the office is necessary to ensure that cases now pending in the Southern District of New York are handled appropriately. This is obviously false," Barr wrote.

Berman was out, but Barr had suffered a loss in this public dogfight. His elegant plan to install Clayton came crashing down around him. Senator Lindsey Graham, chairman of the Judiciary Committee and usually a reliable Trump ally, made clear that Berman's removal was a surprise to him and said he would follow Senate tradition and give New York's two senators—both Democrats—veto power over the nomination. Senators Chuck Schumer and Kirsten Gillibrand said Clayton shouldn't be considered, and that Barr's removal of Berman needed to be investigated.

Barr abandoned his original plans to bring in a political loyalist and appointed Berman's deputy, Audrey Strauss, as the acting U.S. attorney—a victory for career prosecutors in the office and precisely what Berman had requested.

"The moment Berman started objecting, then the plan should've been, 'Never mind, back off,'" said one senior administration official. "But the A.G. pushed ahead with it with disastrous consequences."

By the start of summer, the doctors guiding the administration's coronavirus response felt that their updates were falling on deaf ears. Robert Redfield and others realized the number one, the number two, and the number three priorities for the administration were Trump's reelection campaign. That realization hit home when the White House announced that the president would resume his campaign rallies, starting on June 20 in Tulsa—at an indoor venue, no less, the Bank of Oklahoma Center. Redfield sought out Sean Conley and urged him to dissuade Trump from going.

"This is not in the president's interest," Redfield told the president's physician. "You're putting him at risk. You are his doctor and he can campaign just as easily on Zoom in a way that doesn't put him or others at risk."

Conley sounded somewhat defeated. He was up against a president—and a team of advisers— determined to have Trump connect with his voters. He said something similar to what he had told Redfield in the spring about getting Trump to wear a mask. Doctors try to do their best to give good advice, and sometimes the patient still refuses to take it.

At the president's insistence, Trump campaign aides pressed ahead with the Tulsa rally. Their top priority was to ensure a capacity crowd of nineteen thousand people in the arena. Brad Parscale, who earlier had warned that people might not show up, wasn't going to leave anything to chance, so he authorized roughly $1 million in campaign advertising to drum up a crowd.

The early feedback was positive. Tens of thousands of people signed up for free tickets within hours of the campaign's June 10 announcement of the rally, and the RSVPs kept flowing in from there, totaling hundreds of thousands. The data showed that roughly 150,000 people who lived within one hundred miles of Tulsa had signed up. In the worst-case scenario, Parscale thought, a small fraction of them would actually show up and the arena still would be packed.

The RSVPs kept growing and Parscale, eager to

please Trump, personally kept the president updated on the attendance estimates. On June 15, the campaign manager announced that one million people had signed up for tickets. The tweet was based on internal data but sent impulsively. Parscale would come to regret it.

Meanwhile, officials in Oklahoma were worried about the massive gathering. Tulsa Health Department director Bruce Dart warned publicly that the rally could be a superspreader event. "It's the perfect storm of potential over-the-top disease transmission," Dart said. "It's a perfect storm that we can't afford to have." He urged Tulsa mayor G. T. Bynum to try to postpone the event to a safer time when coronavirus case counts were lower. But the mayor, a Republican, decided to let Trump's event go forward, inaccurately claiming that he did not have the power to stop it. Dart found himself a target of hate mail, threats, and invective from across the political spectrum. Trump opponents warned him that there would be "blood on your hands" if he let the event go forward; Trump supporters warned him that they "pay your salary just as much, if not more, than Trump haters."

A group of Tulsa residents tried and failed to block the Trump rally, arguing in court that the event would dramatically hike the number of coronavirus cases in the area. But the Oklahoma Supreme Court ruled that the Trump campaign had a right to hold the rally with a set of safety precautions: Event staff had to check the temperatures of rally attendees and then provide masks and hand sanitizer for those who wanted them.

At the event site, Trump's advance staff put the finishing touches on the arena and, at Parscale's direction, built a massive stage outside with a jumbotron for an expected overflow crowd of many thousands to watch Trump's speech live. Trump dubbed this rally the "Great American Comeback" and banked on it breathing new life into his campaign. A leased plane flew in a host of surrogates, and film crews were also en route to record soaring moments for campaign ads.

Elsewhere in the country, the Tulsa event seemed an irresponsible spectacle. As Tony Dokoupil asked Senator Jim Lankford, a Republican from Oklahoma, on **CBS This Morning,** "Nobody in this country is holding the kind of indoor, large gathering that the president is planning for tomorrow—not megachurches, not sports leagues—so why put public safety at risk for a political rally?"

Lankford made the argument Trump had been making, which is that thousands of people had been gathering at Black Lives Matter protests, so why can't they gather at a MAGA rally, too?

"This is a gathering like protests, like other events, like shopping, like malls that are open," Lankford told Dokoupil. The senator urged that high-risk individuals take care of themselves and reminded viewers that they could attend a watch party outside the arena or watch on television at home.

"This is an optional event, not a required event by any means," Lankford said.

Tensions were high in Tulsa. The rally had originally been scheduled for June 19 but was changed to June 20 after a backlash for having it on the Juneteenth holiday celebrating the emancipation of slaves. Concerned about violence between Trump supporters and Black Lives Matter protesters, Tulsa police and the Oklahoma National Guard locked down wide swaths of downtown surrounding the arena. Local news coverage played up the possibility of coronavirus spread as well as violent clashes among pro- and anti-Trump demonstrators. Navigating the security perimeter to enter the arena would be difficult, and the forecast was 84 degrees and humid.

As was the case for any presidential event, a large coterie of Secret Service agents, campaign advance staff, and other personnel flew to Tulsa a few days ahead of the rally, mapping out every move Trump would make on the ground and planning the security needed to protect him. In addition, campaign aides erected medical tents around the arena, where staff and volunteers would conduct temperature checks and distribute PPE to those who asked, and doctors and nurses would be on standby to address any emergencies.

On June 20 around noon, hours before the evening rally, under white tents in the shadow of the arena, a group of contract nurses tested campaign staffers,

event officials, and other VIPs for possible coronavirus infection. It was a basic safeguard for the indoor rally, considering the proximity of attendees to
the president. In just two hours of testing, six people
tested positive. One was a senior Secret Service advance agent, and another was a Secret Service officer
assigned to screen rallygoers before they entered the
stadium. It shouldn't have been a shock; Secret Service
personnel rarely wore masks, even though their work
necessitated interacting with strangers. Both had attended a large planning meeting in close quarters
with campaign and other event staff the day before the rally. Dozens of other people may have also
been infected.

When the news about the positive tests was first reported that afternoon, the president was livid. Within
thirty minutes, campaign staff appeared at the nurses'
tent and interrogated the medical staff. Had any
of them discussed the results with reporters? How
had this information gotten out? The health-care
workers administering the tests were insulted. More
curious, however, they were then given a new list of
people who needed to be tested. Some staff said the
new list appeared much shorter than the original.

The campaign immediately clamped down on testing to prevent discovering who else might be infected.
Word was passed throughout the Trump team that
afternoon: remaining staff were not to get tested in
Tulsa, but rather to wait until they returned home to
headquarters in Arlington. "The president wants this

to stop," a campaign staffer told an Oklahoma VIP who had arrived to get tested.

The campaign took another step that made it even easier for the virus to spread among Trump supporters. The BOK Center had purchased twelve thousand stickers that said: "Do Not Sit Here, Please!" to block off seats inside the arena and create safe breathing distance between rallygoers. As arena staff affixed these to nearly every other seat, campaign officials directed them to stop and to remove the stickers that were already placed on chairs. Campaign staff also told arena personnel to remove signs telling attendees how to socially distance inside the building.

Aboard Air Force One on the way to Tulsa, the president received the most enraging news of all: The masses hadn't turned out. On the plane, Trump brooded over cable television footage of sparse crowds, and when he landed, he called Parscale from the Beast, the president's armored vehicle.

"Sir, it's going to be empty," Parscale told Trump.

"Why? What happened?" the president asked.

"It looks like Beirut in the eighties," Parscale said.

"What do you mean?" Trump asked.

"The army's here, the SWAT teams are here, the Secret Service has machine guns out, and you have to walk over three miles. People are passing out. It's hot," Parscale said. "Sir, this is like walking over fire to watch you, and there's just not enough of them. I'm shocked that twelve thousand people showed up. Any other rally in any other situation, with all the advertising we did, this rally would've had a hundred thousand people there easy."

Even that was an overstatement, however. The Tulsa Fire Department later estimated just 6,200 people attended. Virtually nobody was in the outdoor overflow area, where Trump had expected to pay a surprise visit to throngs of supporters who couldn't make it into the packed arena.

Trump put on his game face and strode out onto the big stage in the less-than-half-full BOK Center. After a 110-day, coronavirus-induced dry spell, Trump was ready to rumble. He offered no reconciliation or rapprochement over the health, economic, and racial justice crises engulfing the nation he led. The president mocked health experts and recalled, "I said to my people, 'Slow the testing down,' because as more tests were conducted, more infections were discovered. He uttered a racist term, "Kung Flu," in his list of alternative names for COVID-19. And, referring to the debate over removing Confederate monuments, he cast himself as a protector of "our heritage."

But the lasting takeaway from Trump's Tulsa rally was not anything the president said. It was the empty seats. An image captured by **Washington Post** photographer Jabin Botsford of a lone man holding a red "Make America Great Again" sign in his lap as he watched Trump perform from a vast sea of empty blue seats in the upper bowl of the BOK Center went viral online. The conservative Drudge Report ran the all-caps headline: MAGA LESS MEGA.

It turned out the Trump campaign appeared to have been punked into believing it had one million RSVPs. Users of the social media platform TikTok, as well as Korean pop music fan accounts, claimed to have signed up for hundreds of thousands of tickets to the rally as a prank. Of course, they had no intention of showing up.

Trump was furious. He didn't talk to Parscale for two days, and then exploded on his campaign manager. With Parscale on the phone, Trump delivered a vicious tirade from the Oval Office where other advisers were gathered to listen. He unfurled one presidential f-bomb after another.

"You fucked it up!"

"You fucked me!"

"You fucked up the whole campaign because of it!"

"The worst fucking mistake!"

Parscale sheepishly said, "Sir, there's nothing else I could've done."

The fallout was not merely political. Tulsa had experienced a sharp rise in coronavirus cases in the two days before the June 20 rally, but suffered a record-setting spike in the week that followed. Tulsa County racked up 902 new cases in the week after the event, gaining as many as 200 to 260 new cases each day. Before Trump's visit, the daily count of new cases ranged from 76 to 96. Back at Trump campaign headquarters, staff expressed dismay and fear about having been exposed to the virus. The Trump campaign contracted a medical testing company in Virginia to administer new tests for everyone. Staff were told to keep the testing location a secret, however, to avoid more bad press.

The Secret Service's field office in Tulsa, meanwhile, arranged with a local hospital to have a special testing session off-site on June 23. The session was both to determine if a slew of local agents who assisted with the rally had contracted the virus and to test some local officials who attended the event. In addition, several dozen Secret Service officers who traveled to Tulsa to help provide security and screening were instructed to self-isolate at home for two weeks because they had been exposed to coworkers who tested positive.

Among those who tested positive for coronavirus after attending the rally were Oklahoma governor Kevin Stitt and former presidential candidate Herman Cain. Stitt, who complained of feeling achy mostly, recovered. He insisted he had not contracted the virus at the president's rally, although he, like most attendees, did not wear a mask at the rally. Cain, also maskless at the rally, fell ill a few days later. He was soon hospitalized with COVID-19 and died on July 30.

Throughout the month of June, Trump grew angry and agitated watching Black Lives Matter protests take root across the country. Demonstrations in Seattle and Portland—a pair of Democrat-led cities in Democrat-led states—triggered the president, who complained that "terrorists" were allowed to run roughshod over law-abiding Americans. As he saw it, he needed to call up the cavalry as commander in chief and ride in to save the day. But neither Barr nor Pat Cipollone would green-light Trump's wishes to deploy the military to quell the civil unrest. This sparked constant tension between Trump and his attorney general and White House counsel.

Seattle's Capitol Hill neighborhood was part progressive haven and part tony enclave, with a row of multimillion-dollar houses as well as a funky entertainment district of grunge bars and coffeehouses popular with partiers. In the early days of June, though, the area's Cal Anderson Park and adjoining streets had been converted into an occupied, police-free zone by people protesting Floyd's killing. Protesters named their new camp "CHAZ," for Capitol Hill Autonomous Zone, and later "CHOP," for Capitol Hill Occupied Protest zone. CHOP started as a largely peaceful place, with speeches and music and even a group viewing of a film on systemic racism in the criminal justice system. Seattle mayor Jenny Durkan was concerned about police confronting protesters and someone getting killed, so the city monitored rather than uprooted the encampment. Police boarded up and abandoned a nearby station the week of June 8.

Watching this police retreat on television, Trump vented his disgust with the city's local leaders. On June 10, he tweeted a message to Durkan and Washington governor Jay Inslee: "Take back your city NOW. If you don't do it, I will. This is not a game. These ugly Anarchists must be stooped [**sic**] IMMEDIATELY. MOVE FAST!"

Barr had assured the president that he had a lot of faith in Seattle police chief Carmen Best, explaining to him that she was keeping a close watch on the situation, had plans to clear CHOP if necessary, and was keeping the Feds fully briefed. It's not as if federal buildings were being occupied, Barr told Trump. The situation was fairly contained.

Trump's interest in a military response flared, however, when he turned on Fox News. He brooded watching Tucker Carlson sound dire warnings on his nightly show about "the descent of our nation into chaos and craziness," which prominently featured Seattle as Exhibit A. Carlson claimed invading hordes were overtaking the city and nobody was stopping them. During his June 11 program, Carlson took a moment to jab mockingly at Trump. He said the CHOP organizers were like conquistadors who smartly seized their six-block territory as their own country. Then, Carlson said, "They built a wall around the place just like Donald Trump once said he would do."

Fox found that its reports and commentaries about unrest in Seattle and elsewhere drew sizable attention, especially when paired with ominous images of burning cars and looting rioters. On June 12, Fox's homepage featured an image of a man carrying an assault rifle in front of a Seattle storefront with shattered glass.

But the picture had been digitally altered by splicing together multiple photographic images and putting the man with the rifle—a volunteer working security, in fact—in front of a looted store. Another Fox story on Seattle unrest carried the headline CRAZY TOWN and showed a man running through a street with a car on fire behind him. The image was in fact from a different city, Minneapolis, and had been taken on May 30. When contacted by journalists about the altered or misplaced images, Fox removed them.

Still, the network's coverage—and especially Carlson's hyperbolic warnings—became a significant irritant inside the Justice Department, in no small measure because of how they shaped Trump's thinking. One top law enforcement official said Carlson "kept on waving the bloody shirt on this issue, and even when things were dying down completely, they'd find a cameraman on some street corner and put it as if the whole country was falling apart. And then Carlson started directly attacking [the Justice Department]. I couldn't tell if he was actually parroting the president or the president was parroting him."

Whether or not the images of violence were manufactured didn't matter to Trump. His supporters watching Fox believed America was burning—and the president felt political pressure to show them he was taking care of it. On June 15, Trump talked to Barr in the wake of Carlson's stinging critique. The president asked, wasn't there something he could do to show he was the boss over the protesters? Barr explained to him the state leaders had the authority to call up the National Guard, not the president.

Trump also pushed Cipollone for legal justification for a federal response, including suing Antifa. He often vented to other advisers in June about how ineffective he found Cipollone. In one such gripe session, Trump asked his assistant, Molly Michael, to call Cipollone down to the Oval from his second-floor office. The White House counsel walked in as Trump was still meeting with campaign advisers.

"Yes, Mr. President?" he asked.

Trump looked at Cipollone and said, "What have you been doing all day?"

The other advisers in the room, who had heard Trump getting himself spun up about Cipollone earlier, knew what was coming. **Oh, shit!** they thought to themselves.

"Cities are on fire," Trump yelled. "People are protesting. I want to shut it down. What do you do all day? Why hasn't this stopped. I want it stopped."

Cipollone tried to respond without telling Trump "nothing" or "no."

"Some things are going to happen. We're trying to do some things," Cipollone said, adding that he would leave and call the Justice Department.

Trump, knowing that was unlikely to get him what he wanted, just shook his head.

Over the weekend of June 20, the Capitol Hill district did in fact turn bloody. A nineteen-year-old man was shot there and died, and a thirty-three-year-old man was shot nearby and left in critical condition. For Trump, this was cause to deploy the military. For Carlson, this was an opportunity to crow. In his opening monologue on June 22, Carlson ripped into Trump for "sitting back" and watching the "catastrophe." He compared Trump's do-nothing approach to the parent of a troubled, runaway child making no effort to try to find or help them. At a moment of crisis, Carlson argued, a president needed to act.

Trump fumed at Carlson's broadside. On June 23, the president tweeted a threat to any protesters who tried to occupy the nation's capital as they had in Seattle. "There will never be an 'Autonomous Zone' in Washington, D.C., as long as I'm your President. If they try they will be met with serious force!" Twitter flagged Trump's menacing tweet for violating its standards because it threatened physical harm.

The situation in Seattle steadily grew worse by the end of the next weekend. At about 3:00 a.m. on June 29, Seattle police responding to 911 calls found a white Jeep strafed with gunfire; two teenage boys inside were taken to nearby hospitals. A sixteen-year-old was declared dead soon after arrival, while a fourteen-year-old was in critical condition. The television coverage of the bullet-riddled Jeep in Seattle got the president's attention. Over the next few days, Trump called Barr demanding a massive federal force—military or otherwise—to reclaim CHOP. The attorney general urged the president to hold off because local authorities already had assured him they soon would have the situation resolved.

On July 1, an estimated hundred police officers, wearing body armor and helmets and carrying batons, pushed into the protest zone around 5:00 a.m. Local FBI agents assisted. Soon after the park and nearby streets were fully cleared, Kayleigh McEnany strode into the press briefing room at the White House. "I am pleased to inform everyone that Seattle has been liberated," the press secretary said. "President Trump compelled action."

About a week later, Trump claimed to Fox viewers that the clearing of the CHOP zone was his doing. "One hundred percent," the president told Sean Hannity. "We were going in. We were going in very soon. We let [local officials] know that, and all of a sudden, they didn't want that, so they went in before we got there."

At the Justice Department, Barr and his aides were stunned by the brazenness of the president's claim. "It was bullshit," recalled one official.

Indeed, Durkan denied that Trump had alerted her or other local officials of an imminent federal action. "It just never happened," the mayor told **The Washington Post.** "I don't know what world he's living in."

By the end of June, the number of coronavirus cases and deaths had surged across the Sun Belt. Numbers were on the rise in so-called red states that had voted for Trump in 2016—chief among them, Arizona, Florida, and Texas. The evolving situation, coupled with his humiliating showing in Tulsa, conjured a mood of defeatism for the president as well as for those advising him.

Parscale tried to convince Trump to change course and follow the guidance of the task-force doctors. That way, if infections spread further or the death toll continued to rise, the president could shift blame to them.

"Let the doctors do the work," Parscale advised Trump. "Do whatever Fauci fucking says. Let Fauci take the hit. Don't own it.

"You're going to lose if you don't change," Parscale argued. "You're going to lose."

But Trump wanted to be in charge. "I'm doing this my own way," Trump told Parscale. "I'm going to win."

Yet around this same time, in late June, Trump confided in Kellyanne Conway that the odds were stacked heavily against him. The president simply saw no way out of the pandemic. Plus, he had growing fears about Democrats gaining an edge in mail-in balloting, which had become a popular alternative to in-person voting in many states during the primary elections that spring and, with the pandemic still raging, was poised to be the way tens of millions of Americans voted in the general election.

"There's no way we can win," Trump told Conway. "With this virus and these mail-in ballots and these lockdowns, we can't win."

Conway argued that he still could win. The reason? His opponent was Joe Biden. She and Trump agreed that he could prevail by driving a sharp contrast with Biden, highlighting his nearly five-decade political career and, with the nickname "Sleepy Joe," suggesting to voters that Biden was long past his prime.

Around this time, Chris Christie offered blunt advice to Trump about the state of the race. He told the president he was losing.

"Look, you're running the 2016 campaign again and you can't run the same campaign twice," Christie said. "It just never works. Times are different. You're different. The way people view you is different. Your opponent is different. This doesn't make any logical sense to run the same campaign. You have to run a forward-looking campaign. Incumbents who win are the ones who are talking about tomorrow, not yesterday. All you're doing is talking about yesterday and you've got to stop doing it."

Christie told Trump about a voter he ran into on the boardwalk in Asbury Park in 2013, when he was running for reelection after helping rebuild the Jersey Shore following Hurricane Sandy.

"This guy comes up to me and he says, 'So,

Governor, if I vote for you, what are you going to do?'" Christie said. "And I said, 'Well, you see what I've done. I'm rebuilding the Shore, rebuilding the state.' He goes, 'That's what I got for voting for you last time. What do I get for voting for you this time?'"

Christie told Trump, "You know, that's the way a lot of voters think. They want to know what you're going to do next. They don't want to hear what you did. They lived that and either benefited or not."

Christie advised Trump to reorient his message to voters around the future, such as casting himself as the guy to rebuild America in his second term by expanding manufacturing and repairing infrastructure. He encouraged Trump to do a "thank-you tour" across the country of hospitals, small businesses, and manufacturing plants that made PPE and ventilators.

"The public won't know what to do with Donald Trump running around saying 'thank you' to everybody—and, more importantly, Joe Biden won't know what to do," Christie said. "Right now, he's just hiding in his basement because all you're doing is insulting him. It's the same old Trump playbook. He doesn't have to respond to that, but if you start putting positive things out there, he's going to feel the need to respond. Then he's in trouble because America will not support the really left-wing Democratic agenda, and he's keeping it under the covers right now because he can. You've got to let him get that out."

Trump never ended up implementing Christie's advice.

Trump had been growing angry with the state of his campaign, and not only because he couldn't draw a crowd in Tulsa. Every single national public poll since April showed Biden beating Trump, and the surveys in June showed Biden's lead was increasing—up 10 points in a CNBC poll, up 12 in a Fox poll, up 14 points in a CNN poll.

As he often did at political low points, Trump searched for someone to blame. The easiest target was Parscale, whose rivals had told Trump his campaign manager was in over his head and mismanaging the billion-dollar campaign.

Worse, Trump was coming to believe that Parscale had gotten rich and famous at his expense. The campaign manager had become a veritable MAGA celebrity, and the president was unwilling to share even a watt of his spotlight with others. Trump had also seen a provocative commercial released in May by the Lincoln Project, an anti-Trump political action committee formed by a group of Republican Never Trump political strategists. In the ad, a woman says, "Brad is getting rich. How rich? Really rich. But don't tell Donald. He'd wonder how Brad can afford so much. A $2.4 million waterfront house in Fort Lauderdale. Two Florida condos worth almost a million each. He even has his very own yacht, a gorgeous Ferrari, a sleek Range Rover. Brad brags about using private jets. Oh my, Brad's a star! And why not? Brad's worth every dollar. Just ask him."

Trump playfully confronted Parscale about the ad. "Brad, you've got ass-slapping in your commercials," the president told him, referring to a racy snippet of the Lincoln Project ad. But in conversations with other advisers, Trump revealed he was seething mad about the wealth and notoriety Parscale had attained.

A couple of weeks after the Tulsa rally, Parscale visited the White House and met with Jared Kushner in his small office down the hallway from the Oval. Kushner and Parscale had been friends since working closely on the 2016 campaign, and Parscale had always considered Kushner his closest ally in Trump World. They spoke on the phone daily, sometimes five or six times. They had each other's backs.

This time, however, there was no sense of brotherhood between them. Kushner gave Parscale a cool, emotionless look and said matter-of-factly, "I think we're going to have to make a change."

"What do you mean a change?" Parscale asked. "With me?"

"I think the president's going to want to demote you," Kushner said.

Parscale said he refused to be demoted. He wanted to maintain his title as campaign manager.

"I either quit or get layered," he said.

"Why can't you be demoted?" Kushner asked.

"I can't be demoted," Parscale said.

The conversation ended without resolving Parscale's future.

Ten

The Skunks at the Picnic

President Trump wanted to mark Independence Day with a grand military parade down Constitution Avenue in Washington. He imagined a showcase of American might to draw masses of people to the National Mall in celebration. It would be a signal that the war with the coronavirus—the "invisible enemy," as Trump put it—had been won. A year earlier, he had hosted the "Salute to America" on July 4, 2019, which included tanks on the Mall, a flyover of fighter jets, a speech by Trump at the Lincoln Memorial, and a massive fireworks display. The event was highly controversial because of Trump's use of military assets, but the president wanted to do it again—only much bigger and better.

Mark Esper and Mark Milley only found out about Trump's 2020 plans a few weeks before July 4, fairly late in the planning stages. Mark Meadows and his staff had gone directly to the military's Northern Command to call up more than 70 military aircraft, including fighter jets, as well as bombers and helicopters, to fly over the city and even the White House. The plan also included tanks and other armored vehicles on the White House's South Lawn. Both Esper and Milley were dumbstruck. They strongly opposed using the military as props in Trump's political show once again. It was a waste of money, for one, but it also smacked of authoritarianism. "It's going to look like Berlin" in the 1930s, Esper remarked to associates. He complained to Milley that Trump and Meadows appeared to have learned nothing from the militarization of Lafayette Square on June 1. Milley and Esper were determined not to allow a repeat—certainly not in an election year.

"We cannot do this," Milley said to Esper. "We can't allow this. This is overt politicization of the military."

Esper agreed and got to work brainstorming an alternative to satisfy the president's desire to show off military hardware but without being a political salute to Trump or looking like an occupation of Washington. The defense secretary started doing the math on flight times. His plan, couched as a celebration of the Revolutionary War, was to fly military jets over the great cities of the American Revolution—Boston, New York, Philadelphia, Baltimore, and Washington. In repeated conversations, some of them heated, Meadows pressed Milley and Esper to grant the president's wishes for a military parade instead.

"I don't understand why we can't celebrate our own birthday," Meadows told them. "The president wants this."

"Look, I'm okay with a military parade," Esper told Meadows. "It's fine to celebrate our military, but it has to be done proportionally, tastefully." He urged them to at least scale back the number of planes to fifty and eliminate what he considered the most egregious feature: military might and tanks on the White House lawn.

"Do you guys ever learn?" Milley said. "This is not what we do. This is what North Korea does. This is what Stalin does. We don't do big military parades like this. This is not America. What Secretary Esper is proposing is a good idea, a celebration of the American Revolution."

Meadows ultimately came around. Truth be told, Esper controlled military assets, so the White House would have to go through him to deploy the toys Trump wanted for July 4. The chief of staff backed Esper's alternative and secured the president's sign-off. Behind the scenes, though, Esper discreetly cut the July 4 roster. He got the number of military planes down to thirty from more than seventy. He replaced ominous fighter jets with a traditional airshow favorite, the Blue Angels. If someone at the White House was going to count planes in the sky and complain, Esper thought, let them.

Regardless, Trump had an additional celebration in store. On June 3, he flew to South Dakota to give a speech at the base of Mount Rushmore before a massive fireworks display over the mountain carved to memorialize four past presidents: George Washington, Thomas Jefferson, Abraham Lincoln, and Theodore Roosevelt.

Trump had long eyed Mount Rushmore. South Dakota governor Kristi Noem recalled in a 2018 interview that during her first meeting with Trump in the Oval Office, when she was a congresswoman and he was early in his presidency, "I shook his hand, and I said, 'Mr. President, you should come to South Dakota sometime. We have Mount Rushmore.' And he goes, 'Do you know it's my dream to have my face on Mount Rushmore?'"

"I started laughing," Noem recalled. "He wasn't laughing, so he was totally serious. . . . I said, 'Come pick out a mountain.'"

On July 3, 2020, when Trump arrived before the packed amphitheater at the base of a floodlit Mount Rushmore, Noem introduced the president by stroking his ego. She commended the size of his crowd, at capacity with seventy-five hundred, and compared him to Roosevelt because he "braves the dangers of the arena." When Trump spoke, he delivered an extraordinarily divisive speech to mark a holiday of national unity. He paid tribute to America's legacy of white domination, harshly denounced the racial justice movement, and framed his reelection campaign as a battle to defeat a "new far-left fascism."

"Our nation is witnessing a merciless campaign to wipe out our history, defame our heroes, erase our values, and indoctrinate our children," Trump said. "Angry mobs are trying to tear down statues of our founders, deface our most sacred memorials, and unleash a wave of violent crime in our cities.

"Many of these people have no idea why they're doing this," he continued, "but some know what they are doing. They think the American people are weak and soft and submissive, but no, the American people are strong and proud, and they will not allow our country and all of its values, history, and culture to be taken from them."

On July 9, Trump sat down with his top campaign advisers to discuss an urgent concern: devising a messaging strategy for the general election. Trump had lost ground all spring and by now was trailing Joe Biden by a substantial margin in polls nationally as well as in many of the battleground states. The race had been framed by the media, and therefore in the minds of most voters, as a referendum on the president's handling of the pandemic and his overall leadership. Trump needed to shake things up.

The advisers presented to Trump a slideshow with the latest internal polling. The snapshot was devastating. It showed Biden leading by solid margins in two states Trump had carried in 2016, Michigan and Wisconsin, while six other Trump states were now toss-ups: Arizona, Georgia, Iowa, North Carolina, Ohio, and Pennsylvania. Overall, Biden had 259 electoral college votes to Trump's 193, putting the presumptive Democratic nominee just 11 votes shy of winning the presidency. The campaign's surveys also showed Biden's favorability with voters had improved by 10 percentage points since March, whereas Trump's job approval rating declined by nine percentage points in the same period.

The advisers drilled down into the data. Trump's support had eroded among white independent voters living in suburbs, as well as among nonwhite voters. The percentage declines in Trump's ballot performance were substantial—down 32 points among Black males, 18 points among Black females, 19 points among Hispanic females, 16 points among Hispanic males, 20 points among white suburban independent females, and 13 points among white suburban independent males.

The president's political brain trust tried to get him to focus on going after Biden. They tailored a few key messages aimed at gaining ground with white independent voters, whom the advisers believed Trump could win back with a deliberate and disciplined strategy. They teed up a series of attacks, or "contrasts," in political parlance, that their polling showed would hurt Biden:

"Biden's bad trade deals killed millions of American manufacturing jobs."

"Biden's support of the 'Green New Deal' will increase taxes and kill jobs."

"Biden will protect criminal illegal aliens."

"Biden supported cutting Social Security and Medicare."

The advisers told Trump he should use these lines in every speech, media appearance, and social media post—to repeat them relentlessly as if trying to brainwash voters. But Trump had little patience for the presentation. All he wanted to talk about was Biden hiding in his basement. The president was fixated on the juvenile "Sleepy Joe" caricature of his opponent that he had helped concoct. Trump believed the most effective way to defeat Biden was to go after his stamina and his mental acuity, and to shame the former vice president for following health precautions and campaigning virtually from the safety of his home.

To Trump, Biden oozed weakness. But his political advisers knew that would not be enough to win. If only the president would listen.

The U.S. Postal Service historically has been an apolitical institution, but the Trump administration slowly and quietly consolidated its control over the nation's mail service and its board of governors, culminating in May 2020 with the appointment of

Louis DeJoy, a longtime Republican donor who had supported Trump's 2016 campaign, as postmaster general. On July 10, DeJoy took his first major operational actions when he announced a series of "immediate, lasting, and impactful changes" designed to cut costs.

DeJoy released a memo, with the headline "Pivoting For Our Future," instructing all letter carriers to leave for their routes on time, even if it meant leaving mail behind at distribution centers. In another document, DeJoy said that sorting plants running behind should keep the mail for the next day rather than use overtime—a sea change for postal workers, who had been trained to gather every letter and work overtime or make multiple delivery trips to distribute letters and parcels on time. The new rules prioritized cost cutting and eliminating overtime at the expense of timely delivery, and raised early worries about the Postal Service's ability to deliver and collect ballots from the tens of millions of Americans expected to vote by mail in the upcoming election.

DeJoy's moves seemed to coordinate with Trump's public attacks on the integrity of mail-in ballots. The pandemic had made mail-in balloting not just a last resort but an absolute necessity. Election officials responsible for overseeing the November general election in their counties and states promoted voting by mail in order to protect both election workers' and voters' health.

But Trump, who often saw conspiracies against

him, insisted this was a plot by his enemies to defraud the vote and steal the election from him. On April 8, he tweeted that mail-in ballots are "RIPE for FRAUD." On May 20, he falsely attacked mail-in balloting plans in Michigan and Nevada as "illegal" and incorrectly accused Michigan's secretary of state of mailing ballots to every voter in the state; in fact, she sent applications to request mail-in ballots to all voters. And on May 26, in reference to California's plans to help people vote from home, he tweeted, "There is NO WAY (ZERO!) that Mail-In Ballots will be anything less than substantially fraudulent." He added, "This will be a Rigged Election." This prompted Twitter, for the first time, to tag one of the president's tweets with a warning about its inaccuracy. The social media platform urged its users to "get the facts" about mail-in voting through credible news stories that covered the topic.

Trump's assault on mail-in balloting escalated into the summer. On July 15, when he visited a United Parcel Service hub at Hartsfield-Jackson Atlanta International Airport to showcase his administration's work relaxing environmental regulations for new construction projects, he went off script again about fraudulent ballots.

"Mail-in ballots, be careful. Be careful!" Trump said in his speech to employees of UPS, a private company not responsible for ballot delivery. He went on to level a baseless charge of corruption. "They're going to be rigged," he said, "and there's been tremendous corruption—tremendous corruption on mail-in ballots."

On July 11, **The Washington Post** published a story about Anthony Fauci being sidelined by the White House, which included the following paragraph: "A White House official released a statement saying that 'several White House officials are concerned about the number of times Dr. Fauci has been wrong on things' and included a lengthy list of the scientist's comments from early in the outbreak. Those included his early doubt that people with no symptoms could play a significant role in spreading the virus—a notion based on earlier outbreaks that the novel coronavirus would turn on its head. They also point to public reassurances Fauci made in late February, around the time of the first U.S. case of community transmission, that 'at this moment, there is no need to change anything that you're doing on a day-to-day basis.'"

This was remarkable because White House officials had anonymously shared with reporters Yasmeen Abutaleb, Josh Dawsey, and Laurie McGinley a lengthy, researched list of Fauci's past comments just as they would have about a political opponent. Trump aides were undermining the nation's leading infectious disease expert and the most trusted spokesman for the federal government's pandemic response. This was only the beginning.

On July 12, Dan Scavino posted a cartoon mocking Fauci on Facebook. Scavino wasn't just any White House staffer; he was one of Trump's most loyal and trusted aides, the person the president turned to as a surrogate to push out his more controversial views. Earlier in the year Scavino had been promoted to deputy chief of staff for communications. The image likened Fauci to "Dr. Faucet," with a Pinocchio-like nose drawn to resemble an oversized faucet running water into a sink to drown Uncle Sam, a stand-in for the economy. The temperature was set to "extra cold," and the image included water drops with public health warnings labeled mockingly with exclamation points: "Indefinite lockdown!" "Schools stay closed this fall!" "Shut up and obey!" The cartoon was drawn by the artist Ben Garrison, whose past work had contained anti-Semitic messaging and was popular with the alt-right on social media. In a caption accompanying the cartoon, Scavino wrote, "Sorry, Dr. Faucet! At least you know if I'm going to disagree with a colleague, such as yourself, it's done publicly—and not cowardly, behind journalists with leaks. See you tomorrow!"

Then on July 14, Peter Navarro, who that spring had accused Fauci and Stephen Hahn of having "blood on your hands," published an op-ed in **USA Today** headlined ANTHONY FAUCI HAS BEEN WRONG ABOUT EVERYTHING I HAVE INTERACTED WITH HIM ON. In it, Navarro accused Fauci of downplaying the risk of the virus and of "flip-flopping" on the efficacy of masks. "So when you ask me whether I listen to Dr. Fauci's advice, my answer is: only with skepticism and caution." This was a direct criticism of a colleague in one of the nation's most-read newspapers.

The attacks on Fauci's character and credibility were an unmistakable indication that the president himself wanted to see Fauci's sterling public image tarnished. Trump was jealous that so many Americans trusted and admired Fauci to guide them through the pandemic. He was upset that this horrific catastrophe had produced as its national hero the doctor from Brooklyn and not the president from Queens. As Trump would later complain aloud to reporters at a July 28 news conference, "He's got this high approval rating—so why don't I have a high approval rating, and the administration, with respect to the virus?"

The Fauci-bashing underscored Trump's hostility toward medical expertise and produced a chilling effect among government scientists and public health professionals. Most importantly, it hampered the nation's efforts to combat the virus at the very moment the virus was spreading wildly across the Sun Belt. Thomas Frieden, a former CDC director, said at the time, "It seems that some are more intent on fighting imagined enemies than the real enemy here, which is the virus. The virus doesn't read talking points. The virus doesn't watch news shows. The virus just waits for us to make mistakes. And when we make mistakes, as Texas and Florida and South

Carolina and Arizona did, the virus wins. When we ignore science, the virus wins."

On July 14, the same day Navarro's op-ed published, Fauci spoke at a Georgetown University event and predicted the coronavirus pandemic could reach the level of the 1918 influenza, which infected roughly one third of the world's population. "This is a pandemic of historic proportions," Fauci said. "I think we can't deny that fact. It's something, I think, that when history looks back on it, it will be comparable to what we saw in 1918."

Fauci added, "If you look at the magnitude of the 1918 pandemic, where anywhere from fifty to seventy-five to one hundred million people died, I mean that was the mother of all pandemics and truly historic. I hope we don't even approach that with this, but it does have the makings of the possibility of . . . approaching that in seriousness, though I hope that the kinds of interventions that we're going to be and are implementing would not allow that to happen."

Fauci's comments immediately generated news headlines, and Meadows reacted predictably. He called Francis Collins to scream.

"You've got to get Tony to back down on that," Meadows told Collins. "That is not based on any facts. He's extrapolating. He's scaring people. You're his boss. You've got to make him stop."

It was one of those conversations where Collins had to let Meadows yell, holding the phone away from his ear until the furious chief of staff finished.

"I will certainly talk to Tony and let him know that this seems to cause a pretty strong reaction, and maybe induced a lot of fear, but I think Tony was telling you, from his perspective, what could happen," Collins told Meadows.

Collins had gotten used to Meadows routinely calling to complain when Fauci made comments that he thought undermined Trump's position. In another such instance that summer, Meadows had yelled to Collins, "Fauci's out of control! He's scaring everybody. He's saying that we're not managing this very well. This is doing political damage. He's got to stop making everything always sound so awful."

Collins thought Meadows was generally wrong based on the science and overly sensitive to politics. In this case regarding 1918, however, Collins thought Meadows had a point. He called Fauci and suggested they find a delicate way for Fauci to dial back his 1918 comparison.

"I think the way you said this made it sound like these are equivalent," Collins told Fauci. "We're not quite there yet."

Fauci said his comment was being misinterpreted and decided to try to revisit the topic in his next media appearance. Meanwhile, on July 16, Meadows went on Fox News and rebuked Fauci. He told anchor Martha MacCallum that with regard to Fauci's 1918 comparison, "I can tell you that not only is that false, it is irresponsible to suggest so."

That same day, Fauci made his next appearance,

a virtual conversation with Facebook founder Mark Zuckerberg, who asked him about his 1918 comments.

"I'm glad you brought that up because I want to clarify that. I had used the word 'comparable' and I think that may have been taken out of context, because people would have thought, my goodness, we're having this now, is it going to be the fifty to one hundred million people in 1918?" Fauci said. "No, they're not comparable in that way at all in severity. They're very, very different. I was just talking about . . . we haven't had anything like this really for 102 years."

Fauci had endured his most personally trying week of the awful pandemic year of 2020. He was attacked publicly by his administration colleagues, privately undermined by the White House chief of staff, and had to walk back a public comment. What stung the most was the fact that Navarro could write an editorial attacking him with impunity. In most any corporation, this would be a fireable offense, but not in the Trump White House. Fauci thought to himself, **What am I doing? I'm getting attacked by the people I'm working with? That's crazy.**

Fauci's closest confidante was his wife, Christine Grady, an NIH nurse and bioethicist. She said to him one night that week, as Fauci later told friends, "Tony, do you want to talk about the possibility of you just stepping down?" He did. Together, they weighed the pros and cons of his resigning from the coronavirus task force. Fauci's position at the National Institute of Allergy and Infectious Diseases, where he was responsible for vaccine development, was a permanent civil service job, so he could not easily be fired and had no reason to resign. But he did contemplate removing himself from all things Trump by giving up his position on the task force.

Fauci decided that if he pulled out, he would leave a significant vacuum at the White House. He would no longer be in the Situation Room or on television sharing facts and setting the record straight about science. Fauci proudly referred to himself as "the skunk at the picnic," but if he disappeared, his role might be filled by somebody who instead delivered to the public Trump's preferred happy talk. Ultimately, Fauci concluded that his presence improved things. So he stayed.

On July 14, about two weeks after Jared Kushner first told Brad Parscale he thought Trump would want to "make a change," the presidential son-in-law paid the campaign manager a visit at the campaign's Arlington headquarters. Kushner popped into Parscale's office shortly before a big budget meeting and got right to the point.

"We're demoting you," Kushner told Parscale. "We'd like you to stay in some capacity, to take care of digital infrastructure, but you're out.

"Look," Kushner added, "you know this isn't my decision. It's the president's campaign, and if he loses faith in you, you'll have to make a change. You didn't take this job for your ego. You took this job, hopefully, to help him win, and you need a comfortable candidate. If he's not comfortable, then you can't be in the job."

Kushner valued Parscale's digital know-how and thought he was exceptional at targeting advertisements to subgroups of voters, using data to drive message.

"You're getting the shit kicked out of you all the time in the press," Kushner told Parscale. "Go back to what you're good at. Stay on the team. If Trump wins, you'll be able to say you had a big part of it."

Parscale had known this moment might come, especially after the Tulsa debacle. With Trump mired in the polls behind Biden, Parscale was an easy fall guy, and changing the campaign leadership would, at a minimum, create the impression of change and theoretically give the president a chance to regain his footing.

Still, Parscale panicked. Thoughts raced through his mind. Should he stay on as Kushner wanted, without the title of campaign manager and with a vastly smaller portfolio overseeing digital operations? Or should he resign in protest? He called his wife, Candice.

"Fuck," she told him. "Quit."

"I don't know if I can do that," Parscale said. "It'll be very expensive for me to quit."

Leaving entirely meant Parscale would suddenly be out of the lucrative consulting arrangement he had with the campaign. Millions of dollars in compensation for himself and other campaign advisers—including payments to Kimberly Guilfoyle, the girlfriend of Donald Trump Jr., and to Lara Trump, the wife of Eric Trump—as well as expenses related to the campaign's servers, website, data operation, and other digital infrastructure, flowed through Parscale's private company. It was never disclosed how much Parscale personally pocketed in fees, but rivals in the president's orbit assumed the campaign was funding his lavish lifestyle.

Parscale then called Karl Rove, who had been informally advising Trump and his team. Rove advised Parscale, "Look, just say you're with the man. Act loyal and say, 'I'm still with you.' He's going to probably lose this election anyways and you're going to look even better because it'll look like his biggest mistake was firing you."

Rove also told Parscale, "How you handle this is going to speak volumes about you. If you go away angry, people, whether they like Trump or not, will make judgments about you. . . . But if you take whatever is given to you and handle it with dignity and restraint, people will make a different judgment. So don't be angry. It's unfair. He's not treating you right. This is being done for the wrong reason. But that's him. This isn't about you."

Parscale stayed on as a senior adviser focused on digital and data strategies. Trump appointed Bill Stepien as campaign manager in his place. Stepien, forty-two, was a fixture in Trump World. A former

campaign manager for Chris Christie's guberna-
torial runs in New Jersey and field director on
Rudy Giuliani's 2008 presidential run, he had joined
the Trump campaign in 2016 as national field director. He went on to serve as White House political
director, guiding the president's strategy in the 2018
midterm elections, and then became an outside consultant on Trump's reelection campaign.

In many ways, Stepien was Parscale's opposite.
Whereas Parscale touted his background growing
up in Kansas and living in Texas and Florida as putting him at home with Trump's MAGA supporters,
Stepien was raised in New Jersey and rose up in politics
working in the northeast. Parscale was an imposing
physical presence, at six foot eight with a scraggly red
beard; Stepien was clean-cut, with a generic corporate
look. Parscale styled himself as an expert in consumer
behavior and digital branding; Stepien's skills were in
the nuts-and-bolts of running campaigns, from building field programs to tailoring budgets to analyzing
data. Parscale strived to be a MAGA celebrity and
loved mingling at rallies; Stepien preferred to remain
anonymous, at home watching the New York Mets or
listening to Bruce Springsteen.

When Trump hired Stepien, he told his new
charge that he was concerned about how much his
campaign was spending and directed him to sort out
the budget.

"The most important thing I will do as your manager is to manage the budget, make sure I know where

every dollar is coming in and know where every dollar is going out," Stepien told Trump.

Then he said his first move would be to cut his own salary. Stepien had been making fifteen thousand dollars a month and he told Trump he would cut it by one third, down to ten thousand dollars a month, to set the tone with the staff as they transitioned into a leaner and tighter operation. Trump, always mindful of dollars and cents, and stingy about where his money went—even when it was money he raised from others, as was the case with his campaign—was thrilled.

Trump then got more direct about his worries over the budget.

"Is Brad stealing from me?" Trump asked Stepien, a question he would raise repeatedly.

This was perhaps the greatest transgression any employee could make in Trump's eyes. Stepien resisted the urge to put the knife in Parscale.

"I don't think Brad was stealing from you," Stepien told Trump. "I think Brad spent a lot of money. I think Brad wanted a lot of money. I'm pretty sure Brad can't account for all the money. But was it going right into his pocket? I don't think so."

Stepien was hired with just 111 days remaining until Election Day. Trump was at his lowest point in the campaign's internal polling, running at about 40 percent in the ballot test. The president was at rock bottom. Stepien complained to other aides that the campaign had no formal budget or any document charting anticipated revenue and planned expenses, no metrics or accountability measures; Parscale insisted to allies that of course he kept a budget. There wasn't much management, either. When Stepien called an all-staff meeting on his first day, it turned out to be the first time the staff had ever assembled together in one room.

"In a nutshell, the audience of the campaign wasn't a swing voter in Ohio. It really was the president," a senior campaign official explained. "It was a campaign that was being managed to his expectation and to his audience and to his attention. And as such, the day-to-day management of the operation just wasn't there."

Stepien's first order of business was to elevate his longtime right hand, Justin Clark, to be deputy campaign manager and put him in charge of the budget. He put Clark, who was a lawyer and veteran Republican operative, in an office next door to his own and they met each morning and night to talk about finances. As Clark prepared a budget, he saw that the campaign had been spending millions of dollars on a massive advertising campaign in June and July that wasn't moving the needle with voters. He calculated that if spending continued on the current trajectory, the campaign would be out of money by the first week of October—so broke it wouldn't be able to afford to hold rallies and fly the president to and from them, let alone advertise in battleground states or mobilize voters to turn out.

Money was supposed to give Trump a decisive

advantage over Biden, as the president had spent years leveraging the power of incumbency to attract maximum donations from many wealthy supporters, as well as tapping his grassroots base for small-dollar gifts. But his financial lead over Biden had evaporated by the summer, both because of a surge of Democratic gifts to Biden's campaign and because of the Trump campaign's profligate spending. Based on an analysis of disclosures to the Federal Election Commission, **The New York Times**'s Shane Goldmacher and Maggie Haberman reported that the campaign under Parscale spent $800 million, including $350 million on fundraising operations and more than $100 million on television advertising before the stage in the campaign when most voters historically pay attention. A cascade of small expenses added up, including $156,000 for planes to pull aerial banners and $110,000 for magnetic pouches used at fundraising events to store cell phones and prevent donors from secretly recording Trump's remarks.

Clark walked into Stepien's office and said, "Hey, man, I finished the budget. Good news is we have a budget and I'm pretty sure it's right. Bad news is there's a $115 million hole in it."

"Okay," Stepien said. "What do we do?"

Stepien and Clark instituted a series of cost-cutting measures designed to help stockpile resources they would need in the home stretch in September and October, as well as stringent new guidelines for approving expenses. They significantly pulled back the campaign's planned television advertisements for the month of August and cut down on the number of staffers who traveled to events. And, in a move that saved $3 million at the risk of puncturing the president's ego, they ditched a plan to sponsor and brand a NASCAR race car with Trump's name.

As Trump's new campaign leadership took charge, his pollsters were in the field in battleground states measuring voters' sentiments about what was shaping up to be the key issue in the election: the president's handling of the coronavirus.

In mid- to late-July, Trump met with his political advisers in the Oval Office to hear the results. They were quite discouraging. Trump's ratings had continued to slide downward, with just 40 percent of voters in the campaign's targeted states approving of his handling of the coronavirus and 58 percent disapproving. Asked what issue Trump was more focused on, 65 percent said saving the economy and 7 percent said fighting the coronavirus. But when asked which issue he **should** be more focused on, 50 percent said fighting the coronavirus and 39 percent said saving the economy. As a result of that disconnect, a slim majority, 51 percent, said Trump was not taking the pandemic seriously.

Central to these perceptions, the pollsters found, was Trump's reluctance to wear a mask or to promote wearing them with the public. According to the poll,

70 percent of voters in targeted states supported mandating masks in public spaces, at least indoors. Just 24 percent said masks should not be mandatory. A clear majority of these voters, 59 percent, said they favored Trump issuing an executive order requiring people to wear a face mask in all indoor and outdoor public places. Kushner and Tony Fabrizio used this data to press Trump to change his position. They thought if Trump wore a mask more often in public and more forcefully advocated that his followers do the same, his job approval would rise among the white independent suburban voters he needed to win back to carry some of these battleground states where he trailed Biden.

"To me, this is a no-brainer. Just do it," Kushner told his father-in-law, an argument Fabrizio backed up. "Masks are about showing respect for others. That's how people take them. Whether you believe they work or not, it makes other people more comfortable when people are wearing them."

Kushner's wife had privately conveyed similar points to the president. Ivanka Trump was one of the few West Wing officials to regularly wear a mask and tried unsuccessfully to appeal to her father to lead by example.

In part, Kushner and Fabrizio were trying to counter information Trump had been fed by other advisers over the previous few weeks. Meadows pressed this point strenuously in the Oval meeting. "He can't do it," the chief of staff said. "The base will go against him. He'll lose his base if he does it."

This was the perpetual tension for Trump, who was stuck between fortifying his base with hard-line or controversial policies and rhetoric and appealing to a broader portion of the electorate with more moderate ideas and a more inclusive tone. Yet again, Trump opted to defend his base. His choice was easy and instinctive.

"I'm not going to do it," the president told his team, referring to an executive order mandating masks.

Fabrizio said that even if the executive order idea was a no-go, Trump could still help himself politically by putting a mask on his face.

"Wear a mask," Fabrizio counseled the president. "Voters don't think you take it seriously."

"People tell me it makes me look weak," Trump replied. "People see Biden and he's always wearing a mask and he looks weak. People tell me it doesn't look presidential."

Trump didn't name the "people" telling him this. But the impression of weakness was certainly what he believed. The meeting ended without the change in strategy Kushner and Fabrizio sought.

Sometime in July, White House officials started noticing a new character hanging out in Kushner's office suite: a slight, silver-haired man named Dr.

Scott Atlas. Seemingly overnight, Atlas had become "a blue-badge fixture," as one official described him, referring to the special blue-colored security badge needed for unfettered access throughout the West Wing.

Atlas was a neuroradiologist and health policy expert from the Hoover Institution, a conservative think tank housed at Stanford University. He had attracted Trump's attention during the spring and early summer with frequent appearances on Fox News, where he voiced skepticism of the public health consensus about protective steps needed to slow the virus's spread, criticized lockdowns, advocated for the reopening of businesses and schools, and defended the president's handling of the pandemic. Hope Hicks and Johnny McEntee were impressed by his TV appearances as well and helped bring him to the White House.

Atlas ascended quickly. He was an informal adviser to Trump and Kushner on all things coronavirus. In early August, the president hired him as a special government employee, and by the third week of that month, Atlas appeared with Trump at coronavirus news conferences. He was the only doctor at the president's side, as Fauci and others had largely been forced out of public view by the White House. His lack of experience in infectious diseases and public health did not much matter to Trump, who saw his national television profile and willingness to praise the president as more valuable.

"Scott is a very famous man who's also very highly respected," Trump told reporters on August 16 when he announced Atlas's hiring. "He has many great ideas and he thinks what we've done is really good."

Atlas's arrival was a watershed moment. Trump's attendance at coronavirus task-force meetings had been declining, and he had been spending far less time with Fauci and Deborah Birx than in the spring, but after Atlas came aboard, the president stopped showing up altogether. Instead, Atlas briefed Trump personally on the pandemic. Robert Redfield complained to confidants that Atlas had effectively "iced out" the other doctors from meeting with Trump. Stephen Hahn, too, felt minimized by Atlas. But Birx bore the brunt of Atlas's presence in large part because she was on the White House staff, while Fauci, Redfield, and Hahn all worked under the Department of Health and Human Services.

"He undermined Dr. Birx," a senior White House official recalled, describing Atlas as a "blowhard" who would talk over Birx or try to correct her with a smug delivery. "He was sexist, insulting, condescending, and awful to her. He knew his only value added was he was seen as the right-wing, Fox-friendly version of a doctor and would push stuff that literally wasn't credible. He wanted to scrap our testing strategy and scale it back significantly. He was a snake. He would work his way into the Oval and show up and put things in front of the president."

Pence and Marc Short rationalized that if Atlas was

going to be advising the president, it was better to have him attending task-force meetings than acting as an unguided missile on the outside. Atlas's inclusion immediately created tension around the table. The infectious disease experts were incensed and insulted that a neuroradiologist had been given such prominence, and that he—and not they—was influencing the president's thinking on the virus. Atlas had expertise in reading MRIs and X-rays, but not with contagious pathogens of any kind.

Atlas didn't help matters by seeming to lord his special access to Trump over the other doctors. When he attended his first task-force meetings, Atlas would represent his ideas as official White House policy. He said things like, "This is our policy," or "The president has said so," or "I'm working on the president's talking points." The unmistakable takeaway was that Atlas was Trump's quarterback on COVID-19.

The other doctors would debate Atlas on his rosy assessments about the virus, with Pence listening to both sides of the argument and presiding as chair. "But in the back of my mind, I'm thinking, 'Does this really matter,' because I think the president's already made up his mind he was going to go with Scott Atlas," one of the doctors recalled.

Atlas provided Trump something that Birx, Fauci, and Redfield refused to give him: happy talk about the virus gradually dissipating and life returning to normal. After months of health experts advocating lockdowns and talking about deaths, here was a doctor with a different and far sunnier perspective. Atlas was, as one senior adviser to the president put it, "Somebody, frankly, who had a doctor title but a MAGA perspective." It was easy to see why the president was drawn to him.

At the time, more than 165,000 people in the United States had died from COVID-19, but predominantly in densely populated and urban and suburban areas, concentrated on the two coasts. Smaller communities across large swaths of the country had been relatively unscathed. But in summer, some sparsely populated states like South Dakota were hit with outbreaks for the first time. This was a sign that public behavior in places where residents had been resisting CDC guidelines for reducing the spread, such as social distancing and wearing masks, needed to change.

The other doctors privately scoffed at some of the claims Atlas had made on Fox and then repeated inside the White House. Atlas pushed, among other ideas, the controversial "herd immunity" strategy of letting the virus spread freely among young and healthy populations, whom he said could return to work and resume normal social behaviors, while protecting more vulnerable populations, such as the elderly and people with preexisting conditions. For instance, he argued that schools should reopen by falsely telling the president and members of the task force that young people had nearly "zero risk" of getting COVID-19.

"The science just got totally perverted with Scott in the room," the senior adviser said. "You literally could watch him shrug his shoulders or flick his wrists when he talked about masks. His whole premise was, this is a fat, diabetic person's disease."

Other members of the task force described Atlas bringing falsehoods into the conversation and confusing those around the table, including Pence. Furthermore, one of these members said, Atlas was "single-minded in his efforts to do everything he could to disqualify Tony Fauci's opinions on anything and had, as an ally, Mark Meadows, and the president." Meadows had been a major skeptic of the CDC's aggressive public health pronouncements when he was in Congress. As chief of staff, Meadows had installed Russ Vought—with whom he worked closely when he was on the Hill and Vought worked at the conservative Heritage Foundation—as the director of the Office of Management and Budget to review the CDC's guidance to businesses and schools about steps to reopen. Vought initially held up the recommendations and defanged some before he would agree to its public release. Throughout the summer, Meadows worked tirelessly to align the government's virus guidance with Trump's claim that things were looking good, no matter the reality.

"Mark Meadows was the biggest 'yes' man to hold that position," said one senior public health official. "That includes Nixon's chief of staff,

[H. R.] Haldeman, who went to jail. Even **he's** not as bad as Meadows."

Atlas was key to Meadows's strategy. He had firmly established himself as a charlatan in the eyes of the other doctors. When they warned their White House contacts that Atlas's claims lacked scientific backing, they were told Atlas was there not so much to shape epidemiological policy as to trumpet to the public that the threat of the virus was declining as the campaign entered its final months.

"They liked his message, which was, 'You don't have to worry about controlling the epidemic. Just let it run its course. Just isolate the real old people who are vulnerable. Let the economy roar. Don't shut anything down. Just get the old people out of the way and just let it run its course,'" said a second top White House adviser.

In one of the first task-force meetings he attended, something Atlas asserted so assuredly struck the other doctors as being pulled out of thin air. He began explaining that the country was very close to herd immunity already—or surely would be—once 30 percent of the population became infected. At that level, he said, there would no longer be any risk of continued transmission nationwide. He said more kids needed to get exposed to reach the 30 percent threshold sooner.

"You see why we're not seeing an increase in infections in these cities that were infected in February,

March, April, and May?" Atlas said of early-hit cities on the East Coast. "It's herd immunity."

Birx, Fauci, and Redfield knew that theory was bunk. Most of the time, task-force discussions among the scientists were polite affairs. But both Redfield and Birx got heated when Atlas made this claim, wanting everyone watching to know how ardently they opposed him. Redfield didn't shout, but he raised his voice to keep Atlas from interrupting him. He said that 85 to 95 percent of Americans were going to need to be immune before herd immunity influenced transmission cycles. Birx gave a blow-by-blow of why 30 percent immunity exposure would make little to no difference on transmission. Birx and Redfield both expected more waves of infections to come in those originally hard-hit cities, which indeed came to pass. But to Birx's and Redfield's surprise, Fauci was silent during Atlas's presentation and the ensuing argument, sitting back with his arms crossed. After the meeting broke up, Fauci called Atlas, thinking there might be a chance to persuade him that his theory was wrong.

"Let's talk about this herd immunity thing," Fauci told Atlas. "Scott, you had places that went way up [in case counts] and came down and then went way back up again, so how is that herd immunity?"

Atlas made clear his mind would not be changed. Later, Atlas would claim that he never advocated herd immunity as a response to the pandemic.

Redfield and Birx had wanted Fauci to confront

Atlas in the meeting, but he opted not to. All three concluded that Atlas was a hopeless case and fixed in his ideas, but Redfield and Birx were frustrated that Fauci did not want to square off with him in task-force meetings.

Eleven

Fear and Fantasy

On July 30, President Trump proposed delaying the election, such was his fear of losing. He did not have the power to do so, but nevertheless tweeted, "With Universal Mail-in Voting (not Absentee Voting, which is good), 2020 will be the most INACCURATE & FRAUDULENT Election in history. It will be a great embarrassment to the USA. Delay the Election until people can properly, securely and safely vote???"

The suggestion was laughable. The dates of presidential general elections are determined by the Congress, with power enshrined in Article II of the Constitution. Since 1845, federal law has set the Tuesday after the first Monday of November as the date of the election. In 2020, that would be November 3. No president in history has ever successfully delayed an election, not even in times of war.

More sinister, however, was Trump's assertion that the election would be "the most INACCURATE & FRAUDULENT Election in history." There was simply no basis for that statement. There was no evidence of meaningful voter fraud. And while U.S. intelligence agencies warned that Russia and other countries were attempting to interfere again in the presidential race, there was no indication they had the ability to tamper with voting machines or other election infrastructure to rig the results. At the White House, Trump's aides didn't take what he wrote seriously. They collectively shrugged their shoulders. They saw it as just another tweet that would evaporate.

"That's one of those discussions of how many angels can sit on the head of a pin," one senior White House official recalled. "Anybody who's reasonable, who's involved in it, gave it only a passing thought. Nobody gave it any serious consideration. Nobody. It was just a throwaway comment. It was, like, 'Okay, noted.' Nobody listened to that. Nobody cared about it. Nobody associated with it."

Shortly thereafter, in early August, Trump snapped during a meeting with his campaign advisers. Tony Fabrizio was again presenting the president with poll numbers showing Joe Biden winning because independent voters had flocked away from Trump. Fabrizio believed these voters had reached a breaking point with Trump.

"Mr. President, just look at the data and you can see that the voters are tired," Fabrizio said. "They're tired of the chaos. They're just fatigued. They're really fatigued."

The president jerked his head back and raised his voice.

"**They're** tired? **They're** fatigued? **They're** fucking fatigued?" he asked his pollster. "Well, **I'm** fucking fatigued, too."

The room fell silent for about ten seconds. Then they moved on to another subject. Trump, through a spokesman, denied saying this.

Trump's difference of opinion with Bill Barr about the use of federal forces to quell civil unrest came to a head in dramatic fashion in August. He still felt stung by Barr's resistance to his push to deploy troops in Seattle, and by being upstaged by the city authorities in clearing the protesters there. So he turned his ire south toward Portland. Earlier in the summer, the federal courthouse in Portland was the target of nightly assaults by vandals. And the presence of federal officers to protect the building became a magnet for protesters, drawing thousands of demonstrators against Trump and his administration.

In early August, the crowds shrunk considerably, and Barr was confident there were enough local, state, and federal resources in and around Portland to quell any violence. Yet Trump decided he wanted to deliver a message of power. He summoned Barr to the Oval Office. Trump told his attorney general that he didn't understand why he couldn't just clear the whole area out.

"Why aren't we doing anything about it?" Trump asked.

Barr argued that scenes of unrest could play to Trump's advantage in the campaign.

"It's not like this is a bad thing for you politically because it highlights differences in policing," Barr said.

Trump rejected Barr's analysis, saying the administration needed to take action to stop the protesters and silence his critics.

"It makes me look weak," the president complained.

Barr said the situation was trending toward a calm and controlled standoff. "Look, if it metastasizes and spreads and there's a real issue, maybe we reevaluate how to handle it, but we think we're in a pretty solid position in Portland," he told Trump.

The president's fixation on showing strength against civil unrest played on a loop for a few more rotations. He was sick of the wall of objections Barr was tossing up. He got red in the face and slammed his hand on the Resolute Desk.

"No one supports me," Trump yelled. "No one gives me any fucking support."

The president stormed out of the room, heading to his private dining room next door, where he liked to watch television. Barr glanced over at Mark Meadows and tried to offer some comic relief.

"Well," he quipped, "that went well."

In the first week of August, another senior administration official was wrestling with an announcement he felt he had to make—and one he knew would piss off Trump. As director of the National Counterintelligence and Security Center, Bill Evanina's job was to brief Congress and the public on major disinformation campaigns and cyberattacks by foreign adversaries, as discovered by U.S. intelligence agencies. Earlier that summer, Democratic congressional leaders had accused Evanina of falling short of that responsibility. The accusation stung. Evanina began his job during the Obama administration and stayed on into the Trump administration. While his was a political appointment, Evanina considered himself an objective decades-long public servant.

Evanina knew that malevolent state actors—Russia especially, but also China—were working overtime to sow discord in the United States in 2020, on three simultaneous tracks: the pandemic, George Floyd's killing, and the upcoming election. Russia was using the most active measures—internet trolls, proxies, and other social media tools—to amplify disagreements and conspiracy theories about the virus. They circulated pictures and memes that stoked fear and loathing of both protesters and police. Then came the evidence Russia was working to undermine Biden's candidacy by portraying him as an ailing elderly man and his son Hunter as a thieving operator who made millions trading on his father's office of vice president. Evanina had privately warned members of the congressional intelligence committees about these actions, and, on July 24, he released limited public information about foreign states' goals in the upcoming election.

On July 31, in a private intelligence briefing with lawmakers, House Speaker Nancy Pelosi berated Evanina and told him he was failing the American people because his public statements were so vague as to be nearly meaningless. Pelosi and some of her Democratic colleagues insisted Evanina give the public more than euphemisms about "interference" and say which candidate Russia was really trying to torpedo.

Evanina believed he was boxed in. He wanted to share more information with the public about the U.S. intelligence community's evidence of Russian interference, but he faced sizable, interlocking obstacles. First, some of the information remained classified. Second, some needed to be briefed to the president before it could be shared.

Trump's briefers had increasingly played down the topic of Russia. When they tried to share with him evidence of Russian election interference, Trump had bristled, sometimes telling them they were wrong and shifting attention to other countries, like China, Iran, and North Korea. Back in February, he had fired acting director of National Intelligence Joe Maguire when Maguire's team had briefed Congress on intelligence about election interference, as was its legal responsibility, and explained that Russia had "developed a preference" for Trump winning reelection.

That summer, some of the obstacles Evanina faced in sharing the truth were lifted, including details of the Russian interference efforts. The intelligence community had evidence that Andriy Derkach, a member of the Ukrainian parliament, was a proxy whom Russian intelligence services used to promote and launder bogus stories about Biden to officials and reporters in the United States. One key American on the receiving end of Derkach's misleading narratives was none other than Rudy Giuliani. Trump's personal lawyer had met with Derkach in Ukraine in late 2019 and had been promoting Derkach's information on conservative news outlets. He would later tell Trump he was working on an "October surprise" about Biden family corruption to boost the president's campaign chances.

Evanina felt he could now tell the public more of what U.S. intelligence agencies knew about Russia's campaign to hurt Biden's candidacy. He was eager to refute the Democrats' claim that he was doing Trump's bidding by "soft-pedaling" intelligence.

Director of National Intelligence John Ratcliffe did not try to block Evanina. He just told him to get ready for incoming. Evanina understood, but he proceeded nonetheless, and he felt he had the full endorsement of CIA director Gina Haspel and FBI director Chris Wray. Evanina made his announcement on Friday,

August 7, and included an obvious nod to the president's sensitivities, by leading with China's stake in the U.S. election, before describing Russia's active interference. Evanina noted that intelligence showed the Chinese government considered Trump "unpredictable" and hoped he would lose. He said Iran also opposed a Trump presidency. Unlike Russia, however, China and Iran had not yet launched aggressive measures to hurt Trump. The media—and therefore the president—focused mostly on what Evanina said about Russia's interference campaign. Evanina fully expected to be fired.

Just after 7:00 that evening, the president was at Trump National Golf Club in Bedminster, New Jersey, where he held a hastily arranged news conference to tout falling unemployment numbers. He again vowed that the coronavirus was "going to disappear." Asked about Evanina's report, Trump at first said the intelligence could be true, but then dismissed the idea that Russia was rooting for him.

"I think that the last person Russia wants to see in office is Donald Trump, because nobody's been tougher on Russia than I have, ever," Trump said.

A reporter pointed out that U.S. intelligence agencies disagreed.

"I don't care what anybody says," Trump said.

Moments later, the president urged reporters to reconsider their emphasis on Russia.

"You started off with Russia," Trump said. "Why didn't you start with China?"

That night, Evanina was in a car traveling out of town for the weekend when a friend of his at the White House called.

"I just came out of a meeting. The president is probably going to fire you. It's probably going to happen tonight," the friend told him, saying it was expected after Trump's news conference. "Don't take it personally."

Evanina and his wife were at peace with his likely ousting. They got ready for the Trump tweet. It never came.

Evanina instead took incoming from Democrats. On August 9, Pelosi gave interviews to CNN and Fox News arguing that the administration wasn't telling the whole, unvarnished truth about Russia's fervent efforts to secure a second term for Trump. She complained that it was entirely disingenuous to lump China, Iran, and Russia together when they were "not equivalent," and Russia's efforts were active and serious. And she criticized Evanina for not calling a spade a spade and stating clearly that Trump was Russia's favored candidate.

"The American people need to know what the Russians are doing in this case and the American people believe that they should decide who the next president is, not Vladimir Putin," Pelosi said on Fox.

The next day, Ratcliffe reached out to Evanina to tell him he could stop worrying about the president's reaction. Trump's anger apparently had not reached the level of firing the messenger. "I think you're going to be good," he said.

The morning of Tuesday, August 11, Trump summoned his law-and-order advisers to the White House. The president was incensed about fresh violence by protesters in Portland that weekend. Local police had declared a riot the previous Sunday night after protesters set fires near a police station, set off commercial-grade fireworks, and even used a mortar. Two police officers had sustained minor injuries and sixteen protesters had been arrested. Trump once again wanted to deploy the National Guard or a heavy federal presence to bring the protesters to heel.

The president's team had grown so weary of this all-too-familiar desire. Barr might as well have trudged as he walked into the West Wing, that's how fed up he was. Mark Milley and Stephen Miller were there, too. Mark Esper, who was taking a rare couple of days of vacation with his wife in Myrtle Beach, joined by phone. The president didn't seem to understand that every time he suggested commandeering another state's National Guard, which were under the control of their respective governors, he was proposing invoking the Insurrection Act. His advisers felt as though they had to explain this to him once more.

Barr did most of the talking; Esper had wanted Barr to take the lead because the military should be the course of last resort. Barr proposed that Trump let the team confer with local authorities and then come back to him with a strategy for restoring the peace that did not necessitate a massive federal force, which could appear heavy-handed considering the protest was still relatively small.

"I think it would backfire," Barr told Trump.

Milley was unusually quiet in the meeting, but added his voice at that point to say he agreed with Barr. Eventually, Miller piped up to argue that there would be nothing wrong with a large show of force beating back a small group. He said something along the lines of, "If you only have a few demonstrators and you can handle them, just handle them and it will go away.

"Clearly the city has lost operational control of the situation," Miller added, arguing for invoking the Insurrection Act.

Perhaps it was the number of times Barr had been summoned to the White House for this same discussion, or the number of times he had had to beat back the idea of military troops on American streets, but the attorney general cracked at Miller's suggestion.

"You don't know shit about what you're talking about," Barr said, his voice booming at Miller. "You have never had operational responsibility for anything. For every one of these that works there's a Waco where people are killed." He was referring to the 1993 siege on a religious sect compound in Texas by federal law enforcement and military forces that resulted in a fifty-one-day standoff and nearly eighty people dead.

"Look, we're on the same side here," Miller said to Barr. "We both want to find a way to end these things."

The meeting ended not long after, with the president agreeing to wait to see Barr's proposal.

After quickly consolidating power over the Postal Service by ousting longtime veterans from the institution's leadership and replacing them with loyalists, Louis DeJoy achieved a breakthrough on August 1. More than six hundred massive mail-sorting machines, about 10 percent of those in operation, would be decommissioned starting that day. These machines that helped process the mail were shut down, disassembled, and removed from distribution centers.

It was normal for the Postal Service to decommission aging equipment, but the agency had never removed so many machines at once. Worse still, the changes were coming amid a pandemic, when staffing levels were inconsistent, and ahead of a presidential election expected to flood the Postal Service with tens of millions of ballots. The 671 machines to be removed were spread around the country, but located primarily in high-population areas, and together they had the capacity to sort 21.4 million pieces of mail per hour.

News of this move did not break until two weeks later, on August 13. That is when reporters learned of a formal grievance filed by the American Postal

Workers Union sounding the alarm about the decommissioned machines. This was the only way that postal workers could speak out, because they were barred from discussing internal policy with the public.

The news became a major story that continued for days. Because Trump had been beating his drum to assail mail-in balloting—assuming more Democrats would vote by mail than Republicans and therefore the practice would benefit Biden—the union's filing raised genuine fears that DeJoy was explicitly aiming to prevent votes for Biden from being counted on time.

On August 14, Pelosi and several other Democratic lawmakers wrote to DeJoy demanding answers to questions about "your policies and practices, the specific changes you are proposing, the rationale for those changes, and the potential impacts of those changes." The Postal Service's inspector general also launched an investigation into the complaints Democrats raised against DeJoy. The next day, more than one hundred protesters showed up on a Saturday to the lobby door of DeJoy's apartment in Northwest Washington. Some stuffed phony ballots inside the gate.

On August 16, House Democrats called for DeJoy to testify before Congress. The House Committee on Oversight and Reform scheduled an emergency hearing for the next week, on August 24, to address whether the Trump administration was mucking up the gears of the Postal Service in order to slow down the delivery of mail-in ballots and affect the election. There also were concerns about prescription medications, Social Security checks, and other important items being delayed.

Voting rights activists accused DeJoy of disenfranchising voters with his handiwork. "The slowdown is another tool in the toolbox of voter suppression," said Celina Stewart, senior director of advocacy and litigation with the nonpartisan League of Women Voters. "That's no secret. We do think this is a voter-suppression tactic."

On August 19, Pelosi spoke to DeJoy by phone to ask him point-blank what he was up to. She told reporters after the call that the postmaster general's answers were unsatisfying. She said DeJoy "frankly admitted that he had no intention of replacing the sorting machines, blue mailboxes, and other key mail infrastructure that have been removed."

Faced with the growing public outcry and the looming date of his congressional hearing, DeJoy said that week he was reversing course on some of the cost-saving measures. But when it came to DeJoy, Democrats had adopted a policy of don't trust and definitely verify. Adding to the suspicion, emails later obtained by **The Washington Post** revealed that a top director of Postal Service maintenance operations instructed plant officials on August 18 that "they are not to reconnect/reinstall machines that have previously been disconnected without approval from HQ Maintenance, no matter what direction they are getting from their plant manager."

Whatever the intent, the consequences of DeJoy's moves were plain to see. The Postal Service's general counsel sent letters to forty-six states and the District of Columbia warning that, given the high volume of mail-in ballots, it could not promise that every ballot cast by mail for the November election would arrive in time to be counted. Each state set its own rules for administering elections, including deadlines for sending and receiving absentee or other mail-in ballots. The Postal Service sent a separate and more urgent warning to forty states—which included such key battlegrounds as Florida, Michigan, and Pennsylvania—that their published timetables for voters to return completed ballots did not afford the Postal Service enough time to ensure their delivery. The bottom line: potentially tens of millions of voters were now at risk of not having their votes counted.

Since becoming his party's presumptive nominee in April, Biden had struggled to generate excitement for his candidacy and to prosecute a compelling and comprehensive case against Trump. His lead in the polls was consistent and substantial, yet still most analysts believed his advantage was because of Trump's mismanagement, ineptitude, and squandered opportunities, and not any affirmative steps Biden had taken. Most days, Biden could barely get any oxygen in the news cycle. Trump consumed it all.

Finally, in the third week of August, Biden had the

nation's attention. It was time for the quadrennial Democratic National Convention, originally scheduled to take place in Milwaukee but convened virtually to ensure health safety during the pandemic. The Democrats produced a slick spectacle that for four days straight laid out their case against Trump and for Biden as the healer the country needed to guide it out of crisis.

The convention program was full of cinematic imagery and contrasts. In this virtual format, the opening night's roll call—traditionally a lively affair on the convention floor with each state's delegation casting its votes for the nominee—became a captivating thirty-minute showcase of America's rich diversity. A fisherman in Alaska, a fourth-generation family farmer in Kansas, a bricklayer in Missouri, a registered nurse in New York, and a calamari chef in Rhode Island all appeared on location.

The perfunctory speeches by politicians were choreographed to contrast with Trump and expand Biden's coalition. John Kasich, the former Republican governor of Ohio, stood at a literal crossroads in his suburban Columbus neighborhood as he implored fellow Republicans to follow him in backing Biden. Washington, D.C., mayor Muriel Bowser, who had feuded with Trump earlier over the use of federal officers to clear protesters, spoke from a rooftop looking down on the gleaming yellow letters spelling out "Black Lives Matter" on Sixteenth Street in front of the White House. And former president Barack Obama spoke at the Museum of the American Revolution in Philadelphia, standing against a backdrop of the Constitution itself as he denounced Trump as a threat to its principles.

"I never expected that my successor would embrace my vision or continue my policies," Obama said. "I did hope, for the sake of our country, that Donald Trump might show some interest in taking the job seriously. That he might come to feel the weight of the office and discover some reverence for the democracy that had been placed in his care. But he never did."

The most effective takedown of Trump, however, came from Michelle Obama. Beaming in from the living room of what appeared to be a vacation home on Martha's Vineyard, the former first lady spoke calmly but passionately the night of August 17 about the dark state of the country. She exuded empathy and described a crisis of conscience and of competence.

"Let me be as honest and clear as I possibly can," she said. "Donald Trump is the wrong president for our country. He has had more than enough time to prove that he can do the job, but he is clearly in over his head. He cannot meet this moment. He simply cannot be who we need him to be for us. It is what it is."

"It is what it is." Using Trump's own words from an interview with Jonathan Swan of **Axios** a few weeks earlier, Michelle Obama painfully reminded viewers of Trump's seeming indifference to the soaring COVID-19 death toll. As **Washington Post** columnist Robin Givhan wrote, "She sounded like a wounded citizen. She sounded like a woman in pain. By the end of her speech, her voice was breathy and her eyes began to shine, and it seemed as though she might cry. That she might weep for the future of her country if its citizens couldn't roust themselves from these unfathomable lows and claw their way up toward the light."

Trump needed to change the game.

The week of the Democratic convention, Francis Collins left town to recharge after a grueling few months running the NIH. He relaxed at a house on Chincoteague Island on Virginia's remote Eastern Shore, a little slice of heaven a few hours from Washington known for its wild horses and undeveloped beaches. The NIH director's tranquility was interrupted by a phone call on Wednesday, August 19. It was the White House. The president was on the other line.

Trump began by talking about how great his poll numbers were. This was hardly a concern for the NIH director, of course, never mind that the president's numbers were actually quite low, as Trump's own pollsters would attest. But Collins indulged the president by listening to his spiel. Then Trump changed gears. "You doctors are killing me," he told Collins, according to the account he shared with aides. Trump veered into a tirade about the magical power of convalescent plasma treatments to save the lives of COVID-19 patients. He accused Collins and Anthony Fauci of blocking "what everybody knows" is a life-saving cure. He said they were getting in the way of his being able to announce that convalescent plasma could save lots of lives and they needed to "stop with this resistance."

Collins and Fauci had indeed been blocking a major announcement on convalescent plasma treatment, a process by which antibody-rich blood—donated by people who had recovered from the virus—was given to people fighting an infection. FDA officials were preparing to grant emergency use authorization for the treatment, believing the available data showed there were minimal risks even though the benefits were not yet conclusive. But Collins and Fauci insisted upon collecting more data through clinical trials before the FDA approved its widespread use.

The disagreements had boiled over on a conference call of task-force doctors earlier that month. Stephen Hahn and Dr. Peter Marks, who ran the FDA's Center for Biologics Evaluation and Research, supported issuing an emergency use authorization, as did Robert Redfield and Deborah Birx. They thought that the plasma treatment might or might not provide a modest benefit, but it clearly met the very low standard of safety for an emergency use authorization. That bar required only that the treatment's known and potential benefits outweighed the known risks.

Collins, and to a lesser degree Fauci, objected.

Collins argued that by rushing a decision before additional data were collected, the administration was opening itself to criticism of having politicized the process. When Collins warned that the FDA would feel the wrath of the scientific community, Birx said, "Are you threatening the FDA?" Collins said he was not, but tensions persisted. Hahn and Marks decided to delay the authorization by a couple of weeks to gather more data, a decision Hahn later would come to regret.

On his August 19 call with Trump, Collins preached caution. "Mr. President, you don't want to be in a situation where the FDA is pushed into granting an emergency use authorization without the evidence," he said. "Remember what happened with hydroxychloroquine?"

That triggered Trump into another tirade about how hydroxychloroquine cured people, but the doctors got in the way of its approval.

"We are, right now, about a week away from having the data that I think we could really say is going to be convincing—or not, because it may turn out that this actually isn't helping people," Collins said.

"No," Trump said. "You've got to have the answer by Friday. That's it."

Friday was two days away, and Trump kept up the pressure. He berated Hahn, accusing him of allowing government scientists—the president thought of them as "deep state"—to delay COVID treatments in order to hurt him politically. Meadows encouraged

Trump, saying he was right to keep pressing, and that the scientists "need to feel the heat." Meadows, as well as Adam Boehler, the close ally of Jared Kushner, also personally pressured Hahn during this period.

"You're caving to pressure from the NIH," Meadows told Hahn in one such conversation. "You're allowing them to dictate what you're doing."

"Look," Hahn replied, "we'll make a decision based on the data. We're not caving. We're trying to satisfy legitimate concerns about the data."

The Republican National Convention was the following week, beginning August 24, and it was obvious to the public health professionals that Trump wanted to be able to announce an emergency use authorization for convalescent plasma by then.

By the end of the day Friday, August 21, the data Collins and his NIH team needed to be convinced that convalescent plasma had proved effective for enough patients to justify wide-scale use was not yet in hand. The next day, as the doctors saw more data come in, the evidence of efficacy was unconvincing. Yet an announcement of the emergency use authorization had already been drafted. The FDA press release, traditionally a dull, factual document, had an unusual political pizzazz. Released on August 23, it proclaimed: "Another Achievement in Administration's Fight Against Pandemic."

On August 23, the principals were called to the White House for a special announcement. Beforehand, Trump huddled with Hahn, Collins, Meadows, Alex

FEAR AND FANTASY

Azar, and other advisers in the Oval Office to prepare what they would say. There was no firm evidence of convalescent plasma reducing the rate of deaths, but Marks and his team calculated that based on available data it would reduce the relative risk of death by about 35 percent. Scientists believed the actual rate could vary between 10 percent and 50 percent.

"Why'd you pick thirty-five percent?" Trump asked. "Why don't we say fifty?"

"Well, Mr. President, that would make us a target for criticism," Azar said. He explained that they believed 35 percent would be the safest and most accurate way to describe it.

"I like fifty," Trump said. "Doesn't fifty just sound better to you? Five-zero. Fifty."

"No, the number is thirty-five," Hahn said. "We can't say fifty because that's not what the data show. Thirty-five percent is the number that Peter's team came to."

Trump, fond of overselling when promoting anything, be it one of his golf properties or a trade deal, came back to his 50 percent point two or three additional times, but Azar, Hahn, and others pushed back each time. They ended up using the seemingly more conservative 35 percent number publicly, but even that would prove impossible to defend.

Trump stepped into the press briefing room and announced his administration was authorizing a miracle treatment that could save countless lives. Flanked by Hahn and Azar, the president announced that the FDA had agreed to give emergency permission for doctors to treat COVID-19 patients with convalescent plasma because of what he described as overwhelming evidence that showed that it had an "incredible rate of success" in preventing deaths from the disease.

"Today's action will dramatically expand access to this treatment," Trump said. "We're removing unnecessary barriers and delays. . . . We are being very strong and we are being very forthright, and we have some incredible answers, and we're not going to be held up."

The president told reporters that new studies had proven that treating patients with this blood product laced with antibodies cut the rate of deaths by 35 percent, what Trump called "a tremendous number." Hahn repeated the 35 percent claim in his remarks.

There were inaccuracies in the presentation, which would anger doctors across the country, as well as scientists inside the FDA. The administration's claim relied on a preliminary study by the Mayo Clinic that never claimed to meet the well-established medical standards for assessing the treatment's success rate. The study showed that patients who received the plasma treatment within three days of being hospitalized had lower rates of death over the next thirty days than those patients who got the treatment later. The actual data was statistically interesting but not conclusive. It found the death rate among those who got the earlier plasma treatments was 8.7 percent, while those who had later plasma treatments had a death rate of 11.7 percent. FDA scientists had also warned the study didn't use the standard required for measuring a treatment's verified success. It had not picked patients randomly nor compared patients who received the treatment with patients who received a placebo.

Azar echoed the president, but in language that skirted a conclusion. He did not explicitly claim the plasma treatment cut deaths by 35 percent. "We dream in drug development of something like a thirty-five percent mortality reduction," he said. "This is a major advance in the treatment of patients."

One senior member of the coronavirus task force recalled, "It was just one of those completely disastrous moments that you could hardly believe you were a part of."

The backlash against the venerable FDA was one of the most brutal in its history.

"I watched this in horror," Eric Topol, an expert on clinical trials and the influential director of the Scripps Research Translational Institute, told **The Washington Post** after watching Trump's announcement with Hahn at his side. "These are basically just exploratory analyses that don't prove anything. It's just extraordinary to declare this as a breakthrough." Other health professionals decried what they saw as the FDA's manipulation of science to fit the president's political messaging.

Within roughly twenty-four hours, Hahn

apologized for overstating the evidence of plasma treatment's effectiveness and its ability to save lives. He tweeted the night of August 24, "I have been criticized for remarks I made Sunday night about the benefits of convalescent plasma. The criticism is entirely justified. What I should have said better is that the data show a relative risk reduction, not an absolute risk reduction."

Hahn told others he felt burned by Trump and Meadows. He believed the president's announcement on the eve of the Republican Convention gave the appearance that the FDA's process had been corrupted by politics. Going forward, the FDA commissioner resolved to be better attuned to the political machinations of the White House—even if doing so had a cost for Trump. In particular, Hahn steeled himself for more political manipulation of the highly sensitive vaccine trial process, which the president wanted completed before the election. He was determined never to be put in this position again.

On August 24, Republicans opened their national convention, which would run for four days. Their mission was urgent: to convince voters pessimistic about the state of a country battered by the pandemic, the recession, and racial upheaval that Trump deserved four more years at the helm.

The convention originally had been scheduled to take place in Charlotte. But after Trump publicly feuded over public health restrictions with North Carolina's Democratic governor, Roy Cooper, he moved most of the programming to Jacksonville, Florida, where the Republican governor, Ron DeSantis, was a much more eager and accommodating host. Then Republicans scrapped plans for an in-person convention in a cavernous arena and changed to a hybrid model, setting some of the marquee speeches live before large crowds outdoors.

Kushner and Hope Hicks helped orchestrate the convention, in close consultation with Trump, who micromanaged the speakers' list and choreography. The president was adamant about having high production values. Hicks wanted the event to feel different from the 2016 Republican Convention in Cleveland, where Trump had become the party's unlikely nominee, and saw this convention as an opportunity not merely to amplify the president's MAGA base, but to grow his support beyond it. She asked Tony Sayegh, a longtime GOP operative who had run public affairs at Trump's Treasury Department, to oversee programming, along with Lara Trump.

The Trump team envisioned every night of the convention as a cross between a State of the Union address, in which ordinary Americans sitting with the first lady in the balcony are singled out for their extraordinary achievements, and Tucker Carlson's show. It would be, in their words, "a people's convention." They decided to feature Alice Johnson, whom Trump had released from her lifetime prison sentence over a drug offense and later granted a full pardon; Natalie Harp, a cancer survivor who claimed Trump had saved her life thanks to his "Right to Try" law permitting experimental treatments; Carl and Marsha Mueller, the parents of a humanitarian aid worker who was killed by Islamic State terrorists; and other everyday Americans with diverse testimonials.

At a time of national despair, Trump wanted to project optimism, and programming was planned around themes of "promise," "opportunity," and "greatness." Yet Trump and other speakers also used the platform to inflame culture wars, delivering fiery denunciations of "socialism" and claiming that Americans would not be safe under a Biden presidency. For instance, Mark and Patricia McCloskey, a St. Louis couple who had stood outside their home pointing guns during a Black Lives Matter demonstration, gave a particularly provocative speech warning the American suburbs would fall into dangerous chaos if Democrats were elected.

Trump told aides he wanted the convention to be an entertaining television show. Of course, the president thought of himself as the lead actor and wanted a role each night—akin to his time as star of **The Apprentice**—in addition to his formal acceptance speech. From the White House, he hosted a discussion with frontline workers in the pandemic and with Americans who had been released from prisons overseas, issued a pardon, and conducted a naturalization ceremony.

Trump wanted to deliver his speech on the convention's final night from a special and symbolic venue. Advance staffer Max Miller took the lead on scouting locations steeped in history. Miller and other advisers considered Gettysburg National Military Park at the Civil War battlefield in rural Pennsylvania, but ruled it out because the floodlights required to illuminate the dark field would attract bugs, especially on a hot and steamy August night, and the image still would just be the president in an empty field. They also considered Mount Vernon, the George Washington estate along the Potomac River in Virginia, but it is privately owned, which presented complications. They thought about the National D-Day Memorial honoring the "Bedford Boys" in rural southwestern Virginia, as well as Fort McHenry in Baltimore, which Vice President Pence ended up choosing as the venue for his acceptance speech. Ultimately, Trump decided to give his speech in his own backyard, the South Lawn of the White House, a move that broke yet another norm and swiftly drew complaints about his use of federal property for political purposes.

On August 27, as the South Lawn was being transformed into a campaign rally site for Trump's big acceptance speech, something frightening was occurring at the NIH offices in Bethesda. Anthony Fauci's work demands had become so intense that days would go by before he had a chance to read the bills and other letters that were piling up at home.

So that morning he grabbed the mail stack to bring to the office, figuring he would go through it when he had a spare moment between meetings. When he did, he came across an ordinary-looking envelope. Fauci's name and home address were printed in a strange font, but his mind was racing about his work and he didn't think much of it. He inserted his file opener, tore the seal open, and pulled out the letter. As Fauci unfolded it, powder burst all over his face, on his tie and shirt, and around his office. There was nothing printed on the letter; it was a blank sheet of white paper.

Fauci had investigated enough of these incidences before to know immediately that the powder either was an innocuous hoax or anthrax, meaning he would have to go on ciprofloxacin for a month, or ricin, meaning he likely would die. There was no antidote to ricin.

Since Trump and some of his aides and allies started attacking Fauci earlier that year, the doctor had been receiving threats on his life. He had been provided a round-the-clock government security detail. After opening the envelope with powder, Fauci stayed in his office alone and called out to his assistant to summon the security agents who were standing guard down the hallway, outside Fauci's office suite. They ran in and said to Fauci, "Don't move. Just stay in your office." They called a hazmat team, which quickly arrived on the scene. Agents wearing full protective suits stripped Fauci naked in his office and brought him to a separate room at NIH, where other hazmat agents sprayed him down with a decontaminating chemical. Then they dressed Fauci in a hazmat suit, which ballooned around the diminutive doctor's five-foot-seven frame. They gave Fauci's contaminated clothes to the FBI for testing to determine what the powder was.

Fauci headed to the NIH basement to take a long shower, scrubbing the chemicals out of his skin, and then called his wife, who was with one of their adult daughters at the time, to tell them what had happened. He scared the hell out of them. Like Fauci, his wife, Christine Grady, knew the three possibilities for what had been in that envelope.

Fauci's security detail drove him home, where he waited for four hours for the FBI to complete its tests. He was anxious, wondering whether he might fall dead or just have been inconvenienced for a day. Thinking it might be anthrax, he called in a prescription for ciprofloxacin. Finally, he got the call: No protein was found in the powder. That ruled out anthrax, and it very likely eliminated the possibility of ricin. It had been a hoax. Maybe baby powder. Perhaps flour. It didn't matter. Fauci was safe. He breathed a sigh of relief.

At the White House, meanwhile, an estimated fifteen hundred guests gathered on the South Lawn in violation of social distancing recommendations, and only a small fraction wore face masks. The grand portico of the mansion that had been home to every president since John Adams was illuminated as the backdrop for this most political of speeches. The president spoke from a red-carpeted stage adorned with American flags and bookended by massive campaign signage. Enormous screens erected on the lawn alternately displayed the Trump-Pence campaign logo and propaganda-style campaign videos.

Trump's speech was jarringly dark and divisive. He depicted Biden in the most dangerous and sinister terms and charged that he was beholden to the far-left wing of the Democratic Party, as some sort of "Trojan horse for socialism."

"Joe Biden is not the savior of America's soul," Trump said. "He is the destroyer of America's jobs—and, if given the chance, he will be the destroyer of American greatness."

Trump cast Biden as somehow un-American.

"Your vote will decide whether we protect law-abiding Americans or whether we give free rein to violent anarchists, agitators, and criminals who threaten our citizens," Trump said. "And this election will decide whether we will defend the American way of life or whether we allow a radical movement to completely dismantle and destroy it."

Trump's remarks lasted seventy minutes, among the longest acceptance speeches in convention history, and was followed by fireworks over the

National Mall. Some of the blasts over the night sky bore the president's name, T-R-U-M-P. This was Trump's Washington. The power was his. He didn't plan to relinquish it. It would have to be taken from him.

PART THREE

Twelve

Self-Sabotage

As summer gave way to fall, Deborah Birx hit the road, preaching caution to a nation beleaguered and restless after months of pandemic restrictions. Though her travels took her across the country, she focused on cities and towns in the South and Midwest, where support for President Trump was strong and skepticism of public health guidelines ran deep. In Nashville on July 27, she told Tennessee's governor he should mandate masks and shut down bars. In Little Rock, Arkansas, on August 17, Birx directed residents to stop hosting parties in their backyards. And on a tour of the University of Alabama on September 11, she admonished young men for not wearing masks like many of their female classmates.

Birx's roving public-health safety tour came naturally to her, since she had previously served as a global health ambassador in AIDS hot spots near and far.

She told White House colleagues, "I need to get on the ground to see what they're doing right and what they're doing wrong." But Birx's evangelism jarred with messages coming out of Washington. Trump and his aides pulled the plug on regular virus briefings, blocked many media appearances for Anthony Fauci and other health experts, and carried on campaigning and governing like normal. Trump all but abdicated responsibility for ending the pandemic.

Birx's role was born of necessity. She was still working as the White House coronavirus response coordinator, albeit effectively sidelined by Scott Atlas. Birx figured that if she didn't have the ear of decision-makers in Washington, she would try to shape the views of those in the states. She scheduled meetings with governors and state health officials to brief them on national trends, help them analyze data in their states, outline best practices to slow the spread, and answer questions about how CDC guidelines might apply in their communities or for their industries.

On September 1, Birx traveled to Chicago to meet with Governor J. B. Pritzker and senior members of his team. The conversation was tense. Birx said Illinois was experiencing a spike in infections in many rural counties and showed them a chart with the data. Pritzker thought to himself, **Duh, don't you think we're monitoring our own state?** His chief of staff, Anne Caprara, spoke up.

"I think, Dr. Birx, that part of the problem is that in the rural areas, which tend to be more conservative, they're getting messages from the White House that tell them they shouldn't wear masks and they shouldn't stay in, so all the mitigation efforts that are working in Chicago aren't working in these areas," Caprara said.

"Are you guys doing a public information campaign? Are you showing farmers in the ads?" Birx asked.

"Excuse me?" Caprara said.

"Farmers," Birx said. "Like people outside of Chicago."

Caprara thought, **We have all kinds of other people, too! Not just farmers.** But she went back to the original point about the administration's messaging.

"The problem we are concerned about is that people are hearing from the president that this vaccine is going to show up two to three days before the election," Caprara said. "You guys are already sowing disinformation and discontent and people are mistrusting the vaccine by [the president] talking about it as if it's a political thing."

"What are you talking about?" Birx said. "The president has never said anything like that, nor has anybody in the White House."

In fact, Trump had on multiple occasions in August teased the possibility of a vaccine being tested and approved before the election on November 3. Caprara pulled up a news story about one such comment. The meeting soon ended, and Pritzker and his staff concluded they had wasted their time. They considered Birx's visit to be nothing more than a political tour aimed at generating publicity for the administration. Birx was in fact trying to build support for public health guidelines, but she couldn't escape the distrust sown by the president's own words.

Nor could Birx escape West Wing politics. Earlier in her tour, Birx thought she had a breakthrough with Florida governor Ron DeSantis, one of the laxest state executives when it came to coronavirus restrictions. During a visit to Tampa on July 2, Birx met with DeSantis, along with Vice President Pence and Alex Azar. Birx stressed to the governor the importance of younger people remaining vigilant about social distancing, wearing masks, and getting tested if they've been in large gatherings. At a news conference, DeSantis urged Floridians to avoid what he called the three Cs: closed spaces, crowds, and close contact. He and Birx seemed to be on the same page.

But on August 31, DeSantis hosted Atlas for the day, jetting to Tallahassee, Tampa, and the Villages, a sprawling retirement community in Central Florida. Together the governor and Trump's favorite new doctor argued that children were at low risk for COVID-19 and that schools in the state should reopen with in-person learning.

Birx and Fauci had been far more circumspect about reopening schools, as well as resuming sporting events and other aspects of normal society that necessitated mass gatherings. They urged a cautious strategy of reopening in phases, only if states met certain data benchmarks to contain community spread and ensure public health and safety. But Atlas used his public statements in Florida to assert that he and the governor both shared Trump's strategy to protect vulnerable and high-risk individuals while opening schools and other aspects of society.

Already resentful of Atlas's access to Trump, Birx was angry that Atlas had now cultivated his own ties to governors—and that some of them were listening to him over her. A colleague on the White House coronavirus task force explained why some Republican governors were loath to follow Birx's advice. "They felt like she was gloom and doom and was scaring people," this official said. "They were concerned about keeping the economy moving. That's why a lot of governors didn't want her there. They didn't like her message."

On August 29, John Ratcliffe wrote to the Senate and House intelligence committees announcing that his office would no longer provide in-person briefings about election interference. Since Ratcliffe had proven his loyalty to Trump by defending him during the impeachment hearings, many in the intelligence community widely viewed this new move as more of Ratcliffe's blocking and tackling for the president. Just ten weeks before a presidential election in which U.S. intelligence agencies had concluded Russia was interfering to help Trump, Ratcliffe's decision confirmed that assessment. Despite the intelligence community's statutory duty to keep Congress informed about national security threats, briefers from now on would provide only written summaries. Ratcliffe wrote that this move would help ensure information "is not misunderstood nor politicized."

But as had often happened in his presidency, Trump dispensed with Ratcliffe's summary and spoke plainly.

"Director Ratcliffe brought information into the committee, and the information leaked," Trump said. He invoked House Intelligence Committee chairman Adam Schiff and, without presenting any evidence, added, "Whether it was Shifty Schiff or somebody else, they leaked the information before it gets in. What's even worse, they leak the wrong information. And he got tired of it. So, he wants to do it in a different form, because you have leakers on the committee, obviously, leakers that are doing bad things, probably not even legal to leak, but we'll look into that separately."

Mark Meadows told reporters that information had leaked out of the most recent briefing on this subject and Ratcliffe had to protect sources and methods from being compromised. But officials in Ratcliffe's office did not say what Meadows was referring to. After Bill Evanina's announcement, there had been quite a few news stories in early August about Russia's intelligence agencies using social media and surrogates to undermine Joe Biden's candidacy. Trump had said he thought that information was wrong. Democratic leaders howled at Ratcliffe's new restrictions and accused the executive branch of flouting its duty to the legislative branch.

"This is a shocking abdication of its lawful responsibility to keep the Congress currently informed, and a betrayal of the public's right to know how foreign powers are trying to subvert our democracy," Nancy Pelosi and Schiff said in a joint statement. "This intelligence belongs to the American people, not the agencies which are its custodian. And the American people have both the right and the need to know that another nation, Russia, is trying to help decide who their president should be."

Senator Angus King, an independent from Maine who caucused with Democrats and sat on the Senate Intelligence Committee, was even more exercised. He said a question-and-answer session with intelligence officials was critical for lawmakers to understand the nuances of information, and that a dry written report was no substitute. "It is an outrage," King told **The New York Times.** "It smacks of a cover-up of information about foreign interference in our elections."

James Clapper, the former Obama director of national intelligence, said on CNN that he suspected Ratcliffe was merely trying to avoid talking with Congress about Russian interference, a topic that enraged Trump. By engaging in such conversations, Clapper posited, Ratcliffe would risk "saying something that might incur the wrath of the president."

After twenty-five years in senior leadership roles in

the spy game, Clapper had become persona non grata in the eyes of Trump and his acolytes, ever since early January 2017, when he had briefed President-elect Trump about intelligence showing that Russian president Vladimir Putin sought to help elect him. Clapper's honesty was a cautionary tale to Ratcliffe. As another former senior intelligence official explained, "Ratcliffe didn't want to share the Russia stuff. I think Ratcliffe and Republicans were concerned that what happened to Clapper would happen again."

But key career intelligence officials could not so easily avoid the topic with Trump. Beth Sanner, a deputy director of national intelligence who since April 2017 had personally briefed Trump on the highly classified secrets in the President's Daily Brief, knew firsthand the president's allergic reaction to any intelligence about Russian interference. No matter the context, Trump perceived the information to be some kind of personal accusation or insult. He remained embittered and disgusted by the suggestion that in 2016 he had not won the presidency on his own merit, but instead was lifted to victory by Putin and his nefarious forces.

"Beth was subject to more pressure," the former senior intelligence official said. "She knew what he would want and would not want."

Often when Sanner brought up intelligence about Russia, Trump would bristle. He sometimes would say, "What are the Chinese doing? What are the Iranians doing?" Even though the Russians were far more active during the campaign than the Chinese or Iranians, "He was so sensitive to 'Russia, Russia, Russia,' that he'd get mad at the start and never have a good discussion," recalled one regular attendee.

Some of Trump's aides were worried about how to manage the president's proclivities. Keith Kellogg told colleagues not to emphasize information about Russia at the top of briefings. His mantra was, "Start slow and scale fast."

"Here's how you do it," Kellogg said once. "When you brief the president, you balance it. You don't lead off with something [about Russia] because that will set him off. If you want him to listen to you, you weave it into your story.

"If you start off by throwing gasoline on the top of the fire, we'll get nowhere in these briefings," Kellogg added.

Sanner helped to decide what Trump needed to hear with heavy input from Robert O'Brien and top military leaders. According to the White House, Sanner had decided not to brief Trump on early 2020 intelligence suggesting the Russian military intelligence had paid bounties to Taliban militias to kill U.S. soldiers. O'Brien later said Sanner made that choice because the intelligence hadn't been fully verified; top national security leaders believed the intelligence was flawed and there was no bounty program. But a lot of other unconfirmed intelligence made it into the president's briefings.

The rule in the intelligence community was that

if the president hadn't been briefed on something, it couldn't be shared with the broader government. So, the decision not to brief Trump limited the amount of analysis on that topic for national security decision-makers across the government.

"It would put her in a box," the former senior intelligence official said. "Beth would have to come back and say, 'We won't write this.'"

For Sanner, this caused some professional strife. She had reason to have pride in the intelligence she was presenting to the president. She had previously been the vice-chair of the National Intelligence Council, the group that produced the PDB, so she knew the very officers who were providing the raw material. She also knew a good bit about Russia, having previously worked as a deputy for analysis for Russian and European affairs at the CIA. Briefers were trained to adapt to the president, and Sanner knew her best strategy was to provide the most critical information, but to stay alert to know when Trump had stopped listening. In a rare public speech at a July 2020 intelligence conference, Sanner had stressed the importance of shutting up when your customer stops paying attention.

"Watch your audience and pivot," she told aspiring intelligence analysts. "When they're done, you're done. Ultimately, it's about listening to be heard. You have to really hear people and then adjust yourself."

Labor Day is traditionally when the final stretch of the campaign kicks off in a presidential election, a two-month period after the party conventions during which nominees debate and undecided voters pay serious attention. To get a snapshot of where Trump stood, Tony Fabrizio surveyed voters in the seventeen states that Trump was targeting as major battlegrounds, or at least moderately competitive. He spent September 7, Labor Day, going over the findings with Bill Stepien and two other advisers who saw their influence expand after Brad Parscale's demotion: Justin Clark, the deputy campaign manager who oversaw the budget, legal operations, and other areas; and Jason Miller, a top aide on Trump's 2016 campaign who had returned to the fold as a senior adviser running communications and messaging strategy.

It was not a pretty picture. Biden had the lead in the electoral college and Trump was behind in many key states. Several states that Trump had carried in 2016 were right on the edge, including Arizona, Georgia, North Carolina, and Pennsylvania. Trump's vulnerabilities from earlier in the summer over managing the pandemic had not improved, and he had lost significant ground with independent voters, especially among those under forty-five years old. The president was in serious trouble. Worse still, his campaign was running low on money. Each set of polls across the seventeen states cost several hundred thousand dollars, and, to conserve resources, Stepien and his team had to cut back on future polling.

Jared Kushner tightly controlled which pieces of data were included in slideshows presented to Trump. He told Fabrizio and John McLaughlin, who also was conducting polls for Trump's campaign, "You can't bring him fifty fucking slides because we're not going to get through them. If you bring two or three things to a meeting, that's a good meeting. Focus on the important things and hope he makes a change. You can only have ten slides to make your points."

At this final stage of the campaign, when the president most needed direct advice from the campaign professionals, Fabrizio's access to Trump dried up considerably. Trump was tired of hearing bad news, and Fabrizio wasn't one to sugarcoat what the data showed. He was a realist. Kushner confronted Fabrizio about his lack of positivity.

"You're coming in and giving him negativity, but you're not helping him," Kushner said. "It's just going to make him not listen to you. I'd rather you come in and say, 'This is what people are feeling based on the polls and this is what I'd recommend you do differently,' and he can decide what to do or not. He's got his own instincts and he's a big boy. Your job is to come in and give him ideas and solutions."

Fabrizio summed up his mindset to McLaughlin, a longtime friend and former business partner. "John, our job is to be objective reporters of the data, not to be cheerleaders," Fabrizio said. "That's our first and foremost job. Lord knows, in this operation there are plenty of people that can be cheerleaders."

McLaughlin answered that "being negative without ideas how to move up on the ballot" was not productive, and that he and Fabrizio needed to focus on crafting messages that could help the president gain support.

The polling data wasn't the only setback for Trump. The president had been crusading against mail-in ballots, often making no distinction between absentee ballots proactively requested by voters—how he and members of his family voted—and ballots that some states offered to mail to all registered voters. He suggested all voting by mail was "a total fraud in the making," as he put it in a September 10 tweet, and that the only secure way to vote was in person on Election Day.

But Trump and other Republicans also needed their voters to be enthusiastic about casting ballots by any means necessary. The Trump campaign was spending hundreds of thousands of dollars on Facebook advertisements aimed at encouraging Republican voters to request absentee ballots, vote for Trump, and return them. The campaign had also invested in a robust ground operation in battleground states with teams of grassroots organizers and volunteers contacting voters, knocking on their front doors, and reminding them to fill out and return their ballots. This was a laborious, expensive, and, in Stepien's mind, essential ingredient for the fall campaign.

But campaign data showed that Trump's attacks on mail-in ballots were sometimes confusing voters or dissuading them from voting by mail. The campaign saw a return rate of only 2 or 3 percent of the voters it had contacted, meaning that the overwhelming majority did not actually return mail-in ballots. A normal return rate would have been in double digits, at least.

"Our parade was being rained on," a senior campaign official recalled. "We had these great grassroots teams that were trying to execute that process, but we could have John Smith, local volunteer, knock on someone's door, but if that voter's president is saying, 'Your vote is not going to count,' it doesn't matter a whole lot."

Republican leaders in Congress, who were fighting to maintain their Senate majority and win back the House majority, were also frustrated, believing that Trump's attacks on mail-in ballots were hurting their candidates. In the most competitive states and congressional districts, many more Democratic than Republican voters were requesting and submitting mail-in ballots.

Stepien and House Minority Leader Kevin McCarthy together set up a meeting around this time with Trump to discuss mail-in ballots specifically. They wanted to convince the president to change his message on the topic and to start encouraging his supporters to vote by mail. Stepien and McCarthy came armed with data and PowerPoint slides. But as they began talking in the Oval Office, Trump made clear that he strongly distrusted voting by mail. He said he had long believed Democrats would use mail-in ballots to steal the election from him, though there was no evidence to support that claim. Trump refused to change his tune.

But Stepien and McCarthy convinced the president at least to distinguish between the types of mail-in ballots. He agreed to attack only unsolicited ballots. But that discipline would not last, and soon enough the president would revert to wild generalizations. There was only so much they could do to wean Trump from promoting this conspiracy and likely depressing his own vote count.

The tension between Bill Barr and Trump had been steadily rising all summer over whether or not to deploy troops to suppress the George Floyd protests. In early September, the attorney general sought to create a healthy distance between the two of them. He set out on a nine-city tour, largely to promote a Justice Department program called Operation Legend, which had been launched in early July to provide federal resources to cities experiencing an uptick in violent crime. The program paired federal and local agents to put violent offenders behind bars. In two months' time, the program had achieved a considerable number of arrests and put a modest dent in the murder rates in some cities.

Barr's fall road show, billed as a series of official rather than political events, would indirectly help the president make his case for reelection. Trump thought he was doing a great job already in his speeches and news conferences. Barr privately told his confidants he thought the president was hurting himself with rambling, undisciplined remarks at every outstretched microphone. In public remarks, Trump mostly vented about the injustices he believed he had suffered at the hands of the press, the FBI, and Democrats. When he finally got to talking about his policies, Trump jumbled a lot of topics together and didn't explain how they had helped people. Barr had told Trump that the media were hostile to the president and inordinately emphasized any controversy he generated. He reiterated to Trump that his White House couldn't wing it and needed a more disciplined message strategy in the run-up to the election.

"In a campaign, it's hard enough for Republicans to get their message out—especially for you—but we need to have discipline and every day, every week have a plan of action, and that means we shut up about everything else," Barr told Trump.

Barr practiced what he preached, hoping his appearances promoting Operation Legend would give substance to Trump's claim to be a law-and-order president. It was a tried-and-true political strategy.

On September 9, Barr's tour began in Chicago, one of nine cities where the Justice Department had deployed federal agents—from the FBI, U.S. Marshals Service, and the Bureau of Alcohol, Tobacco, Firearms and Explosives—to assist local police. Speaking in the U.S. Attorney's Office in downtown Chicago, and flanked by federal law enforcement leaders, Barr announced that the coordinated teams of Operation Legend had made more than two thousand five hundred arrests and brought charges against about six hundred defendants. He credited the program with helping reduce Chicago's homicide rate. He said the number of murders in the five weeks after Operation Legend started had declined by 50 percent from roughly the same period before the program.

"I am pleased to report that Operation Legend is working," Barr said. "Crime is down and order is being restored to this great American city."

Barr then visited with Chicago police officers and toured the Englewood neighborhood, which is known as the city's murder capital, with a district commander.

The next day, September 10, Barr made a similar visit to Phoenix, Arizona, a battleground state. He highlighted a huge federal drug bust that had paired the Drug Enforcement Administration with local law enforcement and targeted the transportation networks that Mexican cartels used in major hubs such as Phoenix and other U.S. cities. Barr said the operation netted nearly 1,840 arrests, as well as the seizure of 28,560 pounds of methamphetamine, 284 firearms, and $43.3 million in drug profits.

Local newspapers in Chicago and Phoenix carried stories about Barr's visits. His message about the administration's handiwork locking up violent offenders reached voters there. But on the morning of September 10, almost on cue, Trump tweeted ominously, "If I don't win, America's Suburbs will be OVERRUN with Low Income Projects, Anarchists, Agitators, Looters and, of course, 'Friendly Protesters.'" And that evening, Trump held a campaign rally in Freeland, Michigan, where he alleged that if Biden were elected, terrorists would be welcomed into America and Antifa would rule the suburbs.

"He's promised to flood your state with refugees— and you know that as well as I do, and you see it all the time, from terrorist hot spots around the world, including Syria, Somalia, and Yemen," Trump told his crowd in Michigan.

With a not-so-subtle bit of race-baiting, Trump then accused Biden of wanting to ruin America's suburbs by forcing neighborhoods to allow more low-income housing. He described vicious thugs descending on tranquil mostly white neighborhoods and unleashing "crime like you've never seen before."

"No city, town, or suburb will be safe," Trump said.

The president mimicked the tremulous voice of a suburban housewife talking to her husband. "Say, darling, who moved in next door?" Trump said. "Oh, it's a resident of Antifa. No, thank you. Let's get out of here. Let's get the hell out of here, darling. Let's leave our suburbs. I wish Trump were president. He wouldn't have allowed that to happen."

When his aides relayed Trump's message of the day, Barr shook his head in exasperation. A few days later, Barr tried to explain to Trump that September 10 was an example of failing to highlight his administration's accomplishments, such as Operation Legend.

Trump dismissed this advice out of hand. The president felt Operation Legend was a publicity dud. The name wasn't catchy enough. The name, sadly enough, was in honor of a four-year-old boy named LeGend Taliferro, who had been shot in the face on June 29 while sleeping in bed, during a string of violent shootings in Kansas City, Missouri.

"No one cares about Operation Legend," Trump told Barr. "No one knows what 'Legend' is."

The president was right. He had also made sure no one would hear about Operation Legend. His predictions of anarchy in the suburbs grabbed most of the headlines.

On September 15, Trump notched a rare foreign-policy achievement, welcoming the leaders of Israel, Bahrain, and the United Arab Emirates to the White House to sign agreements normalizing relations among the countries. The so-called Abraham Accords, named after the biblical father of three monotheistic religions, was an important realignment in the region. The three countries had agreed to open embassies in each other's countries and establish economic ties, including allowing commercial air travel between Israel and the Emirates for the first time. Together they formed a bulwark against a common enemy, Iran.

Trump's customary showmanship defined the
elaborate South Lawn signing ceremony, which was
punctuated by the sounding of horns and crashing
of cymbals. Addressing some eight hundred attendees from the South Portico of the White House, just
below the Truman Balcony, Trump declared that the
agreement "sets history on a new course."

"After decades of division and conflict, we mark
the dawn of a new Middle East," Trump said.

Israeli prime minister Benjamin Netanyahu, em-
battled by a corruption scandal at home, was all too
eager to bask in the glow of the American president.
"This day is a pivot of history," he said, standing
alongside Trump on the portico. "It heralds a new
dawn of peace."

In an Oval Office meeting prior to the outdoor ceremony, Trump gifted Netanyahu a large golden key
that he said was "a key to the White House, a key to
our country."

Thanking him, Netanyahu said, "You have the key
to the hearts of the people of Israel."

"This is peace in the Middle East without blood all
over the sand," Trump said.

The grandiose proclamations of Trump and
Netanyahu belied a relatively narrow agreement. In
2017, Trump and Kushner had set out to broker
peace in the Middle East. But the peace plan Kushner
had worked on for years with envoys Avi Berkowitz
and Jason Greenblatt was rejected by the Palestinians.
And the more modest Abraham Accords did not

address the thorniest divide and source of tension in the region—the Israeli-Palestinian conflict. In fact, the Palestinians responded to the agreements among Israel, Bahrain, and the Emirates by launching rockets into Israel from Gaza at roughly the same time as the White House ceremony.

Nevertheless, the agreements broke the dam and gave Kushner, who had long been mocked for being naive enough to think he could bring about peace in the Middle East, a durable accomplishment. Mideast analysts said the Abraham Accords represented a tangible, meaningful diplomatic achievement, albeit something less than the original goal. They said the joint agreements signaled the potential for a broader rapprochement to come, should more Arab states conclude, as Bahrain and the Emirates had, that Iran posed a greater threat to their security than Israel.

That didn't stop Trump from overselling his accomplishment, however. The president suggested to aides, perhaps only half jokingly, that the agreement should be called the "Donald J. Trump Accord." And his campaign took out Facebook ads falsely declaring that Trump had "achieved PEACE in the MIDDLE EAST" and celebrating his nomination for the "Noble Peace Prize," misspelling Nobel. Trump was indeed nominated for the prestigious prize by an anti-immigration crusader whose name was largely unknown in the United States. Christian Tybring-Gjedde, a far-right member of the Norwegian parliament, had nominated Trump for the prize once before, along with a former Dutch politician who had been critical of Islam's treatment of women.

Behind the scenes starting in May and continuing throughout the summer, Robert Redfield pushed to add millions of dollars to the CDC's budget to help distribute the coronavirus vaccines once they had been approved for use. He knew the country sorely lacked a robust public health infrastructure and that the states lacked the money, staff, and expertise to handle the rapid and massive delivery of vaccines necessary to bring an end to the pandemic. Redfield referred to the orderly distribution of millions of doses of vaccines as the "last mile." Several pharmaceutical companies were racing to develop and manufacture vaccines, but that wasn't the end of the road. The last mile was making sure states could safely and efficiently administer shots to their residents.

Other top officials in the administration did not seem to grasp the importance of this. Meadows had been a vocal critic of the CDC when he was in Congress, pushing a bill to reduce its mission and budget by roughly half and to limit its purview to infectious diseases. Meadows had argued the CDC was overstepping by providing its health recommendations on environmental health risks, chronic diseases like obesity and diabetes, and other subjects. As White House chief of staff, Meadows resisted several of Redfield's requests for additional funds during the pandemic. Azar, who oversaw the CDC as the secretary of health and human services, echoed the White House line that the CDC didn't need the additional funds.

Starting in June, as Redfield conferred with congressional appropriators about growing the CDC's budget with supplemental funds, Meadows proactively stepped into the budget discussions to say the White House objected. Redfield learned from a legislative aide that, at Meadows's direction, the White House's legislative affairs staff dive-bombed a negotiated increase for the CDC's budget.

"Meadows just took the money out," the aide told Redfield.

"No, you don't know that," Redfield said, insisting it couldn't be true.

"Yeah," the aide said, "I do know it."

Redfield had been arguing at White House task-force meetings that his focus on the "last mile" was a necessity. He pointed out that with Operation Warp Speed, the government had found money to build factories to ramp up the speed of manufacturing vaccines, which he applauded.

"Just as important as that is for you to get the money to CDC so we can distribute it to the states so they can begin to set up their last mile distribution mechanisms," Redfield told colleagues on the task force. "It's not going to help us to have a bunch of vaccine and still have these states not ready to really function at that high capacity."

Redfield and his team had worked with officials in sixty-four different jurisdictions in all fifty states, all of whom would oversee vaccine distribution, to draft a detailed blueprint for how to get vaccines to their residents. They did tabletop exercises to walk through how local authorities would launch distribution operations, starting as early as January 2021. They had the plans. What was missing was the money to pay for it.

As the discussion over CDC funds continued, Meadows coincidentally called Redfield one day for medical advice. A former constituent of his in North Carolina had a difficult health problem and Meadows asked Redfield what advice he would give. Redfield was more than happy to help. But he took the opportunity at the end of the call to tell Meadows how important the "last mile" money was. Redfield believed Meadows was extremely smart, and had an elephant's memory, able to repeat back to aides what they had said months earlier. Redfield also knew from experience that it was extremely difficult to move Meadows off his stated position. The chief listened politely, but that was it.

Despite this resistance in his own chain of command, Redfield had powerful supporters in Congress in both parties who shared his belief that vaccine distribution funding for the CDC was critical. They included Senator Roy Blunt, the Republican chairman of the Appropriations subcommittee for health and human services, and Senator Patty Murray, the subcommittee's ranking Democrat. Redfield conferred with them privately about gaps in the country's public health system to handle this wartime endeavor.

Agency chiefs or even Cabinet members were not supposed to contradict the president by asking for more money than what was proposed in the budget. Redfield was supposed to keep quiet and be happy with whatever the CDC got. He had been warned by his own staff that Azar and his team were instructing him not to say anything about seeking more emergency funds. "You're not to do this," one Azar aide told a senior Redfield deputy.

But by September, Redfield could no longer be silent. He took a public stand. First, he had a series of private calls with Blunt and Murray to tell them time was running out and the whole country was in trouble if the CDC didn't snag emergency funds in the billions of dollars.

Redfield told one of his deputies, "This is so important that if I get fired by telling Congress what is needed, so be it."

Blunt and Murray went to work. As the subcommittee chairman and a member of Trump's party, Blunt had more sway with the White House, and he made Redfield's mission—getting people safely vaccinated as fast as possible—his own. On September 9, Blunt sent a formal letter to Redfield expressing concern about plans for vaccine distribution and asked in writing a question he already knew the answer to: Did the CDC have enough money to make this happen? Blunt wrote that he feared the CDC would need supplemental emergency funding to achieve this goal. Then Blunt gave Redfield cover to say what he needed to say in public by scheduling a hearing on the matter and calling on the CDC director to testify.

At the hearing, on September 16, Redfield's question-and-answer session with Blunt, Murray, and other senators might as well have been scripted. The senators raised their worries about the speedy delivery of vaccines and the large sums the CDC would need to make it happen, and Redfield answered their probing questions honestly, as required. Redfield incensed the White House by saying that the CDC and its partners needed $6 billion to help states create the infrastructure needed to distribute vaccines. Without it, he testified, the delivery would be jeopardized. The funds had been proposed in pandemic relief legislation that Congress had not yet adopted.

For the White House, the hearing got worse. When Murray asked about the state of the CDC's budget, Redfield revealed that the administration had transferred $300 million from the CDC to the Department of Health and Human Services' public affairs office. Almost all that money was slated to be used for a public relations campaign "to defeat despair and inspire hope" about the virus, ahead of the election, Redfield said. Worse still, he said that the CDC had not been asked to provide scientific expertise for the campaign.

The presentation infuriated Azar, who was ready to fire Redfield.

Redfield also angered Trump when he provided a grim timetable for vaccine distribution that contrasted with the rosy forecasts the president had been giving. The CDC director told the Senate committee that he believed most Americans wouldn't have access to a vaccine until the late spring or summer of 2021, and possibly not until that fall. Trump had been pegging the vaccine rollout to the fall of 2020, around the time of the election.

A top deputy to Azar called Redfield as soon as the hearing broke to ask what in the world he was doing; the CDC director had been instructed not to publicly contradict the president's budget. "I have a higher calling to tell the truth," Redfield replied.

Speaking to reporters that evening, Trump reiterated his timetable, and said that Redfield, despite having spent months planning vaccine distribution with the states, might not have all the facts. "We think we can start sometime in October. So as soon as it's announced, we'll be ready to start," Trump said at the top of his news conference. "We've manufactured all the necessary supplies, so as soon as the FDA approves the vaccine, and as you know we're very close to that, we'll be able to distribute at least one hundred million vaccine doses by the end of 2020, and a large number much sooner than that."

When a reporter pressed Trump about how this squared with Redfield's timeline of mid-2021, the president claimed to reporters that he had called Redfield and that the director had not offered this timeline to him, though Trump had actually not called Redfield that day. "I think he made a mistake when he said that. It's just incorrect information," Trump said. "I think he got the message maybe confused. Maybe it was stated incorrectly."

When another reporter asked the president what the American people should believe, after he had twice contradicted the CDC director's prepared testimony before Congress, Trump, furious by now, cut the reporter off.

"He's contradicting himself," Trump said, referring to Redfield. "You know what I think? I think he misunderstood the . . . I told you. I don't have to go through this. I think he misunderstood the questions. But I'm telling you. Here's the bottom line. Distribution is going to be very rapid. He may not know that. Maybe he's not aware of that. When he said it, I believe he was confused. I'm just telling you. We're ready to go, as soon as the vaccine happens."

Redfield took more arrows. Meadows appeared on Fox News the morning of September 17 and said the CDC director was uninformed and confused.

"If I were a betting man, I would bet on President Trump," Meadows told the hosts of **Fox & Friends.** He added, "I'm not sure where Dr. Redfield got his particular timetable, but it is not based on those that are closest to the process."

The chief of staff's broadside raised the question of who was closest to the process, if not the CDC director.

One September afternoon, amid his scramble to secure more vaccine funding, Redfield paid a visit to Michael Caputo's office at HHS. As they often did when they had some time to kill between meetings, the two men made espresso from a small machine Caputo kept near his desk and chatted about what was going on in the administration. It was a rare moment to relax. Then Redfield noticed a lump on Caputo's neck.

"What's this, Michael?" Redfield asked. "Your lymph node is hard. You have to go to the doctor."

Caputo, fifty-eight, had been under intense stress. He was trying to manage the health department's communications and to somehow spin a positive narrative for the reelection campaign out of the administration's failure to control the virus. He had been on the road with Azar, including a visit to Caputo's hometown of Buffalo in June. They had toured the Roswell Park Comprehensive Cancer Center and promoted, among other things, cancer screenings.

All the while, cancer was spreading in Caputo's neck and he didn't know it. On September 12, Caputo returned home to Buffalo and got an ultrasound. That night, his doctor called. "It looks like cancer," the doctor told Caputo.

Caputo didn't sleep much that night. The next morning, September 13, he sat on the front porch of his Buffalo house, wearing a T-shirt on a sunny Sunday, and recorded a Facebook Live video for friends on his personal Facebook page. It was bizarre. Caputo talked about seeing long shadows on the ceiling of his Washington apartment when he was alone. He claimed he and his family had been threatened and harassed because of his connection to Trump. He warned that "hit squads" were being trained for an armed opposition to a second Trump term. And he encouraged his friends to stock up on ammunition for their guns because it soon could be difficult to procure. Caputo also accused scientists at the CDC and elsewhere in the government of being part of a "resistance unit" working to foil Trump's reelection, though he cited no evidence.

"The scientists—the deep state scientists—want America sick through November," Caputo said. He added, "These people cannot—cannot—allow America to get better, nor can they allow America to hear good news. It must be all bad news from now until the election. Frankly, ladies and gentlemen, that's sedition. They are sacrificing lives in order to defeat Donald Trump."

Under mounting pressure in the media over his odd Facebook soliloquy, Caputo apologized on September 16 to Azar and the HHS staff for embarrassing them. He later told friends that he was in a bad headspace during this livestreaming performance because of his likely cancer diagnosis and because just that morning someone had driven past his house yelling, "Caputo, you're a dead man!" Caputo took a medical leave of absence and moved home to Buffalo to seek treatment for his cancer. His service in the Trump administration was over.

But government scientists still stepped up to help him fight his cancer, despite his insults. Azar arranged for Caputo to get a biopsy at the National Cancer Institute, where the center's director, Dr. Ned Sharpless, treated him and removed his lymph node. Fauci asked two doctors he knew to offer Caputo their medical opinions. Fauci and Redfield, as well as Stephen Hahn, Seema Verma, and Surgeon General Jerome Adams, called Caputo regularly to check in and wish him well. And Admiral Brett Giroir, the assistant secretary for health who oversaw COVID-19 testing, knew a thing or two about cancer, having served as a scientific advisory board member at the MD Anderson Cancer Center. He gave Caputo a pep talk.

"You have to go into your radiation treatments like you own the machine," Giroir said. "Don't go in there weak. Don't go in there with self-pity. Don't go in there like you're gonna die. You go in there like you're the one who's going to throw the switch and you'll get through it."

Thirteen

Stand Back and Stand By

On September 23, about nine minutes into President Trump's news conference from the White House briefing room, a reporter asked whether he would commit to a peaceful transfer of power after the election, "win, lose, or draw." The president's answer was extraordinary, if not surprising.

"We're going to have to see what happens," Trump said. Reviving his assault on mail-in voting, he continued, "You know that I've been complaining very strongly about the ballots. And the ballots are a disaster."

The reporter, Brian Karem of **Playboy** magazine, pressed further. "I understand that, but people are rioting," he said. "Do you commit to making sure that there's a peaceful transferal of power?"

"Get rid of the ballots and we'll have a very

peaceful—there won't be a transfer, frankly. There'll be a continuation," Trump replied. "The ballots are out of control. You know it, and you know who knows it better than anybody else? The Democrats know it better than anybody else."

This exchange lasted less than one minute but represented Trump's most substantial threat yet to the nation's history of free and fair elections and prompted election officials and law enforcement authorities around the country to prepare for an unprecedented constitutional crisis.

Asked about the comments, Joe Biden responded with mocking incredulity. "What country are we in? I'm being facetious," he told reporters. "Look, he says the most irrational things. I don't know what to say."

But the next day, Trump erased any doubt about his seriousness or sincerity by reiterating that he may not honor the results. As he left the White House for a campaign rally in North Carolina, Trump told reporters, "We want to make sure the election is honest, and I'm not sure that it can be."

So serious were the comments, that even Trump's Republican allies in Congress, including Senate Majority Leader Mitch McConnell, felt obliged to issue statements declaring that the winner of the election would be inaugurated on January 20, 2021, as the Constitution requires.

That any official needed to affirm that an orderly transition of power would take place meant the United States was in uncharted territory. Never had

an incumbent president refused to accept the results of an election or obstructed the peaceful transfer
of power.

Despite Trump's equivocations, some of his aides
had begun administering a transition process on his
behalf in accordance with the Presidential Transition
Act. Chris Liddell, a deputy White House chief of
staff, was leading the effort and had begun negotiations with Biden's transition team. On September 4,
the White House issued guidance to all federal departments and agencies outlining transition preparations.

As Bill Barr said at a September 22 news conference in Milwaukee, "What this country has going for
it more than anything else is the peaceful transfer of
power, and that is accomplished through elections
that people have confidence in. And so we should be
doing everything to support that confidence." But the
attorney general's conventions fell on the president's
deaf ears.

As he watched Trump undermine the legitimacy of
the upcoming vote, Senator Mitt Romney couldn't
help but recall his conversations with Trump nearly
four years earlier, when the then president-elect was
considering him to be secretary of state.

"Every time we met, and we met twice in person
and we spoke on the phone more than once, each
time he would begin with, 'You know, I won the
popular vote because of all the illegals that voted in
California,' and, 'I won New Hampshire,'" Romney
recalled. "He said there were hundreds of buses from

Massachusetts that took people to New Hampshire and they voted up there. I didn't argue with him. I just listened and thought this was something he was doing to convince himself."

Both claims were false, of course. In 2016, Hillary Clinton carried New Hampshire and won the national popular vote by nearly three million votes. There was no evidence of widespread fraud in California or New Hampshire or in any other state. As Trump sowed doubt about the 2020 election, Romney naively assumed the president was again trying to satisfy his own outsized ego. He could not imagine Trump was laying the groundwork to actually subvert the election.

"When I heard him say, if I lose to Joe Biden, the worst candidate in the history of the earth, it will be because the election is 'rigged,' I just presumed that's in that category of something he's going to say to himself and a few other people will perhaps believe him and he'll therefore be comfortable at Mar-a-Lago with himself and with his ego in the event that he loses," Romney said.

As for Trump's refusal to commit to a peaceful transfer of power, Romney called this "dangerous for the country and very troubling." When Romney had run for president in 2012, President Obama had authorized his administration to cooperate fully with Romney's transition team, led by former Utah governor Michael Leavitt, because it was important for the country that there be a smooth transition in the event that he lost reelection. But Romney said he suspects

Trump, who was superstitious, was afraid to jinx his chances by making an affirmative statement about a presidential transition.

"As I heard that comment, I thought to myself, oh, he thinks that if he participates in a transition that he's going to get jinxed and that might mean he would lose and that he has to make sure that he doesn't do anything that suggests he can do anything but win," Romney said. "I marked it up to his psyche, but recognized that this comes at a cost in the event he loses."

By early fall, Trump's concerns about vaccine approval morphed into outright paranoia. He imagined a phalanx of powerful officials and institutions aligned to prevent him from announcing a safe vaccine before the election. He suspected that government scientists—and even some of his appointees, including Stephen Hahn—were conspiring to delay the vaccine rollout, and that pharmaceutical companies were in on the con.

There was no evidence of this, but that didn't stop the president venting to advisers and, on occasion, the public. As Trump had told Alex Azar over the phone in August, "These drug companies and Hahn and the FDA. They're going to keep us from having a vaccine before the election. They're going to delay this. You've got to stop them."

"Sure, Mr. President," said Azar. The health secretary had never believed it was possible for manufacturers to develop an effective, fully tested vaccine and get FDA approval before the election, but he sometimes chose to listen to the president rather than challenge him.

Azar was by now familiar with Trump's antipathy toward pharmaceutical companies, which he had long blamed for unfairly driving up the costs of prescription drugs. The president many times had asked Azar to have the government set drug prices—an ironic request considering Azar was a former pharmaceutical executive. "Just like the U.K.," Trump would tell Azar. "Socialize it."

And back in July, Trump had fumed during a meeting about the $2 billion the government had recently agreed to pay Pfizer to buy its coronavirus vaccine. "These evil drug companies," Trump had said. "Why are we giving so much money to these drug companies, who I can't stand?"

Trump ratcheted up his pressure on Azar over vaccines into September. In one conversation, Azar tried to give the president a reality check.

"We are not going to get a vaccine before the election," Azar said. "If we get it by the end of the year, it will be a miracle."

Azar went over the timing for vaccine trials, something he had explained to the president several times before. Patients were chosen randomly. They were given doses in controlled settings. They were carefully monitored. The data tracking their reactions were carefully transcribed and studied.

But the president was impatient. "Putin approved Sputnik and then got the data later," Trump said.

Azar said that scientists worldwide agreed Russia's coronavirus vaccine had been dangerously rushed. It had been approved for widespread use before large trials had been conducted to test reactions from patients and measure the drug's efficacy.

"Mr. President, if we do that, nobody will take the vaccine," Azar said. "We're putting vaccines in people's arms. We have to have the data. If career people at FDA don't sign off on this, we have something people will literally never take."

Dr. Paul Offit, a member of the FDA's vaccine advisory council who served as director of the Vaccine Education Center at Children's Hospital of Philadelphia, observed at the time, "The one thing you can't do—and it's what everybody fears, it's what the pharmaceutical companies fear, it's what everybody on the inside fears—is that the government would, because of political purposes or because other countries put a vaccine out before us, truncate the normal process you'd accept for a safe and effective vaccine."

This was also something that worried Mark Esper, whose office became crucial to Operation Warp Speed. The defense secretary had chosen Army General Gus Perna, whom he had worked with before and trusted totally, as the operation's logistics chief. Esper and

Azar agreed on the plan. When a set of companies hit upon promising vaccines, they would immediately begin mass producing at least two or more vaccines in hopes the drugs would later secure FDA approval after clinical trials. The two men accepted up front that they risked wasting hundreds of millions of dollars on shots that didn't meet the final standard. But they figured they would rather lose money than have to explain to Congress they would need another four months to produce enough vaccine doses for the country. In four months, how many people might die waiting for the vaccine?

By early summer, the plan had been working beautifully. Esper was initially delighted when Perna told him he was authorizing contracts to produce two promising vaccines, and that in preliminary tests they were more than 80 percent effective, far outperforming projections. But the secretary's ebullience then turned to concern. If the president learned they had millions of doses produced, would he or a White House adviser start demanding they administer them to the public before the vaccine had been fully vetted by the FDA?

At the FDA, Hahn had been thinking hard about how to restore people's faith in his agency following the botched August announcement on convalescent plasma. On September 22, Laurie McGinley reported in **The Washington Post** that the FDA was going to set a stricter standard for approving coronavirus vaccines. The FDA would require manufacturers to monitor patients enrolled in late-stage clinical trials for sixty days after they received their second dose of the vaccine, before approving the drug. The scientific goal was to carefully assess long-term immunity. But the political result was that vaccines were unlikely to be approved before the election.

Within thirty minutes of McGinley's story publishing on the **Post**'s website, Mark Meadows called Azar and yelled.

"It's going to take FDA sixty days to rule on an application as a result of this!" Meadows said. "This is going to delay things by sixty days."

"Listen, Mark, this is something FDA leaked before sending to OIRA at OMB," Azar said, referring to the budget office and its regulation-review division, the Office of Information and Regulatory Affairs. "Hahn sent this to manufacturers weeks ago. Then he briefed the media on this guidance before I knew about this."

Azar knew the change had been discussed with Pfizer, Moderna, and other manufacturers in August, but hadn't realized the political impact of the sixty-day monitoring requirement.

"Mark, I told Jared and Brad about these letters weeks ago," Azar said, referring to Jared Kushner and Brad Smith, a coronavirus adviser who was close to Kushner.

"They are not the chief of staff to the president of the United States," Meadows said.

On September 24, at a coronavirus task-force meeting in the Situation Room, Trump complained about the FDA guidance and said the scientists wanted him to fail. He believed that Hahn, having been blasted mercilessly by the scientific community as a Trump enabler over the FDA's convalescent plasma approval, was raising the bar for vaccines—and raising it unfairly high. This was horrible, he said.

"We need a vaccine before the election and this guidance is going to delay that," Trump groaned.

Azar figured Trump had shown incredible leadership in pushing for the fastest vaccine development in history, something about which he could crow, regardless of when the FDA-approved shots were going into arms.

"Mr. President, I need you to understand this," Azar said. "There is no physical way there will be an FDA-approved vaccine by November third. It simply cannot happen. We may get data by then. Then that will be a successful vaccine and you can own that. The pharmaceutical companies will be bragging to heaven about that. That's your win."

Azar told Trump that it wasn't worth griping about the FDA. They had to keep their eyes on the prize: approving a reliable, gold-standard vaccine. "They are the least of our concerns," he added.

The president took it in. He kept his arms folded and nodded. The matter was settled—for now, at least.

As they left the meeting, Smith, the head of innovation at the Centers for Medicare & Medicaid Services, said to Azar, "Mr. Secretary, thank you so much for doing that. That was a home run."

Azar even received praise from his archrival, Seema Verma. "You did a great job on the FDA issue," she wrote him in a text message. "Not easy but hopefully made a big difference." Azar was so bowled over he showed the message to aides.

Trump's fury over the FDA may have subsided, but his rage over Robert Redfield's testimony about the vaccine timeline had not. The president was not alone. Meadows and Azar were angry with Redfield as well. On September 25, CNN reported breaking news: Trump had lost patience with Redfield and he may soon fire the CDC director.

The next morning, just before 7:00, Trump called Redfield on his cell phone. The director was at his home in Baltimore, feeling a tad apprehensive about the conversation to come.

"Are you listening to the news?" Trump asked him.

"I've seen a little," Redfield said.

"Well, it's fake news," Trump said. "You're doing a great job."

Redfield let that soak in. He had a little joke in store for the president.

"You mean, I'm not being fired?" Redfield said, his tone a little impish.

"No, you're doing a great job," Trump insisted.

Redfield looked over at his wife, Joyce, who was listening to the conversation on speakerphone.

"Well, you just broke my wife's heart, because she already called the moving vans," Redfield told the president.

Trump offered a forced laugh. They said goodbye.

But by the next week, Redfield was seriously considering quitting. Unlike many of the president's detractors, Redfield admired Trump as a leader and believed he was unusually gifted in his ability to process a lot of information quickly and make instinctive decisions. He thought Trump's decisions to restrict travel from China in January and from Europe in March had been bold because in each instance he had rapidly overruled his economic advisers. But watching the president and his White House advisers reject science and operate with a campaign-only mindset in the summer and fall, skipping past difficult realities and painting a fantasy in which the virus was on its last legs, took a toll on Redfield. He became uncomfortable with the Emerald City facade.

On September 29, the coronavirus task force gathered in the Situation Room to decide what to do about cruise ships. The no-sail order that Redfield authorized in March and successfully pushed to extend in July was set to expire the next day. Redfield believed infections were likely to spike in the winter months ahead and that resuming travel on cruise ships, which were petri dishes for pathogens, would be irresponsible. He urged the task force to extend the ban until the end of February 2021, at a minimum, by which time some Americans might be vaccinated.

As Redfield advocated for extending the ban, Vice President Pence, who chaired the meeting, nodded and listened politely, but his face was dour. Pence rejected Redfield's proposal and told him he thought it was too draconian and could inflict too much economic pain on cruise lines, which had already laid off workers and taken a massive beating on Wall Street. The Trump administration extended the ban only another month, until October 31, which was what the industry proposed. The Cruise Lines International Association had announced it would voluntarily suspend its cruising business until that date.

Redfield believed that as the CDC director he was legally the final authority on a decision of this nature. Being overruled by Pence made Redfield ask himself, **If I'm not allowed to protect public health, how can I do this job?** He considered resigning if the cruising ban was not extended further.

Redfield spoke with Marc Short. "This is a really important public health issue that I feel has to be done," he said. "I'm not going to be able to do my job if these things aren't operationalized. I feel very strongly about it."

Later that day, **Axios**'s Jonathan Swan reported that Pence had rejected Redfield's push to extend the ban. His story included comments from anonymous sources saying Pence and others in the White House had bowed to a powerful industry's wishes and were rushing to reopen businesses before the election, putting the public at risk. The cruise industry had a major presence in Florida, one of the key battleground states for Trump's reelection.

White House spokesman Brian Morgenstern

rejected that suggestion. "The president, the vice president, and the task force follow the science and data to implement policies that protect the public health and also facilitate the safe reopening of our country," he said in a statement to Swan. "It is not about politics. It is about saving lives."

That statement was misleading, as Pence had rejected the counsel of the top scientist advising him and the data on viral spread on cruise ships. But Redfield refused to give up. Over the next month, he planned how he could hot-wire another extension. He and his staff designed a "conditional" sail order, one that would allow cruise ships to begin a return to sailing in phases, with firm social distancing, testing, and quarantine rules. The order reminded the industry—and the White House—of the studies showing that the virus had rapidly spread aboard a densely populated ship, and often passed from one voyage to the next via infected crew members. The phased plan created substantial and costly hurdles up front. The cruise ships would first have to perform simulated cruises to show they had implemented new measures and were equipped to follow testing protocols for crew and passengers. Only then could a real cruise set sail, albeit with a drastically limited number of passengers.

The White House, facing the risk that Redfield might resign, agreed to the phased-in start. The industry, confronting the high costs of these test runs, voluntarily suspended cruises through the end of the year. Redfield had won.

For Trump, September 26 was a day of celebration. On September 18, Supreme Court justice Ruth Bader Ginsburg, the modern feminist icon, had died at age eighty-seven from complications of pancreatic cancer. Her death presented Trump with the third Supreme Court vacancy of his presidency—and an historic opportunity to shift the court to the right by replacing a liberal hero with a hard-line conservative. Trump had moved quickly, and on September 26 he formally nominated Amy Coney Barrett, a forty-eight-year-old federal judge in Indiana. That Saturday, more than 150 guests arrived at the White House for Trump's Rose Garden announcement. It was a crisp and sunny autumn day in Washington. There was a feeling of invincibility in the air.

Upon arriving, attendees were administered rapid coronavirus tests by White House doctors and waited in a room, wearing masks, for their results. Those who tested negative were told it was safe to remove their masks, so they did. In the Rose Garden, guests mingled, shook hands, and hugged one another. The maskless mixing continued indoors at a reception where guests personally congratulated Barrett.

Attendees included Cabinet members and senior White House officials, Republican senators, Barrett's family, family members of the late justice Antonin Scalia, and other supporters of the president, including Rudy Giuliani, Laura Ingraham, and Chris

Christie. The Reverend John Jenkins, president of the University of Notre Dame, the law school from which Barrett graduated and worked as a professor, flew in from Indiana, where his campus had been reeling from a coronavirus outbreak.

Attendees were seemingly so indifferent to the virus that the gathering resembled a normal event from before the outbreak of the pandemic. To the millions of Americans watching on television as Barrett introduced herself and Trump testified to her qualifications, it appeared there was nothing to worry about.

That weekend Trump had a full schedule of non–socially distanced interactions. After the Barrett event, Trump flew to Middletown, Pennsylvania, where he spoke at an evening campaign rally. The next day, September 27, the president played golf at Trump National Golf Club in northern Virginia, held a news conference at the White House, and hosted a reception for Gold Star parents. Trump also met that weekend with Christie, Giuliani, Kellyanne Conway, Hope Hicks, Jason Miller, Stephen Miller, Bill Stepien, and a few other advisers to prepare for his upcoming debate with Biden.

The Gold Star event the night of September 27 honored the families of fallen service members. Trump gave formal remarks about the Gold Star families in the East Room and then mingled privately with many of them. As with all White House guests who met the president, the Gold Star parents were first tested for the coronavirus and did not disclose any symptoms.

As soon as the reception ended, Trump complained to some of his advisers about having been close to the Gold Star families, a concern he had not had about mingling with Republican officials and friends celebrating Barrett's nomination a day prior.

"You guys are letting people entirely too close to me," the germaphobe president said. "It's so sad, these Gold Star families are telling these stories, they're weeping, they're crying, they want to hug you, and they're all over me. You guys should not let these people close to me. They're way too close.

"If they have COVID," Trump added, "I'm definitely going to get it."

At about 3:30 p.m. on September 27, Candice Parscale called police in Fort Lauderdale, Florida, to report that her husband, Brad, Trump's former campaign manager, had been talking about suicide and may have just shot himself. When officers arrived outside their waterfront home in the Seven Isles neighborhood, they first found Candice on the street, panicked and barefoot wearing a bikini top and a towel wrapped around her waist, having fled her home. She told police that Brad was drunk, had argued with her, made suicidal comments, grabbed a gun, racked the slide, and loaded it in her presence. Afraid for her own safety, Candice said she ran out of the house on foot and heard a possible gunshot, though later assumed Brad had not shot himself because she heard him ranting inside and their dog barking frantically.

Candice told police that Brad drinks, "suffers from PTSD," and had hit her, according to police reports. Candice had several bruises on both arms as well as contusions on her cheek and forehead, which she said she got a few days earlier from an altercation with Brad. She said Brad had been stressed out for the past two weeks and had made suicidal comments over the past week, talking about shooting himself.

Brad Parscale had had a difficult time dealing with his July demotion. He went from being a MAGA celebrity who flew around on Air Force One and had the ear of the president to a castaway in Florida. His proximity to power, intoxicating as it was for so many Trump aides, suddenly was all but nil. Parscale still tried calling Trump every week, but only sometimes got through to the president. The two spoke in late September, a few days before Candice Parscale called police to the house. Brad Parscale told Trump that Stepien and other campaign leaders were "fucking up."

"They're not letting me do what I need to do to help you win," Parscale said. "You asked me to do digital and they're not letting me do it."

Kushner called around this time as well. "We're not sure we made the right decision," he told Parscale. "We need you to come back and [look over] what Bill's doing. We don't think he's making good choices." Kushner told other aides he had exaggerated his concerns about Stepien to Parscale because he wanted to puff up the former campaign manager. He knew Parscale had been distraught and he wanted to keep him involved on the campaign because he valued his data analysis.

Parscale had booked a flight to Washington for Monday, September 28, to return to campaign head-quarters and, as Kushner asked, monitor what Stepien was doing as campaign manager.

But he never made that flight. When police got to his house on September 27, officers out-side contacted him on the phone and asked him to leave. But Parscale stayed. His speech was slurred, and he seemed to be crying, according to police reports. Police called in crisis negotiators and a SWAT team. Police eventually got Parscale to exit the home. "I'm not trying to kill myself," Parscale told officers as he walked down his driveway, barefoot, bare-chested, wearing shorts and a baseball cap, and clutching a can of beer. An officer commanded him multiple times, "Get on the ground." When Parscale stayed stand-ing, the officer tackled him at the waist and pushed him to the ground. Police handcuffed and detained Parscale. "I didn't do anything," Parscale said. Police went inside and secured ten firearms: five handguns, two shotguns, two rifles, and a small revolver. They brought Parscale his phone, shirt, and shoes, and transported him to Broward Health Medical Center under the Baker Act, a Florida law that allows au-thorities to commit people they believe pose a danger to themselves.

The Trump campaign offered support to Parscale initially after his hospitalization. Campaign spokesman Tim Murtaugh issued a statement referring to Parscale as "a member of our family." But later, after the president was briefed on the incident, Murtaugh issued a new statement attempting to capitalize politically on the incident.

"The disgusting, personal attacks from Democrats and disgruntled RINOs have gone too far, and they should be ashamed of themselves for what they've done to this man and his family," Murtaugh said. RINO was an acronym for Republicans in Name Only, a derisive term for Republicans deemed too soft in their support for GOP policies or politicians.

In the weeks leading up to the first presidential debate on September 29 at the campus of Case Western Reserve University in Cleveland, Ohio, Biden spent considerable time practicing—reading briefing books; rehearsing his criticisms of Trump and his defenses of his record; getting used to the ping-pong nature of a two-person debate; training himself to keep his answers to ninety seconds and his follow-up points to thirty seconds; and performing from behind a lectern in mock debates staged by his advisers.

But Trump kept putting off his debate preparation until suddenly the big night was near. Trump's advisers were worried about the president's readiness. Sure, he had sparred incessantly with reporters, but he had not been on a debate stage in four years, and despite winning the election, he was hardly considered a skilled debater. Trump could land a punch, but his advisers knew he struggled to recall facts or to deliver clear and concise messages. Stepien fretted over Trump's ability to recall policy details or recite his accomplishments in a range of areas—not because the president was old or didn't pay attention, but simply because so much had happened over the past four years and he couldn't stick to disciplined talking points.

Lindsey Graham, who had similar concerns, encouraged Trump to avoid nasty personal exchanges with Biden. "The more you talk about issues the better you're going to do," the senator told him. "Sound like the president. Look like the president. Don't take Joe for granted. He'll be fine. You've got to [be] the storyteller on foreign policy, what you're doing, trying to turn around the COVID, marching toward a vaccine—that kind of stuff. Just tell the story of your accomplishments."

To tell that story effectively, Trump needed to study and focus. But his message to the worrywarts on his campaign was, "Guys, I got this."

The weekend of September 26, Trump finally sat for a series of full debate prep sessions. Christie, a former prosecutor and widely considered to be one of the Republican Party's most agile debaters, led the session. He coached Trump to be aggressive in the first thirty minutes of the ninety-minute debate. That was when the most people tuned in and paid the closest attention, and it was a chance to set a tone and framework, with both Biden and the moderator, Chris Wallace of Fox News, for the remainder of the debate.

"That first thirty minutes, you come out there and you are letting people know the kind of president Donald Trump is and the kind of president he will be over the course of the next four years," Christie told Trump.

Christie also advised Trump to stay on offense. "You've got to put him on his heels," he said. "Bait him on Hunter. See if you can get under his skin on Hunter. And don't let him lie about you. If he lies about you, go right back at him."

Conway cautioned against being too aggressive out of the gate and counseled Trump to let Biden hoist himself on his own petard.

"Let Biden speak," she told the president. "Numbers totally fluster Biden. He gets them confused all the time. He will get tired and lose his luster."

In mock exchanges with Trump, Christie played Biden and Conway played Wallace. She was tough with her questions and Christie was brutal with his attacks and interruptions. Together, they were trying to rough up the president so he would be ready.

As Conway told Trump, "There's no debate moderator who's going to be that rude to you. They'll be that challenging, but they won't be officious. And it's good that I'm being angry and getting up in your face. It helps control the temperament."

Trump had invited Giuliani to the sessions, after the former New York mayor called the president asking to be included. Giuliani wanted to help and showed up at the September 27 session armed with talking points about Hunter Biden and his work in Ukraine and China. Giuliani had been pushing stories about Hunter Biden with media outlets and wanted Trump to have ammunition to make the case against his opponent's son.

Giuliani clashed with Christie and Conway. Whereas Christie suggested merely mentioning Hunter Biden as a means to throw Joe Biden off his balance, Giuliani thought Trump should try to litigate his overseas entanglements. Most of the other advisers found Giuliani's advice to be "supremely unhelpful," as one characterized his coaching tips for the president. Though not an official member of the debate team, Giuliani wanted to return for Trump's prep session on September 28, the day before the debate. Aides told Giuliani they would be gathering at 2:00 p.m., though they were scheduled to start at noon. They had tricked Giuliani by giving him the wrong time. He showed up so late he only got to participate in the final half hour of prep.

On September 29, by the time Trump touched down in Cleveland he had become convinced that starting on the offensive and staying there for the entire ninety minutes was the key to beating Biden. The debate devolved into chaos and acrimony from the get-go. Trump repeatedly interrupted Biden, rarely letting him finish a full sentence. He also insulted his opponent, angrily raised his voice, and, yes, lied. Trump's badgering and jeering was so obscene that Wallace pleaded with him multiple times to stick to the debate rules the two campaigns had negotiated and agreed to, and to let Biden speak when it was his turn. At one point, an exasperated Biden begged of Trump, "Will you shut up, man?"

Trump's bullying largely overwhelmed any differences of substance between the candidates. Both men spoke in sweeping and apocalyptic terms about the other. Trump argued that if Biden were elected, the country would experience "a depression the likes of which you've never seen," while Biden said the nation had become "weaker, sicker, poorer, more divided, and more violent" during Trump's presidency.

Heeding Giuliani's advice, Trump pursued a deeply personal attack on Biden. When Biden gave an impassioned defense of the patriotism and heroism of his late son, Beau, who died of brain cancer and had served in the Iraq War, Trump seized the moment as an opening to attack the integrity of his surviving son.

"I don't know Beau," Trump said. "I know Hunter. Hunter got thrown out of the military. He was thrown out, dishonorably discharged."

"That was not true," Biden interjected. "He was not dishonorably discharged."

"For cocaine use," Trump said. "And he didn't have a job until you became vice president."

"None of that is true," Biden said.

"Once you became vice president, he made a fortune in Ukraine, in China, in Moscow, and various other places," Trump said.

Again, Biden interjected: "That is not true."

But Trump kept at it. "He made a fortune and he didn't have a job," he said.

"My son, like a lot of people [watching] at home, had a drug problem," Biden said. "He's overtaken it. He's fixed it. He's worked on it. And I'm proud of him. I'm proud of my son."

Trump may have believed he succeeded in scorching Biden for the troubles of his son, but some of his campaign advisers cringed at the president's clumsy and overly hostile delivery. They feared the exchange showed Biden was a proud and loving father and risked turning off the white independent suburban voters with whom Trump needed to make up ground.

The debate got especially tense on the subject of race. Biden said Trump "has used everything as a dog whistle to try to generate racist hatred, racist division."

"He's just, he's a racist," Biden added of Trump.

Both Wallace and Biden pressed Trump to condemn white supremacists, but the president demurred.

"Give me a name," Trump said. "Who would you like me to condemn?"

"The Proud Boys," Biden interjected, referring to neofascist, male, white nationalist organization whose members had attacked Black Lives Matter protesters that summer.

"The Proud Boys, stand back and stand by," Trump said.

With those eight words, the president sounded a call to arms. Few could imagine then what the Proud Boys and other warriors for the far right had in store.

Fourteen

Nobody's Immune

On September 30, President Trump traveled to Minnesota, a state that traditionally leaned Democratic. He had lost narrowly there in 2016 and was hoping to win it in 2020. As Trump spoke with supporters at a campaign fundraiser in Shorewood, at the Lake Minnetonka home of a wealthy area businessman, Hope Hicks was waiting with other traveling White House aides in a side room. She felt ill. Her symptoms worsened later that evening as she accompanied Trump to a MAGA rally in Duluth. On stage, the president's voice sounded raspy and his speech was shorter than usual. He spoke for only forty-six minutes, while many of his recent rally speeches had stretched well past an hour. Something was amiss.

Hicks talked to Sean Conley, the president's physician, who was traveling with them and told him she wasn't feeling well. But she didn't think she had COVID-19. Like other staff who worked in close contact with the president, Hicks was tested daily for the virus. Her test that morning had come back negative. As she later recounted to friends, Hicks wondered if she might have caught a cold or was just wiped out from all the travel and late-night events she had been doing with Trump and needed a good night's sleep. Conley instructed her to try to rest and self-isolate on the flight home to Washington that evening, so as not to risk infecting others. She sat alone in the president's private office aboard Air Force One. Hicks was discreet; some other aides on the trip were unaware that she had fallen ill or that she had ensconced herself in the forward cabin.

The next morning, October 1, Hicks woke up feeling the same, so instead of rushing into work at 7:30 a.m. as usual, she went back to sleep, hoping to kick the bug, whatever it was. At about 11:00, she went into the White House to take her daily COVID test. The rapid test was positive, so she then took a more reliable PCR test. She got the results shortly after noon. Positive again. Hicks had COVID-19.

She immediately went home to self-isolate and informed Mark Meadows and other key officials about her diagnosis. Word spread quickly among White House staff, who were alarmed because of how much time Hicks spent around Trump and the seniormost members of the administration. Some staffers suddenly started wearing masks around the White House.

Trump was scheduled to depart around 1:00 p.m. for another campaign fundraiser at Trump National Golf Club in Bedminster, New Jersey. Meadows and other aides scrambled to change the flight manifest. Kayleigh McEnany had been scheduled to travel to Bedminster but was pulled from the trip because she had been in close contact with Hicks. Deputy press secretary Judd Deere traveled in her place.

Trump and Meadows did not want Hicks's diagnosis to become public, and the president carried on with his New Jersey trip, where he was slated to raise $5 million for his reelection. The decision to proceed with the fundraiser after the president's extended and recent close contact with an infected person flouted both the CDC recommendations and the advice the White House gave its own staff. What's more, Trump himself wasn't feeling well after sounding hoarse the night before. He could be a vector.

As Dr. Kavita Patel, a practicing physician and former health adviser in the Obama White House, explained at the time, "They knew she was positive and they still let Marine One take off with the president. Why didn't they ground him? That was the break in protocol. The CDC's protocol clearly states that as soon as anybody, i.e., Hope Hicks, was confirmed positive, anybody she came into close contact with for at least forty-eight hours prior should have at least isolated."

In Bedminster, Trump hosted an intimate gathering for the biggest donors. It was held indoors, with guests seated around a large table with the president. Many did not wear masks. The president then spoke outdoors to a few hundred supporters, some of whom wore masks. Many of the attendees were elderly, putting them at high risk if they contracted the virus. On the flight home, Trump talked with his traveling entourage about Hicks's diagnosis and said he would take a test.

Trump also made a virtual appearance that night at the Alfred E. Smith Memorial Foundation Dinner, an annual white-tie charity event in New York that had long been on the political calendar. In a recorded message, Trump proclaimed, "I just want to say that the end of the pandemic is in sight."

Sometime that evening, a White House official confidentially contacted Stephen Hahn to seek information about the FDA approving the compassionate use of monoclonal antibodies for a patient who was a high-level White House individual. Hahn didn't ask for the name of the patient. With compassionate use approvals, the FDA doesn't require a name, but does require some medical information to process paperwork. But Hahn assumed it was for Hicks, since he knew about her diagnosis. It was actually for the president.

Shortly after 8:00 p.m., nearly eight hours after Meadows and other officials learned of Hicks's diagnosis, the public found out—not by a White House announcement, but the reporting of Jennifer Jacobs of Bloomberg News, who had been tipped off by sources. About ninety minutes later, Trump called into Sean Hannity's Fox show, where the president said he had just taken a test and was awaiting his results. He spoke as if he knew he had the virus and was looking to cast blame.

"You know, it's very hard," Trump said. "When you're with soldiers, when you're with airmen, when you're with Marines, and I'm with—and the police officers. I'm with them so much. And when they come over here, it's very hard to say, 'Stay back, stay back.' It's a tough kind of a situation. It's a terrible thing. So, I just went for a test, and we will see what happens. I mean, who knows?"

Suspense built into the night. And then, just before 1:00 a.m., Trump made a dramatic reveal on Twitter: "Tonight, @FLOTUS and I tested positive for COVID-19. We will begin our quarantine and recovery process immediately. We will get through this TOGETHER."

Conley wrote in a memorandum released overnight: "The president and first lady are both well at this time, and they plan to remain at home within the White House during their convalescence. The White House medical team and I will maintain a vigilant watch, and I appreciate the support provided by some of our country's greatest medical professionals and institutions. Rest assured I expect the President to continue carrying out his duties without disruption while recovering, and I will keep you updated on any future developments."

The diagnosis left Trump's advisers and aides in a state of disbelief. The virus hadn't only punctured the president's bubble. It also infected the president himself, as well as his wife. Their minds raced with questions: How did Trump get infected? At the September 26 Amy Coney Barrett announcement? Or at the September 27 Gold Star families event, where he had complained about guests getting too close to him? Or at his recent golf outing or debate prep sessions or campaign rallies or fundraisers, none of which followed social distancing or mask protocols? And who was Patient Zero? Media reports that evening left the impression that Hicks may have given the virus to Trump. But it was just as likely that he gave it to her, and it was also possible that they both got it from someone else. Unlike Hicks and other staff, the president did not get tested every day, so it was possible he had become infected earlier in the week.

Those around the president also fretted about how badly the virus would hit Trump. He was seventy-four years old, had high cholesterol, and at a reported 244 pounds, was considered obese. He made no secret of his cheeseburgers-and-steaks diet or his lack of daily exercise. Trump's age and weight both made him particularly vulnerable to the coronavirus. But Trump had been unusually secretive about his health—resistant to releasing details about his condition and treatments over the years, including the reasons for an abrupt and unannounced visit in

November 2019 to Walter Reed National Military Medical Center. So even White House aides weren't sure whether to believe Conley's assurance that Trump was doing "well."

White House officials also worried about whether they, too, had been infected, considering how lax their workplace had been about virus precautions. And what would become of the campaign? The election was just thirty-three days away. The next scheduled debate was in less than two weeks. How long would the president be grounded? MAGA rallies, after all, were the lifeblood of his campaign. And how would his illness play politically? How could Trump convince voters he could protect their families from the virus if he couldn't protect himself?

The morning of October 2, Meadows stepped outside the West Wing to update a gaggle of reporters on Trump's condition. The chief of staff said the president was "in good spirits." Even now, despite his close interactions with Trump and Hicks, Meadows did not wear a mask. He said defensively, "I've obviously been tested. We're hopefully more than six feet away."

Later that morning, Trump's condition worsened. When Conley checked on him at his bedside, the president had a high fever. A standard pulse oximeter reading showed the level of oxygen in his blood had dropped below 94 percent. A normal reading was 96 to 100 percent, and doctors considered anything lower a warning that could not be ignored. It wasn't definitive, but it was a signal the patient could be on a rapid downward trajectory, and in grave danger. If this trajectory continued and was left unaddressed, it could lead to hypoxia and sudden death. Trump needed supplemental oxygen, stat.

"I was concerned for possible rapid progression of the illness," Conley later told reporters. "I recommended [to] the president we try some supplemental oxygen, see how he'd respond. He was fairly adamant that he didn't need it. He was not short of breath. He was tired. He had the fever. That was about it. After about a minute and only two liters, his saturation levels were back over ninety-five percent. Stayed on that for about an hour, maybe, and it was off and gone."

Conley called other experienced doctors for their opinions about the president's treatment, including Anthony Fauci and Robert Redfield. Having both trained in the military, Conley and Redfield had mutual respect. The younger Conley had learned his profession in the navy and Redfield in the army. Though Conley spoke on the phone with a calm voice, the news he shared alarmed Redfield, who was in his Washington office at the time. Conley told the veteran virologist he was concerned about the significant dip in the oxygen levels in the president's blood. He was giving Trump supplemental oxygen. He also wanted to transport Trump from the White House to Walter Reed immediately because he wanted the intensive second-by-second monitoring that was best provided at a hospital and its critical care at the ready if Trump's condition rapidly worsened.

Redfield asked some detailed questions about the pulse oximeter readings of Trump's oxygen saturation levels. Called SpO2 readings, they measured the amount of oxygen-carrying hemoglobin in the blood relative to the amount of hemoglobin not carrying oxygen. Redfield also urged Conley to consider starting some experimental but promising treatments as soon as possible. He said the president would be a great candidate for monoclonal antibodies, though the promising results seen in some patients were based at that point on very little data, as well as remdesivir. Trump's heavy weight and advanced age meant Conley had to protectively assume that Trump's COVID-19 diagnosis could spiral into the frightening lung problems seen in many severe cases. Though Trump had early in his term tried to get his White House doctors to deny it, he had high blood pressure and hardening of the arteries to his heart. Redfield and Conley agreed that Trump had a strong likelihood of ending up in intensive care. The two doctors discussed the facts clinically, without any trace of panic. Redfield agreed that the president had to get to the hospital soon, and he had to receive the most aggressive treatment Conley could safely order for him.

For Trump, there was an additional motivation to agree to these aggressive steps. If he developed pneumonia and breathing difficulties, he would be unable to communicate and become incapacitated, meaning the vice president would have to temporarily assume his duties.

At the first mention of going to Walter Reed, Trump was resistant. He worried about how weak and vulnerable it would make him—and the country—look. It was bad for the person leading the fight against the virus to actually contract it, he thought, though he had long believed contracting COVID was inevitable. "At some point I'm going to catch it because it's so contagious," he had told aides earlier that fall. But hospitalization would only increase the impression of weakness, he felt. That afternoon, Conley released another memorandum stating that Trump was "fatigued, but in good spirits."

Conley authorized that the president receive a single eight-gram dose of Regeneron's cocktail of two monoclonal antibodies, which was still in the experimental phase but showing great results with reducing the severity of the disease's impact on patients, and he had Trump taking zinc, vitamin D, famotidine, melatonin, and aspirin. Conley's memo mistakenly said Trump received a "polyclonal" cocktail, which was not the case, but a Regeneron official later corrected the error in the doctor's statement.

That evening, Conley pulled another arrow from his quiver and arranged for Trump to receive his first dose of Gilead Sciences' remdesivir, the first of a five-day course of an antiviral therapy that was supposed to prevent spread throughout the body. And the next day Trump was administered dexamethasone, a steroid reserved for more severe illnesses.

The varied and heavy treatments concerned medical

experts. "Suddenly, they're throwing the kitchen sink at him. It raises the question: Is he sicker than we're hearing, or are they being overly aggressive because he is the president, in a way that could be potentially harmful?" Dr. Thomas McGinn, physician-in-chief at Northwell Health, the largest provider in New York State, told **The New York Times.**

Shortly after 6:00 p.m. on October 2, Marine One landed on the South Lawn of the White House and the president walked out of the residence. He was wearing a suit and blue tie, as well as a black mask across his face. He walked out alone, with a notably masked Meadows following behind, as well as a military aide carrying the nuclear codes, known as the football. They loaded into the helicopter and it flew to Walter Reed in nearby Bethesda, Maryland. Trump was hospitalized. The image-conscious president could hardly have wanted footage of him on every media platform in a mask as he was being airlifted to a hospital, not with the election just one month away.

Trump was taken to Ward 71, the palatial presidential suite at Walter Reed where Richard Nixon had battled pneumonia and Ronald Reagan had undergone colon surgery. The suite contained bedrooms, offices, a conference room, as well as a dining room—space not only for Trump to feel at home, but his aides and visitors, too. Meadows stayed with Trump there, sleeping overnight at the hospital.

As Trump got used to his new surroundings, Redfield worried about the president. He knew Trump could easily deteriorate and possibly die. In his life and career, the power of prayer had been sustaining for Redfield in some of the most trying moments of his life. He had prayed when he and his wife had lost a baby in childbirth. He had prayed when he had been working in third-world conflict zones, knowing things could go badly quickly and he might not make it home. That night, Redfield put his fingertips together and prayed hard for Trump. He would do the same the next night and the night after that. Redfield had prayed before about the president, that Trump would embrace wearing a mask and serve as a role model for all Americans. This solemn devotion was not answered. God, Redfield said to himself, must have wanted him to suffer more on that plea.

The morning of October 3, Trump didn't feel so great when he woke up, worse than he had felt the night before, as if the treatments still hadn't fully kicked in. He later said in an interview for this book, "The last thing I want to die of is COVID if I'm president." He explained fearing that if he had died, "that's almost like you're losing to the invisible enemy. We can't do that, so I had an obligation to get better."

That morning, Conley raised the public's suspicion when he gave an astoundingly rosy summary of the president's health. At a press briefing on the steps outside Walter Reed, Conley followed the Trump playbook by focusing on the positive and dodging questions that would reveal that the president's health condition had initially been dire.

"This morning, the president is doing very well," Conley told reporters. "At this time, the team and I are extremely happy with the progress the president has made. Thursday, he had a mild cough and some nasal congestion and fatigue, all of which are now resolving and improving at this time."

He avoided answering some questions several times, including whether the president's oxygen levels ever dropped, a frequent event in worrisome COVID-19 cases. Conley wouldn't say. The skepticism about this dodge—and confusion—ratcheted up shortly thereafter when Meadows spoke to reporters and gave the opposite impression about Trump's prognosis. "The president's vitals over the last twenty-four hours were very concerning, and the next forty-eight hours will be critical in terms of his care," Meadows said. "We're still not on a clear path to a full recovery."

Later Saturday evening, a senior administration official confirmed to reporters that Trump had been given supplemental oxygen at the White House on Friday before going to Walter Reed. It confirmed something else: Conley had intentionally concealed the medical facts. Leaders from the medical community around the country were dismayed.

"Saturday's briefing by President Trump's medical

team was a deliberate exercise in obfuscation, insulting to the public and unbefitting the seriousness of the moment," Dr. Leana S. Wen, who served as Baltimore's health commissioner and was a visiting professor of public health at George Washington University, wrote in a **Washington Post** op-ed.

That evening, the patient had the last word. A little after 7:00, Trump released a video recorded at Walter Reed in which he claimed he was on the mend. "I came here, I wasn't feeling so well, I feel much better now," Trump said. "We're working hard to get me all the way back. I have to be back because we still have to make America great again."

The next day, October 4, Conley held another news briefing outside Walter Reed and admitted to having put a positive spin on Trump's condition. The White House physician finally disclosed that on October 2 Trump's oxygen level had dropped and that he received supplemental oxygen. Conley said he had not shared the information initially because he did not want to cause alarm.

"I was trying to reflect the upbeat attitude that the team, the president, over his course of illness, has had," Conley said. "I didn't want to give any information that might steer the course of illness in another direction. And in doing so, you know, it came off that we were trying to hide something, which wasn't necessarily true. . . . The fact of the matter is that he's doing really well."

Conley's reputation took an immediate hit. As one

former colleague of his in the White House medical unit put it, "Oh, I don't think he can come back from this. You're a doctor; you just can't slant the facts."

Every doctor owed their patients confidentiality about their medical condition, and the outsized stature and micromanaging nature of this particular patient further complicated things for Conley. Few knew the intense pressure Trump and his advisers were putting on Conley. The public expected honest information about the president's health, but Conley was not allowed to say anything his patient did not authorize. So he was forced to dance around several details of his medical condition. On top of that, Conley genuinely felt upbeat, though he could not explain why. Before taking Trump to the hospital, Conley thought there was a high chance he could die.

Conley called Redfield that Sunday to let him know the president was insisting he leave the hospital the next day. Redfield was a bit disturbed to hear this. He strongly urged Conley to find a way to keep Trump there a few more days. As a high school kid, Redfield had had a summer job as a janitor at Walter Reed back when it was called the National Naval Medical Center. From that cleaning job, he knew how enormous and well appointed the presidential suite was. Was there any harm for Trump in hanging there just a little while longer?

"My patient wants to leave," Conley said.

Redfield told him all the medical reasons that it was a bad idea for Trump to leave, which Conley knew already. Redfield stressed that one never knew how well the monoclonal antibodies were going to work, and that a doctor needed time to monitor their effect. Also, he said clinicians had found that patients as old as Trump sometimes experienced the full effect of the virus after five to seven days, and they deteriorated very quickly. Redfield told Conley that leaving the hospital after three nights would be foolhardy.

"It's not going to happen," Conley replied. "He's going to do what he's going to do."

By that Sunday, his third day at Walter Reed, Trump had become bored. It wasn't for lack of activity. He had frequent phone calls from well-wishers and the company of his medical and security teams and several aides, including Meadows and Dan Scavino. Trump was on a strict schedule, with his doctors and nurses giving him intravenous doses of remdesivir and popping in at least every two hours to check his oxygen level, blood pressure, and other vital signs. Outside the hospital, scores of supporters held up signs, waved flags, cheered his name, and honked car horns. More than anything, Trump wanted to project strength and vitality. He was annoyed with Meadows for telling reporters that his health readings were "very concerning," worried the comment gave the impression he was feeble and bedridden. After he spoke on the phone with Rudy Giuliani, Jason Miller, and former campaign manager Corey Lewandowski, the three said in media interviews that, yes, Trump was strong and ready to return to the campaign trail.

In conversations with advisers from his hospital suite, Trump floated a theatrical idea to symbolize his strength, according to Annie Karni and Maggie Haberman of **The New York Times.** When he eventually was filmed leaving the hospital, he could appear frail at first only to then surprise television viewers by ripping open his button-down dress shirt and revealing a Superman T-shirt underneath. Trump also wanted to appear hard at work and posed for photos in his hospital room signing blank pieces of paper. In deference to Trump's psychological need to always appear in complete control, Vice President Pence and military officials were notably quiet during his hospital stay. Nobody gave any public assurances that a plan was in place to ensure continuity of government should the president become incapacitated. They knew that even entertaining that notion would infuriate Trump.

"You would want to hear the secretary of defense, the chairman of the Joint Chiefs of Staff, the vice president say, 'Look, we are going through a situation here. We have it well in hand. Make no mistake, our adversaries should not see this as an opportunity. We are fully prepared to execute all of our authorities,'" remarked David Lapan. But, he added, "the president doesn't want to create an appearance that anybody is in charge except him."

Around lunchtime on October 4, while plotting

with Meadows and Scavino, Trump decided to go for a joy ride. His Secret Service detail leader was alerted that they had an "off-the-record" presidential movement in the works.

Trump teased his supporters that afternoon by sharing a video on social media hinting at his plans for an outing. After thanking the hospital staff, Trump said, "I also think we're gonna pay a little surprise to some of the great patriots that we have out on the street, and they've been out there for a long time, and they've got Trump flags, and they love our country."

Just after 5:00, Trump delivered on his little surprise by riding in his motorcade past the clusters of supporters along Wisconsin Avenue outside Walter Reed. He waved to them from inside a souped-up and armored Chevrolet Suburban, rather than his one-of-a-kind limousine, the Beast. Inside the black vehicle were two Secret Service agents, dressed in masks, protective eye visors, and medical gowns. The agent driving had slowed the SUV to a crawl so everyone could get a good look at the masked commander in chief. Trump's goal: to convince people that, despite everything, he was in good shape and still very much in charge. But the outing alarmed other Secret Service agents and medical professionals, who agreed Trump had improperly endangered the lives of his agents and others involved in the movement for what one physician called "political theater."

"He's not even pretending to care now," one agent said after the president's jaunt.

A former Secret Service member complained that someone should have stepped in to block this plan, if only to protect the president's health. "Where are the adults?" the former agent asked.

Chris Whipple, a student of White House management who published a history of chiefs of staff, pointed his finger directly at Meadows. "You have to wonder if anyone is performing that job, because no competent White House chief of staff would ever have permitted a president with a lethal disease to go take a joyride, thereby threatening the health of the Secret Service," he told **The Washington Post**'s Josh Dawsey. "It's just absolute chief of staff malpractice."

Dr. James Phillips, the chief of disaster medicine at George Washington University who also worked as an attending physician on a contract basis for Walter Reed, took to the president's favorite medium to register his shock at this motorized jaunt.

Phillips tweeted: "Every single person . . . in the vehicle during that completely unnecessary Presidential 'drive-by' just now has to be quarantined for 14 days. They might get sick. They may die. For political theater. Commanded by Trump to put their lives at risk for theater. This is insanity."

Two months later, Phillips would be told he was being removed from Walter Reed's schedule starting in January 2021.

While Trump was hospitalized, his advisers brainstormed how to leverage his situation for maximum benefit in the all-too-near election. As Tony Fabrizio's polls had shown for months, Trump was trailing Joe Biden nationally and in many battleground states in large part because voters disapproved of his handling of the pandemic. Some of Trump's advisers believed his illness, assuming he survived it, could in fact be a political blessing. Bill Stepien, Miller, Hicks, and a few others argued that by catching COVID-19, Trump now had a connection to the many who had suffered and could genuinely and personally testify to the magnitude of the crisis. And Trump's very survival, despite his own comorbidities, could offer hope that the virus could be defeated. These advisers also came up with a watered-down alternative message that still could appeal to voters, should Trump not want to fully pivot from his defiant posture on the virus. Once again, however, Trump rejected the advice of his advisers. He was his own brain trust, and he thought the most important thing he could do was project strength. The president was egged on by others in his orbit—some of whom strategized about how his illness could be proof of his masculinity. They speculated among each other about how to show that, while Trump recovered quickly, COVID would have flattened Biden.

One of the advisers who disagreed with this strength imperative thought, **We're not losing because people don't think he's strong enough. We're losing because people think he doesn't give a shit about them or anything but himself at this point.**

I ALONE CAN FIX IT

On Monday, October 5, Trump got his wish. He was going home. "I will be leaving the great Walter Reed Medical Center today at 6:30 P.M.," he wrote on Twitter. "Feeling really good! Don't be afraid of Covid. Don't let it dominate your life. We have developed, under the Trump Administration, some really great drugs & knowledge. I feel better than I did 20 years ago!"

Trump's medical team backed up their patient. Despite the reservations he and Redfield had privately shared, Conley argued publicly that it was safe for his patient to return to the White House. He told reporters that "the president has continued to improve" and, importantly, that he had "met or exceeded all standard hospital discharge criteria."

"Though he may not entirely be out of the woods yet, the team and I agree that all our evaluations, and most importantly his clinical status, support the president's safe return home, where he'll be surrounded by world-class medical care 24/7," Conley said. He added that considering Trump's full cocktail of experimental drug therapies, "we all remain cautiously optimistic and on guard because we're in a bit of unchartered territory."

Other doctors treating Trump also spoke at the news conference, including Dr. Sean Dooley, who detailed the president's vital signs from that morning, all of them fairly encouraging. His temperature was 98.1, his blood pressure was 134 over 78, his respiratory rate was 17 respirations per minute, and his heart rate was 68 beats per minute.

As Trump prepared to leave Walter Reed, he orchestrated another made-for-television performance to show strength. When Marine One touched down on the South Lawn of the White House at dusk to return the president home, Trump strode off the helicopter and across the lawn with purposeful vigor. He was wearing a dark suit and a blue tie and had a mask across his face. It was dusk. The president ascended the steps to the balcony, where four American flags had been erected. He stood to face the journalists and cameras recording the moment for history. Then Trump, appearing defiant and resolute, removed his mask, saluted, and flashed a thumbs-up.

A film crew on the lawn down below recorded the act for use by Trump's campaign. Later that night, the campaign released a slickly produced propaganda-style video of Trump's dramatic return, set to triumphant orchestral music.

Trump did not go through with the Superman T-shirt stunt he had considered. He later explained to us in the book interview that someone had given him an "incredible shirt," but that he decided it could be disrespectful to people suffering from COVID to make light of his recovery. Still, he would revive the theme later that month once he resumed campaigning, referring to himself as "Superman" and inspiring chants from the crowd of "Su-per-man! Su-per-man!"

Afterward, Trump tried to rub in the fact that he had donned a mask to the subset of his advisers—Jared Kushner, Fabrizio, and others—who had been pleading with him that summer to embrace masks as a means of expanding his political support. "See, I wore the mask like you wanted me to," the president said teasingly to some of them.

Trump returned to a White House ravaged by a virus outbreak, which many officials traced to the Barrett nomination event in the Rose Garden. Hicks did not attend the event, but spent considerable time in close proximity to Trump and others who had. The list of Trump aides and associates who tested positive around this time totaled more than thirty and included Bill Stepien; Kayleigh McEnany; Kellyanne Conway; Stephen Miller; Nick Luna, the president's body man and director of Oval Office operations; Republican National Committee Chairperson Ronna McDaniel; Chris Christie; and Senators Ron Johnson, Mike Lee, and Thom Tillis.

On October 6, Trump settled back into a shortened workday as doctors continued to administer his treatments and monitored his recovery. Bill Barr broke the bad news to Meadows and Trump that John Durham's probe into the origins of the FBI's Russia investigation into Trump's 2016 campaign was still ongoing and would not produce a report before the November election. The so-called October surprise Trump had imagined—dreaming of sending Obama's intel chiefs or former FBI leaders James Comey or Andrew McCabe to jail—was not to be.

For Barr, the lack of a public report was disappointing to say the least. After sixteen months of digging, Durham's team had only a long plea agreement to show for its work. In it FBI lawyer Kevin Clinesmith admitted to altering an email that his department used to win court approval for a secret surveillance warrant on former Trump campaign adviser Carter Page. Trump, who had been salivating in anticipation of some incriminating evidence about Comey or one of his other high-profile enemies, didn't know who Clinesmith was, and neither did most Americans. Barr had hoped this was simply an appetizer before the main course. He had believed one more person was likely to be charged, which would show deeper flaws in the origins of the investigation. But instead, Durham had encountered more problems.

All spring and summer, Meadows had been pestering Barr to get Durham to speed up his work, and Barr had said he was cautiously optimistic there would be a report or some progress by the end of the summer. But when Labor Day rolled around, Barr had asked Durham if he could release a preliminary report they had discussed as a stopgap. Barr had not wanted to be boxed in by Justice Department policy barring public action or comment on politically sensitive cases in the run-up to elections. So, to keep his options open, he had earlier told reporters he didn't feel compelled to follow those rules at that point, as Durham's report would not have anything to do with Biden. Of course, the whole investigation was about vindicating the other candidate, Trump.

Inside the Durham team, Barr's pressure campaign had backfired. On September 10, Nora Dannehy, a well-respected prosecutor and Durham's top aide, had resigned from the probe. A Harvard Law School graduate with decades of politically sensitive federal prosecutions under her belt, Dannehy lent considerable integrity to the probe. Her departure spurred a series of news stories reporting that part of her reason for leaving was dismay at what she considered constant pressure from Barr for a report during the heat of the campaign. Her resignation only intensified suspicion among Democrats that Barr was seeking to raise some preelection red meat for the boss to feed to his base.

Barr was slow to realize the growing reluctance among some members of the Durham team to issue a report or take some public action before the election. Some had been unsettled earlier by what they considered Barr's conclusive rhetoric. That spring, before the results of his department's probe into the matter, he had preemptively called the Russia investigation "one of the greatest travesties in American history." But there was a substantive reason in October that Durham himself concluded he couldn't proceed with the report plan.

Shortly after Dannehy's resignation, Durham called
Barr at headquarters. He told the attorney general
there would be no report he would feel comfortable
releasing before the election. They had lost important momentum on the part of the case that they
had thought might result in charges against a second
official. They had also hit a wall trying to ascertain
whether any U.S. government officials had asked their
British intelligence allies to begin gathering information on Page in the summer of 2016, before the FBI
opened its Crossfire Hurricane investigation. Asking
a U.S. asset or a foreign government to spy on an
American would be a huge violation, but Durham
hadn't yet pieced together what happened. Durham explained to Barr that anything he said in a report now
would just look partial and politically timed. Barr was
disappointed but soon came to agree.

When Barr updated the White House on these
developments, the president was furious. First, he
cursed Barr's name. Then he fired off a barrage of
tweets, starting late in the night on October 6 and
continuing into the next day:

"Can't believe these con men are not yet being
PROSECUTED. Pathetic!"

"Where are all of the arrests? Can you imagine if
the roles were reversed? Long term sentences would
have started two years ago. Shameful!"

"DO SOMETHING ABOUT THIS, THE
BIGGEST OF ALL POLITICAL SCANDALS (IN

HISTORY)!!! BIDEN, OBAMA AND CROOKED
HILLARY LED THIS TREASONOUS PLOT!!!
BIDEN SHOULDN'T BE ALLOWED TO
RUN—GOT CAUGHT!!!"

Trump also retweeted criticisms of Barr from other
Twitter users and shared a meme mocking Barr—a
drawing of comedian Chris Farley, of **Saturday Night
Live** fame, looming over an image of Barr and yelling: "For the love of God, arrest somebody!"

The frequency, ferocity, and late-night timing of
Trump's tweets made people wonder if the president might be suffering some irritability and mania,
common side effects of steroid usage. Among them
was Nancy Pelosi, who speculated in an October 7
interview on ABC's **The View** that "there's something wrong."

"I said yesterday to my colleagues, I said, 'There are
those who say that steroids has an impact on people's
thinking,'" the House Speaker said. "I don't know,
but there are those health-care providers who say that.
Also, if you have the coronavirus, it has an impact as
well. So, the combination is something that should
be viewed."

On October 8, Trump did an interview with Maria
Bartiromo of Fox Business, one of the president's favorite interviewers thanks to her softball questions
and easy praise, in which he attacked Barr for not
delivering to him the heads of his enemies.

"Unless Bill Barr indicts these people for crimes—

the greatest political crime in the history of our country—then we're going to get little satisfaction, unless I win," Trump told Bartiromo. He added, "Bill has got to move," and it would likely go down in history as a "very sad situation."

Fifteen

Somebody's Crazy Uncle

O n October 12, just one week after being released from the hospital, President Trump returned to the campaign trail. Sean Conley issued a memorandum that afternoon stating that Trump had tested negative for the coronavirus "on consecutive days" using a rapid antigen test and was "not infectious to others." Medical experts said that type of test was not accurate enough to ensure a patient was completely free of the virus. Nonetheless, Conley gave the president a green light to travel. Within a few hours Trump touched down in Florida, which his campaign increasingly considered the most important battleground state. As the sun set, Trump stepped off Air Force One at Orlando Sanford International Airport and strode down a catwalk to center stage. He wore his customary dark suit and red tie, his face heavy with makeup and sans mask, and pointed his finger at the sea of supporters spread across the tarmac. He punched his fist in the air and tossed red MAGA caps into the crowd. Trump was back.

Determined to show strength and stamina, and to convince voters everywhere of his vitality, Trump spoke for sixty-five minutes, and though his voice sounded hoarse, his performance was energetic.

"Now they say I'm immune. I feel so powerful. I'll kiss everyone in that audience. I'll kiss the guys and the beautiful women. Just give you a big, fat kiss," Trump said. There was no reason to believe he was immune. In a veiled shot at Joe Biden, whom Trump had mocked for holding virtual campaign events from the basement of his Wilmington home, Trump added, "I don't have to be locked in my basement, and I wouldn't allow that to happen anyway. I wouldn't allow it to happen. When you're the president, you can't lock yourself in a basement and say, 'I'm not going to bother with the world.' You got to get out, and it's risky. It's risky. But you got to get out."

Trump claimed he had fully recovered, but many of his aides remained in self-isolation. Kayleigh McEnany was one of them. In her time as press secretary, she had become a television fixture for Trump's base, appearing practically daily on Fox News and other conservative platforms to promote and defend the president. In her absence, Mark Meadows and Jared Kushner enlisted Alyssa Farah to go on television. As communications director, Farah had been a behind-the-scenes player, devising strategies and crafting messages for McEnany and other officials to deliver. But now Farah was the face of Trump—and the president liked what he saw.

"Alyssa, you're doing great," Trump told Farah during the Florida trip.

Trump liked to give aides reason to doubt their standing with him and pit them against one another. Trump praised Farah in front of many staffers, and, sure enough, word got back to McEnany, who stopped speaking to Farah.

Trump returned to Florida three days later, on October 15, to speak at a nationally televised town hall meeting in Miami moderated by Savannah Guthrie, the co-anchor of NBC's **Today** show. It was the date originally scheduled for the second of three Trump-Biden debates, but the event was cancelled after the president was hospitalized with COVID. Instead, the candidates did simultaneous town hall meetings—Trump with Guthrie on NBC and Biden with George Stephanopoulos on ABC. Trump was especially combative under sharp and persistent questioning from Guthrie. When she pointed out his failure to denounce white supremacy in the first debate, Trump interrupted before she could state her question. "Oh, you always do this," Trump said.

Agitated, he snapped at her. "I denounce white supremacy, okay?"

A few seconds later, he said it again: "Are you listening? I denounce white supremacy."

"It feels sometimes you're hesitant to do so, like you wait a beat," Guthrie said.

"Hesitant?" he replied. "Here we go again. Every time . . . In fact, my people came, 'I'm sure they'll ask you the white supremacy question.' I denounce white supremacy. . . . And frankly, you want to know something? I denounce Antifa, and I denounce these people on the left that are burning down our cities, that are run by Democrats who don't know what they're doing."

"While we're denouncing, let me ask you about QAnon," Guthrie said, referring to a far-right, pro-Trump internet community that spreads false conspiracies, and that the FBI had characterized as a domestic terrorism threat. "It is this theory that Democrats are a satanic pedophile ring and that you are the savior of that. Now can you just, once and for all, state that that is completely not true?"

Trump professed ignorance. "I know nothing about QAnon," he said.

"I just told you," Guthrie replied.

"I know very little," Trump said. "You told me, but what you tell me doesn't necessarily make it fact. I hate to say that. I know nothing about it. I do know they are very much against pedophilia. They fight it very hard. But I know nothing about it."

They went back and forth like this for nearly two minutes, with Guthrie pressing Trump to reject QAnon's most extreme, fringe conspiracies and the president refusing to do so by claiming he had no knowledge of the group.

Guthrie then asked Trump why he had tweeted to his eighty-seven million followers a QAnon conspiracy that President Obama and Biden had orchestrated to have members of the Navy SEALs Team killed to cover up the fake death of Osama bin Laden.

"I know nothing about it," Trump said.

"You retweeted it," Guthrie said.

"That was a retweet," Trump explained. "That was an opinion of somebody. And that was a retweet. I'll put it out there. People can decide for themselves. I don't take a position."

"I don't get that," Guthrie said. "You're the president. You're not, like, somebody's crazy uncle who can just retweet whatever."

"That was a retweet, and I do a lot of retweets," Trump said. "And frankly, because the media is so fake and so corrupt, if I didn't have social media—I don't call it Twitter; I call it social media—I wouldn't be able to get the word out. And the word is—"

"Well," Guthrie interjected, "the word is false."

By the time Trump sparred with Guthrie over QAnon, more than fifteen million Americans already had voted in the election. Local election officials in states that allowed early voting reported record turnout, indicating that for the first time in U.S. history the majority of voters could cast ballots before Election Day.

In Georgia, voters waited as long as ten hours to

cast ballots on the first day of early voting, which was October 12. Nearly 130,000 people voted in person in Georgia that day, a 42 percent increase over the previous first-day record set in 2016. In Michigan, more than one million people had voted by October 14, either in person or by mail, which already was one fourth the total number of voters there in 2016.

This was an extraordinary level of participation, some in person and some by mail, and much of it appeared to be driven by Democratic enthusiasm. In states that reported partisan breakdowns, participation by registered Democrats far outpaced that of registered Republicans. This bore out anecdotally, too. In media interviews, many voters said they cast ballots early because they were determined to seize their first possible opportunity to repudiate Trump.

"Four years of Donald Trump is enough for me," Victor Tellesco, a fifty-year-old suburbanite in Phoenix who voted for the first time, told reporter Jeremy Duda for **The Washington Post.** "Every time I see him on TV, my blood pressure goes up. It just made me feel like I needed to vote this year. I don't know why I've never voted before. But this year, it feels like I needed to vote."

Trump's aides watched the trend with considerable alarm. After hearing that Democrats had a thirty-percentage-point advantage on the first day of early voting in North Carolina, Kellyanne Conway remarked to an associate, "Oh, dear." Bill Stepien and other campaign leaders worried about giving Biden such a huge advantage—not only with the mail vote, but the early vote overall—and leaving too much to chance. What if it rained on Election Day? What if there was snow? The worst-case-scenario line Stepien had repeatedly used with Trump was, "Mr. President, what if we have a hurricane in Florida or some awful storm and so many of our senior voters then can't get out or don't want to get out, but they also don't think they can vote by mail because you say it's a fraud? We're screwed."

With early voting in Arizona well under way, Democrats were recording a massive lead in Maricopa County, which encompasses the Phoenix area and is by far the state's most populous jurisdiction. During a discussion with some on the political team, Kushner observed, "The Republicans have hardly voted."

"Yeah, it's a big gamble," Stepien said. "But the president said, 'Hold on to your ballots.'"

The data coming in from county and state election officials contrasted with the anecdotes Trump and Vice President Pence were picking up as they crisscrossed the country. Their rallies were huge. The enthusiasm of their supporters seemed real. It felt contagious.

On October 15, during a bus tour in Florida, Pence invited Tony Fabrizio on board to chat with him and Marc Short as they rode between stops in the Miami area. The vice president and his chief of staff wanted a personal briefing from the campaign pollster.

"What do you think?" Pence asked.

"Sir, in 2016 we had to draw an inside straight,

and we did," Fabrizio said, using a poker analogy. "In 2020, we've got to draw an inside straight flush, to be honest with you. Every one of these states is on the razor's edge, and a little bit of wind and it goes against us."

"Really?" Pence replied.

"Yes," Fabrizio said.

"But it feels so good out there on the ground," Pence said.

"I understand that, sir," Fabrizio said. "But I'm just telling you what the data says."

They talked about how the still-raging coronavirus was affecting Trump's standing in the polls. Fabrizio said the two states that most troubled him were Arizona and Georgia. Both were reliably Republican, and Trump had carried them comfortably in 2016, but Democrats had worked hard in recent years to register new voters—many of them Black in Georgia and Latino in Arizona—and Biden was bullish on turning both states blue. Fabrizio, who was polling for Senator Martha McSally's reelection race in Arizona and for the National Republican Senatorial Committee's independent expenditure in Georgia, told Pence his recent surveys in both states spelled trouble for Trump. The widespread belief that Trump was leading in both states by a few percentage points was belied by Fabrizio's numbers. He had the presidential race in both states tied.

———

Trump was desperate. His last chance to shake up the race was his second and final debate with Biden, scheduled for October 22. The president needed an October surprise, some shocking revelation that might sully his Democratic foe. Rudy Giuliani tried to engineer one. The **New York Post** published a cover story on October 14 headlined BIDEN SECRET E-MAILS. The tabloid claimed to have reviewed "smoking gun" emails recovered from a laptop allegedly owned by Hunter Biden and obtained by Giuliani's lawyer from a computer repair shop in Delaware where Hunter had dropped it off in April 2019. The story described Hunter's business dealings in China and the large payments he received from Burisma, the Ukrainian energy firm where he was a board member. The so-called smoking gun was a lone email from April 2015 in which a Ukrainian adviser to Burisma appeared to thank Hunter for an offer to meet his father, then the vice president, who at the time had been helping shape U.S. policy on Ukraine.

"Dear Hunter, thank you for inviting me to DC and giving an opportunity to meet your father and spent [**sic**] some time together," the adviser purportedly wrote in the email. "It's realty [**sic**] an honor and pleasure."

If this was a legitimate email, it was hard to say what nefarious deeds it proved. It revealed a company official thanking a board member for offering to arrange or for arranging a meeting with his father. There was no doubt that Hunter was being paid handsomely in a foreign energy sector where he had little experience while his father served as vice president. Burisma had a sizable financial stake in U.S. policy in the region. Surely the company stood to benefit by ingratiating itself with the vice president. There was a long history of corporations, lobbying firms, universities, and other institutions hiring family members of elected officials to try to curry favor with powerful government officials. For all those reasons, Hunter's board compensation created a significant appearance of a conflict of interest, even though Joe Biden said he never discussed his son's foreign work with him.

Still, Trump had hoped to make the Hunter laptop Exhibit A in the Biden corruption case he wanted to argue at the October 22 debate. He started laying the groundwork on the campaign trail. On October 16, Trump said at a campaign rally in Macon, Georgia, that "the Biden family is a criminal enterprise." He added, "Sleepy Joe Biden is the living embodiment of the corrupt political class that enriched himself while draining the economic life and soul from our country." Trump went on to allege—without any evidence—that Biden profited from his son's work with Burisma. "Plenty of it goes to Joe Biden, too," Trump said. "Don't kid yourself. It goes to Joe."

But Trump was disappointed. He and Giuliani had believed the **New York Post** story would be picked up widely in the media, generating big headlines in more credible mainstream outlets like **The New York Times** and **The Washington Post.** But it did not.

In fact, Ben Smith, the **Times**'s media columnist, reported that earlier in October a White House lawyer close to Kushner, Eric Herschmann, and two Trump allies, former deputy White House counsel Stefan Passantino and public relations consultant Arthur Schwartz, tried to pitch an exclusive on the Hunter emails to **The Wall Street Journal.** The three men even furnished a source: Tony Bobulinski, a former business partner of Hunter, who was willing to go on the record with his assertion that Biden had been aware of and profited from his son's work in Ukraine. But the **Journal** did not publish the blockbuster piece the Trump team had envisioned. After doing its due diligence to report out the claims, the **Journal** eventually published a brief story stating that its review of corporate records showed Biden had no role in his son's activities.

Hunter never denied the laptop was his. But the story of the long road it had traveled, allegedly from Biden to Giuliani to the **New York Post,** seemed suspicious to reporters. The **Post** reported it got the material from Giuliani after being tipped off to the laptop's existence by Steve Bannon, the former White House strategist who was then quietly advising Trump's reelection campaign. John Paul Mac Isaac, the owner of a computer repair shop in Wilmington, said that Hunter had dropped off three laptops damaged by liquid and had sought to recover material on them. Mac Isaac would later say in court filings that Hunter neither paid for the repairs nor came to retrieve one of the laptops, making it abandoned property that his shop now owned. Mac Isaac said he shared the hard drive with Robert Costello, a lawyer for Giuliani, and gave a copy of its contents to the FBI.

Trump had long believed that previous Democratic presidents had used the Justice Department to advance their political goals and that he was well within his rights to do the same. Trump had complained bitterly whenever Bill Barr had told him there was no rationale for investigating Obama or indicting James Comey, saying, "These guys, you know if the shoe was on the other foot . . ." So when Giuliani tantalizingly claimed he had smoking-gun emails that linked Biden to his son's foreign profiteering, Trump called Barr sometime in mid-October wanting to discuss Giuliani's "evidence."

Barr had already been down this road with the president and Giuliani and found the idea of returning to it exhausting. In January 2020, at the president's urging, Barr had agreed to have the Justice Department receive—and vet—information Giuliani said he had gathered about Hunter's lucrative role in Burisma and a possible connection to Joe Biden. At the outset, Barr was somewhat guarded about anything Giuliani delivered. The attorney general blamed Trump's lawyer-turned-opposition-researcher for getting the president impeached. After all, it had been Giuliani's promises of getting "dirt" on Biden that had embroiled Trump in his pressure campaign on Ukraine's new president.

Still, Barr had been willing to consider that some small portion of what Trump and Giuliani claimed in January 2020 could be real. One of Giuliani's sources was someone the FBI itself had relied on in the past. So Barr tapped the Republican U.S. attorney in Pittsburgh, Scott Brady, to take in Giuliani's leads and documents, and to figure out whether they stood up. It wasn't an investigation, but a vetting.

Back in February, Lindsey Graham had revealed publicly that the Justice Department had set up a process by which Giuliani could submit information. Barr then confirmed that to reporters, arguing that the Justice Department had an "obligation to have an open door to anybody who wishes to provide us information that they think is relevant." But Barr also said he cautioned Graham that the department had to be circumspect. "We have to be very careful with respect to any information coming from the Ukraine," Barr said he counseled the Senate Judiciary Committee chairman. "There are a lot of agendas in the Ukraine. There are a lot of crosscurrents, and we can't take anything we receive from the Ukraine at face value."

Barr's instincts had been right. While some agents in the FBI believed Brady's assignment was strictly a political mission, it didn't produce any headlines or charges. After reviewing the material, Giuliani's great "case" fell apart. By summer, the Justice Department had concluded none of it could be corroborated or had any basis in real events. "It was nearly all bull-shit," said one former senior law enforcement official.

Giuliani was damaged goods in Barr's eyes for other reasons, too. The attorney general and his deputies had already been given the same defensive briefing that White House officials had received earlier in the year, with the intelligence community warning that Giuliani was being worked and fed some disinformation by a Russian intelligence asset, Andriy Derkach. In October, Giuliani was expecting information from Derkach to figure prominently in the Trump-Biden debate, which he hoped would highlight the ongoing probe into alleged Biden family corruption.

Barr told aides he felt fairly certain that Giuliani had not hit upon something new regarding Hunter that was worth probing. Even if Giuliani had, Trump did not understand that federal criminal investigations were not exactly the all-powerful political weapons he wished them to be. Investigations had a high hurdle to establish a crime, took a long time to complete, and were conducted largely in secret.

But Barr had yet another reason to be tense. He told trusted aides he had assiduously avoided telling Trump anything about an ongoing federal investigation looking into Hunter's finances. The U.S. attorney in Delaware had been probing Biden's son's deals with Chinese officials. After months of probing, prosecutors found evidence suggesting that Hunter had received income that he did not report to the IRS. During the active campaign, however, the federal prosecutors in Delaware put their tax probe of the Democratic nominee's son on ice, avoiding steps that could become public and potentially taint the election. Barr had not told the president any of that.

During his October call with Barr, Trump yet again referenced his hope of finally punishing the enemies that ate at him the most: Comey and others at the FBI whom Trump believed had set him up in 2016 and tried to undermine his presidency. When Trump asked if the Justice Department would ever prosecute his enemies, Barr snapped, saying something to the effect of: "I told you. There's nothing there." Trump did not appreciate Barr's harsh tone. He got off the phone quickly. The president and his longtime Cabinet member would not speak again before the election.

On October 21, the day before the final debate, Giuliani's reputation and credibility took yet another blow. The formerly revered mayor of New York, federal prosecutor, and presidential candidate was punked in Sacha Baron Cohen's parodic movie **Borat 2.** In the film, Giuliani is approached and flattered by a pretty young woman pretending to be a television journalist for a conservative news site, Patriots Report. During the fake interview, which took place in a hotel suite, she fawns over Giuliani. The scene culminates with Giuliani lying on the bed, placing his hands inside his pants, and the actress pretending to flee in shock at Giuliani's romantic overtures.

Baron Cohen, who made a career punking public figures, including Sarah Palin, Dick Cheney, and Ted

Koppel, had sought from the beginning of his **Borat** sequel to nab Giuliani. Not only had he succeeded, but the film's release had coincided with Giuliani's push for an October surprise, generating huge buzz for the film and heightening the embarrassment for the president's key advocate. Giuliani dismissed the scene as a setup, but did not directly deny the events that were filmed, including him patting the bottom of the actress while he lay back on the hotel bed. Predictably, he blamed Trump's foes for the whole incident. "This is an effort to blunt my relentless exposure of the criminality and depravity of Joe Biden and his entire family," Giuliani tweeted on October 21.

Giuliani added, "We are preparing much bigger dumps off of the hard drive from hell, of which Joe Biden will be unable to defend or hide from. I have the receipts."

There were no further dumps. If Giuliani had receipts, he never showed them.

Trump headed into his final debate angry. He was mad at the news media for continuing to intensively cover the ravages of the pandemic. The country's coronavirus death toll continued to climb, above two hundred thousand, and infection numbers soared, especially in the Midwest and Great Plains, where cooler fall temperatures had been forcing people indoors. Trump believed the media were conspiring to sabotage his reelection chances by shining their spotlights on the contagion's spread, despite the fact that the pandemic was the globally dominant news story.

At a rally October 21 in Gastonia, North Carolina, Trump let loose. "That pandemic is rounding the corner. They hate it when I say it," the president proclaimed.

Then, using his derisive nickname for MSNBC to falsely suggest that the cable news network was in bed with the Democratic National Committee, Trump said, "You know you turn onto this MSDNC and fake news CNN, all you hear is, 'COVID, COVID, COVID, COVID, COVID, COVID, COVID, COVID, COVID, COVID, COVID.' That's all they put on, because they want to scare the hell out of everyone."

The next day, as Trump flew to Nashville for the debate, which was held on the campus of Belmont University, his aides discussed another **New York Post** story about Hunter Biden. The story, which was published on October 16, included a text message exchange between Hunter and his father from February 24, 2019, when Hunter was at a rehabilitation facility for his drug abuse and Joe was preparing to announce his campaign for president. Joe wrote to Hunter, "Good morning my beautiful son. I miss you and love you. Dad."

Farah warned campaign advisers against the president using the intimate text messages to suggest there was some corrupt financial relationship between

Biden and his troubled son. She thought bringing the messages up on a presidential debate stage was a low blow and could backfire on Trump.

"Are you kidding me?" Farah told other aides. "We have an addiction crisis in the country. All that shows is Joe Biden is a good father and loves his son."

On the ground in Nashville that evening, shortly before the debate began, Trump orchestrated a stunt designed to rattle Biden and ensure news coverage of it centered on his son. In a move reminiscent of inviting several women who had accused former president Bill Clinton of sexual misconduct to the second debate with Hillary Clinton, Trump trotted out Bobulinski, the former business associate of Hunter, to hold a news conference.

The Bobulinski stunt was a flop. Biden did not appear rattled when the debate began. And when it concluded, there were two main takeaways. This clash had been far calmer than the first debate, in part because of the smooth moderation of NBC's Kristen Welker and new rules that muted the candidates' microphones when they were not answering a question. The two candidates had had starkly divergent stances on the pandemic. Trump was all happy talk, claiming the virus was disappearing and the country was opening, while Biden warned of a "dark winter" to come and called for more aggressive action to control the contagion.

Trump did attack Biden over his son Hunter—though he did not quote the "I love you" text messages—and it didn't seem to move the needle. The election was just eleven days away. The race was static. It was Biden's to lose.

The night of October 24, White House officials confirmed that a new coronavirus outbreak had infected five of Pence's advisers and aides. The outbreak was suspected to have originated with Marty Obst, one of Pence's top outside political advisers, who tested positive after traveling to campaign events earlier that week with the vice president and his staff and security entourage. On October 24, Short tested positive, as did Zach Bauer, the vice president's personal aide, or body man. Both Short and Bauer had been in close contact with Obst on Air Force Two. Two other aides in Pence's office also tested positive. Obst, Short, and Bauer were in close contact with the vice president, but officials said Pence and his wife, Karen, continually tested negative for the virus and would keep up their busy schedule of campaign travel.

Meadows had sought to keep the news secret. Some in the vice president's office suggested that the White House Medical Unit release a statement about Short's diagnosis. Short and others on Pence's staff thought the news would be better received from White House doctors because they could explain why the vice president was authorized to continue campaigning. But Meadows scuttled that idea and ordered the White

House Medical Unit to stand down, threatening to punish the doctors if they released a statement about Short. Trump's chief of staff stressed the White House had no obligation to report to the public the health conditions of members of the staff. More important, though, Meadows and some other White House aides did not want attention on the pandemic in the home stretch of the campaign. Kellyanne Conway strongly disagreed. She counseled Short to do what she had done less than a month earlier, to announce publicly that he had tested positive for COVID. As senior White House officials who appeared regularly on television, they were public people and should be transparent.

"Marc, you've got a big life behind you and a big life ahead of you," Conway said. "You've got to be honest. You're chief of staff to the vice president. You have to tell people."

Conway didn't have to do much convincing. Short already had decided to disclose his diagnosis. Later that night, Pence's spokesman, Devin O'Malley, released a statement to reporters announcing Short's positive test result and that he was self-isolating and had begun contact tracing.

The next morning, October 25, Meadows made an extraordinary admission that the administration had effectively given up on trying to slow the spread of the virus. "We're not going to control the pandemic," Meadows said on CNN. "We are going to control the fact that we get vaccines, therapeutics, and other mitigations."

Biden seized on the comment to bolster his argument that the Trump administration had failed in its pandemic response. "This wasn't a slip by Meadows; it was a candid acknowledgment of what President Trump's strategy has clearly been from the beginning of this crisis: to wave the white flag of defeat and hope that by ignoring it, the virus would simply go away," Biden said. "It hasn't, and it won't."

Back in Washington, a bizarre lack of process unfolded in the final days of October. As Mark Esper was getting ready to fly back from the Mideast late on the night of October 28, he was alerted by Mark Milley that an American citizen and son of a missionary working in Niger had been kidnapped by militia forces from neighboring Nigeria who were demanding a $1 million ransom. Esper and Milley agreed that U.S. hostage negotiators should try to secure the release of the man, Philip Walton, but that they would put Special Forces units on standby in case it turned into a rescue mission and they had to be inserted rapidly into the region. By the time Esper landed back in Washington in the early hours of October 30, U.S. officials had received worrisome intelligence: the militia leaders might be planning to sell Walton to a terrorist group.

"People were nervous," recalled one senior military adviser. "It looked like the soft-core group might trade him to the hard-core group."

At 7:30 a.m. at his Pentagon office that day, Esper got briefed on the situation and was alarmed to learn the president had already green-lit the Special Forces rescue for Walton. Presidents typically received extensive briefings on missions and crises of this magnitude. Esper knew Mike Pompeo was overseas and Robert O'Brien also was out of town, so he questioned who was presenting this very serious set of circumstances and decision options to Trump. To Esper's chagrin, he discovered one key person informing the president had been Kash Patel, a counterterrorism official who sometimes held himself as if he were the national security adviser. In a normal process for something this serious, Meadows should have been calling Esper, Pompeo, and CIA director Gina Haspel to get their feedback. The normal process had been rushed and short-circuited.

Esper wasn't worried about SEAL Team 6 conducting an impeccable extraction. But he was worried about launching a life-or-death mission without knowing whether this Special Forces rescue—just days before the election—was justified and made sense. He couldn't call the White House and trust anything Patel said. He didn't know that O'Brien had participated in briefing the president on the kidnapping and had urged moving fast. So Esper began furiously dialing all the "adults" he did trust—Pompeo, Barr, Haspel, and Chris Wray—so he could find out what they knew about the status on the ground in Nigeria. He reached Wray.

"I hear you are negotiating, and I want to hear how negotiations are going before I send my boys in," Esper told the FBI director. Wray confirmed the talks had gone nowhere and there were worries about what the kidnappers might do next.

For Esper, Wray's assessment was the key. Now he felt on solid ground in agreeing to launch the special operators. But then came a major glitch, thanks to another breakdown somewhere in the White House process. Patel had insisted the countries into which the U.S. forces would have to fly to stage the operation and then conduct the rescue—Niger and Nigeria—had been notified and had approved of the plan. It was not Patel's job responsibility to secure their approval, although senior officials said they were assured by him that this step had been taken. Patel declined to discuss the episode.

As the operators were en route, they had to pause midmission when U.S. military and State Department officials learned Patel had been mistaken. Nigeria had not been notified. The mission had to be paused until the Nigerian government signed off. American forces had come very close to a technical invasion of a foreign country.

Nigerian officials gave the green light and the rescue proceeded successfully. The night of October 31,

Halloween, SEAL Team 6 parachuted into north Nigeria, trekked three miles on foot in the dark, and then surgically took control of the compound where Walton was being held prisoner. The unit of thirty operators killed all but one of the gunmen on the scene and rapidly moved Walton to safety with his family. Yet while Pompeo, Milley, and Esper cheered the flawless rescue, their anger at Patel boiled.

In the final week of campaigning, Biden stuck to his familiar if unimaginative script about the pandemic's dangers, Trump's failures, and the promise to heal a broken nation. The likable yet uninspiring Biden was riding high from the fiery boost he had received from Obama, who had upped the ante by eviscerating Trump at an October 27 rally in Orlando.

"What's his closing argument? That people are too focused on COVID," Obama had said. "He said this at one of his rallies: 'COVID, COVID, COVID.' He's complaining. He's jealous of COVID's media coverage."

Referring to the two coronavirus outbreaks in the White House over the past month, Obama had said, "I lived in the White House for a while. You know, it's a controlled environment. You can take some preventative measures in the White House to avoid getting sick. Except this guy can't seem to do it. He's turned the White House into a hot zone."

Obama had reminded voters of Trump's recent

retweet spreading a false conspiracy theory about Osama bin Laden's assassination, which occurred in 2011 on Obama's order.

"Listen, our president of the United States retweeted a post that claimed that the Navy SEALs didn't actually kill bin Laden," Obama had said. "Think about that. And we act like, 'Well, okay . . . ' It's not okay. I mean, we've gotten so numb to what is bizarre behavior."

As Obama and Biden drove Democrats to the polls early, the Republicans were counting on a massive Election Day turnout, so Trump could lead substantially on Election Night and declare victory before all the early votes were counted. But as Trump jetted from one rally to the next, he and his advisers were so taken by the size and enthusiasm of his crowds that they began to dream big, thinking a real, lasting, and undeniable win might be in the cards. "You thought, damn, he might actually pull this off," one adviser recalled.

Trump and his team thought they were experiencing 2016 all over again. The president flew around the country at a grueling pace, traveling to eleven rallies in the final forty-eight hours. Massive crowds greeted him in such places as Hickory, North Carolina; Rome, Georgia; Scranton, Pennsylvania; Kenosha, Wisconsin; and Grand Rapids, Michigan.

Trump's optimism was reinforced by those traveling with him. Republican National Committee chairwoman Ronna McDaniel and Stepien, who were well informed about state-by-state data and early-vote trends, were circumspect about Trump's path to 270 electoral votes. But Trump's adult children and their spouses, as well as staffers Meadows, McEnany, Farah, Hope Hicks, Derek Lyons, and others, spoke in those final days as if they could already smell victory. They made up what another adviser described as a "traveling Greek chorus" that fed Trump's ego by reveling in the crowd sizes and talking up the possibilities of a landslide win.

In his final days on the stump, Trump decided to add a new name to the long list of foes he attacked at his rallies: Anthony Fauci. He first consulted his political brain trust about whether going after Fauci was a wise idea. Though the president would never admit it, polls soon after the pandemic hit and ever since had shown that Fauci was far more popular with voters than Trump. Before one of his rallies in late October, Trump asked Miller what he thought of going after Fauci from the lectern.

"Say whatever you want to say," Miller told him. "He's out there campaigning against you. The guy's been wrong. He's moved the goalposts on masks. I think the guy's full of shit. He doesn't have to be treated with kid gloves."

As an apolitical public servant, Fauci did not campaign for or against any candidate, though that didn't stop Trump and his aides from thinking of his interviews accurately describing the dangers of the virus as, effectively, the work of a Biden surrogate.

Trump went for it. He started softly, calling Fauci "a Democrat" at a North Carolina rally. But he ratcheted up his attacks on Fauci in subsequent rallies, and by November 1, at a late-night rally in Miami, the crowd knew what was coming when the president started talking about the virus. A "Fire Fauci!" chant broke out. Trump lapped it up. In response, he told his supporters, "Don't tell anybody, but let me wait until a little bit after the election."

But Fauci had a thick skin. As another doctor on the task force put it, "You got so numb to the outrageousness. One more level of outrageous, it barely registered." Fauci was angrier about the White House blocking him from many media appearances. As for Trump, Fauci had all but given up on the president doing the honest or honorable thing some time earlier. So had most of the other doctors. He was a lost cause.

Fabrizio couldn't fathom why the president would choose to make a popular figure like Fauci his punching bag in the closing days of the campaign. It was politically stupid because it risked alienating the white independent voters Trump still needed to attract. As he watched Trump attack Fauci at one of these rallies, Fabrizio sent a text message to Short. He jokingly asked Short if it was safe to assume it had been his "strategic recommendation" to attack Fauci.

"LOL," Short wrote back. He, too, knew how foolish this was.

In Washington, meanwhile, the triumvirate that

had spent so much energy that summer and fall keeping Trump from deploying active-duty troops on the streets of American cities—Esper, Milley, and Barr—were tracking intelligence and social media chatter for any signs of unrest on Election Day. They and their deputies at the Pentagon, Justice Department, and FBI were monitoring the possibility of protests breaking out among supporters on both sides. The trio also were on guard for the possibility that Trump would invoke the Insurrection Act in some way to quell protests or to perpetuate his power by somehow intervening in the election. This scenario weighed heavily on Esper and Milley because they controlled the military and had sworn an oath to the Constitution. Their duty was to protect a free and fair election and to prevent the military from being used for political purposes of any kind.

At around 5:30 p.m. on November 2, the night before the election, Barr called Esper to give the defense secretary a heads-up about something. Trump had told some of his advisers that he planned to contest the election on legal grounds should he fall behind Biden in the vote count. Before polls opened on Election Day, the president already was preparing to lose the official count in key states and to fight it in court.

Barr also relayed to Esper the latest intelligence gathered by the FBI, which showed that if Trump won, significant civil unrest was expected in several cities. Esper thanked Barr for the information and shared it with Milley and other Pentagon officials. Esper, Milley, and Barr were ready for whatever might come the next day. And they knew one thing for certain: the biggest wild card on Election Night would be the commander in chief himself.

Sixteen

The Reckoning

Finally, Election Day had arrived. The morning of November 3, President Trump was upbeat. The mood in the West Wing was good. Some aides talked giddily of a landslide. Several women who worked in the White House arrived wearing red sweaters in a show of optimism, while some Secret Service agents on the president's detail sported red ties for the occasion. Trump's voice was hoarse from his mad dash of rallies, but he thought his exhausting final sprint had sealed the deal. He considered Joe Biden to be a lot of things, but a winner most definitely was not one of them. "I can't lose to this fucking guy," Trump told aides.

At around noon, his detail whisked Trump across the Potomac River to visit his campaign headquarters in Arlington, where Bill Stepien and the campaign's high command gave Trump a briefing in the conference room. Jared Kushner, Mark Meadows, and Kayleigh McEnany joined the president. Stepien outlined what to expect that night—when polls closed in each battleground state, how quickly votes should be tallied, and which states would likely have the first projected winners. The campaign manager explained that due to the huge number of mail-in ballots in many states, it might take long into the night for votes to be counted. Patience was in order.

Four years earlier, Stepien had given a similar Election Day briefing to Trump and told him that the early returns likely would favor Hillary Clinton. For instance, he said then, the first numbers to report out of Florida traditionally were in Democratic strongholds in South Florida, while precincts in the Panhandle, which strongly favored Republicans, reported an hour later because they are in a later time zone. "It's going to be a long night," Stepien had told him in 2016. "Don't be discouraged."

This time, Stepien explained to Trump that the opposite could happen. In many battleground states, the first votes to be recorded were expected to be in-person Election Day votes, which could lean Trump, while mail-in votes, which were likely to heavily favor Biden, were added to the tally later as those ballots were processed. This meant the early vote totals could well show Trump ahead by solid margins.

"It's going to be good early," Stepien told the boss. But, as he cautioned the president, those numbers would be incomplete and the margins likely would tighten later in the evening.

Trump then stepped out of the conference room and into the big open floor of cubicles to give a brief pep talk to scores of assembled staffers, who greeted him with raucous applause. A pool of journalists stood nearby to cover his remarks, and a reporter asked whether he had prepared an acceptance speech or concession speech to deliver that evening.

"No, I'm not thinking about concession speech or acceptance speech yet," Trump said. "Hopefully, we'll be only doing one of those two. And, you know, winning is easy. Losing is never easy. Not for me, it's not."

As Trump thought about winning or losing, the Pentagon brass was focused on keeping the peace. That morning, Mark Esper, Mark Milley, and other defense officials got a briefing on security concerns around the nation. If Trump won, officials expected large crowds of protesters to assemble in Washington, perhaps as many as ten thousand or fifteen thousand people. Law enforcement officials were monitoring cities, including Atlanta, Boston, Los Angeles, Norfolk, Philadelphia, and San Diego, for likely protests.

Meanwhile, White House cooks and ushers were busy preparing to receive hundreds of guests for an Election Night viewing party. Trump's original plan had been to stage his "victory" party at the Trump International Hotel a few blocks away on Pennsylvania Avenue. But that plan had been scotched a few days earlier, as the president's wishes for a celebration at

his luxury hotel ran headlong into the District of
Columbia's public health regulations for coronavirus.
No more than fifty people could gather at an indoor
venue in the city.

Trump's campaign and his White House political
team had nearly four hundred people they wanted to
invite for Election Night, so they moved the party
to the White House, which was on federal property
and therefore not subject to local ordinances. Trump
decided to host his party in the East Room and other
overflow rooms along the Cross Hall of the White
House. The choice of location broke with a solemn
tradition of never using the White House for overt
political purposes, a norm Trump had already tossed
aside in August by holding his Republican National
Convention acceptance speech on the South Lawn.

Trump also used the White House to house his political operation, setting up two "war rooms" with com-
puters, large-screen televisions, and other equipment
where campaign staffers would work monitoring election returns. The larger of the two war rooms was in
government office space in the Eisenhower Executive
Office Building, which was next to the West Wing
and part of the White House campus, where roughly
sixty staffers would have work stations from which
to receive up-to-the-minute information from battleground states and track precinct data. The smaller
war room was in the Map Room, on the ground level
of the White House residence. Steeped in history,
the Map Room took its name from World War II,

when President Franklin Roosevelt turned it into a situation room with maps to track troop movements and to receive classified information on the war's progress. Trump's seniormost aides planned to work through the night in the Map Room, now transformed into the campaign's command center, where Stepien and his top deputies could analyze data and stay close to the president to brief him in person as needed.

Nancy Pelosi had been working toward this night for four years. For her, Election Night in 2016 had been a nightmare, and she was determined not to allow a repeat in 2020. "That night was like getting kicked in the back by a mule over and over again," Pelosi said in an interview for this book. The House Speaker recalled thinking that night about Trump's surprise victory, "It can't be true. It can't be happening to our country."

Pelosi added, "You understand that this is not a person of sound mind. You understand that. You know that. He's not of sound mind. . . . When he first got elected, I was devastated because I thought Hillary Clinton was one of the best prepared people to be president—better than her husband, better than Obama, better than George W. Bush. Maybe not better than George Herbert Walker Bush, because he had been a vice president. I don't think any of the people I just mentioned would deny that she was better qualified, experienced, all the rest of it. So, the idea that he would get elected was shocking. It was shocking."

Mitt Romney had been less shocked by Trump's election—he had watched firsthand as the Republican Party was radicalized by the far right—but was just as determined to prevent a second Trump term. Romney said in an interview for this book that he watched the election returns in California together with his wife, Ann, son Craig, and other family members, and felt a pit in his stomach. The early numbers looked surprisingly good for Trump. Biden was struggling in the quadrennial bellwether of Florida, even in Democrat-rich Miami-Dade County.

"I think he's going to win," Romney recalled telling his family. "Those polls were way off. I think he's going to pull it out."

At the White House, people liked what they were seeing. There was a party atmosphere. Staff hung out in West Wing offices chatting at least until 9:00 p.m. National Security Council officials celebrated in the Roosevelt Room. Meadows served beer and food in the chief of staff's corner office. Another group of aides lingered outside McEnany's office, known as Upper Press. In the residence, scores of guests—Cabinet secretaries, members of Congress, television stars, and other dignitaries—were drinking and milling around, mostly without masks save for Alex Azar, who kept his on. After a few too many swigs of wine and beer, some guests became rather animated as the night progressed.

Upstairs in the first family's private quarters, Trump was glued to the television. He alternated between watching from his bedroom alone and from a family room with Melania, other family members, and some of his most trusted aides, including Hope Hicks. Stepien, Meadows, McEnany, Jason Miller, Stephen Miller, Ronna McDaniel, and other senior advisers were in the Map Room. Members of the president's family—Donald Trump Jr., Ivanka Trump, Kushner, Eric Trump and his wife, Lara, who worked on the campaign—came in and out much of the night, as did a pair of special party guests, Fox News stars Laura Ingraham and Jeanine Pirro.

They all turned to Matt Oczkowski for updates, sometimes as often as every few minutes. As the campaign's top data cruncher, Oczkowski sat in front of a computer and performed real-time analysis of precinct data to stay ahead of state calls and to spot any trouble on the horizon. Oczkowski liked what he saw early on. Florida offered the first good indicators. Trump was overperforming with Blacks and Latinos, especially among Cuban Americans in South Florida. Miami-Dade was going gangbusters for Trump. And turnout among the president's base of rural whites was high. Meadows, meanwhile, paid close attention to precinct returns out of North Carolina, which he had represented in Congress, and he felt confident about Trump's chances there. And early returns out of Pennsylvania were encouraging.

At this point in the evening, Stepien tried to temper

Trump's optimism and keep the president's mind from racing too far ahead of reality. "Stay calm," the campaign manager told him. "We won't know for some period of time."

One Trump confidant who mostly stayed out of the Map Room was Rudy Giuliani. That's because he had set up his own command center upstairs on the party floor. Giuliani sat at a table in the Red Room with his son, Andrew, who worked at the White House in the Office of Public Liaison, staring intensely at a laptop watching vote tallies come in. The Giulianis made for an odd scene, as partygoers swirled around them. After a while, Rudy Giuliani started to cause a commotion. He was telling other guests that he had come up with a strategy for Trump and was trying to get into the president's private quarters to tell him about it. Some people thought Giuliani might have been drinking too much and suggested to Stepien that he go talk to the former New York City mayor. Stepien, Meadows, and Jason Miller brought Giuliani down to a room just off the Map Room to hear him out.

Giuliani went state by state asking Stepien, Miller, and Meadows what they were seeing and what their plan was.

"What's happening in Michigan?" he asked.

They said it was too early to tell, votes were still being counted and they couldn't say.

"Just say we won," Giuliani told them.

Same thing in Pennsylvania. "Just say we won Pennsylvania," Giuliani said.

Giuliani's grand plan was to just say Trump won, state after state, based on nothing. Stepien, Miller, and Meadows thought his argument was both incoherent and irresponsible.

"We can't do that," Meadows said, raising his voice. "We can't."

Some competitive races were falling into place for Republicans. In South Carolina, Lindsey Graham faced a tough challenge from Democrat Jaime Harrison, an impressive candidate who had garnered national attention and raised $109 million, the most ever for a U.S. Senate campaign. But South Carolina, long a bastion of Republicanism, stayed true to form. The race was called early, with Graham winning 54 percent to Harrison's 44 percent.

Trump was watching TV as news networks projected Graham's victory, and within minutes he called his friend.

"You got yours," Trump told Graham. "I've got a fight on my hands."

"Well, Mr. President, hang in there," Graham said. "It's looking pretty good for you."

As the night bore on, some of Trump's advisers began to worry. Public polls, as well as the Trump campaign's internal surveys, had long projected the race was Biden's to lose, and that prediction was bearing out as more precincts reported votes from battleground states. Alyssa Farah stepped away from the party in the East Room and saw McDaniel pacing in the hallway.

"Ronna, good to see you!" Farah said to the Republican National Committee chairwoman.

"Hey, good to see you," McDaniel said. Then, as she turned away, McDaniel said, "Things are not looking good."

Bill Barr had the same feeling. He had shown up for Trump's Election Night party, even though he had thought for months that Trump was destined to become a one-term president. Trump didn't seem able to get out of his own way and deliver a disciplined message, and Barr had warned him of exactly that in April. Barr hung around the party for a bit, but a little after 10:00 decided to call it a night. He went home to get some sleep.

The Pentagon's top two leaders stayed away from Trump's party, still hypervigilant about avoiding any suggestion that they were politicizing the military. Mark Esper and Mark Milley had learned that lesson back on June 1 in Lafayette Square. Milley watched the returns on TV from his home on Fort Myer in Arlington. A history buff, Milley memorialized the night by keeping his own scorecard of states in his journal. At around 10:30, with results from most key states still far too close to call, Milley received an interesting call from a retired military buddy who reminded him of his apolitical role as chairman of the Joint Chiefs of Staff.

"You are an island unto yourself right now," the friend said, according to the account Milley shared with aides. "You are not tethered. Your loyalty is to the Constitution. You represent the stability of this republic."

Milley's friend added, "There's fourth-rate people at the Pentagon. And you have fifth-rate people at the White House. You're surrounded by total incompetence. Hang in there. Hang tough."

Esper was at home in northern Virginia feeling at peace that he had survived this long without getting fired and without having acquiesced to Trump's wishes to order troops to break up domestic protests. The defense secretary had had a target on his back all fall, but Trump had not axed him.

Esper had a scare the night before, November 2, when NBC's Courtney Kube planned to report that Esper was preparing to be fired the day after the election, had updated his resignation letter, and was quietly advising members of Congress about renaming army bases named for Confederate generals as a sort of mic drop to fortify his legacy. Esper believed that if NBC published the story, it would signal he was on the verge of resigning and prompt his premature firing—so he went into overdrive to stop it. He directed his aides to try to convince Kube that her information could be overhyped. It was true that Esper had been consulting with congressional committees about renaming the bases. It also was true that Esper had prepared a resignation letter, as many Trump appointees had, but he had no imminent plans to submit it. In truth, Esper expected Trump would fire him after the election, but was hoping to hold on if he could, at least for a few days after the election. He was worried about what Trump might try to do with the military if he were not at the helm. Esper warned Kube that publishing her story could result in a more compliant acting secretary of defense, which could have worrisome repercussions. The story was held as they tussled back and forth.

Esper was a lifelong Republican and had worked at the conservative Heritage Foundation as well as for Republican senators Bill Frist and Chuck Hagel. But he told his closest colleagues that as he watched TV news anchors cover the election results, he found himself rooting for the Democrat. Esper had worked with Biden and his secretary of state in waiting, Antony Blinken, when he was a senior staffer on the Senate Foreign Relations Committee. He had confidence that they were serious, stable people who cared deeply about shoring up national security. Esper couldn't say the same about Trump. In fact, Trump had privately indicated he would seek to withdraw from NATO and to blow up the U.S. alliance with South Korea, should he win reelection. When those alliances had come up in meetings with Esper and other top aides, some advisers warned Trump that shredding them before the election would be politically dangerous.

"Yeah, the second term," Trump had said. "We'll do it in the second term."

Esper had known that Trump had wanted to fire him ever since their June 3 argument over the

Insurrection Act, but had heard that Mike Pompeo, campaign officials, and other advisers had talked the president out of doing so before the election. They had argued that he couldn't afford to rupture his relationship with a second defense secretary, not after Jim Mattis's rocky departure and the sharp public criticism he later leveled at Trump.

Esper had lived through the strain of the 2000 recounts and the **Bush v. Gore** case. He had repeatedly told his deputies that he wanted this election to be "clean and clear," as in free of any suggestion of corruption and indisputably clear who had won. He had feared anything less might give Trump some shred of a reason to call out troops. Later into the evening, as returns posted in Biden's favor, Esper told a friend, "It looks good." The defense secretary went to bed comforted by signs the country would get a divided and stable government—a Democratic president and, he hoped, a Republican Senate.

At 11:20 p.m. on Fox News, Bill Hemmer was standing before his giant touchscreen in the network's Studio F in New York, guiding viewers through electoral college scenarios when Arizona turned blue on his map. The sudden change in color caught Hemmer off guard. "What is this happening here? Why is Arizona blue? Did we just call it? Did we just make a call in Arizona? Let's see," Hemmer said.

Co-anchor Martha MacCallum said indeed Fox

had called Arizona, a hotly contested battleground state with eleven electoral college votes.

Co-anchor Bret Baier chimed in. "Time out," he said. "This is a big development. Fox News's decision desk is calling Arizona for Joe Biden." Baier added, "Biden picking up Arizona changes the math."

Trump, who had been watching Fox, was livid. He could not fathom that the conservative news network he had long considered an extension of his campaign was the first news organization to call Arizona for Biden. This was a betrayal. His top advisers, who had been in the Map Room at the time, rushed upstairs to see the president. Giuliani followed them up.

"They're calling it way too early," Oczkowski told Trump. "This thing is close. We still think we'll win narrowly—and not just us. Doug Ducey's modeling people show us winning." Ducey, Arizona's Republican governor, and his political team had kept in close contact with Trump's aides.

That hardly reassured the president. "What the fuck is Fox doing?" Trump screamed. Then he barked orders to Kushner: "Call Rupert! Call James and Lachlan!" And to Miller: "Get Sammon. Get Hemmer. They've got to reverse this." The president was referring to Fox owner Rupert Murdoch and his sons, James and Lachlan, as well as Bill Sammon, a top news executive at Fox.

Trump's tirade continued. "What the fuck?" he bellowed. "What the fuck are these guys doing? How could they call this this early?"

Oczkowski again tried to soothe the president. "They're calling this way too early," he said. "This is unbelievable."

Giuliani pushed the president to forget about the Arizona call and just say he won—to step into the East Room and deliver a victory speech. Never mind that Meadows had earlier snapped at Giuliani and said the president couldn't just declare himself the winner.

"Just go declare victory right now," Giuliani told Trump. "You've got to go declare victory now."

Giuliani's interjection of his "just-say-you-won" strategy infuriated Trump's campaign advisers.

"It's hard to be the responsible parent when there's a cool uncle around taking the kid to the movies and driving him around in a Corvette," one of these advisers recalled. "When we say the president can't say that, being responsible is not the easiest place to be when you've got people telling the president what he wants to hear. It's hard to tell the president no. It's not an enviable place to be."

Once they got away from the president, Kushner called Rupert Murdoch. Miller tried Sammon but couldn't reach him. Other Trump aides pitched in, too. Kellyanne Conway reached out to Baier and MacCallum, who were on the air. Hicks, who had worked under Lachlan Murdoch at the Fox Corporation between her White House stints, reached out to Fox Corporation senior vice president Raj Shah, a former Trump spokesman, to track down a number for Jay Wallace, the president of Fox News.

Conway talked to Brian Seitchik, a longtime Trump
adviser based in Arizona, who assured her, "This is irresponsible. Here in Arizona, we just have way too
many votes left to count."

Ducey called the Trump team and was put on
speakerphone. The governor told them that the Fox
call was premature and that, according to his analysis, Trump still had a chance to win because so many
votes remained to be counted.

Typically, most news organizations call states
around the same time because they tend to have similar standards for when it is safe to project winners
and losers. But with Arizona, other major news organizations held back on joining Fox's call. In fact,
Miller received text messages from contacts at other
networks. "I can't believe Fox is doing you guys dirty,"
one of them wrote.

Trump and his family became apoplectic as the
night ticked on and his early leads over Biden in
Pennsylvania and other states kept shrinking. As
additional votes were being counted, Biden inched
closer to Trump. Pennsylvania was too close to call,
as was Georgia. Trump decided to deliver remarks
to his viewing party and came down into the Map
Room, where he yelled at Justin Clark, the deputy
campaign manager.

"Why are they still counting votes?" Trump asked.
"The election's closed. Are they counting ballots
that came in afterward? What the hell is going on?"
Trump, through a spokesman, denied saying this.

The president told Conway he thought something nefarious was at play.

"They're stealing this from us," Trump said. "We have this thing won. I won in a landslide and they're taking it back."

Of course, nobody was taking anything. Election officials were simply doing their duty, counting ballots. But Trump didn't see it that way. He seemed to truly believe he had been winning. As one Trump adviser later explained, "The psychological impact of, he's going to win, people were calling him saying he's going to win, and then somehow these votes just keep showing up."

Eric Trump, who the night before had predicted to friends that his father would win with 322 electoral college votes, flipped out in the Map Room.

"The election is being stolen," the president's thirty-six-year-old son said. "Where are these votes coming from? How is this legit?"

Eric Trump yelled at the campaign's data analysts, as if it were their fault that his father's early leads over Biden were shrinking. "We pay you to do this," he said. "How can this be happening?"

Eric Trump, through a spokesperson, insisted that he did not berate campaign staff, as described by witnesses.

Donald Trump Jr. said, "There's no way we lose to this guy," referring to Biden.

Shortly after 2:00 a.m. on November 4, "Hail to the Chief" played at the East Room party. Out walked Trump, followed by Melania Trump, Vice President Pence, and Karen Pence. Stephen Miller and the speechwriting team had prepared remarks for Trump to deliver, but the president veered from his teleprompter script to instead deliver stream-of-consciousness thoughts.

"We were winning everything and all of a sudden it was just called off," Trump said. He added, "Literally we were just all set to get outside and just celebrate something that was so beautiful, so good."

Trump rattled off states he had won—Florida! Ohio! Texas!—and then claimed he had already won states that were too close to call, including Georgia and North Carolina. He bragged about his leads in some states—"Think of this: We're up six hundred ninety thousand votes in Pennsylvania. Six hundred ninety thousand!"—and falsely claimed to be winning Michigan and Wisconsin.

Neither Trump nor Biden was declared the overall winner because Arizona, Georgia, North Carolina, and Pennsylvania remained too close to call. Yet Trump insisted that he was the actual winner, and that his sweet victory had been somehow snatched from him.

"This is a fraud on the American public," the president said. "This is an embarrassment to our country. We were getting ready to win this election. Frankly, we did win this election. We did win this election. So our goal now is to ensure the integrity for the good of this nation. This is a very big moment. This is a major fraud in our nation. We want the law to be used in a proper manner. So we'll be going to the U.S. Supreme Court. We want all voting to stop. We don't want them to find any ballots at four o'clock in the morning and add them to the list, okay? It's a very sad moment. To me, this is a very sad moment, and we will win this. And as far as I'm concerned, we already have won it."

This was an extraordinary accusation for any political candidate to make about any election, much less for a sitting president to make about the country's most consequential election. Trump was telling the seventy-four million people who voted for him not to trust the results.

Watching from California, Romney was heartsick. "We're in a global battle for the survival of liberal democracy in the face of autocracy and autocratic regimes attempting to dominate the world," he recalled in the interview. "So saying something and doing things that would suggest that in the free nation of the United States of America and the model of democracy for the world, that we can't have a free and fair election would have a destructive effect on democracy around the world, not just to mention here."

Pelosi watched Trump's speech in horror. "It was just a complete, total manifestation [of] insanity," she recalled in the interview.

"It was clear over that four-year period that this was not a person who was on the level—on the level intellectually, on the level mentally, on the level emotionally, and certainly not on the level patriotically," she said. "So for him to say what he said, I wouldn't say was surprising as it might have been if we hadn't seen the instability all along."

In that moment, Pelosi said she thought that if Trump were willing to claim victory when he had not won, there was no telling what he might do in the weeks ahead to try to hold on to power.

"It was a sad night for our country patriotically, constitutionally—forget the politics; that's minor. Patriotically and constitutionally that a president of the United States would say what he said and that there wouldn't be an intervention from his side," Pelosi said. "We knew there was real trouble ahead."

Following his speech, Trump hung around the Green Room next door to the East Room talking to some advisers and VIP guests, asking them what they thought. Ingraham, whose prime-time show was off the air that night because of Fox's special election coverage, was overheard giving the president some advice. Ingraham expressed general doubt that the outcome would change in the days ahead given the historical reluctance of federal courts to intervene in elections, a contrast to what she considered unrealistic scenarios being painted by some others around the president.

"Give up on Arizona," Ingraham told him, apparently confident in her network's decision to project Biden the winner there.

Giving up wasn't in Trump's repertoire. "Fox shouldn't have called it," he told her.

Karl Rove, the former George W. Bush strategist and Fox commentator, had just come off the air when he got a call from a Trump adviser. "He's in a meltdown," the adviser told Rove. "Can you call him and tell him that all is not lost?"

Rove phoned the president and tried to give him a pep talk.

"Hang in there," Rove told Trump. "There's a lot of ballots to be counted and it's not going to be done for some time. You fought a good fight. . . . You're not out yet."

Rove and Trump briefly discussed the state of the race in Arizona. "I know premature calls," he said, reminding the president of the fiasco on Election Night in 2000, when some networks projected Al Gore would win Florida only to have to retract their call a couple of hours later. "Hang in there. You gave it your all. You came down to the end. You upset them in 2016. You can do it again. Just hold on."

Trump then retreated to the Map Room to talk to his campaign team. He stayed up until 4:00 a.m. chewing over the incoming results. The president was fixated on Pennsylvania, where Biden kept cutting into his lead. There were enough votes still to be counted in Philadelphia, which were sure to favor the Democrat, for Biden to overtake Trump. And indeed, Democrats were optimistic that once all the votes were in, Biden would win the state.

Conway and Meadows both preached patience.

"Mr. President, you're ahead in Pennsylvania by

seven hundred thousand votes," Conway told him. "We won Pennsylvania by forty-four thousand votes last time. Just let them count the votes. Let them get through the votes."

Meadows said, "Just count the votes, Mr. President. You probably have enough to keep those leads."

Trump wasn't having any of it. He thought Democrats were rigging the vote totals.

"If I wake up in the morning and they say Trump is ahead by a hundred thousand votes, they'll find a hundred thousand and one votes in the backyard," the president said.

"Mr. President, it stings," Conway said. "It just hurts to have lost Pennsylvania."

"Honey, we didn't lose Pennsylvania," Trump replied. "We won Pennsylvania."

Conway, who often was quick with a rejoinder to lighten the mood at tense moments, invoked the cheap security cameras that some homeowners install at their front doors to monitor for stolen packages or unwanted visitors. "Then your campaign should've invested in Ring and Nest cameras," she quipped.

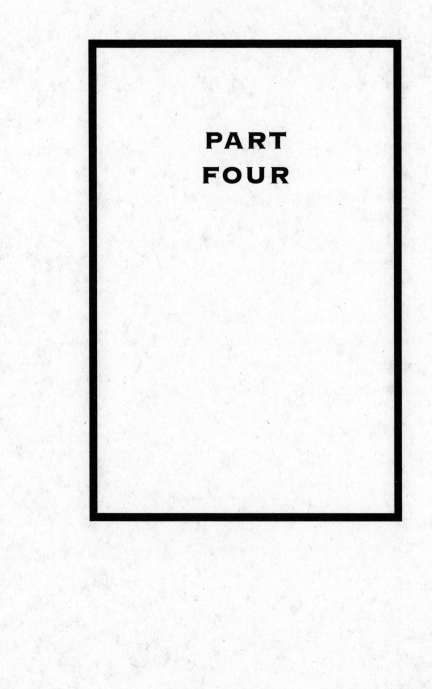

PART
FOUR

Seventeen

The Big Lie

On November 4, the day after the election, President Trump surprised his aides. Joe Biden led handily in the electoral college as well as the popular vote. But with several key states, including Pennsylvania and Georgia, still too close to call, neither Biden nor Trump had been projected the winner. In his 2:00 a.m. speech, Trump had proclaimed that "we already have won it," yet when the president spoke with advisers in private hours later, he suddenly sounded defeatist.

"How did we lose to Joe Biden?" Trump asked. "What happened? What went wrong? Can we still win?"

Most aides responded with variations of the affirmative. "Sure, we can still win," some said. They did not want to dash Trump's hopes, at least not until reality forced their hands. Kellyanne Conway, his adviser with the most experience on political campaigns, offered the president a theory for why he appeared to have come up short.

"Mr. President, it's a convergence of things," she said. "It's the virus, but it's also the mail-in ballots. Your campaign had one and a half billion dollars and you ran out of money. You pulled ads down at the end. I think that's incredibly unfair. I watched you run around the country. You raised so much money only for them to run out of it late in the game."

The president's loss was not even official and already the recriminations had begun. So it went in Trump World. Conway also suggested a message for Trump to push on social media, assuming he would go to court to contest the outcome. "This is very simple," she told him. "All you want to do is say, 'We want to make sure every legal vote is counted and every illegal vote is not counted.' That should be noncontroversial. Biden should retweet that. Ask Joe Biden to retweet it."

"That's genius," Trump said. "If we do that, I'll win."

Conway told Trump that she had just spoken with a smart politico in Georgia who said the presidential race there could go either way by the slimmest of margins, three thousand or five thousand votes.

"How can that be?" Trump asked. "We should be winning Georgia by a landslide."

"You should be, but you're not," Conway said.

"This is crazy," Trump said. "I'm calling the governor. He ruined it."

Georgia bewildered Trump. For the past three decades, the state had voted for Republicans for president. Its governor was Republican, as was its secretary of state, who administered elections. At Trump's final rally there, on the night of November 1 in Rome, a small city in the Appalachian foothills, an estimated thirty thousand people showed up to see him. Their energy was electric. Georgia was MAGA country. Or so Trump thought. Demographic shifts coupled with a massive voter registration and mobilization drive led by Stacey Abrams and other Democrats had turned this red state purple. The story was similar in Arizona. Trump couldn't fathom that Biden had more votes than him there. He asked Lindsey Graham what he thought had gone wrong in Arizona.

"I think you lost Arizona because of John McCain," Graham, who had been the late senator's closest friend in Washington, told Trump. "Beating on McCain went too far and it probably hurt you in Arizona."

Despite Trump's private flashes of realism on November 4, his campaign was defiant. That morning, Jared Kushner, Bill Stepien, Jason Miller, Hope Hicks, and other advisers gathered to strategize, some at campaign headquarters in Arlington and others by phone. Like every presidential campaign since Bush versus Gore in 2000, the Trump team had lined up scores of lawyers and staff on the ground in battleground states ready to mount legal challenges whenever headquarters sent the signal.

In Pennsylvania and Wisconsin, the Trump

campaign believed it had legitimate legal claims that could toss out some votes in Biden's column. The margin in Georgia was close enough that a hand recount was likely, which could put Trump on top. And the campaign's internal model on November 4 had predicted Trump ultimately would eke out a win in Arizona as well as North Carolina. They thought Biden's leads in Michigan and Nevada were insurmountable, but Trump had a pathway to 270 electoral college votes without them.

Miller moved quickly to control the messages emanating from Trump World. The president was preparing to contest the election in courtrooms across the country, and he didn't want any surrogates saying anything detrimental to their efforts. He asked Hicks to hold back any election-related communications from the White House until the campaign got its ducks in a row. Alyssa Farah was booked for an appearance on Fox News the morning of November 4. She had planned to tout the Republican Party's achievements, even though Trump appeared likely to lose, saying something along the lines of, "Results aren't here yet. We're still awaiting them. Republicans have a lot to be proud of. We picked up seats in the House, elected a record number of women, and brought in more Black and Hispanic votes."

But before her TV segment started, Farah got a call from Hicks. "Stand down," Hicks told her. "The campaign's running all messaging going forward. There's a plan here. We appreciate you wanting to be out fighting, but we don't need you." Farah did not appear on the air that day.

By November 5, as a handful of states, including Georgia and Pennsylvania, continued to count mail-in and other ballots, and Biden's total inched up, Trump fired off a series of tweets. His strategy was clear. Shortly after 9:00 a.m., he wrote, "STOP THE COUNT!" Nearly an hour later, he wrote, "ANY VOTE THAT CAME IN AFTER ELECTION DAY WILL NOT BE COUNTED!" And a little over an hour after that, he wrote, "All of the recent Biden claimed States will be legally challenged by us for Voter Fraud and State Election Fraud. Plenty of proof—just check out the Media. WE WILL WIN! America First!"

Trump had his comeback strategy. He would wage a brazen assault on the election, challenging late-counting ballots in courts and trying to pressure judges and state election officials and legislators to stop tabulations. The president believed this was as much a public relations task as a legal one. To be his battle commander, he tapped his deputy campaign manager from 2016, David Bossie, who ran Citizens United, a conservative advocacy group. Bossie was a three-decade veteran of partisan fights against the Clintons and other Democrats, and Trump admired his pugilism.

Though Bossie was technically in charge, Rudy Giuliani asserted himself right away. He showed up at campaign headquarters to crash strategy meetings and spent significant time talking with Trump. Giuliani told the president repeatedly, "They stole this thing." He played to Trump's sense of victimhood and brought any anecdote of alleged voter fraud he could find straight to the president. Giuliani believed Trump's team was ill prepared to go to battle.

The professionals on Trump's campaign thought Giuliani could damage Trump's cause if he made himself the face of the president's legal challenges. They knew Giuliani was undisciplined and that some of his comments sounded, frankly, crazy. They spent this week trying to control and restrain the former New York mayor. "We would sit with him and listen to him," one campaign official recalled. "It was the only way to stop him from running to a TV camera. We assigned a staffer to him to try to contain him, because only bad things were going to come from that."

On November 6, several of Trump's campaign advisers met with the president in the Oval Office to tell him they thought he was likely to lose the recounts he was pursuing. The vote tallies were not going his way. They put Matt Oczkowski on speakerphone to guide Trump through the data. Ticking through the key remaining battleground states, Oczkowski said, "You're going to lose these places."

"I thought we were going to win," Trump said. "Why are they still counting votes coming in after the election? What's going on?"

"We don't know how many votes are left out there," Oczkowski said.

"No," Trump said. "We're winning this. This was stolen."

Then the president got Giuliani on the line.

"You won," Giuliani told him. "They stole this thing."

Trump's campaign team was being realistic, but the president wanted them to keep up the charade that the election had been stolen. He directed his frustration at Justin Clark and Matt Morgan, the campaign's general counsel.

"Why aren't you guys fighting harder? Where's my Roy Cohn?" Trump asked, referring to the late New York lawyer and fixer, who rose to prominence as Senator Joseph McCarthy's chief counsel during his investigations of suspected communists and was a mentor to Trump. The president had earlier made the same appeal to his White House counsel, when seeking to quash the Russia investigation. "I need bulldogs. I need fighters. Democrats fight. We don't fight."

The next day, November 7, Trump's fight seemed all but over. One after another, news organizations declared Biden the winner of Pennsylvania, and with it, the election. It was a Saturday, and the calls rang in while Trump was golfing at his club in Virginia. Giuliani had just finished a bizarre news conference in the asphalt parking lot of Four Seasons Total Landscaping in northeast Philadelphia, near a crematorium and a sex shop, Fantasy Island Adult Bookstore, where he had trumpeted baseless claims of widespread voter fraud.

When Trump returned to the White House, his campaign team was waiting for him in the residence: Stepien, Bossie, Clark, and Miller, as well as White House lawyer Eric Herschmann. They had decided to be straight with the boss about his miniscule chance of overturning the result, though they felt like they were about to be fed to the wolves. They all sat down in the Yellow Oval Room on the private second floor of the White House. The president was still in his golf clothes: dark pants, white polo shirt, black fleece, and white "Make America Great Again" hat. Stepien was the first to speak.

"This is going to be hard," he told Trump. "You have options to pursue. We think they are legitimate options to pursue." But Stepien said the likelihood of success was small.

Stepien and Clark walked through the narrow path to victory that remained. Trump would have to win enough of the few outstanding votes in Arizona and Georgia to pull ahead of Biden in the final counts. He also would have to win a legal challenge in Wisconsin and hope that enough Biden votes were thrown out to carry that state. Although the campaign had cases pending in Pennsylvania, Clark explained that they were unlikely to prevail there.

"This is the path," Clark said. "We have a five to ten percent chance of winning this thing on a straight edge."

Trump had to attend to another matter and left the room for about fifteen minutes. Stepien, Clark, and the others wanted to make sure Trump under-stood what they had told him, so when the presi-dent returned, they repeated themselves. Trump understood—and to their surprise, he didn't show any anger. "He wasn't even displeased, honestly," one of the advisers later recalled. "His attitude was, we'll give it a shot. We'll see what happens. That's what his attitude was. It wasn't, let's get these bastards, or anything like that."

Later that day, Trump spoke by phone with Chris Christie.

"What do you think?" the president asked.

"Look, Mr. President, losing is never easy," Christie said. "It always hurts. I know what it felt like to lose when you're running for the nomination for presi-dent and it hurt. I can imagine how much it hurts to have been president."

But, Christie added, "You've got races in Georgia that we've got to win and you've got a legacy of ac-complishment to protect. And to the extent you con-tinue to fight this, your behavior is going to obscure your accomplishments in office. For the good of your legacy, for the good of your record, you need to just put this behind you."

Christie agreed with Trump that there were likely some voting irregularities but acknowledged that they did not amount to widespread fraud. He had no doubt that the American people had selected Biden to be the next president.

"You don't have to concede in the normal way,"

Christie told Trump. "You don't have to admit that it was a fair and square loss if you don't feel comfortable doing that. But you need to put an end to this."

"Bullshit," Trump said. "I'm not doing it. Chris, if that's all you got, I'm never doing it."

"Sir, that's all I got because it's all anybody has," Christie replied. "Anybody who tells you they've got something more is lying to you. There's nothing to be done here. I would love to have some kind of magic wand I could wave for you to help you through this and get you to the winning side, but we lost."

"No," Trump said. "They stole it. They stole votes all over the country."

Christie then tried to talk some sense into Trump. He asked, "Mr. President, how do we add all these seats in the House [if] the election was being stolen? You tell me they just stole it from you? They allowed the votes to go through for the Republicans in the House?"

"Yes," Trump said.

"Well, that doesn't make any sense, sir," Christie replied. "We don't have any evidence of that."

"Chris, you and I disagree," Trump said.

"I understand that, Mr. President, but I felt like I needed to call you and tell you what I thought," Christie said.

They would not speak again for more than a month. Trump, through a spokesman, denied that he had this conversation.

The next day, November 8, Bossie tested positive for COVID-19. Trump's commander was out. He barely had a chance to start this work before having to self-isolate. Mark Meadows also tested positive that week and had to take a step back. Into the power vacuum around Trump stepped Giuliani.

In the days following the election, the top deputies at the Pentagon, CIA, and FBI were on standby. Not for a terror attack, but for their bosses to get the ax. Trump had told several close allies in October that he wanted to fire immediately after the election the "losers" who weren't sufficiently loyal. At the top of the president's list was Chris Wray—always Wray—and then Mark Esper, Mark Milley, and Gina Haspel. Trump had been talked out of firing them before the election but said there was no reason to keep them around after it, win or lose. Like many retired generals, former White House chief of staff John Kelly had kept in touch with his friends inside the Pentagon and in other corners of the administration. Word of Trump's grumblings had reached his ears. Kelly told Esper to stick to his guns.

"You've got a choice to make," Kelly told him. "Continue to do your job [and risk getting fired]. If you want to survive, you can become a complete sycophant and survive. But what good is life then?"

Like Milley, Esper had decided long ago he had to

set some boundaries with Trump. Both men expected there could be a cost: an unceremonious firing. Kelly understood this, too.

"You're already dead meat," Kelly told Esper.

He told Milley the same: "You're going to get fired."

Both men assumed their ouster was coming.

Meadows, Kushner, and Ivanka Trump knew Trump wanted Esper gone, but they warned him not to also fire Milley. Getting rid of both the civilian and military leaders at the same time would look bad, and removing Milley, the seniormost military officer, might leave the impression the president was threatening the nation's stability. There could be hell to pay for that in the form of a public rejection by the senior brass. As one retired commander said, "Word on the street was: you fire Milley and there will be no one to take the job. You'd have uniform leadership saying they don't want the job."

Speculation swirled in the media that Esper's days were numbered, but there was one story in particular that the defense secretary thought would really tick off the president. On November 7, NBC published Courtney Kube's story, albeit modified, that Esper had tried to have killed. The network reported that Esper had a letter of resignation ready to go, which suggested he was prepared to exit at any moment. Esper stressed he'd had a resignation letter typed up for a while, as did many other Trump appointees. But everybody knew Trump didn't like people to quit on him. Esper was beyond frustrated. He'd hung on for this long. And now he might get axed over what he felt was an unnecessary story. To him, it was a stupid way to get fired.

The morning of November 9, Esper joined a briefing he had requested for his leadership team on "ascertainment." It was a word a lot of people were studying up on, two days after Biden had been pronounced the president-elect. The General Services Administration was the entity that "ascertained" the next president, a determination that would allow Biden's transition team to use government offices and to prepare for a smooth hand-off at the January 20 inauguration. But the GSA chief had not yet agreed to ascertain Biden as the presumed victor because Trump was contesting the election results.

"Look, we're not going to do anything until ascertainment happens," Esper said. "But once it happens, and assuming the polls are right, I want this to be the best transition in history. We're going to do everything we can to make the Biden administration successful."

The rest of the morning whisked by quickly. At around 1:00 p.m., Esper was back in his office when two things happened at once. His chief of staff, Jen Stewart, ran into his office and said, "I just got this email! The president is firing you!" And at precisely the same moment, the phone rang on his desk. Meadows was on the other end of the line.

"I'm calling because, you know, the president's not happy," Meadows began. "He's not happy with your performance."

Meadows continued: "And we don't think you're sufficiently loyal. You're going to be replaced. He's going to announce it this afternoon. You'll be replaced by Chris Miller."

Esper thought to himself: **Who?**

Still processing the "sufficiently loyal" line, Esper responded with words to the effect of, "That's the president's prerogative. My oath is to the Constitution, not to him." With that, the two men hung up.

Esper wondered how much time he had left on the job. Normally, it might have been a few hours. But Trump announced Esper's dismissal with a tweet four minutes later. Milley heard the news and came up to the secretary's suite. The vibe was gloomy. Esper acted professionally and was unemotional, but several staffers looked dazed.

"This is a sad day," Milley said to Esper. "I'm sorry about this."

"I'm just one person in the system," Esper said.

Esper moved through his out-box, signing some documents and finalizing a few action items that had been waiting, including the paperwork to promote two women generals, Laura Richardson of the army and Jacqueline Van Ovost of the air force, to prestigious four-star commands. It was a move Esper and Milley had delayed out of fear that Trump might derail their promotions because they were women; they assumed Biden would approve them.

Some on Esper's team talked about planning a clap out, where officers and staff line the hallways to applaud the departing secretary in a show of support. But an eerie fear took hold. Aides pointed out to Esper that Johnny McEntee, the White House personnel director, had helped install a few hard-core Trump loyalists in the Defense Department who had been complaining the place needed a purge. They feared that these Trump allies would take the names of people who clapped Esper out the door—an enemies list. Esper pulled the plug on a clap out. "Let it go," he said. It was a wonderful tradition, but for Esper it wasn't worth the risk of people worrying about their next promotion. Esper's concerns about protecting his staff weren't exaggerated. When James Anderson resigned the next day as acting undersecretary of defense for policy, the White House asked for a list of political appointees who had participated in his clap out. Esper walked through his suite of offices saying goodbye to people, shaking hands and giving hugs. He thanked each staffer for his or her service. Then he left, walking out the door within an hour and a half.

"It's going to be okay," Milley told the staff. He had been at the Pentagon when Defense Secretary Donald Rumsfeld was replaced by President George W. Bush after the 2006 midterm elections, and was there to greet his successor, Bob Gates. With Esper out, Milley had the task of getting on the phone with several anxious military leaders across the world—the Brits, the French, the Germans, the Chinese. All of them suffered from varying levels of the jitters about Trump.

Was the situation in the White House stable? Milley's mission was to calm everyone down.

Robert O'Brien called Milley a little before 2:00 p.m. to say that Chris Miller would be there very soon and would be joined by Kash Patel. "They'll be at the Pentagon shortly to take over," O'Brien reported. Milley knew Miller a little through the army, and Miller had recently begun work as director of the National Counterterrorism Center. But Milley didn't know Patel, who was in his late thirties and set to become Miller's chief of staff.

At 2:15, Miller arrived. His first moments on the grounds were not reassuring. He tripped coming up the stairs.

Milley walked through some baseline information about the country's current security status. They reviewed continuity of government, key information about nuclear weapons, and hot spots around the world. Miller stressed that there would be no immediate change in policies.

"Just continue what we've been doing, chairman," Miller told Milley.

At 2:30, Milley gathered with the joint chiefs of the army, navy, and air force in the chairman's conference room, known as the Tank, to relay the new acting secretary's message. Steady as she goes. There would be no changes to the national defense strategy.

From the moment he left the meeting at 3:30, and continuing virtually nonstop until the evening, Milley's phone rang repeatedly with concerned callers.

Lawmakers, commanders, retired generals, national security officials—all of them were worried about what Esper's firing portended and what Trump might be planning. They wanted to hear that Milley understood this was a fragile time and to hear him assure them he would hold down the fort.

Adam Smith, the Democratic congressman from Washington State and chairman of the House Armed Services Committee, told Milley, "Risk just went up." In a public statement, Smith said it was "hard to overstate just how dangerous high-level turnover at the Department of Defense is during a period of presidential transition."

Mac Thornberry, the Republican congressman from Texas and the committee's ranking member, who ever since the Lafayette Square incident had been concerned about Trump using the military for political purposes, called to say he was worried about "steadiness" at the Defense Department and wanted to know if Milley thought everything would be okay.

Nancy Pelosi didn't mince words. The House Speaker already had made clear to Milley that she believed Trump was unstable. "We are all trusting you," she told him. "Remember your oath."

Jack Reed, the Rhode Island Democrat and ranking member of the Senate Armed Services Committee, told Milley this was unsettling news. "This is very erratic," said Reed, a regular caller on Milley's cell phone. "I don't know Miller. We're in a high-risk period."

Just a few minutes before 5:00, O'Brien called

Milley again. "Miller is a good guy. He's Special Forces," O'Brien said, alluding to Miller's experience in the Special Operations intelligence unit. "He's a good guy with a good heart. But this is an immense job. Please help him. He's going to need it."

This was the equivalent of warning Milley that Miller might be in over his head, and not exactly comforting. Nor was what came next. Esper's senior military assistant, Lieutenant General Bryan Fenton, called with worrisome news.

"I overheard Ezra Cohen say, 'We have to take Milley out,'" Fenton told Milley.

"Oh great," Milley said.

Ezra Cohen-Watnick was one of three Trump loyalists who had been installed in senior roles at the Pentagon on November 10. Cohen-Watnick, thirty-four, who would later go by the name Ezra Cohen, denied saying anything negative about Milley. He had been named acting under secretary of defense for intelligence, which gave him control of the military's intelligence and counterintelligence operations. At the start of the administration, he had been hired onto the NSC by Michael Flynn and was controversial for both his hawkish ideology and his bureaucratic knife-fighting, as well as for being accused of sharing intelligence reports with his former boss, Congressman Devin Nunes, which Cohen-Watnick had denied. CIA officials complained about working with him. After just seven months on the job, he was pushed out by Flynn's successor, H. R. McMaster. The national security adviser had tried unsuccessfully to remove Cohen-Watnick earlier that year, but later got important backup from Kelly, who had just begun as chief of staff and had received his own warnings about the aide from intel officials. Cohen-Watnick later served as national security adviser to then attorney general Jeff Sessions and then in a pair of Pentagon jobs that did not require Senate confirmation.

As part of a broader shakeup, Tony Tata, sixty-one, was tapped to perform the duties of the under secretary for policy—even though his nomination for that position had previously crumbled when not enough Senate Republicans would support it. Now he was performing the job without Senate confirmation. A retired army brigadier general, Tata had been a frequent guest on Fox News and promoted conspiracy theories, including falsely claiming that President Obama was Muslim and a "terrorist leader," and that the CIA had sought to assassinate Trump.

Late in the evening of November 10, Milley received a call from an old friend. The friend was very concerned about the right-wing acolytes who had just been elevated and enjoyed special access to Trump, warning they were part of a larger cabal willing to cross every line to hold power.

"What they're trying to do here is overturn the government," Milley's friend told him, according to the account Milley shared with aides. "This is all real, man. You are one of the few guys who are standing between us and some really bad stuff. Let me give you some background."

The friend began by describing Michael Ledeen, someone about whom Milley knew very little. Ledeen had deep connections to Flynn, Cohen-Watnick, Patel, Steve Bannon, and Erik Prince, founder of the private military company Blackwater USA, which had changed its name to Academi. He fashioned himself as an expert on information operations and was a neoconservative who had studied Italian far-right leader Benito Mussolini and the rise of fascism. Ledeen had long espoused that Iran was the epicenter of evil and needed to be destroyed. His wife, Barbara Ledeen, a longtime Senate staffer, served as a den mother of sorts for neocon planning sessions at Bannon's home behind the Supreme Court on Capitol Hill, where Patel and Cohen-Watnick were frequent guests. The friend reminded Milley of Bannon's mantra: Burn down the institutions. Milley was shaken. Was there actually a coup plan afoot? He reached out to McMaster for his read.

"What the fuck am I dealing with?" Milley asked him.

"You're dealing with some of the weirdest shit ever," McMaster said. He described the forces animating Trump's political base as a convergence of trouble: extremists who wanted to overturn the U.S. government, followers of the QAnon conspiracy, evangelical Christians, tea party conservatives, and even white supremacists.

Milley felt he had to be on guard for what might come. If someone really wanted to take over the country, he reasoned, they would need the so-called power ministries—the Defense Department, the FBI, and the CIA. Now that some movement acolytes had a toehold in the Pentagon, he would have to watch them closely. But what if more were installed at the FBI and CIA? Milley confided this worry to his closest deputies, though he acknowledged that it sounded slightly crazy.

"They may try, but they're not going to fucking succeed," he told them. "You can't do this without the military. You can't do this without the CIA and the FBI. We're the guys with the guns."

But the president's refusal to concede combined with the installation of Trump loyalists at the top echelons of the Defense Department only made the Pentagon brass more worried about what bizarre order might come down next. They feared some of the president's whisperers, inexperienced and emboldened, might convince him to take rash military action—such as launching a missile strike, withdrawing U.S. forces precipitously from Afghanistan, or even deploying troops in some way related to the election dispute. Strategists by training, Milley and the Joint Chiefs for the army, navy, air force, and Marines began informally planning how they could block a presidential order to use the military in a way they considered illegal, or dangerous and ill-advised.

By design, the U.S. military was run by civilians,

but by law, all orders had to be communicated to the chairman of the Joint Chiefs before they were implemented. Milley knew he had a duty to give the president his military advice, and now he considered how to use that special role to block something impulsive and potentially disastrous.

For the Joint Chiefs, the biggest worry was the revival of one of Trump's hobbyhorses: pulling troops out of Afghanistan, what he had called the "loser" war. A long line of advisers—Mattis, McMaster, Kelly, Mike Pompeo, and former secretary of state Rex Tillerson among them—had repeatedly discouraged this idea from the first time Trump brought it up in 2017. American intelligence units in the region needed military support to keep up their work. The United States had hundreds of millions of dollars' worth of equipment and vehicles on the ground that would have to be methodically removed, or else they could be confiscated by the Taliban and make enemy forces that much better equipped to terrorize civilians and attack the Afghan government. Even if Trump decided to dramatically reduce forces in the region, his generals and top advisers warned him that pulling out of Afghanistan wasn't as simple as putting a bunch of soldiers on a bus and heading out. Withdrawal had to be executed carefully and in stages, protecting each flank and helping the Afghan government remain stable.

Many of Trump's advisers believed they had put this idea to rest. But near the end of Trump's term, some in the White House were urging him to pull out of Afghanistan as quickly as possible, to deliver on a campaign promise he made to end the "endless" wars before his term was up. Pentagon leaders worried about a Saigon situation, with a chaotic last-minute exit and desperate people rushing to a rooftop to catch the last helicopter out.

The Joint Chiefs began preparing for the possibility. If the president ordered a military action they considered a disaster in the making, Milley would insist on speaking to the president before passing on the order, so he could advise against it. Under this plan, if the president rejected Milley's counsel, the chairman would resign to signal his objections. Then, with Milley out of the picture, the Joint Chiefs could demand in turn to give the president their military advice. This would buy time. In informal conversations, they discussed what would happen if they, too, got the brush-off from Trump. They considered falling on their swords, one by one, like a set of dominos. They concluded they might rather serially resign than execute the order. It was a kind of Saturday Night Massacre in reverse, an informal blockade they would keep in their back pockets if it ever came to that.

At the same time, McEntee sent word to political appointees in the White House and federal agencies that if he heard of anyone looking for another job he or she would be fired. Appointees knew the president had lost and they would be out of a job come January, but McEntee wanted them to act as if Trump would stay in office for a second term. If the press caught wind that Trump appointees were looking to jump ship, the jig would be up.

Some senior officials thought McEntee's decree was delusional and damaging to staffers who relied on a steady paycheck to make rent or care for their families. Farah gathered her communications staff and told them not to be afraid to send around their résumés.

"I'm telling you we have so much to be proud of, but you guys need to be thinking about the future," Farah told them. "I'm here to support you in every way. You need to think about having jobs lined up by January twentieth, and I'm here to help."

On November 9, Pfizer announced that its coronavirus vaccine developed in partnership with the German firm BioNTech was more than 90 percent effective in its clinical trials. The vaccine trial still would require a few more weeks of data analysis, peer review, and ultimately a decision about emergency use authorization by the FDA before the drug could be jabbed into people's arms. But this was a landmark moment in the race to end the pandemic.

Trump celebrated the news with a tweet at 7:31 a.m.: "STOCK MARKET UP BIG, VACCINE COMING SOON. REPORT 90% EFFECTIVE. SUCH GREAT NEWS!"

But Trump interpreted the events through the prism of what they meant for him. This triumph of science was, in Trump's mind, a plot to hurt him. The president called Stephen Hahn later that day to accuse the FDA commissioner of conspiring with Pfizer executives to delay the announcement until after the election to deprive him of a "win" before voters cast their ballots. Trump had long nursed this paranoia that the drug companies were going to try to screw him out of his rightful victory in delivering a vaccine to the American people. Hahn told Trump that was categorically false. There was no conspiracy. Hahn said that Pfizer's chief executive had assured him that the company's decision was determined entirely by the timing of the clinical trials.

"Mr. President, they made a scientific decision," Hahn told Trump.

But at 7:43 p.m., Trump tweeted again about the Pfizer news: "The @US_FDA and the Democrats didn't want to have me get a Vaccine WIN, prior to the election, so instead it came out five days later— As I've said all along!"

As Trump continued to allege widespread election fraud, Bill Barr decided it was time to pay him a visit. On November 9, the attorney general had issued a directive instructing U.S. attorneys to review all credible allegations of substantive fraud. They weren't supposed to worry about what Barr had called "onesies or twosies" that wouldn't make any difference in a state's overall vote count, but rather to zero in on allegations of more substantial fraud. Barr was committed to uncovering fraud if it existed but was increasingly concerned that the president's attacks on the vote undermined America's democracy.

Barr hadn't spoken with Trump since mid-October, so as he arrived in the Oval Office to meet with the president, he tried a flattering icebreaker.

"Mr. President, the effort you put in in those last weeks was historic. What a great effort it was," Barr said, according to the account he shared with confidants.

Trump accepted that he'd done a great job on the campaign trail but started in with the fraud. Meadows and Pat Cipollone were in the room, too.

"The election was stolen," Trump told Barr. "I assume you're out there looking at this stuff."

Trump asked Barr about an episode he had been hearing about a lot. Trump had watched parts of a video showing vote counting in Milwaukee on election night, and he complained that it showed truckloads of votes appearing all at once at 3:00 a.m. The president said he had been winning Wisconsin until this flood of suspect votes. "Look at that, they all come in at this time," Trump said. The fact is that voting districts in Wisconsin were required to report absentee ballots all at once. Milwaukee election officials finished counting the city's absentee ballots around 3:00. The video the president cited as "evidence" came from Milwaukee officials livestreaming the recording of those ballots.

As Trump ticked through a list of other "evidence" of fraud, Barr told him, "We're looking into that, Mr. President." He said FBI agents and attorneys were reviewing allegations and he reminded Trump about his directive to investigate fraud. He said the Justice Department was looking at "any specific credible allegations that would have a substantial impact" on the results.

Trump looked skeptical.

"Well, I don't know, there are people saying the Justice Department isn't doing enough," Trump said, his arms folded.

Cipollone tried to assure the president that wasn't true.

"They're doing their job, Mr. President," the White House counsel said. "Let them do their job."

Trump eventually brought up several theories his allies had told him about voting machines being manipulated to skew the count for Biden. Barr listened, but when the president finished, he asked him about how that could physically prove true.

"I think you guys are making a mistake to focus on the machines," Barr said. "It's the one theory you have that can easily be blown out of the water, so you're fighting the wrong battle."

Barr explained what he, Wray, and other top Justice Department officials had been told in an extensive briefing by the Department of Homeland Security's election security team. It was nearly impossible to fake the counts on voting machines because they could be easily audited. If there was a mistake, it would quickly be found.

"These are tabulation machines, Mr. President," Barr said. "You have a stack of paper, they count the paper. You can easily go back and audit every single one because if you had six hundred votes for you and four hundred for Biden, that's going to show up as the number, and it will correlate to the number of pieces of paper, and that's what's going to be shown."

Trump frowned. He didn't buy it.

"What the people are saying about the machines is just silly," Barr said.

Barr told Trump he was willing to have his agents and lawyers jump on every allegation of serious fraud, but so far, he didn't see any allegation that would move the needle on the final call for any state.

Others in the White House had been worried about the president undermining people's confidence in the election results. The unsubstantiated claims from various Trump whisperers were multiplying and metastasizing on social media. Kushner and Ivanka Trump had warned the president he might be going too far in attacking the integrity of the vote. Conway had told him, "You've got to produce evidence." Now Barr was indirectly adding his voice to that chorus.

Barr left the White House, as he later told aides, with a cautiously optimistic feeling. He felt Trump would publicly claim he believed the election was stolen but would be okay with accepting the results and moving on. The president surely would resign himself reluctantly to defeat, Barr thought, if he could maintain it wasn't a "true" defeat.

Around the same time, Trump met separately in the Oval Office with some of his campaign advisers and lawyers, as well as Cipollone and Herschmann. The president wanted to file an election fraud lawsuit directly with the Supreme Court, where conservatives enjoyed a majority after Amy Coney Barrett replaced Ruth Bader Ginsburg. Since he had nominated three of the nine justices, Trump figured the high court owed him. He had a transactional approach to politics and governing.

When Trump asked his lawyers to bring a case to the Supreme Court, some in the room took note when they thought they heard Cipollone say, "Yes, okay." They were perplexed. Herschmann stressed that neither Trump nor the White House could file a brief at the Supreme Court: They did not fit in the very small category of cases that could go directly to the highest court. "That's not a thing," he said. "It's just not happening."

A smaller group gathered later in the Cabinet Room, without the president's company, where Cipollone stressed that of course he would never bless Trump's idea of fighting the election results in the Supreme Court because it was not possible.

"We all know that," Cipollone said. "But we're going to go find some other options to bring him so that we're not just telling him no."

Cipollone was protective of his relationship with Trump, even though tensions between them were rising after the election. His predecessor, Don McGahn, had earned the moniker "Mr. No" for quashing Trump's ideas that were illegal, unethical, or otherwise unsound, often in front of other aides. Trump chafed at McGahn's frequent nos and ultimately tired of dealing with him. They were barely on speaking terms by the time McGahn resigned nearly two years into the administration.

Cipollone was determined to avoid McGahn's fate, so when Trump presented wacky ideas he would nod affirmatively, vow to investigate, or say, "Yes, sir." He didn't want to shut down the president in front of other people and risk embarrassing and angering him as McGahn had, and he was loath to lay out his advice in large groups. When Cipollone later had a private audience with Trump, he would explain why his idea wouldn't work. The problem for Cipollone, as another adviser described it, was, "That initial green light got the president's hopes up. Trump said, 'I thought you said we could do this and now you say we can't. What the fuck?' There was a lot of that." This adviser added, "It was like giving false hope to somebody, letting them latch on and get attached, and someone snatches it away. That builds anger and resentment over time."

Like Barr and Milley, Cipollone saw himself as a guardrail, ensuring the president followed the law and protecting the sanctity of an election. He told

confidants he had to stay on his toes: He knew
Giuliani had unfettered access and would tell Trump
whatever he wanted to hear. If he had said no and the
president fired or sidelined him, who would be left
to counter Giuliani?

In that same week of November 9, Hicks tried to
wean Trump from his claims of a rigged election. In
Trump World, she was considered an A student in the
psychology of DJT, as she called him. More than just
about anyone in the West Wing, Hicks understood
how to manage his moods, appeal to his ego, and
steer him away from his darker impulses. Hicks was
sometimes unsuccessful, but she knew which buttons
to press to have a fighting chance.

Hicks had quietly said to other advisers she thought
Trump's fraud-based challenges were futile, especially
after the race was called for Biden, and many of them
agreed. Larry Kudlow told colleagues he thought
December 14, the date that states were set to certify
their electoral college votes, was the drop-dead moment by which Trump should accept the verdict of
the voters. They thought it best for Trump to concede gracefully and use his remaining time in office
holding events touting his achievements or otherwise
burnishing his legacy. But most would not directly
confront the president about it. Hicks decided to try.

"Look, sir, I'm sorry," she said during an election-
related meeting that week. "I know everybody in the

room is telling you one thing, but I don't think you're doing yourself any favors fighting this election. The networks have called it. You're not going to be able to win it back. There's no way for you to win.

"I'm sorry that everyone's telling you you have a chance and you've got to keep fighting," she continued, "but I just don't want to see you tarnish your legacy."

"You're wrong," Trump told her. "I hear you, but you're wrong. You don't know what all's going on. There's lots of stuff going on. People are telling me about all the evidence. You're wrong."

The two went back and forth about the false conspiracies and baseless allegations the president was hearing from the likes of Giuliani. The massive "dump" of sketchy Biden votes in Wisconsin, the late-night changes in the vote in Pennsylvania when poll observers were barred from watching. Trump insisted this was solid enough evidence to overturn the result.

"Well, then we need to produce the evidence," Hicks said. "If there's evidence, I'm open to a discussion about how to do this tactically and strategically. But we've got to step up to the plate."

Trump didn't want to listen. He tuned out one of his longest-serving advisers, and by Thanksgiving she would pretty much disappear. She would stay on payroll and do some work at the White House but avoided the meetings with the president that normally had filled her days.

On November 13, Trump's aides were scrambling to gin up some tangible proof to show the public that the president was still engaged in the business of running the country. Reporters had started writing articles questioning whether the president had lost all interest in governing, given that he hadn't made a public appearance for six days after the election. His work calendar was largely empty.

The White House team came up with the idea for a presidential work session on the new vaccines that were close to winning FDA approval, to show Trump still had his hand on the wheel. They called in Moncef Slaoui, Gus Perna, and Alex Azar to lead a briefing for Trump on the status of the vaccines. The event was closed to the press. Vice President Pence, Marc Short, Paul Mango, Kushner, Brad Smith, and Adam Boehler also joined.

It was a good thing journalists were not invited. Trump began the session by wailing about how the FDA and drug companies had screwed him. He again complained about the timing of Pfizer's announcement, which Trump believed to be intentional to hurt him in the election. Trump and Meadows had wanted to fire Hahn back in September because he had forced a longer approval process for the emergency use of the vaccines. They were suspicious. By requiring the drug companies to collect sixty days of data from test patients after they got their second vaccine shot, the

FDA had set a timeline that would almost certainly delay the drug's approval until after the election. But the president and his chief of staff had been talked out of removing Hahn, as aides cautioned that firing him—especially before the election—would torpedo confidence in the vaccine and possibly tarnish Trump's own legacy by diminishing his credit for pushing to deliver a vaccine so quickly.

Still, in this November 13 meeting, Trump sounded like he was ready, willing, and eager to fire the FDA commissioner anyway. As Trump attacked Hahn, his top vaccine advisers again emphasized the need to maintain public confidence in the vaccine. Attacking Hahn, they argued, would be counterproductive. The president eventually switched to attacking the sixty-day guidance Hahn imposed for vaccines. Trump looked over at Azar, complaining that he, too, had supported this guidance.

"Alex, you wanted to get that letter out, though," Trump said.

"Mr. President, this information was leaked," Azar said. He said he supported releasing the guidance when that happened. He stressed that it would have been politically foolish to change the time frame after the fact and raise suspicions that the White House was trying to rush the process and or minimize safety.

Slaoui echoed Azar: "We only learned this from the manufacturers, not the FDA." He said that this problem was "all on Hahn."

Trump eventually stopped resisting this point,

while concluding he had been the ultimate victim. He said his critics would have tried any way they could to undermine his amazing success at getting a vaccine so quickly.

"Even if I got the data before the election, they would have just said it was tainted," Trump said, sounding satisfied with his summary. "Now they can't say that."

The president told the group that he planned to make a Rose Garden announcement that day. He was still steamed at Pfizer. And in what would be his first formal public comments since the election, Trump wanted to remind people he was the reason the vaccines were almost ready.

"I wanna hit Pfizer," Trump said. "They did this."

As the group discussed who would speak and in what order, Trump asked, "Where's Hahn?" He was told the FDA commissioner wasn't there.

"Okay, good," Trump said.

Trump pointed at Slaoui's and Azar's masks.

"I can't hear you when you talk through those things," Trump said. "I hate those things."

"Mr. President, they work," Azar said. "The evidence is conclusive that they work."

He described data showing that at one meter distance between two people both wearing masks, the chance of infection was reduced by 72 percent.

"Really?" Trump asked. He genuinely sounded surprised.

"Yes," Azar said.

Trump pondered this for a moment.

"Well, just be sure you take it off when you go to the microphone," he said. "It looks silly."

Several in the group of public health aides assembled for a news conference exchanged looks. The coronavirus had claimed more than 232,000 U.S. lives. And the president, after months of silencing government scientists, still seemed surprised to hear there was a known way to slow down the march of death.

Eighteen

Strange Rangers

On November 12, eight days after Fox News had enraged President Trump by projecting that Joe Biden would carry Arizona, election officials finished tallying the state's more than 3.3 million votes. Biden was declared the winner by just over eleven thousand votes. This was only the second time a Democrat had carried Arizona since Harry S. Truman in 1948; the other was Bill Clinton in 1996.

Trump, predictably, was furious. The next day, November 13, Bill Stepien, Jason Miller, Justin Clark, and the campaign's deputy communications director, Erin Perrine, were in the Cabinet Room going over messaging plans when Dan Scavino interrupted. "Come in here, we've got to talk to you," Scavino said to Clark, one of the campaign's top lawyers. Clark followed Scavino into the Oval Office, where Trump was talking on speakerphone with Rudy Giuliani

about his legal options. Vice President Pence, Pat
Cipollone, Johnny McEntee, and others were in the
room listening.

"They're letting you down," Giuliani told Trump, referring to the campaign's legal team. "They're wrong."

Giuliani zeroed in on the campaign's strategy in
Georgia. "We've got to file a suit today in Georgia—
today," Giuliani told Trump.

"Rudy, I've got Justin here," Trump said, motion-
ing to Clark. "Justin, what do you think of this?"

Clark walked the president through the prescribed
process in Georgia for recounts and explained that the
campaign could not request a recount until after
the state's governor, Republican Brian Kemp, certified the votes. Meanwhile, as Clark explained, the
secretary of state, Republican Brad Raffensperger, already had initiated a statewide audit by hand of the
more than five million votes cast there.

Giuliani then said that the Dominion voting
machines used in Georgia had been rigged so that
votes for Trump were somehow deleted. There was
no evidence to support this conspiracy theory, but
Giuliani spread it to the president as if it were gospel.

"We've got to seize the machines," Giuliani told
Trump.

Cipollone interjected. "I think Justin is saying we're
going to know if these voting machines are working
or not because they're doing a hand recount of those
paper ballots," the White House counsel said.

Giuliani, who also argued that ballots had been

counted in dead people's names, snapped. "The audit isn't going to do anything," he said. Cipollone rolled his eyes.

Clark, who was standing around the Resolute Desk next to Pence, continued with more details about the audit process and the campaign's options when Giuliani, still on speakerphone, interrupted again.

"They're lying to you!" Giuliani told Trump.

"What do you mean lying to him?" Clark asked. "I'm just laying out the process."

"You're lying to him," Giuliani responded.

"You're a fucking asshole, Rudy," Clark said.

The conversation devolved from there into a shouting match. Trump just sat in his chair listening. After a few minutes of this, the president ended the call with Giuliani and turned to Clark: "Hey, just try to work with Rudy." Giuliani, through a spokesman, denied that Clark used an epithet.

Giuliani was not the only close confidant of the president feeding him bogus theories of election fraud. Around this same time, Mark Meadows told Trump that Giuliani's team had asked him to look into allegations that tens of thousands of unregistered "illegal aliens" may have voted in Arizona, which would have been enough to swing the result to Biden. That got the president all riled up. Professionals on the campaign staff investigated Meadows's theory. It did not pan out. The vast majority of the voters he was referring to were U.S. citizens living overseas who had cast ballots legally.

"It was very easy for someone to say, 'Sir, tens of thousands of illegal immigrants voted,' but you had to be the voice in the room who, A, isn't familiar with that, and B, be the bad guy to say, 'No, that's actually wrong,'" another Trump adviser recalled. "As time wore on, the wild claims began to get louder and it just became so much harder to contain."

Meanwhile, there were other Trump efforts afoot to influence the outcome in Georgia. On November 13, Lindsey Graham called Raffensperger in what the secretary of state considered a pressure tactic to get him to help overturn the results by improperly tossing out some legally cast ballots. Raffensperger later told Amy Gardner of **The Washington Post** that Graham had echoed Trump's unfounded claims that Georgia had numerous voting irregularities. He said Graham questioned Georgia's signature-matching law and whether political bias could have prompted poll workers to accept ballots with signatures that didn't match voter registration records. He said Graham also asked him if he had the power to toss out all mail-in ballots for counties found to have higher rates of nonmatching signatures, a suggestion that shocked Raffensperger. Graham denied that he had proposed tossing legally cast votes and claimed he was only trying to understand the signature-matching law and process.

After Giuliani's argument with Clark, Trump tapped Giuliani to oversee his campaign's legal strategy and the communications surrounding it. The president called Clark and said, "Rudy's in charge."

Clark was disappointed, but knew the president had the right to choose his own lawyer. "That's fine," he told Trump. "I'm going to just work on budget and finance on this stuff and make sure no one rips you off."

Giuliani's takeover was immediate. He had already rubbed campaign staff the wrong way by barking orders to them, badgering them to book his travel on private jets or to handle his administrative tasks, and making them listen to theories from him or others, including Sidney Powell, the controversial lawyer for Michael Flynn who would become one of the loudest advocates for the rigged-election conspiracy. Jared Kushner grew increasingly frustrated by Giuliani and would complain to colleagues, "Oh, I have to go deal with the mayor. Rudy has all these ideas about where we can go and what we can do."

Now that Giuliani had the president's permission to run the show, he became even more overbearing. Giuliani's office advised Trump's campaign that he ordinarily would be paid twenty thousand dollars per day for a project of this nature; some campaign officials balked at that estimated fee. Giuliani for the past four years had leveraged his relationship with the president to enrich himself, continuing to take on some wealthy clients who faced Justice Department scrutiny. His clientele included foreign governments and business leaders who sought a special "in" with the Trump administration. While Giuliani claimed he wasn't lobbying the government, some of his clients said they were counting on him as their liaison. One Trump adviser recalled, "When Rudy didn't get attorney general or secretary of state, Rudy threw his hands in the air and said, 'Well, I'll just go make fifteen million dollars a year like I usually do.'"

Giuliani elevated a protégée, Jenna Ellis, thirty-six, who had worked on the Trump campaign's legal team. Ellis had a high opinion of herself. "I'm the Cinderella story of the legal world," she told **The Wall Street Journal.** She marketed herself as a constitutional law expert, though her experience in that realm was largely limited to self-publishing a book in 2015, **The Legal Basis for a Moral Constitution,** in which she argued that the Constitution was designed on the foundation of the Judeo-Christian worldview and that our rights come from God, not government. She had worked as a deputy district attorney handling court violations in a Colorado county but was fired, and later worked at the conservative law firm Thomas More Society, where she represented churches in religious liberty cases. Before December 2020, court records showed that Ellis had not handled an election law case nor appeared in a federal district court, where constitutional matters are weighed.

With Giuliani's blessing, Ellis walked through Trump campaign headquarters telling people they had to answer to her if they wanted to keep their jobs and must no longer take instructions from Stepien or Clark, the campaign manager and deputy campaign manager, respectively. She sent text messages to others saying the same thing. Rank-and-file staffers were shaken by what was happening; one quietly complained to Jason Miller and said, "Hey, Jenna's going crazy." Ellis said this account of her conduct, described by other campaign officials, was "completely false."

Friday the thirteenth of November was a particularly unlucky day for Trump. It marked the start of a nearly unbroken string of court defeats for him. It was an inevitable outcome, of which some Trump advisers had warned. Many of the emergency legal challenges cobbled together by Trump's threadbare legal team lacked evidence, failed to state a legal justification for the sweeping action the campaign sought, or contradicted one another from state to state. Team Trump was simultaneously arguing to continue counting votes in states he was winning and to stop in states he was losing. His campaign lawyers were throwing spaghetti against the wall in hopes some might stick. It was amateur hour.

In Michigan, a state court judge in Wayne County, the state's largest jurisdiction and the home of heavily Democratic Detroit, denied a Republican group's petition to halt the canvassing and certification there, as well as its request for an independent audit. Judge Timothy Kenny wrote that the Republican challengers "did not have a full understanding" of the processing and counting of mailed ballots. "Sinister, fraudulent motives were ascribed to the process and the city of Detroit," he wrote. "Plaintiff's interpretation of events is incorrect and not credible."

In Arizona, the Trump campaign voluntarily withdrew its challenge to the vote tally, as well as a suit it had filed the previous weekend claiming poll workers did not notify in-person voters when electronic ballot tabulation machines detected an "overvote," meaning a voter's choice may have been counted more than once. The Trump campaign admitted in a legal filing that even if the judge had ruled in its favor, tossing the votes in question would not be enough for Trump to overtake Biden in the state.

In Pennsylvania, two judges—in Philadelphia and suburban Montgomery County—rejected the Trump campaign's request to toss out an estimated nine thousand absentee and mail-in ballots as fraudulent.

Kellyanne Conway talked to Trump around this time and told him she thought there were too many cases in too many states for his lawyers to successfully litigate.

"**Bush v. Gore** was about one state, one issue," Conway said, referring to the Florida recount in 2000. "It was cleaner. Gore had his chip on black, Bush had it on red. Someone would win and someone would lose."

Trump insisted to her that he had the facts on his side. "Did you see these crazy things?" he asked.

"Mr. President, you've got to produce evidence," Conway said.

"We have evidence," Trump replied.

"It's not enough," she said.

For Trump, the defeats appeared to have cast a pall. Speaking that afternoon in the Rose Garden, the president for the first time publicly allowed for the possibility that he might not remain in office for a second term. Addressing the possibility of a nationwide lockdown in response to the surging pandemic, Trump said, "This administration will not be going to a lockdown. Hopefully whatever happens in the future, who knows which administration it will be, I guess time will tell. But I can tell you, this administration will not go to a lockdown."

The judiciary was not the only institution discounting Trump's delusions of voter fraud. His own government's top experts on election security did, too. On November 12, Trump had invited a formal declaration of this fact. Just after 11:30 a.m., he tweeted news "analysis" from his new favorite site, One America News Network, which backed up his alternate reality: "REPORT: DOMINION DELETED 2.7 MILLION TRUMP VOTES NATIONWIDE." Trump's tweet went on to claim that Dominion software, used in voting machines in many states, including Pennsylvania, had also switched hundreds of thousands of Trump votes into Biden votes. There was no evidence for this. Chris Krebs, head of a Department of Homeland Security cybersecurity team that had spent months ensuring election systems nationwide were protected from tampering, was flabbergasted. He and his team had created a website called Rumor Control to bat down misinformation about the election coming from foreign actors, but his office had been getting angry calls from the White House to remove some of their fact-based public service announcements because they were rejecting claims the president was himself promoting.

Seeing Trump's tweet that Thursday morning, Krebs and his team felt they couldn't let it stand. His office, joined by an advisory council of election security partners, announced that the 2020 election had been "the most secure in American history." Their joint statement explained how closely the election had been monitored by auditors and cyber teams. Though it never mentioned Trump, the statement included one line in bold font that directly rejected the president's refrain.

"There is no evidence that any voting system deleted or lost votes, changed votes, or was in any way compromised," the statement read.

Krebs understood the consequences. He prepared that day to be fired but come morning he still had a job. Yet on November 17, after Krebs reaffirmed publicly that the election had been secure and fraud allegations were baseless or "technically incoherent," Trump terminated him via tweet.

On Saturday, November 14, legions of Trump supporters from across the country converged on Freedom Plaza, a couple of blocks from the White

House, for a rally protesting the election results. It was billed as a "Million MAGA March," although only tens of thousands attended.

The rally had been heavily promoted in advance, including by Trump, and law enforcement and military leaders were bracing for civil unrest. After attending a security briefing on November 10 about the Million MAGA March, Mark Milley told aides he feared this could be the modern American equivalent of "brownshirts in the streets." Milley was referring to the paramilitary forces and stormtroopers that protected Nazi Party rallies in the 1920s and 1930s and enabled the rise of Adolf Hitler in Germany. Milley told aides the moment reminded him of strange commentary Trump made earlier in his presidency, during a discussion in the Oval Office about NATO and the U.S. alliance with Germany. Trump, who had a strained relationship with German chancellor Angela Merkel, had remarked to his advisers, "That bitch Merkel."

"I know the fucking krauts," the president added, using a derogatory term for German soldiers from World War I and World War II. Trump then pointed to a framed photograph of his father, Fred Trump, displayed on the table behind the Resolute Desk and said, "I was raised by the biggest kraut of them all."

Trump, through a spokesman, denied making these comments.

The group of demonstrators on November 14 included members of the Proud Boys, an extremist group that promotes violence under the auspices of "anti-political correctness" and "anti-white guilt." Some wore flak jackets, helmets, and shirts that read "Stand Back, Stand By," quoting directly Trump's comment from the September debate. The more organized Proud Boys mingled with scores of regular protesters—parents and young people, seniors and flag-toting veterans. They waved MAGA flags as speakers blared Lee Greenwood's "God Bless the U.S.A.," which was Trump's walkout song at his MAGA rallies.

The lineup of speakers included people famous for pushing, and possibly believing, dangerous and salacious falsehoods. Alex Jones, an alt-right activist described by the Southern Poverty Law Center as "the most prolific conspiracy theorist in contemporary America," and Marjorie Taylor Greene, a Republican QAnon adherent just elected to Congress from Georgia, both amplified the fiction that the election had been rigged and that Trump was the rightful victor.

The president of the United States was not scheduled to speak. Trump planned that morning to do what he did most Saturdays: golf. But he asked his Secret Service detail to make a dramatic detour on the drive out to his club in Sterling, Virginia. Just before 10:00, Trump's supporters began cheering and hollering when they realized the presidential motorcade was coming down Pennsylvania Avenue. Many of his fans had to scurry out of the path of the black SUVs and specialized trucks as they passed Freedom Plaza.

The demonstration was largely peaceful, although there were brief but intense clashes throughout the day. Counterprotesters showed up. When some held up orange "Refuse Fascism" posters, Trump fans shouted at them, "U.S.A.! U.S.A.!" As darkness fell, scuffles among activists escalated. Demonstrators on both sides shouted threats and profanity and threw punches and bottles. Police arrested at least twenty people, including four on gun charges. Tensions continued into the night, with altercations occurring at various points across the city. During a melee at a downtown intersection, a man in his twenties was stabbed in the back.

Leaders at the Pentagon and in law enforcement had reason to worry. For most of the year, the nation had been a tinderbox, and Trump was splashing around kerosene with each false claim of a rigged election. Milley's aides remembered the mission the general had outlined for himself after the June 1 Lafayette Square incident: ensure the United States had a free and fair election with no military involvement whatsoever. Sixty-seven days remained until Biden would be sworn in as president. A lot could happen still.

On November 14, Jason Miller arrived at headquarters riled up about what Ellis was telling people. He had a fondness for Giuliani, having worked on communications on his 2008 presidential campaign, but had no tolerance for Ellis's apparent power trip. Miller felt protective of the staff.

Miller found Giuliani and Ellis in the big conference room, along with lawyers Joe DiGenova, Victoria Toensing, and Boris Epshteyn, and a handful of Giuliani associates: his girlfriend, Maria Ryan; his son, Andrew Giuliani; his longtime friend Bernard Kerik, the former New York police commissioner (and convicted felon); and a few twentysomething women who often hung around him and usually wore tight-fitting apparel. The conference room smelled rancid, an aromatic mix of body odor and soiled food—"as if they'd gotten buffalo wings that went bad," as one attendee described it. Garbage cans were overflowing. And nobody was social distancing—another potential Trumpian superspreader event.

This was the all-star team that was supposed to overturn the election for Trump. Miller walked in the room and thought to himself, **What the fuck is this?** The gathering felt like the famous cantina scene from **Star Wars.**

Miller motioned to Ellis and they stepped into the hallway and started laying into each other.

"What the hell are you doing?" Miller asked.

"You're being threatening," Ellis told him. "You're being intimidating to me."

"Jenna, you can't tell people, especially young staffers, that their livelihoods are at stake," Miller said.

"No, no, I never said that," Ellis said.

"Jenna, I have the fucking text messages of you threatening people," Miller said.

"You need to back up," Ellis said. "You're taking a hostile tone with me."

"You're nuts," Miller said. "You're fucking crazy."

"You're being a jerk," Ellis said. "You're being an asshole."

"You're one hundred percent fucking crazy," Miller said. "You're nuts. You can't do this."

"Well, the president told me I'm in charge," Ellis said.

"Really? Let's call him up and ask him who's in charge, because he will not say you're in charge," Miller said. "I'll swear to you he will not say you're in charge. You're not in charge of shit."

Miller stormed out before anyone called the president. Ellis said that after Miller left, Giuliani joked, "Oh, well, good riddance. Better not to deal with that little shit."

Trump caught wind of the altercation and called Miller that night.

"Don't quit," the president told him. "I've got to have you here. I need you on board. People are telling me Jenna's a dictator, bossing people around. She doesn't need to be. Work with Rudy. Do your thing. . . . Just don't quit."

Ellis said she also spoke with Trump that night and said he wanted to keep Miller on the team. The president described Miller as scared of her, according to Ellis, and told her, "Just try not to hurt his feelings so much, okay?"

The next day, November 15, Miller returned to headquarters and met with Giuliani and Ellis. The three tried to make peace.

"I know you guys got into it," Giuliani said. "Look, I'm in charge. Jason's my guy. I love Jason. Jason ran my campaign in 2008. I trust him. And you guys just have to work together."

Ellis, looking at Miller, said, "I think you need to apologize."

"No, I'm not going to," Miller said. "Look, we can work together. Rudy's in charge. We'll roll with that."

Giuliani agreed. "Knock it off," he told Ellis. "We're not going to do any apologies."

Trump continued to insist that he would win Pennsylvania even though Biden already had been declared the winner. Yet in the aftermath of the November 13 ruling, Trump's legal cavalry in the state was retreating. There were two law firms that together had filed four cases on his behalf in Pennsylvania, but in each, numerous lawyers increasingly grew concerned that they were being asked to gin up shoddy claims and were helping undermine confidence in U.S. elections. Porter, Wright, Morris & Arthur formally withdrew from representing the Trump campaign, while a top lawyer at Jones Day, the Trump campaign's longtime legal counsel, notified fellow attorneys by teleconference that the firm would not continue to take part in election-related litigation.

The departure of well-credentialed lawyers only further empowered Giuliani and his associates. Though the Giuliani-Ellis-Powell team dubbed itself "an elite strike force," it included a lawyer who hadn't appeared in court since the 1990s; another whose work largely consisted of domestic abuse, traffic court, and religious-liberty cases; and yet another who gained notoriety for promoting conspiracy theories about a "deep state." Some of them, including their chief strategist, Giuliani, appeared unfamiliar with the legal arguments the team had already made in court filings.

The matter of **Donald J. Trump for President v. Boockvar** was called on the morning of November 17 in Pennsylvania. The day before, Giuliani had been furious to learn that one of the Trump campaign's lawyers had withdrawn the claims of massive fraud from the suit. The other lawyers had chosen to argue only that the campaign had standing to sue, wanting to clear that initial hurdle and then present the voter fraud case at a later hearing.

Giuliani sidelined them and decided he would argue the case himself, appearing in federal court for the first time since the early 1990s, in front of U.S. District Judge Matthew Brann in Williamsport. Based on the detailed nature of his questions, Brann, who had been nominated to the bench by President Obama, appeared to have carefully read all the pleadings from both parties in the case. Stuck arguing the claims the other lawyers framed, Giuliani sounded fuzzy on

Trump's case. He began by stating that Trump was the victim of "widespread nationwide voter fraud." Later, when pressed for evidence, Giuliani acknowledged he was not arguing there had been fraud but rather was seeking to throw out about 680,000 ballots cast in Philadelphia and Pittsburgh—heavily Democratic cities—because, he claimed, Republican observers were not permitted to watch them being counted.

Brann sounded puzzled.

"The poll-watching claims were deleted," he told Giuliani, reminding the lawyer of his own team's amended legal claims. "They're now not before this court, so why should I consider them now?"

After a few moments, Giuliani conceded the poll-watching claims had been struck but said the Trump campaign would refile a third amended complaint to include them again.

Giuliani did eventually articulate his side's lone standing claim: that Republican voters' rights had been violated because Democrat-leaning counties had invited voters to "cure" defective ballots. But then he misspoke when identifying the unfair advantage this gave Biden.

"The Trump campaign has been treated totally differently than the Bush campaign," Giuliani said.

At times the discussion between the lawyers got heated, even though it transpired partially over teleconference. Mark Aronchick, an attorney representing several Pennsylvania counties, accused Giuliani of living in "some fantasy world," making wild allegations that were "disgraceful in an American courtroom," and worst of all, revealing his ignorance of the law.

The hearing stretched for five hours and Brann and Giuliani went round and round on the definition of opacity, which Giuliani said probably meant things that could be easily seen. In a detailed discussion of legal review, Giuliani expressed confusion when the judge asked what legal standard Giuliani believed he should apply in considering the case. "The normal one," Giuliani replied.

"Dismiss this case," opposing counsel Aronchick urged Brann. "Please, dismiss this case. So we can move on."

After the hearing ended, Aronchick told reporters he was "dumbfounded" that a president's legal defense would appear so hapless. "When you're in court, you have to talk about the facts, you have to talk about the law," Aronchick said. He then added a sly reference to Giuliani's Philadelphia news conference: "When you're at Four Seasons Total Landscaping, I guess you can talk about anything."

Brann didn't need many days to reach that precise decision that opposing counsel had suggested. Brann said the Trump campaign's legal argument looked "like Frankenstein's Monster, has been haphazardly stitched together from two distinct theories in an attempt to avoid controlling precedent." He described Giuliani's request to disqualify thousands of Pennsylvania voters' ballots in Democratic-heavy precincts as "unhinged" from his claim that he was defending the basic right of all voters to be fairly counted. The judge said the Trump campaign's request could ultimately disenfranchise millions of Pennsylvanians. "One might expect that when seeking such a startling outcome, a plaintiff would come formidably armed with compelling legal arguments and factual proof of rampant corruption," Brann wrote. "That has not happened. This Court has been presented with strained legal arguments without merit and speculative accusations . . . unsupported by evidence."

After Giuliani's loss, Clark told Trump, "We're going to never win another case because this court decided I don't want the fucking circus coming to town. Every other court has a path to follow."

Trump replied, "Maybe."

As a businessman, Trump had unrelentingly turned to the courts to duke it out with debtors, competitors, contractors, and former staff. Usually he had success wearing people down. But the same tactics did not work when it came to the 2020 election.

Some of Trump's advisers believed the president's amped-up rhetoric gave the courts good reason to issue definitive rulings in short order rather than indulge his conspiracies for weeks on end by allowing his campaign to make lengthy pleadings that would ultimately fail. "Because the president was tweeting and naming names and saying it was stolen and there was fraud, it was too much pressure on the courts to say, 'I don't want to be the place that gives him quarter,'" one of them recalled. "There was no room at the inn."

Trump and Giuliani wanted to get on offense after the defeats in court. They saw the president's campaign to overturn the election as a communications battle as much as a legal one. Miller agreed and thought they needed to convince the public that Trump still had multiple pathways to victory. They decided that Giuliani would hold a news conference on November 19 at the Republican National Committee's headquarters on Capitol Hill.

Giuliani and Miller showed up early at the RNC and strategized in a back room while members of the media set up cameras and took their seats. Giuliani brought along many of the same people who had been with him in the putrid conference room a few days earlier: Ellis, DiGenova, Toensing, Epshteyn, Andrew Giuliani, and some of his young female associates. Powell was also there. Even Giuliani had confessed to others on the team, "Sidney is nuts. She's crazy." But he still wanted her around, in part because his client, the president, was so enamored with what she had to say. The group planned out how the news conference would go. Giuliani and Ellis would speak, and the others would stand beside them, with American flags arrayed behind them.

"Let's have Sidney Powell join us," Giuliani proposed.

"No, Mayor Giuliani, we have some really

compelling evidence to go on, but the Sidney stuff is really far out there," Ellis said.

Miller agreed.

"If we have Sidney join us then people are going to associate us with all of her crazy," Miller said. "Why would we do that?"

"No, no, no," Giuliani said. "Look, I think she has some important things to say."

Trump had put Giuliani in charge. So, Powell would be speaking.

As the legal team stepped into the lights, Miller hung back behind the TV cameras to watch from the same angle as people at home, including the president. For Trump, optics were paramount, and he ingrained this in his aides. Miller later told friends that his first reaction to watching Powell speak was, "Holy shit, what a strange ranger."

Trump's attorneys launched a wholesale assault on the integrity of the election and alleged widespread fraud in Atlanta, Detroit, Milwaukee, Philadelphia, and other cities in which Democratic votes helped Biden carry battleground states. They had no evidence to support their claims, but Giuliani nonetheless said, "We cannot allow these crooks—'cause that's what they are—to steal an election from the American people."

Powell's statement was even more extreme—and absurd. She claimed without evidence that there was a broad conspiracy with roots in Venezuela to rig the U.S. election.

"What we are really dealing with here, and learning more by the day, is the massive influence of communist money through Venezuela, Cuba, and likely China, and the interference with our elections here in the United States," Powell said.

She argued that Dominion voting machines used in Georgia and many other states were programmed to "flip" votes cast for Trump and count them instead for Biden. She said the machines used software that was "created in Venezuela at the direction of Hugo Chavez to make sure he never lost an election."

Powell's purported evidence for this was jaw-dropping, but not in the way she might have hoped. She said the campaign had "a very strong witness"— a Chavez associate who knew how the late Venezuelan leader had deployed Dominion machines to win re-election. Powell said the witness deduced from watching the news on November 3 that the same plot was unfolding in America.

"As soon as he saw multiple states shut down the voting on the night of the election, he knew the same thing was happening here," Powell said.

The Dominion conspiracy theory had spread widely on right-wing websites and social media and had become an obsession of Trump's, but there was not a shred of evidence to support it. In fact, Georgia's hand recount of nearly five million paper ballots affirmed that the Dominion scanners accurately counted the votes.

When reporters asked for evidence of the massive

fraud that the legal team claimed, Ellis said they would produce it later. As the news conference rolled on, streaks of what appeared to be black hair dye mixed with sweat dripped down the sides of Giuliani's face as he spoke.

Miller had been glancing at messages on his phone and knew things had gone poorly. When they went back to their hold room, Miller said to Giuliani, "Look, here's the thing. Everything you said was fine. Everything Jenna said was fine. Sir, Sidney said some crazy shit and it's making a lot of news."

"Oh?" a perplexed Giuliani asked. "What do you mean? But did Fox take it?"

"Yeah, Fox took it, but she was talking about Hugo Chavez and Dominion and all these things," Miller said. "People think we're in fucking crazy town."

"We'll be fine," Giuliani said. "These are concerns. Dominion **is** a foreign company."

Dominion was founded in Canada, but maintained dual headquarters in Toronto and Denver, Colorado. It was not based in Venezuela and had no connection to communist operatives or Chavez, who died in 2013.

Trump was riveted by his lawyers' presentation, but once he heard commentators in the media ridiculing Powell's claims as preposterous, he feared she may have gone a little overboard. He was also unsettled by Giuliani's dripping hair dye.

Some of his White House aides were humiliated. One West Wing staffer recalled watching the news conference with a handful of others and blurting out, "Oh, my God, this is just like a freak show. This is embarrassing."

For Lindsey Graham, who had stuck by Trump's side through so many rough patches, the Giuliani-Ellis-Powell show was the lowest point of the year. Giuliani had assured Graham, "You know we're going to make sure it doesn't go too far." Yet, as Graham told confidants, things undeniably had gone too far with this news conference. Graham thought the president's fate was in the hands of a bunch of people who didn't know what they were doing. He called Trump.

"Mr. President, you need a theory of the case here in each state," Graham said, rather than just alleging fraud "willy-nilly."

Trump told Graham he thought Powell was "over the top."

"It sounds bizarre," Graham said. "You need to get some people who can focus on election law."

Larry Kudlow was worried for his old pal, Giuliani. The two men had served in the Reagan administration together, Kudlow as the number three official at the Office of Management and Budget and Giuliani as the number three at the Justice Department. They considered each other family friends. But Kudlow thought Giuliani was saying things about the election that would likely tarnish his legacy.

Kudlow confided his concerns to several people, including Chris Christie, another longtime Giuliani friend, who was like-minded. Kudlow didn't want to push Giuliani or make him uncomfortable, so he tried to pass messages to Andrew Giuliani. "Tell your dad to be careful," Kudlow told the younger Giuliani. "Tell your dad this is a high-stakes game."

Giuliani disgusted Mitt Romney. The two had been rivals for the Republican presidential nomination in 2008, but both came up short to John McCain. In 2012, Giuliani campaigned for Romney when he was the GOP nominee, and while they were never friends, they respected one another.

"Rudy has such a fine history as a mayor, and his book, **Leadership,** was a bestseller," Romney said in an interview for this book. "I found his participation in something so bizarre and irregular to be virtually incomprehensible. I wondered, how in the world can someone of that stature do something of this nature. And I have to be honest. My concern was not so much with my party. . . . I was again thinking about the cause of democracy."

Romney talked about the diplomatic trips he had taken over the years to Afghanistan and other war-torn places promoting the cause of freedom. "I'm thinking about these places where our sons and daughters have laid down lives to promote freedom and democracy," he said. "And then to see people who are respected globally, like Mayor Giuliani, shred that credibility . . . was extraordinarily disheartening."

The next day, November 20, rivals Alex Azar and
Seema Verma met at the White House to join the
president for an announcement on a sweeping change
in U.S. drug pricing. By executive order, Trump was
forcing pharmaceutical companies to only charge the
U.S. government the lowest price they charged any
other country for prescription drugs. Known as the
Most Favored Nation model, the plan was projected
by the Trump White House to dramatically lower
the prices of certain drugs and to save American taxpayers and Medicare clients more than $85 billion
over seven years.

Any other administration likely would have pursued this change methodically and the announcement would have been hailed as a bold achievement.
But because this was the Trump White House, the
president was scrambling to deliver on his campaign
promise to cut drug prices in his final months in office. For lack of planning, the administration had
short-circuited the process and skipped over some
rule-making steps usually required to push through
such a major change. Legal experts predicted the plan
eventually would get overturned in the courts.

Before the announcement, Azar and Verma arrived
separately to join the president in his private dining
room off the Oval Office, so they could brief him
before the announcement. Verma arrived first and sat
down with Trump at his table. As usual, he had the
television on.

"You know I won," Trump said. "Seema, I won."

Verma later told others that she couldn't believe that after all this Trump still thought he had won. But she knew better than to cross him, so she indulged the boss.

"Well, you did really well with women," Verma replied. "You've done better with women and minorities."

"We're still fighting it," Trump said. "We've got a really good argument. We won. Who knows if the Supreme Court will agree. But we won."

Trump looked up and noticed that Azar had entered the room and was still standing, silently waiting. He tried to engage both Azar and Verma with a new problem that was bothering him.

"What the fuck was with that press conference the other day?" Trump asked. "That was terrible. Birx was just terrible."

On November 19, the same day Giuliani, Ellis, and Powell had been at the RNC, Pence had convened a coronavirus task-force briefing at the White House with Deborah Birx, Anthony Fauci, Robert Redfield, and Jerome Adams, as well as Azar and Verma. With Thanksgiving approaching, Birx had called on every American "to increase their vigilance" and warned against gathering indoors.

"She's a real Negative Nancy," Verma told Trump.

"Should I fire her?" he asked. "Should I get rid of her?"

"At this late date, it's probably not worth the trouble," Verma said.

Azar was silent.

Trump began flipping through his prepared remarks for the drug-pricing order he would soon announce. He noticed a mention of Pfizer. He was still seething that Pfizer had announced that its coronavirus vaccine was ready for use almost immediately after the election. He held a Sharpie in his hand, which he used to edit his remarks.

"Should I say they held back on the vaccine because we're going with Most Favored Nation?" Trump asked. "Should I say that?"

"I wish you wouldn't," Azar said. He counseled Trump to take credit for this major drug-pricing order rather than criticize Pfizer. Otherwise, he warned, "This will become the news, not the policy."

"Is it true they had the data and they didn't look at it before the election?" Trump asked.

The conversation was starting to feel déjà vu, with the president returning to the same points he had made in his meeting with Azar and other medical advisers one week earlier, as if he had completely forgotten the previous discussions about critical elements of his government's coronavirus response.

Azar explained, maybe for the fourth or fifth time, that the FDA guidance required sixty days of data from patients in trials after they received their second vaccine shot. He reminded Trump that Hahn had created this guidance.

"So should I fire Hahn?" Trump asked the pair.

"At this point, it's a distraction," Verma said.

Trump noticed that Azar didn't answer either way.

The health secretary just stood there looking off in the distance.

It was time. Trump and Verma got up from their seats to prepare to go out to the press briefing room.

"You gotta take those fucking masks off," Trump told them.

"I'm the health secretary," Azar said. "I have to wear a mask."

"Once you're at the podium, take it off," Trump said. "Then you can put it back on."

They made a compromise. Azar and Verma would take their masks off when it was their turn to speak, keeping a safe distance at the lectern from each other and from the president.

Azar noted that the masks were very good at preventing the virus from spreading.

"What?" Trump asked as they moved toward the door. "They work?"

On November 22, Christie said on television what many in Trump World had been saying privately. Appearing that Sunday on ABC's **This Week,** the longtime Trump confidant sized up the president's representation.

"If you've got the evidence of fraud, present it. And what's happened here is, quite frankly . . . the president's legal team has been a national embarrassment," Christie told host George Stephanopoulos.

Christie added, "They allege fraud outside the

courtroom, but then they go inside the courtroom, they don't plead fraud and they don't argue fraud. This is what I was concerned about at two thirty in the morning on [election night]. Listen, I've been a supporter of the president's. I voted for him twice. But elections have consequences, and we cannot continue to act as if something happened here that didn't happen. You have an obligation to present the evidence. The evidence has not been presented."

Coming from one of Trump's earliest 2016 endorsers, a former U.S. attorney whom the president had considered naming attorney general or White House chief of staff, this was significant. Christie calling Trump's lawyers "a national embarrassment" generated news headlines. Giuliani had been close with Christie for decades, but was pissed off, feeling as if he had been stabbed in the back. He called him.

"We're friends. What are you doing?" an angry Giuliani asked Christie.

"Rudy, this is ridiculous," Christie replied. "You need to stop."

Giuliani admonished Christie and said he would be embarrassed once he saw all the evidence the Trump team had compiled that proved the election had been rigged.

Christie thought Giuliani was bluffing. He said, "What are you waiting for, man? If there's all this evidence, what are you waiting for? Christmas? Don't wait. Time to put it out there."

This set off Giuliani, who lit into Christie and screamed nonsense into the phone.

"Believe me," Christie said. "I don't like to call the legal team 'a national embarrassment' on television. But it is. You're hanging out with Sidney Powell. Are you kidding me? She's fucking nuts. What's wrong with you? You were U.S. attorney. You were the mayor. You were one of the true national leadership heroes in the last half of the twentieth century. What are you doing?"

"Fuck legacy," Giuliani replied. "Legacy is what happens when you're in the ground. I'm fighting for today."

"Well, if you want us to fight with you, arm us with facts," Christie said. "Let me tell you something. When I was U.S. attorney and you were U.S. attorney, if an [assistant U.S. attorney] came to us with this crock of bullshit, we would have kicked them out of our offices. So act like you're U.S. attorney again, not like you're a lawyer for Donald Trump."

"Stop complaining and shooting off your mouth on TV," Giuliani replied. "Join the legal team and make a difference."

"You're kidding me, right?" Christie said. "No, thank you. I'll pass."

The two men ended the call on bitter terms. The friendship between Christie and Giuliani apparently was a casualty of Trump's quest to retain power. Giuliani, through a spokesman, disputed that this conversation ever happened.

Typically, as soon as an apparent winner is projected in a presidential election, the mammoth undertaking of setting up a new government begins. The president-elect's transition team is provided access to federal agencies, money to pay salaries, and government office space, computer systems, and email addresses. In addition, the labyrinthine process of security clearances and financial disclosures for appointees begins, and those who already have clearances can start receiving intelligence briefings. This taxpayer-funded operation ensures a peaceful transition of power—and, in the modern age of global terrorism, helps safeguard the country at the moment of handover when the government is especially vulnerable.

This did not happen in 2020. After Biden was declared president-elect on November 7, his transition team was set to begin work on Monday, November 9. But the Trump administration refused to formally authorize the transition. This is normally a perfunctory acknowledgment made by the General Services Administration, but the GSA's Trump-appointed administrator, Emily Murphy, would not sign a letter of ascertainment recognizing that Biden was the presumptive president-elect. Murphy's defiance—in alignment with Trump's refusal to concede to Biden and Meadows's insistence that the election was still being contested—created the first transition delay in modern history, other than in 2000 due to George W. Bush and Al Gore's genuine contest in the Florida recount.

As the days ticked by in November, Murphy's refusal to recognize Biden's victory became a critical chokepoint for the incoming president and raised national security concerns. Analysts had concluded that the delay in Bush's transition may have contributed to the government's lack of preparedness for the terrorist attacks of September 11, 2001.

Governors were worried that the incoming Democratic administration would have a late start getting a handle on the pandemic response and delay or botch the vaccine rollout in states. Larry Hogan, who chaired the National Governors Association, and several other governors complained privately that Trump was continuing to contest an election he clearly had lost. But more than Trump's ego was at stake. American lives were on the line. The governors were angry. Hogan conveyed their collective worries to Pence.

"I'm very concerned about the transition," Hogan told the vice president. "Biden has to get up to speed on the coronavirus stuff."

"I know. I know," Pence said. "Look, I can assure you we are going to work together with them. There is going to be a peaceful transition. We are going to make sure they're up to speed and everybody is going to have a smooth handoff. Don't worry about it."

"It doesn't sound like it," Hogan said. "It sounds like the Biden people are telling us nobody is talking to them and it sounds like the president is still saying it's nonsense."

Pence's efforts to calm the waters did not work.

On November 23, after withholding ascertainment for just over two weeks, Murphy finally buckled. Nothing had changed in the election results. Biden was no more certain the president-elect now than he had been on November 7. Murphy had lamented to close confidants, including Mick Mulvaney, that this was uncharted territory. She had argued privately that she needed for Republicans in Congress to give her some political cover to make this uncomfortable decision, yet many of them were parroting the president's election fraud claims. But the public pressure on Murphy to allow the transition to proceed grew so intense that she relented and did her duty. She wrote a highly personal letter to Biden notifying him of the complications she faced in making her decision.

"To be clear, I did not receive any direction to delay my determination," Murphy wrote. "I did, however, receive threats online, by phone, and by mail directed at my safety, my family, my staff, and even my pets in an effort to coerce me into making this determination prematurely. Even in the face of thousands of threats, I always remained committed to upholding the law."

It was not clear—and Murphy didn't say—which events helped the situation mature to the point that she could ascertain who was likely to be the future president. But the day she concluded Biden was the president-elect, more than one hundred national security officials in previous Republican administrations released a letter insisting that the delay in authorizing the transition was weakening the country in the event of a terror attack and putting lives at risk.

Although Murphy had denied that Trump influenced her decision, he asserted that he was the one who gave Murphy the thumbs-up for the transition to begin. He tweeted that although he was still fighting the election results in court, "in the best interest of our country, I am recommending that Emily and her team do what needs to be done with regard to initial protocols, and have told my team to do the same."

Trump was dealing that same week with a transition of his own inside the West Wing. Hope Hicks was receding from her perch as counselor to the president, and now Alyssa Farah had decided to call it quits. Around Thanksgiving, she told Meadows that she wanted to step down as communications director.

"My heart's not in it," Farah told Meadows. "I don't believe in this endeavor. I believe Biden won. We need to give a graceful exit and acknowledge that Biden won."

"I know, I know," Meadows replied. "We're going to get the president there."

Meadows asked Farah to stay on awhile longer, and she agreed to give it at least a few more days. But

Meadows couldn't get the president to acknowledge the reality that he had lost. There wasn't any indication that he had even tried. On December 3, Farah submitted her resignation letter. The next day, she was gone.

Nineteen

Cries of Injustice

As November wound to a close, Bill Barr prepared his team for the inevitable. President Trump was never going to concede, and nor was he, as Barr had hoped, going to tone down his claims of a stolen election. The attorney general warned his deputies to prepare for the president to come hard at the Justice Department. Barr and his top deputies would gather in his office at the end of their day to talk over glasses of scotch or Irish whiskey. Barr spooled out his belief that the Democrats often governed as if the more than 74 million Americans who voted for Trump didn't exist, ignoring their values and dismissing them as troglodytes, while Trump had frittered away his chance to win reelection by refusing to reach out beyond his base. The result was a country as divided as it had ever been in his lifetime. And now, as Barr saw it, Trump had brought the country to a dangerous juncture by undercutting confidence in the election rather than honorably accepting defeat.

After Barr issued his November 9 memo instructing prosecutors to investigate credible allegations of voter fraud, every example had been either baseless or too small to be relevant to the outcome. Barr told his senior deputies that at some point someone was going to have to say that the emperor has no clothes. The question was when.

Other leading Republicans harbored similar concerns. Mitch McConnell feared Trump's false fraud claims were taking hold in some communities and destabilizing the country. The Senate majority leader also saw a short-term political danger: Trump's attacks on the integrity of the election system in Georgia could suppress Republican turnout in the Senate runoff elections scheduled for January 5. The balance of power in the Senate was on the line. If Senators David Perdue and Kelly Loeffler prevailed, Republicans would retain their majority, and McConnell his power. If their Democratic challengers Jon Ossoff and the Reverend Raphael Warnock won, then the Senate's partisan split would be fifty-fifty, and Democrats would have the majority because Vice President-elect Kamala Harris could break any ties in their favor.

At the urging of their senior advisers, Barr and McConnell started talking in mid-November about Trump's insistence on alleging a stolen election. They agreed the results weren't going to be turned around and that Republicans had to accept having lost the White House. Both valued the same principle of democracy, as summed up by one senior Justice official: "You lose. You leave." Barr and McConnell discussed who might get through to Trump and convince him to give up the ghost. One person familiar with their conversations described McConnell asking Barr something to the effect of, "Do you agree with this, Bill? And if not, what can you do about it?"

They agreed it would be too dangerous for McConnell to try to confront Trump. That could backfire and end up harming the Georgia senators. On the other hand, Barr wasn't running for anything; he had the freedom to speak his mind and possibly make a difference. On top of that, Barr had his own reasons to talk some sense into the president. He had thought Johnny McEntee's prohibition on Trump staffers applying for other jobs was despicable, as it put them at risk of not having income for weeks or months after their current paychecks stopped. The attorney general felt a building pressure to put an end to this pretense about a second term.

But while Barr was debating what to do about the president, Trump was rather rapidly souring on him for failing to reveal massive fraud in several states where the president's allies claimed there had been malfeasance. Everything Trump raised fell flat with Barr. Trump had excitedly told him about a video about a water main break allegedly faked to drive witnesses out of an arena in Fulton County, Georgia, where votes were being counted. As the conspiracy theory went, Georgia election workers then pulled eighteen thousand ballots out of suitcases and stuffed ballot boxes with fake votes for Biden, with no election observers present. Barr told Trump he didn't buy it. The "suitcases" were actually the standard boxes that Fulton County used to transport ballots to the central vote tallying center. A water main break had happened hours earlier, state officials said, and had nothing to do with the tallying process the county has followed for years.

Trump also pointed to a Postal Service truck driver who had come forward to report that a supervisor in Erie, Pennsylvania, had instructed staff to improperly backdate ballots that arrived too late for the election. But Barr had reason to discount that as well. That driver had quickly recanted his story in an interview with investigators. Still, Trump continued to push this conspiracy as well as others.

"Sometimes he would show mental awareness that some of this stuff must be bullshit," recalled one senior presidential adviser. But then, like clockwork, Trump would retweet the claims to his followers.

A top former law enforcement official, characterizing the string of allegations Trump and his allies promoted, said, "None of them required extreme investigation. Most of them could be easily disproved."

Although these and other anecdotes of alleged fraud were debunked, Trump complained to aides that Barr had gone soft. To Barr's mind, the president had fallen prey to lightweight acolytes who wanted to prove their loyalty and build their own importance by feeding him fraud allegations. These claims circulated online, but with a few calls, prosecutors found they were easily proven false or impossible.

On November 29, Trump registered his anger at Barr in a venting session with Fox's Maria Bartiromo.

"You would think if you're in the FBI or Department of Justice, this is the biggest thing you could be looking at," Trump said in the Fox interview. "Where are they? I've not seen anything.

"This is total fraud," Trump added. "And how the FBI and Department of Justice—I don't know— maybe they're involved, but how people are getting away with this stuff—it's unbelievable."

Trump then aired the long litany of complaints he had privately raised with Barr, including about John Durham's investigation going nowhere.

"I ask, are they looking at it? Everyone says, 'Yes, they're looking at it,'" Trump told Bartiromo. "Look, where are they with Comey, McCabe, and all these other people?"

Trump wanted to see James Comey and Andrew McCabe locked up.

"Where are they with all of this stuff?" Trump asked. "And what happened to Durham? Where's Durham?"

There it is, Barr told his top advisers after watching Trump's interview. Now he had his answer to the question of when he should try to put an end to this madness. Barr had always believed in taking opportunities when they presented themselves, and Trump had given him an opening by maligning the Justice Department. Barr found a way to weigh in publicly, even though he was aiming to influence the vaunted audience of one. On December 1, Barr met for a lunch interview with Michael Balsamo, the Associated Press reporter who covered the Justice Department. Barr talked with Balsamo about several things, but Balsamo had his scoop after Barr answered a few questions about election integrity. Barr told him that the Justice Department had run to ground each credible claim that had been raised so far and that "to date, we have not seen fraud on a scale that could have effected a different outcome in the election."

That was the money line. Their lunch soon ended, and Balsamo filed his story. This was not some small, off-the-cuff remark at a curbside when a reporter tossed out a question at an official. It was big. The attorney general had deliberately pulled the rug out from under the president.

In an attempt to soothe the sting of this for the president, Barr's office also alerted Balsamo to another scoop he could land first: that the attorney general would be notifying Congress that same day that he had named Durham a special counsel back in October. This was designed to solidify Durham's appointment in the new administration so he could not be fired before finishing his investigation. To Barr and his team, announcing Durham's appointment had a secondary value. They expected the mainstream media would focus on the lack of evidence of fraud but gave some red meat to more conservative news outlets, which they figured would focus on Durham's ability to do his work without any fear.

Barr headed to the White House that afternoon, where he had a previously scheduled 3:00 meeting with Mark Meadows, which Pat Cipollone joined. By then, the AP story, headlined DISPUTING TRUMP, BARR SAYS NO WIDESPREAD ELECTION FRAUD, rocketed onto news sites and the cable news shows that were playing on many White House television screens. Minutes into the meeting, Meadows learned of the Durham appointment and was supremely unhappy.

Surprisingly to Barr, Meadows hated both news developments that day. Cipollone, who had known for a few weeks that Barr was weighing whether to say something publicly about the election results, expressed surprise that Barr had gone so far in definitively knocking down any evidence of game-changing fraud. Meadows warned Barr that the president was going to be livid. Meadows also complained the Durham appointment was just a polite way of signaling he had a special independence and that nothing would come out before the end of Trump's term. Seeming to acknowledge the election outcome, Meadows said that "Biden will just fire him" when he got into office and the public would never learn about what he believed were the FBI's attempts to kneecap Trump's presidency. Then Meadows laid out a new plan: He would fire Durham, so the Trump White

House could get whatever material he had gathered to date and release it. Barr bluffed.

"You can't do that," Barr said. "Only I can do that."

At the end of the meeting with Meadows, Barr conferred with Cipollone upstairs in the White House counsel's office. Word had spread that Barr was in the building and Cipollone got a call. "The president wants to see you," Cipollone told Barr. Barr had a dinner scheduled with Mike Pompeo that evening, so had good reason to bow out, but Cipollone urged him to come see the president; it might be good to speak face-to-face, he said. Barr said he felt his message already had been delivered, so what was the point? Cipollone said it might be better to deal with this right away, and Barr ultimately agreed.

Cipollone and Barr found Trump watching television in his private dining room with Meadows. Eric Herschmann joined them. Trump had the channel tuned to OANN, which had an even more pro-Trump slant than Fox and was airing a hearing about one of the election results the Trump campaign was still disputing. Trump had the remote control in his hand, and it wasn't clear if the hearing was live or recorded. Everything about the president telegraphed that he was in a barely contained rage. His face was reddish, his mouth was pursed tight. He was far from his usual gregarious self. As the attorney general entered, the president seemed physically unable to look at him. Trump's legs and fingers were twitching, drumming on the floor and the table erratically.

Barr put his hands on the back of one of the chairs at the dining table.

"Hello, Mr. President," he said.

"Bill, did you say this?" Trump said, his voice sharp and quick.

"Yeah," Barr said. "I said it."

"How could you say that?" Trump asked.

Barr replied that his statement was true, and that he was merely answering the reporter's question.

"Why didn't you just not answer the question?" Trump said.

Then the president, his voice getting higher, switched oddly to speak of himself in the third person.

"There's no reason for you to have said this!" he said. "You must hate Trump!"

OANN's programming continued to blare. Trump's voice got ever louder. He started yelling. He was so angry his words came out like spit.

"Have you fucking seen this?" the president asked, jabbing his index finger in the direction of the screen.

"Yes, Mr. President," Barr said.

OANN was covering two of Trump's favorite allegations: that illegal and late ballots were backdated in Pennsylvania so they could be counted, and that after-hours ballot stuffing had occurred in Georgia.

"Have you been watching these hearings?" Trump demanded.

Barr told him no.

"How can you say that, then?" Trump said. In other words, how could Barr state there had been no widespread fraud if he hadn't really investigated the claims OANN was reporting?

"We've looked into these things and they're nonsense," Barr said.

"I don't understand why," Trump said. "I've mentioned a few to you. I don't get this at all!"

Trump had papers in front of him purporting to document what he called "the steal." But he was reacting far more to what he was hearing on the television.

Barr told Trump they had looked into the truck driver's claim. "It's complete nonsense," he said.

The same was true with Georgia ballot stuffing. No evidence of that at all.

Trump asked him about the video showing boxes of ballots coming into a central vote-tallying office in Wayne County, Michigan, after polls had closed.

"Mr. President, Wayne County has five hundred precincts, and unlike all other counties, the votes are only counted in one place," Barr said. "Usually they're counted in the precincts, and in Wayne County the ballots are sent into one place for counting and they're initially gone through and they're put in separate piles: Biden, Trump. So you will sometimes see boxes of ballots that are all one candidate because they're being separated in that way, but the fact that people saw boxes going in, it proves nothing, okay?"

The president looked taken aback that Barr could explain such details from memory.

"Those ballots always come in at that time," Barr said of Wayne County's historical practices. "Have any of these people who are telling you this is a problem, have they gone back and looked at the previous patterns?"

Trump switched the topic to another fraud allegation in another state.

"Mr. President, I'm not up here to say there was no fraud," Barr said. "There may very well have been fraud. I suspect there was fraud, maybe more than usual. But there's no evidence of substantial fraud that would change the election, and your problem is you have five weeks. The reason you're sitting where you are today is because you had five weeks for your lawyers to mount a strategy . . . whereby you can turn around the election."

But, Barr said, his lawyers had no coherent strategy or evidence, and they often contradicted their claims from state to state.

"It's been a clown show," he said.

The president was quiet for a moment, then said, "Maybe."

Trump didn't turn off the hearing on the television. It continued to give him something to look at rather than Barr. Trump shifted to his "greatest hits" of grievances with the attorney general. It was a long album. He berated Barr for not coming through for him with any results from Durham and complained that nothing would come out publicly before January 20. Trump believed, as Meadows did, that Barr's decision to appoint Durham as a special counsel would only make him more independent and delay the big reveal he had hoped for. He stared blankly as Barr argued this appointment would ensure the Durham probe's longevity and protect him and his team against being fired by the incoming administration. Trump also re-iterated to Barr that the people who he thought had tried to torpedo his presidency should be in jail.

"What the fuck?" Trump said about the Justice Department's failure to prosecute senior Obama-era officials.

Trump was relentless. He demanded to know what Barr had ever investigated and ever gotten to the bottom of.

Those who worked with Barr described him as a man capable of displaying a wide range of emotions and demeanors in a workplace setting: fuming and dictatorial, calm to the point of appearing robotic, avuncular and generous, viciously funny. At this moment, he was uncharacteristically subdued and even set back on his heels by something he'd never experienced before: Trump directing his fury at him. Normally Barr would go toe-to-toe with Trump when they argued. Earlier that year, when the president brought up an investigation that the Justice Department couldn't discuss, Barr had cut him off. "I've told you!" he had said more than once. "I'm not going to talk to you about that!"

But that wasn't Barr at this meeting. He tried to stay calm and deliberate. And Trump wasn't his normal self either. The president was explosive and crazed. His limbs and torso moved jerkily, as if uncontrolled, and his eyes widened with anger at some of Barr's responses.

Meadows sat silently on the opposite side of the dining room, with his arms crossed, a posture that seemed to say, **This is DOJ's problem.** Cipollone, who had encouraged Barr to attend this horrific meeting, sat quietly most of the time as well, though at one point interjected to tell the president that Barr's department had been dutifully investigating the fraud claims. Herschmann stood for the whole meeting and said nothing. Barr eventually told Trump he was just trying to do his job. He said something to the effect that if the president wasn't happy, he could certainly make a change.

The attorney general left the White House, nearly three hours after he had entered it. Trump continued to stew, telling Meadows he had every reason to fire Barr, and indeed he should fire him. Barr himself had every reason to bail after this apocalyptic scene.

Cipollone feared what would happen if either one of them took that step. Other Republicans who had demurred on the topic or failed to talk sense into the president admired Barr for standing up to him over election fraud conspiracies. Lindsey Graham, who had regular dinners with the attorney general, told friends that Barr was "a stud" for refusing to lend credibility to accusations that had no basis in fact.

A day or two after the meeting with Trump, Cipollone asked Barr to commit to staying on. He hoped to talk down the president. Barr agreed he would stay if the president wanted him to.

In the first week of December, Trump's blizzard of legal challenges melted into slush. The president's daily tally of losses was difficult to ignore. On December 3 alone, his campaign suffered three major defeats. The Wisconsin State Supreme Court, on which Republican judges made up the majority, refused to hear its challenge to Biden's high vote count in heavily Democratic Dane and Milwaukee counties because the Trump campaign had skipped a required procedural step of filing its complaint at a lower court. The Pennsylvania State Supreme Court issued a one-sentence order rejecting a Republican group's plea to reconsider a lawsuit challenging universal voting by mail. And in Arizona, a Maricopa County judge dismissed the state Republican Party chairwoman's claim that the state's vote tally was inaccurate because during the verification process partisan election observers had to stand too far away to make out the signatures on mail-in ballots.

The next day, December 4, the Trump campaign was dealt five additional defeats in key states. More than fifty legal challenges brought by Trump's campaign or his allies had failed or been tossed out of court.

Team Trump could claim just one partial and ultimately pyrrhic victory. In that case, a Pennsylvania court agreed with the Trump campaign that Pennsylvania secretary of state Kathy Boockvar didn't have authority to extend the deadline for people to "cure" their votes by providing proof of identification for certain absentee ballots and mail-in ballots. But the win impacted a small cluster of votes that had been segregated and not yet counted and would not change the outcome in a state Biden had won by tens of thousands of votes.

Judge after judge across the country had turned Trump's lawyers and allies down, saying they either had no evidence for their claims or no legal right to the sweeping remedy they sought. But the president believed the Supreme Court ultimately would help him right this wrong. Trump told several allies that he thought the three justices he had nominated—Neil Gorsuch, Brett Kavanaugh, and Amy Coney Barrett—owed him for their prestigious lifetime positions, and that Kavanaugh should feel especially grateful. After Christine Blasey Ford alleged Kavanaugh had assaulted her, which he denied, some top Republicans urged the president to withdraw Kavanaugh's nomination. "I was told by many Republican senators, 'Cut him loose, sir, cut him loose. He's killing us,'" Trump later told us in an interview. But the president stood by Kavanaugh, and that counted for something in Trump's book.

On December 8, the Supreme Court gave its first view of the 2020 election disputes. Trump's allies had made a last-minute and legally flimsy bid to overturn the Pennsylvania results by asking the federal court to wade into a matter the state's highest court had already decided. The challengers, a group of Republicans led by Congressman Mike Kelly, said the vote count was illegitimate because it was conducted under a 2019 state law that established universal mail voting. Republicans had controlled the legislature when the change was enacted, but the claimants argued the GOP had overstepped its authority. Another irony: Some of the lawmakers challenging the 2019 law to help Trump had publicly urged their own supporters to cast their ballots using the new mail-in procedure. Earlier that day, before the Supreme Court's ruling, Trump sought to pressure the justices to help overturn the election results by appealing to their sense of "courage."

"Now, let's see whether or not somebody has the courage, whether it's a legislator or legislatures, or whether it's a justice of the Supreme Court, or a number of justices of the Supreme Court—let's see if they have the courage to do what everybody in this country knows is right," Trump said at a news conference.

Mitt Romney could not believe Trump had taken it this far. "Normally in our system you can accuse another party of doing something bad if you begin by finding some evidence that they've done something bad," he said later in an interview. "But his intelligence services were saying the election was not rigged. The FBI was saying it was not rigged. I presume Bill Barr was saying it was not rigged. The secretaries of state of the various states were acknowledging that it was a free and fair election. So on what basis did he have any reason to suggest it was rigged other than wanting the outcome that he wanted?"

The U.S. Supreme Court said Team Trump didn't have a case. The justices' decision was so short it could have been put on a block stamp. "The application for injunctive relief presented to Justice Alito and by him referred to the Court is denied," the order read.

This did not bode well for subsequent challenges. Also, on December 8, Texas attorney general Ken Paxton, a Republican, filed a broad and some argued fatally flawed complaint with the Supreme Court. He asked the justices to perform some legal jujitsu: grant one state the legal standing to intervene in the elections of other states. He asked the court to overturn Biden's vote counts in Georgia, Michigan, Pennsylvania, and Wisconsin on the grounds their allegedly flawed elections had violated the rights of Texans.

Trump called the Paxton case "the Big One." He and his allies watched closely for news, and it came in short order. On December 11, the court issued an unsigned order that read in part: "The State of Texas's motion for leave to file a bill of complaint is denied for lack of standing under Article III of the Constitution." Case dismissed.

That night, Trump and his aides scurried to decode what the decision meant, and then to explain the loss to the president's base. Kayleigh McEnany went on Fox to assail what she characterized as the cowardice of the court. Though she had received a law degree from Harvard and should have known better, the White House press secretary falsely alleged that allowing one state to intervene in the elections of another would be a step to "enforce the Constitution."

"There's no way to say it other than they dodged," McEnany said. "They dodged. They hid behind procedure and they refused to use their authority to enforce the Constitution. . . . This was on standing, dismissed on standing. None of the justices gave a view on the facts of the case."

Trump tweeted, "It is a legal disgrace, an embarrassment to the USA!!!" He repeated a false claim by Texas lieutenant governor Dan Patrick that no court has yet judged any of Trump's legal challenges "on its merit." The problem was the courts decided most of the cases had no merit and no evidence to consider.

Early the next morning, Trump added to the confusion by retweeting praise of Justices Samuel Alito and Clarence Thomas and shared part of Sean Hannity's summary of the ruling: "Justices Alito and Thomas say they would have allowed Texas to proceed with its election lawsuit."

Either Trump was intending to obscure how the two conservative justices had ruled or his lawyers had not explained to him the meaning of the Supreme Court's order. Alito and Thomas made a separate statement in which they did not dissent from their fellow justices. Instead, they simply registered their concern that the court should not automatically block cases like the one Texas brought. But they agreed Trump's particular case would not have been granted remedy.

On December 8, Mark Milley felt his internal alarm bells going off. He was in his office in the Pentagon and got a report that Kash Patel had been unexpectedly recalled from his trip to Asia with Chris Miller. He heard the military had considered dispatching a gray tail—a military plane—to bring Patel home. That suggested a heck of a lot of urgency. As Milley recounted the moment to aides, he made some calls and learned that Patel had been summoned back to Washington by the White House, but his contacts didn't know why.

Milley had never trusted Patel, and had ample reason since the October rescue snafu. But Patel obviously made others uncomfortable, too. Sometimes in meetings with Miller, when Patel left the room, the acting defense secretary would visibly let his shoulders down, as if he could finally speak freely.

Because the recall involved Patel, and because of the circumstances of that late-night call after the election, Milley was highly suspicious. This came at a moment when there were rampant rumors and media reports with aides speculating that Trump was going to fire Chris Wray or Gina Haspel or both. Milley was close to Haspel so he called her.

"Gina, what are you hearing?" Milley asked, meaning about Trump firing her.

Haspel, by dint of decades of intelligence work, rarely showed much emotion.

"I'm always on the ropes," she deadpanned, noting that she was constantly at odds with the cabal of people around Trump and this time was no different.

On December 11, with the rumors circulating, Haspel decided to take the temperature at the White House. That day, after several weeks away, she appeared for the president's routine briefing. While helping provide some context for the intelligence he was receiving, she took her opportunities to remind Trump of how effective the CIA had been on her watch. What Haspel didn't know is that Trump was fully ready to install Patel as deputy director at the CIA, replacing Vaughn Bishop temporarily. Then, once Patel was aboard, Trump could fire Haspel, allowing Patel to ascend to acting director of the agency.

Other administration officials said Meadows had a burr under his saddle about Haspel. The two were not personally close and Meadows would complain to them that Haspel kept him out of the loop on some intelligence matters. He also questioned her loyalty to Trump and indicated he wanted a more politically supportive leader at the CIA who might, for instance, help uncover what he and Trump suspected were political efforts on the part of intelligence officials to harm his campaign in 2016. Enter Patel, whose ace in the hole was his loyalty to Trump, not his résumé. He had worked as a national security prosecutor but had no substantive intelligence background other than serving as a staffer to then chairman of the House Intelligence Committee Devin Nunes, which is how he had gotten to know Meadows.

After Trump's intelligence briefing finished and Haspel left the Oval, the president asked Vice President Pence and Cipollone whether he should remove the CIA director. Pence was usually deferential to Trump on sensitive topics such as personnel and mostly offered his advice in private. "Give us the room," the vice president would say when he wanted to talk with the president without aides hearing him and risking that details of the conversation might leak to the press. But this time, Pence spoke up strongly in Haspel's defense, with Cipollone and Keith Kellogg still in the room.

"Gina's done a lot for this nation," Pence told Trump. "I don't agree with removing her.

"She's done a lot of heavy lifting," he added, referring to her record on capturing or taking out terrorists.

When it was his turn to weigh in, Kellogg was more plainspoken with Trump: "She killed a lot of bad guys."

Pence also refuted the argument Meadows had been making about loyalty. "Mr. President, she's done what you've asked her to do," the vice president said.

Cipollone, a prudent lawyer, hung back. Though generally a fan of Haspel's, he let Pence do most of the talking in the meeting. Trump ultimately decided that day to put his Patel plan on ice and keep Haspel in her position.

Down the hall in the chief of staff's office, Meadows told Haspel he had offered the deputy CIA director job to Patel. She was unaware that the president had originally planned to do exactly this and that he had just decided against it. Haspel made clear that she would resign noisily rather than let Patel become her number two.

"I won't stand for that," Haspel told Meadows. "I'd like to then tender my resignation to the president myself."

Before it came to that, however, Trump had backed off the idea of replacing Haspel.

Milley had heard from his contacts about Haspel's dramatic Friday at the White House. He wasn't convinced that the idea of installing Patel in a top job like CIA director or FBI director was entirely dead, but he was hoping he might help kill it for good. He had an opportunity the next day, Saturday, December 12: the annual Army-Navy football game. The cadets and midshipmen gathered at Army's Michie Stadium in West Point, New York, and Milley and other brass flew up for the big game, as did Trump. After Milley joined Trump on the field for the commander in chief to perform a coin toss to start the game, they retired to the president's viewing box. Other guests included Meadows, McConnell and Kevin McCarthy, and Patel and Miller, who had returned from Asia as well.

Meadows was talking to Trump in a whisper, but as Milley later told aides, he could hear some of the exchange. The president said, "Yeah, I want you to take care of that." Meadows nodded and said, "Oh, yes, Mr. President. I'll take care of that."

Milley, who had been on edge for four days since Patel's recall, decided to play the rube and try to flush out what was going on.

"Hey, Kash," Milley hollered from across the box. "So, what are you going to take? CIA or FBI? Which one is it?"

Milley said it loudly, for everyone in the box to hear. Trump looked at Milley, a slight frown on his face. Meadows stared over, too.

"It's all in the papers, Kash," Milley said, faking his information. "Which are you doing?"

"Oh Chairman! Chairman!" Patel said, waving him off and seeming to adopt a pose of mild embarrassment. "Come on. Stop! Stop!"

Milley didn't care how awkward this was. He put everyone on notice that he was watching their moves. Meadows, with a look of consternation on his face, pulled Milley aside to try to interrupt what was becoming a scene.

"What's going on? Are you guys getting rid of Wray or Gina?" Milley asked Meadows. "Come on, Chief. What the hell is going on here? What are you guys doing?"

"Don't worry about it," Meadows said. "Just some personnel moves."

"Just be careful," Milley said. He didn't say this in a supportive way. It was more like a warning. Milley wanted Meadows to know that he was watching. Did anyone think the leaders of the U.S. military were idiots? He wanted the White House to understand that he was drawing hard boundaries, and that Patel and his pals weren't going to get the guys with the guns.

On the same day, December 12, thousands of Trump supporters flocked again onto the streets of downtown Washington to display their strong opposition to the election results. It was another in the series of "Stop the Steal" rallies. The crowd included a heavy representation of QAnon supporters and Proud Boys, whose leader, Enrique Tarrio, posted a picture of the White House on the right-wing social media platform Parler, claiming he had received a "last minute invite to an undisclosed location." A White House spokesman said Tarrio was taking a public tour of the mansion's Christmas decorations.

The opening of the rally felt like a cacophonic religious revival for Trump worshippers. The stage speeches had been organized in part by Jericho March, a Judeo-Christian group that had formed to fight for what it believed to be Trump's rightful return to a second term and had been named in honor of the triumphant battle of Jericho. In the biblical story of Joshua, the righteous Israelites were said to have marched around the city for six days and performed other ceremonies until the walls fell and they were able to conquer the city of Canaan. Here, too, Trump's righteous warriors set out to march around the Capitol and monuments until they could reclaim their government. Preachers gave chest-thumping sermons. A man dressed in all-white garb took the stage and held up a ritual Jewish horn, which the Israelites sounded to begin their march. Called a shofar, it resembled a steer's horn but was decorated with red, white, and blue paint. The Jericho March leader said it had been made especially for Donald Trump.

"President Trump, come get your shofar and lead us to another four years!" the man said. "Amen!"

MAGA celebrities on hand included conspiracy theorist radio host Alex Jones and Trump adviser Katrina Pierson, both of whom were known for inflammatory rhetoric. Pierson promised that the Trump warriors gathered downtown would stop Biden from becoming president. "We will utilize that system to the very end. And if that does not work, we will take our country back," she said.

The founder of the "Stop the Steal" movement, Ali Alexander, told the demonstrators to get ready to take action to protect their government and that if, "heaven forbid," the electoral college certified Biden as the winner on December 14, their fight would move to Congress. He said they should all stand ready to take up this fight on January 6, when Congress was scheduled to officially certify the electoral college results. Alexander said that Alabama congressman Mo

Brooks planned to object to House certification and warned other Republicans to join him "or we will throw them out of office."

The crowd favorite—and the one whose appearance most rattled his former colleagues in the firmament of the U.S. government—was Michael Flynn, whom Trump had pardoned on November 25. Flynn wore a red polo shirt and a blue blazer with a flag-motif handkerchief knotted around his neck, a kind of revolutionary's ascot. He led the MAGA fans in prayer before ebulliently insisting that Trump would remain in office for a second term. Acknowledging that "we're in a crucible moment in the history of the United States of America," Flynn said the president was counting on them.

"Don't get bent out of shape," he said. "There are still avenues." He added, "The courts aren't going to decide who the next president of the United States is going to be. We the people decide."

Marine One, presumably carrying the president, along with two decoy helicopters, flew overhead as Flynn spoke.

"There he is," Flynn said. "He's a sneaky guy. But he's a fighter!"

One of Flynn's fellow generals watched the event on television, shaking his head at the zaniness of what he was hearing. "Mike, you've gone off the deep end," the general said to himself. "This is psychotic."

Though the rhetoric was amped up, the protests that day were largely peaceful and calm. Later that night, however, D.C. police struggled to keep the Trump supporters separated from anti-Trump protesters, especially near Black Lives Matter Plaza and near Harry's Bar downtown, which the Proud Boys had used as a gathering point. At least four people were stabbed in scuffles nearby. The organizers of Jericho March weren't involved. They insisted they were people of peace and faith.

In locations across America around this time, Trump supporters were acting out with threatening and dangerous behavior. In Gwinnett County, Georgia, a Dominion Voting Machines contractor was accused of treason and found a noose outside his house, after a video accusing him of vote manipulation spread online. Gabriel Sterling, a top election official in Georgia, who is Republican, pleaded with Trump to tell his supporters to stop their violence and intimidation.

"It's all gone too far," Sterling said in an emotional news conference on December 2. "You need to step up and say this . . . stop inspiring people to commit potential acts of violence. Someone's going to get hurt. Someone's going to get shot. Someone's going to get killed. And it's not right."

Sterling's plea did not douse the passions of Trump's backers. In Michigan three days later, a state Biden carried by 154,000 votes, protesters picketed outside the home of Secretary of State Jocelyn Benson. She had just finished wrapping her portico with Christmas lights and was about to watch **How**

the Grinch Stole Christmas with her four-year-old son when about two dozen protesters picketed her home, some of them carrying guns and chanting "Stop the Steal!"

"Ever since the president first tweeted at me and every time there is an additional attempt to spread false information, you see an uptick in the threats," Benson told **The New York Times.** "And now apparently, they're in front of my house, in the dark of night, in this very private, quiet residential neighborhood. We are concerned not only for the safety of my family, but my neighbors as well."

Other election officials and state legislators in Arizona, Georgia, Michigan, Pennsylvania, Wisconsin, and other states reported receiving threatening emails and voice-mail messages. Michigan state representative Darrin Camilleri told the **Times** he had received an email that said, "Be prepared to take your last meal," and another that read, "We're looking forward to bring[ing] back firing squads."

Finally, on December 14, the electoral college convened with electors gathered in every state and in the District of Columbia to officially affirm their election results. This was the moment when McConnell and some other senior Republicans believed the results would truly be final. By the end of a daylong cascade of ceremonial votes, Biden received 306 electoral votes to Trump's 232. In an address to the nation that night, Biden said, "In this battle for the soul of America, democracy prevailed. We the people voted.

Faith in our institutions held. The integrity of our elections remains intact, and now it's time to turn the page, as we've done throughout history."

The next day, December 15, McConnell tried to put an end to Trump's election-fraud shenanigans. Rising on the Senate floor to deliver a speech, the majority leader said, "Many of us hoped that the presidential election would yield a different result, but our system of government has processes to determine who will be sworn in on January 20. The electoral college has spoken. So today, I want to congratulate President-elect Joe Biden."

Trump and his supporters were not ready to turn the page. They shifted their attention to the next date on the calendar: January 6, when Congress was slated to certify the electoral college results. Already, some House Republicans, led by backbencher Brooks, were planning to object to certification from five states where Trump had alleged fraud: Arizona, Georgia, Nevada, Pennsylvania, and Wisconsin. Shortly after his floor speech congratulating Biden, McConnell privately urged fellow Senate Republicans not to sign on to this effort to reverse the election outcome because he said it would be futile. McConnell also spoke by phone with Biden, who had called to thank him for the congratulations and vowed to work together on issues where they could find agreement.

Trump was furious and called McConnell. Animated and angry, the president cursed at the Senate leader. Trump made clear McConnell's offer of congratulations to Biden was so disloyal he might as well have declared a mutiny. McConnell, equally firm, said this was the result dictated by the constitutional process and had to be accepted. "The electoral college is the final word," McConnell told Trump.

McConnell was quite familiar with the president's profanities, and at peace with the outcome. But Trump would not rest. He wanted to keep fighting to subvert the vote, but Trump would have to do so without the support of the Senate's top Republican. This acrimonious call would be the last time the two men spoke for the remainder of Trump's presidency.

After his caustic meeting with Trump on December 1, Barr knew it was probably time to go. He wanted to make sure his exit was dignified, without the president taking cheap shots at his expense, but Barr also didn't want to resign in a manner that would be interpreted as a break with Trump and injure the president politically. The attorney general had been on a high wire for two years and had to figure out how to dismount under extreme pressure. Barr was tired, and the closer the calendar got to Christmas, the more he longed for a work-free holiday, so he set his sights on leaving before then. He had confidence in the team he was leaving behind, including Deputy Attorney General Jeff Rosen and Principal Associate Deputy Attorney General Rich Donoghue. There weren't that many days left to hold down the fort, but Barr thought they would handle it well.

Over the weekend of December 12, Barr decided that he would talk to Trump on Monday, December 14, about leaving. That Sunday night, he wrote a resignation letter he expected would eventually become public. But there was only one person it needed to impress—Trump—and Barr dutifully emphasized the president's accomplishments as well as his strength as a leader.

On Monday, Barr went to the White House and directly to Cipollone's office and said he wanted to speak to the president alone. They entered the Oval Office together and found Meadows with Trump. Cipollone and Meadows excused themselves. The conversation between Trump and Barr was nothing like their last meeting two weeks prior, according to the account Barr shared with some of his senior deputies. The attorney general came bearing a gift, which helped: a letter full of praise. But in this opening conversation, he was clear-eyed.

"I think you know how much I've supported your administration and your policies," Barr began. "I've tried to help you be a successful administration that way."

"Yes, yes," Trump replied, nodding his head.

"You and I have had a good relationship for most of that time. It's been strained recently and I think we're butting heads a lot and I'd rather not end our

relationship with a blowup or have it further deteriorate," Barr said. "I would just as soon leave now, and
I wrote a letter that expresses my feelings about what
we've been able to accomplish."

Trump was listening closely. He was immediately
intrigued. The president knew that resignation letters could pack a punch. He had felt victimized two
years earlier when Jim Mattis quit as defense secretary
with a headline-making resignation letter effectively
denouncing Trump's worldview.

"Let me see it," Trump told Barr.

After scanning it, the president said, "Hmmm . . .
This is a good letter."

In very short order, Trump called Meadows and
Cipollone back into the Oval.

"Bill wrote this great letter," Trump told them,
and showed each of them. "He'd like to leave now."

As his advisers read over the glowing letter, they
complimented Barr. The attorney general wanted to
stay until December 23 to wrap up some work. The
four of them talked for a moment about replacements
and Barr suggested elevating Rosen to be acting attorney general, backed by Donoghue as acting deputy
attorney general. Trump nodded. That sounded fine
to him.

The meeting was going so smoothly. Not one hiccup
or sharp note. Trump looked relieved, those briefed on
the meeting said. With Barr, he had a Cabinet member he had liked so much, and seemed to personally

enjoy, yet they ended up on a collision course over the election. Barr had a lot of credibility and things could only end badly if they stayed together.

The White House released Barr's letter, and every paragraph delighted Trump. It opened by suggesting that they had met that day to discuss the ongoing election fraud investigations—not exactly true—and Barr stressed the importance of continuing those probes. Then he got to the meat: "I am proud to have played a role in the many successes and unprecedented achievements you have delivered for the American people."

Barr then sounded a note that Trump loved perhaps the most, describing the many slings and arrows the president took from his enemies yet was still standing, unfazed.

"Your record is all the more historic because you accomplished it in the face of relentless, implacable resistance," Barr wrote. He condemned "a partisan onslaught against you in which no tactic, no matter how abusive and deceitful, was out of bounds. The nadir of this campaign was the effort to cripple, if not oust, your Administration with frenzied and baseless allegations of collusion with Russia."

Here, when it came to the Mueller investigation, the two men stood on common ground. "Few could have weathered these attacks, much less forge ahead," Barr wrote, but Trump did.

The president tweeted his praise for the departing attorney general that night: "Our relationship has been a very good one, he has done an outstanding job!"

Barr had pulled it off. He left the Trump administration without a nasty tweet or a knock-down, drag-out fight amplified by the leaks of scheming courtiers. He felt he had done this quite deftly. He didn't know how brilliantly he had timed it.

Flynn's former military colleagues thought they were long past being shocked by his bizarre behavior after he joined Trump's campaign and his administration. He had taken money from the Turkish government while seeking a White House job, lied to the FBI about his conversations with a Russian ambassador on his fourth day as national security adviser, and then claimed prosecutors had coerced him to falsely admit to lying. But on December 17, the military brass he used to work alongside were floored anew when the retired lieutenant general asserted in a television interview that Trump had won the election, and urged him to seize voting machines and declare martial law if necessary to "rerun" the election.

In his Newsmax TV interview with Greg Kelly at about 4:00 that afternoon, Flynn said there was precedent for deploying military troops for this purpose when in fact there was none.

"Number one, President Trump won on the third of November," he said. "First of all, he needs to appoint a special counsel immediately. He needs to seize all of these Dominion and these other voting machines that we have across the country. . . . Clearly there is a foreign influence that is tied to this system and it goes back to China, likely goes to Russia, likely goes to Iran. . . . There's been problems all over the country with them.

"The president has to plan for every eventuality because we cannot allow this election and the integrity of our election to go the way it is," Flynn added. "He could also order, within the swing states, if he wanted to, he could take military capabilities and he could place them in those states and basically rerun an election in each of those states. It's not unprecedented. . . . These people out there talking about martial law like it's something we've never done. Martial law has been instituted sixty-four times."

Late the next day, December 18, Flynn showed up at the White House with Sidney Powell to outline for the president this very plan. They were joined that Friday evening by Emily Newman, a former Trump administration official, and Patrick Byrne, the former CEO of online retailer Overstock.com. A promoter of conspiracy theories, Byrne had left his executive position and had dated a woman who was a Russian agent.

Herschmann spotted Powell walking into the West Wing and became suspicious. He trailed the foursome into the Oval Office, filing in behind them and sitting in the back of the room while they took seats in front of Trump at the Resolute Desk.

Powell proceeded to tell Trump that she believed he had been the victim of manipulated voting machines and a foreign influence campaign. She said he should issue an executive order to seize voting machines in key states, and name her a special counsel to investigate. From a clutch of papers, she waved the affidavit she had boasted about at the Republican National Committee news conference, a sworn statement from a person she said was a direct witness to the manipulation of Dominion machines in a Venezuela election to ensure Hugo Chavez's victory. She did not give a clear explanation of how this person witnessed anything incriminating or corrupt about the 2020 U.S. presidential election.

Herschmann objected, saying he didn't follow Powell's claims. They were about foreign interference, and very different from the legal challenges that Rudy Giuliani and other Trump campaign lawyers had been making in dozens of courts. The campaign argued in those cases that Democrats had changed or flouted voting rules, leading some counties and states to overcount Biden votes.

Powell told Herschmann that Giuliani had failed to grasp the source of the fraud—"until now."

With that, Herschmann called out to an aide outside the Oval for someone to get Cipollone to join them immediately. The White House counsel arrived and was surprised to find people in the Oval he did not recognize. He asked Byrne: "Who are you?"

Cipollone listened as Powell claimed a massive and vague conspiracy to flip votes for Biden in Georgia, Michigan, and Pennsylvania. Flynn echoed her.

Herschmann debated the Georgia county Powell mentioned; it was one Trump actually had won. That didn't make sense. Powell said the innards of the machines would show how the counts were corrupted. Cipollone warned this foursome the president had no legal grounds to seize machines. Flynn disagreed, saying Cipollone didn't understand the president's broad authority.

The meeting, first described in detail by Jonathan Swan of **Axios,** turned ugly fast. The attendees cursed and hurled insults at one another. The tenor of the conversation did not befit the serious work normally conducted in the Oval Office, not even in Trump's unorthodox one. But that's how deep the West Wing had sunk, and how desperate Trump had become for a rescue plan, four days after the states certified their vote results for the electoral college. By this point, the president had almost entirely ceased doing the business of running the country. Instead, he was taking meetings with people who had wild theories.

The Powell-Flynn-Byrne team told Trump that his other advisers were not loyal enough and not fighting hard enough for him. Flynn shouted that the people denying this extensive fraud by Dominion machines—at that moment, he was directing his anger at Cipollone and Herschmann—were "quitters."

Herschmann was equally disgusted. "Why the fuck do you keep standing up and screaming at me?" he said to Flynn. "If you want to come over here, come over here. If not, sit your ass down."

Flynn backed off for a bit. But eventually he started yelling again, this time at Cipollone. He called him a "capitulator" and a "weakling." Cipollone snorted. Powell insisted she had evidence the election was dirty, and she was willing to fight for the president and prove his case. She and Flynn argued that the Department of Justice couldn't be trusted to handle this.

The meeting eventually dragged on for hours and drew in more people. Trump dialed campaign lawyer Matt Morgan and Robert O'Brien to bring them into the discussion at various times. The scene was chaotic. The din grew louder as people spoke over each other. O'Brien, who was speaking from his home after about 8:00 p.m., was asked by one of the White House lawyers whether he had any national security information regarding Powell's claim of foreign governments hijacking voting machines. O'Brien, who could hardly believe this was a serious question, responded that he saw no evidence or intelligence of such foreign manipulation. When someone soon after tried to add Giuliani to the conference call, O'Brien was inadvertently dropped from the line. Nobody called him back, and O'Brien, content to be liberated from the discussion, did not attempt to rejoin it.

Trump took a break and left the Oval to go to his dining room for a while, but then resumed the discussion from the residence. By this time, Giuliani had made his way to the White House in person. Herschmann told Powell she should tell Giuliani to his face what she told them in the Oval: that

Giuliani hadn't known what he was doing and only just recently figured out the source of the fraud.

Trump never took the steps Flynn and Powell had urged. And the Giuliani-Powell relationship appeared to have suffered a break. Giuliani had figured out that Powell lacked any supporting evidence for some of her claims. And he complained to his associates that "Sidney doesn't play well in the sandbox."

When **The New York Times** reported on December 19 that a tempestuous meeting in the Oval had included a discussion of naming Powell as a special counsel on election fraud, Giuliani quickly distanced himself and Trump from Powell. He asserted she had not been part of Trump's legal team for the past five weeks and did not speak for the president.

"She's a fine woman, a fine lawyer," Giuliani told Newsmax host Sean Spicer, who had been Trump's first White House press secretary. "But whatever she's talking about, it's her own opinions. I'm not responsible for them, the president isn't, nor is anybody else on our legal team."

Twenty

Hitting a Dead End

Pesident Trump's time in office was running out when, on December 22, he granted a pre-Christmas wave of pardons. The president continued to undo the Mueller investigation's most important prosecutions by pardoning two people who pleaded guilty to lying to investigators: George Papadopoulos, a former national security adviser to Trump's 2016 campaign, and Alex van der Zwaan, a lawyer who had married into one of Russia's wealthiest families and had worked with former Trump campaign officials Paul Manafort and Rick Gates. Trump also granted mercy to four Blackwater guards convicted in connection with opening fire on Iraqi civilians, as well as three former Republican members of Congress who had pleaded guilty or been convicted on corruption charges. These acts of clemency fit a pattern; by this point in his presidency, according to one legal tally, 88 percent of pardons went to people who had personal ties to the president or who furthered his political aims.

Trump had been using most of his remaining time trying to overturn the election, calling state election officials and state legislators to pressure them to block certification of Joe Biden's wins. Much of his attention was focused on Georgia. Throughout December, Trump had been ratcheting up pressure on Georgia's leaders to somehow toss out enough Biden votes to overturn the Democrat's razor-thin victory. He had accused Secretary of State Brad Raffensperger and Governor Brian Kemp of disloyalty for not requiring signature verification, which Trump said would "expose the massive voter fraud in Georgia" and result in Republican victories.

On December 23, Trump made a call to Frances Watson, the chief investigator in Raffensperger's office, who was probing allegations of ballot fraud in Cobb County, in the Atlanta suburbs. Watson had met a day earlier with Mark Meadows, who flew to Georgia to observe firsthand the ballot-signature audit. On the call, Trump told Watson that Meadows had asked him to call her. The president claimed that "something bad happened" and urged Watson to identify "dishonesty" in the state's vote tally, stressing to her that she would earn praise if she did so.

"The people of Georgia are so angry at what happened to me," Trump told Watson. "They know I won, won by hundreds of thousands of votes. It wasn't close."

Trump added, "Hopefully when the right answer comes out you'll be praised. . . . People will say, 'Great.'"

Watson sounded flattered to get a call from the president—"Quite frankly, I'm shocked that you would take time to do that," she told him—and thanked him profusely for his interest in her and her team's work. But she also was cautious. She did not offer or reveal any details of her open investigation. Trump offered her some investigative tips, though. He recommended she try to match ballot signatures with older signatures on file, a strategy that Trump allies believed would increase the number that had to be rejected.

"I hope you're going back two years as opposed to just checking, you know, one against the other because that would just be sort of a signature check that didn't mean anything," Trump said.

The president also urged her to look at votes in Fulton County, which encompasses most of the city of Atlanta and is Georgia's most populous county. Nearly 45 percent of Fulton's one million residents are Black, and the county is one of Georgia's most solidly Democratic.

"If you can get to Fulton, you're going to find things that are going to be unbelievable, the dishonesty that we've heard from, just good sources, really good sources," Trump told Watson. He added, "Fulton is the mother lode, you know, as the expression goes."

Watson did not engage Trump on the details of his requests. "Well, Mr. President, I appreciate your comment," she said. "And I can assure you that our team, and the [Georgia Bureau of Investigations], that we're only interested in the truth."

Trump's call to Watson was especially brazen. Experts in criminal law said his attempt to pressure the investigator was inappropriate and may have constituted obstruction of a state investigation. And Trump's continued assault on the integrity of Georgia's elections was taking a demonstrable toll on the state's Republican senators in their runoff campaigns. David Perdue's and Kelly Loeffler's seats—and with them, the GOP's Senate majority—were in jeopardy. The party's internal polling showed the way to win was with a "checks and balances" message, meaning Perdue and Loeffler would need to campaign as Republican counters to the incoming Democratic administration's power. To do so credibly, however, the senators had to acknowledge Biden's victory. Unfortunately for the Republican senators, the leader of their party was saying the opposite and wanted them to do the same. With Trump claiming widespread fraud and refusing to concede, many of his voters would not believe Biden was the next president. Worse still for Perdue and Loeffler—and for Mitch McConnell, who was desperate to remain majority leader—many Georgia Republicans were skeptical about the value of voting in the January 5 runoff because they believed the president when he said the system was rigged.

Trump wasn't alone in propagating these doubts. Lin Wood, a prominent Atlanta attorney and Trump ally, had been urging Georgia Republicans not to vote in elections with Dominion machines. At a "Stop the Steal" rally on December 2 in Alpharetta, Wood had appeared with Sidney Powell and told the crowd, "Don't be fooled twice. This is Georgia. We ain't dumb. We're not going to vote on January 5 on another machine made by China. You're not going to fool Georgians again." Michael Flynn had made the same claim in his December 17 interview on Newsmax TV, calling the Georgia runoffs "fake elections." "You can't have another election on the same system," Flynn said. "It's a broken system, and we cannot allow a system that's tied to foreign powers to be used to vote for the president or any election, any elected office in our country."

After McConnell's easy reelection win in November, he dispatched some of his field staffers to Georgia to assist in the runoff campaigns. One of McConnell's most talented young operatives settled in northwest Georgia, a bastion of hard-core conservatism where voters had just elected Marjorie Taylor Greene. This was Trump Country. McConnell kept in close contact with the operative as he and his team canvassed door-to-door in the area. On one such phone call, the operative said, "Leader, they're very confused."

"What are you hearing?" McConnell asked.

"They don't think their votes are going to count," the operative said. "They don't trust the system."

Mark Milley's task to protect against Trump and his people manipulating the military had become considerably more difficult with Mark Esper and Bill Barr gone and new loyalists installed at the Pentagon. Milley told confidants he would never openly defy the president; that would be illegal and violate his own sense of duty. But he was determined to plant flags. As Milley had once told Meadows, during one of their many discussions about Trump's wishes to show off the military's might, "I'm not moving, just so you know. You're dealing with a thick-headed Irish guy from Boston. I'm stubborn as shit, and I'm not going to move. It's just the way I am."

Milley, who had considered resigning in the summer, had consulted with lifelong friends and peers he trusted, both in the military and in academia, throughout the rest of the year. Former defense secretary Bob Gates, a mentor, warned Milley the days ahead might be hard, but implored him not to back down. "Stick to it," Gates said. "Don't quit. Steel your back. It's not going to be easy, but you're the right guy in the right place and at the right time. Thank God you're there." Gates had told Esper the same thing at his low point, counseling both men that resigning would give Trump an easy way out and advising them to stay unless or until the president fired them.

As the president amped up his rhetoric, Milley fine-tuned his antennae for trouble. He monitored the horizon for some stealthy move by Chris Miller, Kash Patel, or Ezra Cohen-Watnick, or for an outbreak of violence in the streets. On New Year's Eve, military chiefs received an update on how local law enforcement was preparing for a spate of pro-Trump rallies planned in Washington on January 6. The Pentagon was tracking as many as ten planned events centered around Black Lives Matter Plaza, the White House, and the Capitol. The D.C. Metropolitan Police Department requested the Defense Department provide about 340 D.C. National Guard troops for extra support beginning that next week, hoping to assign about 300 to traffic control on the streets and crowd control in the Metro subway, and to place about 40 on standby at Joint Base Andrews as part of a quick-reaction force in case of emergency.

Meantime, Republicans on Capitol Hill were divided over whether to try to contest the election results on January 6. More than 140 Republicans in the House, roughly two thirds of the GOP members, were planning to do so, even though a bedrock conservative, Barr, had announced the Justice Department found no voter fraud that could change the outcome. Their fealty to Trump was so strong that they rejected the facts in front of them.

In the Senate, Josh Hawley of Missouri became the first to announce that he planned to vote to oppose certifying the electoral college vote and force an ugly floor debate over the integrity of the election. The freshman senator, jockeying for position to run for president in 2024, garnered national headlines that he surely hoped would endear him to Trump's supporters—and that infuriated McConnell. On December 31, McConnell said on a conference call with Senate Republicans that he would vote to certify and that he considered it "the most consequential I have ever cast" in his thirty-six years in the Senate.

Milley was not alone in his anxiety about the coming days. Other senior leaders in the administration and in Congress were concerned about whether Trump might try to use the powers of the FBI, the CIA, and especially the military to try to stay in office. Starting on December 31, some of them called Milley seeking comfort.

"Everybody's worried about coups, attempted coups, overseas stuff in Iran," one congressman told Milley. "There's high tension."

"The military's going to stay out of politics," Milley responded. "We don't determine the outcome of the election. We don't pick the people in power. Everything's going to be okay. We're going to have a peaceful transfer of power. We're going to land this plane safely. This is America. It's strong. The institutions are bending, but it won't break."

Milley would repeat a version of the same pledge to various government officials many times during this period.

"Our political leadership will be determined by the American people," Milley told another member of Congress. "We will obey lawful, legal orders from a duly constituted government, period. And at twelve o'clock on the twentieth of January, there will be a president and he will be certified by the legislature."

The general's steady assurances over the phone masked his internal worry. Signs of the country's division kept flaring like little brush fires in the inauspicious first days of the new year. On January 1, police in San Francisco found a spray-painted message at Nancy Pelosi's home. One or more vandals had sprayed the words "Cancel Rent" on the House Speaker's garage door and left in her driveway what appeared to be a pig's head in a pool of fake blood.

The next day, police in Louisville, Kentucky, found spray-painted messages on McConnell's home. "WERES MY MONEY" was sprayed on the front door, while "MITCH KILLS POOR" was sprayed over his front window. McConnell had just blocked a vote on a House bill that would have increased the size of stimulus payments in the most recent COVID relief bill.

On January 2, violence also broke out in Salem, Oregon, where police clashed with pro-Trump demonstrators, including members of the Proud Boys, who were objecting to the election results as well as coronavirus restrictions.

In Wisconsin that day, five hundred National Guard members were being drawn up to help support local police maintain order amid protests expected for the upcoming arraignment of Kyle Rittenhouse, an Illinois teen charged with fatally shooting two people during civil rights demonstrations in Kenosha. Rittenhouse had come to Kenosha offering to help defend local business owners from protesters who took to the streets after police there shot and paralyzed Jacob Blake, a twenty-nine-year-old Black man.

And in Washington, security preparations for the January 6 protests continued. Ten groups had filed applications for protest marches and rally sites, and police estimated 15,000 protesters would descend on the nation's capital to object to the election results. Some 7,000 law enforcement officers, on top of roughly 340 D.C. National Guard members, were ready to keep the peace. One piece of good news: Leading anti-Trump activists were urging their followers not to show up to counterprotest, which presumably would cut down on skirmishes.

At the same time, Pentagon leaders and other national security officials were closely watching an uptick in aggressive rhetoric from leaders in Iran, where a significant date was approaching. January 3 would mark the one-year anniversary of the killing of Iranian general Qassim Soleimani by U.S. forces. In the days leading up to January 3, Iranian officials had been making threats about seeking revenge for the death of their Quds Force commander. In a routine morning meeting on January 2, Milley and his colleagues conferred about Iran's saber-rattling, including a speech by Iranian president Hassan Rouhani the night before in which he seemed to make a thinly veiled threat on Trump's life.

"Trump . . . will soon be deposed not just from office but from life," Rouhani said. "The disappearance of the criminal Trump will bring quiet and stability to the region and throughout the world. He perpetrated many crimes but the economic embargo on Iran and the assassination of [Qassim] Soleimani are crimes we cannot forgive." He added that Iran's payback would come "at a time and place that it sees fit."

Rouhani's statement stumped U.S. officials. Iran's leader could have been issuing a bona fide threat of assassination, a tough-sounding but ultimately hollow threat to impress his own citizenry, or a chest-beating tease about Trump losing reelection. Late in the day January 2, Robert O'Brien called for a meeting at the White House with Trump the following day to discuss the Iranian threats. The dangers overseas—and the ad-hominem nature of the Iranian leader's comments—had forced Trump to cut short his holiday vacation at Mar-a-Lago to return to the White House.

Given everything that was going on, Milley had to keep one eye on Iran and the other on Washington. The Joint Chiefs of Staff chairman was concerned that day, having taken stock of the increasingly unhinged tone of Trump's tweets just before midnight the night before. Trump repeatedly complained about all the ways the election had been corrupt. As the president told it on Twitter, he had actually won Georgia, but Stacey Abrams intervened to stop him; changes in state election laws made the entire results both illegal and invalid; and the vote count in Wisconsin should have been tossed out. Trump insisted he had lost due to massive fraud, continuing to push theories of manipulated Dominion machines, illegal ballot dumps, and other conspiracies. By now, more than eighty judges of both political parties had concluded the president had no leg to stand on. But recent polls showed two thirds of Republican voters believed the election was illegitimate.

Milley told close aides that listening to the president was like reading George Orwell's **1984.** "Lies are truth. Division is unity. Evil is good," the general said, mimicking the dystopian novel.

But it was Trump's call to action that most worried Milley. "January 6th. See you in D.C.," the president wrote to his Twitter followers. Trump had been steadily promoting the event like a celebrity boxing match, and roughly ten days earlier had reminded his fans to come to Washington: "Be there, will be wild." On OANN, a steady drumbeat of advertisements aired promoting the upcoming march. "The cavalry is coming," one read. "Time not to be silent," read another.

Milley told his staff that he believed Trump was stoking unrest, possibly in hopes of an excuse to invoke the Insurrection Act and call out the military. He had also shared his concerns with a few trusted peers. They and several others were worried, too. The night of January 2, Milley got a heads-up from a former defense secretary that all ten living former secretaries of defense had reached the same conclusion. They were about to publish an opinion piece in **The Washington Post** warning the current Pentagon leaders they should never allow the military to be used to settle election disputes or interrupt the peaceful transfer of power.

A student of history, Milley saw Trump as the classic authoritarian leader with nothing to lose. He described to aides that he kept having this stomach-churning feeling that some of the worrisome early stages of twentieth-century fascism in Germany were replaying in twenty-first-century America. He saw parallels between Trump's rhetoric of election fraud and Adolf Hitler's insistence to his followers at the Nuremberg rallies that he was both a victim and their savior.

"This is a Reichstag moment," Milley told aides. "The gospel of the Führer."

After states certified their election results on December 14, they sent their electoral college votes to Congress to be counted and affirmed on January 6. This event had long been a ceremonial formality, officiated by the vice president, acting in his or her capacity as president of the Senate. In this case, Vice President Pence was set to certify Biden's victory. As painful as that might be, there was precedent: Vice

President Al Gore had certified George W. Bush's win in 2001 and Vice President Walter Mondale had done the same for Ronald Reagan in 1981.

But Trump imagined a different scenario. The president became convinced that Pence had the power to refuse to accept votes from such key states as Arizona, Georgia, and Pennsylvania, and to send them back citing concerns with the tallies. Then, Republicans in those state legislatures could maneuver on his behalf to somehow overturn the election results, or at least delay the ultimate outcome.

Most lawyers and constitutional scholars believed this would be illegal; the vice president had no such authority. But not Trump's lawyers. Rudy Giuliani and Sidney Powell told the president that this junk legal theory was no slam dunk but had potential. A litany of other outside voices, whom Meadows put on the phone with the president or invited into the Oval Office for meetings in late December and early January, echoed their agreement. They included Flynn, MyPillow founder Mike Lindell, and Mark Martin, a former chief justice of the State Supreme Court in Meadows's home state of North Carolina. One after another, they told Trump that Pence not only had the power but the duty to take this drastic step. The vice president was the guy to right this wrong.

Other senior administration officials blamed Meadows for neglecting his gatekeeper role. "The president was exposed to crazy people spouting lunatic theories about the election and his ability to overturn it. That is all Meadows," one of them recalled. "He's going to pick up the phone and call people, or crazy people are going to call him, but you can limit that. You've got to get him exposed to the right people, the right dissenting voices, and channel it. Meadows did none of that. He reinforced [Trump's] instincts."

Trump told his aides several times, "The lawyers are saying we can do this. We need Mike to be strong. We've got to do something about it."

Trump irrationally expected that Pence—a model of complicity, a man he had selected as vice president in part because he could be trusted to never cross the president or challenge his authority—would boldly overturn America's two-hundred-year-old system of laws in service to his president. Trump was forcing Pence to choose between defying the Constitution—many parts of which he had memorized—and his lame-duck leader.

"It's the ultimate irony that a guy who acted like a total sycophantic pussy for four years, Trump wants him to be the Six Million Dollar Man at the end," one of Trump's advisers later remarked. "Well, shit, the guy hasn't stood up to anybody for four years and now you want him to stand up illegally, unconstitutionally to the United States Senate and the House of Representatives? Are you nuts? Have you looked at Mike Pence?"

Ever since being nominated as vice president, Pence had provided nothing but subservience to and fawning praise of Trump. He had sounded at times like a robot as he extolled Trump's virtues in virtually every public appearance, from his "broad-shouldered leadership" to his "clear vision." For Pence to reject Trump's wishes in their final month in office would be unprecedented.

Something else motivated the president at this time. The Lincoln Project aired a viral ad in mid-December that featured a haunting voice-over by a deep-voiced man: "The end is coming, Donald. Even Mike Pence knows. He's backing away from your train wreck, from your desperate lies and clown lawyers. When Mike Pence is running away from you, you know it's over. Trying to save **his** reputation, protect **his** future.

"Oh, there's one last thing, Donald," the narrator continued. "On January sixth, Mike Pence will put the nail in your political coffin when he presides over the Senate vote to prove Joe Biden won. It's over, and Mike Pence knows it."

The ad, the brainchild of top-flight Republican strategists who were proud Never Trumpers, aired only in the D.C. media market, and during commercial breaks on **Fox & Friends.** Its target audience was just one man—the president—and its aim was to prey on his paranoia about disloyalty.

It worked. Trump was furious about the ad and told Pence to send the Lincoln Project a cease-and-desist letter. Pence ignored the president's order, not wanting to draw more attention to the ad. But Pence actually wanted to fulfill Trump's wishes. A graduate of law school who also had practiced law, Pence knew enough about the Constitution to understand that his role on January 6 was merely ceremonial. He felt fairly sure there was no legal way for him to do what Trump wanted him to do. Yet Pence still was open to that possibility and explored whether any defensible option existed. Pence met regularly with Marc Short and the vice president's counsel, Greg Jacob, to hash over the extensive legal research they had conducted into his constitutional powers and historical precedent. Pence also consulted his outside counsel, Richard Cullen, and huddled with the Senate parliamentarian to understand his obligations. Pence also called Lindsey Graham, just in case the senator saw any workaround.

"No," Graham said.

"Really?" Pence asked.

"I'd tell you if I could, but I don't. I've had my people look at it," Graham replied. "Mike, I'm no constitutional lawyer, but common sense tells you you can't do this."

Some of the professionals working for Trump, including Pat Cipollone, tried to talk sense into the boss.

"Tell the vice president he needs to send the votes back. He needs to do it," Trump told Cipollone during a meeting in the president's private dining room in early January.

"He can't do that," Cipollone said. "It's not a constitutional role for him."

Walking out of the meeting, Keith Kellogg said to

Cipollone, "Pat, you need to go back in there. You need to keep pounding away at it."

"I'm not going back in there," Cipollone said. The White House counsel knew there was little he or anyone else could do to change Trump's mind.

As part of his job, Milley had developed close relationships with several lawmakers, including Senator Angus King. Their friendship had been forged at Milley's confirmation hearing in 2015 to become the army's chief of staff. King had asked Milley if he would be able to give his forceful advice when it ran counter to the administration's position.

"I want to underline the importance of that question," King said. "All of your experience, all of your knowledge, all of your wisdom that you have accumulated over the years are of no value if you do not share them. And you will be operating in the highest levels of our government in a situation that often can be intimidating. And I want to encourage you to remember that question, and when in doubt, speak up."

Milley had answered without hesitation. "Senator, I can guarantee that," he said. "I have been in a lot of combat, and I will be intimidated by no one."

A mutual respect grew between Milley and King, and in 2020 they spoke privately about their concerns over Trump's unhinged behavior. Because Milley was on high alert about January 6, he had been monitoring

Dataminr, an app that tracked specific news reports or Twitter alerts on subjects of one's choosing. Milley was checking it several times a day, looking for any sign of election protests, plans for civil unrest, or nutty calls for martial law that Flynn may have stirred up. The general knew that a small spark could set off a blaze.

Sometime in the first couple of days of January, Milley saw disconcerting chatter on Dataminr. Pro-Trump rhetoric was interlaced with calls for violence. He saw references to smuggling guns and other weapons into Washington to "stop the steal." He also saw unsettlingly personal and specific threats. One message said something along the lines of "Let's burn Senator McConnell's house down while he's in it." This wasn't inconceivable, not after McConnell's home in Kentucky had been vandalized.

"We are coming to kill you. Just wait a few days," read another message, which appeared to be aimed at members of Congress who supported certifying the election.

It was unclear whether the social media chatter represented a serious threat. Still, Milley shared with King what he was seeing. On January 2, King called Mitt Romney, knowing the Utah Republican was a likely target of Trump sympathizers. King told Romney what his senior Defense Department contact had heard. Concerned, Romney then told his wife, Ann, who was more alarmed.

"Mitt, you can't go back," Ann Romney told her

husband. She called his Senate staff and said she was fearful for his safety.

Mitt Romney tried to reassure her. "It's the Capitol and I'm careful and I do have precautions and security. I'll be very, very careful," he told his wife. He said he had a responsibility to go back to Washington and certify the election. He had to help the country move on.

Romney solidified his plans to fly to Washington while his aides arranged for some additional security to protect him at the Capitol. "What gave me a sense that there could be trouble in Washington was that the president had called for people to come to 'stop the steal,'" he recalled in an interview. "There would be normal people across the broad spectrum, but there would also be extremists, [and] there could well be violence."

Trump was not only stirring chaos on social media and calling his supporters to the streets. On January 2, the president called Raffensperger to repeatedly coerce Georgia's secretary of state to "recalculate" the statewide vote tally to put him on top. It was an egregious abuse of power, legal scholars said, and possibly a criminal act.

"All I want to do is this," Trump told Raffensperger. "I just want to find 11,780 votes, which is one more than we have. Because we won the state."

Trump repeated his request: "So what are we going to do here, folks? I only need 11,000 votes. Fellas, I need 11,000 votes. Give me a break. You know, we have that in spades already."

On the call, which was arranged by Meadows, Trump was rambling and at times nonsensical. He alternately berated and flattered Raffensperger, who along with his office's general counsel, Ryan Germany, tried to explain to the president that his assertions were based on debunked conspiracy theories and that Biden's 11,779-vote victory in Georgia was fair and accurate.

"The people of Georgia are angry, the people of the country are angry, and there's nothing wrong with saying that, you know, um, that you've recalculated," Trump said.

"Well, Mr. President, the challenge that you have is, the data you have is wrong," Raffensperger said.

Trump had tried to call Raffensperger eighteen times before he finally reached him on January 2. The president's calls kept being rerouted to interns because staff in the secretary of state's office thought they were prank calls. Raffensperger and his staff were upset by Trump's nonsensical claims and unrelenting pressure in the hour-long call. The secretary of state's office had recorded the conversation, but did not intend to release it, until Trump forced their hands. Shortly before 9:00 a.m. the next day, January 3, Trump tweeted that he had spoken to Raffensperger and "he was unwilling, or unable, to answer questions such as the 'ballots under table' scam, ballot destruction, out of state 'voters', dead voters, and more. He has no clue!"

After seeing Trump's tweet, Raffensperger authorized that the taped conversation be shared with **Washington Post** reporter Amy Gardner, who later that day published an account of the call, along with a full audio recording. The undeniable sounds of Trump's mafia tactics immediately drew condemnations.

Raffensperger would later explain that Trump only had himself to blame for the audio's release. "If President Trump wouldn't have tweeted out anything and would have stayed silent, we would have stayed silent as well. And that would have just been a conversation between him and I, man to man, and that would have been fine with us," Raffensperger said in an interview with Brendan Keefe of WXIA, Atlanta's NBC affiliate. "But he's the one that couldn't, you know, had to put it out on Twitter. And so if you're going to put out stuff that we don't believe is true, then we will respond in kind."

At the White House, some loyal Trump advisers blasted Meadows for having arranged the call. By not shielding the president from such a conversation, they thought, the chief of staff had committed political malpractice. Larry Kudlow and Meadows had been friends of long standing, but the economic adviser was furious that Trump had been allowed to be in such a compromised position.

"Mark, did you think for one minute that that call would not be leaked in its entirety?" Kudlow said to Meadows. "Are we children here or are we adults? . . . What were you thinking?"

Meadows responded sheepishly, "I couldn't stop the president. I tried, but I couldn't stop him."

On January 3, officials from the Justice Department, Defense Department, Department of Homeland Security, and local law enforcement gathered on a conference call to discuss security preparations for the January 6 events. One official reviewing the latest intelligence said there were no clear indications of an attack but warned that hotel occupancy rates and the number of incoming buses suggested that the crowd would be slightly larger than the pro-Trump demonstrations in Washington in November and December. A Homeland Security operations chief said his agency had picked up chatter of some folks traveling to Washington with intent to do violence but concluded the overall threat from these protests wasn't significant.

A domestic security briefer told the group, "Our biggest concern is when the sun goes down, just like what happened on 12 December and 14 November." At those rallies, fights broke out at night between pro-Trump demonstrators and counterprotesters. O'Brien advised that security in and around the White House had been increased and that he believed the Secret Service had the complex well buttoned up, though he said there could be serious danger if counterprotesters showed up to bedevil the pro-Trump crowd.

That afternoon, the op-ed from the ten living defense secretaries—including Dick Cheney, Donald Rumsfeld, and Jim Mattis—was published on the **Washington Post** website. The piece never mentioned Trump's name and yet it was all about him. It raised the possibility of Trump using the military to interfere in the transition and issued a not-so-subtle threat to Miller, the acting defense secretary, and Trump's newly installed toadies.

"Efforts to involve the U.S. armed forces in resolving election disputes would take us into dangerous, unlawful and unconstitutional territory," the former secretaries wrote. "Civilian and military officials who direct or carry out such measures would be accountable, including potentially facing criminal penalties, for the grave consequences of their actions on our republic."

At about 5:30 p.m., top military and national security officials convened in the Oval Office to meet with Trump about the Iranian threats. Meadows, O'Brien, Cipollone, Miller, Milley, Patel, and Mike Pompeo were there. The president wanted to reopen a decision that Miller had just issued to return the USS **Nimitz,** one of the navy's largest aircraft carriers, to its home base in California. Trump, who always wanted to look tough, hoped to send a message to the Iranians by routing the aircraft carrier back to patrolling the Arabian Sea. The conversation was rational and without any drama or vitriol. Most of the generals agreed that's what should happen. Trump so ordered it.

General Frank McKenzie of the U.S. Central Command was especially pleased. He had earlier made a special request that the carrier remain in theater amid the threats of revenge on Americans on the anniversary of Soleimani's killing and had been surprised when Miller proceeded to ignore him and withdraw the ship. The easiest target for Iranian attackers would be U.S. troops in the region, he thought, and the **Nimitz** could provide significant support in staving off such an assault. The conversation in the Oval then shifted to public relations. How would the government explain the decision to turn the aircraft carrier around? They decided it would send a strong message if they were clear the change was due to Iran's threats.

At the tail end of the meeting, in an exchange that lasted about ninety seconds, Trump shifted the topic to the upcoming protests. He turned to look at Miller. "You've got enough guys and you're all set for the sixth of January?" he asked.

"Oh yes, Mr. President," Miller replied. "We've got a plan."

Trump nodded.

"Just make sure it's all safe," Trump said.

Milley thought this was pretty benign and that Trump sounded genuine. Still, when the meeting wrapped up, he approached Miller privately. Milley wanted to be clear that when Trump said "you're all set," he was referring only to National Guard capabilities.

"There's nothing else set, right?" Milley asked.

Miller told him, yes, the National Guard was all the president meant. Nothing else was in the works.

On January 4, Pentagon officials received a morning update on preparations for January 6 and learned the FBI had no credible reports of dangerous threats, but that the crowd estimate had risen to twenty thousand based on hotel occupancy levels. The weather forecast was a clear day without rain, not what law enforcement officials hoping for a low turnout wanted to hear.

Homeland Security officials reported that the two main points of protest would be at the Capitol and at the Ellipse near the White House. Washington D.C. National Guard Commander William Walker said his team was helping D.C. police man key checkpoints, and D.C. police seemed to believe they had enough Guard support. The Secret Service asked for five military civil support teams to help them in and around the White House. The FBI flagged in a briefing later that afternoon that agents had seen an increase in violent rhetoric on social media, just as Milley had on Dataminr, but there was nothing specific they could act on.

At the White House, meanwhile, staffers were preparing for Trump to address the "Save America" rally at the Ellipse on January 6. Advance staff considered the best places to hang signs and mapped out where the president would stand and what the camera angles might be. Secret Service officers prepared how and when to safely move the president from the White House to the rally space. It was one thing for the president to encourage his supporters to gather in solidarity with his quest to overturn the election; it was another for him to take the stage and make the event his own. Some of Trump's advisers objected.

"Holy cow," Kudlow told Meadows when he found out Trump would be speaking. "We shouldn't go near it."

"It's going to be okay," Meadows assured him. "It's going to be okay."

On January 4, Trump was due in Dalton, Georgia, for a massive nighttime rally with Perdue and Loeffler on the eve of the runoff. But the president's mind was not on the Senate and whether Republicans would retain their majority. It was on whether he could retain his power. Before departing late that afternoon, Trump met in the Oval Office with Pence, who had just returned from a campaign trip earlier in the day to Georgia. They were joined by Giuliani and John Eastman, a law professor with solid conservative credentials, having clerked for Supreme Court justice Clarence Thomas and served as dean of the Chapman University School of Law.

Eastman had a history with Trump. He had been

encouraging the president earlier in the year to end birthright citizenship by executive order, something Barr had worked repeatedly to prevent from happening. When Barr had argued to Trump that an order taking people's citizenship away retroactively would never stand up in court, the president said he knew a legal scholar who claimed the opposite. Eastman argued that the president could clarify by executive order that citizenship does not extend to children born of parents who were only temporarily visiting the United States.

In the run-up to January 6, Eastman had argued that Pence could conceivably object to certification and send electoral votes back to states and force state legislatures to review the votes. This helped get Trump all spun up, though even Eastman realized this was merely a theory, not a likely outcome. But Trump, always optimistic about his chances, eagerly pursued Eastman's legal theory. In the January 4 meeting with Pence, Trump introduced Eastman to the vice president.

"This guy's a really respected constitutional lawyer," Trump said. "He thinks you have more authority. Let's talk it through."

Eastman discussed two historical examples of vice presidents intervening during certification. The first was from 1801, when then vice president Thomas Jefferson presided over the certification of his own election as president. There was a dispute over certifying Georgia's slate of electors because a page was missing due to a clerical error. Jefferson refused to wait and simply accepted electors from Georgia in his favor. This was an imperfect analogy, however, because Jefferson's victory in Georgia was never in dispute. Furthermore, the Twelfth Amendment, which passed in 1804, clarified the process, and the Electoral Count Act of 1887 clarified it even further.

Eastman's second example was from 1961. Then vice president Richard Nixon was presiding over his own loss to John F. Kennedy as president. This was the first presidential election since Hawaii became a state. Hawaii sent Congress two slates of electors, one for Nixon who was initially thought to have won, and a second for Kennedy, who prevailed narrowly in a recount. Nixon wanted to count the slate for Kennedy—a magnanimous gesture to help heal the country since Kennedy was the clear winner overall—and asked Congress if there were any objections. There were none, so Nixon certified the Kennedy slate from Hawaii. Though 1961 presented a very narrow and unique situation, Eastman oddly argued that Nixon set a precedent for vice presidents choosing which electors to certify, as if that empowered Pence to unilaterally dismiss electors from some states that Biden won.

Pence, who was accompanied by Jacob and Short, calmly and politely refuted Eastman's arguments. He explained why the Jefferson and Nixon examples were in no way analogous to the current moment. The vice president called the Hawaii case a red herring, arguing that sending electors back to the states would be fruitless because the states already had certified their election results. Pence walked Trump through the overall analysis Jacob had provided based on extensive research: There was simply no legal way for him to reject the electors or otherwise act unilaterally to overturn the election. The Constitution would not permit it.

After the meeting, Eastman acknowledged to Giuliani, "There's no chance any of this is going to happen." Later, Eastman would deny that Pence had refuted his arguments.

Trump was unconvinced by Pence's presentation. He soon walked out of the Oval and boarded Marine One to begin his trek to Dalton. On the trip, Donald Trump Jr. got Trump riled up again about Pence. The president's eldest son did not believe the vice president was fighting hard enough to keep Trump in office. "He's weak," Trump Jr. told his father.

Graham traveled with the president and tried to counter the Pence hate. "He can't do what you're asking him to do," Graham told Trump. "If Al Gore tried this, we would have all been rioting in the streets."

Trump responded by suggesting Gore wasn't smart enough to try to block certification. "They didn't think about it," he said.

"Oh, okay," Graham said facetiously.

When Trump took the rally stage in Dalton, he was supposed to be motivating his supporters to vote for Perdue and Loeffler. Instead, he gave them reason to doubt the integrity of the state's elections. The very first words out of the president's mouth were: "I want to thank you very much. Hello, Georgia. By the way, there's no way we lost Georgia. There's no way. That was a rigged election. But we're still fighting it, and you'll see what's going to happen."

"I've had two elections," he added. "I won both of them. It's amazing. I actually did much better on the second one."

None of that was true. The rally devolved from there into a classic Trump grievance fest. About eight minutes into his remarks, the president threatened the man who had stood by him more faithfully than anyone.

"I hope Mike Pence comes through for us, I have to tell you," Trump said. "I hope that our great vice president comes through for us. He's a great guy. Of course, if he doesn't come through, I won't like him quite as much. No, Mike is a great guy. He's a wonderful man and a smart man and a man that I like a lot, but he's going to have a lot to say about it."

After days of privately pressuring Pence to do what the law would not allow, Trump had turned on him publicly. The president's comments disgusted some senior White House officials. One of them recalled, "Pence had been such a loyalist during the whole four-year period. My God. We all took bullets for the guy, but Pence went out straightening misstatements and taking bullets on everything. How the president could go after Pence as disloyal was insane to me. And you had these outside nutjobs—I don't even want to call them conservatives; I'll say Trumpists—who were picking on Pence. That made my blood boil."

In Colorado that night, Mike Luttig, a former federal appeals court judge, a lifelong conservative, and a respected expert on the Constitution, was having dinner with his wife at their getaway home. The phone rang and Cullen, Luttig's good friend, was on the other end of the line, calling from his home in Virginia, where it was about 9:00.

"We've got an issue," Cullen said, pausing briefly. "It's John Eastman."

The Pence team was shaken by Eastman's insistence to Trump about the vice president's authority to block certification. Short had looked up Eastman's biography and saw that he had once clerked for Luttig. He knew Luttig had an esteemed pedigree and his views were influential in conservative circles. Short and Cullen discussed the Eastman problem and his connection to Luttig.

When Cullen called, Luttig said he knew Eastman as a former clerk, but added, "Richard, I don't even know what you're talking about."

"Did you know John Eastman's advising the president?" Cullen asked.

The former judge was curious. He said he had not known that. On what in particular?

"He's advising the president that the vice president

doesn't have to accept the electoral college vote," Cullen said.

Luttig had been very open about his opinion of the law: Pence had no choice but to accept the state-certified election counts. But he found this new information a strange development: Eastman, a legal scholar Luttig respected, was telling Trump there was some legal reason Pence could not certify the vote.

Luttig asked Cullen, "The president is killing the vice president based on Eastman's advice, right?"

"Right," Cullen said. "And it's coming to a head tomorrow."

"Now look, John is a brilliant constitutional scholar. Whatever John is telling the president has some basis in the law," Luttig said. But a scholarly analysis of historical precedents and Senate rules was a vastly different enterprise than giving a client legal advice that would hold up in court, Luttig said. And Eastman was a scholar, not normally in the business of advising clients.

The two friends said good night and planned to talk again in the morning.

It was barely 6:00 a.m. in Colorado on January 5 when Cullen called back.

"Okay, here's the deal," he told Luttig. "The V.P. has to make the decision today and has to confront the president.

"Is there anything you can do to help the vice president?" Cullen asked.

"Well, I've been thinking about it overnight," Luttig said. "I don't know what I could do.

I ALONE CAN FIX IT

"Look, of course you can tell the vice president that I said he has no choice under these circumstances but to accept the electoral college vote."

"I know that," Cullen said. "I'll do that, of course. But I've already told him that."

Luttig paused.

"When does the vice president need me to do something?" Luttig asked.

"Immediately," Cullen said.

Luttig's mind was racing. And then he had an idea. "Well, Richard, I guess I could tweet something," he said.

Cullen said that would be very helpful. A piece of legal advice offered in a public forum by a judge heralded in conservative circles would give Pence some backup with Trump.

Luttig chuckled at himself in this important moment. He wasn't a technological Luddite, but he wasn't a regular tweeter either. He couldn't give a legal opinion in 240 characters, so he would need to connect the tweets. He asked his son to send him some instructions for creating a thread. Then he sent a draft of what he would write to Cullen. He didn't want to tweet something Pence wouldn't approve.

Cullen shared it with Short and then wrote back to Luttig by email.

"Okay, the vice president would appreciate this," Cullen said.

Luttig drafted each thread and, at 9:53 a.m. Eastern time, hit the blue "Tweet" button.

"The only responsibility and power of the Vice President under the Constitution is to faithfully count the electoral college votes as they have been cast," Luttig wrote. "The Constitution does not empower the Vice President to alter in any way the votes that have been cast, either by rejecting certain of them or otherwise. How the Vice President discharges this constitutional obligation is not a question of his loyalty to the President."

Later in the day on January 5, more danger warnings emerged about what was in store for Washington. The ever-watchful Milley got a call from Senator Dan Sullivan in the early afternoon. The Alaska Republican and former Marine said he had just finished a run on the National Mall, where he had seen groups of protesters gathering ahead of the next day's demonstrations. Sullivan sensed trouble brewing.

"What's the plan for security?" Sullivan asked Milley. "I heard in the news that the D.C. National Guard is being called up. Crowd control is a difficult mission. And these are good people," he said of the Trump supporters in town, some of whom had come all the way from Alaska. "The troops need to be prepared and we don't need any Kent States," Sullivan added, referring to the 1970 shooting of unarmed college students at an antiwar protest by members of the Ohio National Guard that left four dead.

Later that day, Romney went to the Salt Lake City

International Airport to catch a flight to Washington, despite his wife's concerns for his safety. Two days earlier, Romney had issued a statement calling the push to block certification—a dozen Republican senators, led by Ted Cruz of Texas, had since joined Hawley in this gambit—an "egregious ploy" that "may enhance the political ambition of some, but dangerously threatens our Democratic Republic." At the airport, Romney was working on his iPad as he waited in the terminal to board his flight when a maskless woman approached.

"Why aren't you supporting President Trump?" she asked, holding out her cell phone to record video of the interaction.

"I do support President Trump in things I agree with," Romney said.

The woman asked if Romney was going to support Trump's claims about the "fraudulent votes."

"No, I'm not," Romney said. "We have a Constitution and the constitutional process is clear and I will follow the Constitution, and then I will explain all that when we meet in Congress."

Romney then stood up and walked away. A man told him, "Your legacy is nothing." And the woman said, "You're a joke. Absolute joke."

On board the plane, Romney discovered many of the other passengers were Trump supporters en route to Washington, presumably for the next day's protests. At one point in the flight, a woman cried out to other passengers to tell the senator "what we think." A large group of passengers then chanted, "Traitor! Traitor! Traitor!" One of them shouted, "Resign, Mitt!"

Videos of Romney's terminal interactions and of the onboard heckling were posted on Twitter and went viral.

A little later that evening, the Georgia results came in. It was a bloodbath for Republicans. Warnock defeated Loeffler by 93,550 votes, and Ossoff defeated Perdue by 54,944 votes. The Democrats had taken the Senate. Too many Republican voters believed their vote wouldn't count and stayed home. It was just as McConnell feared, and he was now the minority leader.

Graham called Trump that night to let him know that he planned to vote the next day to certify the presidential election results. Trump was upset and appealed to Graham to join Cruz, Hawley, and the other rebels set on objecting. But Graham wouldn't have it.

"Mr. President, I've been very supportive of you challenging, but there's no more asphalt on the highway," Graham told him. "We've come to an end here."

Twenty-one

The Insurrection

As the sun rose over Washington on January 6, electricity hung in the air. The big day had come. Thousands of President Trump's supporters began gathering at the Ellipse to stake out a good spot from which to see the president, who was scheduled to address the "Save America" rally around noon. Organizers had obtained a federal permit for thirty thousand people, but it looked as if the crowd would be even larger than that. Thousands more prepared to make their way toward the Capitol to protest the certification of Joe Biden's election.

At the White House, Trump set the tone for the day with an 8:17 a.m. tweet: "States want to correct their votes, which they now know were based on irregularities and fraud, plus corrupt process never received legislative approval. All Mike Pence has to do is send them back to the States, AND WE WIN. Do it Mike, this is a time for extreme courage!"

Many of Trump's advisers knew this would never actually happen. They chalked the president's tweet up to theater. Vice President Pence could have the courage of a lion, but there was no doubt he would fulfill his constitutional duty and preside over the pro forma certification of Biden's win. As one senior official recalled, "All of us knew this was the endgame. The clock had run out. By January sixth, it was game over. . . . We knew we would take the blows. This was date certain. The vice president knew this."

As Nancy Pelosi left her luxury condo building in Georgetown, she greeted her security agents who would drive her to the Capitol. "This is going to be quite a day," the House Speaker said to them. She kept the rest of her thoughts to herself, but later recalled thinking, "I know the Republicans will try some stunts. But at the end of the day, Joe Biden will be the president of the United States—the ascertained future president." She was prepared for Republicans to try some parliamentary shenanigans to slow down the certification.

In the Oval Office later that morning, Trump huddled with some aides and family members. The president went in and out of the dining room to check on TV coverage, hoping to gauge the size of the crowd at the Ellipse. Stephen Miller was there going over the remarks he and his team had prepared for the president to deliver at the rally. Trump read some of the lines aloud. Mark Meadows, Keith Kellogg, and Eric Herschmann were there, too, as were Donald Trump Jr., Ivanka Trump, Eric Trump, and Kimberly Guilfoyle. Trump talked about his rally as well as what he thought might happen at the Capitol when lawmakers convened. Some of those around him encouraged his fantasy of Pence the hero stepping in to overturn the election. Guilfoyle, referring to the growing crowd at the Ellipse, told the president, "They're just reflecting the will of the people. **This** is the will of the people."

Ivanka Trump did not agree and was upset about what Rudy Giuliani and others had been advising her father. At one point that morning, she said, "This is not right. It's not right."

Trump called Pence, who was spending the morning at his Naval Observatory residence before heading to the Capitol. Pence again explained to Trump the legal limits on his authority as vice president and said he planned to perform his ceremonial duty, as prescribed by the Constitution. But Trump showed him no mercy.

"You don't have the courage to make a hard decision," Trump told Pence.

Ivanka Trump, standing next to Kellogg near the grandfather clock in the back of the room, had a hard time listening to her father badger the vice president to do something she knew was not possible. "Mike Pence is a good man," she said quietly to Kellogg.

"I know that," he replied. "Let this ride. Take a deep breath. We'll come back at it."

After hanging up with Pence, Trump went back into the dining room to check on the crowd on TV. Kellogg subtly suggested to Ivanka Trump that she follow him. "Go back in there and talk to your dad," he said.

Ivanka Trump already had been thinking about how she might calm her father and convince him to see the situation rationally. She then spoke with the president but was unpersuasive. Trump had given Pence instructions and was hell-bent on getting him to follow through.

Meanwhile, at the U.S. Capitol Police headquarters near Union Station, Chief Steven Sund had gathered with some of his assistant chiefs, commanders, and other senior aides in their command center to monitor protests that day. They took their assigned stations around an enormous U-shaped desk, with the chief at the top of the U, facing a wall of screens playing live video feeds of protesters gathering around the city, including at various portions of the Capitol grounds and entrances. The images would help them coordinate with commanders on the ground.

A twenty-five-year veteran of security planning for major D.C. events and protests, Sund suggested a technician pull up on the center screen the live broadcast of the crowds gathering at the Ellipse for the Save America rally. It was a chilly day in Washington, the temperature barely hitting 40 degrees, but at the Ellipse, Trump's supporters were energetic and bois- terous. Despite the permit for thirty thousand, police estimated there could be as many as forty thousand people assembling.

Just before 11:00 a.m., the police commanders heard Giuliani onstage telling the crowd the many reasons Pence should not certify the election results that afternoon: "criminality" in the vote tallies; "cor- rupt" voting machines; states "begging" for a recount; the "unconstitutionality" of an 1800s election law. But then Giuliani said a phrase, best known from the HBO series **Game of Thrones,** that caught a few of the commanders' attention: "Let's have trial by combat." Why was Giuliani suggesting a fight to the death?

Standing onstage with Giuliani was John Eastman. He spoke next, but the two functioned as a tag team. Screaming into the microphone, Eastman alleged that election officials stored ballots "in a secret folder in the machines" until late on election night and, once polls closed and officials determined who had voted and who had not, could "match those unvoted ballots with an unvoted voter and put them together in the machine" to give Biden just enough votes to win. This was a new far-fetched theory for which the Trump team had no evidence, yet the crowd ate it up. So did Giuliani, who grinned widely and flashed a thumbs-up.

Mo Brooks, the Alabama congressman who was

among the first to say he would try to block certification, said from the stage, "Today is the day American patriots start taking down names and kicking ass!" The crowd roared with approval.

Under a large tent backstage at the rally, Trump hung out with his entourage of family, aides, and Secret Service agents before stepping out to deliver his speech. There was a party atmosphere. Laura Branigan's 1982 hit "Gloria" boomed over the loudspeakers. Trump Jr. filmed the scene with his cell phone to post on Instagram. "I think we're T-minus a couple of seconds here, guys, so check it out. Tune in if you're livestreaming," the president's son said. He turned the camera to Meadows and called him "an actual fighter," then turned it to Guilfoyle. After realizing she was being filmed, she began dancing to the music and implored Trump's supporters to "have the courage to do the right thing—fight!"

Ivanka Trump was spotted in the tent, too, tending to her father. Melania Trump had chosen not to attend the Save America rally, telling aides she was not sure it was a good idea for her to participate. The first lady was busy that morning overseeing a scheduled photo shoot of rugs and other décor items in the residence for use by the White House Historical Association. Yet the first daughter, who typically was just as careful as the first lady about when and where she appeared in public, attended, which surprised other White House officials.

"You who curates your image, you who looks down

on many of the rest of us, what are you doing there? Honestly," a Trump adviser remarked about Ivanka Trump's presence.

Ivanka Trump did not appear onstage, however. Rally organizers repeatedly had asked her to give a speech, but she declined. The first daughter told aides she had become increasingly uncomfortable with efforts to overturn the election results. Yet she told them she decided to attend because she had hoped to calm the president and help keep the event on an even keel.

At noon, Trump took the stage. Sund and his team at Capitol Police headquarters turned up the volume a bit and heard the thundering applause. At the Pentagon, Mark Milley was watching on television from his office as well, deeply disturbed by the rhetoric. He told aides he thought the whole scene was a national embarrassment.

Trump opened his speech as he often began campaign rallies, boasting about the throngs of people who had come to see him and complaining that the media didn't fairly cover his immense popularity. Then he got into the reason they were all there.

"Our country has had enough," Trump said. "We will not take it anymore, and that's what this is all about. To use a favorite term that all of you people really came up with, we will 'stop the steal.' Today I will lay out just some of the evidence proving that we won this election, and we won it by a landslide."

Trump repeated more lies about the election

outcome and then paused to praise Giuliani and Eastman for both doing a "fantastic job. I watched. That's a tough act to follow, those two."

Trump said of Giuliani, "He's got guts, unlike a lot of people in the Republican Party. He's got guts. He fights." And of Eastman, he said, "John is one of the most brilliant lawyers in the country, and he looked at this and he said, 'What an absolute disgrace that this could be happening to our Constitution.' He looked at Mike Pence, and I hope Mike is going to do the right thing. I hope so. I hope so, because if Mike Pence does the right thing, we win the election."

Trump added, "States want to revote. The states got defrauded. They were given false information. They voted on it. Now they want to recertify. They want it back. All Vice President Pence has to do is send it back to the states to recertify and we become president, and you are the happiest people. I just spoke to Mike. I said, 'Mike, that doesn't take courage. What takes courage is to do nothing. That takes courage.' And then we're stuck with a president who lost the election by a lot, and we have to live with that for four more years. We're not going to let that happen."

Trump concluded his speech by urging his supporters to march to the Capitol and suggesting he would join them. He said, "Mike Pence is going to have to come through for us," and that "it is up to Congress to confront this egregious assault on our democracy."

"We're going to walk down to the Capitol and we're

going to cheer on our brave senators and congress-
men and women," Trump said. He added, "We're
going to try and give our Republicans—the weak
ones, because the strong ones don't need any of our
help—we're going to try and give them the kind
of pride and boldness that they need to take back
our country."

At noon, the same time Trump began speaking
at his rally, police reported that roughly three
hundred members of the Proud Boys were outside
the Capitol. About twenty minutes into the speech,
Capitol Police received reports about suspected bombs
in Capitol Hill: suspicious packages at the Supreme
Court and near the Democratic National Committee
headquarters as well as a pipe bomb with a timer
found outside the Republican National Committee
headquarters. Police in that area also soon after found
an unoccupied red pickup truck with Alabama tags
containing a handgun, an M4 Carbine assault rifle,
loaded magazines of ammunition, and components
to make eleven Molotov cocktails with mason jars,
lighters, rags, and other ignitable substances.

At the Capitol Police's command center, Sund and
his team had turned their attention to the bomb threats
and muted Trump's speech so commanders could confer with officers in the field. They did not hear Trump
urge his supporters to march on the Capitol, but
within a few minutes of his call, thousands of people

started walking down Pennsylvania and Constitution avenues toward the Capitol.

They were pouring into the streets to join the first pack of Trump's supporters who had already hit the barricades hard on the Capitol's western front. That first and more organized group had arrived at 12:45, while the president was still speaking at the Ellipse. They clearly intended to force their way up to the building. It was easy to do, as the outer barricades had very few officers stationed nearby, so the streaming crowds quickly knocked over the temporary fencing that resembled bike racks and stormed onward toward the foundation and series of outdoor steps and patios. Many rushed toward the raised platform that had been partially set up for Biden's inauguration, just two weeks away.

Even from their command center several blocks away from the Capitol, Sund and his team could sense a level of preparation on the part of the protesters. Some of the men leading the first charge and snaking their way up the hill were barking into walkie-talkies in their hands. Many wore backpacks, and some had on battle helmets and bulletproof vests.

At around the same time, Pence arrived at the Capitol to begin the day's proceedings, set to start at 1:00. Just as his motorcade deposited him on the building's eastern front, the vice president's office released a three-page letter to members of Congress signed by Pence outlining his interpretation of his legal duties and the limits of his power as presiding officer. In it, Pence wrote, "I share the concerns of millions of Americans about the integrity of this election" and that he would ensure they "receive a fair and open hearing."

But, Pence added, "As a student of history who loves the Constitution and reveres its Framers, I do not believe that the Founders of our country intended to invest the Vice President with unilateral authority to decide which electoral votes should be counted during the Joint Session of Congress, and no Vice President in American history has ever asserted such authority. Instead, Vice Presidents presiding over Joint Sessions have uniformly followed the Electoral Count Act, conducting the proceedings in an orderly manner even where the count resulted in the defeat of their party or their own candidacy."

Pence cited his own "careful study of our Constitution, our laws, and our history," and quoted from Michael Luttig's tweeted legal analysis in his letter. The vice president vowed to hear objections raised by senators and representatives, and then to count the votes of the electoral college "in a manner consistent with our Constitution, laws, and history." His final words: "So Help Me God."

Outside the Capitol, the pro-Trump protest was quickly morphing into a battle scene. Demonstrators so outnumbered law enforcement that hundreds of Capitol Police officers on the western front of the complex had no chance of holding the crowds away from the grounds. They retreated to create a tighter blockade around the Capitol's grand external balconies and steps, all with the goal of keeping people away from the immediate building. This was no ordinary political protest. It was a riot. Many of those crashing through the outer barricades were wearing military gear, carrying Trump flags, and some were wielding pipes, batons, and cans of bear spray as weapons. A few had climbing gear, and some even brought night goggles and fire-retardant gloves. Some engaged in hand-to-hand combat with the police officers, who chose not to fire on the crowd for fear of triggering gruesome violence.

By 12:58, Sund knew his officers were getting slammed and they wouldn't be able to stop the onslaught shoving its way toward the halls of Congress. He needed to declare an emergency and call in reinforcements. He called the House Sergeant at Arms, Paul Irving, requesting he and the Senate Sergeant at Arms, Michael Stenger, approve the emergency declaration and call in the National Guard immediately. Irving said he would get back to him after "running it up the chain," presumably getting approval from Pelosi and Mitch McConnell.

By the time Trump finished his speech about 1:10, the police's command over the escalating crisis on the Capitol grounds was rapidly breaking down; captains and commanders in charge of relaying instructions to officers abandoned their supervisor posts and rushed to lend a hand to their officers getting crushed on the battle lines. Captain Thomas Lloyd, stationed inside the Capitol, ran down the steps to help officers hold the waist-high fencing that rioters were trying to yank out of their hands. As he joined his compatriots, Lloyd landed a few punches on the faces of rioters on the opposite side. Sund had moments earlier called D.C. Metropolitan Police for emergency backup; D.C. Chief Robert Contee III dispatched two armed tactical teams to the scene and they arrived in their bright yellow vests at 1:13.

Inside the Capitol, the joint session was under way in the House Chamber. Lawmakers from both chambers began considering electoral vote counts state by state, in alphabetical order, but were interrupted by a Republican objection to Arizona's tally and soon disbanded. Senators returned to the Senate Chamber for debate, where at 1:35 McConnell rose to strenuously condemn the move by some of his Republican brethren to block certification.

Reading from a carefully prepared text, McConnell said, "The Constitution gives us here in Congress a limited role. We cannot simply declare ourselves a National Board of Elections on steroids. The voters, the courts, and the states have all spoken. They've all spoken. If we overrule them, it would damage our republic forever. This election, actually, was not unusually close. Just in recent history, 1976, 2000 and 2004 were all closer than this one. The electoral college margin is almost identical to what it was in 2016. [If] this election were overturned by mere allegations from the losing side, our democracy would enter a death spiral. We'd never see the whole nation accept an election again. Every four years would be a scramble for power at any cost."

McConnell and most of his colleagues, who were seated at their desks on the Senate floor and engaged in the certification debate, did not know about the mayhem building outside. But Mitt Romney had been more attentive than others, after getting the tip-off from Angus King and being harassed on his flight to Washington. Romney's phone buzzed with a text message from aide Chris Marroletti.

"I'm not liking what's happening outside the Capitol," Marroletti wrote to his boss. "There are really big, violent demonstrations going on. I think you ought to leave."

"Let me know if they get inside the Capitol and I will go to my hideaway," Romney texted back.

Meanwhile, Sund called Irving four more times to check on the holdup in getting an emergency declaration. He was losing patience. At 1:50, with violent renegades on the cusp of breaking into the building, two momentous decisions came down in unison. A D.C. police commander on the scene officially declared a riot, and Sund called General William Walker, commander of the D.C. National Guard, and told him he needed his soldiers to come help immediately.

Just outside the Capitol, the first fatality was recorded at 2:05. Kevin Greeson, a fifty-five-year-old Trump supporter from Alabama who had joined the protest, died after suffering a heart attack.

Sund got the emergency declaration from his bosses at 2:07, after rioters were already at the Capitol's windows and doors trying to beat them open. At 2:10 the first rioter, Dominic Pezzola, a forty-three-year-old member of the Proud Boys from upstate New York, entered the Capitol by breaking through a window and climbing inside. A stream of Trump warriors followed him.

In the Senate Chamber, where Pence was presiding at the rostrum, Romney was the first to move. After Marroletti texted him, "They're inside the Capitol," Romney walked off the floor and started to make his way alone toward his small hideaway office in the Capitol. He ran into Capitol Police Officer Eugene Goodman, who was guarding the area outside the chamber. "Go back in," Goodman instructed Romney. "There are people not far. You'll be safer inside." Romney turned around and returned to his desk on the Senate floor.

Senator James Lankford was in the middle of arguing against certifying the vote given that the public had so many concerns about fraud, when officers rushed in, guns drawn, and began shutting the main doors to the chamber to protect the senators inside. At 2:13, Pence's Secret Service detail removed the vice president from the Senate floor and took him through a side door to his ceremonial office nearby, along with his wife, Karen, their daughter Charlotte, and his brother, Greg, a congressman from Indiana. The Pences were hurried across one of the Capitol's many ornate marble hallways to get there, but the path proved eerily close to danger. One or two minutes later, marauders chanting Pence's name charged up the stairs to that precise landing in front of the hallway, and a quick-thinking Goodman led the rioters in a different direction, away from the Senate Chamber. Had Pence walked past any later, the intruders who called him a traitor would have spotted him.

The Senate immediately went into recess. The C-SPAN feed providing live footage of the proceedings was shut off. The same was happening at the other end of the building, where plainclothes Capitol Police agents barricaded the door to the Speaker's Lobby just off the House Chamber to keep the marauders from charging in. The House adjourned at 2:20. Pelosi had been presiding when her security team yanked her from the rostrum. "I thought they were just switching off because of mischief," she later recalled. "I didn't know it was because of real danger."

Capitol Police officers whisked away the leaders of both Houses of Congress to an undisclosed safe location in the Hart Senate Office Building. Other lawmakers were evacuated, too, although the process of getting to safety proved chaotic.

"We're walking down the tunnels and there happened to be two officers there and we said, 'Where are we going?'" Romney recalled. "They said, 'Well, I'm sure the senators know.' I said, 'Well, I'm a senator and I don't know.' We didn't know where we were supposed to go."

At the White House, Trump was back in his private dining room watching everything unfold on television. Aides, including Dan Scavino and Kayleigh McEnany, popped in and out to join him. The president was riveted. His supporters had heeded his call to march on the Capitol with "pride and boldness." For Trump, there was no more beautiful sight than thousands of energetic people waving Trump flags, wearing red MAGA caps, and fighting to keep Trump in power.

"He thought, 'This is cool.' He was happy," recalled one aide who was with him that afternoon. "Then when it turned violent, he thought, 'Oh, crap.'"

Lindsey Graham said, "It took him a while to appreciate the gravity of the situation. The president saw these people as allies in his journey and sympathetic to the idea that the election was stolen."

As rioters marauded through the Capitol, it was clear who they were looking for. Some of them shouted "Hang Mike Pence!" Trump didn't exactly throw them off the hunt. At 2:24, the president tweeted, "Mike Pence didn't have the courage to do what should have been done to protect our Country and our Constitution."

Trump also tried to call Senator Tommy Tuberville, a newly elected Alabama Republican who was helping lead the effort to block certification, but misdialed and reached Senator Mike Lee, a Utah Republican. Lee passed his phone to Tuberville. Trump was trying to urge Tuberville to continue making objections, but Tuberville was short with him. "Mr. President, they just took the vice president out," Tuberville said. "I've got to go."

At this moment, Pence was still in his ceremonial office with his family and aides—protected by Secret Service, but vulnerable because the second-floor office had windows that could be breached and the intruding thugs had gained control of the building. Tim Giebels, the lead special agent in charge of the vice president's protective detail, twice asked Pence to evacuate the Capitol, but Pence refused. "I'm not leaving the Capitol," he told Giebels. The last thing the vice president wanted was the people attacking the Capitol to see his twenty-car motorcade fleeing. That would only vindicate their insurrection.

The third time Giebels asked Pence to evacuate, it was more of an order than a request. "They're in the building," Giebels said. "The room you're in is not secure. There are glass windows. I need to move you. We're going."

At 2:26, after a team of agents scouted a safe path to ensure the Pences would not encounter trouble, Giebels and the rest of Pence's detail agents guided them down a staircase to a secured subterranean area that rioters couldn't reach, where Pence's armored limousine awaited. Giebels asked Pence to get in one of the vehicles. "We can hold here," he said.

"I'm not getting in the car, Tim," Pence replied. "I trust you, Tim, but you're not driving the car. If I get in that vehicle, you guys are taking off. I'm not getting in the car."

The Pences then made their way to a secured underground area to wait out the riot.

Back at the White House, Kellogg was worried about Pence's safety and checked in with Zach Bauer, Pence's body man, who said they were in the Capitol basement. Kellogg then went to find Trump.

"Is Mike okay?" the president asked him.

"The Secret Service has him under control," Kellogg told Trump. "Karen is there with the daughter."

"Oh?" Trump asked.

"They're going to stay there until this thing gets sorted out," Kellogg said.

Trump said nothing more. He didn't express any hope that Pence was okay. He didn't try calling the vice president to check on him. He just stayed in the dining room watching television.

Around this time, Kellogg ran into Tony Ornato in the West Wing. Ornato, who oversaw Secret Service movements, told him Pence's detail was planning to move the vice president to Joint Base Andrews.

"You can't do that, Tony," Kellogg said. "Leave him where he's at. He's got a job to do. I know you guys too well. You'll fly him to Alaska if you have a chance. Don't do it."

Pence had made clear to Giebels the level of his determination and Kellogg said there was no changing it.

"He's going to stay there," Kellogg told Ornato. "If he has to wait there all night, he's going to do it."

Ornato, through a spokesman, denied having this conversation.

Once in his secure area, Pence kept in close contact with McConnell, Pelosi, Chuck Schumer, and Kevin McCarthy, making sure the congressional leaders were safe. Later that afternoon, Marc Short, who was with Pence, called Meadows to let him know the vice president was protected and that it was their intention to stay put and finish their work that evening as soon as it was safe. Meadows said he thought it was appropriate for Pence to continue his work, though did not communicate any well wishes from Trump.

Sund's effort to secure the Capitol with military reinforcements hit a major snag. Though the Capitol Police chief had received approval to ask the D.C. National Guard Commander for reinforcements, he was shocked to learn that, on that day, Walker didn't have permission to dispatch them. Only the top official at the Pentagon could make that order. A few days earlier, Chris Miller, the acting defense secretary, had signed a memo instructing that only he could approve use of the D.C. National Guard, an apparent hangover from the intense criticism Defense Department leaders had received the previous June for the military's role in the clearing of Lafayette Square.

A little before 2:30, D.C. mayor muriel Bowser's homeland security director launched an urgent conference call connecting the mayor, Contee, Sund, and Walker. Top staff working for Army secretary Ryan McCarthy dialed in from across the river. Sund joined the call in progress and told the two army lieutenant generals working under McCarthy that his officers were in a dire crisis and needed help immediately. But the McCarthy aides, Walter Piatt and Charles Flynn, who coincidentally was Michael Flynn's brother, sounded reluctant. Piatt said he didn't like the "visual" of National Guard members standing sentry in front of the Capitol, and he would prefer Guard soldiers take up posts elsewhere around the city to relieve D.C. police so police officers could instead respond to the Capitol. As they both stood over a desk phone set on speaker, Flynn concurred with Piatt, saying it would not be his military advice to McCarthy to deploy the Guard without a plan. Flynn would later seek to conceal that he was on the call; when he ultimately admitted he was part of the discussion, he said he could not recall exactly what he had said.

Contee, who by that point had already sent more than one hundred of his officers to help the Capitol Police, was stunned. Sund was pleading for help. He had just told Piatt and Flynn that armed rioters had breached the Capitol and that shots had been fired inside the building. And they were talking about optics and planning duty assignments.

"Wait, wait," Contee said. "Steve, are you requesting National Guard assistance at the Capitol?"

"I am making urgent, urgent, immediate request for National Guard assistance," Sund said, his voice barely controlled.

"And are you turning down the Chief's request?"

Contee asked the lieutenant generals on the other side of the Potomac River.

Piatt said no, they weren't rejecting Sund's request, but rather explaining their objections and concerns. He said they would have to talk to McCarthy. They hung up.

Elsewhere in the Pentagon, more senior leaders had rushed into Miller's office suite to try to get a handle on the rapidly deteriorating situation. It was about 2:30. The acting secretary was there as were Army chief of staff James McConville; National Guard chief Dan Hokanson; Kash Patel; Bryan Fenton, the senior military adviser to Miller; and Milley, who had just been yanked out of a meeting with Christine Wormuth, a Biden transition team official. They stood around the room taking in the facts. The crowd outside the Capitol was estimated at twenty-five thousand, some of them armed and many of them violent.

Just then, McCarthy entered the room breathing heavily; he had run from his own office. McCarthy gave Miller and the group a rapid update from the phone call his aides had just had with Sund and Contee. Police at the Capitol were badly outnumbered by rioters, engaged in hand-to-hand combat, and losing the fight to secure the Capitol. As many as eight thousand protesters had pounded their way through barricades and were streaming through the halls of Congress.

The Pentagon leaders were aghast.

"What do you think, Chairman?" Miller asked Milley.

"Get on the phone with the A.G. right now and get every cop in D.C. down there to the Capitol this minute, all seven to eight thousand of them," Milley said. He recommended Hokanson mobilize the entire D.C. National Guard and send out a call for National Guard reinforcements from the nearby states of Maryland, Delaware, Pennsylvania, and Virginia.

The discussion was briefly interrupted when, on a television in Miller's office, a news flash reported that shots had been fired in the Capitol. At 2:44, Ashli Babbitt, a thirty-five-year-old Air Force veteran and Trump supporter from California, was shot by a Capitol Police officer as she tried to break into the Speaker's Lobby and refused a command to stop.

At the Maryland State House in Annapolis, Governor Larry Hogan was a step ahead of them. When protesters first breached the police line at the Capitol, an aide pulled Hogan out of a Zoom meeting he was having with Japan's ambassador to the United States, and the governor quickly ordered the Maryland State Police superintendent to mobilize 280 troopers in its rapid-deployment force to grab their riot gear and drive immediately to the Capitol.

Hogan then directed the adjutant general of the Maryland National Guard to begin calling up one thousand of its members. He knew they would not be able to cross state lines and enter the District of Columbia without approval from Miller, but he anticipated the ask would come, and wanted Guard forces ready at the border for a speedy deployment. "I don't want to wait around," Hogan said.

Hogan soon got a call from Congressman Steny Hoyer, the number two House Democrat, who was from Maryland. Hoyer was in the Hart Building with Pelosi, Schumer, Kevin McCarthy, and other leaders. He spoke fast and his tone conveyed urgency.

"Governor, we need your help right now," Hoyer said. "The Capitol Police have been overrun. What can you do to help us? Can you send in the police? Can you send in the National Guard?"

"Calm down, Steny," Hogan said. "I have nearly three hundred state police on the way to the Capitol right now as we speak, and I've activated the National Guard, everybody we had available, a thousand soldiers. But we don't have authorization to go in."

Hoyer yelled across the room at Schumer. "Hey, Chuck! Chuck! Hogan says he doesn't have authorization."

Hoyer then tells Hogan, "Chuck says you do have authorization."

"Steny, I'm telling you, I don't care what Chuck says, I've been told by the Department of Defense that we don't have authorization," Hogan said.

They ended the call.

Most lawmakers had been evacuated from the Capitol for their own safety, but most of their staffers were left to fend for themselves as armed mobs of violent rioters started to roam through hallways and in and out of offices. Some of them punched and kicked doors. They yelled, "Stop the steal!" As if trapped in a building with multiple active shooters, Hill staffers suffered the terror of not being sure if they would live or die. Many of them were in their twenties and thirties—part of a generation of Americans who had grown up with the scourge of mass gun violence and had learned in school what to do in active-shooter situations.

In Pelosi's office suite, eight of her staffers hunkered down undetected in a small conference room as invaders trashed her offices, rifled through the papers on her desk, and yelled, "Where are you, Nancy?"

Pelosi later recalled in her interview for this book that the most traumatic part of the siege for her was hearing that after she had been evacuated her aides remained in serious danger. "Much of my staff were under a table, in the dark, locked up in rooms, silent for more than two hours because these people were banging on the doors trying to find the Speaker because they were going to do whatever they were going to do," she said. "They're young people who come with their idealism to Capitol Hill to be involved in public service for the life of our country. Patriotic."

On the Senate side, McConnell's aides were just as terrified. A top McConnell staffer who had left the Senate Chamber after McConnell was evacuated by his security team began walking quickly toward the Rotunda and came face-to-face with a U.S. Capitol Police officer sprinting in the opposite direction. The two made eye contact, then the officer yelled: "Run!"

The staffer wasn't sure what he was running from and which way he should go to safety. He darted down a side hallway lined with offices and realized he didn't have his office key with him. He jiggled one locked doorknob, then another. A co-worker poked his head out of the office of McConnell's speechwriter. The fleeing staffer lunged inside, pushing the co-worker back in as he did.

Within minutes, the McConnell aides heard the shouts and footfalls of rioters getting louder, as well as unexplained screams. A text alert from Capitol Police blared on every phone in the room: "Due to security threat inside: immediately, move inside your office, take emergency equipment, lock the doors, take shelter." Some of McConnell's aides piled a sofa and tables against the door as quietly as they could, ever fearful they'd be discovered.

It was terrifying. The senior McConnell staffer began texting and then calling a friend he thought could help: Will Levi, who had recently been Bill Barr's chief of staff at the Justice Department. He told Levi that the Capitol Police had lost control of the building. Countless staffers were in hiding but who knew when rioters would break down their doors. If backup did not arrive soon, the McConnell staffer told him, people could die.

Levi called FBI deputy director David Bowdich, who was then monitoring the protests in the command center in the FBI's Washington Field Office. Bowdich knew protesters from the Ellipse had been

aggressively skirmishing with police around the perimeter but was surprised when Levi reported they
were now running roughshod through the Capitol.

Bowdich normally would seek an invitation from
the Capitol Police to send FBI agents onto the Capitol
grounds, but he decided there was no time. He dispatched an FBI SWAT team from the Washington
office, then two more, to the Capitol. He instructed
the first team to start by securing the safety of lawmakers and staff on the Senate side, and follow-up
teams would try to help regain control of the entire
building. Speed was key, so he told them to skip the
standard step of meeting off-site to coordinate.

"Get their asses over there. Go now," Bowdich
said to the first SWAT team's commander. "We don't
have time to huddle."

After first evacuating congressional leaders to the
secure area of the Hart Building, Capitol Police decided to err on the side of caution and transported
leaders, including Pelosi, McConnell, Schumer, and
Kevin McCarthy, to Fort McNair, an army post
in Southwest Washington where the Potomac and
Anacostia rivers meet.

At the Pentagon, Miller's office was a hub of activity. At 2:45, the acting defense secretary had a group
conference call with acting attorney general Jeffrey
Rosen to urge he deploy all law enforcement officers
at his disposal. Miller stressed they had to make an
immediate show of presence at the Capitol. Milley
said the National Guard had to move as soon as

possible, too, though he acknowledged that it would surely take longer to move troops into action than police forces.

At 3:04, Ryan McCarthy transmitted the decision to call up National Guard units from D.C. and neighboring states. The Guard units would begin to arrive on the Capitol grounds about two and a half hours later—which the Pentagon considered lightning speed.

Lawmakers were horrified as they hid from rioters. People who appeared to be maniacs—some wearing horns, carrying zip ties, and chanting about hanging the traitors—were coursing through the halls of Congress waving Confederate and neo-Nazi flags. A mob had taken over the Senate floor.

At 3:15, Dan Sullivan called Milley. "This is really fucked up down here," the Republican senator said. Milley told him there was confusion about how to deploy troops to the Capitol.

Sullivan told Milley the senators were safe in a secure location and there was a tentative plan by Capitol Police to evacuate them by bus from the Capitol complex. Sullivan, who had military training, thought the movement would put them in more danger. "I'm going to tell them it's a bad idea," Sullivan told Milley. "Can I mention that the chairman of the Joint Chiefs agrees?"

"Yes," Milley said. The plan never came to be.

At 3:22, Adam Smith called Milley to say, "We need to clear the Capitol. Bring overwhelming force.

The mob has overwhelmed us." The Democratic congressman said some members were in their hide-away offices and people were freaking out.

At 3:33, Pelosi and Schumer together called Miller, who had other Pentagon leaders standing by listening. The two had a firm message to deliver. There was high anxiety in their voices. They sounded angry, though not panicked.

"We want action now," one of them said. "We must have active-duty troops."

Milley spoke up: "We have the Guard coming."

Miller explained that the FBI and other federal law enforcement were on their way.

Pelosi and Schumer said that wasn't enough. They needed active-duty troops to get control of the situation. This was a matter of life and limb.

"The country is at stake," Pelosi said.

Miller said soldiers were on their way. He didn't explain how long it would take for troops to arrive.

At 4:00, Pence called Miller from his secure location. The vice president was calm. He had no anxiety or fear in his voice. Pence delivered a set of directives to the defense chief.

"Get troops here; get them here now," the vice president ordered. "We've got to get the Congress to do its business."

"Yes, sir," Miller said.

Pence emphasized they needed to act with all possible speed. It was the sternest Miller or the other Pentagon officials listening had ever heard Pence.

He sounded like a commander in a firefight, issuing orders upon which lives depended. The voices overheard in the background of Pence's end of the call were far more animated and anxious. Lots of people were talking, perhaps his family members or his aides. But Pence sounded resolute.

"Get the Capitol cleared," he told Miller. "You've got to get down here. You've got to get the place cleared. We've got to do what we have to do."

"Yes, sir," Miller answered.

As Pence gave orders to the military, the actual commander in chief was effectively AWOL. Trump spent the afternoon glued to the television watching the drama unfold.

After his tweet castigating Pence for his lack of courage amid the height of the attack, Trump had issued two tweets that many of his aides felt still missed the mark. In neither did Trump call on his supporters to leave the Capitol. At 2:38 p.m., Trump wrote, "Please support our Capitol Police and Law Enforcement. They are truly on the side of our Country. Stay peaceful!" And at 3:13, Trump tweeted, "I am asking for everyone at the U.S. Capitol to remain peaceful. No violence! Remember, WE are the Party of Law & Order—respect the Law and our great men and women in Blue. Thank you!"

As soon as she saw on the television in her second-floor office that the rioters were inside the Capitol,

Ivanka Trump said to her aides, "I'm going down to my dad. This has to stop." She spent several hours walking back and forth to the Oval trying to convince the president to be stronger in telling his supporters he stood with law enforcement and ordering them to disperse. Just when Ivanka Trump thought she had made headway and returned upstairs, Meadows would call her to say the president still needed more persuading. "I need you to come back down here," Meadows would tell her. "We've got to get this under control." He would clear the room of other aides and say, "I only want Ivanka, myself, and the president in here." This cycle repeated itself several times that afternoon. As another presidential adviser said, "Ivanka was described to me like a stable pony. When the racehorse gets too agitated, you bring the stable pony in to calm him down."

Other White House officials also pleaded with Trump to condemn the violence unequivocally. One after another, they urged the president to implore the thousands of rioters laying siege to the Capitol under his name to stand down and go home.

"You need to tweet something," Kellogg told Trump. "Nobody's going to be watching TV out there, but they will be looking at their phones. You need to tweet something."

"Once mobs get moving, you can't turn them off," Kellogg added. "Once they start rolling, it's hard to bring it under control. But you've got to get on top of this and say something."

Kevin McCarthy, who had been trying to reach Trump at the White House, finally succeeded and asked him to publicly and forcefully call off the rioters. Trump falsely claimed that the attackers were members of Antifa. McCarthy told the president that in fact they were his own supporters.

"Well, Kevin, I guess these people are more upset about the election than you are," Trump said, according to the account that Republican congresswoman Jaime Herrera Beutler said McCarthy gave her.

Other advisers who were away from the White House tried to call Trump, but he didn't take their calls. They figured he knew what they were going to say, and he didn't want to hear it. Plus, he was busy watching TV.

Chris Christie called the White House intending to tell Trump, "Are you crazy? What are you doing? You're the president of the United States . . . You've got to stop this." But when Trump didn't take his call, the former New Jersey governor went on TV and tried to deliver his message to the president through the screen.

"I've been spending the last twenty-five minutes or so trying to get the president on the phone myself to say this to him directly," Christie said during ABC's breaking news coverage. "The president caused this protest to occur. He's the only one who can make it stop. The president has to come out and tell his supporters to leave the Capitol grounds and to allow the Congress to do their business peacefully. And anything short of that is an abrogation of his responsibility. He spoke to this crowd, his son spoke to this crowd, and sent them on their way. I don't know that they anticipated this was going to be the result, but it doesn't matter whether they did or they didn't. This is the result of their words, and now their words must put a stop to this."

Kellyanne Conway tried to talk to Trump and left a message with his office, asking that her name be added to the chorus of people calling on the president to do something.

"This is really bad," Conway said. "People are going to get hurt. Only he can stop them. He can't just tweet. He's got to get down there."

Alyssa Farah, watching on television from Florida, was heartbroken and reached out several times to Meadows, her former boss. "You guys have to say something," she told Meadows. "Even if the president's not willing to put out a statement, you should go to the [cameras] and say, 'We condemn this. Please stand down.' If you don't, people are going to die."

Some other White House officials felt helpless as they watched the horror unfold. Larry Kudlow watched the riot on television from his second-floor West Wing office. At one point, Chris Liddell came in to join him. They were horrified, but they didn't believe there was anything they could do to stop it. These were two of the most powerful people in the government, yet what could they do if the president refused to act? Kudlow drew a parallel in that moment to his publicized battle with alcoholism and cocaine addiction in the 1990s. Kudlow later told others he realized on January 6 that he had no control, just like how in his youth as a Wall Street trader he thought he was the master of the universe until he crashed and burned and it dawned on him he wasn't the master of anything.

More junior staffers felt just as hopeless. Sarah Matthews, twenty-five, was a deputy press secretary, working under McEnany, and had put her name to countless defenses of the president as his mishaps and statements landed him in crisis after crisis. But the Capitol insurrection was one she could not stomach defending. She had gone to the Ellipse that morning to watch Trump speak and was thrilled to see so many supporters turning out for the president. After getting back to the West Wing, she huddled outside McEnany's office with a few colleagues and watched the crowds arrive at the Capitol. They were excited to see so many demonstrators but knew things had turned ugly when protesters started clashing with police and rushing through the barricades and up the Capitol steps.

Matthews appealed to two of her more senior colleagues, McEnany and Ben Williamson, an adviser to Meadows, that she thought Trump needed to say something along the lines of, "I support peaceful protesters but violence is never the answer and attacking law enforcement is unacceptable and those who are doing that need to stop." But Trump's tweets fell short of that. He gave no call to action to leave.

Frustrated that her advice was being ignored, Matthews headed down to the Lower Press area. Emotional and physically shaking, she told some press staff colleagues, "Oh, my gosh, we're not saying what we need to say right now."

Graham wanted to get through to the president as well. He had an idea: call Ivanka Trump. The senator rang the first daughter on her cell phone numerous times until she finally picked up.

"You need to tell him to tell these people to leave," Graham told her.

"We're working on it," Ivanka Trump replied.

On Capitol Hill, most of the senators, along with about fifty staff members, were together in a large undisclosed room secured by Capitol Police. They had several televisions on to watch live news coverage of the siege under way around them. Tensions were high. Romney was as upset as he'd ever been. He went up to Josh Hawley and Ron Johnson, two of the dozen Republican senators objecting to certification, and confronted them.

"This is what you have caused," Romney said to them both.

Romney later recalled, "I was angry that in the cradle of democracy . . . a process which is the center of the democratic process was being interrupted and attacked."

At 4:05 p.m., Biden came on the screens to deliver

remarks from Wilmington. The senators stopped what they were doing and silently watched. Trump still had not appeared on camera since the siege began, but the president-elect stepped in to try to calm the nation.

"At this hour, our democracy is under unprecedented assault, unlike anything we've seen in modern times," Biden said. He added, "What we're seeing are a small number of extremists dedicated to lawlessness. This is not dissent. It's disorder. It's chaos. It borders on sedition. And it must end now. I call on this mob to pull back and allow the work of democracy to go forward."

Biden added, "The words of a president matter, no matter how good or bad that president is. At their best the words of a president can inspire. At their worst, they can incite. Therefore, I call on President Trump to go on national television now to fulfill his oath and defend the Constitution and demand an end to this siege."

Watching from their secure room, the senators stood and applauded—Republicans and Democrats both. "It was like, wow, we have a leader who said what needed to be said," Romney recalled.

At 4:17, Trump posted on Twitter a video of remarks to the nation that he had recorded in the Rose Garden after hours of pleading from those closest to him. He began by repeating his fraudulent line that the election was rigged.

"I know your pain. I know you're hurt," Trump said. "We had an election that was stolen from us.

It was a landslide election and everybody knows it, especially the other side. But you have to go home now. We have to have peace. We have to have law and order."

Then the president said: "We have to have peace. So go home. We love you. You're very special. You've seen what happens. You see the way others are treated that are so bad and so evil. I know how you feel, but go home, and go home in peace."

Finally, Trump told the rioters to "go home," which was the message Ivanka Trump had spent two hours prodding him to give. Yet he also told people who had just tried to stage an insurrection on his behalf, "We love you." The president's message was jarringly inconsistent. He had recorded three takes, each time veering off the script his speechwriters had prepared for him. The version released was the most palatable option.

Watching from her desk, Matthews was upset. Trump had not even bothered to distinguish between peaceful protesters and violent insurrectionists. He said he loved them all. That, to her, was unacceptable. So she packed up the things on her desk, threw the half a dozen pairs of heels she kept stashed under her desk into a big bag, and headed home early. She knew in her heart she would not return. A few hours later, after consulting with loved ones, she resigned.

As the sun began to go down over the city, the Capitol still was not secure. Bowser had declared a 6:00 p.m. curfew. The rioters continued to dangerously roam the building. A third casualty occurred at 4:26, when Rosanne Boyland, a thirty-four-year-old Trump supporter from Georgia, was trampled to death by fellow insurrectionists trying to push through a police line at an entrance to the Capitol. And a fourth casualty would be recorded the next day, when Capitol Police officer Brian Sicknick, forty-two, died from two strokes the day after confronting rioters who had attacked him with a powerful chemical spray they called "Bear shit."

At 4:39, Miller gave Meadows an update on the status of removing protesters from the Capitol complex. McConnell came onto the call at different points and sounded furious.

"I want it clear," the Senate leader demanded. "I want it cleared out now. The Senate needs to get its business done."

Miller tried to manage expectations, saying it would take time for members to be able to return to the Capitol. He explained they had to deploy teams to check for explosive devices everywhere and it could take until the morning.

"Let me just sum it up," McConnell said. "We're going back in session at eight o'clock in prime time. If you haven't secured the entire area, you have to secure the two chambers, because we're going to go back on the air in prime time and let the American people know that this insurrection has failed."

Pelosi also was insistent the House return to session that evening. At one point, defense officials suggested to her they transport House members by bus to Fort McNair and hold their session there, since it could more easily be secured than the Capitol, she later told us.

"No, you're not," Pelosi said. "We're going back to the Capitol. You just tell us how long it will take to get rid of these people. We're coming back to the Capitol."

Pence, who had been in close contact with McConnell, Pelosi, and other congressional leaders throughout the afternoon, agreed. He, too, was adamant that both the Senate and House return to session as soon as possible and finish its work that evening.

"We need to get back tonight," he said on a call with congressional leaders and defense and security officials. "We can't let the world see that our process of confirming the next president can be delayed."

At 4:40, more than an hour after Hogan had first called Maryland National Guard units to prepare to enter Washington, he got a call from Ryan McCarthy.

"Governor, are you able to send some National Guard units to D.C.?" the army secretary asked.

"Yeah, we're ready to go," Hogan replied. "We've been waiting for the authorization."

Hogan took McCarthy's question to be the green light he needed. Despite Milley recommending the

Pentagon call up neighboring National Guard units immediately, McCarthy hadn't gotten around to it until more than two and a half hours after the Capitol was breached. About 750 Guard soldiers from Maryland would soon begin arriving, along with 620 from Virginia.

By 6:00, the Capitol was cleared of rioters but not fully secure. Explosive teams were sweeping for bombs and were nearly done. But they still expected it would take another ninety minutes to give the all-clear for lawmakers to return.

At 6:01, Trump tweeted again: "These are the things and events that happen when a sacred landslide election victory is so unceremoniously & viciously stripped away from great patriots who have been badly & unfairly treated for so long. Go home with love & in peace. Remember this day forever!"

At Fort McNair, meanwhile, about 150 National Guard members secured the entrances to the base, which was being treated as a continuity of government site since the congressional leaders were there. They were getting the extra protection typically provided when the country was under attack.

At 6:30, Pence called Miller back, with McConnell, Pelosi, McCarthy, and Schumer on the line. They worked out a timeline for returning to certify the election results. Pence wanted to begin as soon as possible. At 7:15, Miller told the leaders that members were cleared to return. Pence then announced that the Senate would come back into session at 8:00.

At no time that Wednesday since the Capitol siege began did these government and military leaders hear from the president. Not even the vice president heard from Trump.

The recently departed Mark Esper watched the horror play out all afternoon on television, first from the gym and then from his home. He watched rioters tromping through the same halls of the Capitol that he had walked as a Senate aide. Esper was disgusted to see vandals sullying this house of democracy. A little after 7:00 p.m., he registered his outrage in a trio of tweets. Though he did not name Trump, Esper left little doubt that he considered his former boss responsible.

"This is not how citizens of the world's greatest and oldest democracy behave," Esper wrote. "The perpetrators who committed this illegal act were inspired by partisan misinformation and patently false claims about the election. This must end now for the good of the republic."

John Kelly, who in the two years since leaving the White House had largely shied away from criticizing Trump on the record, typed out an email to Josh Dawsey of **The Washington Post.** He said he was heartbroken and horrified by the day's events. He praised McConnell's remarks as "words for the ages" and Biden's speech as "presidential," though had no praise for Trump's.

"What we need to do going forward—what we have to do as a people—not as Democrats or Republicans or independents, but as Americans, is to ask ourselves how did we ever get to this place," Kelly wrote. "We need to look infinitely harder at who we elect to any office in our land. At the office seeker's character, at their morals, at their ethical record, their integrity, their honesty, their flaws, what they have said about women, and minorities, why they are seeking office in the first place, and only then consider the policies they espouse."

At 8:06 p.m., an emotional Pence called the Senate back into session. "To those who wreaked havoc in our Capitol today, you did not win," the vice president said. "Violence never wins. Freedom wins, and this is still the people's house. And as we reconvene in this chamber, the world will again witness the resilience and strength of our democracy, for even in the wake of unprecedented violence and vandalism at this Capitol, the elected representatives of the people of the United States have assembled again on the very same day to support and defend the Constitution of the United States."

As Pence got to work doing precisely what Trump had ordered him not to do, Romney thought to himself, "High personal cost. Five years of praising the president in every possible way, both visually and verbally, to instead have all of that flipped upon him and be criticized by the president had to be a reversal of historic proportion."

The floor debate picked up where it left off, with Arizona's electoral votes. And although some Republicans continued to object, they were fewer in number than before the siege. Lankford, who had been in the process or trying to block certification when Pence was evacuated and the proceedings abruptly suspended, changed his mind and implored his Republican colleagues to join him in voting to certify Biden's victory.

Various senators took turns delivering speeches from their desks. They all condemned the violence, even if some still objected to certifying the vote.

Graham gave an animated speech in which he appeared to be grieving for a friend who had lost his way.

"Trump and I, we had a hell of a journey. I hate it being this way," Graham said. "All I can say is count me out. Enough is enough. I tried to be helpful."

When it was Romney's turn, he had sharp words not only for the president but also for some of his fellow senators.

"We gather today due to a selfish man's injured pride and the outrage of his supporters whom he has deliberately misinformed for the past two months and stirred to action this very morning," Romney said. "What happened here today was an insurrection, incited by the president of the United States. Those who choose to continue to support his dangerous gambit by objecting to the results of a legitimate, democratic election will forever be seen as being complicit in an unprecedented attack against our democracy.

"They will be remembered for their role in this shameful episode in American history," Romney continued. "That will be their legacy."

In the end, six Republican senators objected to the counting of Arizona's electoral votes and seven objected to counting Pennsylvania's.

In the House, where Pelosi gaveled the session to order an hour later, at 9:00, the Republican resistance was greater still. One hundred twenty-one House members, nearly two thirds of the Republican conference, voted against counting Arizona's votes, and even more, 138, voted against counting Pennsylvania's.

Pelosi could hardly believe it. "That they, in the middle of the night, would say, 'We still want to [object to] Pennsylvania,' just showed you the total cavalier disregard they had for our country," she recalled. They weren't beholden to country, she said, but to Trump, "this insane person spreading this insanity." Maybe the House Republicans feared him, maybe they agreed with him, Pelosi said, "or they were just in a cult."

Senators made their way to the House Chamber to reconvene their joint session. At 3:24 a.m., with Pence presiding, the Congress completed its duty and voted to confirm Biden's 306 to 232 electoral win. Pence formally declared him the next president of the United States.

Trump and his allies in Congress who voted not to certify the results "actually thought that someone could get out there and disrupt the constitutional

process of the United States of America and perpetuate this guy in office," one of the president's top advisers said. "They underestimated their own country and
the people in power. They underestimated the strength
of the legislature. They underestimated the vice president to do his duty, Georgia representatives, the
judiciary. They didn't understand their own country."

Trump stayed silent through much of the evening.
Twitter that night took the extraordinary step of suspending his accounts temporarily, citing that his messages had violated its civic policies against spreading
misinformation. Facebook soon followed. The truth
was he had violated those policies hundreds of times
before January 6. But the brutality and threat to the
country that Trump's misinformation had fomented
deeply shook the leaders of both social media giants.
The ban on Trump on both platforms would become permanent.

Jason Miller worked with Trump, suddenly de-
prived of his megaphone, and the first lady to draft
a statement that Scavino would release on the president's behalf once the outcome was official. For
Trump, conceding to Biden was out of the question.
But Miller pressed him to, at a minimum, commit to
an orderly transition of power. After January 6, there
could no longer be a peaceful one. But he argued that
the country needed to be assured that Trump would
not try any more gambits in his two weeks remaining
in office.

On that, Trump agreed. His statement read, "Even

though I totally disagree with the outcome of the election, and the facts bear me out, nevertheless there will be an orderly transition on January 20th. I have always said we would continue our fight to ensure that only legal votes were counted. While this represents the end of the greatest first term in presidential history, it's only the beginning of our fight to Make America Great Again."

Twenty-two

Landing the Bad Boy

On January 7, officials awoke across Washington to assess the damage. Democracy had prevailed. President-elect Biden's victory was official. But there were still two weeks until Biden's inauguration. President Trump remained a danger. A deep unease coursed through the administration. There were discussions overnight and into the morning about the possibility of the Cabinet invoking the Twenty-fifth Amendment and of the Congress rushing to impeach and remove him from office. A handful of Trump aides resigned the night of January 6, and many more contemplated doing so on January 7.

In these uncertain times, three top advisers to the president had begun having regular check-ins. Mark Milley, Mark Meadows, and Mike Pompeo would hop on the phone each day to compare notes about what each was hearing and collectively survey the horizon for trouble.

"The general theme of these calls was, come hell or high water, there will be a peaceful transfer of power on January twentieth," recalled one senior official. "We've got an aircraft, our landing gear is stuck, we've got one engine, and we're out of fuel. We've got to land this bad boy."

Although concern had been building since just before the election, the events of January 6 gave the trio reason to don crash helmets. Milley, who had been more on edge than the others, told aides he saw the calls as an opportunity to keep tabs on Trump.

Pompeo was an original Trump hire, having joined the administration on Day One as CIA director, and then subsequently having been so liked by Trump that he was promoted to secretary of state. In both jobs, he cultivated a reputation as an absolute Trump loyalist. In the fall of 2020, however, Pompeo started privately confiding in others that he was concerned about the crackpot advisers Trump was listening to. Pompeo and Milley both lived at Fort Myer and conferred regularly. Shortly before the election, Pompeo visited Milley's home and they had a heart-to-heart. Sitting at the general's kitchen table, Pompeo said, "You know the crazies are taking over," according to people familiar with the conversation.

"Look, none of it fucking matters," Milley said. "We've got to bring it on home. There's gonna be an election. We've got to make sure it's a free and fair election."

Pompeo and Milley had shared the same persistent worry that Trump might try to use the military to help him hold on to power if he lost the election. But Milley was adamant about stopping that. "This military's not going to be used," he assured Pompeo.

After the siege on January 6, there was reason for them to be on higher alert. Same for Meadows. On their check-in call on January 7, Pompeo said, "The two of you realize it's just us and Pat [Cipollone] now, right? We have to stay steady," according to people familiar with the conversation.

Meadows said, "The president is very emotional. He's in a really bad place. . . . He's extremely angry."

Pompeo, through a person close to him, denied that he made the comments attributed to him in his meeting with Milley and in his call with Meadows and Milley, and said they are not reflective of his views.

The three of them agreed to remain in close contact through the remainder of Trump's presidency. It was extraordinary that the secretary of state, the chairman of the Joint Chiefs of Staff, and the White House chief of staff would need to do such a thing, but this was no ordinary time.

News stories reported that Robert O'Brien also contemplated resigning. The national security adviser was unsettled by what had happened at the Capitol and by Trump's role in it. He was one of the few Trump appointees to praise Vice President Pence, publicly breaking with the president. On the evening of January 6, O'Brien tweeted, "I just spoke with Vice President Pence. He is a genuinely fine and decent man. He exhibited courage today as he did at the Capitol on 9/11 as a Congressman. I am proud to serve with him."

But O'Brien did not seriously consider quitting. However, the news reports led a chorus of senior national security officials both current and past, as well as Mitch McConnell, to appeal to O'Brien to stay on the job. O'Brien's deputy, Matt Pottinger, resigned on January 7, after weeks of preparing to relocate his family out West. Losing O'Brien, too, would have left the National Security Council gutted. O'Brien's callers said they feared a power vacuum that would make the United States vulnerable to a foreign attack.

One person who notably did not have to consider resigning on January 7 was Bill Barr, who had left the administration two weeks prior. "Bill Barr—he is one smart guy," one Trump adviser said. "He could have been at that rally on January 6. That was one smart move. He probably looks in the mirror every day and says, 'Bill, you are one smart guy.'"

As appalled as he was by the Capitol siege, at first Barr reserved judgment about Trump's role in the violence. Barr told confidants he thought Trump could have salvaged his reputation if he had instantaneously said something definitively condemning the attack, showing he had never intended it to be violent. But then he saw the president's first instinct had been to do nothing to call off his supporters. The delay had cost him.

Free to speak his mind now that he was no longer in Trump's employ, on January 7 Barr issued a public statement directly condemning his former boss. "Orchestrating a mob to pressure Congress is inexcusable. The president's conduct yesterday was a betrayal of his office and supporters," Barr said.

Cipollone also was considering quitting. The afternoon of January 6, it started dawning on the White House counsel and his deputies that Trump could conceivably be charged with a crime for setting off the deadly riot. There were a lot of ifs about whether that was likely. But one thing was guaranteed: sprawling investigations. Congress was sure to examine what had led to and allowed this violent breach of the Capitol, including the president's role in instigating it. More important, thousands of felonies had occurred on the Capitol grounds. A police officer and four rioters had been killed. Hundreds of officers had been injured. The FBI was about to launch the largest investigation in its history. Any good prosecutor would examine closely what the president, Donald Trump Jr., Rudy Giuliani, and others had said at the rally. Had they egged the mob on to the Capitol? If so, what was their intent? They could be accused of sedition, a charge not leveled at a president in a century. Some in the White House worried that Trump, his son, and his lawyer were also at serious risk of being charged with inciting a riot. It would be difficult to prove. Intent was key, and a very high bar. But not impossible.

A discussion arose inside the White House about whether the president could prospectively pardon Giuliani and Trump Jr.—and perhaps even himself—to eliminate the risk of being charged. Cipollone told Meadows that was a step too far. It would smack of—and quite possibly constitute—obstruction of justice. Cipollone wouldn't have any of it. He threatened to resign if the president issued any such pardons. Not only that, but he said he and many of his senior lawyers would resign en masse, and then he would hold a news conference announcing their strong objections. The news conference threat was the death knell for the discussion. The White House could not afford to take any more public shaming. Cipollone won, giving the White House counsel and his deputies the upper hand.

Still, Cipollone believed what Trump did on January 6 was galling and could damage his own reputation. He had faithfully supported the president but did not want to look like he was condoning this behavior. He called McConnell for advice about whether to resign.

"It's a tough call," McConnell said, "but I think your country needs you to stay where you are until January twentieth."

Jared Kushner also pressed Cipollone to stay. Along with Ivanka Trump, Kushner had been a primary driver of the president granting clemency to people who were wrongfully convicted, had already served lengthy sentences, or had compelling personal stories. And the White House counsel's office had taken charge of vetting and approving the pardons. If Cipollone and his deputies resigned with only two weeks remaining in the administration, the pardons Kushner wanted would likely fail to get through.

"You took an oath to the country," Kushner told Cipollone. "This is your service. If you leave, do you think the country's safer or not safer? Let's stay to the end. You don't run when it gets tough. It's our job to see this through."

Cipollone and his team stayed. He might have gotten a great headline in the media had he resigned on principle. But McConnell told him he was grateful to him for taking the reputational risk of staying. Friends said Cipollone dryly told them in the days after he decided to stay that his main job was to "make sure bad things don't happen." Cipollone's decision seemed to elevate his internal stock. As another top Trump adviser explained, "People begged them to stay another two weeks to finish out the term. Once they stayed, they rightly believed they had a lot more power."

"The president tells them something they don't want to do—nope, they're not doing it," the adviser continued. "Pat was able to basically say no. He could dig his heels in where it really mattered to him. He felt they had veto power."

Two Cabinet members decided to quit: Education Secretary Betsy DeVos and Transportation Secretary Elaine Chao, who is married to McConnell. Both had served from the start of the administration and had stuck by Trump through many scandals. Chao had literally stood at Trump's side, dutifully smiling, during an August 2017 news conference in which he said "both sides" were to blame for the violence and a woman's death at a white supremacist rally in Charlottesville, Virginia. For both women, January 6 was the breaking point.

In her resignation letter to Trump, DeVos wrote, "We should be highlighting and celebrating your Administration's many accomplishments on behalf of the American people. Instead, we are left to clean up the mess caused by violent protesters overrunning the U.S. Capitol in an attempt to undermine the people's business. That behavior was unconscionable for our country. There is no mistaking the impact your rhetoric had on the situation, and it is the inflection point for me."

The education secretary added, "Impressionable children are watching all of this, and they are learning from us. I believe we each have a moral obligation to exercise good judgement and model the behavior we hope they would emulate. They must know from us that America is greater than what transpired yesterday."

Chao had discussed with McConnell what she should do. She felt the way many did. Trump had made working for him a liability to their professional reputations. Chao and others didn't want to stain their résumés. McConnell had told both O'Brien and Cipollone that their respective jobs—overseeing the nation's security and making sure the White House followed the law—were too critical to walk away from. But he thought his wife could leave the Department of Transportation without jeopardizing the country's stability.

The other Cabinet secretaries stayed, as did most top West Wing staff. As one senior official remarked, "If we all left, there wouldn't be any adults in the building, and that would make it worse."

Trump had made the nation's leaders choose. Not just whether to stay or go. But whether to preserve democracy or devolve toward authoritarian rule, whether the truth mattered or not, whether the end justifies the means. Tensions were running high. Congresswoman Liz Cheney, the number three–ranking House Republican who had close ties to several military and national security leaders, called Milley on January 7 to check in.

"How are you doing?" he asked her.

"That fucking guy Jim Jordan. That son of a bitch," Cheney said, referring to one of Trump's staunchest allies in the House. She described being together with Jordan during the siege. "While these maniacs are going through the place, I'm standing in the aisle and he said, 'We need to get the ladies away from the aisle. Let me help you.' I smacked his hand away and told him, 'Get away from me. You fucking did this.'"

Historian Doris Kearns Goodwin, who worked in

Lyndon Johnson's White House and closely studied many presidents, including Abraham Lincoln, said, "I have spent my entire career with presidents and there is nothing like this other than the 1850s, when events led inevitably to the Civil War.

"I do think that history will look back on this election and it will be a badge of dishonor for the people who objected without evidence," Goodwin said. "And you have to measure, for what purpose are they doing that? Is it ambition to be on the side of Trump? Is it party identification? This is a critical moment in our history."

On Capitol Hill, leaders in both parties were alarmed by Trump's state of mind and fearful of what he might do in his remaining days as president. Nancy Pelosi felt Trump had lost his sanity yet had access to the nuclear launch codes. The morning of January 8, the House Speaker called Milley. It was mostly a one-way conversation, with the chairman of the Joint Chiefs of Staff on the receiving end.

"This guy's crazy," Pelosi said of Trump. "He's dangerous. He's a maniac. We have deep concerns."

Pelosi reminded Milley of the oath he swore to the Constitution and asked him to review precautions for preventing an unstable president from initiating war by ordering a nuclear strike.

"Ma'am, I guarantee you that we have checks and balances in the system," Milley told her. He walked her through the process of nuclear release authorities.

"Ma'am, I guarantee you these processes are very good," he said. "There's not going to be an accidental firing of nuclear weapons."

"How can you guarantee me?" Pelosi asked.

"Ma'am, there's a process," he said. "We will only follow legal orders. We'll only do things that are legal, ethical, and moral."

This was something Pentagon and Justice Department officials had discussed several times. The president had the legal authority to launch a preemptive nuclear strike if nuclear missiles were heading, for instance, from Russia toward U.S. targets. But launching such a strike would not be legal—and the Pentagon could block it—if the risk were not imminent. The president would instead have to go to Congress to get authorization. Democratic lawmakers, however, were worried about a controversial legal opinion on military aggression authored by the Justice Department in 2018. It concluded the president had broad authority to bypass Congress to conduct limited strikes on foreign countries if he determined it was in the national interest and posed little risk of escalation, as Trump had done in Syria.

Speaking with Milley, Pelosi reiterated her assessment of Trump as deranged and dangerous—she already had publicly called on Pence and the Cabinet to invoke the Twenty-fifth Amendment and warned that if they did not the House would try to impeach him—but he resisted chiming in. Milley tried to stay professional.

"I'm not going to characterize the president," Milley told her. "That's not my place. That's not my duty."

After their call ended, Pelosi informed Democratic House members about her conversation with Milley. "The situation of this unhinged President could not be more dangerous," she wrote in a letter to her caucus.

At least a few senior Republican lawmakers privately shared Pelosi's concerns, though they were afraid of saying so in public. One of them recalled thinking at the time that Trump had "reached a new level of almost derangement after he lost the election. You know, we had this bizarre behavior all along, sort of contained, but a lot of heroic people at various points over the four years—and then, boom! All of the guardrails were gone."

In the days following January 6, the president and vice president were not on speaking terms. On January 7, Pence worked from home at the Naval Observatory. On January 8, he went to the White House and worked out of his West Wing office. Pence typically would ask staff in the mornings if the president had come down from the residence yet, and if he had, head straight to the Oval Office to see him. But not on January 8. The two men stayed in their separate offices.

"God, this is a fracture," Keith Kellogg, one of the few administration officials with loyalties to both

Trump and Pence, told colleagues. "We've got to fix this."

Not everyone around Pence was so eager to make amends. Marc Short was furious with the president for having left the vice president out to dry. Just about everything that had transpired over the past week disgusted Short—Trump's irrational refusal to acknowledge that the Constitution did not grant a vice president the power to overturn election results; his threats to Pence at the Georgia rally and then at the Ellipse; his tweet saying Pence lacked the courage to do what was right; and, most of all, his delay in telling his supporters chanting "Hang Mike Pence" to stand down and go home.

Trump was in the wrong, clearly, but was not about to apologize to Pence. In Trump's book, apologizing was a sin, an admission of weakness. So, Kellogg, O'Brien, and Kushner brainstormed how to bring the president and vice president back together, short of an apology. O'Brien proposed having Trump award Pence the Presidential Medal of Freedom, the nation's highest civilian honor, one that President Obama had bestowed upon Vice President Biden in their final days in office. The others liked the idea. They thought the award could recognize Pence's work chairing the coronavirus task force, though they knew it would be interpreted as a postinsurrection peace treaty. The three thought this could repair the relationship.

O'Brien broached the idea with Short. Short told him that if the president wanted to do this, that would be terrific, but that neither he nor the vice president would ask for the medal, and nor did they want to be seen as lobbying for it.

The plan was put on ice, and it was unclear whether Trump ever found out about it. Kushner and Ivanka Trump had another idea. Ivanka Trump felt strongly that her father and Pence needed to reconcile and asked the president if he would sit down with the vice president. He agreed and told her to have Pence come by the private dining room. Ivanka Trump, Kushner, and Short then met with Pence to make sure he was comfortable with the plan. He was ready to talk to Trump. Pence had surprised West Wing officials by his Reaganesque demeanor and sunny disposition around the office in the wake of the president's betrayal.

On the afternoon of January 11, Pence went in to see Trump. Kushner joined them. They spoke for about ninety minutes. Advisers to both the president and vice president described the conversation as cordial but would not characterize it further.

At the same time Kushner was trying to broker peace between the president and vice president, he also was trying to convince his father-in-law to stop stewing and start celebrating. Specifically, he wanted Trump to maximize his final days in office by burnishing his legacy, what so many advisers had been recommending for months.

Kushner hadn't been around the White House on January 6 or in the days leading up to the Capitol siege. He and his close adviser Avi Berkowitz had been in the Middle East negotiating another peace accord aimed at destabilizing Iran, this one between Qatar and Saudi Arabia. Saudi Arabia had agreed to end a yearslong blockade and reopen its borders and air space to Qatar. On January 4, the breakthrough had been announced. On January 6, Kushner and Berkowitz had been flying over the Atlantic en route to Washington. They thought to themselves, **We're done. We were diplomats. We crushed it. We put a ton of wins on the board, we made peace deals to make the world safer and create new hope.** Then they touched down in Washington and saw that all hell had broken loose, and Kushner went into what one colleague called "Mr. Fix-It mode." Kushner wanted Trump to take Air Force One on the road and give speeches touting his accomplishments across a range of policy areas—to remind Americans that he was a president who did much more than just complain about losing the election.

"Let's take a victory lap on all the things you've done and leave with your head held high," Kushner told his father-in-law. He suggested he visit the southern border and talk about immigration enforcement and newly constructed portions of the border wall.

"Talk about how you've rebuilt the military, gotten us out of wars, made peace deals," Kushner said, also suggesting an event to promote the coronavirus vaccines. "Look, I think this Warp Speed vaccine is one of your greatest accomplishments and one of the greatest accomplishments in our country in the last century."

Lindsey Graham was encouraging the same thing. Despite his "count me out" declaration from the Senate floor the night of January 6, Graham had almost immediately sidled up next to Trump again. He called the president and said, "I like you. I don't think you meant to incite a riot. You're not stupid. What good comes from inciting a riot? I think it got out of hand. I think it's going to be part of your legacy and you need to come to grips with this happening on your watch. You need to start repairing the damage."

Graham then spent a full day at the White House working with Kushner and Meadows to sketch a series of "legacy" events to help Trump get out from under January 6 and to keep him focused and busy until Inauguration Day on January 20. The last thing they wanted was Trump holed up in front of a television brooding. Like Kushner, Graham encouraged Trump to make a visit to the border and show off the wall. "Mr. President, you need a plan here," he said. "Just show people you're not sitting in the corner. The border is a good thing. You should be proud of what you've accomplished there."

Trump, however, was almost entirely fixated on the fallout from January 6. He was isolated and vengeful. With only days of his term left, many staffers were emptying out their offices in the West Wing and Trump lashed out at some of those who remained. Despite their tête-à-tête, he remained furious at

Pence and was angry that Democrats were planning to impeach him. The president also was upset with Giuliani and instructed aides not to pay his lawyer's legal fees.

One of Trump's advisers tried to cast blame on Giuliani and others on the legal team for trying to take advantage of him at a moment of extreme weakness. "They capitalize on people's vulnerabilities," this adviser said. "A desperate person is the most vulnerable to falsehoods and willing to believe what people tell them if it's something they want to hear." Still, this adviser felt Trump allowed himself to be susceptible: "He's not a victim. He's an adult. He makes his own decisions. He knows the difference between right and wrong."

This was one of the central characteristics of so many of Trump's advisers, their readiness to find someone or something else to blame for Trump's actions.

Trump agreed to get out of town. After six days out of public view, on January 12, the president touched down in the Rio Grande Valley of Texas, where he toured a new portion of wall in Alamo and gave a speech touting his immigration policy. Graham traveled with him. On the flight down, the president asked what January 6 felt like.

"It's going to be one of those big days in American history," Graham told him. "They'll be talking about this after we're all dead and gone."

At the wall, Trump included a few paragraphs in his speech addressing the insurrection. He warned against the effort by Democrats in Congress to hold him accountable.

"The impeachment hoax is a continuation of the greatest and most vicious witch hunt in the history of our country and is causing tremendous anger and division and pain, far greater than most people will ever understand, which is very dangerous for the U.S.A., especially at this very tender time," he said.

Also, during the trip Trump claimed his remarks at the Ellipse encouraging his supporters to march to the Capitol had been thoroughly analyzed and "everybody to the T thought it was totally appropriate."

It was just like Trump's "perfect phone call" with the Ukrainian president and the pandemic he had "totally under control." Predictably, Trump's comments about the siege became the headline that day. His aides threw their hands in the air. They could choreograph as many victory tour stops as they wanted, but it would be impossible for anyone to look at Trump without thinking of January 6.

"The media's not going to let us have, 'Wow, last week was really terrible, but Trump went to Texas today to wrap up the presidency.' It just wasn't happening," one aide remarked. "He could climb over that [border] fence himself and they are not taking the images of people at the Capitol off the TV."

The next day, January 13, the House voted to impeach Trump. It was a historic moment. Trump became the first president to be impeached twice. Yet it felt anticlimactic because there had been no doubt that the Democrat-controlled House would take this course.

"He must go," Pelosi said from the floor during the proceedings. "He is a clear and present danger to the nation that we all love."

Unlike in Trump's first impeachment, which had almost no Republican support, ten House Republicans, including Cheney, voted with Democrats to impeach him for inciting a riot with false claims of a stolen election. The final margin was sizable, 232 to 197, but Trump was unlikely to be removed from office prematurely. He had just seven days remaining in his term, and the Senate trial was not expected to begin until right after the inauguration. It seemed unlikely that enough Republicans there would join with Democrats to convict Trump. Indeed, in February, forty-three of fifty Senate Republicans would vote to acquit him of those crimes, allowing Trump to avoid conviction.

Ahead of Biden's inauguration, Washington was converted into a fortress city. A huge swath of the city was fenced off with tall metal barricades. Downtown businesses boarded their windows. Upwards of twenty thousand National Guard forces descended on the capital from across the country, on top of the massive patchwork of federal and local law enforcement personnel. Thousands of Trump supporters were organizing on social media to return to

Washington for what some called "the week of siege." Leaders across the city were determined to prevent a repeat of January 6.

On January 14, dozens of military and law enforcement leaders gathered at Fort Myer for a drill exercise. They took over a large gymnasium and mapped out the city on the floor to imagine where people might congregate, where security forces would be staged, which buildings snipers would occupy, and which intersections would be accessible.

Milley helped lead the drill and, in an initial smaller meeting with the more senior leaders, laid out the stakes:

"Here's the deal, guys: These guys are Nazis, they're boogaloo boys, they're Proud Boys. These are the same people we fought in World War II," Milley told them. "Everyone in this room, whether you're a cop, whether you're a soldier, we're going to stop these guys to make sure we have a peaceful transfer of power. We're going to put a ring of steel around this city and the Nazis aren't getting in."

He proceeded to pepper everyone with detailed questions. How many snipers would be here? How many there? What was their response time? What were their rules of engagement? How would they communicate with other forces? He posed a question to law enforcement leaders that, after January 6, was not entirely hypothetical: "So, if a guy shows up with horns, a painted face, wearing bear skins, and tries to take your weapon, what do you want our soldiers to do?"

Milley's point was to make everyone uncomfortable, to make them think through every possibility and plan for a worst-case scenario. One of the failings of January 6 was the lack of imagination on the part of the law enforcement and military agencies who shared responsibility for protecting the nation's capital. Those officers and their intelligence units did not expect that Trump's rally supporters would suddenly become violent, crazed rioters.

"The pain of preparation is much less than the pain of regret," Milley told the group.

As Trump was consumed by the insurrection and its aftermath, including his impeachment, criminal justice reform advocates and lawyers who had been trying unsuccessfully for weeks to get the president to focus on clemency applications started to panic. This group included Alice Johnson, a sixty-five-year-old Black woman and convicted drug offender, who had become the face of Trump's criminal justice reform efforts after he commuted her life sentence in 2018. Johnson and other advocates represented people who had been sentenced to years in prison for petty drug crimes or who had been unfairly tried and convicted, locked up even after witnesses recanted or evidence used at trial had been proven unreliable or flawed. Although they had an advocate in Kushner, they had struggled to get Trump's attention since the November election. Their clock was about to run out.

Trump liked granting pardons. He had long relished this unchecked power of his office. Many of the pardons he had issued earlier in his presidency were for political allies, such as Joe Arpaio, the former sheriff of Maricopa County, Arizona. Advisers said he genuinely looked forward to bestowing this "gift" of mercy upon deserving people, yet had done so mostly for people personally connected to him. In late December, Trump had delivered clemency to twenty-nine people, most of them well connected, including former Trump campaign advisers Paul Manafort and Roger Stone, as well as Kushner's father, Charles Kushner.

But the community that Johnson cared about—people who were neither famous nor fairly punished—still hadn't received Trump's mercy. Cipollone and other lawyers in his office were responsible for vetting clemency applications and had to sign off on and prepare the final paperwork for pardons. But after January 6, the White House lawyers had become fanatical about trying to fend off last-minute attempts by the president's allies to get Trump to do anything—including issuing controversial pardons—that could embarrass him and the administration.

"After January sixth, there is genuine panic almost nothing will happen, because Pat is furious with the president, fed up, and only wants to deal with the most solid, vetted, and noncontroversial cases," a Trump adviser said.

On January 13, Cipollone spread the word to

the president's staff and emissaries for pardon applicants that no more pardons would be granted after January 15. If they hadn't made it to the White House counsel's team for vetting and approval by that date, they weren't going to happen. Johnson was near tears upon hearing this news. She told colleagues she had a list of dozens of people practically rotting in prison, totally deserving of their freedom, who now would never even get a look. Kushner and Ivanka Trump were also upset and resolved to get more applications vetted. The couple pressed Trump to prioritize pardons. Meanwhile, outside lawyers involved in the process were surprised by Cipollone's deadline. They reminded him that in January 2001, President Clinton had issued pardons in the middle of the night before George W. Bush's inauguration, up until 2:00 a.m. in fact. Why couldn't Trump?

Over the weekend of January 16 and 17, Trump dug in, spending numerous hours going over the highlights of nearly four hundred applicants. Cipollone, Kushner, and Ivanka Trump weighed in with pros and cons. The president vacillated between who should and should not get his mercy, and even offered to pardon people who hadn't applied. He took phone calls from people advocating on behalf of a client or a friend. In some cases, once he decided to grant his mercy, Trump called the person's relative or lawyer to share the good news ahead of time.

Just before midnight on January 20, the White House announced that Trump would issue clemency to 143 candidates, a widely diverse group. Nonviolent drug offenders, one of Kushner's priorities, made up nearly one third of the list. But politicians convicted of misconduct and corruption, as well as officials embroiled in the Mueller investigation and those with special ties to Trump, made up just as large a share.

The most controversial pardon went to Steve Bannon, Trump's on-again, off-again adviser, who had been charged the previous year with defrauding donors to a charity that had been established to privately fund the wall on the southern border. Rapper Lil' Wayne also received a pardon. A last-minute advocacy campaign by rapper Snoop Dogg convinced Trump to commute the sentence of Death Row Records cofounder Michael "Harry-O" Harris. Trump also extended a pardon to Republican megadonor Elliott Broidy, who had pleaded guilty to lobbying the Trump administration for foreign governments without registering as a foreign agent.

The list was so hastily assembled that the paperwork bore multiple errors about the specific cases and key information was misspelled or missing altogether. Many of those winning Trump's mercy never even filed a petition for consideration with the Department of Justice, which was the standard process for pardon applicants. The vast majority who succeeded had a powerful friend who knew someone they could call in the White House or were brought to the president's attention by advocates like Johnson. Most of the fourteen thousand applicants who did follow the normal Justice Department process were sidelined and remained in limbo.

It has long been an American tradition that on Inauguration Day the outgoing president receives the incoming one, even if the departing leader has just lost a bruising campaign to his successor. Hands are shaken. Pleasantries are exchanged. When the new president swears his oath of office, his predecessor is sitting right beside him observing, approving. This is how power has been peacefully transferred over so many years. This was the beauty of democracy.

On Inauguration Day 2017, Barack and Michelle Obama were disturbed to be turning over the White House—the people's house—to Donald and Melania Trump. They had watched Trump's campaign and feared his bleak vision for America. But they abided by tradition. The country deserved nothing less. As Michelle Obama wrote in her memoir, **Becoming,** "Sitting on the inaugural stage in front of the U.S. Capitol for the third time, I worked to contain my emotions. The vibrant diversity of the two previous inaugurations was gone, replaced by what felt like a dispiriting uniformity, the kind of overwhelmingly white and male tableau I'd encountered so many times in my life." When she realized this wasn't just bad optics, but perhaps the new reality, she wrote, "I made my own optic adjustment: I stopped even trying to smile."

On January 20, 2021, as Biden took office, the Trumps were nowhere to be seen. They didn't even bother going through the motions as the Obamas had done four years earlier. Instead, they fled the capital before the festivities began. As he left the White House early that morning, the outgoing president told a small crowd, "We will be back in some form. Have a good life."

Trump then staged a farewell rally at Joint Base Andrews before boarding Air Force One en route to West Palm Beach. In his remarks, Trump never once uttered the names of Biden or Vice President-elect Kamala Harris, even though they were written into his prepared script. And he made clear that he did not intend to cede the political stage.

"I will always fight for you," Trump said. "I will be watching. I will be listening. And I will tell you that the future of this country has never been better. I wish the new administration great luck and great success. I think they'll have great success. They have the foundation to do something really spectacular."

The Trumps then boarded Air Force One, and as the presidential jet taxied down the runway and took off, the loudspeakers at his rally blared Frank Sinatra's "My Way." During the flight to Florida, in his final minutes as president, Trump granted a full pardon for Albert Pirro, the ex-husband of his Fox News loyalist Jeanine Pirro. It was announced just as Trump's motorcade deposited him at Mar-a-Lago.

Trump's Andrews event was sparsely attended.

Many of his once-close Republican allies eschewed the farewell to attend Biden's inauguration, including Pence and McConnell. Pence had said goodbye to Trump the day before, in the Oval Office. The scene was awkward.

"Hey, Mike, are you flying away? Where are you going?" Trump asked.

"I'm going to Indiana," Pence said.

"Okay, I'll see you later," Trump said.

Trump then told Pence, "You did a good job," and they shook hands.

Aides watching could sense the frostiness between the two men. "There was a coolness," one recalled. "They didn't know whether to hug, shake hands, pat on the back, say, 'See you later.' That feeling when you don't know what to say."

At the Capitol on January 20, Pence and his wife, Karen, sat respectfully at the platform as the ceremony got under way. They were the lone representatives of the outgoing administration. At 11:48 a.m., Joseph Robinette Biden Jr. raised his right hand and swore the oath to serve his nation and to preserve, protect, and defend the Constitution. His wife, Jill Biden, in a striking peacock-green dress and matching coat, held a large family Bible from the late 1800s.

The oath took less than two minutes and then came shouts of hurrah and applause. The Bidens embraced, and then the new president hugged his son Hunter and his daughter Ashley. The former presidents, former first ladies, congressional leaders, and other VIPs seated on the platform seemed to share a collective moment of pinch-me relief. The Trump era was over.

A number of musical artists performed, and Amanda Gorman, the National Youth Poet Laureate of 2017, read "The Hill We Climb," her paean to the nation's triumph over a threatening four years of chaos and division:

> We've seen a force that would shatter our nation
>   rather than share it
> Would destroy our country if it meant delaying
> Democracy
> And this effort very nearly succeeded
> But while democracy can be periodically delayed
>   it can never be permanently defeated.

Soon the ceremony was over, and it was time for old friends to greet one another. Milley had been seated directly behind the Obamas and the three of them chatted, sharing a moment of levity. Michelle Obama asked Milley how he was feeling.

"No one has a bigger smile today than I do," he told her. "You can't see it under my mask, but I do."

The "bad boy" that Milley, Pompeo, and Meadows had worried about landing finally was on the ground. The peaceful transfer of power had been completed.

Harris, now the vice president, paused to thank Milley profusely. "We all know what you and some others did," she said. "Thank you."

It was time for the Bidens to make their way down the parade route that now was practically a hermetically sealed street topped off by razor wire. Milley kept looking at his phone, receiving security updates. The city was a "ring of steel," just as he had said it would be, and there were no signs of trouble.

As Milley recounted to aides, he got home that night to his house high atop Fort Myer and took in his most perfect view. From his front lawn, he could stare down over the monuments to America's great presidents—Washington, Jefferson, and Lincoln—and to Martin Luther King Jr., as well as to the hard-fought wars that enshrined the country's commitment to democracy. He saw the White House in the foreground and the Capitol off in the distance.

Looking out over the capital city at peace, Milley thought to himself, **Thank God Almighty, we landed the ship safely.**

Epilogue

S eventy days had passed since Donald Trump left Washington against his will. On March 31, 2021, we ventured to Mar-a-Lago, where he still reigned as king of Republican politics. We arrived late that afternoon for our audience with the man who used to be president and were ushered into an ornate sixty-foot-long room that functioned as a kind of lobby leading to the club's patio. A model of Air Force One painted in Trump's proposed redesign—a flat red stripe across the middle, a navy belly, a white top, and a giant American flag on the tail—was proudly displayed on the coffee table facing the entrance. It was a prop disconnected from reality. Trump's vision never came to be; the fleet now in use by President Biden still bears the iconic baby blue–and–white livery designed by Jacqueline Kennedy.

"Used to be" is not a phrase anyone dares use to describe the president inside his Palm Beach castle. Here, beneath the gold-leaf ceiling of winged griffins and crystal chandeliers, Trump still rules, surrounded day and night by applauding fans, obsequious courtiers, and dutiful servants. At the perfectly manicured Mar-a-Lago, none of the disgrace that marked the end of his presidency pierces Trump's reality. Here, he and his aides work to maintain the gospel according to Trump, with the most important revelations being that Donald Trump was the greatest president of all time and was unjustly denied a second term.

Trump had invited us to Mar-a-Lago to interview him for this book. He had declined an interview for our first book about his presidency, and when **A Very Stable Genius** was published in January 2020, attacked us personally and branded our reporting a work of fiction. But Trump was quick to agree to our request this time. He sought to curate history.

As we sat for the interview, the former president's press secretary presented us copies of a bound volume: **1,000 Accomplishments of President Donald J. Trump: Highlights of the First Term.** On the back cover is an American flag, the presidential seal, and Trump's thick, jagged signature. The book totals 92 pages and is organized with chapters dedicated to the economy, tax cuts, deregulation, trade, and so on.

Trump walked into the room flanked by a couple of plainclothed Secret Service agents, a much smaller detail than he once had as president. He wore his customary dark suit and tie, his face covered with bronze makeup. He sat in his preferred position, a plush armchair of ivory brocade facing the entrance where guests arrive, with us on a sofa to his right. Behind him was a huge window looking out to the Atlantic Ocean; in front of him, the patio facing Lake Worth.

"This is the biggest, the best, the most acreage, the most everything—the ocean, the lake, it fronts both," the ever-boasting Trump said. "Mar-a-Lago is ocean-to-lake. Did you know that? Mar-a-Lago, ocean to lake. It's the only place. See that window? That window, when that was built, is the largest pane of glass in the world, okay?"

Trump started the interview by pointing out his enduring and unrivaled power within the Republican Party. He explained that he didn't intend to follow the path of former presidents, who largely bowed out of the nitty-gritty of party politics. He was proud to say he genuinely enjoys this sport he found so late in life, and believes he plays it better than anyone else. The parade of Republican politicians flocking to Mar-a-Lago all spring to kiss his ring had both energized him, he said, and proved the value of his stock.

"We have had so many, and so many are coming in," Trump said. "It's been pretty amazing. You see the numbers. They need the endorsement. I don't say this in a braggadocious way, but if they don't get the endorsement, they don't win."

But future elections were not front and center in his mind. A past election was. Trump was fixated on his loss in 2020, returning to this wound repeatedly throughout the interview.

"In a certain way, I had two presidencies," he said.

In the first, when the economy was roaring, Trump argued that he had been unbeatable, never mind that his approval rating was never higher than 46 percent in the Gallup poll during his first three years as president.

"I think it would be hard if George Washington came back from the dead and he chose Abraham Lincoln as his vice president, I think it would have been very hard for them to beat me," Trump said.

Then, he lamented, came his second presidency: the pandemic killed his chances.

Trump seemed determined as well to convince us that he actually had won, and handily, had it not been for the many people who had wronged him—the "evil people" who conspired to deny him his rightful second term.

"The greatest fraud ever perpetrated in this country was this last election," Trump said. "It was rigged and it was stolen. It was both. It was a combination, and Bill Barr didn't do anything about it."

Trump faulted not only his attorney general, but Vice President Pence for lacking the bravery to do what was right.

"Had Mike Pence had the courage to send it back to the legislatures, you would have had a different outcome, in my opinion," Trump said.

"I think that the vice president of the United States must protect the Constitution of the United States," he added. "I don't believe he's just supposed to be a statue who gets these votes from the states and immediately hands them over. If you see fraud, then I believe you have an obligation to do one of a number of things."

The irony was lost on Trump, however, that one of the central reasons he had prized Pence as his number two was his resemblance to a statue standing adoringly at his side.

Trump then invoked the nonanalogous example he had latched on to: "Thomas Jefferson was in the exact same position, but only one state, the state of Georgia. Did you know that? It's true. 'Hear ye, hear ye . . .'—was much more elegant in those days. It was, 'Hear ye, hear ye, the great state of Georgia is unable to accurately count its votes.' Thomas Jefferson said, 'Are you sure?' They said, 'Yes, we are sure.' 'Then we will take the votes from the great state of Georgia.' He took them for him and the president."

Trump continued, "So I said, 'Mike, you can be Thomas Jefferson or you can be Mike Pence.' What happened is, I had a very good relationship with Mike Pence—very good—but when you are handed these votes and before you even start about the individual corruptions, the people, the this, the that, all the different things that took place, when you are handed these votes . . . right there you should have sent them back to the legislatures."

Later in the conversation, Trump again expressed his disappointment in Pence. "What courage would have been is to do what Thomas Jefferson did [and said], 'We're taking the votes,'" he said. "That would have been politically unacceptable. But sending it back to these legislatures, who now know that bad things happened, would have been very acceptable. And I could show you letters from legislators, big-scale letters from different states, the states we're talking about. Had he done that, I think it would have been a great thing for our country." But, he surmised, "I think he had bad advice."

Trump argued that he stands apart from the presidents before him by the loyalty and intensity of his supporters. "There's never been a base that screams out, with thirty-five thousand people, 'We love you! We love you!'" he said. "That never happened to Ronald Reagan. It never happened to anybody. We have a base like no other. They're very angry. That's what happened in Washington on the sixth. They went down because of the election fraud. . . . The one thing that nobody says is how many people were there, because if you look at that real crowd, the crowd for the speech, I'll bet you it was over a million people."

What was Trump's goal on January 6? What did he hope his supporters would do after he told them to march on the Capitol?

He chose to remark again on the size of the crowd. "I would venture to say I think it was the largest crowd I had ever spoken [to] before," Trump said. "It was a loving crowd, too, by the way. There was a lot of love. I've heard that from everybody. Many, many people have told me that was a loving crowd. It was too bad, it was too bad that they did that."

Pressed again, Trump said he had hoped his supporters would show up outside the Capitol but not enter the building. "In all fairness, the Capitol Police were ushering people in," Trump said. "The Capitol Police were very friendly. They were hugging and kissing. You don't see that. There's plenty of tape on that."

Trump didn't mention the countless other video recordings showing horrific violence—that of a riotous mob shoving a police officer to the ground, later threatening to shoot him with his own gun, or that of an insurrectionist bashing a flagpole into another police officer's chest, or that of yet another officer howling in pain as his torso was compressed in a closing revolving door.

"Personally, what I wanted is what they wanted," Trump said of the rioters. "They showed up just to show support because I happen to believe the election was rigged at a level like nothing has ever been rigged before. There's tremendous proof. There's tremendous proof. Statistically, it wasn't even possible that [Biden] won. Things such as, if you win Florida and Ohio and Iowa, there's never been a loss."

He was referring to conventional wisdom that historically the winner of the presidential election has carried that same trio of states that Trump won. This was one of the traits that had led Trump to the White House on full display: his extraordinary capacity to say things that were not true. He always seemed to have complete conviction in whatever product he was selling or argument he was making. He had an uncanny ability to say with a straight face, things are not as you've been told or even as you've seen with your own eyes. He could commit to a lie in the frame of his body and in the timbre of his voice so fully, despite all statistical and even video evidence to the contrary.

At various points in our interview, Trump presented other examples of what he called proof the election had been stolen from him.

"Take all of the dead people that voted, and there were thousands of them, by the way. We have lists of obituaries," Trump argued. "If you take the illegal immigrants that voted. If you take this—Indians that got paid to vote in different places. We had Indians getting paid to vote! Many, many different things, all election changing."

Trump zeroed in on large cities in Michigan and Pennsylvania, both of which he lost to Biden, that are home to many Black people and historically vote heavily Democratic. "Look, everyone knows that Detroit was so corrupt. Everyone knows that they literally beat up people there, they hurt people to get the vote watchers out, our vote watchers, Republican vote watchers," he said. He added, "Philadelphia, highly corrupt in terms of elections. There were tremendous irregularities that went on there, including the fact that you had more votes than you had voters."

He was still fixated on the debunked water main

conspiracy in Fulton County, Georgia. "They say, 'Water main break!,' everyone leaves—everyone leaves—and then you have these people go in with two or three other people, all their people, run to the table where ballots are . . . this table which had a skirt on it, opened the skirt and took out the ballots and started stuffing the ballot boxes," he said. "It was reported on every newscast."

In his discussion of the "stolen" election, Trump grew more animated and specific about the long list of advisers and allies he considered disloyal. He said that Barr failed him as attorney general for not buying the conspiracy and for not dispatching the FBI to investigate Fulton County's vote-tallying process. To Trump's mind, Barr had become too exhausted to act in his final months on the job. Trump also posited that Barr had grown too sensitive to media criticism, worried about his depiction as a loyal marionette who did the president's bidding, that he backed away from properly investigating voter fraud.

"Bill Barr changed a lot," Trump said. "He changed drastically, and in my opinion, he changed because of the media. The media is brilliant. I give them credit. I get it better than anybody that's ever lived. Bill Barr came in because he was really legitimately incensed at what they were doing to me and the presidency on the Mueller hoax. . . . He did a good job on the Russian hoax, right? And then as time went by, and what I should have done is said, 'Bill, thank you very much. Great job.'"

The Department of Justice, he continued, "is loaded up with radical left, and Bill Barr was being portrayed as a puppet of mine. They said he's my 'personal lawyer,' 'he'll do anything,' and I said, 'Here we go. . . .' He got more and more difficult, and I knew it. You know why? Because he's a human being. Because that's the way it works."

Trump listed Barr's sins: He didn't charge James Comey or Andrew McCabe; he didn't announce an investigation into Hunter Biden; and he didn't bring an end to John Durham's probe of the origins of the Russia investigation before the election. Trump speculated that Barr was motivated by personal pique rather than reality when he announced on December 1 that the Justice Department had uncovered no evidence of widespread voter fraud that could change the election outcome.

"Barr disliked me at the end, in my opinion, and that's why he made the statement about the election, because he did not know," Trump said. "And I like Bill Barr, just so you know. I think he started off as a great patriot, but I don't believe he finished that way."

Trump said he was also disappointed by federal judges—especially the three conservative justices he had nominated to the Supreme Court—for ruling against his campaign in the scores of lawsuits it filed or, in the case of the high court, declining to take the case. When we asked whether he needed better lawyers, considering so many courts had ruled there was not substantiated evidence of fraud nor merit to the cases brought before them, Trump said his legal team was not to blame.

"I needed better judges. The Supreme Court was afraid to take it," Trump said, suggesting that justices might have declined to intervene in the election out of fear of stoking violence. Referring to the election result, Trump added, "It should have been reversed by the Supreme Court. I'm very disappointed in the Supreme Court because they did a very bad thing for the country."

Trump singled out Justice Brett Kavanaugh, suggesting that he should have tried to intervene in the election as payback for the president standing by his nomination in 2018 in the face of sexual assault allegations. "I'm very disappointed in Kavanaugh," he said.

Trump's chagrin was evident in many of his answers. He emphasized his feelings of victimhood.

"I had two jobs: running our country, and running it well, and survival," Trump said. "I had the Mueller hoax. I had the witch hunt. It's one big witch hunt that's gone from the day I came down the escalator," a reference to his 2015 campaign launch event in the lobby of New York's Trump Tower.

"Nobody's ever gone through what I have," Trump added. "They got me on all phony stuff."

Trump found fault with most of his fellow Republican leaders, past and present. Still clearly vexed by the ghost of the late Arizona senator John

McCain, Trump without prompting brought up the party's 2008 presidential nominee, whom he had attacked for years.

"John McCain was a bad guy," he said of the decorated prisoner of war. "He was a bully and a nasty guy, bad guy. A lot of people disliked him. Last in his class in Annapolis. All that stuff, but he was a bad guy. I say it to you. I don't care. Does it affect me? I won Arizona, okay? By a lot. Didn't turn out that way in terms of the vote, but I won Arizona. Everyone knows it. He didn't affect me. I won the first time. I won it the second time."

Trump, who in fact lost Arizona to Biden, continued with this fix. "You know, I did three rallies in Arizona," he said. "I never had an empty seat." Governor Doug Ducey, who withstood Trump's pressure to overturn the result, was "not a loyal party member," according to the former president. "I think Ducey is a terrible Republican," he said. "Ducey did everything he could to block voter integrity, to block people from making sure the vote was accurate."

Trump also complained about former House Speaker Paul Ryan, whom he labeled a "super-RINO"—Republican in name only. And he said Mitch McConnell has "no personality" nor a killer political instinct. He faulted McConnell for refusing to eliminate the filibuster to ram through Republican legislation and for not persuading Senator Joe Manchin, the moderate Democrat from West Virginia, to switch parties.

"He's a stupid person," Trump said of McConnell. "I don't think he's smart enough."

"I tried to convince Mitch McConnell to get rid of the filibuster, to terminate it, so that we would get everything, and he was a knucklehead and he didn't do it," Trump said.

Trump said he wished he had had partners in Congress like Meade Esposito, who was the head of the Democratic Party machine in Brooklyn from the late 1960s to the early 1980s. Esposito, who counted Trump and his late father, Fred Trump, as business associates, was known for his patronage and commanded respect.

"Nobody would ever talk back to Meade Esposito. Meade Esposito didn't have a RINO like a Mitt Romney, you know, or as I said, Ben Sasse, who's a lightweight," Trump said, invoking two Republican senators who sometimes criticized him. He added, "Mitch McConnell compared to Meade Esposito, it's like a baby compared to a grownup football player with brains on top of everything else."

Esposito had run a citywide patronage system that doled out important jobs to loyalists and people providing gifts and favors. The party boss gained a fearsome reputation for his intimidation tactics and connections to organized crime. Amid an investigation of his work, Esposito retired in 1983; he was convicted on a corruption charge in 1987.

Other presidents attend to philanthropic interests, write memoirs, and curate presidential libraries after leaving office. But not Trump. Many of his Palm Beach days have followed the tempo and style he set back in Washington, a reflection of his addiction to the twenty-four-hour news cycle and appetite to maintain political relevance. In the morning hours, he spends time alone in his private quarters watching television and making phone calls to allies and friends. Many days he plays a round of golf at one of his nearby clubs. And in the afternoons, he puts on his suit, applies his makeup, and emerges for meetings with whichever politicians or acolytes have made the pilgrimage to Mar-a-Lago.

The original owner of Mar-a-Lago, cereal heiress Marjorie Merriweather Post, had hoped her ocean-front mansion would serve as a Winter White House after her death. In 1985, Trump purchased the property from the U.S. government and used it as a private residence before turning it into a members-only club in 1995. Merriweather Post's wish indirectly came true during Trump's presidency, as he spent many winter weekends and the Thanksgiving and Christmas holidays there. He also received some foreign heads of state at Mar-a-Lago. But in early 2021, Trump had turned his club into a political base camp for his potential comeback.

Trump made no secret of his interest in perhaps running for president in 2024. Would he choose Pence again as his running mate?

"Well, I was disappointed in Mike," Trump said. "But, you know, I'll be making a decision at some point. I will say this: Based on the polls, those polls are great, the Republican Party loves Trump. Ninety-seven percent!"

When we pointed out that Pence is said to be interested in running for president, too, Trump seemed to welcome the competition. "It's a free country, right?" he said. "It's a free country."

But Trump all but ruled out running with Chris Christie, who had been runner-up to Pence in his 2016 veepstakes, and Nikki Haley, the former ambassador to the United Nations who had criticized Trump's attempts to subvert the vote in repeated interviews with Tim Alberta of **Politico.**

"Chris has been very disloyal, but that's okay," Trump said. "I helped Chris Christie a lot. He knows that more than anybody, but I helped him a lot. But he's been disloyal."

As for his former ambassador, Trump said he was rebuffing her outreach. "Nikki Haley wants to come here so badly," he said. "She did a little nasty couple of statements. . . . She has been killed by the party. When they speak badly about me, the party is not happy about it. It's pretty amazing. There's not been anything like this."

Over the years, Trump rarely has expressed misgivings. But he regrets his response to protests last summer in Minneapolis, Portland, Seattle, and other cities. "I think if I had it to do again, I would have brought in the military immediately," he said.

Trump had no such second thoughts about his handling of the pandemic. He said he had been "very tough" in protecting the country by restricting travel, first from China and then from Europe. He said he did so against the wishes of his top medical advisers; in fact, most of them agreed with the restrictions before he made his decision, according to participants in the discussions and their contemporaneous notes. But he correctly said he pushed scientists at the FDA "at a level that they have never been pushed before" to get vaccines approved in record time.

"I think we did a great job on COVID and it hasn't been recognized," Trump said, noting that other countries saw spikes in COVID-19 infections in the months after he left office. "The cupboards were bare. We didn't have gowns. We didn't have masks. We didn't have ventilators. We didn't have anything. . . . We brought in plane loads. We did a great job."

When we asked Trump why he encouraged people to believe things that weren't true or to distrust science and the media, he delighted in talking about the scientific smarts in his family's genes.

"First of all, I'm a big person," he said. "Do you know this? My uncle, Dr. John Trump, I think he was at [the Massachusetts Institute of Technology] longer than any other professor. Totally brilliant man . . . He had numerous degrees. So that's in the genes. I always go with that stuff. But it's a little bit in the genes and Dr. John Trump, he was a great guy. My father's brother. No, I'm a big believer in science. If I wasn't, you wouldn't have a vaccine. It depends. Are you talking about disinformation or are you talking about lies? There is a more beautiful word called disinformation."

When we pressed him on whether a president should be expected to be honest all the time, given his long record of exaggerating successes, downplaying pitfalls, and spreading misinformation, Trump said, "I want to be somebody that's optimistic for our country. I think it's very important."

Trump ridiculed Anthony Fauci as a self-promoter and lamented the doctor's high popularity. He said the widespread praise for Fauci was undeserved, and mocked Fauci's frequent request of people to call him by his first name.

"A highly overrated person," Trump said. "He's a nice guy. I got along great with him. 'Please call me Tony,' I call him. 'Please call me Tony.' He's a great promoter, but he was wrong on everything."

Trump also trashed Deborah Birx and said she was far too restrictive.

"She was a lot of work, a real diva with the scarves and shit," he said. "If it were up to her, we wouldn't be meeting tonight. This place would be totally closed. You wouldn't have three hundred people having dinner outside and schools open. . . . If it were up to her, everything would be closed forever."

"She's a woman I always liked, but in the end I jettisoned her and I didn't take her advice," he said, adding: "She loves publicity almost as much as Fauci. I got some real beauties."

Trump credited himself with turning government officials into household names, but said it also had a negative consequence. The incredible excitement of his administration, he said, drove media interest in chronicling disputes and differences of opinion among his staff, creating a false impression that his administration was chaotic.

"You have people that have never been stars before and all of a sudden **The Washington Post** is calling. **New York Times** is calling. CNN would love to have lunch with you. 'Come up and meet our editorial staff!,'" Trump said. "All of these people are calling. You are a regular person in government. If you were [in the] Jimmy Carter [administration], you're not calling these people. If you were [in the] Bush [administration], you're not calling these people. With Trump, everybody becomes a star. I'm the greatest star-maker in history."

Our interview with Trump was scheduled for one hour but stretched to two and a half. His press secretary chimed in every thirty minutes to let him know how long we had been speaking and to give him an opening to end it, but Trump seemed to enjoy the conversation and kept talking. Clusters of club members traipsed through the room before dinner on the Moorish-tiled patio overlooking the lagoon. Service staff gingerly arranged tables around the room's perimeter for the buffet—a spread of jumbo gulf shrimp and fresh Wellpoint oysters over ice here, a bananas Foster station there.

Some of Trump's friends breezed past to greet him, interrupting the interview. Laura Ingraham stopped by and urged the former president to tune into her Fox show that night at 10:00. She said she would be talking about his former medical advisers. A few nights earlier, CNN had aired a documentary featuring critical comments by Birx, Fauci, and other members of Trump's coronavirus task force.

"We're really going to put it to the doctors. You should watch," Ingraham told Trump. Dressed in the classic Palm Beach attire of a bright-striped blouse and sherbet-colored slacks, Ingraham was one of the few women at the club that night wearing pants; the vast majority wore cocktail dresses and stiletto heels.

Then Kimberly Guilfoyle, the girlfriend of Trump's eldest son, paraded through, with a full face of makeup. She told her small clutch of guests to go out to the patio to take their seats and she would join them soon. Then she hovered nearby our interview to say hello to the former president.

Guilfoyle's approach seemed cautious and formal, unlike someone greeting her boyfriend's father. She had recently bought a mansion with Donald

Trump Jr. in nearby Jupiter, but she had other reasons to claim good standing in Trump's world. Guilfoyle had been a major fundraiser for Trump's campaign and promoted the claim that the election had been rigged. She asked Trump to please come by her dinner table later, where she would sit with Trump Jr., so she could introduce her friends to him.

"They're **huge** supporters of yours," Guilfoyle stressed. Trump nodded and smiled, telling her he would swing by.

Congressman Dan Crenshaw, a Texas Republican and former Navy SEAL, also came by, interrupting the interview to tell Trump that life in Palm Beach was obviously agreeing with him.

"You look great, sir," Crenshaw said. "What's your secret?"

As more dinner guests with plates began queuing up in the room to visit the raw bar and other food stations, Trump finally decided it was time to wrap up our conversation. He invited us to stay for dinner and instructed the maître d' to find us a table. Then the former president stepped onto the veranda and into the last of the day's sun. Right on cue, the dinner guests immediately stood up at their tables to applaud him. He took it all in, smiling. Just another Wednesday night at Mar-a-Lago. And off he went, table by table, to greet friends.

Later in the evening Trump returned to check on us. He wanted to make sure we were comfortable. His gallantry seemed genuine.

"Good conversation," Trump said. "I'm getting the word out."

The interview, he said, was "a great honor." He offered to do another if we needed to ask anything else and shrugged off the mention of how many hours he had already spent answering our questions.

"I enjoyed it actually," Trump said, a twinkle in his eye. "For some sick reason I enjoyed it."

Acknowledgments

We first extend our appreciation to the many people who were willing to share their accounts from this tumultuous time. We cannot name them here, but each helped us immeasurably in telling the full story of a historic year. Some suffered and chafed in their service to President Trump and could have decided to pack up their memories and put this challenging period behind them. Many public officials sought to serve their country when the stakes couldn't have been higher, and when safeguarding Americans was often in conflict with fulfilling the demands of the president. We are grateful to them for helping us document this consequential year.

This project would not have been possible without the generous support and commitment of our editors at **The Washington Post.** We thank our former executive editor, Marty Baron, whose commitment to shining a light on the powerful and unearthing truths not only propelled our newsroom but also fortified a free press as it came under attack. We are grateful to Steven Ginsberg, a guide and touchstone for the **Post**'s gripping coverage of the Trump administration and a critical advocate and inspiration for this deeper examination. We owe a debt as well to Cameron Barr, who ably led our remote newsroom after Marty's retirement and kept our mothership sailing steadily forward amid a pandemic. We also thank Dave Clarke, Dan Eggen, Matea Gold, Tracy Grant, Lori Montgomery, Kat Downs Mulder, Krissah Thompson, and Peter Wallsten for the support and wisdom they lent to our reporting and this endeavor.

Our work has been lifted and inspired by the very best journalists in America, our colleagues at the **Post** whose probing coverage of President Trump in this final year paved our path. We are grateful to them for their keen insights and friendship, and for shouldering the work when we were absent. Special thanks to Yasmeen Abutaleb, Devlin Barrett, Bob Costa, Alice Crites, Aaron Davis, Josh Dawsey, David Fahrenthold, Amy Gardner, Anne Gearan, Tom Hamburger, Shane Harris, Rosalind Helderman, Seung Min Kim, Dan Lamothe, Toluse Olorunnipa, Ashley Parker, Damian Paletta, Beth Reinhard, Missy Ryan, Lena Sun, and Matt Zapotosky.

We have had the good fortune to find stability and unsurpassed vision at the **Post.** Carol came to the paper in 2000 and Philip in 2005, and we consider ourselves lucky to work in a newsroom that seeds excellence in its journalism and nurtures collegiality in its journalists. The **Post**'s mission flourishes because of an unbroken chain of leaders committed to the public good and our democracy. These values were first enshrined by Katharine Graham and protected by Don Graham and Katharine Weymouth. Jeff Bezos and Fred Ryan have championed and built upon the Graham family legacy with their determination to uphold the highest journalistic principles, hold the powerful to account, and expand the **Post**'s reach.

We also are fortunate at the **Post** to work with a diligent group of public relations professionals, especially Cindy Andrade, Kris Coratti, Molly Gannon, and Shani George, who dedicate themselves to ensuring our journalism finds a broad audience on many platforms. We also are indebted to Alma Gill, Sam Martin, Elliot Postell, and Liz Whyte for giving us the tools to do our best work.

We thought we knew all the reasons it was wonderful to have Ann Godoff as our book editor, but to partner with her again to make sense of this horrific year was a special privilege. Ann is a maestro who can conduct several symphonies at once, a ferocious competitor, and a steadfast champion of the deep reporting that infuses these pages. As the finest editors do, she demands of her writers what feels all but impossible, convinces them they can, and mounts the same Herculean effort on their behalf. William Heyward lent his considerable talent, intellectual firepower, and narrative instincts to this project. The superlative team at Penguin Press, including Casey Denis,

Aly D'Amato, Tess Espinoza, Katie Hurley, Jane Cavolina, Gary Stimeling, Do Mi Stauber, Mike Brown, Alice Dalrymple, Kate Griggs, Will Jeffries, John Jusino, Lorie Young, Nicole Celli, Chelsea Cohen, Amanda Dewey, Gloria Arminio, Claire Vaccaro, and Yuki Hirose helped perfect and polish these pages. And the estimable Sarah Hutson, Matthew Boyd, and Colleen McGarvey helped maximize the reach of our reporting.

Elyse Cheney is our brilliant literary agent, but far more than that to us both. She has been an integral part of our work throughout, giving us hours upon hours of her support and sage advice on everything from our narrative arc to our jacket design. Her level of commitment to us and to our work has been invaluable, impressive, and moving. We are grateful for Elyse and her team, including Allison Devereux, Claire Gillespie, Isabel Mendia, and Natasha Fairweather.

A number of other people played essential roles in this project. Julie Tate, our longtime collaborator and friend, once again gave her all to stress test our manuscript. The rigor of her work is unparalleled. Kimberly Cataudella and Aaron Schaffer conducted essential research. Cynthia Colonna transcribed many of our interviews. Melina Mara, our friend and **Post** photojournalist, shot our author portraits.

We have now spent five years in the trenches with scores of journalists at the top of their game, who each toiled and sacrificed to bring truth to the American public with unflinching professionalism. Our work builds upon and benefits from our competitors, of which there are too many to list here. This has been the most challenging and exhilarating period in American journalism during our lifetimes, and we are in awe of their contributions amid threats against them and disinformation.

Rucker

To my mother, Naomi, who raised me with unconditional love and endowed me with the character and courage to achieve my goals, thank you. You afforded me countless opportunities and empowered me to follow my passions and overcome my trepidations. I could never be the author or the man I am today without the sacrifices you made.

My exceptional sister, Clara, has become as loving a mother as she is gifted a professional. She and Karen have created a nurturing home for Lee, my sweet and inquisitive nephew, who brings joy to my life. Our late grandparents, Bunny and Helen, brave champions of peace, equality, and justice, would be proud.

Thank you to Carol Leonnig for her unbending determination and devotion to our endeavor. I was not sure how our partnership would evolve after we wrote **A Very Stable Genius,** for we had no intention of writing a sequel, but I am so glad we did, and that we did it together. Carol brought intelligence and shrewd intuition to our undertaking, and her penetrating questioning deepened our reporting. She never wavered in her commitment to our mission, no matter what it required, and history is richer for it.

I had the great fortune to cover the final year of the Trump presidency as part of the fiercest White House reporting team in the news business: Josh Dawsey, Anne Gearan, Seung Min Kim, David Nakamura, Toluse Olorunnipa, and Ashley Parker, led by our deft and dedicated editors, Dan Eggen and Dave Clark. Our many collaborations made me a stronger journalist, and our lively Zooms helped me get through months of lockdown. Special thanks to Dan, my direct editor for nearly a decade. His rigor, instincts, and energy have been at the heart of our Trump coverage since even before the famous escalator ride.

I am lucky to work in a newsroom where collegiality is the creed. Thank you as well to Dan Balz, Jabin Botsford, Bob Costa, Jose Del Real, Amy Gardner, Ann Gerhart, Tammy Haddad, Shane Harris, Roz Helderman, Tracy Jan, Jenna Johnson, Mary Jordan, Al Kamen, Paul Kane, Annie Linskey, Sally Quinn, Damian Paletta, Lisa Rein, Lois Romano, Eli Saslow, Maralee Schwartz, Valerie Strauss, Kevin Sullivan, Karen Tumulty, and Matt Viser for your warm friendship during the pandemic.

It has been a privilege to work with the all-star team at NBC News and MSNBC. Thank you to Kasie Hunt, Rashida Jones, Rachel Maddow, Andrea Mitchell, Elena Nachmanoff, Joy Reid, Jesse Rodriguez,

Stephanie Ruhle, Katy Tur, Nicolle Wallace, Brian Williams, and so many others. I am indebted to the inimitable Alan Berger and his crack team at Creative Artists Agency for making it all possible.

To Yamiche Alcindor, Peter Alexander, Peter Baker, Michael Bender, Geoff Bennett, Kaitlan Collins, Jeremy Diamond, Maggie Haberman, Hallie Jackson, Jonathan Karl, Annie Karni, Weijia Jiang, Tamara Keith, Carol Lee, Jonathan Lemire, Jeff Mason, Zeke Miller, Kelly O'Donnell, Katie Rogers, April Ryan, Mike Shear, Eli Stokols, Cecilia Vega, Kristen Welker, and so many others, thank you for being wonderful colleagues on the White House beat and for your companionship on the road.

To Luis Gabriel Cuervo, Liz Dooghan, Borja Gracia, Anna Gregory, Mari Fer Merino, Justin Mills, Ryan Ozimek, John Petersen, Sarah Strom, and April Warren, who have been my D.C. family at Sunday night "Noche" dinners, thank you for your love and nourishment. To Marc Adelman, Adrienne Arsht, Michael Barbaro, Andrew and Liz Cedar, Luke Frazier, Rick Guinne, Garrett Haake, Joel Johnson, Evelyn Kramer, Matt Lachman, Elyse Layton, Tom Lee, Lisa Lerer, Will and Addar Levi, Dafna Linzer, Rebecca Livengood, Sara Murray, Leslie Pope, Adam and Rachel Presser, Julia Pudlin, Maeve Reston, Matt Rivera, Tim Runfola, Graves Spindler, Rachel Streitfeld, Keith Urbahn, Burden Walker, Nate Wenstrup, Alicia Widge, and David Wishnick, thank you for always being there.

Leonnig

I want to thank the people who have now held me
together through the grueling work of three books.
The first is John Reeder. Words don't convey how
lucky I feel to have chosen him as my life partner.
Unflappable, ethical, and centered, he reminds me
what is important and helps me get there. He brings
the lattes, the pep talks, the love. With him in my
corner, it is all possible.

To my wonderful daughters, Elise and Molly. You
grew into even more beautiful people inside and
out while this work was in progress. I stand stunned
at what you and your friends have accomplished
amid all the challenges this last year brought. Your
determination, smiles, and even your TikTok dances
brightened the hardest days lashed to the laptop. You
make your father and me so proud.

To my work partner, Phil Rucker. I was also incredibly lucky to partner with him, and even after having
done this once before, I remain in awe of the rigor,
creativity, and integrity he brought to each aspect
of our work together for this second book. Readers
across the country know what a graceful writer he
is and rightfully count him among the best White
House reporters in a generation. But working with
him under incredible pressure, I got to experience the
grace he has as a person, the hard extra mile he is willing to travel to give and be the very best.

I thank my treasured family. To my mother, Dolly

Leonnig, for cheering me with her gourmet cooking, flower arrangements, and visits on the porch with her grandchildren. To Ronnie Reno, for loving my mom and always setting the example. To sister Brooke and brother Henry, for the love I feel across the miles. To my late father, Harry Leonnig, for showing me how fun it can be when you love your work. To my extended Reeder clan, I am so glad to call you my family.

Where would I be without my wonderful friends? Special thanks to my indomitable CCDC crew for being on speed dial for me and my family and enriching our life: Caity and Michael Callison, Michelle and Steve Dolge, Julie and Andy Maner, Lisa Rosenberg and Frank Gorman, Liz Wieser and Phil Inglima, and Kristin and Peter Willsey. I'm deeply grateful for the friendship of Jodi Moraru, Paige Williams, the Hanleys, Resches, Slades, Scalzos, and Teems, and equally indebted to my wonderful pals from the ornament club, book club, cool group, and the Bryn Mawr posse. Thanks to those who have always supported and cheered my work, too many to name, with an atta girl when our paths crossed or a Facebook like on a story I shared. Special mention: Mike Raibman and Mona Benach. I hope to thank all of you soon.

The Washington Post, the hometown paper where I had always wanted to work, turned out to be a great place for the kind of reporting I loved. It now also holds so many people who feel like family. I thank them for making it a joy to go to work. In addition to the great **Post** colleagues we mentioned above, thank you to Dan Balz, Bob Barnes, Tammy Haddad, Sari Horwitz, Colby Itkowitz, Greg Jaffe, Tracy Jan, Natalie Jennings, Paul Kane, Michael Kranish, Michelle Lee, Nick Miroff, Dana Priest, Mike Semel, Robert Samuels, Ian Shapira, Julie Tate, Craig Timberg, Karen Tumulty, and Katie Zezima.

Finally, thank you to the producers and hosts at NBC News and MSNBC, including Savannah Guthrie, Hallie Jackson, Rachel Maddow, Andrea Mitchell, Joy Reid, Stephanie Ruhle, Ali Velshi, Nicolle Wallace, Brian Williams, Alex Witt, as well as Sarah Baker and Jesse Rodriguez. This smart team shines a light day in and day out on the best reporting in the country, and brings that informed conversation to more Americans. I'm honored to join them.

Notes

Chapter One: Deadly Distractions

17 **Redfield had told them:** CBS, **CBS This Morning,** October 2018, John Dickerson.

23 **American intelligence agencies had learned:** Eric Schmitt et al., "For Trump, a Risky Decision on Suleimani Is One Other Presidents Had Avoided," **New York Times,** January 3, 2020, www.nytimes .com/2020/01/03/world/middleeast/suleimani -iran-iraq-strike.html.

23 **The intelligence was, in the assessment:** Press Gaggle with Secretary of Defense Dr. Mark T. Esper and Chairman of the Joint Chiefs of Staff General Mark A. Milley, January 6, 2020, www .defense.gov/Newsroom/Transcripts/Transcript/ Article/2051321/press-gaggle-with-secretary -of-defense-dr-mark-t-esper-and-chairman-of -the-join.

26 **Trump would later regale:** Kevin Liptak, "Trump Recounts Minute-by-Minute Details of Soleimani Strike to Donors at Mar-a-Lago," CNN, January 18, 2020, www.cnn.com/2020/01/18/

politics/trump-soleimani-details-mar-a-lago/
index.html.

27 **In early January, U.S. intelligence agencies:**
Greg Miller and Ellen Nakashima, "President's
Intelligence Briefing Book Repeatedly Cited Virus
Threat," **Washington Post,** April 27, 2020, www
.washingtonpost.com/national-security/presidents
-intelligence-briefing-book-repeatedly-cited-virus
-threat/2020/04/27/ca66949a-8885-11ea-ac8a
-fe9b8088e101_story.html.

32 **Even the high-level Chinese delegation:** David
Nakamura, "After Epic Trade Fight, Trump Puts
Chinese Leaders' Patience to the Test in Marathon
White House Ceremony," **Washington Post,**
January 15, 2020, www.washingtonpost.com/
politics/after-epic-trade-fight-trump-puts-chinese
-leaders-patience-to-the-test-in-marathon-white
-house-ceremony/2020/01/15/fea4b2c6-37c9
-11ea-bf30-ad313e4ec754_story.html.

34 **Trump passed word to his aides:** Maggie
Haberman, "Trump Was Not Watching as the
Articles Were Read on the Senate Floor," **New York
Times,** January 16, 2020, www.nytimes.com/live/
2020/trump-impeachment-01-16#trump-was-not
-watching-as-the-articles-were-read-on-the-senate
-floor.

Chapter Two: Totally Under Control

49 **The CDC publicly announced:** Centers for
Disease Control, "First Travel-Related Case of
2019 Novel Coronavirus Detected in United
States," CDC Newsroom, January 21, 2020,

www.cdc.gov/media/releases/2020/p0121-novel
-coronavirus-travel-case.html.

53 **The Spanish flu had infected:** Centers for Disease Control, "History of 1918 Flu Pandemic," www.cdc.gov/flu/pandemic-resources/1918 -commemoration/1918-pandemic-history .htm.

66 **Later intelligence would confirm:** Mai He et al., "Cremation-Based Estimates Suggest Significant Under- and Delayed Reporting of COVID-19 Epidemic Data in Wuhan and China," www .medrxiv.org/content/10.1101/2020.05.28 .20116012v2.full.pdf.

68 **And he declared:** Erica Werner et al., "Trump Administration Announces Mandatory Quarantines in Response to Coronavirus," **Washington Post,** January 31, 2020, www.washingtonpost .com/us-policy/2020/01/31/trump-weighs-tighter -china-travel-restrictions-response-coronavirus.

68 **Before the markets closed:** Fred Imbert, Yun Li, and Thomas Franck, "Stock Market Updates Friday: Dow Drops 600, Coronavirus Fears Grow, Apple Loses 4%," CNBC, January 31, 2020, www .cnbc.com/2020/01/31/stock-market-live-updates -dow-down-100-amazon-up-10percent-to -1-trillion.html.

Chapter Three: Seeking Revenge

70 **Two days later, Trump strode:** Ashley Parker and Josh Dawsey, "The Surprises at Trump's State of the Union Were Carefully Planned," **Washington Post**, February 5, 2020, www.washingtonpost

.com/politics/the-surprises-at-trumps-state-of
-the-union-were-carefully-planned/2020/02/05/
d4561646-4835-11ea-ab15-b5df3261b710_story
.html.

74 **Trump's rash and retaliatory dismissal:**
William H. McRaven, "Opinion: William
McRaven: If Good Men Like Joe Maguire Can't
Speak the Truth, We Should Be Deeply Afraid,"
Washington Post, February 21, 2020, www
.washingtonpost.com/opinions/william-mcraven
-if-good-men-like-joe-maguire-cant-speak-the
-truth-we-should-be-deeply-afraid/2020/02/21/
2068874c-5503-11ea-b119-4faabac6674f_story
.html.

74 **In early February, around the time:** "Presidential
Approval Ratings—Donald Trump," Gallup,
https://news.gallup.com/poll/203198/presidential
-approval-ratings-donald-trump.aspx.

82 **They said Shea felt pressure:** Statement for
the Record: Assistant United States Attorney
Aaron S. J. Zelinsky, House Judiciary Committee,
June 24, 2020, www.congress.gov/116/meeting/
house/110836/witnesses/HHRG-116-JU00
-Wstate-ZelinskyA-20200624-U7.pdf.

82 **One of the prosecutors:** Statement for the Record:
Assistant United States Attorney Aaron S. J.
Zelinsky, House Judiciary Committee, June 24,
2020.

83 **In a sign of how little:** Timothy Bella, "'Cannot
Allow This Miscarriage of Justice!': Trump Blasts
Sentencing Recommendation for Roger Stone,"
Washington Post, February 11, 2020, www

.washingtonpost.com/nation/2020/02/11/trump
-stone-sentencing.

85 **"I think it's time to stop":** Attorney General Bill
Barr's Interview with ABC News: Transcript, ABC
News, July 2020, https://abcnews.go.com/Politics/
attorney-general-bill-barrs-interview-abc-news
-transcript/story?id=71696291.

91 **He was fuming:** Yasmeen Abutaleb, Ashley Parker,
and Josh Dawsey, "Inside Trump's Frantic Attempts
to Minimize the Coronavirus Crisis," **Washington
Post,** February 29, 2020, www.washingtonpost.com/
politics/inside-trumps-frantic-attempts-to-minimize
-the-coronavirus-crisis/2020/02/29/7ebc882a-5b25
-11ea-9b35-def5a027d470_story.html.

Chapter Four: The P-Word

100 **"We're dealing with":** "Dr. Fauci: Coronavirus
Now at 'Outbreak' and 'Likely Pandemic
Proportions,'" MSNBC, March 2, 2020, www
.msnbc.com/msnbc/watch/dr-fauci-coronavirus
-now-at-outbreak-and-likely-pandemic
-proportions-79827013761.

102 **The next day, Trump toured:** "President Trump
Visits NIH Vaccine Research Center," National
Institutes of Health, **NIH Director's Blog,**
March 3, 2020, https://directorsblog.nih.gov/
potus-lab-visit_3-3-21.

103 **This was a move to please:** Abby Goodnough,
"Trump Administration Sharply Curtails Fetal
Tissue Medical Research," **New York Times,**
June 5, 2019, www.nytimes.com/2019/06/05/us/
politics/fetal-tissue-research.html.

103 **he wanted them to reverse the ban:** Amy Goldstein, "Trump Ban on Fetal Tissue Research Blocks Coronavirus Treatment Effort," **Washington Post,** March 18, 2020, www.washingtonpost.com/health/trump-ban-on-fetal-tissue-research-blocks-coronavirus-treatment-effort/2020/03/18/ddd9f754-685c-11ea-abef-020f086a3fab_story.html.

109 **On March 3, she tested:** "Placer County Announces Death of Patient with COVID-19," County of Placer, March 4, 2020, www.placer.ca.gov/6438/Death-of-patient-with-COVID-19.

113 **He had recently dined:** Seung Min Kim and Josh Dawsey, "Trump Picks Mark Meadows to Be New White House Chief of Staff," **Washington Post,** March 6, 2020, www.washingtonpost.com/politics/trump-picks-mark-meadows-as-new-white-house-chief-of-staff/2020/03/06/c669d3fe-6010-11ea-8baf-519cedb6ccd9_story.html.

121 **Futures for the Dow Jones:** Philip Rucker, Ashley Parker, and Josh Dawsey, "Ten Minutes at the Teleprompter: Inside Trump's Failed Attempt to Calm Coronavirus Fears," **Washington Post,** March 12, 2020, www.washingtonpost.com/politics/trump-coronavirus-teleprompter-speech/2020/03/12/81bc8a3a-647a-11ea-acca-80c22bbee96f_story.html.

124 **"The crowds & lines":** Governor J. B. Pritzker (@GovPritzker), Twitter, March 14, 2020, 10:50 p.m., https://twitter.com/govpritzker/status/1239021033191018497?lang=en.

125 **"Respirators, ventilators, all of the equipment":** Jonathan Martin, "Trump to Governors on

Ventilators: 'Try Getting It Yourselves,'" **New York Times,** March 16, 2020, www.nytimes.com/2020/03/16/us/politics/trump-coronavirus-respirators.html.

126 **"We have an invisible enemy":** Philip Rucker, "Americans Kept Wondering What the President Wanted Them to Do About Coronavirus. Finally, Trump Offered Some Guidance," **Washington Post,** March 16, 2020, www.washingtonpost.com/politics/americans-kept-wondering-what-the-president-wanted-them-to-do-about-coronavirus-finally-trump-offered-some-guidance/2020/03/16/e58d8200-6793-11ea-9923-57073adce27c_story.html.

Chapter Five: Rebelling Against the Experts

138 **"I say that you are a terrible reporter":** Paul Farhi, "NBC's Peter Alexander Asked Trump to Reassure Americans About Coronavirus. Trump Berated Him Instead," **Washington Post,** March 20, 2020, www.washingtonpost.com/lifestyle/media/nbcs-peter-alexander-asked-trump-to-reassure-americans-about-coronavirus-trump-berated-him-instead/2020/03/20/f7452a80-6ada-11ea-b313-df458622c2cc_story.html.

140 **On March 29, the president announced:** Philip Rucker, "Trump Beats a Retreat on Opening the Country as Coronavirus Data, Images Show Dark Reality," **Washington Post,** March 29, 2020, www.washingtonpost.com/politics/trump-coronavirus-guidelines-easter-elmhurst/2020/03/29/c15c21f2-7215-11ea-87da-77a8136c1a6d_story.html.

142 **The volunteers worked out:** Peter Baker et al., "Kushner Puts Himself in Middle of White House's Chaotic Coronavirus Response," **New York Times,** April 2, 2020, www.nytimes.com/ 2020/04/02/us/politics/jared-kushner-coronavirus -trump.html.

143 **But because of his exalted status:** Baker et al., "Kushner Puts Himself in Middle."

145 **Unbeknownst to Birx:** Philip Rucker et al., "34 Days of Pandemic: Inside Trump's Desperate Attempts to Reopen America," **Washington Post,** May 2, 2020, www.washingtonpost.com/politics/ 34-days-of-pandemic-inside-trumps-desperate -attempts-to-reopen-america/2020/05/02/e99911f4 -8b54-11ea-9dfd-990f9dcc71fc_story.html.

152 **"Without any basis":** Matt Zapotosky, "Barr Calls Current Restrictions 'Draconian' and Suggests They Should Be Revisited Next Month," **Washington Post,** April 9, 2020, www.washingtonpost.com/ national-security/attorney-general-william-barr -fox-news-coronavirus/2020/04/09/dfda1f94 -7a12-11ea-a130-df573469f094_story.html.

154 **"It's Fauci's fault":** Robert Costa et al., "Trump's May Days: A Month of Distractions and Grievances as Nation Marks Bleak Coronavirus Milestone," **Washington Post,** May 31, 2020, www.washingtonpost.com/politics/trumps-may -days-a-month-of-distractions-and-grievances-as -nation-marks-bleak-coronavirus-milestone/2020/ 05/31/123e7e6a-a120-11ea-81bb-c2f70f01034b _story.html.

154 **On April 14, he formally:** Betsy Klein and Jennifer Hansler, "Trump Halts World Health Organization Funding over Handling of Coronavirus Outbreak," CNN, April 15, 2020, https://edition.cnn.com/2020/04/14/politics/donald-trump-world-health-organization-funding-coronavirus/index.html.

156 **They also warned:** Josh Rogin, "Opinion: State Department Cables Warned of Safety Issues at Wuhan Lab Studying Bat Coronaviruses," **Washington Post,** April 14, 2020, www.washingtonpost.com/opinions/2020/04/14/state-department-cables-warned-safety-issues-wuhan-lab-studying-bat-coronaviruses.

157 **Now they were adding:** Rogin, "Opinion: State Department Cables Warned of Safety Issues."

157 **"A lot of people are":** David Jackson and Kim Hjelmgaard, "Trump Says US Investigating Whether Coronavirus Spread After China Lab Mishap but Cites No Evidence," **USA Today,** April 18, 2020, www.usatoday.com/story/news/world/2020/04/18/trump-us-investigating-whether-coronavirus-spread-china-lab/5158551002.

158 **That was not normal:** Charles Schmidt, "Did the Coronavirus Leak from a Lab? These Scientists Say We Shouldn't Rule It Out," **MIT Technology Review,** March 18, 2021, www.technologyreview.com/2021/03/18/1021030/coronavirus-leak-wuhan-lab-scientists-conspiracy.

159 **Later research would establish:** Rafi Letzter, "The Coronavirus Didn't Really Start at That Wuhan 'Wet Market,'" **Live Science,** www

.livescience.com/covid-19-did-not-start-at-wuhan
-wet-market.html.

161 **But Trump, who famously said:** Philip Rucker
et al., "'What Do You Have to Lose?': Inside
Trump's Embrace of a Risky Drug Against
Coronavirus," **Washington Post,** April 6, 2020,
www.washingtonpost.com/politics/what-do-you
-have-to-lose-inside-trumps-embrace-of-a-risky
-drug-against-coronavirus/2020/04/06/0a744d7e
-781f-11ea-a130-df573469f094_story.html.

Chapter Six: Refusing to Mask Up

176 **Shortly after the CNN story:** Jeremy Diamond,
Jamie Gangel, and Tami Luhby, "White House
Officials Are Discussing Plans to Replace HHS
Secretary Alex Azar," CNN, April 26, 2020,
www.cnn.com/2020/04/25/politics/white-house
-health-and-human-services-secretary-alex-azar/
index.html.

181 **After the CDC issued guidance:** Centers for
Disease Control, "Use Masks to Slow the Spread
of COVID-19," February 16, 2021, www.cdc.gov/
coronavirus/2019-ncov/prevent-getting-sick/diy
-cloth-face-coverings.html.

182 **"Somehow sitting in the Oval Office":** Daniel
Victor, Lew Serviss, and Azi Paybarah, "In His
Own Words, Trump on the Coronavirus and
Masks," **New York Times,** October 2, 2020, www
.nytimes.com/2020/10/02/us/politics/donald
-trump-masks.html.

183 **"Since I don't have the coronavirus":** Felicia
Sonmez, "Pence Meets with Mayo Clinic Patients,

Staff While Not Wearing Face Mask," **Washington Post,** April 28, 2020, www.washingtonpost.com/politics/pence-meets-with-mayo-clinic-patients-staff-while-not-wearing-face-mask/2020/04/28/57c4200c-897e-11ea-9dfd-990f9dcc71fc_story.html.

183 **Two days later second lady:** Talia Kaplan, "Karen Pence Defends Husband After Backlash for Not Wearing a Mask at Mayo Clinic Visit," Fox News, April 30, 2020, www.foxnews.com/media/karen-pence-defends-vp-mike-pence-not-wearing-mask.

183 **Before the trip:** Paul Farhi, "Pence's Staff Threatens Action Against Reporter Who Tweeted About Visit to Clinic Without Surgical Mask," **Washington Post,** April 30, 2020, www.washingtonpost.com/lifestyle/media/pence-staff-threatens-action-against-reporter-who-tweeted-about-visit-to-clinic-without-surgical-mask/2020/04/30/27c63056-8b0a-11ea-9dfd-990f9dcc71fc_story.html.

183 **In a rare public:** Annie Karni, "Pence Visits Ventilator Plant in Indiana, This Time Wearing a Mask," **New York Times,** April 30, 2020, www.nytimes.com/2020/04/30/us/politics/coronavirus-pence-mask.html.

184 **"I didn't think it was necessary":** John Wagner and Hannah Knowles, "Pence Acknowledges He Should Have Worn a Mask During His Mayo Clinic Visit," **Washington Post**, May 4, 2020, www.washingtonpost.com/politics/pence-acknowledges-he-should-have-worn-a-mask-during-his-mayo-clinic-visit/2020/05/04/

7cbe5c0e-8e03-11ea-a9c0-73b93422d691_story
.html.

186 **"He will always protect American citizens":**
Erik Wemple, "Opinion: Kayleigh McEnany
Fails to Reframe Her Famous Coronavirus
Gaffe," **Washington Post,** May 7, 2020, www
.washingtonpost.com/opinions/2020/05/07/
kayleigh-mcenany-fails-reframe-her-famous
-coronavirus-gaffe.

189 **But subsequent reporting by Dan Diamond:**
Dan Diamond, "Trump Officials Interfered
with CDC Reports on Covid-19," **Politico,**
September 11, 2020, www.politico.com/news/
2020/09/11/exclusive-trump-officials-interfered
-with-cdc-reports-on-covid-19-412809.

191 **For the germaphobe president:** Nicholas Wu,
"Trump Kicks Out Chief of Staff for Coughing
During an Interview," **USA Today,** June 17,
2019, www.usatoday.com/story/news/politics/
onpolitics/2019/06/17/trump-kicks-out-mulvaney
-coughing-stephanopoulos-abc-interview/
1475364001.

192 **In fact, Trump continued:** David Nakamura,
Carol D. Leonnig, and Josh Dawsey, "Trump
Flouts Coronavirus Protocols as Security Experts
Warn of Need to Protect President from a Lethal
Threat," **Washington Post,** May 8, 2020, www
.washingtonpost.com/politics/trump-flouts
-coronavirus-protocols-as-security-experts-warn-of
-need-to-protect-president-from-a-lethal-threat/
2020/05/08/3a6a9cec-9136-11ea-a9c0-73b93422
d691_story.html.

192 **He procured hundreds of thousands:** Carol D. Leonnig, Elizabeth Dwoskin, and John Hudson, "As U.S. Discouraged Mask Use for Public, White House Team Raced to Secure Face Coverings from Taiwan for Senior Staff," **Washington Post,** April 15, 2020, www.washingtonpost.com/politics/ as-us-discouraged-mask-use-for-public-white -house-team-raced-to-secure-face-coverings-from -taiwan-for-senior-staff/2020/04/15/27d815d2 -7ac5-11ea-a130-df573469f094_story.html.

204 **On May 10, which was Mother's Day:** Glenn Kessler and Salvador Rizzo, "Trump's Mother's Day Tweetstorm Accusing Obama of Crimes," **Washington Post,** May 12, 2020, www .washingtonpost.com/politics/2020/05/12/ trumps-mothers-day-tweet-storm-accusing-obama -crimes.

211 **On May 20, the U.S. government:** Aakash B, Guy Faulconbridge, and Kate Holton, "U.S. Secures 300 Million Doses of Potential AstraZeneca COVID-19 Vaccine," Reuters, May 21, 2020, www.reuters.com/article/us-health-corona- virus-astrazeneca/u-s-secures-300-million-doses -of-potential-astrazeneca-covid-19-vaccine-id USKBN22X0J9.

Chapter Seven: Bunkers, Blasts, and Bibles

217 **A white officer:** Richard A. Oppel Jr. and Kim Barker, "New Transcripts Detail Last Moments for George Floyd," **New York Times,** July 8, 2020, www.nytimes.com/2020/07/08/us/george-floyd -body-camera-transcripts.html.

218   **"There is no gray":** "Minneapolis Mayor Jacob Frey Speech Transcript After Minnesota Police Officer Kills Man," Rev, May 26, 2020, www.rev.com/blog/transcripts/minneapolis-mayor-jacob-frey-speech-transcript-after-minnesota-police-officer-kills-man.

220   **He had wanted to know:** Matt Zapotosky and Devlin Barrett, "Justice Dept. Will Not Charge Police in Connection with Eric Garner's Death," **Washington Post,** July 16, 2019, www.washingtonpost.com/national-security/justice-dept-will-not-charge-police-in-connection-with-eric-garners-death/2019/07/16/f5188d84-a761-11e9-86dd-d7f0e60391e9_story.html.

222   **"It was so fast":** "Floyd's Brother: Trump 'Didn't Give Me the Opportunity to Even Speak,'" MSNBC, May 30, 2020, www.msnbc.com/politicsnation/watch/george-floyd-s-brother-says-trump-didn-t-give-him-the-opportunity-to-even-speak-in-conversation-84136517515.

223   **Instead Trump focused:** Peter Baker, "Trump Tweets and Golfs, but Makes No Mention of Virus's Toll," **New York Times,** May 24, 2020, www.nytimes.com/2020/05/24/us/politics/trump-coronavirus-death-toll.html.

224   **"There's maybe a fundamental problem":** Ashley Parker, "For a Numbers-Obsessed Trump, There's One He Has Tried to Ignore: 100,000 Dead," **Washington Post,** May 28, 2020, www.washingtonpost.com/politics/for-a-numbers-obsessed-trump-theres-one-he-has-tried-to-ignore-100000-dead/2020/05/27/0a9c58ee-9f63-11ea-9590-1858a893bd59_story.html.

224 **Between May 27 and May 29:** Keith L. Alexander and Meryl Kornfield, "Among More Than 400 Arrested During Protests in the District, Most Cases Involve Curfew Violations and Burglary," **Washington Post,** June 16, 2020, www .washingtonpost.com/local/public-safety/among -more-than-400-arrested-during-protests-in-the -district-most-cases-involve-curfew-violations -and-burglary/2020/06/14/ef7e2e82-ac93-11ea -94d2-d7bc43b26bf9_story.html.

226 **Additional demonstrators had scaled:** Clarence Williams, Perry Stein, and Peter Hermann, "Demonstrations for George Floyd Lead to Clashes Outside White House," **Washington Post,** May 30, 2020, www.washingtonpost.com/ local/public-safety/demonstration-for-george -floyd-shuts-down-dc-intersection/2020/05/29/ af7b5d40-a1f9-11ea-b5c9-570a91917d8d_story .html.

227 **Trump also claimed:** Maggie Haberman, "Trump Threatens White House Protesters with 'Vicious Dogs' and 'Ominous Weapons,'" **New York Times,** May 30, 2020, www.nytimes.com/2020/ 05/30/us/politics/trump-threatens-protesters-dogs -weapons.html.

228 **Indeed some in the public arena:** Philip Rucker, "As Cities Burned, Trump Stayed Silent—Other Than Tweeting Fuel on the Fire," **Washington Post,** May 31, 2020, www.washingtonpost.com/politics/ as-cities-burned-trump-stayed-silent-other-than -tweeting-fuel-on-the-fire/2020/05/31/4fc8761a -a354-11ea-b619-3f9133bbb482_story.html.

229 **That weekend, Tom Rath:** Rucker, "As Cities Burned, Trump Stayed Silent."

236 **Trump had been mulling a plan:** Ashley Parker, Josh Dawsey, and Rebecca Tan, "Inside the Push to Tear-Gas Protesters Ahead of a Trump Photo Op," **Washington Post,** June 1, 2020, www .washingtonpost.com/politics/inside-the-push -to-tear-gas-protesters-ahead-of-a-trump-photo -op/2020/06/01/4b0f7b50-a46c-11ea-bb20-ebf 0921f3bbd_story.html.

241 **"You have to dominate":** "Transcript of Trump's Call with Governors: 'Dominate . . . or You'll Look Like a Bunch of Jerks,'" San Jose **Mercury News,** June 2, 2020, www.mercurynews.com/2020/ 06/02/transcript-of-trumps-call-with-governors -dominate-or-youll-look-like-a-bunch-of-jerks.

252 **D.C. Metropolitan Police Chief Peter Newsham:** Aaron C. Davis et al., "Officials Familiar with Lafayette Square Confrontation Challenge Trump Administration Claim of What Drove Aggressive Expulsion of Protesters," **Washington Post,** June 14, 2020, www.washingtonpost.com/ politics/officials-challenge-trump-administration -claim-of-what-drove-aggressive-expulsion-of -lafayette-square-protesters/2020/06/14/f2177e1e -acd4-11ea-a9d9-a81c1a491c52_story.html.

252 **Both Newsham and DeMarco:** Tony Jackman and Carol D. Leonnig, "National Guard Officer Says Police Suddenly Moved on Lafayette Square Protesters, Used 'Excessive Force' Before Trump Visit," **Washington Post,** July 27, 2020, www .washingtonpost.com/nation/2020/07/27/

national-guard-commander-says-police-suddenly
-moved-lafayette-square-protesters-used-excessive
-force-clear-path-trump.

252 **But the part of his account:** Jackman and
Leonnig, "National Guard Officer Says Police
Suddenly Moved on Lafayette Square Protesters."

Chapter Eight: Staring Down the Dragon

254–255 **That night, Esper instructed:** "Message to
the Department—Support to Civil Authorities,"
U.S. Department of Defense, June 3, 2020, www
.defense.gov/Newsroom/Releases/Release/Article/
2206224/message-to-the-department-support-to
-civil-authorities.

257 **Esper noted that:** "Secretary of Defense Mark
Esper Press Conference Transcript: Does Not
Support Military Response to Protests," Rev, June 3,
2020, www.rev.com/blog/transcripts/secretary-of
-defense-mark-esper-press-conference-transcript
-does-not-support-military-response-to-protests.

268 **The FDA announced:** Food and Drug
Administration, "Coronavirus (COVID-19) Update:
FDA Revokes Emergency Use Authorization
for Chloroquine and Hydroxychloroquine,"
June 15, 2020, www.fda.gov/news-events/press
-announcements/coronavirus-covid-19-update
-fda-revokes-emergency-use-authorization
-chloroquine-and.

273 **"Whatever Trump's goal":** Mike Mullen, "I
Cannot Remain Silent," **Atlantic,** June 2, 2020,
https://www.theatlantic.com/ideas/archive/2020/
06/american-cities-are-not-battlespaces/612553.

273   **"Donald Trump is the first president":** Jeffrey Goldberg, "James Mattis Denounces President Trump, Describes Him as a Threat to the Constitution," **Atlantic,** June 3, 2020, www.theatlantic.com/politics/archive/2020/06/james-mattis-denounces-trump-protests-militarization/612640.

274   **The nonpartisan military:** Carol D. Leonnig and Dan Lamothe, "How Mattis Reached His Breaking Point—and Decided to Speak Out Against Trump," **Washington Post,** June 5, 2020, www.washingtonpost.com/politics/how-mattis-reached-his-breaking-point--and-decided-to-speak-out-against-trump/2020/06/05/6aafd548-a69e-11ea-bb20-ebf0921f3bbd_story.html.

276   **"We are still struggling with racism":** Mark Milley, National Defense University 2020 Class Graduation Address, June 11, 2020, www.americanrhetoric.com/speeches/markmilley nationaldefenseuniversitygraduationremarks.htm.

276   **"I should not have been there":** Dan Lamothe, "Pentagon's Top General Apologizes for Appearing Alongside Trump in Lafayette Square," **Washington Post,** June 11, 2020, www.washingtonpost.com/national-security/2020/06/11/pentagons-top-general-apologizes-appearing-alongside-trump-lafayette-square.

Chapter Nine: A Sea of Empty Seats

282   **Trump had significant business:** Eric Lipton and Benjamin Weiser, "Turkish Bank Case Showed

Erdogan's Influence with Trump," **New York Times,** October 29, 2020, www.nytimes.com/ 2020/10/29/us/politics/trump-erdogan-halkbank .html?smid=tw-share.

282 **On June 18, as Barr's office:** Shayna Jacobs, "Before His Ouster, U.S. Attorney Refused to Join Justice Dept. Rebuke of New York Mayor," **Washington Post,** June 22, 2020, www.washingtonpost.com/ national-security/before-his-ouster-us-attorney -refused-to-join-justice-dept-rebuke-of-new-york -mayor/2020/06/22/46b485f0-b4c5-11ea-a8da -693df3d7674a_story.html.

285 **He urged Berman:** Opening Statement of Geoffrey S. Berman Before the House Judiciary Committee, July 9, 2020, https://judiciary.house .gov/uploadedfiles/opening_statement_geoffrey_s ._berman.pdf?utm_campaign=4107-519.

287 **"I cherish every day":** Devlin Barrett, "Trump Administration in Standoff with Manhattan U.S. Attorney Who Investigated the President's Associates," **Washington Post,** June 19, 2020, www.washingtonpost.com/national-security/ trump-administration-replaces-manhattan-us -attorney/2020/06/19/acae9348-b298-11ea-8758 -bfd1d045525a_story.html.

288 **"Your statement also wrongly":** Rosalind S. Helderman et al., "Trump Ousts Manhattan U.S. Attorney Who Investigated President's Associates," **Washington Post,** June 20, 2020, www.washington post.com/politics/geoffrey-berman-us-attorney -william-barr-trump/2020/06/20/fcbfa3b4-b30f -11ea-8758-bfd1d045525a_story.html.

291   **"It's the perfect storm":** Noah Weiland, "Tulsa Officials Plead for Trump to Cancel Rally as Virus Spikes in Oklahoma," **New York Times,** June 16, 2020, www.nytimes.com/2020/06/16/us/politics/trump-coronavirus-rally.html.

291   **Trump opponents warned:** Joshua Partlow, "Threats and Invective Hurled at Health Director Who Sought to Postpone Trump's Tulsa Rally, Emails Show," **Washington Post,** September 21, 2020, www.washingtonpost.com/politics/threats-and-invective-hurled-at-local-health-director-who-sought-to-postpone-president-trumps-rally-in-tulsa-emails-show/2020/09/21/b383d5ae-f756-11ea-a510-f57d8ce76e11_story.html.

292   **A leased plane flew:** Jonathan Swan and Margaret Talev, "Exclusive: Trump Plots Virus-Era, Made-for-TV Mass Festival," **Axios,** June 18, 2020, www.axios.com/trump-tulsa-rally-mass-crowds-convention-test-f2fd68a6-6427-4908-ae84-6f25ac0ccd1f.html.

292   **As Tony Dokoupil asked:** "Oklahoma GOP Senator James Lankford on President Trump's Upcoming Tulsa Rally," CBS News, June 19, 2020, www.cbsnews.com/video/oklahoma-gop-senator-james-lankford-on-president-trumps-upcoming-tulsa-rally/#x.

294   **Had any of them discussed:** Josh Dawsey and Carol D. Leonnig, "In Wake of Trump's Tulsa Rally, His Campaign Is Still Contending with the Fallout," **Washington Post,** July 1, 2020, www.washingtonpost.com/politics/in-wake-of-trumps-tulsa-rally-his-campaign-is-still

-contending-with-the-fallout/2020/07/01/ee8e
6530-b9b5-11ea-bdaf-a129f921026f_story.html.

295 **Campaign staff also told:** Joshua Partlow and
Josh Dawsey, "Workers Removed Thousands of
Social Distancing Stickers Before Trump's Tulsa
Rally, According to Video and a Person Familiar
with the Set-Up," **Washington Post,** June 27,
2020, www.washingtonpost.com/politics/workers
-removed-thousands-of-social-distancing-stickers
-before-trumps-tulsa-rally-according-to-video-and
-a-person-familiar-with-the-set-up/2020/06/27/
f429c3be-b801-11ea-9b0f-c797548c1154_story
.html.

296 **Even that was an overstatement:** Giovanni
Russonello, "Trump's Tulsa Rally Attendance:
6,200, Fire Dept. Says," **New York Times,** June 22,
2020, www.nytimes.com/2020/06/22/us/politics/
trump-rally-coronavirus.html.

296 **And, referring to the debate:** Philip Rucker
and Robert Costa, "Trump Rallies in Red-State
America—and Faces a Sea of Empty Blue
Seats," **Washington Post,** June 20, 2020, www
.washingtonpost.com/politics/at-a-time-of
-national-crisis-and-division-trump-chooses-to
-prepare-for-a-fight/2020/06/20/5ebf3306-b296
-11ea-856d-5054296735e5_story.html.

296 **The conservative Drudge Report:** Michael D.
Shear, Maggie Haberman, and Astead W. Herndon,
"Trump Rally Fizzles as Attendance Falls Short
of Campaign's Expectations," **New York Times,**
June 20, 2020, www.nytimes.com/2020/06/20/
us/politics/tulsa-trump-rally.html.

297 **Of course, they had no intention:** Taylor Lorenz, Kellen Browning, and Sheera Frenkel, "TikTok Teens and K-Pop Stans Say They Sank Trump Rally," **New York Times,** June 21, 2020, www .nytimes.com/2020/06/21/style/tiktok-trump -rally-tulsa.html.

297 **Before Trump's visit:** Sean Murphy, "Health Official: Trump Rally 'Likely' Source of Virus Surge," **Washington Post,** July 8, 2020, www .washingtonpost.com/health/health-official-trump -rally-likely-source-of-virus-surge/2020/07/08/b17f 557c-c159-11ea-8908-68a2b9eae9e0_story.html.

298 **In addition, several dozen:** Carol D. Leonnig and Joshua Partlow, "Dozens of Secret Service Officers and Agents Told to Self-Quarantine After Trump's Tulsa Rally," **Washington Post,** June 24, 2020, www.washingtonpost.com/politics/dozens-of-secret -service-officers-and-agents-told-to-self-quarantine -after-trumps-tulsa-rally/2020/06/24/22c08b36 -b55f-11ea-aca5-ebb63d27e1ff_story.html.

298 **He was soon hospitalized:** John Wagner, Robert Costa, and Annie Gowen, "Herman Cain, Former Republican Presidential Hopeful, Has Died of Coronavirus, His Website Says," **Washington Post,** July 30, 2020, www.washingtonpost.com/politics/ herman-cain-former-republican-presidential -hopeful-has-died-of-the-coronavirus-statement -on-his-website-says/2020/07/30/4ac62a10-d273 -11ea-9038-af089b63ac21_story.html.

298 **Demonstrations in Seattle:** Jordan Muller, "Trump Calls Protesters 'Terrorists,' Pledges 'Retribution' for Tearing Down Statues," **Politico,**

June 26, 2020, www.politico.com/news/2020/ 06/26/trump-retribution-protesters-statues -340957.

300 **Carlson claimed invading hordes:** Charles Creitz, "Tucker Carlson Compares Seattle Protesters to Conquistadors: 'They Planted a Flag and They Stole' That Land," Fox News, June 11, 2020, www.foxnews.com/media/tucker-carlson -seattle-protesters-like-spanish-conquistadors.

301 **When contacted by journalists:** Jim Brunner, "Fox News Runs Digitally Altered Images in Coverage of Seattle's Protests, Capitol Hill Autonomous Zone," **Seattle Times,** June 12, 2020, www.seattletimes.com/seattle-news/politics/ fox-news-runs-digitally-altered-images-in-coverage -of-seattles-protests-capitol-hill-autonomous-zone.

303 **At a moment of crisis:** James Walker, "Tucker Carlson Criticizes Trump over 'Wrong Answer' to Seattle CHAZ," **Newsweek,** June 23, 2020, www .newsweek.com/tucker-carlson-criticizes-trump -wrong-answer-seattle-chaz-1512690.

303 **Twitter flagged Trump's menacing tweet:** Twitter Safety (@TwitterSafety), Twitter, June 23, 2020, 2:46 p.m., https://twitter.com/TwitterSafety/ status/1275500569940176897?s=20.

304 **"I am pleased to inform":** "Press Secretary Kayleigh McEnany White House Press Conference Transcript," Rev, July 1, 2020, www.rev.com/ blog/transcripts/press-secretary-kayleigh-mcenany -white-house-press-conference-transcript-july-1.

304 **"We were going in":** "Trump Takes Swipes at Biden in Explosive 'Hannity' Interview," Fox

News, July 9, 2020, www.youtube.com/watch?v= b7b1NMMoqR4.

304 **"I don't know what world":** Greg Sargent and Paul Waldman, "Opinion: Trump Told Hannity a Story About Threatening Seattle. The Mayor Says It Never Happened," **Washington Post,** July 10, 2020, www.washingtonpost.com/opinions/2020/07/ 10/trump-told-hannity-story-about-threatening -seattle-mayor-says-it-never-happened.

Chapter Ten: The Skunks at the Picnic

314 **"And he goes":** Michael Klinski, "Mount Trumpmore? It's the President's 'Dream,' Rep. Kristi Noem Says," **Sioux Falls Argus Leader,** April 24, 2018, www.argusleader.com/story/news/ 2018/04/24/president-donald-trump-mount -rushmore-trumpmore/544597002.

314 **She commended the size:** Jonathan Martin and Maggie Haberman, "How Kristi Noem, Mt. Rushmore, and Trump Fueled Speculation About Pence's Job," **New York Times,** August 8, 2020, www.nytimes.com/2020/08/08/us/politics/kristi -noem-pence-trump.html.

318 **In another document:** Jacob Bogage, "Postal Service Memos Detail 'Difficult' Changes, Including Slower Mail Delivery," **Washington Post,** July 14, 2020, www.washingtonpost.com/ business/2020/07/14/postal-service-trump-dejoy -delay-mail.

319 **"They're going to be rigged":** "Trump Tells UPS Workers to 'Be Careful' with Mail-In Ballots," **Washington Post,** July 15, 2020, www

.washingtonpost.com/video/politics/trump
-tells-ups-workers-to-be-careful-with-mail-in
-ballots/2020/07/15/1389aa21-f636-448c-835c
-030035379cff_video.html.

320 **They also point to public reassurances:** Yasmeen
Abutaleb, Josh Dawsey, and Laurie McGinley,
"Fauci Is Sidelined by the White House as He
Steps Up Blunt Talk on Pandemic," **Washington
Post,** July 11, 2020, www.washingtonpost.com/
politics/2020/07/11/fauci-trump-coronavirus.

321 **The cartoon was drawn:** Katie Rogers, "Aide Posts
Cartoon Mocking Fauci as White House Denies
Undermining Him," **New York Times,** July 14,
2020, www.nytimes.com/2020/07/14/us/politics/
fauci-scavino-cartoon-white-house.html.

322 **"So when you ask me":** Peter Navarro, "Anthony
Fauci Has Been Wrong About Everything I
Have Interacted with Him On," **USA Today,**
July 14, 2020, www.usatoday.com/story/opinion/
todaysdebate/2020/07/14/anthony-fauci-wrong
-with-me-peter-navarro-editorials-debates/
5439374002.

323 **"When we ignore science":** Philip Rucker
et al., "Rancor Between Scientists and Trump
Allies Threatens Pandemic Response as Cases
Surge," **Washington Post,** July 17, 2020, www
.washingtonpost.com/politics/rancor-between
-scientists-and-trump-allies-threatens-pandemic
-response-as-cases-surge/2020/07/17/d950e9b6
-c777-11ea-a99f-3bbdffb1af38_story.html.

323 **On July 14, the same day:** "A Conversation
with Anthony Fauci," Georgetown University

Global Health Initiative, July 14, 2020, https://globalhealth.georgetown.edu/events/a -conversation-with-anthony-fauci.

323 **"It's something, I think":** Kelly Taylor Hayes, "'We Have a Serious Situation Here': Fauci Calls COVID-19, Like 1918 Flu, 'Pandemic of Historic Proportions,'" FOX5 New York, July 15, 2020, www.fox5ny.com/news/we-have-a-serious -situation-here-fauci-calls-covid-19-like-1918-flu -pandemic-of-historic-proportions.

323 **"I hope we don't even":** Morgan Chalfant, "Meadows Says Fauci Wrong to Compare Coronavirus to 1918 Pandemic," **The Hill,** July 16, 2020, https://thehill.com/homenews/ administration/507763-meadows-says-fauci-wrong -to-compare-coronavirus-to-1918-pandemic.

324 **He told anchor Martha MacCallum:** Chalfant, "Meadows Says Fauci Wrong to Compare Coronavirus."

325 **"No, they're not comparable":** "Mark Zuckerberg & Dr. Fauci Interview Transcript July 16," Rev, July 17, 2020, www.rev.com/blog/ transcripts/mark-zuckerberg-dr-fauci-interview -transcript-july-16.

332 **A cascade of small expenses:** Shane Goldmacher and Maggie Haberman, "How Trump's Billion-Dollar Campaign Lost Its Cash Advantage," **New York Times,** September 7, 2020, www.nytimes .com/2020/09/07/us/politics/trump-election -campaign-fundraising.html.

336 **Hope Hicks and Johnny McEntee:** Yasmeen Abutaleb et al., "The Inside Story of How Trump's

Denial, Mismanagement and Magical Thinking Led to the Pandemic's Dark Winter," **Washington Post,** December 19, 2020, www.washingtonpost .com/graphics/2020/politics/trump-covid -pandemic-dark-winter.

339 **For instance, he argued:** Yasmeen Abutaleb and Josh Dawsey, "New Trump Pandemic Adviser Pushes Controversial 'Herd Immunity' Strategy, Worrying Public Health Officials," **Washington Post,** August 31, 2020, www.washingtonpost .com/politics/trump-coronavirus-scott-atlas-herd -immunity/2020/08/30/925e68fe-e93b-11ea -970a-64c73a1c2392_story.html.

Chapter Eleven: Fear and Fantasy

344 **Since 1845, federal law:** Alexander Burns, "Why Trump Has No Power to Delay the 2020 Election," **New York Times,**" July 30, 2020, www.nytimes .com/2020/07/30/us/politics/trump-postpone -election.html.

349 **Evanina had privately warned:** "Statement by NCSC Director William Evanina: 100 Days Until Election 2020," Office of the Director of National Intelligence, July 24, 2020, www.dni .gov/index.php/newsroom/press-releases/item/ 2135-statement-by-ncsc-director-william-evanina -100-days-until-election-2020.

350 **He would later tell Trump:** Shane Harris, Ellen Nakashima, and Josh Dawsey, "Russia Is Trying to 'Denigrate' Biden While China Prefers 'Unpredictable' Trump Not Be Reelected, Senior U.S. Intelligence Official Says," **Washington**

Post, August 7, 2020, www.washingtonpost.com/
national-security/seeing-trump-as-unpredictable
-china-would-prefer-he-not-win-reelection
-intelligence-official-says/2020/08/07/98e1ad8c
-d8e0-11ea-aff6-220dd3a14741_story.html.

351 **Unlike Russia, however:** "Statement by NCSC
Director William Evanina: Election Threat Update
for the American Public," Office of the Director
of National Intelligence, August 7, 2020, www
.dni.gov/index.php/newsroom/press-releases/
press-releases-2020/item/2139-statement-by-ncsc
-director-william-evanina-election-threat-update
-for-the-american-public.

351 **Asked about Evanina's report:** "08/07/20:
President Trump Holds a News Conference," Trump
White House Archived, August 7, 2020, www
.youtube.com/watch?v=VhCb7QIEJAU; "Donald
Trump Press Conference Transcript August 7: Talks
Stimulus, Economy, Executive Orders, Beirut," Rev,
August 7, 2020, www.rev.com/blog/transcripts/
donald-trump-press-conference-transcript-august
-7-talks-stimulus-economy-beirut.

352 **And she criticized Evanina:** "Pelosi: Russia Is
24/7 Interfering in Election," CNN, August 9,
2020, www.cnn.com/videos/politics/2020/08/09/
sotu-pelosi-russia.cnn.

352 **"The American people need":** Nancy Pelosi
(@SpeakerPelosi), Twitter, August 9, 2020,
2:16 p.m., https://twitter.com/SpeakerPelosi/
status/1292525252338163712?s=20.

355 **The 671 machines:** Jacob Bogage and Christopher
Ingraham, "Here's Why the Postal Service Wanted

to Remove Hundreds of Mail-Sorting Machines," **Washington Post,** August 20, 2020, www .washingtonpost.com/business/2020/08/20/postal -service-mail-sorters-removals.

356 **On August 14, Pelosi:** Letter from House Speaker Nancy Pelosi et al., to Postmaster General Louis DeJoy, August 14, 2020, www.speaker.gov/sites/ speaker.house.gov/files/20200814_Letter_Joint PelosiSchumerLofgrenKlobucharCBMPetersto PMGreElectionPrep.pdf.

356 **Some stuffed phony:** Kolbie Satterfield (@KolbieReports), Twitter, August 15, 2020, 8:42 a.m., https://twitter.com/KolbieReports/ status/1294615470004469760?s=20.

356 **The House Committee on Oversight and Reform:** Letter from Committee on Oversight and Reform Chairwoman Carolyn B. Maloney to Postmaster General Louis DeJoy, August 16, 2020, https://oversight.house.gov/sites/democrats .oversight.house.gov/files/2020-08-16.CBM %20to%20DeJoy-PMG%20reWitnessInvite.pdf.

357 **"That's no secret":** Erin Coz et al., "Postal Service Warns 46 States Their Voters Could Be Disenfranchised by Delayed Mail-In Ballots," **Washington Post,** August 14, 2020, www .washingtonpost.com/local/md-politics/usps -states-delayed-mail-in-ballots/2020/08/14/ 64bf3c3c-dcc7-11ea-8051-d5f887d73381_story .html.

357 **Adding to the suspicion:** Bogage and Ingraham, "Here's Why the Postal Service Wanted to Remove Hundreds of Mail-Sorting Machines."

358 **Postal Service sent a separate:** Coz et al., "Postal Service Warns 46 States."

359 **A fisherman in Alaska:** Matt Stevens and Isabella Grullón Paz, "Democratic National Convention's Roll Call Showcases Voices from Across America," **New York Times,** August 19, 2020, www.nytimes .com/2020/08/19/us/politics/dnc-roll-call.html.

359 **John Kasich, the former Republican:** Jackie Borchardt, "Where Were the Crossroads from John Kasich's Democratic Convention Speech? We Found Them," **Cincinnati Enquirer,** August 19, 2020, www.cincinnati.com/story/news/politics/ 2020/08/19/where-were-two-paths-john-kasichs -dnc-speech-crossroads/3394783001.

361 **"That she might weep":** Robin Givhan, "Michelle Obama's Speech Was Like an Empathetic Neighbor Expressing Sorrow for What Our Country Has Become," **Washington Post,** August 18, 2020, www.washingtonpost.com/lifestyle/style/michelle -obama-convention-speech-necklace-vote/2020/ 08/18/bd07fb74-e0e4-11ea-8181-606e603bb1c4 _story.html.

367 **"These are basically":** Carolyn Y. Johnson et al., "Trump Touts FDA's Emergency Authorization of Convalescent Plasma as Historic Breakthrough, but Scientists Are Doubtful," **Washington Post,** August 23, 2020, www.washingtonpost.com/ health/2020/08/23/trump-convalescent-plasma -okay.

367 **Within roughly twenty-four hours:** Matthew Perrone and Deb Riechmann, "FDA Chief Apologizes for Overstating Plasma Effect on Virus," **Washington Post,** August 25, 2020, www.washingtonpost.com/politics/fda -commissioner-says-he-overstated-effects-of -virus-therapy/2020/08/25/38c603dc-e6da-11ea -bf44-0d31c85838a5_story.html.

370 **For instance, Mark and Patricia McCloskey:** Philip Rucker and Dan Balz, "Trump Looks to Republican Convention for Campaign Reboot," **Washington Post,** August 22, 2020, www .washingtonpost.com/politics/trump-convention -reboot/2020/08/22/498f1bec-e417-11ea-b69b -64f7b0477ed4_story.html.

374 **The president spoke:** Philip Rucker et al., "Trump Attacks Biden and Casts Himself as an Insurgent in His Acceptance Speech," **Washington Post,** August 28, 2020, www.washingtonpost .com/elections/2020/08/27/republican-national -convention-live-updates.

Chapter Twelve: Self-Sabotage

379 **In Little Rock:** Monica Alba, "Birx Goes on the Road to Push Her Pandemic Message," NBC News, September 25, 2020, www.nbcnews.com/ politics/white-house/birx-goes-road-push-her -pandemic-message-n1241085.

382 **At a news conference:** Autumn Bell, "Vice President Pence, Gov. DeSantis Urge Floridians to Stay Vigilant Amid COVID-19 Pandemic," WTXL Tallahassee, July 2, 2020, www.wtxl.com/ news/local-news/vice-president-pence-gov-desantis -urge-floridians-to-stay-vigilantv-amid-covid-19 -pandemic.

383 **But Atlas used:** Cindy Krischer Goodman, "DeSantis Brings White House Adviser to Back School Reopenings. But Atlas Denies Promoting 'Herd Immunity' Strategy," **South Florida Sun Sentinel,** August 31, 2020, www.sun-sentinel .com/coronavirus/fl-ne-covid-ron-desantis-scott -atlas-20200831-afjkwrnk75hr3jloiyvnslfxie-story .html.

384 **Ratcliffe wrote that:** Jake Tapper and Zachary Cohen, "Top Intelligence Office Informs Congressional Committees It'll No Longer Brief In-Person on Election Security," CNN, August 29, 2020, www.cnn.com/2020/08/29/politics/office -of-director-of-national-intelligence-congress -election-security/index.html.

385 **"It is an outrage":** Nicholas Fandos and Julian E. Barnes, "No More In-Person Election Briefings for Congress, Intelligence Chief Says," **New York Times,** August 29, 2020, www.nytimes.com/2020/ 08/29/us/politics/election-security-intelligence -briefings-congress.html.

385 **By engaging in such conversations:** Tapper and Cohen, "Top Intelligence Office Informs."

388 **"When they're done":** Natasha Bertrand, "Trump's Intel Briefer Breaks Her Silence," **Politico,** July 6, 2020, www.politico.com/news/2020/07/06/ trump-intelligence-briefer-breaks-silence-349936.

391 **The Trump campaign was spending:** Nick Corasaniti, "As Trump Attacks Voting by Mail, His Campaign Tells Supporters to Request Absentee Ballots," **New York Times,** September 2, 2020, www.nytimes.com/2020/09/02/us/elections/as

-trump-attacks-voting-by-mail-his-campaign-tells
-supporters-to-request-absentee-ballots.html.

393 **The program paired:** "Attorney General
William P. Barr Announces Launch of Operation
Legend," U.S. Department of Justice, July 8,
2020, www.justice.gov/opa/pr/attorney-general
-william-p-barr-announces-launch-operation
-legend.

395 **Barr said the operation:** AZFamily.com news
staff, "Attorney General William Barr Visits
Phoenix to Announce Nationwide Drug Bust,"
AZFamily.com, September 10, 2020, www
.azfamily.com/news/attorney-general-william-barr
-visits-phoenix-to-announce-nationwide-drug
-bust/article_9d2b7450-f37e-11ea-9815-07d4
a02f8e36.html.

398 **Addressing some eight hundred attendees:**
Michael Crowley, "Israel, U.A.E., and Bahrain Sign
Accords, with an Eager Trump Playing Host," **New
York Times,** September 15, 2020, www.nytimes
.com/2020/09/15/us/politics/trump-israel-peace
-emirates-bahrain.html.

399 **The president suggested:** Peter Baker et al., "Israel
and United Arab Emirates Strike Major Diplomatic
Agreement," **New York Times,** August 13, 2020,
www.nytimes.com/2020/08/13/us/politics/trump
-israel-united-arab-emirates-uae.html.

399 **And his campaign took:** Jamie Ross, "Team
Trump Misspells 'Nobel' in Campaign Ad
Celebrating Meaningless Peace Prize Nomination,"
Daily Beast, September 11, 2020, www
.thedailybeast.com/trump-team-misspells-nobel

-in-campaign-ad-celebrating-meaningless-peace
-prize-nomination.

404 **Worse still, he said:** Amy Goldstein and Sean
Sullivan, "CDC Director Says Coronavirus
Vaccines Won't Be Widely Available Till the Middle
of Next Year," **Washington Post,** September 16,
2020, www.washingtonpost.com/health/cdc
-director-says-coronavirus-vaccines-wont-be
-widely-available-till-the-middle-of-next-year/
2020/09/16/209fecf6-f827-11ea-be57-d00bb9bc
632d_story.html.

405 **"We've manufactured all the necessary
supplies":** "Donald Trump Says CDC Director
'Confused' About Covid-19 Vaccine Timetable,"
Guardian, September 17, 2020, www.youtube
.com/watch?v=VlBd7zxfhhs.

406 **He added, "I'm not sure":** Morgan Chalfant,
"Meadows Disputes CDC Director's Vaccine
Timeline," **The Hill,** September 17, 2020,
https://thehill.com/homenews/administration/
516855-meadows-disputes-cdc-directors-vaccine
-timeline.

408 **recorded a Facebook Live video:** "Top HHS
Spokesman Shares Conspiracy-Laden Rant in
Facebook Live," CNN, September 16, 2020, www
.cnn.com/videos/politics/2020/09/16/caputo
-facebook-live-cdc-valencia-ip-vpx.cnn.

408 **And he encouraged his friends:** Sharon
LaFraniere, "Trump Health Aide Pushes Bizarre
Conspiracies and Warns of Armed Revolt," **New
York Times,** September 14, 2020, www.nytimes
.com/2020/09/14/us/politics/caputo-virus.html.

408 **Under mounting pressure:** Sharon LaFraniere, "Trump Health Official Apologizes for Facebook Outburst," **New York Times,** September 15, 2020, www.nytimes.com/2020/09/15/us/michael -caputo-coronavirus.html.

Chapter Thirteen: Stand Back and Stand By

410 **The president's answer:** Michael Crowley, "Trump Won't Commit to 'Peaceful' Post-Election Transfer of Power," **New York Times,** September 23, 2020, www.nytimes.com/2020/09/23/us/politics/trump -power-transfer-2020-election.html.

411 **"The ballots are out of control":** "Donald Trump White House Press Briefing Transcript September 23," Rev, September 23, 2020, www.rev .com/blog/transcripts/donald-trump-white-house -press-briefing-transcript-september-23.

411 **This exchange lasted less:** Philip Rucker, Amy Gardner, and Annie Linskey, "Trump's Escalating Attacks on Election Prompt Fears of a Constitutional Crisis," **Washington Post,** September 24, 2020, www.washingtonpost.com/ politics/trump-election-transition-crisis/2020/ 09/24/068d2286-fe79-11ea-8d05-9beaaa91c71f _story.html.

416 **It had been approved:** Ewen Callaway, "Russia's Fast-Track Coronavirus Vaccine Draws Outrage over Safety," **Nature,** August 11, 2020, www .nature.com/articles/d41586-020-02386-2.

416 **Dr. Paul Offit, a member:** Yasmeen Abutaleb et al., "Trump's Den of Dissent: Inside the White House Task Force as Coronavirus Surges," **Washington**

Post, October 19, 2020, www.washingtonpost
.com/politics/trumps-den-of-dissent-inside-the
-white-house-task-force-as-coronavirus-surges/
2020/10/19/7ff8ee6a-0a6e-11eb-859b-f9c27abe
638d_story.html.

418 **But the political result:** Laurie McGinley and
Carolyn Y. Johnson, "FDA Poised to Announce
Tougher Standards for a Covid-19 Vaccine That
Make It Unlikely One Will Be Cleared by Election
Day," **Washington Post,** September 22, 2020,
www.washingtonpost.com/health/2020/09/22/fda
-covid-vaccine-approval-standard.

420 **On September 25:** Jeremy Diamond, Nick
Valencia, and Sara Murray, "Trump Has Lost
Patience with CDC Head After Series of Mixed
Messages," CNN, September 25, 2020, www.cnn
.com/2020/09/25/politics/redfield-trump-cdc
-morale/index.html.

423 **"The president, the vice president":** Jonathan
Swan, "Scoop: CDC Director Overruled on
Cruise Ship Ban," **Axios,** September 29, 2020,
www.axios.com/scoop-white-house-overruled-cdc
-cruise-ships-florida-91442136-1b8e-442e-a2a1
-0b24e9a39fb6.html.

423 **The White House, facing the risk:** "Framework
for Conditional Sailing and Initial Phase Covid-19
Testing Requirements for Protection of Crew,"
U.S. Department of Health and Human Services
and Centers for Disease Control and Prevention,
October 30, 2020, www.cdc.gov/quarantine/pdf/
CDC-Conditional-Sail-Order_10_30_2020-p.pdf.

427 **Candice told police:** Incident/Investigation Report, Ft. Lauderdale Police Department, September 27, 2020, www.flpd.org/home/show document?id=6114.

428 **When Parscale stayed standing:** "Video of Brad Parscale Being Taken into Custody Released by Fort Lauderdale Police," WPLG Local 10, September 28, 2020, www.youtube.com/watch?v =U86UEfo3Dv0.

429 **RINO was an acronym:** Ashley Parker and Josh Dawsey, "Police Report of Suicide Threat by Former Trump Campaign Manager Includes Domestic Abuse Allegations," **Washington Post,** September 28, 2020, www.washingtonpost.com/ politics/parscale-suicide-threat-abuse/2020/09/ 28/34644958-01aa-11eb-8879-7663b816bfa5 _story.html.

433 **At one point, an exasperated:** Anne Gearan, Philip Rucker, and Annie Linskey, "Trump Incessantly Interrupts and Insults Biden as They Spar in Acrimonious First Debate," **Washington Post,** September 30, 2020, www.washingtonpost .com/politics/debate-trump-biden/2020/09/30/ 722499a8-0274-11eb-b7ed-141dd88560ea_story .html.

433 **When Biden gave an impassioned defense:** "Donald Trump & Joe Biden 1st Presidential Debate Transcript 2020," Rev, September 29, 2020, www.rev.com/blog/transcripts/donald-trump -joe-biden-1st-presidential-debate-transcript -2020.

Chapter Fourteen: Nobody's Immune

438 Trump and Meadows did not want: Jennifer Jacobs and Josh Wingrove, "Trump Kept Regular Schedule After Learning Close Aide Hope Hicks Had Covid," Bloomberg, October 2, 2020, www.bloomberg.com/news/articles/2020-10-02/trump-kept-regular-schedule-after-learning-close-aide-had-covid.

438 As Dr. Kavita Patel: Philip Rucker et al., "Invincibility Punctured by Infection: How the Coronavirus Spread in Trump's White House," **Washington Post,** October 2, 2020, www.washingtonpost.com/politics/trump-virus-spread-white-house/2020/10/02/38c5b354-04cc-11eb-b7ed-141dd88560ea_story.html.

439 In a recorded message: Maggie Haberman and Michael D. Shear, "Trump Says He'll Begin 'Quarantine Process' After Hope Hicks Tests Positive for Coronavirus," **New York Times,** October 1, 2020, www.nytimes.com/2020/10/01/us/politics/hope-hicks-coronavirus.html.

439 Shortly after 8:00 p.m., nearly eight hours: Jennifer Jacobs (@JenniferJJacobs), Twitter, October 1, 2020, 8:09 p.m., https://twitter.com/JenniferJJacobs/status/1311820562587619333?s=20.

440 "Rest assured I expect": "Read the Letter from White House Physician Dr. Sean Conley About Trump's Covid Diagnosis," NBC News, October 2, 2020, www.nbcnews.com/politics/donald-trump/read-letter-white-house-physician-dr-sean-conley-about-trump-n1241771.

442 **Later that morning, Trump's condition:** Christina Morales, Allyson Waller, and Marie Fazio, "A Timeline of Trump's Symptoms and Treatments," **New York Times,** October 4, 2020, www.nytimes.com/2020/10/04/us/trump-covid -symptoms-timeline.html.

443 **"Stayed on that":** "President Trump's Doctors Provide Update from Walter Reed," Rev, October 4, 2020, www.rev.com/transcript-editor/shared/ td0F6VmlQb-4CvMXxugZSFOOwxNoFqiYg _G52pk0zPm2IsiTK3ONR5_vsXTuSZih _TeHULcUbhcHOd9g5AUyOTGNLnI ?loadFrom=PastedDeeplink&ts=75.65.

445 **Conley's memo mistakenly:** "Memorandum from Trump's Doctor on COVID-19 Treatment," Associated Press, October 2, 2020, https://apnews .com/article/virus-outbreak-melania-trump -archive-f1ef1f03cdd92fa83618ed34a3ea5ddb.

446 **Dr. Thomas McGinn:** Katie Thomas and Roni Caryn Rabin, "Use of Dexamethasone to Treat Trump Suggests Severe Covid-19, Experts Say," **New York Times,** October 4, 2020, www.nytimes.com/ 2020/10/04/health/trump-covid-treatment.html.

448 **Later Saturday evening:** Carol D. Leonnig and Robert O'Harrow Jr., "White House Physician Sean Conley Draws Scrutiny for Rosy Assessments of Trump's Health," **Washington Post,** October 7, 2020, www.washingtonpost.com/politics/sean -conley-trump-health/2020/10/04/af63a16e-0653 -11eb-a166-dc429b380d10_story.html.

448 **"Saturday's briefing by President Trump's medical team":** Leana S. Wen, "Opinion: The

Medical Briefing on Trump's Health Was an Insulting Exercise in Obfuscation," **Washington Post,** October 3, 2020, www.washingtonpost.com/opinions/2020/10/03/medical-briefing-trumps-health-was-an-insulting-exercise-obfuscation.

449 **"We're working hard":** "Trump in New Video from Hospital: 'Wasn't Feeling So Well, I Am Feeling Much Better Now,'" FOX 7 Austin, October 3, 2020, www.facebook.com/FOX7Austin/videos/870871296991591.

452 **In conversations with advisers:** Annie Karni and Maggie Haberman, "Trump Makes First Public Appearance Since Leaving Walter Reed," **New York Times,** October 10, 2020, www.nytimes.com/2020/10/10/us/politics/trump-white-house-coronavirus.html.

452 **But, he added:** Philip Rucker, Ashley Parker, and Josh Dawsey, "Even from His Hospital Rooms, Trump Tries to Convince Public He's in Charge," **Washington Post,** October 5, 2020, www.washingtonpost.com/politics/trump-hospital-in-charge-virus/2020/10/05/a052f37c-0744-11eb-9be6-cf25fb429f1a_story.html.

454 **"Where are the adults?" the former agent:** Josh Dawsey, Carol D. Leonnig, and Hannah Knowles, "Secret Service Agents, Doctors Aghast at Trump's Drive Outside Hospital," **Washington Post,** October 4, 2020, www.washingtonpost.com/politics/2020/10/04/trump-hospital-drive-criticism.

454 **"It's just absolute chief of staff":** Rucker, Parker, and Dawsey, "Even from His Hospital Rooms."

457 **Then Trump, appearing defiant:** Peter Baker and Maggie Haberman, "Trump Leaves Hospital, Minimizing Virus and Urging Americans 'Don't Let It Dominate Your Lives,'" **New York Times,** October 5, 2020, www.nytimes.com/2020/10/05/us/politics/trump-leaves-hospital-coronavirus.html?action=click&module=RelatedLinks&pgtype=Article.

459 **In it FBI lawyer:** Matt Zapotosky and Ann E. Marimow, "Ex-FBI Lawyer Admits to Falsifying Document in Probe of Trump's Campaign," **Washington Post,** August 19, 2020, www.washingtonpost.com/national-security/kevin-clinesmith-fbi-pleads-guilty/2020/08/19/6c0dec54-e0a0-11ea-8dd2-d07812bf00f7_story.html.

460 **Of course, the whole investigation:** Devlin Barrett and Matt Zapotosky, "Prosecutor Resigns from U.S. Attorney's Investigation into Origins of Trump-Russia Probe," **Washington Post,** September 11, 2020, www.washingtonpost.com/national-security/nora-dannehy-john-durham-trump-russia/2020/09/11/8bf49890-f466-11ea-b796-2dd09962649c_story.html.

460 **Her resignation only intensified:** Edmund H. Mahony, "Nora Dannehy, Connecticut Prosecutor Who Was Top Aide to John Durham's Trump-Russia Investigation, Resigns Amid Concern About Pressure from Attorney General William Barr," **Hartford Courant,** September 11, 2020, www.courant.com/news/connecticut/hc-news-john-durham-dannehy-resignation

-20200911-20200911-xcsapnq7g5e63kvtw5aqi
7cv34-story.html.

460 That spring, before the results: Aaron Blake, "'One of the Greatest Travesties in American History': Barr Drops All Pretense About Ongoing Probe of Russia Investigation," **Washington Post,** April 9, 2020, www.washingtonpost.com/politics/ 2020/04/09/one-greatest-travesties-american -history-barr-drops-all-pretense-about-ongoing -probe-russia-investigation.

461 "Where are all": Trump War Room (@TrumpWarRoom), Twitter, October 6, 2020, 7:06 p.m., https://t.co/w2s8LdiRu0.

462 "For the love of God": Lisa Matassa (@Lisa_Matassa), Twitter, October 6, 2020, 9:01 p.m., https://twitter.com/Lisa_Matassa/ status/1313645583819780097?s=20.

462 "I said yesterday": "Transcript of Pelosi Interview on ABC's **The View,**" Nancy Pelosi, Speaker of the House, October 7, 2020, www.speaker.gov/ newsroom/10720.

Chapter Fifteen: Somebody's Crazy Uncle

464 Medical experts said: Kayleigh McEnany 45 Archived (@PressSec45), Twitter, October 12, 2020, 5:20 p.m., twitter.com/PressSec45/status/ 1315764217249771526?s=20.

465 Determined to show strength: Annie Karni and Maggie Haberman, "Votes and Vitality in Mind, Trump Addresses Rally in Florida," **New York Times,** October 12, 2020, www.nytimes.com/ 2020/10/12/us/politics/trump-rally-florida.html.

465 **"You got to get out":** "Donald Trump Campaign Rally Sanford, Florida, Transcript October 12: First Rally Since Diagnosis," Rev, October 12, 2020, www.rev.com/blog/transcripts/donald -trump-campaign-rally-sanford-florida-transcript -october-12-first-rally-since-diagnosis.

466 **Trump returned to Florida:** "Donald Trump NBC Town Hall Transcript," Rev, October 15, 2020, www.rev.com/blog/transcripts/donald -trump-nbc-town-hall-transcript-october-15.

468 **Guthrie then asked Trump:** Aaron Blake, "As Trump's Chief Conspiracy Theory Suffers a Major Blow, He Reaches for More Desperate Ones," **Washington Post,** October 14, 2020, www.washingtonpost.com/politics/2020/10/14/ trumps-chief-conspiracy-theory-suffers-major -blow-he-reaches-more-desperate-ones.

468 **In Georgia, voters waited:** Michelle Ye Hee Lee, Haisten Willis, and Amy Gardner, "Long Lines Mark the First Day of Early Voting in Georgia as Voters Flock to the Polls," **Washington Post,** October 12, 2020, www.washingtonpost.com/ politics/georgia-early-vote-lines/2020/10/12/ f8ffcd8c-0ca9-11eb-8a35-237ef1eb2ef7_story .html.

469 **Nearly 130,000 people:** "Record Turnout on First Day of Early Voting in Georgia," Georgia Secretary of State Brad Raffensperger, https://sos.ga.gov/ index.php/elections/record_turnout_on_first_day _of_early_voting_in_georgia.

469 **"Every time I see him":** Amy Gardner and Elise Viebeck, "Across the Country, Democratic

Enthusiasm Is Propelling an Enormous Wave of
Early Voting," **Washington Post,** October 14,
2020, www.washingtonpost.com/politics/early
-voting-2020-election/2020/10/14/500c22ce
-0d90-11eb-8a35-237ef1eb2ef7_story.html.

473   **He added, "Sleepy Joe":** "Donald Trump Macon,
Georgia, Rally Speech Transcript October 16,"
Rev, October 17, 2020, www.rev.com/blog/
transcripts/donald-trump-macon-georgia-rally
-speech-transcript-october-16.

474   **In fact, Ben Smith:** Ben Smith, "Trump Had One
Last Story to Sell. The **Wall Street Journal** Wouldn't
Buy It," **New York Times,** October 25, 2020, www
.nytimes.com/2020/10/25/business/media/hunter
-biden-wall-street-journal-trump.html.

474   **After doing its due diligence:** Andrew Duehren
and James T. Areddy, "Hunter Biden's Ex-Business
Partner Alleges Father Knew About Venture," **Wall
Street Journal,** October 23, 2020, www.wsj.com/
articles/hunter-bidens-ex-business-partner-alleges
-father-knew-about-venture-11603421247?mod
=lead_feature_below_a_pos1.

474   **Mac Isaac would later say:** Ken Dilanian and
Tom Winter, "Here's What Happened When NBC
News Tried to Report on the Alleged Hunter Biden
Emails," NBC News, October 30, 2020, www
.nbcnews.com/politics/2020-election/here-s-what
-happened-when-nbc-news-tried-report-alleged
-n1245533.

476   **Back in February, Lindsey Graham:** Darlene
Superville, "Graham: DOJ Has Process to Review
Giuliani's Ukraine Info," Associated Press,

February 9, 2020, https://apnews.com/article/
d13ceede5c2618cf52340c08b21eae08.

476 **"There are a lot of agendas":** Michael Balsamo,
"Barr: Justice Dept. Is Collecting Ukraine Info
from Giuliani," Associated Press, February 10,
2020, https://apnews.com/article/d617dc21b3f
0db0553dd2a52206fcb75.

477 **In October, Giuliani:** Shane Harris et al.,
"White House Was Warned Giuliani Was Target
of Russian Intelligence Operation to Feed
Misinformation to Trump," **Washington Post,**
October 15, 2020, www.washingtonpost.com/
national-security/giuliani-biden-ukraine-russian
-disinformation/2020/10/15/43158900-0ef5
-11eb-b1e8-16b59b92b36d_story.html.

479 **Not only had he succeeded:** Josh Rottenberg,
"Rudy Giuliani Is in the New 'Borat.' Here's What
to Know About His Controversial Scene," **Los
Angeles Times,** October 21, 2020, www.latimes
.com/entertainment-arts/movies/story/2020-10
-21/rudy-giuliani-borat-sequel.

479 **"This is an effort":** Rudy W. Giuliani
(@RudyGiuliani), Twitter, October 21, 2020,
5:42 p.m., https://twitter.com/RudyGiuliani/
status/1319031310074171394?s=20.

479 **Giuliani added, "We are preparing":** Giuliani
(@RudyGiuliani), Twitter, October 21, 2020,
5:42 p.m.

479 **The country's coronavirus death toll:** Sarah
Mervosh, Mitch Smith, and Apoorva Mandavilli,
"A Third Surge of Coronavirus Infections Has
Now Firmly Taken Hold Across Much of the

United States," **New York Times,** October 21, 2020, www.nytimes.com/live/2020/10/20/world/ covid-19-coronavirus-updates#a-third-surge-of -coronavirus-infections-has-now-firmly-taken -hold-across-much-of-the-united-states.

480 **Then, using his derisive nickname:** Alexander Burns, "Trump in North Carolina: 'All You Hear Is Covid, Covid, Covid, Covid, Covid,'" **New York Times,** October 21, 2020, www.nytimes .com/2020/10/21/us/elections/trump-in-north -carolina-all-you-hear-is-covid-covid-covid-covid -covid.html.

480 **The story, which was published on October 16:** Emma-Jo Morris and Gabrielle Fonrouge, "Text Messages Show Raw and Intimate Exchange Between Joe and Hunter Biden," **New York Post,** October 16, 2020, https://nypost.com/2020/10/ 16/texts-show-raw-intimate-exchange-between -joe-and-hunter-biden.

481 **Trump was all happy talk:** Alexander Burns and Jonathan Martin, "In Calmer Debate, Biden and Trump Offer Sharply Different Visions for Nation," **New York Times,** October 22, 2020, www.nytimes.com/2020/10/22/us/politics/debate -presidential-recap.html.

482 **Two other aides:** Philip Rucker and Josh Dawsey, "Pence's Chief of Staff, Marc Short, Tests Positive for the Coronavirus," **Washington Post,** October 25, 2020, www.washingtonpost.com/politics/pences -chief-of-staff-marc-short-tests-positive-for-the -coronavirus/2020/10/24/c89c90bc-166d-11eb -bc10-40b25382f1be_story.html.

484 **"It hasn't, and it won't":** Philip Rucker, Josh Dawsey, and Amy B Wang, "White House Signals Defeat in Pandemic as Coronavirus Outbreak Roils Pence's Office," **Washington Post,** October 25, 2020, www.washingtonpost.com/politics/pence -coronavirus-outbreak/2020/10/25/923bb382 -16d5-11eb-befb-8864259bd2d8_story.html.

487 **The likable yet uninspiring Biden:** Aaron Blake, "In Scathing Speech, Obama Embraces His Inner Trump Troll," **Washington Post,** October 27, 2020, www.washingtonpost.com/politics/2020/ 10/27/scathing-speech-obama-embraces-his-inner -trump-troll.

490 **In response, he told his supporters:** "Trump Suggests He Might Try to Fire Fauci After the Election," CNBC, November 2, 2020, www.cnbc .com/2020/11/02/trump-suggests-he-might-try -to-fire-fauci-after-the-election.html.

Chapter Sixteen: The Reckoning

495 **"No, I'm not thinking":** "Remarks: Donald Trump Speaks with Staff at Campaign Headquarters—November 3, 2020," Factbase, https://factba.se/transcript/donald-trump-remarks -campaign-hq-arlington-va-november-3-2020.

511 **"And as far as I'm concerned":** "Donald Trump 2020 Election Night Speech Transcript," Rev, November 4, 2020, www.rev.com/blog/ transcripts/donald-trump-2020-election-night -speech-transcript.

Chapter Seventeen: The Big Lie

521 **Bossie was a three-decade veteran:** Maggie Haberman, "Trump Campaign Will Name David Bossie, a Political Combat Veteran, to Lead Its Ballot Battles Team," **New York Times,** November 6, 2020, www.nytimes.com/live/2020/ 11/06/us/trump-biden#trump-campaign-will -name-david-bossie-a-political-combat-veteran-to -lead-its-ballot-battles-team.

530 **It was a move Esper and Milley:** Eric Schmitt and Helene Cooper, "Promotions for Female Generals Were Delayed over Fears of Trump's Reaction," **New York Times,** February 17, 2021, www.nytimes.com/2021/02/17/us/politics/ women-generals-promotions-trump.html.

533 **In a public statement:** Dan Lamothe et al., "Trump Administration Upends Senior Pentagon Ranks, Installing Loyalists," **Washington Post,** November 10, 2020, www.washingtonpost.com/ national-security/defense-department-election -transition/2020/11/10/5a173e60-2371-11eb -8599-406466ad1b8e_story.html.

534 **CIA officials complained:** Kenneth P. Vogel and Eliana Johnson, "Trump Steps In to Keep 30 -year-old NSC Aide," **Politico,** March 14, 2017, www.politico.com/story/2017/03/trump-national -security-mcmaster-overrule-236065.

535 **The national security adviser:** Eliana Johnson, Nahal Toosi, and Ali Watkins, "McMaster Dismisses Another Flynn Hire from National Security Council," **Politico,** August 2, 2017,

www.politico.com/story/2017/08/02/mcmaster
-national-security-council-241264.

535 **Cohen-Watnick later served:** Helene Cooper, "Aide Ousted from White House Reappears Again in Administration Job," **New York Times,** May 11, 2020, www.nytimes.com/2020/05/11/us/politics/ezra-cohen-watnick-pentagon.html.

535 **A retired army brigadier general:** Em Steck et al., "Top Pentagon Nominee Pushed Conspiracy Theories That Former CIA Director Tried to Overthrow Trump and Even Have Him Assassinated," CNN, June 23, 2020, www.cnn .com/2020/06/23/politics/kfile-tata-conspiracy -theory/index.html.

539 **At the same time, McEntee:** Jake Tapper (@jaketapper), Twitter, November 9, 2020, 1:39 p.m., https://twitter.com/jaketapper/status/ 13258705916619035138?s=20.

540 **The vaccine trial:** Carolyn Y. Johnson, "Pfizer's Coronavirus Vaccine Is More Than 90 Percent Effective in First Analysis, Company Reports," **Washington Post**, November 9, 2020, www .washingtonpost.com/health/2020/11/09/pfizer -coronavirus-vaccine-effective.

549 **His work calendar:** Betsy Klein, "Trump's Public Schedules Show Little Interest in Work as He Protests Biden's Legitimate Election," CNN, November 11, 2020, www.cnn.com/2020/11/11/ politics/donald-trump-schedule-election/index .html.

551 **a Rose Garden announcement:** "Donald Trump Rose Garden Press Conference on COVID-19

Vaccine Transcript," Rev, November 13, 2020, www.rev.com/blog/transcripts/donald-trump-rose -garden-press-conference-on-covid-19-vaccine -transcript-november-13.

Chapter Eighteen: Strange Rangers

553 **Biden was declared the winner:** Luis Ferré-Sadurní, Jennifer Medina, and Eileen Sullivan, "Biden Flips Arizona, Further Cementing His Presidential Victory," **New York Times,** November 12, 2020, www.nytimes.com/2020/11/ 12/us/biden-wins-arizona.html.

556 **He said Graham questioned:** Amy Gardner, "Ga. Secretary of State Says Fellow Republicans Are Pressuring Him to Find Ways to Exclude Ballots," **Washington Post,** November 16, 2020, www.washingtonpost.com/politics/brad -raffensperger-georgia-vote/2020/11/16/6b6cb 2f4-283e-11eb-8fa2-06e7cbb145c0_story .html.

557 **Giuliani's office advised Trump's campaign:** Michael S. Schmidt and Maggie Haberman, "Giuliani Is Said to Seek $20,000 a Day Payment for Trump Legal Work," **New York Times,** November 17, 2020, www.nytimes.com/2020/11/ 17/us/politics/giuliani-trump-election-pay.html.

557 **While Giuliani claimed:** Kenneth P. Vogel, Michael S. Schmidt, and Katie Benner, "Giuliani Mixes His Business with Role as Trump's Lawyer," **New York Times,** October 18, 2019, www.nytimes .com/2019/10/18/us/politics/giuliani-business .html.

558 **Giuliani elevated a protégée:** Mark Maremont and Corinne Ramey, "How Jenna Ellis Rose from Traffic Court to Trump's Legal Team," **Wall Street Journal,** December 3, 2020, www.wsj.com/articles/how-jenna-ellis-rose-from-traffic-court-to-trumps-legal-team-11607038900.

558 **She had worked as a deputy district attorney:** Jesse Paul, "Jenna Ellis, President Trump's Lawyer, Was Fired from Weld County DA's Office for 'Mistakes,' Records Show," **Colorado Sun,** December 15, 2020, https://coloradosun.com/2020/12/15/jenna-ellis-weld-county-district-attorneys-office.

558 **Before December 2020:** Jeremy W. Peters and Alan Feuer, "How Is Trump's Lawyer Jenna Ellis 'Elite Strike Force' Material?," **New York Times,** December 3, 2020, www.nytimes.com/2020/12/03/us/politics/jenna-ellis-trump.html.

560 **"Plaintiff's interpretation of events":** Beth LeBlanc, "Judge Rejects Request for Wayne County Audit, Halt to Election Certification," **Detroit News,** November 13, 2020, www.detroitnews.com/story/news/politics/2020/11/13/judge-rejects-bid-wayne-county-audit-halt-election-certification/6278120002.

560 **The Trump campaign admitted:** Danielle Haynes, "Trump Campaign Walks Away from Arizona Elections Lawsuit," United Press International, November 13, 2020, www.upi.com/Top_News/US/2020/11/13/Trump-campaign-walks-away-from-Arizona-elections-lawsuit/1701605293993.

561 Addressing the possibility: Andrew Restuccia, "Trump Says 'Who Knows Which Administration' Will Be in Power Next Year," **Wall Street Journal,** December 2, 2020, www.wsj.com/livecoverage/ latest-updates-biden-trump-election-2020/card/ cS7Mi6nroEt7RnchpBnG.

562 "There is no evidence": "Joint Statement from Elections Infrastructure Government Coordinating Council & the Election Infrastructure Sector Coordinating Executive Committees," Cybersecurity & Infrastructure Security Agency, November 12, 2020, www.cisa.gov/news/2020/ 11/12/joint-statement-elections-infrastructure -government-coordinating-council-election.

564 Many of his fans: Marissa J. Lang et al., "After Thousands of Trump Supporters Rally in D.C., Violence Erupts When Night Falls," **Washington Post,** November 15, 2020, www.washingtonpost .com/dc-md-va/2020/11/14/million-maga-march -dc-protests.

568 Porter, Wright, Morris & Arthur formally withdrew: Rachel Abrams, David Enrich, and Jessica Silver-Greenberg, "Once Loyal to Trump, Law Firms Pull Back from His Election Fight," **New York Times,** November 13, 2020, www .nytimes.com/2020/11/13/business/porter-wright -trump-pennsylvania.html.

569 Though the Giuliani-Ellis-Powell team: Maremont and Ramey, "How Jenna Ellis Rose."

570 At times the discussion: Jon Swaine and Aaron Schaffer, "Here's What Happened When Rudolph Giuliani Made His First Appearance in Federal

Court in Nearly Three Decades," **Washington Post,** November 18, 2020, www.washingtonpost .com/politics/giuliani-pennsylvania-court -appearance/2020/11/18/ad7288dc-2941-11eb -92b7-6ef17b3fe3b4_story.html.

571 **He then added a sly reference:** Jeremy Roebuck, "Rudy Giuliani's Courtroom Showing in Pa. Election Fight Left Many Scratching Their Heads. Trump Backers Praised It as 'Brilliant,'" **Philadelphia Inquirer,** November 18, 2020, www.inquirer.com/news/rudy-giuliani-trump -pennsylvania-election-results-lawsuits-matthew -brann-federal-court-20201118.html.

572 **"That has not happened":** Memorandum Opinion, **Donald J. Trump for President Inc. et al. v. Kathy Boockvar et al.,** United States District Court for the Middle District of Pennsylvania, November 21, 2020, www.courtlistener.com/ recap/gov.uscourts.pamd.127057/gov.uscourts .pamd.127057.202.0_1.pdf.

575 **"As soon as he saw multiple states":** "Trump Campaign News Conference on Legal Challenges," C-SPAN, November 19, 2020, www.c-span.org/ video/?478246-1/trump-campaign-alleges-voter -fraud-states-plans-lawsuits.

575 **In fact, Georgia's hand:** Philip Rucker, Amy Gardner, and Josh Dawsey, "Trump Uses Power of Presidency to Try to Overturn the Election and Stay in Office," **Washington Post,** November 19, 2020, www.washingtonpost.com/politics/trump -uses-power-of-presidency-to-try-to-overturn -the-election-and-stay-in-office/2020/11/19/

bc89caa6-2a9f-11eb-8fa2-06e7cbb145c0_story
.html.

579 **Legal experts predicted:** Yasmeen Abutaleb,
"Trump Pushes Last-Minute Drug Pricing Rules
Likely to Face Big Legal Challenges," **Washington
Post,** November 20, 2020, www.washingtonpost
.com/health/2020/11/20/trump-drug-price-rules.

582 **"If you've got the evidence":** "'This Week'
Transcript 11-22-20: President-elect Biden Chief
of Staff Ronald Klain and Dr. Moncef Slaoui,"
ABC News, November 22, 2020, https://abcnews
.go.com/Politics/week-transcript-11-22-20
-president-elect-biden/story?id=74345705.

585 **Murphy's defiance—in alignment with:** Lisa
Rein, Jonathan O'Connell, and Josh Dawsey, "A
Little-Known Trump Appointee Is in Charge of
Handing Transition Resources to Biden—and She
Isn't Budging," **Washington Post,** November 8,
2020, www.washingtonpost.com/politics/trump
-gsa-letter-biden-transition/2020/11/08/07093acc
-21e9-11eb-8672-c281c7a2c96e_story.html.

587 **She wrote a highly personal letter:** Lisa Rein,
"Under Pressure, Trump Appointee Emily Murphy
Approves Transition in Unusually Personal Letter
to Biden," **Washington Post,** November 23, 2020,
www.washingtonpost.com/politics/gsa-emily
-murphy-transition-biden/2020/11/23/c0f43e84
-2de0-11eb-96c2-aac3f162215d_story.html.

587 **"To be clear, I did not":** "Read GSA Administrator
Emily Murphy's Letter to President-elect Joe
Biden," **Washington Post,** November 23,
2020, www.washingtonpost.com/context/read

-gsa-administrator-emily-murphy-s-letter-to
-president-elect-joe-biden/a615a8b4-29b4-4628
-8a9c-7e87fc2430dd/?itid=lk_readmore_manual
_10.

588 **But the day she concluded:** "Read the Statement
from 100-Plus Former National Security Officials,"
Washington Post, November 23, 2020, www
.washingtonpost.com/context/read-the-statement
-from-100-plus-former-national-security-officials/
a559eb00-6e6c-4671-ab49-7bc9ccb967dc.

589 **On December 3, Farah submitted:** Ashley
Parker, "Farah Resigns as White House
Communications Director in Tacit Nod to
Trump's Loss," **Washington Post,** December 3,
2020, www.washingtonpost.com/politics/trump
-farah-resign/2020/12/03/1623fa7a-3598-11eb
-a997-1f4c53d2a747_story.html.

Chapter Nineteen: Cries of Injustice

593 **Still, Trump continued:** Shawn Boburg and
Jacob Bogage, "Postal Worker Recanted Allegations
of Ballot Tampering, Officials Say," **Washington
Post,** November 10, 2020, www.washingtonpost
.com/investigations/postal-worker-fabricated
-ballot-pennsylvania/2020/11/10/99269a7c-2364
-11eb-8599-406466ad1b8e_story.html?no_nav
=true.

594 **"And what happened":** Talia Kaplan, "Trump:
DOJ 'Missing in Action' on Alleged Election
Fraud," Fox News, November 29, 2020, www
.foxnews.com/politics/trump-doj-missing-in
-action-alleged-election-fraud.

595 Barr told him that the Justice Department: Michael Balsamo, "Disputing Trump, Barr Says No Widespread Election Fraud," Associated Press, December 1, 2020, https://apnews.com/article/barr-no-widespread-election-fraud-b1f1488796c9a98c4b1a9061a6c7f49d.

595 This was designed: Charlie Savage, "Barr Makes Durham a Special Counsel in a Bid to Entrench Scrutiny of the Russia Inquiry," **New York Times,** December 1, 2020, www.nytimes.com/2020/12/01/us/politics/john-durham-special-counsel-russia-investigation.html.

602 Trump continued to stew: Matt Zapotosky, Josh Dawsey, and Devlin Barrett, "Trump Is Said to Be Livid at Barr, with One Official Suggesting Termination Possible," **Washington Post,** December 2, 2020, www.washingtonpost.com/national-security/trump-barr-election-fraud/2020/12/02/5717626c-34e2-11eb-a997-1f4c53d2a747_story.html.

603 The president's daily tally: Rosalind S. Helderman, Emma Brown, and Elise Viebeck, "Trump's Losses Stack Up Further as Wisconsin Supreme Court Declines to Hear Campaign Challenge to Election Results," **Washington Post,** December 3, 2020, www.washingtonpost.com/politics/wisconsin-supreme-court-trump-lawsuit/2020/12/03/ee481942-3596-11eb-a997-1f4c53d2a747_story.html.

603 And in Arizona: Maria Polletta, "Judge Rejects Arizona Republican Party's Attempt to Overturn Election Results; GOP Vows Appeal," **Arizona**

Republic, December 4, 2020, www.azcentral
.com/story/news/politics/elections/2020/12/04/
arizona-judge-rejects-republican-effort-overturn
-state-election-results/3821578001.

603 **More than fifty:** Rosalind S. Helderman and
Elise Viebeck, "'The Last Wall': How Dozens of
Judges Across the Political Spectrum Rejected
Trump's Efforts to Overturn the Election,
Washington Post, December 12, 2020, https://
www.washingtonpost.com/politics/judges-trump
-election-lawsuits/2020/12/12/e3a57224-3a72
-11eb-98c4-25dc9f4987e8_story.html.

604 **But the win impacted a small cluster:** Mick
Stinelli, "Trump Campaign Wins Case on Pa.
Voter ID Deadline," **Pittsburgh Post-Gazette,**
November 12, 2020, www.post-gazette.com/
news/crime-courts/2020/11/12/trump-campaign
-election-2020-presidential-pennsylvania-lawsuit
-ballots-late-identification/stories/202011120132.

605 **Another irony:** Robert Barnes and Elise
Viebeck, "Supreme Court Denies Trump
Allies' Bid to Overturn Pennsylvania Election
Results," **Washington Post,** December 8, 2020,
www.washingtonpost.com/politics/courts
_law/supreme-court-trump-pennsylvania-election
-results/2020/12/08/4d39e16c-397d-11eb-98c4
-25dc9f4987e8_story.html.

606 **"The application for injunctive relief":** Order in
Pending Case, Kelly, **Mike, et al., v. Pennsylvania,
et al.,** Supreme Court, December 8, 2020, www
.supremecourt.gov/orders/courtorders/120820zr
_bq7d.pdf.

606 **On December 11, the court:** Robert Barnes, "Supreme Court Dismisses Bid Led by Texas Attorney General to Overturn the Presidential Election Results, Blocking Trump's Legal Path to a Reversal of His Loss," **Washington Post,** December 11, 2020, www.washingtonpost.com/politics/courts_law/supreme-court-texas-election-trump/2020/12/11/bf462f22-3bc6-11eb-bc68-96af0daae728_story.html.

608 **As Milley recounted the moment:** Jennifer Griffin (@JenGriffinFNC), Twitter, December 8, 2020, 8:42 a.m., https://twitter.com/JenGriffinFNC/status/1336305053754421255?s=20.

611 **Before it came to that:** Jonathan Swan, "Scoop: Gina Haspel Threatened to Resign over Plan to Install Kash Patel as CIA Deputy," **Axios,** January 16, 2021, www.axios.com/kash-patel-cia-gina-haspel-757b92c0-82a5-457b-bde8-d0d683ee222e.html.

613 **A White House spokesman:** Reuters Staff, "Proud Boys Leader Wasn't Invited to White House, Took Public Tour: Spokesman," Reuters, December 12, 2020, www.reuters.com/article/us-usa-election-protests-proud-boys/proud-boys-leader-wasnt-invited-to-white-house-took-public-tour-spokesman-idUSKBN28M0V2.

614 **"We will utilize that system":** Emily Davies et al., "Multiple People Stabbed After Thousands Gather for Pro-Trump Demonstrations in Washington," **Washington Post,** December 12, 2020, www.washingtonpost.com/local/trump-dc-rally-maga/2020/12/11/8b5af818-3bdb-11eb-bc68-96af0daae728_story.html.

616 **"You need to step up":** "Georgia Election Official Gabriel Sterling: 'Someone's Going to Get Killed' Transcript," Rev, December 1, 2020, www.rev.com/blog/transcripts/georgia-election-official-gabriel-sterling-someones-going-to-get-killed-transcript.

616 **She had just finished:** Katie Shepherd, "Armed Protesters Alleging Voter Fraud Surrounded the Home of Michigan's Secretary of State," **Washington Post,** December 7, 2020, www.washingtonpost.com/nation/2020/12/07/michigan-sos-benson-armed-protest.

617 **"And now apparently":** Nick Corasaniti, Jim Rutenberg, and Kathleen Gray, "As Trump Rails Against Loss, His Supporters Become More Threatening," **New York Times,** December 8, 2020, www.nytimes.com/2020/12/08/us/politics/trump-election-challenges.html.

618 **Shortly after his floor speech:** Nicholas Fandos and Luke Broadwater, "McConnell Congratulates Biden and Lobbies Colleagues to Oppose a Final-Stage G.O.P. Effort to Overturn His Victory," **New York Times,** December 15, 2020, www.nytimes.com/2020/12/15/us/politics/mitch-mcconnell-congratulates-biden.html.

622 **It opened by suggesting that:** "Read William Barr's Resignation Letter to President Trump," **Washington Post,** December 14, 2020, www.washingtonpost.com/context/read-william-barr-s-resignation-letter-to-president-trump/2b0820cb-3890-498a-bd46-c1b248049c70.

623 **In his Newsmax TV interview:** Solange Reyner, "Michael Flynn to Newsmax TV: Trump Has

Options to Secure Integrity of 2020 Election," Newsmax TV, December 17, 2020, www.newsmax .com/politics/trump-election-flynn-martiallaw/ 2020/12/17/id/1002139.

625   **She said he should:** Maggie Haberman and Zolan Kanno-Youngs, "Trump Weighed Naming Election Conspiracy Theorist as Special Counsel," **New York Times,** December 19, 2020, www .nytimes.com/2020/12/19/us/politics/trump -sidney-powell-voter-fraud.html.

625   **With that, Herschmann called:** Jonathan Swan and Zachary Basu, "Bonus Episode: Inside the Craziest Meeting of the Trump Presidency," **Axios,** February 2, 2021, www.axios.com/trump-oval -office-meeting-sidney-powell-a8e1e466-2e42 -42d0-9cf1-26eb267f8723.html.

628   **When The New York Times reported:** Haberman and Kanno-Youngs, "Trump Weighed Naming Election Conspiracy Theorist."

Chapter Twenty: Hitting a Dead End

629   **Trump also granted mercy:** Maggie Haberman and Michael S. Schmidt, "Trump Pardons Two Russia Inquiry Figures and Blackwater Guards," **New York Times,** December 22, 2020, www .nytimes.com/2020/12/22/us/politics/trump -pardons.html.

630   **The president claimed:** Amy Gardner, "Trump Pressured a Georgia Elections Investigator in a Separate Call Legal Experts Say Could Amount to Obstruction," **Washington Post,** March 11, 2021, www.washingtonpost.com/politics/trump-call

-georgia-investigator/2021/01/09/7a55c7fa-51cf
-11eb-83e3-322644d82356_story.html#click=
https://t.co/5J07XsWeSl.

630 **"The people of Georgia are so angry":** Charles Davis, "Trump Pressured Another Georgia Elections Official, Frances Watson, to Uncover Nonexistent Voter Fraud," **Business Insider,** March 10, 2021, www.businessinsider.com/transcript-trump-pressures-another-georgia-elections-official-to-find-fraud-2021-3.

633 **At a "Stop the Steal" rally:** Joey Garrison, "'They Have Not Earned Your Vote': Trump Allies Urge Georgia Republicans to Sit Out Senate Runoffs," **USA Today,** December 2, 2020, www.usatoday.com/story/news/politics/elections/2020/12/02/trump-allies-urge-georgia-republicans-sit-out-senate-runoffs/3800126001.

635 **In the Senate, Josh Hawley:** John Wagner and Rosalind S. Helderman, "Hawley's Plan to Contest Electoral College Vote Certification Ensures Drawn-Out Process," **Washington Post,** December 31, 2020, www.washingtonpost.com/politics/congress-election-vote-certification-objection/2020/12/30/4dce936c-4ab6-11eb-839a-cf4ba7b7c48c_story.html.

636 **On December 31, McConnell:** Jonathan Swan, "McConnell Calls January 6 Certification His 'Most Consequential Vote,'" **Axios,** December 31, 2020, www.axios.com/mcconnell-calls-jan-6-certification-his-most-consequential-vote-323cd74c-7dfa-4420-bd32-32a36398dadc.html.

637 **"WERES MY MONEY" was sprayed:** Stephanie Wolf, "Louisville Home of Sen. Majority Leader Mitch McConnell Spray Painted," 89.3 WFPL, January 2, 2021, https://wfpl.org/mitch-mcconnells-louisville-home-spray-painted-with-wheres-my-money.

639 **"Trump . . . will soon":** Neta Bar, "In Thinly Veiled Threat, Rouhani Says Trump 'Nearing the End of His Life,'" **Israel Hayom,** January 3, 2021, www.israelhayom.com/2021/01/03/in-thinly-veiled-threat-rouhani-says-trump-nearing-the-end-of-his-life.

640 **more than eighty judges:** Rosalind S. Helderman and Elise Viebeck, "'The Last Wall': How Dozens of Judges Across the Political Spectrum Rejected Trump's Efforts to Overturn the Election," **Washington Post,** December 12, 2020, www.washingtonpost.com/politics/judges-trump-election-lawsuits/2020/12/12/e3a57224-3a72-11eb-98c4-25dc9f4987e8_story.html.

641 **They were about to publish:** Ashton Carter et al., "Opinion: All 10 Living Former Defense Secretaries: Involving the Military in Election Disputes Would Cross into Dangerous Territory," **Washington Post,** January 3, 2021, www.washingtonpost.com/opinions/10-former-defense-secretaries-military-peaceful-transfer-of-power/2021/01/03/2a23d52e-4c4d-11eb-a9f4-0e668b9772ba_story.html.

644 **"The end is coming":** "Pence," Lincoln Project, December 8, 2020, www.youtube.com/watch?v=HxBPqCHFCcc.

644 **Pence ignored the president's order:** Mike Allen, "The Swamp Wins," **Axios,** January 20, 2021, www .axios.com/newsletters/axios-am-f813b85e-e4e4 -4b39-aea4-4340375df10e.html?chunk=2&utm _term=twsocialshare#story2.

646 **"Senator, I can guarantee that":** Committee on Armed Services, U.S. Senate, Hearing to Consider the Nomination of General Mark A. Milley, USA, to Be Chief of Staff of the Army, July 21, 2015, www.armed-services.senate.gov/imo/media/doc/ 15-64%20-%207-21-15.pdf.

649 **"Well, Mr. President, the challenge":** Amy Gardner and Paulina Firozi, "Here's the Full Transcript and Audio of the Call Between Trump and Raffensperger," **Washington Post,** January 5, 2021, www.washingtonpost.com/politics/ trump-raffensperger-call-transcript-georgia -vote/2021/01/03/2768e0cc-4ddd-11eb-83e3 -322644d82356_story.html.

649 **Shortly before 9:00 a.m. the next day:** Brendan Keefe (@BrendanKeefe), Twitter, January 4, 2021, 2:47 p.m., https://twitter.com/BrendanKeefe/ status/1346191481179148288?s=20.

650 **The undeniable sounds:** Amy Gardner, "'I Just Want to Find 11,780 Votes': In Extraordinary Hour-Long Call, Trump Pressures Georgia Secretary of State to Recalculate the Vote in His Favor," **Washington Post,** January 3, 2021, www .washingtonpost.com/politics/trump-raffensperger -call-georgia-vote/2021/01/03/d45acb92-4dc4 -11eb-bda4-615aaefd0555_story.html.

650 **"If President Trump wouldn't have":** Brendan Keefe (@BrendanKeefe), Twitter, January 4, 2021, 2:47 p.m., https://twitter.com/BrendanKeefe/status/1346181358092222467?s=20.

652 **"Civilian and military officials":** Carter et al., "Opinion: All 10 Living Former Defense Secretaries."

659 **"I hope Mike Pence":** "Donald Trump Rally Speech Transcript Dalton, Georgia: Senate Runoff Election," Rev, January 4, 2021, www.rev.com/blog/transcripts/donald-trump-rally-speech-transcript-dalton-georgia-senate-runoff-election.

664 **Two days earlier:** "Romney Statement on Certification of Presidential Election Results," Mitt Romney, U.S. Senator for Utah, January 3, 2021, www.romney.senate.gov/romney-statement-certification-presidential-election-results.

665 **One of them shouted:** Jaclyn Peiser, "Trump Supporters Heckle Romney, Chanting 'Traitor' on Flight to D.C.," **Washington Post,** January 6, 2021, www.washingtonpost.com/nation/2021/01/06/romney-airport-flight-heckled-trump.

665 **A little later that evening:** "Georgia Senate Runoff Election Results 2021," NBC News, March 6, 2021, www.nbcnews.com/politics/2020-elections/georgia-senate-runoff-results.

Chapter Twenty-one: The Insurrection

670 **But then Giuliani said:** "Rudy Giuliani Speech Transcript at Trump's Washington, D.C. Rally: Wants 'Trial by Combat,'" Rev, January 6, 2021, www.rev.com/blog/transcripts/rudy-giuliani

-speech-transcript-at-trumps-washington-d-c
-rally-wants-trial-by-combat.

671 **After realizing she was being filmed:** Ali
Swenson, "Video of Trump Family in Tent was
Filmed Before Capitol Riot," Associated Press,
January 8, 2021, https://apnews.com/article/fact
-checking-afs:Content:9916360242.

671 **The first lady was busy that morning:** Kate
Bennett, "Melania Trump and Adult Trump
Children Avoid the Spotlight After One of Nation's
Darkest Days," CNN, January 11, 2021, www.cnn
.com/2021/01/08/politics/melania-trump-white
-house-capitol-riot/index.html.

674 **Police in that area:** "Alabama Man Charged with
Possession of Eleven Molotov Cocktails Found
Near Protest at U.S. Capitol," U.S. Attorney's
Office, January 8, 2021, www.justice.gov/usao
-dc/pr/alabama-man-charged-possession-eleven
-molotov-cocktails-found-near-protest-us-capitol.

676 **His final words:** Aaron Glantz, "Read Pence's Full
Letter Saying He Can't Claim 'Unilateral Authority'
to Reject Electoral Votes," **PBS NewsHour,**
January 6, 2021, www.pbs.org/newshour/politics/
read-pences-full-letter-saying-he-cant-claim
-unilateral-authority-to-reject-electoral-votes.

678 **Reading from a carefully prepared text:** "Mitch
McConnell Senate Speech Transcript January 6:
Rejects Efforts to Overturn Presidential Election
Results," Rev, January 6, 2021, www.rev.com/
transcript-editor/shared/_BVl6g_r_ZHl4d0d
8oIEIgxEKf9aCpcassr2QQRLz9GCqZd22ybzoq

_ZrGp8D3L6nVb6YIYZTGjOgxSTld6Rb TbtCfo?loadFrom=PastedDeeplink&ts=101.07.

679 **Just outside the Capitol:** "Alabama Man Was Among 4 Who Died During Siege on US Capitol," Associated Press, January 7, 2021, https://apnews .com/article/alabama-arrests-violence-ab2cd 813876bab778df07a991ba2379d.

680 **A stream of Trump warriors:** Dominic Pezzola and William Pepe, Indictment, U.S. District Court for the District of Columbia, www.justice .gov/opa/page/file/1362646/download.

681 **Had Pence walked past:** Ashley Parker et al., "How the Rioters Who Stormed the Capitol Came Dangerously Close to Pence," **Washington Post,** January 15, 2021, www.washingtonpost.com/ politics/pence-rioters-capitol-attack/2021/01/15/ ab62e434-567c-11eb-a08b-f1381ef3d207_story .html.

682 **Lindsey Graham said:** Ashley Parker, Josh Dawsey, and Philip Rucker, "Six Hours of Paralysis: Inside Trump's Failure to Act After a Mob Stormed the Capitol," **Washington Post,** January 11, 2021, www.washingtonpost.com/politics/trump-mob -failure/2021/01/11/36a46e2e-542e-11eb-a817 -e5e7f8a406d6_story.html.

682 **"Mr. President, they just took the vice president":** Kyle Cheney, "Tuberville Says He Informed Trump of Pence's Evacuation Before Rioters Reached Senate," **Politico,** February 11, 2021, www.politico.com/news/2021/02/11/ tuberville-pences-evacuation-trump-impeachment -468572.

686 **And they were talking about optics:** Dan Lamothe et al., "Army Falsely Denied Flynn's Brother Was Involved in Key Part of Military Response to Capitol Riot," **Washington Post,** January 20, 2021, www.washingtonpost.com/ national-security/flynn-national-guard-call -riot/2021/01/20/7f4f41ba-5b4c-11eb-aaad -93988621dd28_story.html.

686 **"I am making urgent":** Carol D. Leonnig et al., "Outgoing Capitol Police Chief: House, Senate Security Officials Hamstrung Efforts to Call in National Guard," **Washington Post,** January 10, 2021, www.washingtonpost.com/politics/sund -riot-national-guard/2021/01/10/fc2ce7d4-5384 -11eb-a817-e5e7f8a406d6_story.html.

688 **At 2:44, Ashli Babbitt:** Jon Swaine et al., "Video Shows Fatal Shooting of Ashli Babbitt in the Capitol," **Washington Post,** January 8, 2021, www.washingtonpost.com/investigations/2021/ 01/08/ashli-babbitt-shooting-video-capitol.

690 **In Pelosi's office suite:** Joe Heim and Valerie Strauss, "As U.S. Capitol Attack Unfolded, Some Hill Staffers Remembered Their School-Shooting Drills," **Washington Post,** January 14, 2021, www.washingtonpost.com/education/hill-staffers -school-shooting-drills/2021/01/14/3fe783d0 -55e7-11eb-a931-5b162d0d033d_story.html.

691 **Some of McConnell's aides:** Karoun Demirjian et al., "Inside the Capitol Siege: How Barricaded Lawmakers and Aides Sounded Urgent Pleas for Help as Police Lost Control," **Washington Post,** January 10, 2021, www.washingtonpost

.com/politics/inside-capitol-siege/2021/01/09/
e3ad3274-5283-11eb-bda4-615aaefd0555_story
.html.

697   **Kevin McCarthy, who had been:** "Herrera Beutler
Again Confirms Conversation with McCarthy
Regarding January 6 U.S. Capitol Attack," Jaime
Herrera Beutler, U.S. Congresswoman, Feb. 12,
2021, https://jhb.house.gov/news/documentsingle
.aspx?DocumentID=402083.

697   **"I've been spending the last twenty-five
minutes":** Matt Arco, "Christie Says Trump
Must 'Tell His Supporters to Leave the Capitol
Grounds,'" NJ.com, January 6, 2021, www.nj.com/
politics/2021/01/christie-says-trump-must-tell-his
-supporters-to-leave-the-capitol-grounds.html.

702   **The president's message:** Parker, Dawsey, and
Rucker, "Six Hours of Paralysis."

703   **A third casualty:** Evan Hill, Arielle Ray, and
Dahlia Kozlowsky, "Videos Show How Rioter
Was Trampled in Stampede at Capitol," **New York
Times,** January 15, 2021, www.nytimes.com/
2021/01/15/us/rosanne-boyland-capitol-riot
-death.html.

703   **Capitol Police officer Brian Sicknick:** Peter
Hermann and Spencer S. Hsu, "Capitol Police Officer
Brian Sicknick, Who Engaged Rioters, Suffered
Two Strokes and Died of Natural Causes, Officials
Say," **Washington Post,** April 19, 2021, www
.washingtonpost.com/local/public-safety/brian
-sicknick-death-strokes/2021/04/19/36d2d310
-617e-11eb-afbe-9a11a127d146_story.html.

Chapter Twenty-two: Lag the Bad Boy

714 **On the evening:** Robert C. O'Brien (@robert-cobrien), Twitter, January 6, 2021, 6:03 p.m., https://twitter.com/robertcobrien/status/1346955563968524289?s=20.

719 **In her resignation letter:** "Betsy DeVos Resignation Letter," **Washington Post,** January 7, 2021, www.washingtonpost.com/context/betsy -devos-resignation-letter/cfd93504-2353-4ac3 -8e71-155446242dda.

722 **Democratic lawmakers, however:** Charlie Savage, "Trump Had Power to Attack Syria Without Congress, Justice Dept. Memo Says," **New York Times,** June 1, 2018, www.nytimes .com/2018/06/01/us/politics/trump-war-powers -syria-congress.html.

729 **Also, during the trip:** Philip Rucker and Josh Dawsey, "Trump Defiant and Unapologetic About His Role in Inciting Capitol Mob Attack," **Washington Post,** January 12, 2021, www .washingtonpost.com/politics/trump-defiant -mob/2021/01/12/b93231bc-54f8-11eb-a817 -e5e7f8a406d6_story.html.

730 **"He is a clear and present danger":** Mike DeBonis and Paul Kane, "House Hands Trump a Second Impeachment, This Time with GOP Support," **Washington Post,** January 13, 2021, www.washingtonpost.com/politics/house -impeachment-trump/2021/01/13/05fe731c -55c5-11eb-a931-5b162d0d033d_story.html.

730   **Downtown businesses boarded:** Missy Ryan et al., "Security Footprint Grows in Nation's Capital Ahead of Inauguration," **Washington Post,** January 13, 2021, www.washingtonpost .com/national-security/2021/01/13/national -guard-inauguration-security.

733   **In late December:** Matt Zapotosky et al., "Trump Pardons Charles Kushner, Paul Manafort, Roger Stone in Latest Wave of Clemency Grants," **Washington Post,** December 23, 2020, www .washingtonpost.com/national-security/charles -kushner-paul-manafort-roger-stone-trump -pardons/2020/12/23/05cf013a-456d-11eb-975c -d17b8815a66d_story.html.

735   **But politicians convicted:** Rosalind S. Helderman, Josh Dawsey, and Beth Reinhard, "Trump Grants Clemency to 143 People in Late-Night Pardon Blast," **Washington Post,** January 20, 2021, www.washingtonpost.com/ politics/trump-pardons/2021/01/20/7653bd12 -59a2-11eb-8bcf-3877871c819d_story.html.

735   **Most of the fourteen thousand:** Beth Reinhard et al., "The Cottage Industry Behind Trump's Pardons: How the Rich and Well-Connected Got Ahead at the Expense of Others," **Washington Post,** February 5, 2021, www.washingtonpost .com/politics/trump-pardons-lobbying/2021/02/ 05/896f0b52-624b-11eb-9430-e7c77b5b0297 _story.html.

737   **Biden or Vice President-elect Kamala Harris:** Josh Dawsey, Ashley Parker, and Philip Rucker, "'Have a Good Life': Trump Leaves for Florida

in Low-Key Farewell," **Washington Post, January 20, 2021,** www.washingtonpost.com/ politics/trump-farewell-florida/2021/01/20/ c6ca8a82-5b50-11eb-a976-bad6431e03e2_story .html.

Epilogue

744 **In the first, when the economy:** "Presidential Approval Ratings—Donald Trump," Gallup, https://news.gallup.com/poll/203198/presidential -approval-ratings-donald-trump.aspx.

755 **But Trump all but ruled out:** Tim Alberta, "Nikki Haley's Time for Choosing," **Politico,** www .politico.com/interactives/2021/magazine-nikki -haleys-choice.

ABOUT THE AUTHORS

CAROL LEONNIG is a national investigative reporter at **The Washington Post,** where she has worked since 2000, covering Donald Trump's presidency and previous administrations. She won the 2015 Pulitzer Prize for her reporting on security failures and misconduct inside the Secret Service. She also was part of the **Post** teams awarded Pulitzers in 2018, for reporting on Russia's interference in the 2016 presidential election, and in 2014, for revealing the U.S. government's secret, broad surveillance of Americans. Leonnig is an on-air contributor to NBC News and MSNBC and the author of **Zero Fail: The Rise and Fall of the Secret Service.**

PHILIP RUCKER is the senior Washington correspondent at **The Washington Post** and led its coverage of President Trump and his administration as White House Bureau chief. He and a team of **Post** reporters won the Pulitzer Prize and George Polk Award for their reporting on Russia's interference in the 2016 presidential election. In 2021, the White House Correspondents' Association honored Rucker with the Aldo Beckman Award for overall excellence in White House coverage. Rucker joined the **Post** in 2005 and previously has covered Congress, the Obama White House, and the 2012 and 2016 presidential campaigns. He serves as an on-air political analyst for NBC News and MSNBC and graduated from Yale University with a degree in history.